Seventh Edition

Introduction to Educational Research

Craig A. Mertler
University of West Georgia

C. M. Charles
Professor Emeritus, San Diego State University

PEARSON

Boston Columbus Indianapolis New York San Francisco Upper Saddle River
Amsterdam Cape Town Dubai London Madrid Milan Munich Paris Montreal Toronto
Delhi Mexico City Sao Paulo Sydney Hong Kong Seoul Singapore Taipei Tokyo

Editor-in-Chief: *Paul A. Smith*
Managing Editor: *Shannon Steed*
Series Editorial Assistant: *Matthew Buchholz*
Vice President, Director of Marketing: *Quinn Perkson*
Marketing Manager: *Jared Brueckner*
Production Editor: *Paula Carroll*
Editorial-Production Service: *Omegatype Typography, Inc.*
Manufacturing Manager: *Megan Cochran*
Electronic Composition: *Omegatype Typography, Inc.*
Interior Design: *Omegatype Typography, Inc.*
Cover Designer: *Elena Sidorova*

For related titles and support materials, visit our online catalog at www.pearsonhighered.com

Between the time website information is gathered and then published, it is not unusual for some sites to have closed. Also, the transcription of URLs can result in typographical errors. The publisher would appreciate notification where these errors occur so that they may be corrected in subsequent editions.

Library of Congress Cataloging-in-Publication Data

Mertler, Craig A.
   Introduction to educational research / Craig A. Mertler, C. M. Charles.—7th ed.
      p. cm.
   Includes bibliographical references and index.
   ISBN-13: 978-0-13-701344-9 (pbk.)
   ISBN-10: 0-13-701344-2 (pbk.)
  1. Education—Research—Methodology. I. Charles, C. M. II. Title.
   LB1028.C515   2011
   370.72—dc22

                                               2009041843

Printed in the United States of America

10 9 8 7 6 5 4 3   B-R 13 12 11 10

www.pearsonhighered.com

ISBN-10: 0-13-701344-2
ISBN-13: 978-0-13-701344-9

About the Author

Craig A. Mertler is currently a professor and director of the doctoral program in school improvement in the College of Education at the University of West Georgia. He teaches doctoral courses focused on the application of action research to promote school improvement and reform, and also teaches quantitative research methods, introductory statistical analysis, multivariate statistical analysis, and educational assessment methods. He is the author of five books, four invited book chapters, 15 refereed journal articles, two instructors' manuals, and numerous nonrefereed articles and manuscripts. He has also presented numerous research papers at professional meetings around the country, as well as internationally. He conducts workshops for in-service educational professionals on classroom-based action research and on the broad topic of classroom assessment. His primary research interests include classroom-based action research, professional learning communities, and assessment practices of classroom teachers. Before teaching and researching at the university level, he taught high school biology and earth science, and also coached track and volleyball. In his leisure time, he enjoys travelling with his family and playing golf.

Dr. Mertler can be reached at the following:

Doctoral Program in School Improvement
Room 251 Education Center
College of Education
Carrollton, GA 30118
cmertler@westga.edu
http://coe.westga.edu/edd

*In memory
of my father, Chuck . . .
for helping me to understand why it's important
to always take pride in my work!*

—C. A. M.

Contents

CHAPTER 4

Locating Published Research   62

PART THREE
Conducting Your Own Research Project   98

CHAPTER 9

PART FOUR
Procedures and Exemplars of Research as Differentiated by Tradition   190

CHAPTER 10

Qualitative Research Methods   190

CHAPTER 14   **Mixed-Methods Research Designs**   318

PART FIVE
Procedures and Exemplars of Research as Differentiated by Practicality   336

CHAPTER 15   **Action Research**   336

FOR WHOM THIS BOOK IS INTENDED

The seventh edition of *Introduction to Educational Research* is designed specifically for educators who are new to research and seeking advanced degrees in graduate studies. Most users will be in-service teachers, administrators, special education personnel, coaches, and counselors, but the book is also appropriate for graduate students not yet actively teaching. No prior familiarity with the principles, procedures, or terminology of educational research is required in order to fully profit from this book.

WHAT'S NEW IN THIS EDITION

The reviewers of the sixth edition of this book are to be thanked for providing substantial guidance regarding ways to improve the book as it went into this seventh edition. Reviewers cited several "needs" for the book in order to improve its effectiveness for students taking their initial course in educational research methods. I greatly appreciated their suggestions, and took them to heart. The needs identified by the reviewers included the following:

- A reorganization of the classification of the various approaches to conducting research
- The inclusion of a more thorough example of a research proposal
- An enhanced presentation of qualitative research, including material on narrative research, as well as discussions and examples of qualitative data collection and analysis
- More information on the topic of single-subject research designs and studies

Users familiar with the previous edition of this book will see several changes, the most substantial of which are intended only to enhance the previous editions of the text and to make the learning experience much more meaningful for students. Major changes, along with the potential benefits of those changes, include the following:

- This edition of the text is substantially enhanced through its integration with My EducationLab for Research. Every chapter contains margin icons that correlate chapter topics to assignments and activities within the MyEducationLab for Research website.

Benefit: MyEducationLab for Research is an interactive learning website that helps students strengthen skills that are essential to understanding and producing good research.

- Chapter 10 ("Qualitative Research Methods") has been revised substantially. It now includes a detailed discussion of narrative research, in addition to ethnographic research. Examples of published research studies for both types of qualitative research have been included. In addition, greater detail and examples related to qualitative data collection and data analysis have been provided.

Benefits: Students will gain a more thorough understanding of the nature of qualitative research, with in-depth discussions of ethnographic and narrative research, as well as brief overviews of grounded theory research, phenomenology, case studies, and historical research. The presentations of data collection and data analysis—along with the incorporated examples—will help students to better envision the process of conducting qualitative research, will make them better consumers of qualitative research, and will enable them to plan and conduct their own original qualitative research studies.

■ More information about single-subject research designs has been added to Chapter 13 ("Experimental, Quasi-Experimental, and Single-Subject Designs"). An additional published example of single-subject research has also been included.

Benefits: Given the popularity and appropriateness of single-subject research in the areas of special education and counseling, its enrichment in this chapter will allow students to better comprehend this methodological technique. The added discussions of specific types of single-subject research designs will undoubtedly help students see their practical applications. The addition of the sample published article utilizing a single-subject design will enable students to see the application of these types of designs in a real-world context.

■ "Action Research" (Chapter 15) and "Evaluation Research" (Chapter 16) now appear as separate chapters. Additional detail and discussion have been provided for both types of research. In addition, these two approaches to research now appear in their own section ("Part Five: Procedures and Exemplars of Research as Differentiated by Practicality").

Benefits: The biggest benefit of splitting these two methodological techniques into separate chapters is that more thorough coverage has now been provided for both. New to the chapter on action research is a discussion of the rigor of action research, which is crucial because some critics mistakenly believe that it is not rigorous. New to the chapter on evaluation research are overviews of various approaches to conducting program evaluations, including objectives-oriented, management-oriented, consumer-oriented, expertise-oriented, adversary-oriented, and naturalistic- and participant-oriented approaches. These discussions will enable students to see the potential applications of evaluation research, perhaps in their own settings.

■ The chapter titled "Designing a Research Project" (formerly Chapter 6) has been moved to become Chapter 8 (and, therefore, immediately precedes Chapter 9, "Preparing a Research Report").

Benefits: The main benefit of moving this chapter is that it is now more closely connected with Chapter 9. Both of these chapters deal with issues related to writing up various aspects of research studies. With the discussions and techniques provided, students should be able to see the chapter on proposal development and the chapter on writing a final research report as being interconnected scientific writing activities.

■ In Chapter 10 through Chapter 16, all new examples of published research studies have been included, for a total of 10 new studies in this edition.

Benefits: The obvious benefit of the examples of published studies is that students can read and engage in interactive discussions about the application of specific methodological techniques and research designs in a practical context. These articles reinforce the skills and concepts taught in each of the chapters, and also provide students a context within which to "practice" their skills as consumers of published research.

Minor revisions include the following:

■ Chapter 2 ("Types of Educational Research and Corresponding Sources of Data") includes a slight reclassification of the various approaches to research.

Benefit: This reclassification puts action research and evaluation research into their own category, based on practical application of research methods. Often, students view action and evaluation research as completely separate from more "traditional" approaches to conducting research. In reality, they often use these traditional approaches, but in a changed context (from a purely research context to one that has real, practical implications).

■ Chapter 7 ("Analyzing Research Data and Presenting Findings") has been revised to include more details regarding the analysis of qualitative data.

Benefit: Similar to the content added to Chapter 10, the additional discussions of qualitative data analysis in this chapter will enable students to have a better and deeper appreciation for the complex process of analyzing these types of data.

■ Brief discussions of the use of SPSS and Excel have been included in Chapter 7 ("Analyzing Research Data and Presenting Findings").

Benefit: Many programs, courses, and institutions across the country instruct students on the use of SPSS and/or Excel as a means for analyzing quantitative data. The inclusion of brief discussions of these software programs, along with several screen captures, will support that instruction within the context of a course in educational research methods.

■ A new sample research proposal has been included in Chapter 8 ("Designing a Research Project").

Benefit: I believe that the included sample research proposal will better meet the needs of instructors and their students, who need to see all aspects of a well-developed research proposal.

■ Wherever appropriate, "Applying Technology" sections have been updated.

Benefit: In our technologically driven world, it is important to support the content of the book with technology supplements. These sections have been revised and updated in order to be as current as possible at the time of printing.

SPECIAL FEATURES

This book has several special features that increase the appeal and value to readers and also facilitate the instructor's presentation of material.

SEQUENCED TO ASSIST DOING RESEARCH

As with the previous edition, the book remains organized to help you plan and conduct your first educational research projects. By proceeding through chapter contents and by completing the in-text exercises as well as the developmental activities, you will simultaneously prepare a research plan on a topic of importance and learn how to obtain and analyze data, answer research questions and test hypotheses, and prepare a proper report of your projects.

READABILITY: ORGANIZATION AND STYLE

This seventh edition demonstrates continued refinement in clarity and readability, a trait that many users consider to be a major strength. Throughout, unfamiliar terms are highlighted, and clear definitions are provided. Many examples are provided to make concepts and applications more understandable. At the same time, the material is kept concise, resulting in a book that covers essential concepts without overwhelming the reader.

PEDAGOGICAL FEATURES

In keeping with the main purpose of helping students clearly understand and apply research concepts, many pedagogical features have been included in the book.

■ Chapter Previews provide accurate anticipation of what is to be covered.
■ Chapter Targeted Learnings provide lists of key understandings students will acquire.

- Chapter organizers offer graphic depictions of contents and organization of the chapters.
- In-text application exercises give periodic breaks for students to respond to new information.
- Chapter summaries help students comprehend chapter contents succinctly.
- Current status sections help students see the progress they have made and what comes next.
- Lists of important terms provide opportunities for review and self-testing.
- End-of-chapter activities enable practice, reflection, and discussion.
- Appendix of statistical concepts reviews and expands statistical concepts and procedures introduced in other chapters.
- Expanded glossary offers easy reference to research terminology.

REPRINTED RESEARCH REPORTS

Ten reprinted journal articles are included that exemplify various types of research. These published research articles have been specially selected to serve as exemplars to orient and encourage students who wish to conduct similar types of research. Guided activities and questions for discussion are provided to help students analyze the articles.

GLOSSARY

A glossary of more than 250 terms important in educational research has been provided for easy student reference. The terms are highlighted in boldface when first appearing in the text. This is one of the most comprehensive glossaries presented in any educational research textbook.

SUPPLEMENTS AND LEARNING AIDS

The following supplements provide an outstanding array of resources that facilitate learning about educational research. For more information, ask your local Pearson Education representative or contact the Pearson Faculty Field Support Department at 1-800-526-0485. For technology support, please contact technical support directly at 1-800-677-6337 or http://247.pearsoned.com. Instructor supplements can be downloaded from the Instructor Resource Center at www.pearsonhighered.com/irc.

RESOURCES FOR INSTRUCTORS

Instructor's Manual (S. Kim MacGregor, Louisiana State University)

The Instructor's Manual includes a wealth of interesting ideas, activities, and test items designed to help instructors teach the course. The Instructor's Manual is available for download from the Instructor Resource Center at www.pearsonhighered.com/irc.

PowerPoint Presentation

Ideal for classroom presentations and student handouts, the PowerPoint Presentation created for this text provides dozens of ready-to-use graphic and text images. The PowerPoint Presentation is available for download from the Instructor Resource Center at www.pearsonhighered.com/irc.

RESOURCES FOR STUDENTS

MyEducationLab for Research is a dynamic online learning environment for students located at www.myeducationlab.com that helps students master course content. MyEducationLab for Research is easy to use. Wherever the MyEducationLab for Research logo appears in the margins, readers can follow the simple instructions to access the MyEducationLab for Research resource that corresponds with the chapter content.

You will find two types of activities in the MyEducationLab for Research materials:

■ *Activities and Applications.* Give students opportunities to understand the content of *Introduction to Educational Research* more deeply and to practice applying content. Instructors may choose to assign these activities or use them in class. Feedback for these activities is available only to instructors.

■ *Building Research Skills activities.* Give students scaffolded practice to strengthen skills that are essential for understanding research. Feedback is provided to help students further develop skills for reading research articles.

PURPOSES OF THE BOOK

This book has two main purposes that receive attention simultaneously. The first is to provide knowledge about educational research, sufficient for a clear understanding of the following:

■ The ethical and philosophical principles adhered to in research
■ The nature of research and the scientific process it employs
■ Research questions, hypotheses, and hypothesis testing
■ The various types of research and their purposes, traits, and designs
■ The characteristics, sources, and collection of data
■ Procedures for analyzing qualitative and quantitative data
■ Published research, where it is found in the library, and how it is interpreted

The second purpose of this book, a purpose that has been made preeminent in this edition (as well as in its previous editions), is to help graduate students conduct their own research. Toward that end, specific guidance is provided in the following areas:

■ Identifying satisfactory topics for research
■ Framing research questions and subquestions
■ Stating research hypotheses and null hypotheses
■ Identifying the type of research called for in various topics
■ Preparing a research proposal for a selected topic
■ Conducting a thorough library search of literature
■ Analyzing types of research appropriate for investigating selected topics
■ Identifying needed data, their sources, and the procedures by which data are collected
■ Analyzing data appropriately
■ Answering research questions and testing hypotheses
■ Stating findings and drawing conclusions
■ Preparing research reports

ORGANIZATION OF THE BOOK

In keeping with the purposes of helping students organize and undertake research while simultaneously acquiring fundamental knowledge about research, the book is organized into five parts.

Part One: Orientation to Educational Research

Chapter 1.   Educational Research: Its Nature and Rules of Operation

Chapter 2.   Types of Educational Research and Corresponding Sources of Data

Part One clarifies the nature of research, explains its rules of operation, identifies standard types of educational research, and reviews the sources of data employed in those types of research.

Part Two: Preliminary Skills Needed for Conducting Research

Chapter 3.   Selecting, Refining, and Proposing a Topic for Research

Chapter 4.   Locating Published Research

Chapter 5.   Interpreting and Summarizing Published Research

The skills addressed in Part Two include selecting, refining, and proposing a topic for research; locating published research in the library; and interpreting, summarizing, and annotating published research.

Part Three: Conducting Your Own Research Project

Chapter 6.   Procedures and Tools for Gathering Data

Chapter 7.   Analyzing Research Data and Presenting Findings

Chapter 8.   Designing a Research Project

Chapter 9.   Preparing a Research Report

You will be shown how to design your own research projects with a process that clarifies the procedures and tools you will need for gathering data in your investigations; explains how to analyze qualitative and quantitative research data, present findings, and draw conclusions; and takes you step by step through preparing an appropriate research report.

Part Four: Procedures and Exemplars of Research as Differentiated by Tradition

Chapter 10.   Qualitative Research Methods

Chapter 11.   Survey Research

Chapter 12.   Nonexperimental Quantitative Research

Chapter 13.   Experimental, Quasi-Experimental, and Single-Subject Designs

Chapter 14.   Mixed-Methods Research Designs

Part Four provides details about how major traditional approaches to conducting research—ethnographic research, narrative research, survey research, correlational research, causal-comparative research, experimental and quasi-experimental research, single-subject research, and mixed-methods research—are planned and conducted. Published research reports that exemplify these types of research are reprinted in the chapters.

Part Five: Procedures and Exemplars of Research as Differentiated by Practicality

Chapter 15.   Action Research

Chapter 16.   Evaluation Research

Part Five provides details about how two very important types of research, as defined by their immediate practicality—action research and evaluation research—are planned and conducted. Published research reports that exemplify these types of research are also re-printed in the respective chapters.

HOW TO USE ASPECTS OF EACH CHAPTER

As with the previous edition, chapters are formatted to include standard sections to help organize a research framework.

Preview

Presented at the beginning of each chapter, the Preview provides a brief but thorough overview of what is to come in the chapter. These Previews help you anticipate and focus on the major topics presented in the chapter.

Targeted Learnings

After examining the Preview, you are directed to look especially for information related to specific chapter topics. These Targeted Learnings are repeated at the ends of chapters and are helpful for review and self-testing.

Chapter Information Organizer

A graphic organizer is presented in each chapter to outline its organization and content. The organizers are helpful by providing an overview to facilitate learning as well as a vehicle for review.

The Body of the Chapter

Here, the information, examples, and other explanations that convey chapter contents are presented. Interspersed within the body of the chapter are *application exercises* that require you to interpret or make realistic applications of what you have learned. These exercises are intended to enliven the reading, keep you actively involved, and reinforce what has been learned.

Applying Technology

This section contains relatively brief presentations or discussions related to chapter topics and incorporates technology and related websites that support the content of the chapter. Rather than reiterate chapter material, the Applying Technology section contains specific information that can exemplify or extend the content being discussed. Typically, these sections emphasize technology and web resources and applications. Some chapters contain multiple Applying Technology sections.

MyEducationLab for Research

This edition of the text is substantially enhanced through its integration with **MyEducationLab for Research,** an interactive learning website that helps students practice and strengthen skills that are essential to understanding and producing good research. As you can see from the list comprising the left-hand navigation bar (as well as below), thorough topic coverage is presented:

- Introduction to Educational Research
- Selecting and Defining a Research Topic

- Reviewing the Literature
- Preparing and Evaluating a Research Plan
- Selecting a Sample
- Selecting Measuring Instruments
- Survey Research
- Correlational Research
- Causal-Comparative Research
- Experimental Research
- Single-Subject Experimental Research
- Descriptive Statistics
- Inferential Statistics
- Qualitative Data Collection
- Narrative Research
- Ethnographic Research
- Case Study Research
- Qualitative Research: Data Analysis and Interpretation
- Mixed Methods Research
- Action Research
- Preparing a Research Report
- Evaluating a Research Report

For each of the topics listed, two basic resources can be found.

- *Assignments and Activities.* These activities provide opportunities to understand educational research more deeply and to practice applying concepts.
- *Building Research Skills.* These assignments help students to practice skills that are essential for understanding research.

Features of MyEducationLab for Research that correspond with chapter content are specifically highlighted in the chapters. These margin notes indicate opportunities for you to practice and reinforce students' understanding of educational research concepts and topics.

Chapter Summary

A brief résumé is presented at the end of each chapter that reiterates the major points covered in the body of the chapter. These summaries help readers tie the information together succinctly.

List of Important Terms

Following the chapter summary, a list of important terms discussed in the chapter is presented. Because definitions of the terms are not provided, the list is useful for review, discussion, and student self-testing. Definitions appear in the glossary near the end of the book.

Your Current Status

This section appears in select chapters and follows the list of important terms. It provides a cumulative look at the progress the reader has made through the specific chapter. This knowledge reinforces learning and fosters a sense of accomplishment.

Activities for Thought and Discussion

At the end of each chapter are additional activities that call on students to interpret or apply information presented in the chapter. Students are encouraged to explore the activities individually or in groups. The topics and their interpretations can be used for lively and informative class discussions.

Answers to Chapter Exercises

Suitable answers are presented for the in-text exercises included in the chapter. Alternative answers not presented are often correct; disagreement concerning answers provides students with a valuable opportunity for discussion and exploration of concepts in greater depth.

References and Recommended Readings

In-chapter references are cited in this section. Also included are works that have not been cited but that relate to the chapter contents and are recommended for additional supplemental reading.

STATISTICAL PROCEDURES

Fundamental statistical concepts and procedures appropriate for beginning students of educational research are presented as needed in various chapters. They are explained in relation to the analysis of specific research data and clarified through many examples, thus, they are not intimidating to the reader. In-depth coverage of statistical topics is presented in the Appendix.

APPENDIX

Following the final chapter of the text, an Appendix is presented that presents an overview of statistical concepts and treatments in more depth than is offered elsewhere in the text. That information is assembled in the Appendix for reference or more advanced study.

GLOSSARY

Research terminology introduced in the text is listed and defined in the glossary.

ACKNOWLEDGMENTS

We would like to acknowledge the contributions of several individuals who made the work on this edition proceed quite smoothly. We would like to thank the staff at Pearson Education—in particular, Shannon Steed, our editor, for her feedback and support. Thank you to S. Kim MacGregor, who revised and updated the new edition of the Instructor's Manual. We would also certainly be remiss if we did not acknowledge the valuable comments and suggestions provided by the reviewers of this seventh edition: Debbie Hahs-Vaughn, University of Central Florida; S. Kim MacGregor, Louisiana State University; Maureen Mack, University of Wisconsin–Eau Claire; David Pugalee, University of North Carolina, Charlotte; and Tandra Tyler-Wood, University of North Texas.

In addition, we would like to thank the following reviewers who have kindly analyzed previous editions of the text and have offered many valuable comments and suggestions over the years: Beate Baltes, National University; Julie Bao, Shippensburg University; Li-Ling

Chen, California State University at East Bay; Kevin D. Crehan, University of Nevada at Las Vegas; Laura J. Shea Doolan, St. Joseph's College; Charlotte Webb Fair, University of Wyoming; Alvirda Farmer, San Jose State University; Jane A. Goldman, University of Connecticut; Laura D. Goodwill, University of Colorado at Denver; Bryan W. Griffin, Georgia Southern University; Robert L. Hale, Penn State University; Joseph Khazzaka, University of Scranton; Vicki LaBoskey, Mills College; Alex G. Ober, Western Maryland College; Linda Parker, McDaniel College; Pietro J. Pascale, Youngstown State University; William T. Phelan, University of Massachusetts; Steven Pulos, University of Northern Colorado; Sylvia Roberts, City College of New York; Sam Securro, Marshall University; Dale G. Shaw, University of Northern Colorado; Lowell Wade Smith, Tennessee State University; William B. Ware, University of North Carolina at Chapel Hill; Nedra Skaggs Wheeler, Western Kentucky University; Douglas C. Wiseman, Plymouth State College; and Terrence D. Wong, Marquette University.

Educational Research

Its Nature and Rules of Operation

PREVIEW

This chapter presents four clusters of information fundamental to educational research:

- The nature of educational research
- The value of the scientific method in answering perplexing questions
- The process by which educational research is done
- The operating rules for conducting educational research

You will see that research is a careful, systematic, patient investigation that does the following:

- Employs the scientific method, which seeks facts and relationships
- Follows a research process that obtains, analyzes, and interprets data
- Adheres to operating rules of legality, ethics, and established research procedures

TARGETED LEARNINGS

This chapter describes the nature of educational research, explains why the scientific method is valuable in answering perplexing questions about education, outlines the process by which educational research is conducted, and identifies the operating rules for conducting research. As you read the chapter, look especially for information related to the following questions:

1. What *sources of information* do people usually consult first for answers to difficult questions? Why are those first sources of information often of so little value?
2. What is meant by *scientific method*?
3. What is *research*? How is educational research similar to and different from research in the natural sciences?
4. What is the *general procedure* by which research is done?
5. What are the legal, ethical, philosophical, and procedural *operating rules* for conducting educational research? What is an example of each?
6. Why should the operating rules of educational research be thought of as unwritten law?

CHAPTER INFORMATION ORGANIZERS

This chapter and those that follow present *information organizers,* graphic frameworks that show the organization and contents of the chapter. They are provided to help you see the chapter organization and coverage as a whole and to anticipate information you will encounter. You will also find the organizers helpful for reviewing chapter contents.

AN EXAMPLE: NEW QUESTIONS ABOUT ELMWOOD'S SCHOOLS

To facilitate an introduction to educational research and the agreements by which it operates, let us consider the fictitious example of the Elmwood Urban School District, serving a city that in recent years has been undergoing dramatic change. Once a predominantly Anglo community, Elmwood has grown to reflect wide racial, ethnic, and cultural diversity. More than 70 different languages are spoken by students in Elmwood schools. Many of those students do not speak English well, and some of their parents do not speak English at all. In many ways Elmwood is richer because of this growing mix of cultures and viewpoints, but the changes

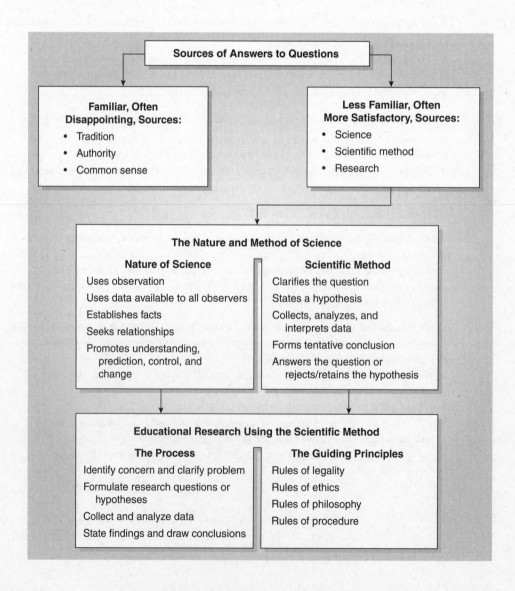

have also brought difficulties. Gangs have formed. Some ethnic groups do not get along well with others. Overall academic achievement has declined, with certain groups performing well below national norms. Dropout rates have increased. Parents and students complain more frequently about racism, insensitivity, lack of fairness, and inappropriate curricula.

In an attempt to improve conditions, Elmwood district's community coordinating council has asked the superintendent to prepare a formal report on achievement, curriculum, and race relations in Elmwood schools. This effort will first require that a number of answerable questions be posed, of which the following might be examples:

- How does student achievement in Elmwood compare with that of other urban areas?
- Which segments of the student population are achieving at levels that are less than expected?
- What is causing the lower-than-expected rates of achievement?
- What is the transiency rate of students? How does it compare with transiency rates 10 and 20 years ago?
- What relationship, if any, exists between students' English language proficiency and their success in school?
- Which areas of the present school curriculum are of most benefit to Elmwood's students? Which are of least benefit?
- Would Elmwood students profit from instructional procedures different from those presently used?
- What are Elmwood students' thoughts about school and its value?
- What are the students' major concerns about school? What are their parents' major concerns about school?
- How well do students of various ethnic groups interact and get along with each other?
- What might be done to improve ethnic and racial relations?
- What are Elmwood students' lives like outside of school?

Positing such questions is an important first step in addressing Elmwood's concerns. But having done that, how does one go about finding answers to the dozens or hundreds of such questions that might be asked about Elmwood schools, students, and the broader community?

SEEKING ANSWERS TO QUESTIONS

Whenever pressing questions arise, human nature prompts us to try to find answers as quickly as possible, and the sources we usually consult first are those most convenient to us—tradition, authority, and common sense. *Tradition* refers to how we collectively have judged, reasoned, and behaved in the past. Elmwood school personnel remember that the district's curriculum was considered to be exemplary many years ago, well delivered and well received. Tradition, therefore, tells them that the Elmwood curriculum needs no change, that something else must be at fault. This answer may possibly be correct, but present concerns suggest strongly that while the curriculum was effective in the past, it is no longer meeting the needs of Elmwood students.

When tradition fails to provide a suitable answer, we look next to *authority,* seeking the opinions of insightful experts who, we hope, know what is best. This source remains popular. Witness the variety of bandwagons schools have jumped onto—and almost as quickly off of—as new problems arise in the schools. Elmwood district officials would almost certainly look to school districts in Los Angeles, Atlanta, New York, Miami, or elsewhere in hopes of finding answers to its problems. But Elmwood may find that Atlanta recommends one solution, while Chicago recommends another that is entirely different. Chances are that because no other urban area is closely similar to Elmwood, recommendations from elsewhere will not prove satisfactory.

With authoritative answers plentiful but not particularly helpful, Elmwood school personnel may decide to work things out for themselves, using a *commonsense* approach. Although human reason can be formidable, as evidenced by incredible accomplishments in technology and culture, it is clear that common sense also misses the mark regularly, as is equally evident from the social and economic difficulties in which we find ourselves. Good reasoning is dependent on reliable information. Without that, it is subject to serious error. Unfortunately, Elmwood personnel do not presently seem to have the reliable information needed for making sound educational decisions.

So after all is said and done, Elmwood district's council will probably find that no matter where it turns for help, sooner or later it will have to find its own solutions to its pressing problems. It will have to identify the specific concerns it wishes to address, formulate and clarify the questions it wants answered, obtain reliable information for answering those questions, and based on those answers, determine the changes that may, and may not, be needed.

But how can reliable information be obtained? Life swamps us with information, most of it irrelevant to our concerns. Of the information that interests us, a great portion comes from media whose stock in trade is the sensational. Much also comes from people and organizations with axes to grind and agendas to advance. No small amount comes from our own personal experience, which is sometimes objective and useful, but not always so. With information from these readily available sources, almost everyone in make-believe Elmwood has already formed conclusions about Elmwood schools—what is good and bad about them, what the students and teachers are like, what is wrong with the curriculum, what is holding students back, and why the entire enterprise is better or worse than it used to be. But in the absence of reliable, objective information, citizens' conclusions may or may not be correct.

The crucial task for Elmwood then—and coincidentally for any person or group intending to conduct research—is to obtain information that is reliable and valid. This is best accomplished by using what is called the *scientific method*.

THE SCIENTIFIC METHOD

Today we take for granted a level of comfort and convenience undreamed of only a few decades ago. We are among the best-fed, best-clothed, best-housed, and healthiest people the world has ever known. Exchange of information occurs with speed and accuracy beyond belief. Mobility is such that any part of the earth can be reached within hours. These advances in health and technology have been brought about through use of the scientific method of thinking.

The **scientific method** is a specific strategy used to answer questions and resolve problems. Essentially, it focuses on discovering valid facts and relationships. We should note that the term *fact* does not mean the same thing as truth. Facts are not immutable; they are merely agreements concerning observations made by impartial people who are judged to be competent to observe. For example, if competent people measure the heights of the players on Elmwood High School's basketball team and find the average height to be six feet two inches, then that average height is considered to be a fact. However, if two new players enroll who are each seven feet tall, the previous average will no longer be fact; a new fact will replace it. The key point is that fact depends on observation and, when possible, accurate measurement. Fact is not established through speculation, hunch, or inner vision.

Facts by themselves can often help us understand conditions and events. If we desire to know what Elmwood's schools, curricula, teachers, and students were like 100 years ago, we can uncover a great number of facts that allow us to piece together a fairly accurate picture. But facts in and of themselves do not always provide answers to questions that intrigue us. It may be necessary to go further and search for relationships among various facts. We may wish to know, for example, why certain groups of students continually outdo other groups in achievement. To answer this question we seek out cause–effect relationships, such as traits or conditions (the cause) that produce higher or lower scholastic achievement (the effect). Or we may want to know how we can organize and implement an effective race-relations program in Elmwood schools. Here we seek out means–end relationships; knowing the desired end (improved relationships among various groups), we seek the means to bring it about.

Relationships among facts—the most powerful quality of science—give us the ability to predict, control, and even change human behavior and aspects of the world in which we live. If we can determine how traditional ethnic group values correlate with student behavior, we can *predict* with some accuracy how certain students are likely to behave in school. If we can determine that a new discipline system causes students to exhibit higher incidence of positive behavior, we can *control* the amount of disruptive classroom behavior, thus allowing students to gain more from their educational experience. And if we determine that students learn better when taught by a new instructional approach, we can teach in ways that permanently *change* (in this case increase) the amount of student learning.

The discovery of such valuable relationships is more likely to occur when the scientific method of thinking and problem solving is used. What is this method? In 1938, the American philosopher John Dewey described his concept of the scientific method, depicting it as a procedure for thinking more objectively. He presented the procedure as a series of steps, shown in the following list. As you will see later, these steps parallel the procedures followed in conducting research.

1. Clarify the main question inherent in the problem.
2. State a hypothesis (a possible answer to the question).
3. Collect, analyze, and interpret information related to the question and hypothesis.
4. Form conclusions derived from the information analyzed.
5. Use the conclusions to verify or reject the hypothesis.

Although Dewey's popularization of the scientific method has helped us think more productively, it would be misleading to suggest that researchers always follow the steps he described exactly. Many research problems are simply interesting questions that nag at people's minds and can be answered without using a hypothesis (Dewey's step 2). Collecting, analyzing, and interpreting data (Dewey's step 3) is always done in research, but sometimes may be the first or second step taken rather than the third. Such could be the case if someone had an interest in the life of Elmwood's first superintendent of schools and, after finding out a good deal about him or her, decided to do further research into that person's life. Despite exceptions such as these—and they are numerous—Dewey's scientific method remains useful both in conducting research and in helping neophytes understand the research process.

RESEARCH AND THE SCIENTIFIC METHOD

How closely does the research process mirror the scientific method, and why does it follow the scientific method at all? To understand the relationship between research process and scientific method, let us explore more closely the nature of research and how it is done.

THE MEANING OF RESEARCH

The word **research** comes from the French *rechercher* ("to search after or to investigate") and is defined as "a careful, systematic, patient investigation undertaken to discover or establish facts and relationships." We would do well to remember the words *careful, systematic,* and *patient investigation,* because they emphasize that research is more than a hurried process of looking up information in reference books. Research is called for when one is confronted with a question or problem that has no readily available answer. One must obtain information and make sense of it in order to answer the problematic question.

Many topics of great human interest can be explored scientifically, but others cannot. In **scientific research,** information is obtained by using the senses to observe objects and events. Not all topics can be investigated in this manner. For example, scientific research is of little value in exploring the major questions in philosophy, religion, and ethics. Such questions as, What is truth? What is the nature of God? and How should people treat each other? are certainly explored vigorously, but as they cannot be approached through impartial observation, they cannot be investigated scientifically.

Exercise 1.1

To what extent do you believe the following activities involve a careful, systematic process? Indicate (H) high, (M) medium, or (L) low for each activity.

_____ **1.** Finding the year in which Elmwood Urban School District was established

_____ **2.** Preparing student achievement profiles for the nation's 10 largest urban school districts

_____ **3.** Identifying the ethnic group affiliations of 100 students randomly selected from Elmwood schools

_____ **4.** Describing the daily lives of 10 randomly selected students from Elmwood schools

_____ **5.** Developing instructional activities that best promote achievement in Elmwood's high school students

THE PROCESS OF EDUCATIONAL RESEARCH

myeducationlab for research

To check your understanding of terminology related to educational research, go to the "Introduction to Educational Research" section of **MyEducationLab for Research** and then click on *Assignments and Activities*. Complete the exercise titled "Defining Key Terms."

Educational research is typically carried out in a manner using the following steps. (Note the parallel with Dewey's scientific method.)

A Concern Exists

A concern is identified for which there is no ready answer. The concern may have arisen because of a need, an interest, a requirement, or a commissioned work, and may have been present for a long time or may have arisen unexpectedly. For example, Elmwood educators have identified a disturbing pattern of academic achievement in Elmwood schools—students from certain ethnic groups seem to progress more rapidly than others, despite the educators' efforts to provide equal educational opportunity for all.

The Concern Is Addressed

After being identified, the concern is addressed by the following procedure:

Step 1.   The concern is clarified and stated succinctly, after which it becomes known as the **research problem.** In large-scale research, as would be called for in Elmwood schools, a number of smaller, more manageable concerns are also clarified. All told, a number of problems may be identified for research.

Step 2.   One or more main **research questions** are posed to guide an investigation into each of the problems. If the use of research questions is not appropriate, one or more **hypotheses** may be stated for each problem. Often an investigation makes use of both research questions and hypotheses. Research questions indicate what the researcher actually hopes to determine—for example, What are the achievement levels in 10th-grade English and algebra among students whose primary affiliations are in the following ethnic groups: (group names are stated)?

Hypotheses differ from research questions in that hypotheses are statements that can be tested statistically. Often they do not indicate what the researcher truly expects to find. The following statement is an example of a hypothesis: No differences exist in the average achievement levels in 10th-grade English and algebra among students whose primary ethnic affiliations are as follows: (groups are named).

Both research questions and hypotheses are useful in orienting research, and both receive additional attention in subsequent chapters.

Step 3.   When research questions or hypotheses have been stated, information (referred to as **data**) pertinent to them is sought from various sources such as people, records, physical objects, environments, social settings, journal articles, books, and other printed materials.

Step 4.   As data are accumulated, they are summarized, organized, and analyzed. Statistical treatments are normally used to analyze numerical data, whereas verbal logic is used to analyze narrative data. (These analytical procedures are introduced in Chapters 7 and 10 through 16 and are more fully developed in the Appendix.) The steps taken to obtain, summarize, organize, and analyze information are called the **procedures** of the study. Once data are analyzed, they are presented as the **findings** of the study.

Step 5.   When the findings have been stated, researchers endeavor to interpret the meanings of those findings in terms of the original research questions or hypotheses. The interpretations they finally make are called the **conclusions** of the study.

In summary, the research process usually includes the following activities:

- Identifying the matter about which concern exists
- Clarifying the specific problem on which the research will center
- Formulating research questions or hypotheses concerning the central problem
- Carrying out procedures by which data are collected, summarized, and analyzed
- Stating the findings determined through data analysis
- Drawing conclusions related to the original research questions or hypotheses

But let us remember that in practice these phases do not always occur so neatly as this summary might suggest, nor are they always accomplished in the sequence shown.

Exercise 1.2

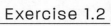

José Gomes investigated the reading achievement of seventh-grade Vietnamese, Cambodian, Korean, and Filipino students who had been in the United States for four years or less. Identify each of the following from his research as (P) problem, (Q) research question, (H) hypothesis, (PR) procedure, (F) finding, or (C) conclusion.

 1. The mean raw score for Korean students was 78.7.

2. Average achievement for Korean students was two months above grade level.

 3. Twenty-five students were randomly selected from each ethnic group.

4. The purpose of this study was to investigate comparative reading achievement of seventh-grade students from selected ethnic groups.

 5. A two-year average difference was found between the highest-achieving and the lowest-achieving group.

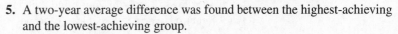

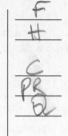

6. Average performance in reading was above the level anticipated.

7. No difference exists in reading achievement among seventh-grade students of selected ethnic groups.

8. The hypothesis was rejected.

9. The median test scores are shown in Table 23.

10. What differences, if any, exist in reading achievement among seventh-grade students of Vietnamese, Cambodian, Filipino, and Korean descent who have been in the United States for four years or less?

RESEARCH AND EDUCATIONAL RESEARCH

To this point, the terms *research* and *educational research* have been used interchangeably. Scientific research follows the same general process regardless of the discipline in which it is employed, whether in biology, astronomy, forestry, sociology, psychology, education, or elsewhere. Educational research is, therefore, simply scientific research applied to educational matters. As previously noted, for research to be considered scientific, its data must come from the observation of objects and events, and those same observational opportunities must be accessible to all interested individuals.

How can the scientific method be used to address the concerns about Elmwood schools? Suppose Elmwood wants to identify the student population groups whose scholastic achievement is lagging and then pinpoint the causes of low achievement, so that groups in need can be better served. Using a scientific approach, one must obtain reliable information for establishing pertinent facts, such as by administering achievement tests to students, in conjunction with interviewing them and observing their behavior. Once data are collected and facts established, relationships can be explored—in particular, causative relationships that might indicate factors responsible for the low achievement of certain groups. This search for relationships might lead one to consider language proficiency, work expectations outside the home, and the value students and parents place on education. All could be explored objectively.

RULES OF OPERATION IN EDUCATIONAL RESEARCH

The research process, though it can occur in a rambling manner, is best done systematically by following certain operating rules. As we proceed, we will see that by following these rules, researchers can credibly obtain reliable information from which to draw valid conclusions. We will see, further, that the rules are neither obscure nor difficult to follow. Before we examine the operating rules of research, let us be mindful of what R. S. Peters wrote regarding educational research in *The Philosophy of Education* (1973):

> There must be respect for evidence and a ban on "cooking" or distorting it; there must be a willingness to admit that one is mistaken. . . . To learn science is not just to learn facts and to understand theories; it is also to participate in a public form of life governed by such principles of procedure. (p. 25)

Peters's words help explain why the **operating rules of research** are emphasized so strongly. You would do well to think of these 13 rules as laws to be followed scrupulously. Indeed, two of them actually are law. Before progressing beyond this chapter, you should fix these rules so firmly in your mind that any violation of them will immediately raise a flag of caution. The 13 rules have to do with protection of people involved, maintaining participant confidentiality, beneficence, honesty, accurate disclosure, significance of the

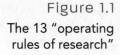

Figure 1.1

The 13 "operating rules of research"

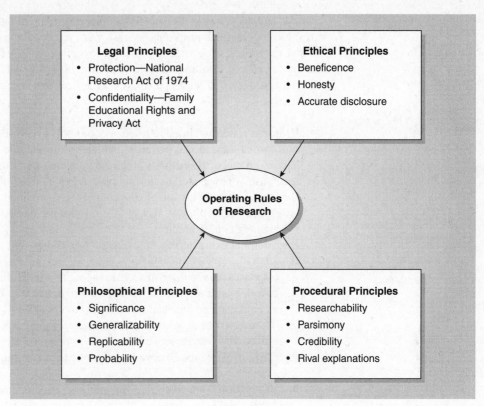

research, generalizability, replicability, probability, researchability, parsimony, credibility, and rival explanations. We can think of these rules as the guiding principles of research. For consideration here, the principles are grouped into four categories—legal, ethical, philosophical, and procedural, as summarized in Figure 1.1.

LEGAL PRINCIPLES

Legal requirements of protection and confidentiality are placed on research in which humans are used as **participants** (people being studied). Researchers may not violate these restrictions.

Rule 1: Protection

The National Research Act of 1974 ensured protection of individuals invited to participate in research studies. The **principle of protection** does not allow research to place individuals in physical danger, nor does it permit inquiry, without advised consent of the participants involved, into personal matters considered sensitive in nature. The intent of the law is to protect individuals against physical, mental, or emotional harm.

Rule 2: Confidentiality

The Family Educational Rights and Privacy Act (known as the Buckley Amendment), also passed in 1974, put into law the **principle of confidentiality.** Without express permission to the contrary, the anonymity of human research participants is to be maintained.

To ensure compliance with laws of protection and confidentiality, colleges and universities where research is conducted have established institutional review boards (sometimes referred to as "human subjects review boards") whose function is to examine proposed research and make sure participants' rights are not violated. The review board does not have to evaluate all research proposals because many, especially in education, pose no physical, mental, emotional, or degradational danger to participants. Specifically exempt by law from having to undergo institutional review (meaning it is all right to proceed without a review board's approval or at least approval of the full review board) are the following kinds of research:

1. Research conducted in established or commonly accepted educational settings, involving normal educational practices, which would include research on administration, classroom practices, methods of teaching, instructional strategies, classroom management, use of new materials, testing procedures, and the like

2. Research involving the use of educational tests, provided information from those tests is recorded in such a way that individuals are not named or readily identifiable (thus maintaining confidentiality)

3. Research involving survey or interview procedures, but such research is not allowed if
   a. Responses are recorded in such a manner that individual students can be identified
   b. A participant's responses could place him or her at risk of civil or criminal liability or could damage financial standing or employability
   c. The research deals with sensitive aspects of the participant's behavior, such as illegal conduct, drug use, sexual behavior, or use of alcohol

4. Research involving the observation of public behavior, but such research is not allowed if
   a. Observations are recorded in such a manner that individuals are readily identifiable
   b. Recorded information could put the participant at risk of civil or criminal liability or could damage his or her financial standing or employability
   c. The research deals with sensitive aspects of the participant's behavior, such as illegal conduct, drug use, sexual behavior, or use of alcohol

5. Research involving the collection or study of existing data, documents, records, pathological specimens, or diagnostic specimens, if these sources are publicly available or if the information is obtained in such a way that no potential risk is foreseen for individual participants

Most educational research topics fall within permissible areas, and the only legal prohibition to be observed is that of confidentiality. Graduate research topics therefore seldom have to be reviewed by the entire institutional review board. Oftentimes, even when sensitive topics such as drug use are proposed for investigation, the research will be allowed by the institutional review board if participants give their written consent.

If there is any question about the legality or ethics of proposed research, it is best to check with the institutional review committee or the institution's grants officer before proceeding.

ETHICAL PRINCIPLES

Ethics have to do with moral aspects of research. Although not stipulated in law, researchers must be scrupulously ethical if their work is to have credibility. Operating rules in this category relate to beneficence, honesty, and accurate disclosure.

Rule 3: Beneficence

The **principle of beneficence** indicates that educational research is done to garner knowledge and shed light on the human condition. It is never conducted as a means of doing harm to individuals or groups or to denigrate, cast blame, find fault, deny opportunity, or stifle

PEARSON
myeducationlab
for research

To apply your understanding of research ethics, go to the "Introduction to Educational Research" section of **MyEducationLab for Research** and then click on *Building Research Skills*. First, read the articles authored by Hamre and Pianta and by Wolcott, and then complete the exercise titled "Understanding Research Ethics."

progress. The researcher's aim is always to increase understanding and, where possible, to promote opportunity and advancement for the population at large.

Rule 4: Honesty

The **principle of honesty** is absolutely essential in the research process. This is such an obvious requirement that it might seem unnecessary to mention it. However, with dismaying frequency we hear of important research data being "fixed" to yield findings the researcher had hoped for or else suppressed because they contradicted what was desired. Such dishonest manipulation of data is inexcusable and renders the research meaningless or dangerously misleading.

Occasionally bona fide researchers risk loss of reputation and career by tampering with data. This shows how high the stakes can be in certain research, especially when large grants of money or questions of career advancement are involved. The temptation to alter data may even arise in research at the graduate level. That temptation, if experienced, must be put aside without hesitation.

Once the process of data collection is under way, data should be reported exactly as obtained; no data are to be suppressed, no alterations made in them, and no exceptions made in the procedures by which they are collected. If for any reason these stipulations cannot be followed, the entire research process should be terminated and replanned.

Rule 5: Accurate Disclosure

The **principle of accurate disclosure** indicates that individuals selected to serve as participants in research must be informed accurately about the general topic of research and any unusual procedures or tasks in which they will be involved. They should receive assurance that their names will be kept confidential and that they will not be subjected to unusual discomfort or risk. In school research that involves entire classes, it is sufficient to inform (and obtain permission from) the head administrator rather than the students. If the research involves an unusual procedure, teaching method, set of materials, or the like, it may sometimes be necessary to obtain written consent from the students' parents and from the governing board of the school district.

Note that accurate disclosure does not mean full disclosure. Full disclosure would provide participants with all the details of the research, which might introduce the possibility of error that would render the research invalid. For example, one group of participants might, because of information they receive, try harder than another, or believe they are superior or inferior and behave accordingly, or think they are receiving special treatment, good or bad, that is not being given to other groups. As a result, the research findings might differ from what would otherwise have been the case. For that reason, researchers try to provide equally to all participants knowledge of the topic, any importance, and any general requirements.

Following these guidelines, if one wanted to investigate the relative effects of two different sets of materials in teaching composition to high school students whose English capability is below national norms, accurate disclosure might be akin to the following: "We are going to investigate two different sets of instructional materials to see which works better for the students in our schools. Both sets of materials are considered to be good and are published by reputable companies. You will not undergo any unusual activities or testing procedures, and you will be under no risk of harm whatsoever. Your names will be kept strictly confidential."

Figure 1.2 shows an example of a cover letter that accompanied a survey as part of a research study. Notice that, at a minimum, the letter addresses the principles of protection, confidentiality, beneficence, and accurate disclosure.

Related to the concept of accurate disclosure are the notions of assent and consent. Once potential research subjects have been informed of the nature of their participation in a research study, they must agree to participate. As you saw in Figure 1.2, this is relatively straightforward in the case of survey research. Individuals who want to participate simply

Figure 1.2

Sample cover letter demonstrating adherence to crucial principles of research

Purpose of the study

Accurate disclosure

Anonymity, confidentiality, honesty

Protection

Dear Ohio Teacher,

I am currently conducting a Web-based survey research study titled "**Teachers' Perceptions of the Influence of No Child Left Behind on Instructional and Assessment Practices,**" the purpose of which is examine how (or if) NCLB has affected the ways in which teachers assess the academic learning of their students.

Your superintendent has granted approval for teachers in your district to participate in the study as one of 150 randomly selected school districts in Ohio. The purpose of this e-mail message is to ask for your participation in the study. I am asking you to participate in the study by simply completing the survey as honestly and openly as you can. The survey should only take about 10–15 minutes to complete. When you have completed the survey, simply click on the **SUBMIT** button located at the bottom of the page to send your responses to me. Please make sure you submit your responses only once! Additionally, please complete the survey by **September 30, 2005.**

Please be assured that your responses will be anonymous. There will be no way for me to determine the origin of your responses. You will not be contacted for any further information. No one other than you will know if you have or have not participated in this study. Additionally, no individual information will be shared; only aggregate results will be reported. Finally, due to the Web-based nature of the survey, there exists a minimal chance that your responses could be intercepted by individuals not involved with this study while being transmitted.

Your participation in this study is voluntary. By completing and submitting the survey, you are giving your consent to participate. Please be assured that your decision to participate or not participate in this study will have no impact on your relationship with your respective school district. If you do not wish to participate, simply disregard this message. If you have any questions regarding this survey study, I may be contacted at mertler@bgnet.bgsu .edu. You may also contact the Chair, Human Subjects Review Board, Bowling Green State University, (419) 372-7716 (hsrb@bgnet.bgsu.edu) if any problems or concerns arise during the course of the study.

I would like very much for you to participate in the study by completing the brief survey which can be found by clicking on the following link:

http://edhd.bgsu.edu/mertler/nclbsurveya.php

In advance, thank you very much for your participation in this research endeavor and best of luck in the remainder of your school year!

Best Regards,

Craig A. Mertler

Craig A. Mertler, Ph.D.
Associate Professor of Assessment and Research Methodologies

APPROVED – BGSU HSRB
EFFECTIVE 8/22/05
EXPIRES 8/14/06

complete the survey and return it. If not, they simply do not complete the survey. (In Figure 1.2, refer to the portion in the fourth paragraph that reads, "Your participation in this study is voluntary. By completing and submitting the survey, you are giving your consent to participate.") However, in other types of research (e.g., experimental, causal-comparative, correlation, and qualitative research), it is important to have potential subjects' agreement to participate *in writing.* This is known as **consent.** Adults (i.e., individuals over the age of 18) are provided a form that gives a complete description of their potential participation, similar to the survey research cover letter. However, they are then required to sign and date the form in order to formalize, and establish a record of, their agreement to participate in the study. In the case of minors (i.e., individuals under the age of 18), they must give their **assent.** The rationale for the difference in terminology is that adults are able to "consent" to participate in research (assuming they are not cognitively impaired), meaning that they can *decide for themselves* whether they want to participate. Children cannot legally give consent to participate in research; the parent or legal guardian must give permission for the child to participate. However, in addition, the researcher must have a procedure for securing the child's agreement, or assent, to participate.

Exercise 1.3

For each of the following, indicate the research operating rule(s) complied with or violated: (P) protection, (C) confidentiality, (B) beneficence, (H) honesty, or (AD) accurate disclosure.

 1. Jones's research assistant inadvertently mentioned the names of three high school students identified by Jones as alcohol abusers.

 2. Noting poor test performance by a bright student and realizing the performance did not reflect the student's ability, Jones changed the score to what he believed the student should have made.

 3. Jones informed the students, though not in detail, of the nature of the research in which they would be involved.

4. In the outdoor performance trials one of the participants succumbed to heat prostration and had to be hospitalized overnight.

PHILOSOPHICAL PRINCIPLES

Philosophical principles have to do with the anticipated value of a particular investigation as regards significance (importance), generalizability (findings applicable elsewhere), replicability (repeatable by others), and probability (the understanding that research findings are considered probabilities, not certainties).

Rule 6: Significance

The topic of any research other than that done purely for personal interest should be justified in terms of the **principle of significance**—that is, whether the research findings are likely to contribute to human knowledge or be useful elsewhere. Research, to be taken seriously, must show promise of being worth the time, effort, and expenditures entailed. This applies to research done in graduate degree programs as well. Graduate research topics are not acceptable if they are trivial or superficial or if their potential findings are likely to be inconsequential. It is the researcher's responsibility to justify the research under consideration. Ordinarily this can be done by pointing to the educational importance of a topic, establishing a need for information about it, and showing that the research has the potential to supply needed information.

Rule 7: Generalizability

The **principle of generalizability** means that the findings of research can be applied, or generalized, to other individuals and settings. For example, suppose an investigation is being done into the learning styles of Elmwood students who have immigrated to this country during the past two years from Central America. If the research is to have maximum value, the findings should do more than illuminate learning style patterns of the students in the sample; they should also promote an understanding of similar students attending schools elsewhere.

But how does one predict whether, or to what extent, research findings might be generalizable? Indications of potential generalizability can be forecast by analyzing the proposed research locale, participants involved, time required, and treatments and measurements used. But a far more valuable predictor of generalizability is the degree to which the sample of individuals being studied (e.g., 70 sixth-grade students in Elmwood) represents the larger population to which the sample belongs (e.g., 20,000 sixth-grade students nationwide). Close correspondence between sample and population is assumed when participants are randomly selected from the larger population. This does not guarantee but does vastly improve the likelihood that the sample is representative of the population. When that is not possible (as it would not be for students attending Elmwood schools, who are already there and are, thus, preselected), then participants are scrutinized to see if their socioeconomic status, language ability, gender, age, and background seem consistent with those of the larger population.

The principle of generalizability, although normally of great importance, does not apply in all research. Most types of qualitative research (as described in Chapters 2 and 10) are done to learn about a particular event or group of people at a particular place at a particular time. The purpose is to provide understanding, not to predict what might happen elsewhere. One might be able to discover what Elmwood's first school was like, but that information could not, without considerable support, be generalized to the historical development of school systems in other cities, whose populations might have been dissimilar in culture, religion, language, wealth, customs, and other traits.

Similarly, action research (described in Chapters 2 and 15) is by definition pertinent only to the solution of a particular problem in a particular place. It is not done to help resolve concerns in other locations, though in some instances it might do so. If Mr. Branca decides to develop and test a community awareness project for his students in high school civics, he does not do so with the thought that his efforts will be noted across the country. His concern is to find something that works for him and his students in Elmwood Lincoln High School.

Rule 8: Replicability

We often hear of new findings in medicine or physics or biology that have important implications for human well-being. Occasionally we later hear that those same findings have become suspect because other scientists, when repeating the original research, obtained different findings.

The **principle of replicability** requires that any research be repeatable, for that is a prime means of establishing credibility. Research is made replicable by keeping records of exactly what was done, and why, in each phase of the investigation. Another researcher who follows the same recipe ought to come up with the same results. If not, the original research should be strongly questioned. Educational research is not often replicated, but the anticipation that it might be should remind researchers to be circumspect in procedure and report.

Rule 9: Probability

Both beginning researchers and those who wish to make use of published research findings should understand the **principle of probability**—that educational research rarely turns up hard-and-fast answers to the questions it explores. Research, especially quantitative research, deals in probabilities, likelihoods, or the best answers among a variety of possibilities. *It almost never provides certainty.* This point will become clearer later when we consider statistical procedures for analyzing and interpreting data. Many of those procedures make reference to probability levels. A researcher might find, for example, that the average reading level of Latino students entering Elmwood's sixth-grade classes is "fifth year–eighth month, plus or minus three months." This finding would mean that while the average measured reading level was "fifth year–eighth month," potential errors inherent in sample selection and testing make it very unlikely that measurements will be absolutely accurate, and further, that the likely margin of error extends three months on each side of the "fifth year–eighth month" average.

Probability as related to data analysis is explained in detail in the Appendix. For the time being, remember that research conclusions hinge not on absolute certainty but on probability. For research findings to be taken seriously, there must be a very strong probability that if the research were repeated numerous times, the findings would almost always be approximately the same.

PROCEDURAL PRINCIPLES

Procedural rules of research pertain to the selection of researchable topics, parsimony (keeping everything as succinct as possible), credibility (ensuring believability), and acknowledgment that rival (alternative) explanations might be made for the study's findings.

Rule 10: Researchability

It is difficult for most graduate students to determine whether a topic that interests them is consistent with the **principle of researchability,** that is, whether it can be approached and resolved through established research procedures. A preliminary test of researchability includes four questions: (1) Can the scientific method be used to investigate the topic under consideration? (2) If the answer to the first question is no, can the topic be limited or reworded to make it researchable? (3) If the topic statement is, or can be made, approachable through the scientific method, is it possible to obtain required data? (4) Can the topic be investigated within existing constraints of time, facilities, distance, money, and other such practical matters? Let us consider each of these questions briefly.

Question Concerning Scientific Method. We have noted that science depends on reliable information. To what degree do you believe reliable information could be obtained for the following questions?

1. What are the grade point averages among students that comprise five different ethnic groups attending Elmwood's secondary schools?
2. Does spirituality affect student academic performance at the secondary school level?
3. What are the comparative effects of teaching spelling using two different methods at the third-grade level?
4. To what extent are students' attitudes toward school affected by the value that their parents and grandparents have placed on education?

As you can see, reliable information could easily be obtained for questions 1 and 3 but not for question 2 (because agreement could not be reached concerning the existence, definition, or measurement of spirituality, which is not to say that spirituality does not exist). Question 4 presents nearly insurmountable difficulties, in that it would be next to impossible to obtain reliable information about the extent to which a given group of parents and grandparents might value education. Questions 1 and 3 would, therefore, be considered researchable, whereas questions 2 and 4 would not.

Question Concerning Rewording the Topic.   Topics that are not researchable can often be reworded to make them researchable. Consider question 2. If the researcher restated the question as follows, it would easily be researchable: "What is the relationship between school achievement and frequency of church attendance among students at the secondary level?" Both achievement and church attendance could be determined objectively, making the topic approachable through the scientific method. However, frequency of church attendance can hardly be considered synonymous with spirituality, if that is what the researcher wants to explore.

Question Concerning Availability of Data.   Even when research topics can be stated in a manner approachable through science, they may still be unresearchable because needed data are unavailable. Consider this question:

> To what extent is student compliance with teacher expectations related to the compliance levels displayed by parents of those students during the parents' own childhoods?

Levels of compliance shown by parents when they were children would be extremely difficult to ascertain.

Question Concerning Practicality.   Even when data are available for a topic, many practical matters can render the topic unresearchable. Consider this question:

> What is the relationship between patterns of behavioral compliance among first-grade students and the grade point averages of those same students when they graduate from high school?

This study could certainly be done, but only if one were willing to spend 12 years on it, hardly practical for most people.

Rule 11: Parsimony

In science the **principle of parsimony** holds that the simpler a theory is, the better it is, provided it adequately explains the phenomena involved. This simpler-is-better principle applies equally to research: Given a topic's guiding questions or hypotheses, the best research procedures are those that most *simply* and *efficiently* obtain necessary data and provide proper analysis. In research, more is not better. The principle of parsimony reminds us that research should be guided by questions or hypotheses stated as clearly and simply as possible. Only necessary data should be collected, and the process should be kept efficient. Data analysis should be to the point. Findings resulting from that analysis should be reported clearly and the conclusions stated succinctly. This is not to imply that research is a simple endeavor, or that all statements can be made in three-word sentences. Complexity is almost always present in research and its interpretation. Nevertheless, research should be kept as clear, simple, efficient, and to the point as conditions allow.

Rule 12: Credibility

It is an absolute waste of time to conduct research that, when completed, lacks credibility. Nothing is gained by doing so; in fact, much is lost. Fortunately, almost all research remains credible if it is conducted according to the established procedures of research, which help ensure significance, reliability, and validity.

The **principle of credibility** is established as follows: First, the topic selected must be significant and researchable. Second, the operating principles of research explored in this chapter must be followed. Third, reliable and valid data must be obtained (*reliable* means consistent, and *valid* means on target). Fourth, appropriate methods must be used to analyze the data. Fifth, findings must be supported by the data. And, sixth, conclusions related to research questions or hypotheses must be logically persuasive and reported clearly and accurately.

Rule 13: Rival Explanations

In some ways, reporting one's research is like throwing down a dare. Although not saying so in words, the researcher implies, "Here are my findings and my explanation of them; I dare you to find fault with what I say or come up with a better explanation." According to the **principle of rival explanations,** researchers should always anticipate that others will scrutinize their methods and make interpretations different from their own. For that reason, researchers should take measures to forestall criticism and other possible interpretations. This can be accomplished by following procedures properly, accounting for undesired influences (called *confounding variables*), analyzing data appropriately, pinpointing possible *bias,* and foreseeing and ruling out alternative interpretations. If alternate possibilities cannot be explained, they can be acknowledged in discussions of the findings. Ideally, investigators should feel complimented if their research attracts attention, but not if rival interpretations are clearly superior to their own. That would suggest they had not been meticulous in conducting, analyzing, and reporting their efforts.

Exercise 1.4

Indicate which research principles have been observed or violated in the following: (S) significance, (G) generalizability, (RE) replicability, (PR) probability, (RS) researchability, (PS) parsimony, (C) credibility, or (RV) rival explanations.

_____ **1.** For his master's thesis in education, Altamura wanted to study genealogical family roots in Italy.

_____ **2.** Professor Allen complimented Altamura's revised research plan as one of the most concise and direct she had ever seen.

_____ **3.** Norton wanted to repeat an earlier experiment on learning but found that the documentation available was insufficient.

_____ **4.** Professor Allen told Norton, "The differences you found could as easily have been due to motivation as to intelligence."

_____ **5.** Norton wrote, "The data firmly prove the existence of a full year's difference in achievement."

_____ **6.** Professor Allen determined that Norton's conclusions were not valid.

WHY STUDY EDUCATIONAL RESEARCH?

The act of studying and learning about the educational research process is valuable to the professional lives of educators, regardless of the setting in which you work. It is vitally important for educators at all levels to have a sound understanding of research methods for two basic reasons. First, at some point in your professional career, it may be highly beneficial for you to design and conduct, or otherwise become involved in, some sort of research study, as you will see in the next section. Second, having a foundational understanding of the research process enables you to be a more discriminating consumer of published research studies, helping you identify a particular study's strengths and weaknesses and determine the extent to which its findings may, or may not, apply to your setting.

Additionally, there are several common purposes—or *practical applications,* if you will—for studying educational research, including, but not limited to, the following:

- Writing grant proposals (including their evaluation components)
- Completing theses and dissertations

- Reading primary and secondary sources more critically
- Reviewing professional literature as a means of thinking more critically, and possibly more reflectively, about issues and problems related to your setting (e.g., your classroom or your students)
- Conducting more formal research projects

These are just a few of the ways in which studying educational research can inform your professional practice.

EDUCATORS AS RESEARCHERS

You may be wondering, in view of the requirements and rules considered so far, whether genuine research can be carried out by educators, and if so, whether such research can shed light on topics of educational concern. Rest assured that educators can, even while busy on the job, do research of quality and importance. Indeed, it is now considered that practical inquiry undertaken by educators is more likely to lead to classroom change than formal research conducted by research specialists (Richardson, 1994). In truth, educators have rarely found traditional educational research to be of much practical use (Foshay, 1994); they prefer action research into matters directly related to their work. Radebaugh (1994) contends that educational research should not be left to experts but should involve educators much more extensively; educator-conducted research is especially powerful in shedding light on topics such as educators' personal and professional lives and the problems educators regularly encounter in their work (Fleischer, 1994; Goodson, 1994). A considerable measure of recent opinion proposes that teaching should, itself, be viewed as ongoing action research, where teachers routinely raise questions about their work with learners, collect data, interpret it, and share their conclusions with fellow teachers (Cochran-Smith, 1995).

Educators have shown an aversion to doing more formalized educational research, considering it unrealistically esoteric, especially regarding statistical analysis and hypothesis testing. With today's desktop computers, statistical computation is no longer a concern. Moreover, Ornstein (1995) points out that newer concepts of research into teaching rely on storytelling, narrative, autobiography, language, and dialogue, all of which affirm the wisdom of teachers while allowing them to share their knowledge using ordinary language. Flake, Kuhs, Donnelly, and Ebert (1995) explain that, when compared to research conducted in universities, research based on educational practice is usually the more meaningful—the questions addressed are more appropriate to education, the investigations more straightforward, and the findings more valid for school practice.

Thus, be assured that not only can you involve yourself successfully in meaningful educational research, it is likely that any investigation you conduct will be more beneficial than formal research to your work in education and probably more beneficial to other educators as well. You may even wish to involve your students as coresearchers in your investigations, which seems to help them take more ownership for their learning (Pearson & Santa, 1995).

DEVELOPMENTAL ACTIVITY

Guiding Principles of Research

A common project for students enrolled in a research methods course is to develop their own research proposals or final research reports. Integrated throughout Chapters 1 through 9 are "developmental activities" designed to help you navigate the stages in formulating a research proposal. These activities follow the overarching theme of research proposal development, focusing on various aspects of research you must consider and strategic decisions you must make when planning a research study of your own design. Furthermore, these activities are intended to lead you step-by-step through the process, as demonstrated by the following list of topics addressed in each chapter.

- Chapter 1—Guiding Principles of Research
- Chapter 2—Type of Research
- Chapter 3—Research Topic Refinement
- Chapter 4—Locating Published Research
- Chapter 5—Reviewing Published Research
- Chapter 6—Data Collection Decisions
- Chapter 7—Statistical Analysis Decisions
- Chapter 8—Planning for Your Research
- Chapter 9—Preparing to Write Your Report

In this chapter you read about the 13 guiding principles for research. Although important considerations during all phases of a study, they are probably most important during the planning stages and actual development of your proposal. In the early stages of developing a research proposal, the budding researcher begins by considering a general topic and then gives thought to various related principles. Respond to the following issues to help you with these considerations.

1. A possible topic or problem I am thinking of researching

   _____

2. Potential harm to participants in my study

   _____

3. My proposal for resolving these potential sources of harm

   _____

4. Potential violations of confidentiality

   _____

5. My proposal to address these potential violations

   _____

6. My methodology for adhering to the *ethical* principles

   _____

7. Ways to maintain the *philosophical* principles

   _____

8. Ways to adhere to the *procedural* principles

   _____

9. Reason my proposed topic for research is or is not eligible for "exempt" status

   _____
   _____

CHAPTER SUMMARY

Educational research, a careful, systematic, patient investigation, leads to new knowledge through use of the scientific method, which involves clarifying a problem, formulating research questions or hypotheses, obtaining pertinent information, analyzing data, describing the findings, and drawing conclusions that answer the questions or test the hypotheses. Rather strict operating procedures are followed in scientific investigations to ensure that participants are protected, information is reliable,

data are analyzed properly and reported accurately, and findings and conclusions are persuasively drawn from the data.

Several operating principles orient the research process, including (1) the legal principles of participant protection and confidentiality; (2) the ethical principles of beneficence, honesty, and accurate disclosure to participants; (3) the philosophical principles of significance, generalizability, replicability, and probability; and (4) the procedural principles of researchability, parsimony, credibility, and rival explanations.

Traditionally, educators have been reluctant to involve themselves in educational research, believing it to require sophisticated skills that only highly trained professional researchers possess. That view has changed dramatically in recent years. Educators can and do conduct research into meaningful educational topics. Research design and data analysis and interpretation no longer present obstacles. Not only can educators successfully conduct research, but also the findings they make are often of great value, both to themselves and to fellow educators.

LIST OF IMPORTANT TERMS

assent	principle of beneficence	principle of rival explanations
conclusions	principle of confidentiality	principle of significance
consent	principle of credibility	procedures
data	principle of generalizability	research
educational research	principle of honesty	research problem
findings	principle of parsimony	research question
hypothesis	principle of probability	scientific method
operating rules of research	principle of protection	scientific research
participants	principle of replicability	
principle of accurate disclosure	principle of researchability	

YOUR CURRENT STATUS

You now have a preliminary understanding of the nature of educational research. You recognize the general tasks involved in conducting research, the major characteristics of the scientific method, and the operating principles researchers are expected to follow. You are now ready to examine the sources of data used in educational research. Before proceeding to that topic in Chapter 2, try your hand at the following activities presented for thought and discussion.

ACTIVITIES FOR THOUGHT AND DISCUSSION

1. Here once more are the questions presented at the beginning of the chapter. Check yourself to see how well you can answer them.
   a. What sources of information do people usually consult first for answers to difficult questions? Why are those first sources of information often of so little value?
   b. What is meant by scientific method?
   c. What is research? How is educational research similar to and different from research in the natural sciences?
   d. What is the general procedure by which research is done?
   e. What are the legal, ethical, philosophical, and procedural operating rules for conducting educational research? What is an example of each?
   f. Why should the operating rules of educational research be thought of as unwritten law?

2. Recall or turn to the chapter information organizer presented at the beginning of the chapter. Without looking in the chapter, explain briefly what you now understand about each item in the organizer.
3. Suppose you wanted to investigate the effects of two different methods of teaching reading to third-grade students. How would you comply with the principles of (a) accurate disclosure, (b) significance, (c) replicability, and (d) rival explanations?
4. Suppose you wanted to investigate the after-school activities of adolescent students from various ethnic groups. How would you comply with the principles of (a) protection, (b) confidentiality, (c) beneficence, (d) significance, and (e) credibility?
5. In terms of intent, procedure, and results, compare science with a nonscientific endeavor such as philosophy or religion.

ANSWERS TO CHAPTER EXERCISES

1.1. 1. L 2. M 3. L 4. H 5. H

1.2. 1. F 2. F/C 3. PR 4. P 5. F 6. F/C 7. H/C 8. C
9. F 10. Q

1.3. 1. C 2. H 3. AD 4. P

1.4. 1. S/G 2. PS 3. RE 4. RV 5. PR 6. C

REFERENCES AND RECOMMENDED READINGS

Akers, W., & Schubert, W. (1992). Do the right thing: Ethical issues and problems in the conduct of qualitative research in the classroom. *Teaching and Learning, 6*(2), 19–24.

Best, J., & Kahn, J. (2006). *Research in Education* (10th ed.). Boston: Allyn & Bacon.

Cochran-Smith, M. (1995). Color blindness and basket making are not the answers: Confronting the dilemmas of race, culture, and language diversity in teacher education. *American Educational Research Journal, 32,* 493–522.

Dewey, J. (1933). *How We Think.* Boston: Raytheon Education.

Dewey, J. (1938). *Logic: The Theory of Inquiry.* New York: Holt, Rinehart, & Winston.

Family Educational Rights and Privacy Act of 1974. Washington, DC: Family Educational Rights and Privacy Office.

Feigl, H., & Broadneck, M. (1953). *Readings in the Philosophy of Science.* New York: Appleton-Century-Crofts.

Flake, C., Kuhs, T., Donnelly, A., & Ebert, C. (1995). Teacher as researcher: Reinventing the role of teacher. *Phi Delta Kappan, 76,* 405–407.

Fleischer, C. (1994). Researching teacher-research: A practitioner's retrospective. *English Education, 26,* 86–126.

Foshay, A. (1994). Action research: An early history in the United States. *Journal of Curriculum and Supervision, 9,* 317–325.

Gall, M., Borg, W., & Gall, J. (2003). *Educational Research: An Introduction* (7th ed.). Boston: Allyn & Bacon.

Goodson, I. (1994). Studying the teacher's life and work. *Teaching and Teacher Education, 10,* 29–37.

Krathwohl, D. (1994). A slice of advice. *Educational Researcher, 23,* 29–32, 42.

Lederman, N. (1992). Students' and teachers' conceptions of the nature of science: A review of the research. *Journal of Research in Science Teaching, 29,* 331–359.

McMillan, J. (2004). *Educational Research: Fundamentals for the Consumer* (4th ed.). Boston: Allyn & Bacon.

McMillan, J., & Schumacher, S. (2006). *Research in Education: Evidence Based Inquiry* (6th ed.). Boston: Allyn & Bacon.

National Research Act of 1974. Bethesda, MD: National Commission for the Protection of Human Subjects.

Ornstein, A. (1995). The new paradigm in research on teaching. *Educational Forum, 59,* 124–129.

Padak, N., & Padak, G. (1995). *Guidelines for Planning Action Research Projects: Research to Practice.* Kent: Ohio Literacy Resource Center.

Pearson, J., & Santa, C. (1995). Students as researchers of their own learning. *Journal of Reading, 38,* 462–469.

Peters, R. S. (1973). Aims of education—a conceptual inquiry. In R. S. Peters (Ed.), *The Philosophy of Education* (pp. 11–29). London: Oxford University Press.

Radebaugh, B. (1994). Democratizing educational research or why is our nation still at risk after ten years of educational reform? *Thresholds in Education, 20*(2–3), 18–21.

Reichardt, C. (1992). The fallibility of our judgments. *Evaluation Practice, 13,* 157–163.

Richardson, V. (1994). Conducting research on practice. *Educational Researcher, 23*(5), 5–10.

Strometz, D., & Skleder, A. (1992). The use of role-play in teaching research ethics: A validation study. *Teaching of Psychology, 19,* 106–108.

Types of Educational Research and Corresponding Sources of Data

PREVIEW

This chapter introduces the principal types of educational research, differentiated on the basis of the following:

- Usefulness
- Research tradition and methodology
- Questions addressed
- Practicality

Differentiated in terms of its immediate usefulness, research can be categorized two ways:

- Basic research
- Applied research

Differentiated in terms of methodology used, as defined by tradition, research is classified as one of the following:

- Qualitative research
- Quantitative research

Those classifications can be further broken down as follows:

- Experimental research
- Nonexperimental research

Differentiated in terms of methodology used, as defined by the questions addressed, research can take many forms, including the following:

- Ethnographic research
- Narrative research
- Survey research
- Correlational research
- Causal-comparative research

Differentiated in terms of practicality, research is identified as one of the following:

- Action research
- Evaluation research

The chapter also explains three elements of data collection:

- Sources of data
- Procedures in obtaining data
- Types of data

TARGETED LEARNINGS

This chapter introduces the principal types of educational research—two types differentiated on the basis of *usefulness*, four differentiated on the basis of the *research methodology employed*, several on the basis of the *research questions addressed* (which are explored in detail in Chapters 10 through 15), and two differentiated on the basis of *practicality*. The data sources, data characteristics, and procedures of each type of research are examined. Finally, terminology important in understanding research procedures and data is presented and defined. As you read the chapter, look especially for information that answers the following questions:

1. How do the concepts of *usefulness, methodology, questions addressed,* and *practicality* serve to differentiate among types of educational research?
2. Describe various types of educational research whose methodology is determined by questions addressed.
3. What are the differences between *primary* and *secondary* data sources? Which, if either, is more valued in research?
4. What are the seven procedures commonly used in obtaining data?
5. What is meant by the terms *external criticism, internal criticism, reliability,* and *validity*?

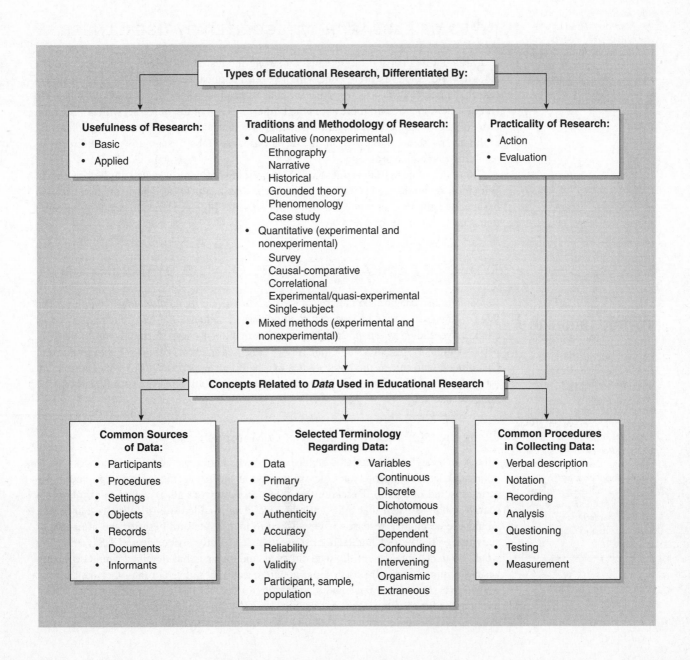

In Chapter 1 we saw that the purpose of educational research is to help find answers to perplexing questions that have no immediate solutions and that those answers often lead to improvements in education. We saw that research employs scientific procedures for obtaining valid information, clarifying facts, and exploring relationships among those facts. We saw further that educators can, and often do, conduct research within their institutional settings.

TYPES OF EDUCATIONAL RESEARCH

PEARSON
myeducationlab)
for research

To check the development of your understanding of terminology related to educational research, revisit the "Introduction to Educational Research" section of **MyEducationLab for Research** and then click on *Assignments and Activities.* Complete the exercise titled "Defining Key Terms."

Research is categorized in a number of ways. Best and Kahn (2006) note that various writers present their own systems of categorization, which indicates the absence of a standardized classification scheme. In this book, types of research will be differentiated according to (1) whether the research is done with immediate usefulness in mind, (2) the traditional, overall methodology employed, and (3) the practicality of the research.

TYPES OF RESEARCH CATEGORIZED BY USEFULNESS

Research is often carried out to satisfy a strong interest about people, practices, and the natural world. Such research, done with no useful application in mind, is called **basic research.** This type of research is done to satisfy a need to know, just as researchers use the Hubble telescope to learn more about the farthest reaches of the universe, with no intention of resolving an immediate social or personal problem. Basic research is often conducted in the natural sciences but seldom in education, where most research is aimed directly at resolving immediate problems.

Research done to find useful solutions to pressing problems is called **applied research.** With few exceptions, this is the type of research done in education. The distinction between basic and applied research is informative but provides little guidance in selecting research topics or designing research.

TYPES OF RESEARCH DIFFERENTIATED BY TRADITION

PEARSON
myeducationlab)
for research

To check your understanding of the differences between qualitative and quantitative research, go to the "Introduction to Educational Research" section of **MyEducationLab for Research** and then click on *Building Research Skills.* First, read the articles authored by Hamre and Pianta and by Wolcott, and then complete the exercise titled "Recognizing the Characteristics of Quantitative and Qualitative Research."

Research is also categorized in terms of the *traditional general methodology* it employs. The three different categories of **research methods** used in educational research are *qualitative, quantitative,* and *mixed methods.* Any given investigation is characterized by one of these labels. Additionally, research studies are further classified as *experimental* or *nonexperimental.* Quantitative and mixed-methods studies can be either experimental or nonexperimental (or both). For reasons you will learn about later, a qualitative research study can only be nonexperimental.

Qualitative, Quantitative, and Mixed-Methods Research

All research can be differentiated on the basis of whether its methodology produces mostly numerical data (e.g., scores and measurements) or mostly narrative data (e.g., verbal descriptions and opinions). Research that relies on narrative data is called **qualitative research,** while research that relies on numerical data is called **quantitative research.** We would use qualitative research if we wished to investigate and describe the after-school activities of a group of high school students that recently arrived from El Salvador. We would try to document carefully who did what, and the data thus obtained would be mostly verbal, acquired through observation, notation, and recording. On the other hand, if we wished to assess the language and mathematics abilities of those same students, we would use quantitative research. We would administer tests that yield numerical scores we could analyze statistically. At times, qualitative and quantitative methods are used in the same

Table 2.1 Experimental Research		
Two Equal Groups	**Taught Differently**	**Results Compared**
Group A	Normal instruction	Achievement?
Group B	Computers used	Achievement?

study. Studies where it is appropriate to use both qualitative and quantitative methods are known as **mixed-methods research.**

Experimental and Nonexperimental Research

Though not often used in school settings because it disrupts normal groupings and teaching methods, **experimental research** can, more persuasively than any other type of research, show cause–effect relationships. It is this knowledge of cause and effect that enables us to predict and control events. The classical methodology of experimental research is as follows: Two or more groups are selected at random from a large population. Those groups, say, group A and group B, are given different treatments. Group A might receive normal instruction while group B receives instruction that involves extensive use of computers. After a time, the two groups are tested to see whether differences in learning have occurred. If differences are found, they are said to be the *effect* of the new treatment, while the new treatment (use of computers) is considered to be the *cause.* This is commonly called a **cause–effect relationship.**

Experimental research is carefully designed to control the influence of all variables except those whose specific relationship is being explored (types of variables will be discussed later in Chapter 3). Experimental methods may be appropriately used in quantitative and mixed-methods research studies. Experimental research can be illustrated as in Table 2.1.

Nonexperimental research is used to (1) depict people, events, situations, conditions, and relationships as they currently exist or once existed; (2) evaluate products or processes; and (3) develop innovations. In these cases, experimentation is not appropriate or else is not used because the independent (causative) variables, such as gender or ethnicity, cannot be manipulated—that is, varied—by the researcher to see whether a resultant change is produced in the dependent variable. The average person equates scientific research with experimentation, a view that is often correct in the natural sciences. But in education and the social sciences, experimentation is difficult to accomplish. Therefore, in education, nonexperimental research is the rule rather than the exception. Nonexperimental methods may be appropriately used in any type (i.e., qualitative, quantitative, and mixed methods) of research study.

TYPES OF RESEARCH DIFFERENTIATED BY METHODOLOGY

Several types of research are traditionally identified based on the nature of methods used, as determined by the questions researchers are seeking to answer. Those types include ethnography, narrative, historical, grounded theory, phenomenology, case study, survey, causal-comparative, correlational, experimental, quasi-experimental, single-subject, and mixed-methods research. While not all of these types of research are addressed below, you will read much more about each in later chapters. For the time being, let us consider the following example research questions.

1. What is a typical week like in the lives of five selected students attending Elmwood's Lincoln High School?

2. What cultural, ethnic, and linguistic groups made up Elmwood schools' student population in 1955, and how successful were those groups academically?
3. How do Elmwood's teachers and students view its overall school climate?
4. What is the relationship between English vocabulary proficiency and school achievement among Elmwood students?
5. What is the effect of bilingualism on school achievement among Elmwood students?
6. Can cultural sensitivity training improve interpersonal relationships among Elmwood's students of diverse ethnic backgrounds?
7. Can a schoolwide disciplinary system be designed to improve the overall behavior of students in Elmwood's Cutter Elementary School?
8. How effective is Elmwood's bilingual education program in promoting scholastic achievement?

Each of these questions calls for a different type of research, as shown in the following explanations.

Question 1: What is a typical week like in the lives of five selected students attending Elmwood's Lincoln High School?

This question calls for **ethnographic research,** which documents and explains social behavior within groups. Unlike other types of research, ethnography explores behavior holistically within a social setting of customs, values, and styles of communication. Data sources are people, objects, environments, and communication patterns inherent in the context under study. Findings are usually presented in narrative form, sometimes enhanced by graphic illustrations. This type of research is nonexperimental, largely qualitative, and is heavily dependent on investigator perception and skill in making observations and interpretations.

Question 2: What cultural, ethnic, and linguistic groups made up Elmwood schools' student population in 1955, and how successful were those groups academically?

This question calls for **historical research,** which explores conditions, situations, events, or people of the past. Historical research is nonexperimental and may be qualitative, quantitative, or a combination of the two. It is typically guided by research questions and uses as sources of data original documents, newspaper accounts, photographs and drawings, historical records, locales, objects, and people who have some knowledge of the time and place under investigation. Findings from historical research are normally presented in narrative form illuminated by numerical, categorical, and graphic illustrations.

Question 3: How do Elmwood's teachers and students view its overall school climate?

This question calls for **survey research,** which is done to describe the characteristics of a population as it currently exists. Survey research is nonexperimental and can be either qualitative, quantitative, or a combination of the two. Hypotheses are frequently used in survey research, as are research questions. The major source of information is a sample of individuals, usually selected in order to represent a larger population. Findings are presented in narrative form enhanced by numerical, categorical, and graphic illustrations.

Question 4: What is the relationship between English vocabulary proficiency and school achievement among Elmwood students?

This question calls for **correlational research,** which can explore the degree of correlation between two or more variables. In correlational research, data are obtained from the individuals serving as participants in the study. At least one pair of measures must be obtained for each of the people involved. To answer the foregoing question, we need to obtain a measure of each person's vocabulary proficiency (one of the variables) and a measure of each person's achievement level (the other variable). Those measures—probably numerical—give us a pair of scores for each student. From that information we can calcu-

Table 2.2   Correlational Research

A Single Group	Two Traits Measured	Relationship between Traits
Several individuals	English vocabulary School achievement	Might range from none to high

late the degree of relationship—the *correlation*—that exists between vocabulary proficiency and academic achievement for the sample. Correlational research, which is quantitative and nonexperimental, may strongly suggest cause–effect relationships but cannot demonstrate them nearly so convincingly as can experimental research. We must be cautious when inferring cause–effect from correlations. In themselves, correlations merely show that two traits covary with each other. For example, student intelligence and grade point average (GPA) are known to be correlated, which means that people high in one tend to be high in the other, and vice versa, though not always. But this does not say that either of the traits necessarily "causes" the other. It is foolish to suggest that a high GPA causes one to be more intelligent. Our minds tell us that intelligence is very likely an important contributing factor to high GPA, but so are motivation, perseverance, and good study habits.

In addition to suggesting possible causation, correlations give us the valuable ability to predict one of the variables from the other. If we know that 16-year-old Kareem is very intelligent, we can predict that he will probably graduate with a high GPA. If a university admissions official looks at Kareem's high GPA on his transcript, that official can predict with some certainty that Kareem is quite intelligent and has the capability to do well in college. Correlational research is illustrated in Table 2.2.

Question 5: What is the effect of bilingualism on school achievement among Elmwood students?

This question calls for **causal-comparative research,** which explores the influence of a preexisting condition—in this case bilingualism—on a variable such as learning. This type of research can suggest causality more persuasively than correlational research, but less persuasively than experimental research. For the question posed here, the researcher first randomly selects a group of monolingual students and a group of bilingual students, making sure that the two groups are otherwise as similar as possible, especially in ability and curriculum experienced. Then academic achievement of the two groups is measured. Finally, assuming that other factors are equal between the groups—an assumption that is tenuous in this case—any difference in scholastic achievement (the effect) can be attributed to bilingualism (the cause). This is not considered to be experimental research because the independent variable (bilingualism) cannot, except over long periods of time, be altered (manipulated) by the researcher, as is essential in experimental research. Causal-comparative research is nonexperimental and quantitative and uses data obtained from the people involved. It can be illustrated as in Table 2.3.

Question 6: Can cultural sensitivity training improve interpersonal relationships among Elmwood's students of diverse ethnic backgrounds?

This question calls for experimental research, which might be designed as follows: A number of students are randomly selected from the population and then randomly assigned

Table 2.3   Causal-Comparative Research

Otherwise Equal Groups	Hypothesized Causal Factor	Observed Effect
Bilingual group A	Bilingualism	Achievement?
Monolingual group B	Monolingualism	Achievement?

to two groups. None of the students has previously undergone cultural sensitivity training. One group (the experimental group) is given sensitivity exercises—an example of what is meant by "manipulating the independent variable." The second group (the control group) is given "placebo" exercises, activities believed to have no effect on participants except to make them think they are receiving special attention, as is the experimental group. After the sensitivity training is completed, the two groups are assessed to see if differences become apparent in individuals' relationships with others.

Experimental research, which is usually quantitative, focuses on independent and dependent variables, called *cause* and *effect,* respectively. The *independent* (causal) variable in this question is cultural sensitivity training. The *dependent* (effect) variable is interpersonal relationships. If the two sample groups are originally very similar, and if other cautions to be described later are satisfied, then subsequent changes in interpersonal relationships tentatively may be attributed to the effects of sensitivity training.

Experimental research is difficult to conduct in education because in true experiments students are randomly assigned to groups receiving the different treatments. However, random assignment is impractical where students already belong to classes that cannot be reconstituted easily. Even when possible, many parents object to their children being "experimented on." Yet, as we have noted, experimental research is highly valued because it indicates cause–effect relationships more convincingly than any other type of research.

Exercise 2.1

Identify each of the following possible research projects as (B) basic or (A) applied; (E) experimental or (NE) nonexperimental; and (QA) qualitative or (QN) quantitative. Three or more labels should be applied to each research example.

_____   1. LaToyne Marshall, a retired teacher, becomes interested in describing the present-day lives of community residents who were his students in Cutter Elementary School at least 30 years ago.

_____   2. Nativadad Rojas, bilingual coordinator for Elmwood schools, wants to determine how achievement is affected by instructing students part of the day in their native language.

_____   3. Teachers at Fairfield High School want to produce and field-test an instructional packet on cultural diversity they believe will benefit all students at their school.

_____   4. Alana Hopkins, a teacher at Magnolia Middle School, wants to determine, as a requirement for her master's degree, whether a relationship exists between school achievement and the number of schools previously attended by Magnolia students.

TYPES OF RESEARCH BASED ON PRACTICALITY

A third means of categorizing research focuses on the practicality of the research findings. In this interesting category the two approaches to research presented here—that is, action research and evaluation research—often utilize specific techniques that have already been discussed. The difference, however, lies in the overarching goal of the research.

In **action research,** educators attempt to solve or address an immediate, local-level problem or research question. Often, the question may be of great interest to those directly involved in the investigation (i.e., its findings will likely have an immediate and practical use), but may not be to anyone else. Action research may use qualitative (e.g., narrative) methods, quantitative (e.g., causal-comparative) methods, or perhaps even mixed methods. It is critical to note that what classifies a study as action research is not the type of traditional method(s) employed, but rather the guiding purpose or reason underlying the research study.

Evaluation research is very similar to action research in that traditional methods are used to actually conduct the research study, but its overall goals are more situation-specific. Evaluation research is done for the purpose of making judgments about educational programs, curriculum, or interventions. Typically, these judgments result in more formalized decisions, and these decisions are oftentimes financially oriented. For example, an evaluation research study, utilizing a causal-comparative approach, might be employed in order to make a decision about the continuation of an after-school intervention program as a means of reducing neighborhood vandalism. If the study shows the program to be ineffective, it would likely be decided that the program would no longer be funded. In contrast, if it was found to directly reduce vandalism, funding would likely persist.

Continuing our previous scenario, consider the final two example research questions. Each question calls for a very practical approach in order to collect data that, when analyzed, will enable the researcher to provide answers.

Question 7: Can a schoolwide disciplinary system be designed to improve the overall behavior of students in Elmwood's Cutter Elementary School?

This question calls for action research, done to improve conditions within a particular setting without concern for applying the findings elsewhere. If the Cutter Elementary School faculty is worried about classroom discipline and wishes to make improvements at their school, then action research might be undertaken to identify the specific problems, formulate possible solutions, apply those solutions, and evaluate the results, all while keeping records that document problems, procedures, and results. Action research can be illustrated as in Table 2.4.

Question 8: How effective is Elmwood's bilingual education program in promoting scholastic achievement?

This question calls for evaluation research, done to make judgments about the quality of particular programs, procedures, materials, and the like. In Elmwood schools, evaluation research can determine the value of the bilingual program in terms of student learning and teacher satisfaction. Data in evaluation research are obtained by assessing student performance, analyzing materials, and interviewing teachers, students, administrators, parents, and community members. The data collected are then compared against a set of criteria used to indicate quality. The bilingual program, for example, might be judged against criteria such as student learning, ease of implementation, cost-effectiveness, availability and quality of materials, student and teacher morale, and high level of commitment from parents, teachers, and students.

Table 2.4   Action Research

Undesirable Condition	New Development Implemented	Result Evaluated
Unruliness	New discipline system	Better behavior?

Exercise 2.2

Label each of the following research topics as (ET) ethnographic, (H) historical, (S) survey, (C) correlation, (A) action, (EV) evaluation, (CC) causal-comparative, or (EX) experimental. In some cases more than one label can be correctly applied.

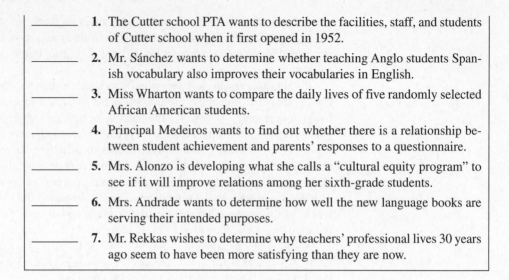

_____ **1.** The Cutter school PTA wants to describe the facilities, staff, and students of Cutter school when it first opened in 1952.

_____ **2.** Mr. Sánchez wants to determine whether teaching Anglo students Spanish vocabulary also improves their vocabularies in English.

_____ **3.** Miss Wharton wants to compare the daily lives of five randomly selected African American students.

_____ **4.** Principal Medeiros wants to find out whether there is a relationship between student achievement and parents' responses to a questionnaire.

_____ **5.** Mrs. Alonzo is developing what she calls a "cultural equity program" to see if it will improve relations among her sixth-grade students.

_____ **6.** Mrs. Andrade wants to determine how well the new language books are serving their intended purposes.

_____ **7.** Mr. Rekkas wishes to determine why teachers' professional lives 30 years ago seem to have been more satisfying than they are now.

Given the foregoing overview of standard types of educational research, let us consider the sources and requirements of the data they employ.

PRIMARY AND SECONDARY SOURCES OF RESEARCH DATA

The information researchers obtain about people, settings, objects, and procedures is called **data,** which can be recorded in verbal or numerical form. Data are obtained from two broad sources of information, called **primary sources** and **secondary sources.** Information from those sources is correspondingly called **primary data** and **secondary data.** Usually a third type of information is sought as well—reports of previous investigations related to the matter under consideration.

Primary data sources are highly valued because the firsthand information they supply tends to be more accurate than information obtained from secondary sources. Examples of primary data sources are physical objects, original reports, records, and eyewitness accounts. In studying Elmwood schools, primary data sources would include test scores, demographic records, attendance records, minutes of meetings, transcripts of testimony, photographs, instructional materials, student informants, parent informants, teacher informants, and transcripts of hearings. Although the primary data obtained from such sources are prized for accuracy, they nevertheless can be erroneous. It is well established that personal reports about the same incident usually differ, sometimes substantially.

Secondary data sources provide reports or interpretations of primary data from people who did not directly experience the events under consideration. Examples of secondary data sources are hearsay testimony, histories (not autobiographical), selected compilations, encyclopedia entries, newspaper reports, and analyses and interpretations of events not experienced firsthand. Secondary data sources are quite valuable and, at times, highly accurate—sometimes even more accurate than primary sources—but they are subject to errors of interpretation, emphasis, memory, and personal bias and are, therefore, generally considered less reliable than primary sources. In research involving Elmwood schools, secondary data sources might include newspaper accounts of meetings and incidents, editorials, radio and television reports, abstracts of hearings and court cases, what students say their parents believe, and what parents say their children experience and believe.

Additional information sought by researchers includes the findings made in other investigations similar to their own. Researchers always review the literature to see if they can find such related studies. The information thus obtained is used for the following purposes: (1) to orient, guide, and define the limits of a study; (2) as secondary data possibly useful in the topic under investigation; and (3) as primary data in what are called meta-analytical studies, which analyze numerous existing studies to draw new conclusions. Usually, however, the questions, procedures, and findings in studies similar to one's own provide only context and guidance for research.

SPECIFIC SOURCES OF RESEARCH DATA

Data in educational research are obtained from several different sources, including participants, procedures, settings, objects, records, documents, and informants.

Participants, as we have noted, are individuals from whom data are obtained. They often, but not always, comprise a **sample,** which is a group of individuals chosen to represent the population at large.

Procedures are formalized ways of operating in the educational setting—the way things are done. How lessons are presented and how homework is assigned are two examples of procedures from among hundreds in education.

Settings are the specific environments within which educational behavior occurs. Examples include classrooms, athletic fields, libraries, laboratories, playgrounds, and homes.

Objects are inanimate things such as books, supplies, materials, and artifacts.

Records are highly summarized reports of performance, expenditures, and the like, kept for later reference.

Documents are written papers and reports in their entirety, such as journal articles, technical papers, and curriculum guides. Photographs, drawings, and other illustrations are also considered documents.

Informants are people, other than participants in the study, from whom opinion, informed views, and expert testimony are obtained.

Exercise 2.3

For the following indicate the most likely source of data: (P) participant, (PR) procedure, (ST) setting, (O) object, (R) record, (D) document, or (I) informant.

_____ **1.** Study of old textbooks

_____ **2.** Average achievement scores in 1957

_____ **3.** Observations of how primary teachers begin the day

_____ **4.** Children's playgrounds

_____ **5.** A comparative analysis of secondary school curriculum guides

_____ **6.** What students say about self-directed work

_____ **7.** What one "insider" says about the value of faculty meetings

_____ **8.** School districts' mission statements

_____ **9.** Live testimony before a committee

_____ **10.** The group's reading level today, as yet undetermined

PROCEDURES AND TOOLS USED IN COLLECTING DATA

Data are collected from the sources just listed by means of seven general procedures: verbal description, notation, recording, analysis, questioning, testing, and measurement.

Verbal description is a data collection procedure used in the study of settings, procedures, and behaviors. It depends on observation and is a written or spoken depiction of what is observed. It attempts to capture fairly complete pictures. Verbal description is indispensable in researching topics where measurement and numerical representation are not feasible. It is the primary method used to obtain data in ethnographic research and is frequently used in historical and descriptive research as well. It enables researchers to capture full pictures of situations and dynamics within and among schools, classrooms, teachers, administrators, parents, community members, and students both inside and outside of school (Zaharlick, 1992).

Notation refers to making tally marks or brief written notes about people, objects, or other data sources. One sees a particular behavior and makes a note of its occurrence. One examines a textbook and lists its characteristics. One finds important information in a document and summarizes contents and bibliographical information. Notation is tied to observation. One observes and makes notes about what is seen or heard.

Recording refers to capturing scenes and interactions by means of cameras or audio or video recorders. Recordings are replete with detail that might go unnoticed until scrutinized. Data obtained in recordings must be converted to words, scores, or tally marks before they can be analyzed properly.

Analysis, which should not be confused with statistical analysis of data, involves breaking entities down into constituent parts in order to determine their composition, how they are organized, and how they function. Many sources can be accessed through analysis, but this procedure is especially useful in obtaining data about objects, relics, documents, and procedures, as follows.

Objects routinely analyzed include products made by students—art, handicrafts, handwriting, timed tests, constructions, portfolios, and the like—as well as those made by teachers and others concerned with education, examples of which include textbooks, curricula, guides, instructors' manuals, supplementary materials, and discipline systems.

Relics, which are objects recovered from prior times, are invaluable sources of data in historical research. For example, over a half century ago, all the inhabitants of the mining town of Bodie, California, abruptly departed when the mining operation closed. The weather at Bodie was so inhospitable that no one wanted to stay. Rather than try to move the town, the populace simply left their homes, stores, shops, buildings, and school more or less intact, with furniture, merchandise, supplies, and equipment in place. Now restored and protected, the ghost town of Bodie is replete with relics from which researchers have pieced together a detailed picture of life and education there in earlier times.

Documents analyzed in research include published papers, curriculum guides, newspaper accounts, photographs and other illustrations, transcripts of proceedings, and the like. Documents provide much of the data used in descriptive and historical research.

Procedures related to education are also analyzed to determine who does what, when, and with what effect. Analysis of procedures was used by both Kounin (1971) and Jones (1987) in their pivotal studies on the relationship between instructional procedures and classroom discipline. By analyzing classroom procedures, Kounin and Jones identified those that facilitated or inhibited student attention and work, and from that knowledge new procedures were developed that reduced the incidence of classroom misbehavior.

Questioning involves researchers asking questions directly of participants or informants. Questioning is not done haphazardly, but in a carefully planned manner. It uses both surveys and personal interviews, which can be carried out through correspondence, telephone contact, or personal contact, as follows.

Surveys are used in educational research to gather responses on such matters as opinions about education, attitudes toward the school system, home reading habits, and teachers' perceptions of their workloads. Surveys typically make use of questionnaires whose formats and contents are carefully prepared and refined before final use. Surveys stick scrupulously to the written format and do not provide for probing or clarifying.

The personal **interview** is organized around a predetermined set of questions but allows the questioner to provide encouragement, ask probing questions, and request additional information. The interview can obtain more useful information than the questionnaire, but the reliability of that information can be suspect. Respondents are easily influenced by the interviewer's manner, encouragement, and requests for clarification, so that a person's responses to the same questions may vary substantially from one interviewer to another (Smith, 1992).

Testing, which calls on participants to perform cognitive or psychomotor tasks, is probably more frequently used to collect educational research data than any other method. Most tests are administered in written form, but many are administered orally. They usually yield a numerical score, but not always. Sometimes they provide ranked or categorical data and sometimes only verbal data. Validity (accuracy) and reliability (consistency) are matters of great concern in testing; therefore, research that makes use of tests must give close attention to the validity and reliability of test instruments used.

Measurement is used to obtain data by checking performance or status against an established scale. Testing, one means by which measurement is done, is often used synonymously with measurement, but measurement is the broader and more inclusive term and is used herein to refer to data obtained by means of scales other than tests. Examples of measurement include determining height and weight, blood pressure, number of books read, distance run, time spent on lesson segments, and hours spent watching television.

Exercise 2.4

Which of the following data collection procedures is best associated with each of the numbered items: (N) notation, (D) description, (A) analysis, (Q) questioning, (T) testing, or (M) measurement?

_____   **1.** Granger administered the Stanford Achievement Test.

_____   **2.** Morris carefully studied samples of student art work.

_____   **3.** Torres found the names in court records.

_____   **4.** Nguyen mailed out 1,000 questionnaires.

_____   **5.** Truk spoke with each of the top administrators.

_____   **6.** Michaels kept detailed accounts of classroom interactions.

_____   **7.** Oliphant wanted to determine students' pulse rates during final examinations.

QUALITIES REQUIRED IN RESEARCH DATA

Research conclusions cannot be taken seriously if there are questions about the quality of the data from which the conclusions are drawn. Researchers, therefore, scrutinize data to make sure they are authentic, believable, valid, and reliable.

AUTHENTICITY AND BELIEVABILITY OF QUALITATIVE DATA

Researchers use two informal, unstructured means of assessing data for authenticity and believability. These two means, used primarily with qualitative data, are called the tests of *external criticism* and *internal criticism.*

External criticism has to do with determining whether the data come from legitimate sources. Unwritten and using no statistical calculations, this test is one of analysis and judgment. Let us suppose researcher Ms. Jordan, investigating past funding and expenditures of Elmwood schools, has discovered an unusual letter in Elmwood's archives. Bearing the signature of Dr. Lehman, a former superintendent of schools who recently died in a mental institution, the letter is one of confession, in which Dr. Lehman admits falsifying over a period of five years both attendance and achievement records, in order to obtain increased federal funding for Elmwood schools. According to the letter, the admission of wrongdoing was made to assuage feelings of guilt and to set the record straight.

Ms. Jordan has the obligation of determining whether the information is legitimate. In applying the test of external criticism, she must satisfy a variety of questions. Is this letter genuine, or is it a fake? Can the signature be verified as that of Dr. Lehman? Was it really written on the date indicated, when Dr. Lehman was already a resident in the mental institution? If so, how did the letter get in the archives? Is there evidence that Dr. Lehman had enemies who wished to discredit him and might have attempted to do so in this manner?

While authenticity of data is fundamentally important, educational researchers do not often encounter situations that raise questions about authenticity of data. That is, there is relatively little likelihood of encountering fabricated scores or informants who misrepresent facts intentionally. Still, there remains the question of believability of the data, which calls for application of internal criticism.

Turning to **internal criticism,** even if Ms. Jordan concludes that Dr. Lehman wrote the letter, she must still decide whether the information is believable. Researchers do regularly encounter information of questionable veracity. Ms. Jordan must, therefore, apply a second test to the letter she has found, called *internal criticism,* which concerns data accuracy and lack of bias. Let us assume she determined that the signature on the letter was similar to that of Dr. Lehman in his declining years. Ms. Jordan knows that even legitimate sources can provide erroneous data. People do not perceive things exactly the same, nor do they always remember events similarly. Their recollections may be slanted by existing bias, and sometimes they believe imagined scenarios to be true. Ms. Jordan applies the test of internal criticism by asking pertinent questions. Did Dr. Lehman have his facts correct? Might he have believed he falsified records when in fact he did not? Was Dr. Lehman known to have made other unusual assertions? Do other experts believe that Dr. Lehman could have obtained funding through the misrepresentations he admits?

All researchers should ask themselves similar questions about the data they acquire. Is the source legitimate? Do the data come from real people, objects, or events? Are the data accurate? Is there possibility of bias? Such questions are usually answered through corroborating evidence from another source—in this case perhaps from a colleague who worked closely with Dr. Lehman at the time in question.

Additional techniques can also be used to establish the accuracy and believability of qualitative data. **Member checking** involves sharing summarizations of analyzed data with participants in order to gauge the accuracy of the interpretations made by the researcher. These summarizations could be preliminary, or perhaps final, research reports, or even some earlier step in the analytical process (prior to finalizing the results of a study). **Triangulation** is a process of utilizing multiple data collection techniques (e.g., interviews and observations, as opposed to a single data collection strategy) or multiple data sources (again, instead of one) in order to gain a clearer, stronger, and deeper understanding of the topic being studied. Data resulting from these multiple techniques or sources are then cross-checked in order to examine similarities or differences in the data.

VALIDITY AND RELIABILITY OF QUANTITATIVE DATA

Data must not only be authentic and believable but are worthless unless they are also valid and reliable. Quantitative data are **valid** to the extent they depict or deal directly with the topic under consideration. For example, data in the form of scores made on geometry tests are valid if they have to do with knowledge of geometry rather than some other ability (such as reading, which could unduly affect understanding of written directions and responses to word problems). Information about Scotch-Irish migration patterns in the United States is valid if it depicts movements of the Scotch-Irish rather than English or other immigrants contemporaneous with the Scotch-Irish.

Data are **reliable** to the extent they are consistent. Geometry test scores are reliable if individuals make approximately the same scores when again taking the test. Research data are considered reliable if there is consistency among the reports provided by different observers. On the other hand, if information about a topic is inconsistent—if it varies noticeably from test to test, observation to observation, or competent person to competent person—it is considered unreliable and is, therefore, of no value to the researcher. The concepts of validity and reliability will be discussed in greater detail in Chapter 6.

Exercise 2.5

Which of the following labels can best be associated with each of the numbered scenarios: (P) primary data source, (S) secondary data source, (E) external criticism, (I) internal criticism, (R) reliable data, or (V) valid data?

_____ **1.** Determination that data obtained from Mr. Collins's new algebra test did in fact have to do mainly with knowledge of algebra

_____ **2.** Students from whom information was obtained when Mr. Collins's test underwent validation procedures

_____ **3.** Parents who reported their children's comments on what they liked about Mr. Collins's test

_____ **4.** Test data obtained from a selected group of students that were almost the same the second time they took Mr. Collins's test as when those students first took his test a week earlier

_____ **5.** Mr. Collins explaining how he constructed his test

_____ **6.** A lead story that appeared in the local newspaper concerning what students and administrators said about Mr. Collins's new algebra test

_____ **7.** Determination that Mr. Collins did author the new test, as he claimed

_____ **8.** Verification of Mr. Collins's conclusions by two independent authorities

TREATMENT AND PRESENTATION OF DATA

Once data are obtained, they are treated and presented in various ways. They may simply be identified, listed, described, or given as written narrative. Data presented in these ways can show the condition or status of people, objects, or processes, and are common in ethnographic, historical, and descriptive research. But data may often be analyzed further for confidence testing, hypothesis testing, and to show comparisons, trends, relative placement of scores, differences among groups, relationships among variables, or effects produced by different treatments or conditions. Data analysis is described in its various forms in Chapters 7, 10 through 16, and the Appendix.

ADDITIONAL TERMINOLOGY RELATED TO DATA

So far, we have considered the labels used to differentiate among types of research, noted the sources of data used in research, and become acquainted with some of the necessary qualities of data. At this point, additional important concepts related to data are introduced.

APPLYING TECHNOLOGY

More about Variables and Questions

Dr. William Trochim, a professor at Cornell University, has developed an extensive online research methods textbook (www.socialresearchmethods .net/kb/index.htm). His electronic text, titled *Research Methods Knowledge Base,* is an excellent resource and may prove very beneficial as a supplement to readers throughout this text. Dr. Trochim's e-text is organized into six major sections:

- Foundations of research
- Sampling
- Measurement
- Research design
- Data analysis
- Writing up research

Considering topics addressed in this chapter, Dr. Trochim provides a discussion of the various types of variables encountered in educational research. His discussion is quite good, as he presents specific examples of the classifications of variables (www.socialresearchmethods.net/kb/variable.htm). He is also quite frank in confessing that he had much difficulty in learning the distinction between independent and dependent variables—a problem often encountered by graduate students.

A discussion of types of data, specifically qualitative and quantitative, is also presented (www .socialresearchmethods.net/kb/datatype.htm). The discussion focuses on the distinction between qualitative and quantitative data but also enlightens future researchers as to the "intimate relationship" shared by these two types of data. This is a "must read" for all researchers, as it will surely improve understanding of the basic nature of data.

Although it may not be specifically mentioned in subsequent chapters, Dr. Trochim's knowledge base can be an excellent supplement for topics covered later in this text.

PARTICIPANTS, SAMPLES, AND POPULATIONS

Researchers obtain data from participants in order to learn about populations. People and other living things, when being studied in research, are referred to as *participants.* Participants are usually, but not always, members of *samples,* which are groups of individuals selected from a larger population. (Sometimes a single participant is studied in depth.) A **population** contains all the individuals within certain descriptive parameters, such as location, age, or sex. For example, a population might be all the 10-year-olds in the world, all the third-grade students in the United States, all the teachers in Elmwood, or all the parents and guardians of students attending Cutter Elementary School.

Researchers usually want to learn about entire populations, but it is impractical to study a population unless it is quite small—there are simply too many individuals to deal with. Therefore, researchers use samples drawn from the larger population. In order for their findings to apply to the entire population, the sample must fairly accurately represent the population. Random selection of participants from the population is a preferred method for establishing samples, but random selection is not often practical in educational research because it disrupts preestablished classes. When random selection is not possible, or for some reason is not appropriate, other procedures are used to select samples, which are discussed in Chapter 6.

DEVELOPMENTAL ACTIVITY

Type of Research

In the developmental activity at the end of Chapter 1, you began your process of planning a research study by thinking of a possible research topic, considering potential pitfalls you might encounter along the way, and brainstorming various ways to overcome them. Another important decision that you must make as a researcher in the early stages of planning a research study is to determine what type (or types) of research might be most appropriate in order to adequately address your topic. Consider the topic with which you began working in Chapter 1 and answer the following questions:

1. A possible topic or problem I am thinking of researching

    _____

2. The type of research that seems most appropriate to my chosen topic (*check one*)

    ☐ Ethnographic research
    ☐ Historical research
    ☐ Descriptive research
    ☐ Correlational research
    ☐ Action research
    ☐ Evaluation research
    ☐ Causal-comparative research
    ☐ Experimental research

3. The reason that I chose that particular type of research and why I think it is most appropriate for my topic

    _____

    _____

4. Other types of research (if any) in the preceding list that *might* also seem appropriate for my topic include:

    _____

    _____

5. Based on my responses to questions 3 and 4, possible criticisms by experienced researchers of my topic using these approaches

    _____

    _____

6. Based on my responses to the preceding questions, type of research that would be most appropriate

    _____

    _____

CHAPTER SUMMARY

Types of educational research, sources of data, and means of obtaining data are intertwined. For individuals new to research, the most useful way of differentiating types of research is by the nature of the research questions addressed. Types of research thus differentiated include ethnographic, historical, survey, correlational, causal-comparative, experimental, action, and evaluation. Other labels that serve to differentiate among types of research are basic, applied, quantitative, qualitative, experimental, and nonexperimental.

Research information obtained about people, places, things, interactions, and the like is called *data*. Important concepts related to data include authenticity (genuineness), accuracy, reliability (consistency), validity (on target), primary (firsthand), secondary (secondhand), participants (people being studied), sample (a group of participants selected from, and representative of, a larger population), population (all the individuals within selected parameters), and variable (a characteristic that tends to differ from person to person or item to item).

Various procedures are used to obtain research data. Seven common procedures are notation, recording, description, analysis, questioning, measurement, and testing.

LIST OF IMPORTANT TERMS

action research	historical research	quantitative research
analysis	internal criticism	questioning
applied research	interview	reliability (of data)
basic research	measurement	research method
causal-comparative research	member checking	sample
cause–effect relationship	mixed-methods research	secondary data
correlational research	nonexperimental research	secondary source
data	notation	survey
ethnographic research	population	survey research
evaluation research	primary data	triangulation
experimental research	primary source	validity (of data)
external criticism	qualitative research	

YOUR CURRENT STATUS

To your previous knowledge of the nature, principles, and procedures of educational research, you have added knowledge of various types of educational research, as defined by usefulness (basic or applied), traditional methodology (quantitative, qualitative, or mixed methods; experimental or nonexperimental), and practicality (action or evaluation). You know what is meant by data, recognize the differences between primary and secondary data, and can identify many of the major data sources. You under-

stand the concepts of authenticity, accuracy, reliability, and validity and recognize their importance in research. Finally, you understand the meanings of the terms *population, sample,* and *participant.* You are now ready to move on to a consideration of how one selects, refines, and proposes a topic for research. Before proceeding to Chapter 3, please take time to complete the following activities for thought and discussion.

ACTIVITIES FOR THOUGHT AND DISCUSSION

1. Suppose you wanted to investigate the effects of two different methods of teaching reading to third-grade students.
   a. Which of the eight types of research would be indicated?
   b. What would be the independent and dependent variables in your research?
   c. Identify your likely sources of primary data.
2. Suppose you wanted to compare the history and development of an urban school (Cutter) with that of a rural school (Greenleaf).
   a. What type of research would be called for?
   b. Name important primary and secondary sources of data.
   c. Would you orient your research by means of research questions, hypotheses, or both? Give examples.
   d. To what approximate degree do you believe this research would be qualitative, as contrasted with quantitative research?

3. Here are the questions presented at the beginning of the chapter. How well can you answer them?
   a. How do the concepts of *usefulness, methodology, questions addressed,* and *practicality* serve to differentiate among types of educational research?
   b. Describe eight types of educational research differentiated by questions addressed?
   c. What are the differences between *primary* and *secondary data sources*? Which, if either, is more valued in research?
   d. What are the seven procedures commonly used in obtaining data?
   e. What is meant by the terms *external criticism, internal criticism, reliability,* and *validity*?
4. Recall or turn to the information organizer presented at the beginning of the chapter. Without looking in the text, explain briefly what you now understand about each item in the organizer.

ANSWERS TO CHAPTER EXERCISES

2.1. 1. B/NE/QA 2. A/E (NE)/QN 3. A/NE (E)/QA (QN)
4. A/NE/QN

2.2. 1. H 2. EX 3. ET 4. C 5. A 6. EV 7. H/EV

2.3. 1. O 2. R 3. P 4. ST 5. D 6. P 7. I 8. D 9. I 10. P

2.4. 1. T 2. A 3. N 4. Q 5. Q 6. D 7. M

2.5. 1. V 2. P 3. S 4. R 5. P 6. S 7. E 8. I

REFERENCES AND RECOMMENDED READINGS

Best, J., & Kahn, J. (2006). *Research in Education* (10th ed.). Boston: Allyn & Bacon.

Brandt, R. (1992). On research on teaching: A conversation with Lee Schulman. *Educational Leadership, 49*(7), 14–19.

Crowl, T. (1993). *Fundamentals of Educational Research* (pp. 3–9). Madison, WI: WCB Brown & Benchmark.

Edyburn, D. L. (1999). *The Electronic Scholar: Enhancing Research Productivity with Technology.* Upper Saddle River, NJ: Merrill.

Gay, L. R., Mills, G. E., & Airasian, P. (2006). *Educational Research: Competencies for Analysis and Application* (8th ed.). Upper Saddle River, NJ: Merrill.

Howe, K. (1992). Getting over the quantitative-qualitative debate. *American Journal of Education, 100*(2), 236–256.

Jones, F. (1987). *Positive Classroom Discipline.* New York: McGraw-Hill.

Kounin, J. (1971). *Discipline and Group Management in Classrooms.* New York: Holt, Rinehart, & Winston.

Lederman, N. (1992). You can't do it by arithmetic, you have to do it by algebra! *Journal of Research in Science Teaching, 29,* 1011–1013.

Lytle, S., & Cochran-Smith, M. (1992). Teacher research as a way of knowing. *Harvard Educational Review, 62,* 447–474.

Sawin, E. (1992). Reaction: Experimental research in the context of other methods. *School of Education Review, 4*(Spring), 18–21.

Schmidt, T. (1992). Assessment and evaluation of technology in education—The teacher as a researcher. *Computing Teacher, 20*(1), 9–10.

Smith, J. (1992). Interpretive inquiry: A practical and moral activity. *Theory into Practice, 31*(1), 100–106.

Smith, M. (1987). Publishing qualitative research. *American Educational Research Journal, 24*(2), 173–183.

Trochim, W. M. (2002). *The Research Methods Knowledge Base* (2nd ed.). Available at http://socialresearchmethods.net/Kb/index.htm

Winkler, K. (1992). Researchers leave labs, flock to schools for a new look at how students learn. *Chronicle of Higher Education, 39*(8), 6–7.

Zaharlick, A. (1992). Ethnography in anthropology and its value for education. *Theory into Practice, 31*(1), 116–125.

Selecting, Refining, and Proposing a Topic for Research

PREVIEW

This chapter introduces five clusters of research skills important to graduate students:

1. Choosing a topic for research
   - Identification of promising topics
   - Selection of a specific topic to investigate
   - Refinement of the selected topic

2. Stating the problem to be investigated
   - Purpose of the study—what it is supposed to accomplish and how
   - Importance of the study—why it is worth pursuing, what it can contribute
   - Limitations of the study—restrictions that limit its scope
   - Special terms that are used in the study

3. Orienting the research
   - Formulating research questions—what one hopes to discover or resolve
   - Formulating hypotheses—forecasts of results of the study

4. Identifying variables
   - Distinguishing between the various classifications of variables

5. Preparing the research proposal
   - Organization and presentation—how to put a proposal together

TARGETED LEARNINGS

This chapter introduces five important clusters of research skills. The first cluster includes identifying, selecting, and refining a promising topic for research. After the topic is refined, it becomes known as the *problem*. The second cluster includes *stating the problem* in a way that describes the purpose of the study, explaining why the problem is important, identifying the limitations that affect the study, and defining special terms that will be used. The third cluster includes phrasing *research questions* and *hypotheses* that can serve to guide the investigation, and the fourth cluster explains several classifications of variables. The fifth cluster deals with how one organizes and presents *research proposals.* As you read the chapter, look especially for information related to the following:

1. Where can good educational research topics be found?
2. What should one keep in mind when selecting a topic for research?
3. Why do modifications and refinements usually have to be made in research topics after they have been selected?
4. What are the purposes of research questions and hypotheses?
5. How are research questions and hypotheses best stated?
6. What are the similarities and differences between research questions and hypotheses?
7. What is the distinction between a research topic and research problem?
8. What is meant by the term *variable* and what are the distinguishing characteristics of various types—*continuous, discrete, independent, dependent,* and *confounding variables*?
9. What is a research proposal and how is it prepared and presented?

To begin explaining the learning skills involved in doing research of one's own, we start by exploring how potentially fruitful research topics are identified, selected, refined, and ultimately presented as research proposals.

Where to find good research topics

All educators have concerns about educational matters and many questions for which they would like to find answers. They might like to know whether biculturalism facilitates, impedes, or has no discernible effect on school learning. They might like to determine whether computers can, as is often claimed, actually improve teaching and learning. They might like

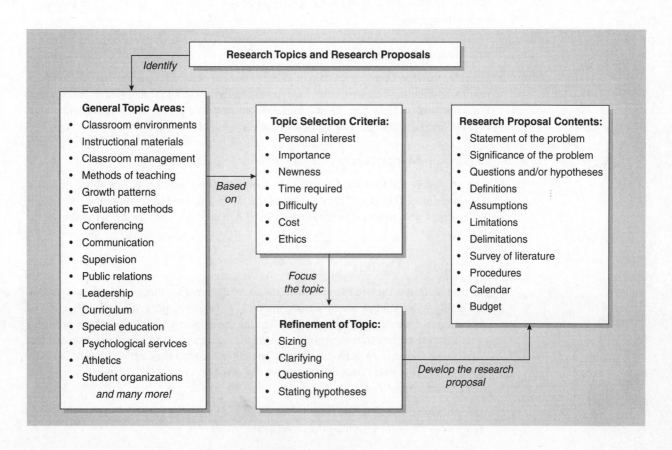

to learn about the degree to which certain achievement tests correspond to or differ from the curricula and materials used in their school. They might want to determine how to help beginning teachers be more successful during their first years, and how to help experienced teachers avoid burnout, which seems to be the fate of so many.

Concerns such as these can suggest innumerable topics for research, and personal concerns are one of the best places to look for good research topics. But there are other excellent sources as well (see Ginsburg, McLaughlin, & Plisko, 1992). Pick up any education journal and you are likely to find several potential topics. Ask teachers what bothers them about teaching or what they would most like help with; their answers will identify a number of topic ideas. Or go to the university library and leaf through a recent volume of the *Education Index* or the *Current Index to Journals in Education*. There you will find hundreds of topics that call for further investigation. Many of these topics will be especially interesting to teachers, while others will appeal to administrators, counselors, psychologists, librarians, and other professionals working in schools.

TOPICS FOR TEACHERS, COUNSELORS, AND OTHER EDUCATORS

Teaching offers a broad range of good topics to be researched. Reflect on the imaginary Elmwood school district. The following are only a few of the topics that could be investigated there.

Classroom Environment

Consider the numerous aspects of the physical and psychosocial environments in Elmwood classrooms. What impact might they have on student learning, behavior, attitude, interests, assumption of responsibility, relations with one another, and relations with the teacher? How could those classrooms make better use of time, movement, grouping, and management of materials?

Instructional Materials

Consider to what degree textbooks and other printed materials are appropriate for Elmwood's multicultural makeup. Are they consistent with the racial and ethnic balance that Elmwood values? How familiar and useful do teachers find the materials? Do the materials hold student attention, provide enjoyment, allow for creativity, and spur achievement?

Classroom Management

How efficiently are Elmwood classrooms operated? How satisfactory are the methods of managing student behavior? Do the routines currently practiced make efficient use of time? Are teachers able to teach as they would like? Are students able to learn without undue distraction?

Instructional Methods

There remains a great need for research into how different teaching methods and teacher personality styles affect learning among students of various ethnic groups. However, a note of caution: Research comparing different racial and ethnic groups moves onto sensitive ground. Proposed research must follow the legal requirements discussed in Chapter 1 and avoid suggesting, even inadvertently, that one ethnic group is somehow inherently better than another. Given that caution, let us note that teachers are always interested in new and workable information on

- Factors that motivate and hold attention
- Effective means of giving directions, cues, and signals

- The best methods of teaching to reach stated goals and objectives
- Effective teaching methods and strategies—their nature, timing, and delivery
- Ways of providing effective oral and written feedback for student work efforts

The Relation of Human Growth Patterns to Education

Although much information is available on human intellectual, social, physical, and emotional growth and development, relatively little research has been done into teaching strategies that best match or promote

- Individual interests and learning preferences
- Individual rates of learning
- Concerned, responsible, and self-disciplined behavior
- Natural student attentive behavior and teachable moments
- Classroom esprit de corps, joy, and pride in learning

Special Populations

Educators at all levels are experiencing increasing need for research on effective strategies for students with special or exceptional needs. This is a body of research that is always growing, due, at least in part, to the increasing number and diversity of special needs students. More sound research on effective classroom adaptations for learners with special needs will benefit all educators.

Evaluation

More information is needed about the effects that grades, grading systems, and evaluative feedback have on student motivation, stress, attitude, and achievement. More information is needed on authentic assessment and on other nontraditional means of assessing student growth.

Conferencing

Research is needed on how to maximize the value and improve the efficiency of personal conferences among teachers, students, and parents.

TOPICS FOR ADMINISTRATORS

Administrators experience many of the same concerns as teachers, and, in addition, they always need more reliable information and better procedures related to topics such as the following.

Effective Communication

There is an increasing need for better styles of communication and links among teachers, students, parents, other administrators, and the general community.

Effective Supervision

Administrators are always on the lookout for better ways of motivating, guiding, assisting, and supporting quality teaching in faculties where personalities and competencies are diverse.

Effective Public Relations

Administrators need to know effective strategies for obtaining the support of, and high regard from, parents and the community.

APPLYING TECHNOLOGY

Sources for Research Topics

The idea for a research topic is the first real decision facing a student engaging in the research process. The student's areas of interest often provide the best starting point. Initial interest in a topic may serve as the driving force behind the development of the research study. However, there are also several sources of information students may advantageously use to identify and evaluate initial topics (Edyburn, 1999).

Individuals who are knowledgeable in a particular field are excellent sources of information, and e-mail serves as an efficient means of contacting them with initial questions. One might request further information on a topic or the names of important researchers or research articles that address the topic. One note of caution, however: Be sure to ask your contact person specific questions; a student should not submit an e-mail request such as, "Please send me everything you have done related to . . ." (Edyburn, 1999). If you are lucky, this may be the beginning of an important professional relationship.

Browsing the Web can also provide valuable information regarding possible research topics. An excellent source of current topics and issues in all fields of education is *Education Week* (www .edweek.org/ew/index.html). Available in print form as well, *Education Week* touts itself as "America's education newspaper of record." Other online education newsletters, magazines, and articles can be located using the wide variety of search engines on the Web. *Search engines* organize websites by keywords. The results of a search for a specific topic will yield a list of related websites ranked in terms of relevance to the topic keyword(s). Commonly used search engines, listed with their respective URLs, include the following:

- DogPile (www.dogpile.com)
- Excite (www.excite.com)
- Go.com (www.go.com)
- Google (www.google.com)
- Google Scholar (www.scholar.google.com)
- Yahoo! (www.yahoo.com)
- WebCrawler (www.webcrawler.com)
- Ask Jeeves (www.ask.com)

Of course, one of the best sources for research topic ideas is professional, scholarly literature. In essence, this huge body of research literature consists of published research studies on just about every topic imaginable. Several searchable databases exist for locating published research studies, including ERIC (www.eric.ed.gov), EBSCOhost (www .ebscohost.com), and PsycINFO (www.apa.org/ psycinfo). Databases of scholarly research literature are discussed in more detail in Chapter 4.

Many *professional associations* operate websites and include links to other Web pages. These sites may be useful in identifying an initial topic or in narrowing the focus of a research topic. The premier professional association in education is the American Educational Research Association (AERA). AERA is divided into 12 divisions, based on broad disciplines. In addition, there are numerous special interest groups (SIGs). The AERA Web page can be found at www.aera.net. Other prominent professional associations include the following:

- American Psychological Association (www.apa .org)
- Association for Supervision and Curriculum Development (www.ascd.org)
- Association for Educational Communications and Technology (www.aect.org)
- Council for Exceptional Children (www.cec .sped.org)
- International Society for Technology in Education (www.iste.org)
- National Education Association (www.nea.org)
- Phi Delta Kappa (www.pdkintl.org)

Additionally, the U.S. Department of Education (ED) maintains a list of professional organizations and links to their websites. The list currently includes over 30 professional organizations and can be found online (www.ed.gov/about/contacts/gen/ othersites/associations.html).

Internet discussion groups can also be invaluable sources of information regarding ideas for and additional questions about research studies. A series of these discussion forums, or *LISTSERVs*, is maintained by AERA. The topical discussions take place via e-mail messages sent to everyone who has subscribed to a particular LISTSERV. As shown in the following list, AERA maintains one general LIST, 12 division LISTs, and one LIST for graduate students.

ERL-L	General discussion LIST for AERA	
AERA-A	Division A: Administration	
AERA-B	Division B: Curriculum Studies	
AERA-C	Division C: Learning and Instruction	
AERA-D	Division D: Measurement and Research Methodology	
AERA-E	Division E: Counseling and Human Development	
AERA-F	Division F: History and Historiography	
AERA-G	Division G: Social Context of Education	
AERA-H	Division H: School Evaluation and Program Development	
AERA-I	Division I: Education in the Professions	
AERA-J	Division J: Postsecondary Education	
AERA-K	Division K: Teaching and Teacher Education	
AERA-L	Division L: Politics and Policy in Education	

AERA-GSL Graduate Students List

In order to subscribe to any of the LISTSERVs, one simply sends an e-mail message to listserv@asu.edu using the following message format:

SUB list-name your-first-name

your-last-name

For example, if Mary Smith would like to subscribe to the research methodology LISTSERV, she would send the following e-mail message:

SUB AERA-D Mary Smith

AERA also maintains a *hypermail archive* of all LISTSERV activity, organized by division. Some divisions have topic discussions archived as far back as 1993. To access the AERA LISTSERV archive, simply point your browser to http://lists.asu.edu/archives/index.html. Then click on the appropriate division to access the archived discussions.

Effective Leadership

Administrators are continually searching for more effective ways of organizing, directing, encouraging, supporting, and otherwise getting the best from teachers, students, and support staffs in their schools.

TOPICS FOR OTHER EDUCATORS

We have noted only a few of the educational concerns that persist in schools, and, as you can see, they offer a multitude of possible research topics. Your interest may lie in yet another aspect of education—perhaps curriculum, special education, counseling, psychological services, athletics, the arts, or student organizations. Whatever the case, you will have no difficulty identifying a concern related to education that you will find enjoyable to research. Your own interests and needs are your best guides to good topics.

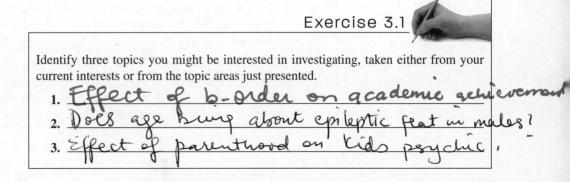

Exercise 3.1

Identify three topics you might be interested in investigating, taken either from your current interests or from the topic areas just presented.

1. Effect of b-order on academic achievement

2. Does age bring about epileptic feat in males?

3. Effect of parenthood on kids psychic.

PRELIMINARY CONSIDERATIONS IN SELECTING TOPICS

When first identifying a research topic of interest, you should evaluate it as follows:

1. You should have a *personal interest* in the topic you select. Perhaps the topic is new and intriguing or one that you associate with pleasant experiences. Perhaps it is one that has caused you unpleasant concern. Any topic that repeatedly suggests itself to you should be strongly considered.

2. The topic should be *important* and should make a difference in some aspect of education. If it does not, it should not be pursued, even if it interests you personally.

3. The *newness* of a research topic may affect your enthusiasm and satisfaction. Although there is value in repeating previous research—to validate methods and see if findings hold true over time—it is ordinarily more exciting to explore topics that may lead to new information.

4. In selecting research topics, always give attention to the amount of *time* the investigation will require. Compare that against what you have available. Other things being equal, you should select a topic that can be completed in a relatively short time.

5. Reflect on the *difficulty* of researching the topic. Many extremely interesting topics are difficult or impossible to research for a number of reasons. You would find it difficult to do a descriptive study of education among the Eskimos of Siberia and impossible to determine what happens to students' brain cells as they learn mathematics.

6. Consider the *monetary costs* that investigating your topic would entail. If you would have to pay for costly supplies, materials, travel, and consultant services, find a different topic. There are many good topics you can investigate with very little expense.

7. A final consideration has to do with *ethics*. As pointed out in Chapter 1, it is unethical and sometimes illegal to conduct research that slanders, does physical or psychological harm to, implants undesirable ideas in the minds of, or otherwise mistreats human or animal participants.

Exercise 3.2

A. Which of these considerations is most probably being overlooked in contemplating the following five topics: (PI) personal interest, (I) importance, (N) newness, (T) time, (D) difficulty, (C) cost, or (E) ethics?

   _T, D_   1. The effects of early childhood trauma on later school learning

   _PI_   2. Graduate student involving herself in a research project about which she cares nothing

   _E I_   3. The average income of male students versus the average income of female students enrolled in teacher education classes

   _I N_   4. An experiment to explore the effects of active involvement on learning, a topic already discussed in more than 1,000 studies

   _C E_   5. The effect on learning in classrooms where the temperature is kept excessively hot or cold

B. Evaluate each of the three topics you selected in Exercise 3.1 against the seven considerations just presented. Reword your topics as you see fit.

   1. _____

   2. _____

   3. _____

REFINING THE RESEARCH TOPIC

myeducationlab for research

To help you better understand research topics and problems, go to the "Selecting and Defining a Research Topic" section of **MyEducationLab for Research** and then click on *Building Research Skills*. First, read the articles authored by Hamre and Pianta and by Wolcott, and then complete the exercise titled "Identifying Research Problems in Research Reports."

Once a topic has been selected, it usually must be refined before it can be researched effectively and efficiently. Most topics are at first too broad, too narrow, too vague, or too complex. Such defects are corrected by refining the topic.

First, the topic must be properly *sized,* that is, reduced—or occasionally expanded—in scope. Graduate students typically select topic ideas that are too broad to be dealt with efficiently, especially under constraints of time and resources. Such topics must be pared down so that the research can be accomplished expeditiously. Occasionally, a research topic is too narrow. In that case, the topic must be fleshed out. Examples of overly broad or narrow topics are presented later in this chapter.

Second, the topic may need to be *clarified,* reworded so that it states clearly and unambiguously the matter to be investigated, the variables to be investigated, and the participants, if any. Examples of how topics can be reworded are also presented later in the chapter.

Third, a series of *research questions* or one or more *hypotheses,* or both, should be stated. Such questions and hypotheses orient the study, add cohesiveness, and are essential in helping resolve the primary concern that prompted the investigation.

Research questions and hypotheses are both valuable in orienting research, and each offers an advantage the other does not. The advantage of research questions is that their several subquestions serve as guideposts and markers that, as they are reached, keep the research on track and ultimately lead to a successful conclusion. The advantage of hypotheses is that they can be tested statistically, thereby adding credibility to the research findings. Remember that researchers do not say that a hypothesis is true, correct, or proved, only that it is retained or supported or else rejected or not supported. Guidance for composing research questions and hypotheses is given later in the chapter. Once these refinements have been made, what has heretofore been called the *research topic* becomes known as the *research problem.*

SOME NECESSARY TERMINOLOGY

myeducationlab for research

To check your understanding of the different types of hypothesis statements, go to the "Selecting and Defining a Research Topic" section of **MyEducationLab for Research** and then click on *Assignments and Activities*. Complete the exercise titled "Writing Research Hypotheses." This will provide good exposure to stating both null and directional research hypotheses.

Before proceeding to a discussion of how to regulate the size of a topic, it will be helpful to examine the meanings of some terms and phrases that you will encounter often: *topic, broad topic, narrowing the topic, amorphous topic, clarifying the topic, problem, problem statement, research question, subquestions, hypothesis, research hypothesis, null hypothesis,* and *theory.*

The topic refers to the matter to be investigated. The topic is usually stated as a sentence fragment, such as

- Successful teaching practices for multiethnic students
- School success and age of entry into kindergarten
- Using computers in the classroom to increase student achievement

A **broad topic** has no specific definition but generally means that a topic is too large in scope for the time or resources available. Examples of topics too broad to be pursued by a graduate student in education include

- The formulation and field-testing of a new English curriculum for bilingual students in the elementary schools
- What teachers' lives are like outside school
- The factors that affect learning among culturally diverse students

Even if adequate expertise were available for investigating these topics, which is unlikely, the investigations would require far more time and resources than are available to graduate students.

Narrowing the topic refers to paring the topic down to manageable size. The previous broad topics might be narrowed down to

- A program for developing English language vocabulary among bilingual students at the third-grade level
- Leisure activities of elementary teachers and the amount of time spent on them
- Hispanic students' perceptions of factors that interfere with success in school

An **amorphous topic** is stated so vaguely that it cannot be understood without further clarification. Examples of amorphous topics include

- Using the library to confront students' primary views of their lives
- Daily family routines and students' involvement in the school setting
- Administrators' compulsions and teachers' stress factors

In these examples, one gets no sense of what the research is actually aimed at or how it might be carried out.

Clarifying the topic involves changing the wording to make the topic statement understandable. The preceding topics could be clarified as

- Using bibliotherapy to improve attitude toward school among middle school students with low self-concept
- The relationship between home chore assignments and the degree of responsibility shown in school by fifth-grade students
- Teachers' opinions concerning the nature and frequency of required staff meetings

The **problem,** as previously noted, is the term used for a topic that has been refined appropriately for research. The preceding topics, as clarified, would be called problems if accompanied by research questions or hypotheses.

A **problem statement** is a sentence or paragraph that explains the purpose of a given investigation. Problem statements are presented in future tense in research proposals and in past tense in research reports, as shown in the following examples of problem statements for a research proposal and a research report, respectively.

The purpose of this study will be to develop and subject to preliminary testing a program for English-language vocabulary development among third-grade bilingual students.

The purpose of this study was to develop and subject to preliminary testing a program for English-language vocabulary development among third-grade bilingual students.

Problem statements are usually presented in one sentence, which often makes the statement a bit cumbersome to read, as in the examples just presented. Though infrequent, it is perfectly acceptable to state the problem in two or more shorter sentences, as follows:

The purpose of this study will be to construct and test an English vocabulary program.

The program will be designed for use in third-grade classrooms and will be field-tested in five selected classes in Elmwood schools.

A **research question** is the fundamental question inherent in the research topic. Such questions, normally supplemented by a number of subquestions, are often employed to guide the research process. For a topic such as using bibliotherapy to improve student attitude, a main research question could be:

What is the influence of bibliotherapy on attitudes toward school among students with low self-esteem?

Subquestions are questions subordinate to the research question. Their effect is complementary and cumulative; as the subquestions are answered, the main question is also ultimately answered. The following three examples show subquestions that might be asked in the investigation involving bibliotherapy.

1. In what ways has bibliotherapy been used to help students deal with problems in their lives?
2. What have been the positive and negative results of bibliotherapy?
3. What specific books might have bibliotherapeutic value for adolescent students with a low self-concept?

Hypotheses are succinct statements that forecast the findings of the study. They usually make predictions about future events, existing differences among groups, or existing relationships among variables. Hypotheses are of three types: *directional research hypotheses, nondirectional research hypotheses,* and *null hypotheses* (Charters, 1992).

A **research hypothesis** is a statement of what the investigator truly expects to find in the study. An example of a research hypothesis might be

Students with low self-concept who participate in a program of bibliotherapy will show improvement in their attitudes toward school.

This hypothesis is called **directional** because it indicates the direction of the results—in this case, a positive direction (improvement). It would also be a directional hypothesis if it stated that participating students would show a deterioration in attitude (a negative direction). A research hypothesis can also be **nondirectional**—for example,

Students with low self-concept who participate in a program of bibliotherapy will show changes in their attitudes toward school.

This research hypothesis is called nondirectional because it does not specify the direction of change, but only that change will occur. The change could be positive or negative.

The third type of hypothesis, the **null hypothesis,** states that no effect will occur, or that no differences or relationships will be found, even if that is not what the investigator expects to find. The following example demonstrates a null hypothesis:

Students with low self-concept who participate in a program of bibliotherapy will show no change in their attitudes toward school.

This statement would also be a research hypothesis if "no change" was what the investigator did expect to find, but in this example there would be little point in conducting research to try to show that bibliotherapy is of no value. Sometimes, however, investigators do set up research to demonstrate that no change, difference, or relationship is occurring. For example, suppose you hoped to show that the achievement of physics students taught with inexpensive equipment was just as high as that of students taught with expensive equipment. You would state a null hypothesis, believing or hoping it would be supported by the data.

There is a reason, however, for using null hypotheses even when they do not state what the investigator expects to find. Generally speaking, it is easier to disprove a statement than to prove it. And remember, in most cases researchers hope to "disprove"—or, more accurately, find inadequate support for—the null hypothesis.

Consider the following: Suppose you implement your bibliotherapy program. You hypothesize that at the end of the year, Elmwood students who complete your program will demonstrate an overall better attitude toward school than will matched groups of students attending other schools in your area. Note that this is a directional research hypothesis, not a null hypothesis. In order to *retain* your hypothesis as it is stated, your students must almost always outperform students in other schools. You might repeat this investigation five times and find each time that your students are better. Even then you cannot be certain that the results will not be different next time. For reasons discussed in the Appendix, for you to retain the research hypothesis, you must project that similar differences will occur at least 95 percent of the time, given hundreds of repetitions of the study.

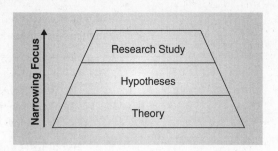

Figure 3.1

Structural view of theory, hypotheses, and research studies

But suppose you stated the hypothesis in the null form, saying that after students completed your program, no difference would exist in attitude toward school between your students and those attending the other schools in your area. Now if you do find a difference, you have greater confidence in rejecting the null hypothesis. Again, for reasons explained in the Appendix, you need to project, on average, only six "differences between groups" out of every 100 repetitions of the study in order to reject the null hypothesis. Tests of significance are designed so that even finding many compliances with a hypothesis statement does not provide compelling evidence that it is correct. But only very few contradictions of your statement are required to suggest it is incorrect. For that reason, researchers state hypotheses in the null form and then see if they can find contradictions to those hypotheses.

In many cases, researchers do not limit themselves to just a null hypothesis or a research hypothesis. Instead, they use both (Gay, Mills, & Airasian, 2006). In the example just considered, the investigator might state a null hypothesis and then pair it with a directional research hypothesis indicating the expected finding. The reason for doing this would be, first, to reject the hypothesis of no difference in attitude toward school and, second, to begin building the case that since a difference does seem to exist, it is very likely that the difference is being caused by the bibliotherapy program. It must be understood, however, that rejecting the null hypothesis does not, in itself, provide verification of the research hypothesis (McMillan & Schumacher, 2006). How hypotheses are tested for significance is explained in the Appendix.

A **theory** is an overall explanation of *how* things are or of *why* things are as they are. The term is defined here because many people confuse the terms *theory* and *hypothesis*. *Theory* is the much broader term: It explains but does not predict. It would be improper to say, "My theory is that these two boys will turn out to be behavior problems when they reach sixth grade." Hypotheses, on the other hand, do predict, and they can be drawn from theory. Take as an example psychologist Jean Piaget's theory of human intellectual development—his explanation of how the intellect is formed (Piaget, 1947/1950). From the basis of Piaget's theory, one can hypothesize, or make predictions, about how children will behave as their intellects develop, and then ultimately test that hypothesis in a research study (see Figure 3.1).

Exercise 3.3

A. Indicate whether each of the following is most in keeping with the definition of (RQ) research question, (SQ) subquestion, (DRH) directional research hypothesis, (NRH) nondirectional research hypothesis, (NH) null hypothesis, or (T) theory.

RQ NH   **1.** What do Elmwood's high school students believe to be true about the nature and frequency of sexual harassment by and among their peers?

NH   **2.** No overall difference exists in job satisfaction among teachers at different grade levels.

T DRH   **3.** One's sense of morality grows out of socialization and feedback from others.

S Q   **4.** To what degree do eighth-grade teachers look forward to going to work each day?

DRH   **5.** Students given a year's course in Latin will develop better English vocabularies than will students who do not study Latin.

DRH   **6.** Students given a year's course in Latin will develop English vocabularies that are inferior to those of students who do not study Latin.

NRH   **7.** Students taught algebra through method Z will reach different achievement levels than those taught algebra through method X.

B. Answer the following (T) true or (F) false.

T   **1.** Hypotheses are statements that predict occurrences or relationships between or among variables.

F   **2.** Null hypotheses cannot be tested statistically.

T   **3.** Null hypotheses assume that no differences originally existed among samples drawn from the same population.

T   **4.** If the null hypothesis is rejected, one can conclude either that the sample was not accurately drawn or that differences now observed between groups have resulted from variables intentionally or unintentionally introduced during the investigation.

F   **5.** Null hypotheses are usually statements of what the investigator really expects to find.

F   **6.** A directional research hypothesis should be tested for significance before it is tested in the null form.

F   **7.** Nondirectional research hypothesis and null hypothesis are different names for statements that say the same thing.

F   **8.** Hypotheses are more valuable in orienting almost all kinds of research than are research questions.

An example of the process of narrowing the focus of a research topic is depicted in Figure 3.2.

VARIABLES AND EDUCATIONAL RESEARCH

When formally stating research questions and hypotheses, it is imperative to carefully and deliberately identify the key variable(s) to be studied. **Variables** are sets of data that differ from one individual, object, or procedure to another, such as physical height, achievement scores, family incomes, styles of teaching, and varieties of books. A trait that does not differ from individual to individual is called a **constant.** The number of variables extant is enormous. Variables are of different types, including continuous, discrete, and dichotomous variables; independent and dependent variables; and several kinds of confounding variables.

CONTINUOUS, DISCRETE, AND DICHOTOMOUS VARIABLES

Variables can be continuous, discrete, or dichotomous. **Continuous variables** show gradational differences; individuals possess more or less of the same trait, which varies in small increments along a continuum. Examples of continuous variables are height and weight. At the fictitious Elmwood Schools introduced in Chapter 1, we could identify several

Figure 3.2

Example of the process of narrowing a broad research topic to arrive at specific research questions and hypotheses

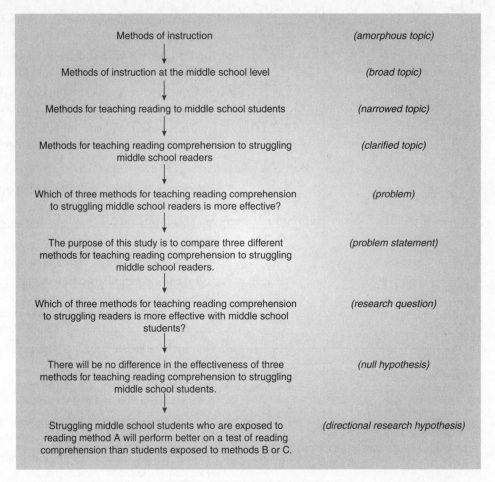

examples of continuous variables, such as "achievement" and "language proficiency" (as measured by standardized tests). **Discrete variables** are categorical in nature. Individuals may be classified into one of several categories. Examples of discrete variables are socioeconomic status, ethnicity, and ratings such as high–medium–low. At Elmwood Schools, specific discrete variables would include "ethnic group membership" and "type of instruction received." **Dichotomous variables** are simply special cases of discrete variables where there are only two possible categories—for example, handedness (right, left) and sex (male, female). Examples of specific dichotomous variables from the Elmwood example might include "school district"(Elmwood, other urban districts) and "language spoken" (English, non-English).

It is critical to note that a single variable *could* be continuous or discrete, depending on *how* the researcher chooses to measure or collect data on the variable. Consider the previous example of socioeconomic status (or SES). The researcher could ask the following question of participants:

To the nearest thousand dollars, what is your total annual household income?

Participants could then respond with precise dollar amounts, such as $26,000, $55,000, or $94,000. On the other hand, the researcher might only want to broadly categorize participants in terms of SES (e.g., low, medium, high). In this case, she would have to predetermine her "cut-off" points. For purposes of her study, she might arbitrarily decide to establish the separation between low and medium SES at $25,000 and between medium and high at $75,000. Her question of participants might then resemble the following:

Based on your total household income, in which of the following categories would you place yourself?

_____   Low (<$25,000)
_____   Medium ($25,000–$74,999)
_____   High (>$75,000)

Notice that more precise data is collected with the first form of the question, but this type of question is more difficult for people to answer. The second question, while not as precise, poses an easier task for the participant. Both result in the collection of SES data; they are just measured differently.

INDEPENDENT AND DEPENDENT VARIABLES

Independent and dependent variables play important roles in experimental and causal-comparative research. The terms *independent* and *dependent* are always linked together: You cannot have an independent variable without a dependent variable, and vice versa. The **independent variable** precedes in time and exerts influence on the **dependent variable,** which may change when influenced by the independent variable. For example, level of intelligence (independent variable) may influence how quickly students learn (dependent variable), or different methods of teaching (independent variable) may influence students' enjoyment of school (dependent variable). In the Elmwood Schools example, the two levels of the independent variable "school district" (Elmwood versus other urban districts) might be compared in order to determine if differences exist with respect to "student achievement" (the dependent variable).

CONFOUNDING VARIABLES

Confounding variables are traits or conditions, whose presence may or may not be recognized by the researcher, that may taint research outcomes. Types of confounding variables include (1) **intervening variables** (innate traits such as motivation and intelligence of participants); (2) **organismic variables** (relatively permanent physical traits that cannot be changed easily, such as poor eyesight, hearing, or coordination); and (3) **extraneous variables** (temporary conditions in nature, such as fatigue, distraction, excitement, discomfort, and test anxiety). Confounding variables must be controlled if research results are to be valid. Otherwise, conclusions drawn from research studies in which their effects were not controlled would very likely be misleading.

REGULATING THE SIZE OF RESEARCH TOPICS

As mentioned, most graduate students at first select problems that are much too broad to be investigated within existing constraints of time, skill, and resources. Occasionally, they select topics that are too narrow; those topics need to be broadened to make them worthwhile. How does one get a sense of the proper size of a topic in order to pare it down or flesh it out to acceptable dimensions? This "sizing" is best approached by anticipating what must be done to investigate a problem.

In Chapter 1 we noted that research begins with the identification of a concern for which there is no readily available solution but for which a solution might be found. To obtain and process information so that the concern might be resolved, one follows a sequence of research steps. Assuming a topic has been selected and posed as a problem, the investigation will involve the following tasks:

1. *Reviewing the literature.* Some topics have had almost nothing written about them; others may have been covered extensively in journal articles, reference works, and other publications, all of which should be examined. Researchers, therefore, use the library to check indexes and other references, a process described in detail in Chapters 4 and 5. To help decide whether a given topic is of a size feasible for investigation, it is a good idea to consult a library reference book entitled *Resources in Education,* plus either the *Education Index* or the *Current Index to Journals in Education,* which will give you an idea of how much has been published on the topic. You should hope to find 20 to 50 recent publications related, but not identical, to your topic. But if you find hundreds, the review of literature might become overwhelming. In that case you might narrow the topic further or do only a selected review of the literature.

2. *Organizing the study.* This step gives you the clearest picture of what researching a proposed topic is likely to entail. Some studies are easy to organize, whereas others are difficult because they involve many arrangements, selection procedures, permissions, approvals, and the like. Think through what will be necessary to enable you to complete the investigation.

3. *Collecting and analyzing data.* Collecting good data is usually the most difficult—at least the most worrisome and time-consuming—part of conducting research. Statistical analysis, which once frightened beginners, is now easily done with computers. Data must be obtained in the appropriate kind and quantity, paralleling the investigation's research questions and hypotheses. You may have to prepare questionnaires, tests, or other assessment devices. It may be necessary to obtain published tests. You may need access to records from schools and elsewhere. Graduate students operate within stringent limitations of time and money, and their research skills are not yet sophisticated. Anticipating as precisely as possible the procedures involved in data collection will give you a good idea of whether a particular research topic can be investigated, given your constraints.

Foreseeing the Research Report Format

When reporting research, one follows conventions that make reading easier and allow critical analysis of the topic, procedures, findings, and conclusions. The components of a research report, as shown in the following list, generally parallel the steps by which the research is conducted and, thus, provide further insight into the time and labor requirements of the topic you select.

1. *Introduction.* This section specifies the topic and tells why it is worth investigating. In reports such as graduate theses the introduction may also contain a statement of the problem, hypotheses, research questions, definitions of terms, and limits placed on the study.

2. *Review of related literature.* This component is not difficult to accomplish but may be very time-consuming, especially when there is a vast amount of literature related to your topic.

3. *Method.* The **method** spells out how the study was designed and how data were obtained and analyzed. Listing the procedures followed is easy enough but actually carrying them out may involve an enormous amount of work. It is best to select a topic about which data can be obtained and analyzed easily. With the availability of computers and statistics programs, statistical treatments of the data no longer present a significant obstacle. This section includes the following components:

a. *Design.* The type of research that will be conducted, including how the variables and participants are arranged in order to test the predicted outcomes

b. *Subjects (participants).* A thorough description of who your participants are, including where they are from, how they were selected, how many were selected, and what will be required of them during your study

   c. *Instrumentation.* Descriptions of how the data will be collected and how the quality of the data (i.e., its validity and reliability) will be ensured

   d. *Procedures.* Describes the sequence of all major activities that must be conducted during the study

   e. *Data analysis.* The specifications of how the resulting data will be analyzed

4. *Findings.* Often called results, this section summarizes the new information that has been discovered. Findings are reported verbally, graphically, and/or numerically.

5. *Conclusions and discussion.* The researcher clarifies the meaning of the new information discovered and uses that information to answer the research questions and to retain or reject the hypotheses. Also included are the investigator's speculations and other discussions about the study and conclusions reached.

THE VALUE OF CONVENTIONAL PROCEDURES AND REPORTS

Attempting to foresee the research and report requirements helps greatly in selecting a topic, limiting it, and investigating it to a conclusion. From beginning to end, a prime goal should be to conduct and report research in a manner that quietly implies, "Here is my research; find fault with it if you can." This attitude explains why it is so necessary to select a topic of importance, refine it, follow established research conventions, and report the work clearly.

Exercise 3.4

Evaluate each of the following potential topics for research at the graduate level. Mark them as V (too vague), B (too broad), N (too narrow), C (too affected by constraints), or R (about right).

___B___ **1.** An investigation of the social problems evident among students attending Elmwood's public schools

___R___ **2.** An investigation of the relative effectiveness of two different systems of discipline in selected sixth-grade classrooms

___V/B___ **3.** An investigation of six Filipino students' global behavior as a function of the interplay of their values, social contexts, and familial patterns

___R___ **4.** A comparison of the after-school responsibilities of selected sixth-grade students from three different ethnic groups

___B___ **5.** Views that students of diverse ethnic groups hold of teachers and other adults

___BC___ **6.** The effect that monetary payment for improved grades has on high school achievement of white students

___BC___ **7.** Around-the-clock shadowing of 10 selected Elmwood high school teachers

___R___ **8.** Improvement in written composition among selected high school sophomores as a function of same-day analysis and feedback concerning their written work

___N___ **9.** An experiment to add 10 words to the vocabulary of an inner-city student

REFINING THE TOPIC: AN ILLUSTRATIVE CASE

We have noted that the research topics selected by graduate students are at first usually too broad, too vague, or too narrow and therefore must be refined before they can be researched. The case of Jan is presented to illustrate the process of sharpening research topics into research problems.

JAN'S CONCERN ABOUT STUDENTS' ENTRY AGE TO KINDERGARTEN

Jan, a kindergarten teacher, has long believed that students who have already reached age 5 when they enter kindergarten do better throughout their subsequent school years than students who enter kindergarten while only 4 years old. She believes, therefore, that it is a bad idea to enroll children in kindergarten before they reach age 5. She thinks doing so harms the children, which she wants to demonstrate in her study. In fact, the topic she has submitted for approval is "The bad effects of early entry into kindergarten." Jan's thesis adviser tells her that the topic cannot be researched in its stated form. To help her, the adviser presses Jan to state exactly what she means by "bad effects." Jan replies that the children have trouble in later grades.

What kind of trouble, the adviser wants to know.

Emotional problems, Jan maintains. She says the children cry a great deal, get upset easily, don't show much responsibility, and generally act like babies.

The adviser asks Jan how she knows that early-entry students behave like that, and Jan says all the teachers in her school are aware of it and that she has heard many of them comment on the problem. The adviser wants to know if early-entry students all behave that way (not all, Jan says) and if they do so only in primary grades.

No, they do so throughout school, Jan maintains, claiming that most of the problem students in sixth grade entered kindergarten at age 4.

The adviser asks Jan if she believes she could, for three randomly selected schools, divide sixth-grade students into two groups: those who had begun school at age 4 and those who had begun at age 5. Jan says she could, that records were available in the schools, and that she is sure the respective building administrators would be interested.

On what basis would Jan compare the two groups, the adviser wanted to know.

On how well they are doing in sixth grade, Jan answers. When pressed to be more specific, Jan mentions learning, behavior, personal relations, and emotionality.

The adviser points out that Jan's topic is too large and unwieldy and that it needs to be narrowed. The adviser asks what would be at the heart of Jan's concern if she had to select only two variables to measure in the students? Jan identifies reading ability and overall maturity.

How would she assess reading ability? From achievement test records, Jan decides. And how would she assess maturity? After considerable thought and discussion, Jan decides she could prepare a rating scale with categories such as responsibility, personal relations with others, emotionality, and self-assurance. She could ask teachers to rate the students in her sample, using the scale.

The adviser asks Jan to restate her topic. After two more discussions, Jan states her topic: "The effects of entry age into kindergarten on later student learning and emotional maturity."

The adviser approves that topic, contingent on Jan's obtaining permission from school district officials to pursue the investigation and her obtaining access to pertinent school records.

Pending permission and access, Jan is directed to prepare a research question and subquestions for the topic. Jan submits the following, which are approved.

Research Question

How do sixth-grade students who entered kindergarten at age 4 compare with those who entered kindergarten at age 5 in reading achievement and social maturity?

Subquestions (questions subordinate to the main research question)

1. By what rationales of intellectual and social growth might one predict reading and maturity differences between the groups?
2. What existing research, if any, tends to confirm or deny the existence of such differences?
3. What is the average reading level of "older students" (those who entered kindergarten at age 5)?
4. What is the average reading level of "younger students" (those who entered kindergarten at age 4)?
5. What is the average maturity level of older students, as judged by their present teachers?
6. What is the average maturity level of younger students, as judged by their present teachers?
7. What is the average incidence of "problem behavior episodes" among older students?
8. What is the average incidence of "problem behavior episodes" among younger students?
9. Does gender seem to influence achievement and behavior in the two groups?

PREPARING A RESEARCH PROPOSAL

for research

To check your understanding of the various aspects of a research proposal, go to the "Selecting and Defining a Research Topic" section of **MyEducationLab for Research** and then click on *Assignments and Activities*. First, read the research proposal provided, and then complete the activity titled "Reviewing Research Proposal B." This exercise provides you with an opportunity to closely examine the components of a proposal.

The example of Jan illustrates something of the process of selecting an appropriate research topic and then through reworking and refinement making it researchable. Jan still has an important task to accomplish before proceeding with her investigation: compose and submit a research proposal that includes (1) a statement of the problem; (2) the significance of the problem; (3) the research questions or hypotheses; (4) definitions, assumptions, limitations, and delimitations; (5) a survey of existing literature; (6) the general procedure to be followed; (7) a time calendar; and, possibly, (8) a budget. Let us note briefly what each of these elements entails.

1. *Statement of the problem.* As mentioned earlier, an explanation of the purpose of the study, usually a simple declarative statement that is kept short but identifies the key elements of the proposed study. For example:

> The purpose of this study is to determine whether age of entry into kindergarten has an effect on students' subsequent school learning and behavior.

2. *Significance of the problem.* Statement that explains why the problem merits investigation, including why it is worth the time, effort, and expense involved in carrying it out. For example:

> Many teachers have long believed that children who enter kindergarten at age 4 are not sufficiently mature intellectually or emotionally to work on equal terms with students who enter kindergarten at age 5. They believe they see in those students differences in learning and social behavior that persist through the elementary grades. This study is designed to yield evidence that will substantiate or negate such concerns about age of entry to kindergarten.

3. *Research questions or hypotheses.* Posed to guide the study and lead to resolution of the central concern. The following research question, research hypothesis, or null hypothesis would be suitable for Jan's study:

Research question—How do sixth-grade students who entered kindergarten at age 4 compare with those who entered kindergarten at age 5 regarding reading achievement and social maturity? (This main research question is accompanied by subquestions, such as those presented for Jan's research.)

Research hypothesis—Students who entered kindergarten at age 4 will in sixth grade show lower reading achievement and lower levels of social maturity than will students who entered kindergarten at age 5.

Null hypothesis—No differences exist in reading achievement and social maturity between sixth-grade students who entered kindergarten at age 4 and sixth-grade students who entered kindergarten at age 5.

4. *Definitions, assumptions, limitations, and delimitations.* The investigator defines terms that are unclear or that have special meanings (insofar as such terms can be anticipated early in the study; modifications may be made later). In Jan's study, the term *social maturity* would be defined, as would *reading achievement* and such special terms as *younger students* and *older students.*

The investigator also states any known **assumptions** that are being made but cannot be proved. Examples in Jan's study would include the assumption that social maturity can be judged through instances of student behavior and that teachers are competent to make valid judgments about student behavior.

Limitations refer to conditions outside the investigator's control that affect data collection. Jan's limitations would include the availability of records needed to show age of entry to kindergarten, sixth-grade achievement scores in reading, and objections that might arise from parents and administrators.

Delimitations are the boundaries purposely put on the study, usually to narrow it for researchability. Jan's study was delimited to certain identifiable students in certain schools and concerned only age of kindergarten entry, social maturity, and achievement in reading.

5. *Survey of the literature.* For the research proposal, one need not conduct a full review of the literature. It is advisable, however, to *survey* the literature—that is, examine appropriate references and indexes to determine the amount and kind of literature that must later be reviewed. It is also important to scan titles of articles to see if any deal directly with the topic under consideration.

6. *General procedures.* The investigator presents a preliminary listing of the steps to be undertaken in obtaining permission, selecting participants, composing questionnaires or selecting tests or similar materials, obtaining data, summarizing and analyzing data, and presenting findings and drawing conclusions. Of course, not all details of these steps, nor even all of the steps themselves, can be totally foreseen.

7. *Time calendar.* The time line, with dates and deadlines, is superimposed, figuratively if not literally, on the list of procedures. Time is of the essence in most research, especially research in graduate degree programs, where an investigation often must be completed in as little as five or six months. A time calendar is therefore of great help for keeping on track and on time.

8. *Budget.* Depending on the type of investigation to be undertaken, it is often a good idea to prepare a budget that indicates direct and indirect costs. *Direct costs* are those that you will have to pay out of pocket for such things as tests, other materials, transportation, and clerical help. *Indirect costs* are those that someone (preferably not you) will have to pay for items such as utilities, space, computer access, custodial services, and the like. Indirect costs are normally provided to graduate students by the institutions in which they are enrolled.

DEVELOPMENTAL ACTIVITY

Research Topic Refinement

Up to this point, you have been working with a general topic area or possible topic for your proposed research study. Based on the considerations of Chapter 1 and the determination of the most appropriate type of research for your topic or problem you made in Chapter 2, it is now time to refine—and further specify—your topic. In addition to refining your topic, you will begin to specify your research questions or hypotheses. Carefully consider your topic as you respond to the following:

1. A possible topic or problem I am thinking of researching

   _____

   _____

2. A *broader* research topic within my general topic area

   _____

   _____

3. A more *narrow* research topic within my general topic area

   _____

   _____

4. After *careful* consideration of my responses to items 1, 2, and 3, I believe that my topic is researchable as stated (*check one*)

   _____ yes   _____ no (if "no," you'll need to focus your topic before you go any further)

5. The problem statement for my proposed study

   The purpose of this study will be to _____

   _____

6. I intend to use hypotheses to guide this research study *(check one and provide explanation)*

   yes _____

   My hypotheses (both null and research)

   _____

   _____

   _____

   no _____

7. My research question(s)

   _____

   _____

8. Possible *assumptions* for my study

   _____

   _____

9. Possible *limitations* for my study

   _____

   _____

10. Possible *delimitations* for my study

    _____

    _____

CHAPTER SUMMARY

Research begins with the selection and refinement of a suitable topic for investigation. When refined and clarified, the topic becomes known as the problem. The problem, in turn, may be supplemented with additional information and presented as a proposal for research.

There is no dearth of topics for research in education. Various indexes and other references attest to the enormous range of possibilities, but the most fruitful topics for graduate research usually lie in personal concerns about aspects of education. Certain cautions and considerations should be kept in mind when selecting a topic. Key considerations include one's personal interest and the topic's importance, relative newness, amenability to time constraints, and ease of management. The topic should be inexpensive to investigate, and it must incorporate impeccable standards of ethics at all times.

Once a research topic is selected, it ordinarily must be refined by limiting its scope, wording it clearly, and supplementing it with research questions or hypotheses that guide the investigation and help resolve its central questions. The difficult matter of regulating topics so they will be of a suitable size for graduate-level investigation can be managed by foreseeing the tasks that research requires. It is also helpful at this time to anticipate the format required for the final research report.

Research usually focuses on variables, which are sets of data that show ranges of difference in people, objects, and procedures. Terms used for variables include *continuous* (a wide range), *discrete* (several categories), *dichotomous* (two categories), *independent* (a manipulated variable), *dependent* (changes in accord with changes in the independent variable), and *confounding* (variables not subjected to research but which may taint research findings).

When a topic has been refined into a problem, graduate students are usually asked to prepare and submit for approval a research proposal that includes a statement of the problem; commentary on the significance of the problem; research questions or hypotheses; certain definitions, assumptions, limitations, and delimitations of the problem; a brief survey of the literature; a description of probable procedures for organizing the study and obtaining and analyzing data; a calendar, or time line, for accomplishing various aspects of the research process; and sometimes a budget that lists direct and indirect costs.

LIST OF IMPORTANT TERMS

amorphous topic
assumptions
broad topic
clarifying the topic
confounding variable
constant
continuous variable
delimitations
dependent variable
dichotomous variable

directional (research hypothesis)
discrete variables
extraneous variable
hypotheses
independent variable
intervening variable
limitations
method
nondirectional (research hypothesis)
null hypothesis

organismic variable
problem
problem statement
research hypothesis
research question
subquestions
theory
variable

YOUR CURRENT STATUS

Building on what you already know about the nature of educational research and its purposes, types, and data sources, you have now become acquainted with where and how one finds and selects a worthwhile research topic, refines the topic to make it researchable and manageable, supplements the topic with useful research questions or hypotheses, and prepares a research proposal. Your next task is to learn how to locate published reports in the research library, the topic of Chapter 4. Before proceeding, please respond to the activities for thought and discussion.

ACTIVITIES FOR THOUGHT AND DISCUSSION

1. Name, in order of importance to you, five considerations you would keep in mind when selecting a topic for possible research. *[handwritten: Time? money how long has been researched? ...]*

2. For an investigation into bibliotherapy as a means to improve the attitude toward school of students with low self-concept, complete the following questions:

   RESEARCH QUESTION   Can bibliotherapy be used to help _____?

   SUBQUESTIONS

   a. In what ways has bibliotherapy been used _____?
   b. What have been the positive and negative _____?
   c. What books, suitable for early adolescent readers _____?
   d. To what extent do students freely select _____ ?
   e. How do students react to _____?
   f. What changes in _____?

3. Look back at the three topics you selected in Exercise 3.1 as interesting possibilities for research. For one of those topics (a) compose a directional research hypothesis and (b) compose a null hypothesis. Discuss your efforts with others in the class.

4. For that same topic, outline on a single page a brief research proposal that contains the elements normally included in research proposals. Discuss with others in the class.

5. See how well you can answer the questions presented at the beginning of the chapter.
   a. Where can good educational research topics be found?
   b. What should one keep in mind when selecting a topic for research?
   c. Why do modifications and refinements usually have to be made in research topics after they have been selected?
   d. What are the purposes of research questions and hypotheses?
   e. How are research questions and hypotheses best stated?
   f. What are the similarities and difference between research questions and hypotheses?
   g. What is the distinction between a research topic and research problem?
   h. What is meant by the term *variable* and what are the distinguishing characteristics of various types—*continuous, discrete, independent, dependent,* and *confounding variables*?
   i. What is a research proposal and how is it prepared and presented?

6. Recall or turn to the organizer presented at the beginning of the chapter. Without looking in the text explain the chapter contents as suggested by the organizer.

ANSWERS TO CHAPTER EXERCISES

3.2. 1. D 2. PI 3. I 4. N 5. E

3.3A. 1. RQ 2. NH 3. T 4. SQ 5. DRH 6. DRH 7. NRH

3.3B. 1. T 2. F 3. T 4. T 5. F 6. F 7. F 8. F

3.4. 1. B 2. R 3. V/B 4. R 5. B 6. C 7. C 8. R 9. N

REFERENCES AND RECOMMENDED READINGS

Best, J., & Kahn, J. (2006). *Research in Education* (10th ed.). Boston: Allyn & Bacon.

Charters, W. (1992). *Understanding Variables and Hypotheses in Scientific Research.* (Report No. ISBN 0-86552-115-8). Eugene, OR: ERIC Clearinghouse on Educational Management. (ERIC No. ED 342 056).

Current Index to Journals in Education. (1969 to present). Phoenix: Oryx Press.

Edyburn, D. L. (1999). *The Electronic Scholar: Enhancing Research Productivity with Technology.* Upper Saddle River, NJ: Merrill.

Encyclopedia of Educational Research (6th ed.). (1992). New York: Free Press.

Gall, M., Borg, W., & Gall, J. (2003). *Educational Research: An Introduction* (7th ed.). Boston: Allyn & Bacon.

Gay, L. R., Mills, G. E., & Airasian, P. (2006). *Educational Research: Competencies for Analysis and Application* (8th ed.). Upper Saddle River, NJ: Merrill.

Ginsburg, A., McLaughlin, M., & Plisko, V. (1992). Reinvigorating program evaluation at the U.S. Department of Education. *Educational Researcher, 21*(3), 24–27.

Lesourd, S. (1992). A review of methodologies for cross-cultural education. *Social Studies, 83*(1), 30–35.

Mann, T. (1987). *A Guide to Library Research Methods.* New York: Oxford.

McMillan, J., & Schumacher, S. (2006). *Research in Education: Evidence Based Inquiry* (6th ed.). Boston: Allyn & Bacon.

Piaget, J. (1950). *The Psychology of Intelligence.* M. Percy and D. Berlyne, (Trans.). London: Routledge and Kegan Paul. (Original work published 1947).

Review of Research in Education. (1973 to present). Washington, DC: American Educational Research Association.

Wittrock, M. (Ed.). (1986). *Handbook of Research on Teaching* (3rd ed.). New York: Macmillan.

4

Locating
Published Research

PREVIEW

This chapter explores using the university research library to locate two types of sources:

■ Secondary (not firsthand) sources of information, such as

Encyclopedias	Yearbooks
Reviews of research	Handbooks of research
Scholarly books	Magazine and newspaper articles

■ Primary (firsthand) sources of information, such as

Journal articles	Conference papers
Dissertations	Monographs
Scholarly books	Technical reports
Digest of Educational Statistics	

Locating sources of information is accomplished through the following:

■ The use of published journals, such as

Resources in Education	*Dissertation Abstracts International*
CIJE	*Psychological Abstracts*
Mental Measurements Yearbook	

■ The use of online indexes, such as

ERIC descriptors	Education Research Complete
PsycINFO	Education Index
EBSCOhost	

■ Computer-assisted searches of library resources

TARGETED LEARNINGS

In Chapter 3 you learned how to identify a research problem, refine it for investigation, formulate appropriate questions and hypotheses, and compose a research proposal. In this chapter you will learn how to use the research library to access major sources of information related to a given topic. As you read this chapter, look especially for information having to do with the following questions:

1. Why are secondary sources a good place to begin looking for information on a topic?
2. What are four specific examples of secondary sources?
3. How are primary sources located in a library?

4. Which library holdings are usually considered to be primary sources of information?
5. What are three specific examples of directories to primary sources?
6. What advantages do computer searches of the literature offer over manual searches?

USING THE RESEARCH LIBRARY

All researchers explore the literature for material about their topic, first to see what has already been done and second to profit from findings, cautions, and suggestions made by other researchers. The guidance from this review helps keep the research on course toward a satisfactory conclusion.

The skills of locating information in a library are best learned not from reading about the library but from actually using its resources. Therefore, this chapter does not go into great detail about important library references and indexes. Instead you will find them listed and briefly described, accompanied by a guide for their use. Although this chapter is relatively short, remember that in order to grasp the potential of the research library—and to ready yourself for conducting your own research—you must take the time to personally explore the library's resources, using the specific details described in this chapter for guidance.

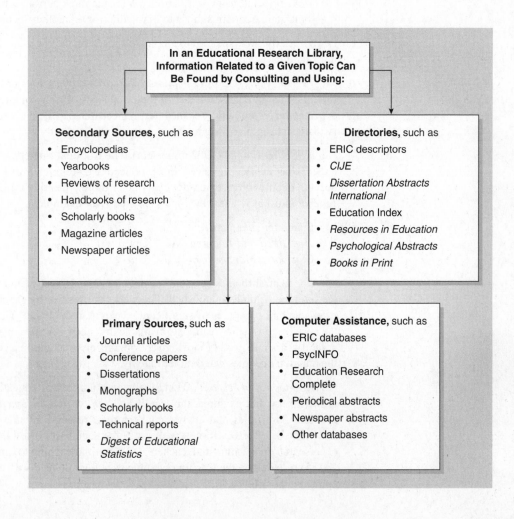

In an Educational Research Library, Information Related to a Given Topic Can Be Found by Consulting and Using:

Secondary Sources, such as
- Encyclopedias
- Yearbooks
- Reviews of research
- Handbooks of research
- Scholarly books
- Magazine articles
- Newspaper articles

Directories, such as
- ERIC descriptors
- *CIJE*
- *Dissertation Abstracts International*
- Education Index
- *Resources in Education*
- *Psychological Abstracts*
- *Books in Print*

Primary Sources, such as
- Journal articles
- Conference papers
- Dissertations
- Monographs
- Scholarly books
- Technical reports
- *Digest of Educational Statistics*

Computer Assistance, such as
- ERIC databases
- PsycINFO
- Education Research Complete
- Periodical abstracts
- Newspaper abstracts
- Other databases

Secondary Sources in the Library

All research libraries contain a number of **secondary sources** of information. *Secondary* means that these sources do not provide firsthand or eyewitness accounts. Rather, they provide expert compilations, analyses, and interpretations of primary information by other individuals. As a rule, it is best to leave primary sources aside at first and begin a literature search by examining secondary sources, which indicate trends and general conclusions. They usually contain extensive bibliographies of primary source materials. The secondary sources you will find profitable include encyclopedias of research, yearbooks and handbooks of research, reviews of research, scholarly books, and sometimes magazine and newspaper articles.

This all have a but. Why? [handwritten marginal note]

- *Reference* books such as handbooks, yearbooks, and encyclopedias give the best overall coverage of various topics but tend to become dated three or four years after publication. *So is obsolete?* [handwritten note]
- *Reviews of research* provide the best compilations and critiques of research on selected topics, but the topic selection is limited, and the material begins to become dated three or four years after publication.
- *Scholarly books* offer the best overviews and in-depth analyses of certain topics, but the topics are typically few in number and treated in great detail, as is the case with single-theme works, or else are many in number and treated more superficially, as with textbooks. (Note that scholarly books are considered primary sources if they report an investigator's own work and conclusions.)
- *Magazine and newspaper* articles offer the most current information about particular topics but are more subject to bias and error than other secondary sources.

Let us briefly note specific examples of some of the more useful secondary sources of information.

1. *The Encyclopedia of Educational Research* (1992). This prime source of research information about a large number of topics consists of four volumes with articles written by experts who review, analyze, and interpret research pertinent to broad topics. This reference is a key starting place when reviewing research literature.

2. *NSSE Yearbooks* (1902 to present). The National Society for the Study of Education (NSSE) has, every year since 1902, produced two volumes, Part 1 and Part 2, each of which deals in depth with research done on one or more education topics. The titles of the *NSSE Yearbooks* usually reveal the topics covered—for example,

> *Education and the Brain* (Vol. 77, pt. 2)
> *The Gifted and Talented* (Vol. 78, pt. 1)
> *Classroom Management* (Vol. 78, pt. 2)

The central themes selected for new volumes reflect matters of particular concern at the time the volume is published. The works are written by experts in the topic areas, and extensive bibliographies of significant research are included. The works provide some of the very best in-depth treatments available, but each volume covers only a few topics, and several years may pass before a given topic receives attention a second time, if ever. Thus, the material becomes dated rather quickly.

3. *Handbooks of research.* Handbooks on a number of educational topics are available in the library. For example, the *Handbook of Research on Teaching* (third edition, 1986) provides 35 articles that analyze and interpret research related to five areas: (1) theory and methods of research on teaching; (2) the social and institutional context of teaching; (3) research on teaching and teachers; (4) adapting teaching to differences among learners; and (5) research on the teaching of subjects and grade levels. Extensive bibliographies accompany the articles.

This reference was, for a few years after its publication, one of the best for research topics having to do with teachers and teaching. But because so much research has been done since the 1986 edition, this resource is dated for most current topics. When the new edition appears, the handbook will again be one of the most valuable references available to educational researchers.

The following are among the many excellent handbooks of research on specific topics in education:

Handbook of Research on Early Childhood Education
Handbook of Research on Educational Administration
Handbook of Research on Language Development
Handbook of Research on Curriculum
Handbook of Research on Math Teaching and Learning
Handbook of Research on Multicultural Education
Handbook of Research on Music Teaching and Learning
Handbook of Research on Science Teaching

4. *Review of Research in Education.* Published yearly, this reference provides expert critical review and analysis of important research on selected topics. The articles typically include more research citations than the articles in a reference such as *The Encyclopedia of Educational Research.* The articles, written by expert researchers, vary in number in each issue. Volumes tend to emphasize one to three current issues. The 1984 volume, for example, emphasized various aspects of human development and education of the handicapped, whereas the 1990 volume emphasized mathematics and science instruction and parental choice of schools, and the 1994 volume emphasized teaching knowledge and practice and equity issues in educational access and assessment.

5. *Review of Educational Research.* This quarterly publication, as the title indicates, contains reviews of research on selected topics in education. The reviews are quite complete, and the authors provide extensive bibliographies.

6. *Educational Leadership.* Widely read by professors, school administrators, and school district personnel who work in curriculum and supervision, this journal is published by the Association for Supervision and Curriculum Development. Periodically, the journal presents reviews of recent research literature on given topics. These reviews are accurate but nontechnical and reveal the current status of the topic reviewed.

7. *Scholarly books.* Books written by academicians can, on occasion, be of great value to researchers. They are generally of two types: single-theme books and textbooks. **Single-theme books** go into great depth in addressing a particular matter and can provide much insight into the topic's nature and history. Usually these books present the author's interpretations of what others have done. They are, therefore, considered secondary sources, although sometimes they report a scholar's own research, in which case they are considered primary sources. Single-theme books tend to be technical and detailed. Often they report a scholar's views, interpretations, and speculations; in those cases, the author's biases are usually evident. Bearing this caveat in mind, investigators should not overlook this source of potentially valuable information.

Textbooks, in contrast to single-theme books, usually treat a great many topics, although rarely in much depth. They can be of considerable value in depicting the history, stages, and trends within various topics. Textbook authors are selective in the references they include, which means that most textbook bibliographies are short but of high quality.

Books in Print (annual editions) is the best source for identifying books that are of recent publication or that have stood the test of time, listing books by author, title, and topic and indicating where the book can be obtained. Summaries of a few selected books are given. University libraries, unfortunately, do not quickly acquire recent books. Acquisition time is slow and financial considerations preclude the purchase of many books. If you need to obtain a book your library does not have, it can often be acquired on interlibrary loan from one university to another. It may be more convenient to purchase a needed book through booksellers or by writing or calling the publisher directly. WOW

8. *Magazine and newspaper articles.* Especially important for some topics, newspapers and magazines often report the latest occurrences, findings, and controversies. If cited as literature related to a research topic, articles from these sources must be carefully evaluated for accuracy, completeness, and lack of bias. Remember that they are written by reporters who rarely have scholarly backgrounds in the topics presented, and their presentations may not have been subjected to scrutiny by authorities before publication. Moreover, the popular media thrive on controversy, and their articles are rarely presented in a calm, evenhanded manner. Nevertheless, magazines and newspapers sometimes provide the most up-to-date information available.

LOCATING SECONDARY SOURCES

The library's main catalog is used to locate encyclopedias, yearbooks, handbooks, and scholarly books. The main catalog formerly consisted of drawers of index cards, one card for each book or series of books, containing complete bibliographic information and a Library of Congress number or other code that indicated the material's location in the library. A few libraries still retain card catalogs, but most have converted to computer cataloging. Now, instead of leafing through drawers of cards, you use a computer terminal and follow on-screen directions to locate reference materials. The computer screen shows the source you are seeking and provides a full bibliographic citation and the source's location in the library.

Reference books such as the *Encyclopedia of Educational Research, Review of Research in Education,* and various handbooks are shelved in the library's main reference section. Other secondary sources, such as certain abstracts, journals, and yearbooks, may be bound and shelved in the stacks or put onto microfiche and kept in the microfiche reading room. If you have trouble locating guides or resources, ask a librarian for assistance; librarians are most helpful.

Newspaper stories related to given topics can now be located and reviewed on library computers via *Newspaper Abstracts,* an index that abstracts articles published since 1989 in 25 major regional, national, financial, and ethnic newspapers. "Education" is one of approximately 20 topic categories for which abstracts are provided. Your library also keeps contents of various newspapers on microfiche, available in the microfiche reading room.

Similarly, magazine articles related to given topics can be located and reviewed in *Periodical Abstracts.* Topic coverage, including education, is the same as for *Newspaper Abstracts.* Ask a librarian for directions. Your library keeps a selection of periodicals on microfiche or bound in original form and shelved.

PRIMARY SOURCES IN THE LIBRARY

After exploring secondary sources, you should examine primary sources in order to judge original research for yourself and to obtain more current information than is normally available in reference works. Common primary sources are journal articles, monographs, and papers presented at conferences. You can locate **primary sources** through specialized indexes, bibliographies, abstracts, and reviews of research. The Educational Resources Information Center (ERIC) provides marvelous assistance in locating primary sources through its listings and abstracts of published research.

■ **Abstracts** (summaries) of original works can be found in publications such as *Psychological Abstracts* and ERIC's *Current Index to Journals in Education (CIJE).* Published without evaluation or comment, abstracts help you decide whether the original publication merits further examination.

- *Reviews,* listed previously as a secondary source, provide extensive bibliographies of journal articles and other publications that can be consulted as primary sources.
- *Indexes* are especially valuable because they list primary sources of information such as monographs and journal articles that would otherwise be difficult to locate. Several excellent indexes, many of which can be accessed through computers, are available in research libraries.

Exercise 4.1

Indicate whether each of the following is most likely a (S) secondary source or (P) a primary source of information.

_____ **1.** Professor Oldshanks's report of his own research on the aging process

_____ **2.** Professor Oldshanks's in-depth analyses of other investigators' research on the aging process

_____ **3.** Dr. Apodaca's book that criticizes the treatment of Hispanic students in Texas schools

_____ **4.** The published article "How We Improved Multicultural Understanding in Elmwood Schools," written by the director of the project

_____ **5.** The book entitled *A Review of Progress in Bilingual Teaching*

_____ **6.** A conference address, "Stress and the Workplace: One Teacher's Personal Perspective"

SPECIFIC DIRECTORIES OF PRIMARY REFERENCES

Several printed and online directories can help locate primary sources. Some list articles for a variety of topics whereas others are more specialized.

The ERIC Database

The Educational Resources Information Center, or **ERIC,** publishes the most widely used indexes for locating education materials printed since 1981. (For articles published before 1981, consult a reference called *The Education Index.*) ERIC (www.eric.ed.gov) consists of 16 regional clearinghouses and four adjunct houses that locate, catalog, abstract, and index research articles and other documents. Each clearinghouse is responsible for one of the following subject areas: (1) adult, career, and vocational education; (2) counseling and personnel services; (3) reading and communication skills; (4) educational management; (5) handicapped and gifted children; (6) languages and linguistics; (7) higher education; (8) information resources; (9) junior colleges; (10) elementary and early childhood education; (11) rural education and small schools; (12) science, mathematics, and environmental education; (13) social studies/social science education; (14) teacher education; (15) tests, measurements, and evaluation; (16) urban education; (17) art education; (18) United States–Japan studies; (19) literacy education for limited-English-proficient adults; and (20) matters related to Chapter 1 (federal law regarding instructional assistance for disadvantaged students). ERIC publishes a thesaurus of descriptive terms and two indexes that provide abstracts and complete citations of materials reviewed.

1. The ***Thesaurus of ERIC Descriptors*** is a book that lists the specific topics and labels under which various articles and documents are indexed. It is mainly used for accessing ERIC abstracts via computer, a topic to which we shall return.

2. *CIJE (Current Index to Journals in Education)* is the ERIC index that cites and presents abstracts of articles published in education and closely related fields. Two bound volumes of new citations are published each year, and supplements are issued each month. The bound volumes of *CIJE* are typically shelved with the general reference books or in the education section of the library. Most larger libraries provide computer access to *CIJE* on CD-ROM (compact disk with read-only memory), which, as will be described later, provides wonderful benefits to the researcher.

3. *RIE (Resources in Education)* is the ERIC index that cites and abstracts documents such as papers read at conferences, descriptions of new programs, technical reports, reports from federally funded programs, selected books, and much original research that has not been published elsewhere, specifically in academic journals. *RIE* is shelved in bound form and is also accessible via the library computer. Until recently, the materials indexed were not usually available in libraries and had to be ordered from the addresses provided in the citations. Increasingly, libraries are making *RIE* materials directly available to researchers, predominantly in the form of microfiche.

Both *CIJE* and *RIE* are available and searchable via the Internet (see Applying Technology: "Searching ERIC Online" on pages 72–75).

PsycINFO

PsycINFO (www.apa.org/psycinfo) is an abstract database of psychological literature from the 1800s to the present. It can certainly serve as an essential tool for researchers, as it contains bibliographic citations, abstracts, cited references, and descriptive information to help researchers locate published research across a wide variety of scholarly publications in the behavioral and social sciences.

Education Research Complete

Education Research Complete (www.ebscohost.com/thisTopic.php?marketID=1&topicID=639) is an online resource for education research, maintained by EBSCOhost, that offers the world's largest and most complete collection of full-text education journals. It is a bibliographic and full-text database covering scholarly research and information relating to all areas of education. Topics covered include all levels of education, from early childhood to higher education, and all educational specialties, such as multilingual education, health education, and testing. Education Research Complete also covers areas of curriculum instruction as well as administration, policy, funding, and related social issues. The database provides indexing and abstracts for more than 1,870 journals, as well as full text for more than 1,060 journals. This database also includes full text for 133 books and monographs and full text for numerous education-related conference papers.

Abstracts Publications

Some journals specialize in publishing short abstracts of unpublished papers and of previously published articles. The following are among the most useful for educational researchers:

1. *Psychological Abstracts* is the monthly publication of the American Psychological Association. It provides summaries of works selected from almost 1,000 publications, including journals, technical reports, and monographs. Some of the articles have to do with psychological aspects of teaching, learning, counseling, child development, and the learning process.

2. *Child Development Abstracts and Bibliography* is published three times per year and provides summaries of articles on child development selected from approximately 200 publications. Book reviews are included, as are extensive bibliographies. The publication is organized into six categories, of which two—"Cognition, Learning, and Perception" and "Educational Processes"—are related to education in the school setting. This source is especially valuable to researchers interested in child development and early childhood education.

3. DAI *(Dissertation Abstracts International)* provides abstracts of doctoral dissertations completed each year in more than 300 universities in the United States and Europe. The abstracts are grouped into nine different subject areas, or volumes. Volume VII, *Education,* is of most interest to educational researchers. The abstracts are complete, indicating what the researcher was attempting to explore, the procedures applied, and the results obtained. Doctoral dissertations have been relatively little used in educational research, despite the fact that they often contain some of the most recent and reliable scholarly information available.

Social Science Citation Index

SSCI *(Social Science Citation Index)* lists research reports having to do with education, social science, and behavioral science. This index provides the valuable service of indicating where a given author has been cited by other authors in later research, which provides one indication of how important the research was considered to be by later investigators. In addition, the index provides bibliographic citations for the articles that made reference to that particular author. For example, if Jones in 1975 published research on multicultural education, the *SSCI* would provide a list of reports published later that made reference to Jones's work.

Digest of Educational Statistics

This reference book is unlike other sources in that it does not list, review, or analyze research. It nevertheless may be of much value in a particular investigation. Researchers often need reliable statistics concerning such matters as the number of students in bilingual education, the percentages of the national school population that belong to various ethnic groups, and the amount of money each state spends on students, teachers, and buildings, for example.

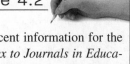

Exercise 4.2

Indicate the index or source that would most likely contain recent information for the needs presented below: (N) *NSSE Yearbooks,* (C) *Current Index to Journals in Education,* (D) *Dissertation Abstracts International,* (H) *Handbook of Research on Teaching,* (RI) *Resources in Education,* (S) *Digest of Educational Statistics,* (E) *Encyclopedia of Educational Research,* or (SS) *Social Science Citation Index.*

_____ **1.** You have lost the title of an important article.

_____ **2.** You want a copy of a paper presented at a major convention.

_____ **3.** You want to know your state's ranking on expenditures per student.

_____ **4.** You want to know what sorts of topics doctoral students in England are researching.

_____ **5.** You want to look at a research review book published this year.

_____ **6.** You need a reference book devoted specifically to research on teaching.

_____ **7.** You want to read analyses of educational research into many different topics.

_____ **8.** You want to know how much influence a given report might have had on later research.

LOCATING PRIMARY SOURCES

Journal articles and unpublished documents are normally found in bound volumes on library shelves or on microfiche adjacent to the microfiche readers. Very recent articles are shelved in the current reading room prior to being bound. Specific articles and documents are identified and located through the indexes described earlier, either manually or, in most libraries, by means of computer.

The Computer Search

Computers greatly facilitate the search procedure by covering great quantities of information rapidly, by surveying many different **databases,** and by limiting the searches in accord with selected **descriptors,** such as key words and dates of publication. Examples of general databases include *Newspaper Abstracts* and *Periodical Abstracts,* which provide abstracts of stories and articles via computer. Among the major education-related indexes accessible through library computer terminals are the following:

Education Index
Education Research Complete
Exceptional Child Education Resources
PsycINFO
Current Index to Journals in Education
Resources in Education
Psychological Abstracts
Sociological Abstracts
Social Science Citation Index
Dissertation Abstracts International
Books in Print

Most libraries have these indexes available online; some may make them available on CD-ROM. In some cases, depending on your library, you may need to check out the compact disk from the librarian and use it in a computer equipped with a CD-ROM player. These disks contain the same information as do the bound volumes of the indexes, and they are updated every few months to keep them current.

As previously mentioned, ERIC is the most widely used index for locating published educational materials, although databases such as Education Research Complete and PsycINFO have very large collections that are gaining increasing popularity. Most online databases can be searched in similar fashion. As an example, specific information regarding an online search of ERIC is provided in the Applying Technology feature titled "Searching ERIC Online" on pages 72–75.

DEVELOPMENTAL ACTIVITY

Locating Published Research

Now that you have specified your research topic, it is time to begin reading and learning more about it. The best source for further information on your chosen topic is previously conducted—and preferably *published*—research. It is important to approach your search for published research in an organized manner, maintaining records as you proceed. Keep this in mind as you respond to the following:

1.   A possible topic or problem I am planning to research *How comparison of siblings can creat problem for chn.*

2.   The main question or hypothesis for my study _____

3. Secondary sources that I consulted for information _Eric,_ _psychinfo, psycharticles._

4. Database(s) used to search for *primary* sources _Erics Computer_ _Psychinfa, psycarticles lib._

5. The search descriptors that I used (*list single descriptors, and any combinations of descriptors, in the order in which they were searched*):

_or_ _____

and _____

with

6. A summary of the results of my search using these descriptors

Search Number	Descriptor(s) Used	Number Retrieved

APPLYING TECHNOLOGY

Electronic Journals

In addition to the major divisions of AERA (American Educational Research Association) that you read about in Applying Technology: "Sources for Research Topics" in Chapter 3, AERA also supports the existence of many *special interest groups* (*SIGs*). The more than 150 AERA SIGs "provide a forum within AERA for the involvement of individuals drawn together by a common interest in a field of study, teaching, or research when the existing divisional structure may not directly facilitate such activity" (www.aera.net/Default.aspx?menu_id=26&id=274). One of these SIGs, "Communication of Research," maintains a website (http://aera-cr.asu.edu), which includes a second page containing links to over 50 electronic journals (or *e-journals*). This page, titled "Open Access Journals in the Field of Education" and found by pointing your Web browser to http://aera-cr.asu.edu/ejournals, has included only links to e-journals that are

■ Scholarly
■ Peer-reviewed
■ Full-text
■ Accessible without cost

These last two factors are key for the beginning researcher. First, access to full-text articles means that you can view, read, and download them directly on your Web browser—there is no need to go to the library to retrieve these articles. Second, because a goal of the SIG is to promote free worldwide access to scholarship in education, all articles in these e-journals are available free of charge—there are no subscription fees, as there usually are with print journals, or fees of any other kind.

A sampling of the e-journals to which links are provided by the "Communications among Researchers" SIG includes

■ *Action Research International*
■ *Advancing Women in Leadership Journal*
■ *Bilingual Research Journal*
■ *Contemporary Issues in Early Childhood*
■ *Early Childhood Research and Practice*
■ *Current Issues in Education*
■ *Educational Insights: Electronic Journal of Graduate Student Research*
■ *Educational Technology and Society*
■ *The Electronic Journal of Science Education*
■ *International Education Journal*
■ *Journal of Technology Education*
■ *The Ontario Action Researcher*
■ *Practical Assessment, Research and Evaluation*
■ *Reading Online: An Electronic Journal of the International Reading Association*
■ *Teaching English as a Second Language*

APPLYING TECHNOLOGY

Searching ERIC Online

As we have seen up to this point, the Internet provides wonderful resources researchers can advantageously use to facilitate their research endeavors. The development of CD-ROM technology has made the process of locating published research much easier. Prior to that, one had to scan nearly every volume of *CIJE* and *RIE* in order to locate published work relevant to a given topic. However, today's researchers are able to locate relevant articles and other documents without even *going* to the library. The entire ERIC database (including both *CIJE* and *RIE*) is available and searchable online at www.eric .ed.gov.

The main page for this site is shown in Figure 4.1. One simply clicks on "Advanced Search" to arrive at the common search page, shown in Figure 4.2.

Notice that, initially, one can search for up to three terms in ERIC, although more rows can be added. Furthermore, notice that the search can be conducted based on one of several criteria (located in the drop-down menus, or *selection buttons*), including searching by Keyword, Author, and Title. Most searches are conducted by Keyword, at least during the initial stages.

To consider a concrete example, suppose we wanted to locate published research on the topic of teachers' classroom assessment practices. We might search under the terms "educational assessment" and "classroom techniques" (see Figure 4.2). Notice that located next to the "Search for:" button is another selection button containing Boolean operators, which are keywords that enable the retrieval of terms in specific combinations. The most common operators are AND and OR. If AND is used, only those documents containing *both* keywords as descriptors will be retrieved (i.e., a more narrow search); if OR is used, *every* document with *either* of these two keywords as descriptors will be retrieved (i.e., a broader search). Using AND for our example, we search for documents that contain both "educational assessment" *and* "classroom techniques." We then click on Search to search the database. Results are shown in Figure 4.3.

First, you will notice that ERIC retrieved 2,625 documents containing these two descriptive keywords, entirely too many to search through. By clicking on Search Within Results, you can reduce the number of citations returned by adding more

Figure 4.1

Main page for ERIC website

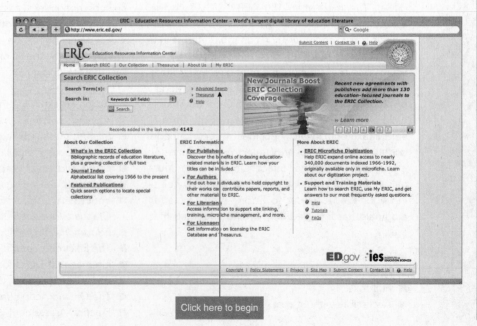

Click here to begin

Figure 4.2

ERIC advanced search page

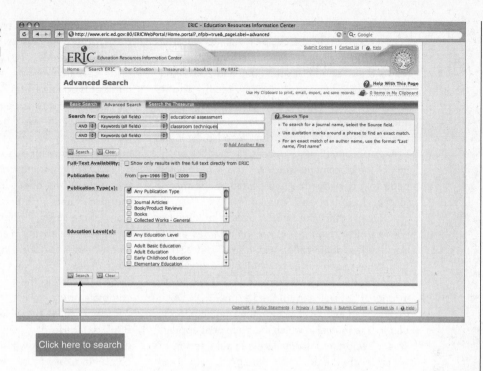

Click here to search

Figure 4.3

Results for search shown in Figure 4.2

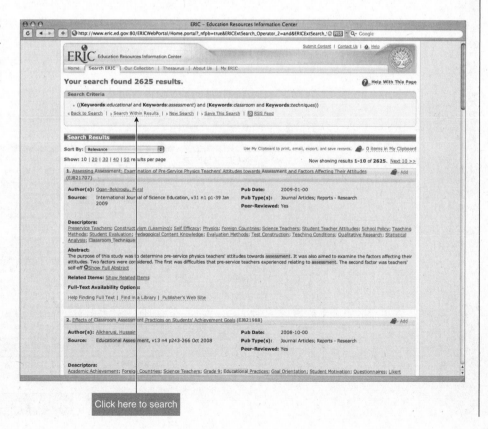

Click here to search

(continued)

descriptors or by focusing the years of publication. For purposes of this search, the focus was narrowed by searching only for documents available in full text and published between 2005 and 2009—thus reducing the number of citations returned to 43 documents (see Figure 4.4). The documents are initially screened by the user for relevance by examining the titles. If you are interested in exploring a given document more closely, simply click on the title of the document, which will take you to a new page that provides the entire citation information for that document (see Figure 4.5).

Recall that the ERIC accession number (ED500752 in Figure 4.4) not only serves as the document's identification within ERIC but also informs the researcher as to whether the document was published in an academic journal (EJ) or exists in one of several unpublished forms (ED). Documents listed as EJ will include the citation information for the journal in which the document appears. This is important information you will need in order to locate the article on the appropriate library shelves.

Documents listed as ED may have originally been written as papers to be presented at academic conferences, position papers, technical reports, research reports, and so on. The accession number is again of vital importance here, because all ED documents appear on microfiche and *are cataloged by the six-digit ED number.* This number is the *only* means of locating the correct microfiche in your library's microfiche stacks.

Also of great importance to the researcher is the abstract, the brief summary of the contents of the document, including the results and conclusions of the study, if appropriate. Only by reading the document abstract can the researcher really be sure whether to obtain the full document for complete review. It is always best to study the abstract prior to investing the time required to locate the complete article.

Because of the flexibility of the searchable ERIC database, it does take some practice and experience to work with it effectively. The idea of combining keywords in a single search—or even combining keywords with authors' names and so

Figure 4.4
Results for narrowed search

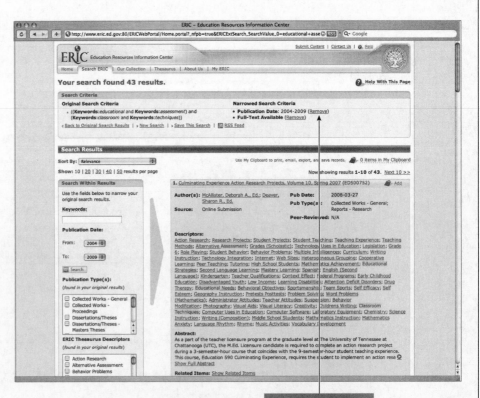

Narrowed search criteria

Figure 4.5

Document
citation
from ERIC

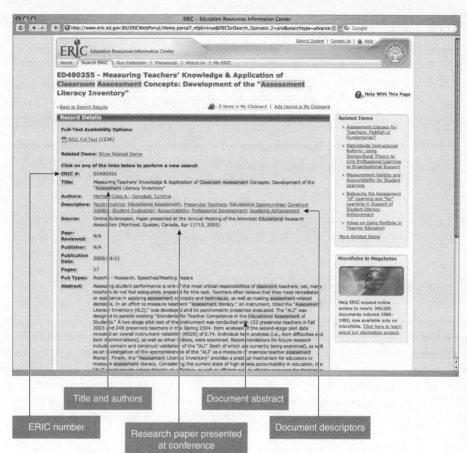

Title and authors

Document abstract

ERIC number

Research paper presented
at conference

Document descriptors

on—can be a little intimidating to the beginning re-searcher. However, novice researchers should not hesitate to "experiment" with searches of ERIC. Online access to the ERIC database is certainly a valuable research tool of which all researchers—at any level of experience—should take advantage.

As you can see, computer searches can save considerable time compared to manual searches. However, they only give you citations and, at best, brief abstracts of the original work. You must still go to the library stacks or microfiche room because the abstracts do not contain important details that you require; the summaries are presented only to help you to decide whether the original is worth finding and reading.

A word to first-time computer searchers: Think of your first attempts as learning experiences. Most people, especially those not accustomed to using computers, make mistakes, need assistance, and have to start over again more than once. To ease initiation into a computer search, start small and learn how the process is done. If possible, get an experienced user to walk you through the process. Take notes to help you feel secure when you begin to work on your own. Although the procedure may at first seem intimidating, it is easily learned and will save you many, many hours of hard work.

NOT JUST FOR CONDUCTING RESEARCH—VALUABLE SOURCES FOR PROFESSIONAL DEVELOPMENT

Although your primary and immediate focus may be on learning about and actually conducting graduate-level research, it is important to realize that you may have a long career in education or an education-related field. The sources of information, both primary and secondary, that have been presented and discussed in this chapter will continue to be excellent and invaluable sources of up-to-date research. True professionals continue to develop in their respective fields throughout their careers. These individuals maintain membership in professional organizations and continue to read journals and other sources of current information specific to their disciplines. As current or future members of your respective professions, you too should avail yourselves of such opportunities.

CHAPTER SUMMARY

It is important to review existing literature related to the topic you wish to research in order to learn more about the topic, determine the contexts in which the topic might have been researched previously, and obtain guidance that will help your research efforts.

When you use the university library to review research literature, begin with secondary sources, such as the *Encyclopedia of Educational Research, Review of Research in Education,* and *NSSE Yearbooks,* which contain excellent reviews and summaries of research done on various topics, plus extensive bibliographies that can direct you to good primary sources.

To find primary sources, next consult directories such as the *Current Index to Journals in Education, Psychological Abstracts,* and *Dissertation Abstracts International,* all of which provide summaries of the materials indexed. The summaries will suggest whether the original source is worth reading carefully, and the index will provide the bibliographic citation for locating the article, conference paper, monograph, dissertation, or technical report that interests you.

LIST OF IMPORTANT TERMS

abstracts	ERIC	*RIE*
CIJE	*Newspaper Abstracts*	secondary sources
DAI	*NSSE Yearbooks*	single-theme books
database	*Periodical Abstracts*	*SSCI*
descriptor	primary sources	*Thesaurus of ERIC Descriptors*

YOUR CURRENT STATUS

Chapter 3 showed you how to select a research topic, refine the topic into a problem, and compose a proposal for research. In Chapter 4 you have learned to locate secondary sources of research information related to a given topic or problem and to use various indexes to locate primary sources, a process facilitated by library and home computers that can search the ERIC database and other indexes with amazing speed. You are now ready to learn how to interpret and annotate materials you have located that are important to your research, the topic of Chapter 5. First, however, please respond to the following activities for thought and discussion.

ACTIVITIES FOR THOUGHT AND DISCUSSION

1. From perusing the research literature, what do you consider the most valuable traits of secondary sources? What do you consider to be the major limitations of secondary sources?

2. Describe what you consider to be the advantages and disadvantages of a computer search of ERIC and other databases, as compared to a manual search.

3. Based on what you discovered in the *CIJE* article abstracts, why is it often necessary to locate and read the original articles or papers rather than rely on the information in the abstracts?

4. Here are the questions presented at the beginning of the chapter. See how well you can answer them.
   a. Why are secondary sources a good place to begin looking for information on a topic?
   b. What are four specific examples of secondary sources?
   c. How are primary sources located in a library?
   d. Which library holdings are usually considered to be primary sources of information?
   e. What are three specific examples of directories to primary sources?
   f. What advantages do computer searches of the literature offer over manual searches?

5. Recall or turn to the chapter information organizer you saw at the beginning of the chapter. Without looking in the text, explain your understanding of each element of the organizer.

ANSWERS TO CHAPTER EXERCISES

4.1. 1. P 2. S 3. P/S 4. P 5. S 6. P

4.2. 1. C 2. RI 3. S 4. D 5. N 6. H 7. E 8. SS

REFERENCES AND RECOMMENDED READINGS

Alkin, M. (Ed.). (1992). *Encyclopedia of Educational Research* (6th ed.). New York: Macmillan.

Batt, F. (1988). *Online Searching for End Users: An Information Sourcebook*. Phoenix: Oryx Press.

Books in Print. (1995). New Providence, NJ: R. R. Bowker.

Burek, D. (Ed.). (1992). *Encyclopedia of Associations* (26th ed.). Detroit: Gale.

Buttlar, L. (1989). *Education: A Guide to Reference and Information Sources*. Englewood, CO: Libraries Unlimited.

Child Development Abstracts and Bibliography. (1927 to date). Chicago: University of Chicago Press.

Completed Research in Health, Physical Education and Recreation Including International Sources. (1958 to date). Washington, DC: American Alliance for Health, Physical Education and Recreation.

Current Index to Journals in Education. (1969 to date). Phoenix, AZ: Oryx Press.

Dissertation Abstracts International. (1955 to date). Ann Arbor, MI: Xerox University Microfilms.

Education Index. (1929 to date). New York: H. W. Wilson.

Edyburn, D. L. (1999). *The Electronic Scholar: Enhancing Research Productivity with Technology*. Upper Saddle River, NJ: Merrill.

Exceptional Child Education Resources. (1969 to date). Arlington, VA: Council for Exceptional Children.

Houston, J. (Ed.). (1990). *Thesaurus of ERIC Descriptors* (12th ed.). Phoenix, AZ: Oryx Press.

Huck, S. (2004). *Reading Statistics and Research* (4th ed.). Boston: Allyn & Bacon.

Husén, T., & Postlethwaite, T. (Eds.). (1994). *The International Encyclopedia of Education: Research and Studies*. New York: Pergamon.

National School Law Reporter. (1955 to date). New London, CT: Croft Educational Services.

The New York Times Index. (1913 to date). New York: New York Times.

Physical Education/Sports Index. (1978 to date). Albany, NY: Marathon Press.

Psychological Abstracts. (1927 to date). Washington, DC: American Psychological Association.

Readers' Guide to Periodic Literature. (1900 to date). New York: H. W. Wilson.

Rehabilitation Literature. (1940 to date). Chicago: National Society for Crippled Children and Adults.

Resources in Education. (1966 to date). Washington, DC: Superintendent of Documents, Government Printing Office.

Review of Educational Research. (1931 to date). Washington, DC: American Educational Research Association.

Review of Research in Education. (1973 to date). Washington, DC: American Educational Research Association.

Social Science Citation Index. (1973 to date). Philadelphia: Institute for Scientific Information.

Social Sciences Index. (1974 to date). New York: H. W. Wilson.

Sociological Abstracts. (1952 to date). San Diego, CA: Sociological Abstracts.

Subject Index to the Christian Science Monitor. (1960 to date). Boston: Christian Science Monitor.

Thomas, R. (Ed.). (1990). *The Encyclopedia of Human Development and Education: Theory, Research, and Studies.* New York: Pergamon.

Wegner, L. (1992). The research library and emerging information technology. *New Directions for Teaching and Learning, 51 (Teaching in the information age: The role of educational technology)*, 83–90.

Wittrock, M. (Ed.). (1986). *Handbook of Research on Teaching* (3rd ed.). New York: Macmillan.

Interpreting and Summarizing Published Research

PREVIEW

This chapter provides practical suggestions to help you review, interpret, and annotate published literature related to your topic. Included are suggestions to help you rapidly peruse reports to determine the following:

- Topic and purpose
- Type of report
- Findings and conclusions

Also included are guidelines on how to do the following:

- Skim information
- Summarize information
- Make annotated citations

Most reports, by type, are status reports, group comparison reports, or relationship reports. Interpretation of these reports often requires some knowledge of statistical analysis techniques:

- For status reports
  Mean, median, mode   Norms
  Standard deviation   Percentiles

- For group comparison reports
  Chi-square   Analysis of variance
  Difference between means   Statistical significance

- For relationship reports
  Coefficient of correlation   Statistical significance

TARGETED LEARNINGS

In Chapter 4, you learned how to locate and use some of the most valuable secondary and primary sources of information in the research library. In this chapter, you will find suggestions on how to peruse published reports, interpret their contents, summarize them quickly, and make effective notes for bibliographic needs. As you read the chapter, be sure to look for information related to the following questions:

1. Why should research reports be skimmed rapidly before they are read carefully?
2. What specifically does one look for when skimming reports?
3. What entries should one make on note cards when annotating published reports?
4. What are the three general types of research reports encountered in published literature?
5. What characterizes the three different types of research reports?

6. What common analysis terminology—verbal and/or statistical—is usually associated with each of the three types of reports?
7. Why do the different types of research reports utilize different verbal and statistical procedures to analyze their data?
8. What two different meanings does the term *significance* have in the context of research?
9. Why is the term *significant* often misleading to uninformed readers of research?

You have already familiarized yourself with the major sources and locations of published research, the first phase in learning to use the library profitably. You are now ready to undertake the second phase, which involves accurately interpreting the published information in the sources you locate. This phase is accomplished by learning three skills: (1) how to read and summarize the material, (2) how to identify the type of report and interpret statistical analyses you might encounter, and (3) how to enter annotations on summary cards to maximize their value and ease of use.

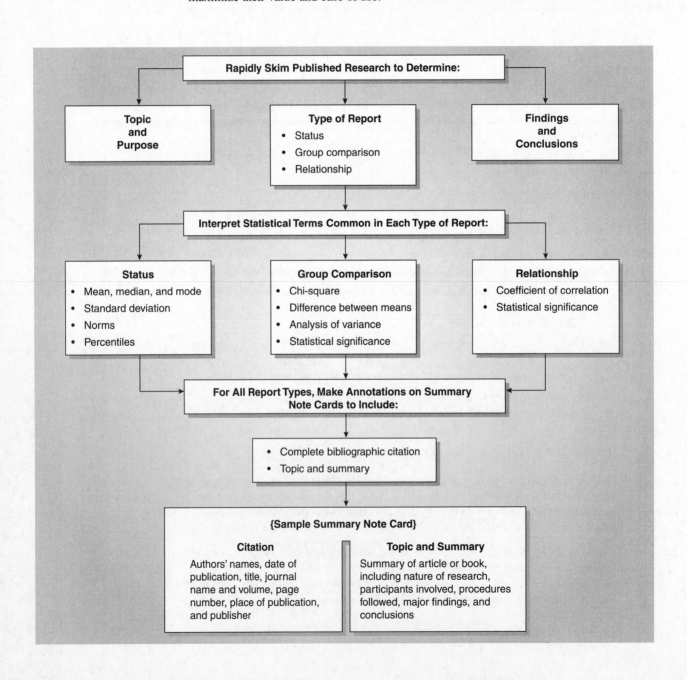

Rapidly Skim Published Research to Determine:

Topic and Purpose

Type of Report
- Status
- Group comparison
- Relationship

Findings and Conclusions

Interpret Statistical Terms Common in Each Type of Report:

Status
- Mean, median, and mode
- Standard deviation
- Norms
- Percentiles

Group Comparison
- Chi-square
- Difference between means
- Analysis of variance
- Statistical significance

Relationship
- Coefficient of correlation
- Statistical significance

For All Report Types, Make Annotations on Summary Note Cards to Include:

- Complete bibliographic citation
- Topic and summary

{Sample Summary Note Card}

Citation

Authors' names, date of publication, title, journal name and volume, page number, place of publication, and publisher

Topic and Summary

Summary of article or book, including nature of research, participants involved, procedures followed, major findings, and conclusions

READING RESEARCH REPORTS

Research literature comes in various forms now familiar to you, such as references, handbooks, reviews, journal articles, technical reports, and scholarly books. After becoming able to locate relevant information, how does one effectively employ it? The first step is learning how to *skim* the material quickly to ascertain its nature and the researcher's conclusions.

SKIMMING THE INFORMATION

You know how to find a number of published reports related to almost any educational topic you choose. Because so much material is available, you need to be able to move through it quickly. The summaries presented in indexes such as *CIJE* and in journals such as *Psychological Abstracts* provide immeasurable help in pinpointing materials of value to your topic. However, summaries and abstracts omit many important details and can by no means replace reading the original material.

   To move rather quickly through quantities of reports, you should practice skimming the materials so that you can quickly determine what the study is about and what the author concludes. By using this strategy, you can expeditiously obtain information and further identify reports that have direct bearing on your topic.

DETERMINING WHAT THE MATERIAL IS ABOUT

To pinpoint the focus of the article, look quickly for a title and an introduction. The title should clearly indicate the topic. Despite some exceptions, most researchers use descriptive titles for their reports, as in the following example of a citation whose title is self-explanatory.

   Cipielewski, J., & Stanovich, K. (1992). Predicting growth in reading ability from children's exposure to print. *Journal of Experimental Child Psychology, 54*(1):74–89.

In contrast, the following fictitious examples of titles would leave one guessing.

   Onward and upward in educational research

   The golden egg of bilingual education

These two titles suggest that the reports have something to do with educational research and bilingual education, but little else is indicated.

   Once you have examined the title, you are ready to scan the introduction of the report, which may be labeled as such. If not labeled, the first paragraph or two usually introduces the report and tells why the topic is considered important.

IDENTIFYING THE WRITER'S CONCLUSIONS

To find the conclusions presented by the writer of the report, look for an abstract, summary, or a section near the end of the report entitled "Findings," "Conclusions," or "Discussion." If there is no such heading, the conclusions are usually presented in the final paragraphs of the report or article.

   Some journals—the exceptions rather than the rule—present an abstract at the beginning of the article. This is helpful to readers because it provides a brief synopsis of the article. If there is no abstract at the beginning, flip to the end of the article to see if there is a summary, which will indicate concisely what the article is about along with its conclusions.

CAUTIONS TO KEEP IN MIND

As you skim documents that describe (1) ethnographic research (such as patterns of interaction among teachers), (2) historical research (such as the backgrounds of the first teachers in Elmwood schools), or (3) action research (such as development of a special spelling program for Cutter Elementary School students), remember that the conclusions presented in such reports may be correct for the specific groups and locales investigated, but that does not necessarily make them applicable elsewhere.

On the other hand, if you are reading technical reports of research funded by grants or reports published in research journals, most of the information you encounter will be intended for wide dispersion and will have been subjected to close scrutiny by experts in their respective fields who judge the research methodology, analysis of data, and appropriateness of conclusions. When reports meet these criteria, the results can nearly always be generalized to similar locales and populations. This is not to say that the conclusions are invariably correct, nor that you should *never* analyze critically the methods and conclusions of reports published in prestigious journals. But the likelihood is great that researchers reporting those investigations have followed established procedures, analyzed the data appropriately, and formulated conclusions that follow from the analyses and seem logically correct.

SUMMARIZING THE REPORTS

Suppose you read a journal article reporting a large study on high school students' attitudes toward the use of alcohol, gleaning the following information:

> Lazerus surveyed 2,000 high school students in four eastern states concerning their attitude toward the use of alcohol . . . and found that 42 percent approved of the use of alcohol in general, but that only 17 percent approved of their parents using alcohol.

In what form should you make your notations so they will be most accurate and useful? Good notations should not only summarize information, as the preceding entry does, but also indicate the *topic* and include a *complete bibliographical citation*. If you do a preliminary search via computer, you can print out the citations, thus ensuring completeness and accuracy. If you do a manual search, it is very important that your notes are clear and complete. It is irritating and a frustrating waste of time—not to mention a sometimes unrealistic task—to have to go back later to find an item of information that was omitted or written illegibly. Plenty of software programs are available to help you maintain your bibliographic citation information (see later in this chapter Applying Technology: "Writing a Review of Literature" on pages 86–87).

If you have note-taking software and a laptop computer, the computer can enter, organize, and rearrange your notes in a number of ways. If you do not have that capability, it is suggested that you enter your summary notes on 5 × 8-inch index cards, placing each reference on a separate card. These cards are large enough to hold a good deal of information, and they are easy to store, organize, regroup, and retrieve. Index cards are valuable even if you have used a computer to print out citations and summaries. Simply cut and tape the citations onto the cards. But keep in mind that the article abstracts seldom contain all the details you need for your research. Those important notations must be made by hand.

One helpful suggestion is to write the topic of the report in the upper-right-hand corner of the card and the author's name and date of publication in the left-hand corner, which will help you more easily group cards by topic, publication date, or alphabetized authors' names. This will save time when you begin organizing your references and preparing your bibliography.

An article citation *must* include all of the following:

- Author's name
- Date of publication

Figure 5.1

Summary note card
for a journal article

> Cruise, P., & Fisher, S. (2002)   <u>Teachers' Attitudes toward No Child Left Behind</u>
>
> Cruise, P., & Fisher, S. (2002). A descriptive study of elementary teachers' attitudes toward NCLB legislation. *The Journal of Research in Education, 18*(3), 145–156.
>
> Cruise and Fisher (2002) surveyed elementary-level teachers throughout the Midwest in an attempt to describe their current attitudes toward the No Child Left Behind (2001) legislation. The authors collected their data through the use of a self-developed survey, adapting many items from existing surveys into their own survey. The survey consisted primarily of Likert-scaled items, but also included several open-ended items. Evidence of validity included a content review of their original instrument by five individuals with expertise in survey design and two individuals employed at state departments of education. Reliability of their resulting data was calculated using Cronbach's alpha coefficient (α) and was equal to .89. Five thousand five hundred teachers were randomly selected from state department of education databases across 11 states. One thousand nine hundred eighty-three ($n = 1,983$) usable surveys were returned, for a return rate of 36%.
>
> Results included the fact that the majority of teachers believe in the overall purpose of NCLB but disagree with the ways in which it is being implemented. Specifically, teachers agreed with statements that NCLB has forced them to change the focus of their classroom instruction and that both teachers and students are experiencing greater levels of stress due to various requirements of the law. Findings also seemed to indicate that teachers may not have a clear understanding of the overall impact of the legislation. Recommendations for teacher professional development, focusing on improving teachers' understanding of the law and its probable influence on classroom instruction, are discussed.

- Title of article
- Name of journal
- Volume of journal and issue (issue optional)
- Page numbers of the article

A book citation must include the following:

- Author's name
- Year of publication
- Title of book
- City where published
- Name of publishing company

As previously mentioned, make sure to record the citation correctly in its entirety. Make sure, also, that you enter notational information accurately, and if you quote material directly, indicate so clearly. Your card for a journal article might look similar to Figure 5.1. Note the author, date, topic, complete citation, and notes about principal findings. (All aspects of this particular entry are fictitious.)

Exercise 5.1

From the following fictitious information, write note cards in the manner suggested:

_____ **1.** James F. Roberts did research on teacher partnering that showed that men are somewhat lazier than women when it comes to doing menial tasks. That finding was reported in his 1995 book, *Unequal Teacher Partners,* which was published in New York by the Domestic Press.

> **2.** Cecilia A. González studied role acceptance in teacher partnering. In her article "Parameters of Teacher Role Acclimatization," published in the July 1993 (Vol. 4, pp. 12–18) *Journal of Teacher Partnering,* González reported that she found no gender differences in teachers' ability to adjust to new roles in the partnering process.

INTERPRETING THE STATISTICAL INFORMATION YOU ENCOUNTER

Researchers use words and phrases in special ways to express concepts clearly with an economy of language, but the special terms are usually confusing to people not schooled in research. If you are to understand the research reports you read, you must have a grasp of the fundamentals of this research language, especially having to do with statistics, significance, and conclusions.

Suppose you read the following statements in a report: "The difference between the groups was not significant." "The coefficient of correlation was .85." "The standard error of the mean was 1.72." What would these statements mean to you? If you are a beginner in research, they would mean little or might even be misleading.

Chapter 7 and the Appendix present considerable information about statistical terms and procedures. However, certain terms must be introduced here if you are to read research reports—even their conclusions—with adequate understanding. You can learn the meanings of these terms more easily when they are presented in relation to types of research findings. These types of findings generally consist of one or more of the following:

1. The *status* of one or more groups—say, a school, a community, a peer group, the 11th grade in Elmwood High School. This status describes people, places, events, objects, and the like as they now exist or once did. Status reports are typically appropriate for qualitative and survey research studies.

2. *Comparisons* between two or more groups. Again, this might involve schools, communities, grade levels, gender, ethnic groups, and so forth. These comparisons demonstrate the existence and nature of differences that might exist between or among groups—differences such as preferences, lifestyles, achievement, rates of learning, or access to resources. These differences may exist inherently in the groups or may have been produced by introducing a variable that caused one group to become different from the other. Reports of this type are appropriate for nonexperimental research studies (such as causal-comparative studies), as well as for experimental, quasi-experimental, and evaluation studies.

3. *Covarying relationships* between two or more sets of measurements (such as between scores of language ability on the one hand and reading ability on the other) obtained from the same group of individuals. Such relationships, when confirmed, enable you to predict one of the variables from the other, and the relationships may *imply*—although they can never irrefutably demonstrate—the existence of cause and effect between the variables. Correlational reports are, of course, appropriate for correlational studies, another type of nonexperimental quantitative research.

Let us examine some of the terms you can expect to encounter in reports that present these three different types of findings.

STATUS REPORTS

Status reports provide descriptions of current or previous conditions. Often status studies are qualitative in nature and do not employ statistical procedures; the findings in qualitative research are ascertained through verbal logic and are presented as verbal statements. Such is often the case for ethnographic and historical research. But other status studies are quantitative in nature and involve numbers and testing. In those reports, you are likely to encounter the use of the following types of descriptive statistics and terms.

Raw Numbers or Raw Scores

Raw numbers or **raw scores** are numerals that indicate counts of individuals (e.g., 35 adolescents) or scores made on tests before they are converted in any way (e.g., 78). You can expect to see entries such as the following:

> Elmwood High School was opened in 1874, with *32* students attending grades 8 through 12. Today it serves *2,750* students, grades 9 through 12.

> Samuel's raw score on the math section of the Stanford Achievement Test was *43*. Raw scores of other students in Samuel's class ranged from a high of *45* to a low of *6*.

Terms That Indicate Typicality or Central Tendency

Three terms are commonly used to depict what is average or typical for a group of raw numbers or scores:

1. Mean, symbolized by M or $\bar{X}$. The mean is the arithmetic average of a group of raw scores or other measurements that are expressed numerically. Commonly thought of as synonymous with the term *average,* the mean is calculated by adding the raw scores together and then dividing the sum by the number of scores.

2. Median, symbolized by *Mdn* or *Md*. The median is the point halfway between the highest and lowest scores of a particular array (group of scores). In other words, it is the value that separates the bottom 50 percent of scores from the upper 50 percent of scores. The median is determined by arranging the scores in order from lowest to highest and then counting halfway through the number of scores. For example, the median for the following array of scores would be 4:

> 1, 2, 2, 3, 4, 6, 12, 13, 13

If there is an even number of scores in the array, the median is the arithmetic average of the two middle scores. The median in the following array would be 7.5 (the average of 7 and 8):

> 4, 5, 5, 7, 8, 9, 10, 10

The median is less affected than is the mean by unusually high or low scores (also known as *extreme scores*) and for that reason is frequently the method of reporting information such as average personal income or price of housing. Its usefulness in educational research is limited.

3. Mode, symbolized by *Mo,* is simply the most frequently occurring score. The mode has no other use in statistics.

Terms That Indicate Spread or Diversity

Researchers are interested not only in what is average for a group but also in the dispersion of values within that group—that is, how spread out the scores or measurements are. Dispersion is often expressed in the following terms:

1. Range, which is the group spread from the highest through the lowest score or measurement. It is calculated by subtracting the lowest score from the highest score. For example,

APPLYING TECHNOLOGY

Writing a Review of Literature

Writing a review of literature is an integral part of any formal proposal or design of a research study. A literature review involves the "systematic identification, location, and analysis of documents containing information related to the research problem" (Gay, Mills, & Airasian, 2006). Once you have obtained documents related to your topic, you must analyze them for several reasons:

■ To determine what has already been done
■ To learn about specific research strategies, procedures, and instruments that have been shown to be effective in researching your topic
■ To form the basis for interpreting your results (Gay, Mills, & Airasian, 2006)

However, you must avoid the temptation to include everything you have found in your search for published literature. Additionally, a literature review is *not* simply a compilation of summaries of articles, one after another. On the contrary, a literature review is an opportunity for you to demonstrate your ability to "recognize relevant information . . . and to synthesize and evaluate it" according to the overall purpose and goals of your study (Taylor, 1998).

Writing the literature review is quite honestly not an easy task. There is no "recipe" for developing the actual written review. It will likely take several iterations of written drafts, perhaps organizing and reorganizing the analysis of your related literature. Although no formula exists for this important research activity, several websites offer many suggestions that can be especially helpful. Purdue University has developed an Online Writing Lab (http://owl.english.purdue.edu/oldindex.html) that includes links to several helpful pages, many of which incorporate activities for understanding and reinforcement:

■ Paraphrase: Write It in Your Own Words (http://owl.english.purdue.edu/handouts/research/r_paraphr.html)
This page explains what paraphrasing is and why it is an important skill in technical writing; it includes an example containing an original passage, a legitimate paraphrase, and a plagiarized version. It also provides six steps to effective paraphrasing.

■ Quoting, Paraphrasing, and Summarizing (http://owl.english.purdue.edu/handouts/research/r_quotprsm.html)
Building on the previous page, this one offers explanations of the differences between quoting, paraphrasing, and summarizing published work. A brief sample essay is included, along with guiding instructions for writing a summary of the piece—a good activity.

■ Avoiding Plagiarism (http://owl.english.purdue.edu/handouts/research/r_plagiar.html)
This page defines *plagiarism* (the unacknowledged use of someone else's work or ideas) and provides examples that might be considered plagiarism, as well as others not considered to be objectionable. The site also provides specific examples documenting when credit should be given to an author. Included is an activity that provides sample situations in which the reader must decide the degree to which there exists a risk of plagiarism.

Also affiliated with the development of a written review of literature is the associated list of references, which must follow a prescribed format. In education, the preferred guidelines are provided by the *Publication Manual of the American Psychological Association* (6th ed.), commonly referred to as the "APA Manual." Because the citation of electronic sources of information continues to evolve, and because citation formats may change as technologies change, the American Psychological Association has provided this information at its website on a page titled "Electronic References" (www.apastyle.org/manual/related/electronic-sources.pdf).

Finally, as previously mentioned, it is important to maintain accurate records of all of the sources you reference in your literature review. This can be a time-consuming and tedious task, but for obvious reasons it is a crucial part of the research process. However, several types of bibliographic software can simplify the task by automating the creation of stand-alone bibliographies or bibliographies within your research paper (Gay, Mills, & Airasian, 2006). Software titles include EndNote (www.endnote.com), TakeNote!, Bookends Plus 5 (www.sonnysoftware.com/bookends/bookends.html), Bibliography Builder (www.risinc.com/rminfo_bib .asp),

and Reference Manager (www.risinc.com). As an example, EndNote comes complete with over 2,800 predefined reference citation styles and works with your word processing program to enter citations from your EndNote database directly into a document. Additionally, EndNote can store Web pages containing full-text articles and can automatically start your Web browser, taking you directly to that page. It essentially becomes the "card catalog of the electronic library" (Gay, Mills, & Airasian, 2006). Although it takes some time and effort to learn how to use bibliographic software effectively, it can certainly simplify the research process by making this aspect a less careless procedure.

the range of an array of scores from the highest at 45 to the lowest at 15 would be 30: 45 − 15 = 30. The concept of range has no further application in research statistics.

2. Standard deviation, symbolized *SD* or *s*. Standard deviation indicates the divergence of scores away from the mean of the group. Standard deviation is a concept not encountered in ordinary experience and is, therefore, difficult to describe empirically. It is analogous to the concept of an *average* deviation, which indicates how much each score, on average, differs from the mean. But average deviation is not a stable measure, statistically speaking; therefore, standard deviation, a stable and widely applicable measure, is used instead. Mathematically, standard deviation is closely associated with the normal curve. If a group of scores or measurements is normally distributed, 68.26 percent of them fall between plus one standard deviation and minus one standard deviation from the mean. The area beneath the normal curve between −1.96 and +1.96 standard deviations includes 95 percent of all scores, and the area between −2.58 and +2.58 standard deviations includes 99 percent of all scores (see Figure A.3 in the Appendix). These relationships are illustrated and further explained in Chapter 7 and the Appendix.

Converted, or Transformed, Numbers and Scores

Raw scores are frequently converted or transformed into comparable scores to make them more understandable and more easily compared. For example, educators frequently work with **norms,** charts that show what is typical for certain ages, groups, or grade levels. It is important to remember, however, that once raw scores have been converted, they cannot be treated as if they were still raw scores. For example, converted scores cannot be averaged in an effort to obtain a composite (i.e., overall) converted score. Converted scores you are likely to encounter in research reports include the following:

1. Grade equivalents are shown in **grade norms** that accompany standardized achievement tests. They indicate the average scores made on a particular standardized test by students at different grade levels in various localities. The grade levels are further divided into months; they might, for example, show the mean score for students at seventh grade, sixth month; fourth grade, third month; and so on. Let us assume that Manuel, a second grader, has a raw score on a standardized reading test equal to 22, which, when compared to the norms accompanying the test, is seen to have a grade level equivalency of 3.3 (third grade, third month). A research report that contains this information might say that Manuel's reading level was 3.3. This does not imply that Manuel should be moved to the third grade, however. It simply indicates that Manuel's current level of reading ability is above the norm, or average, for second-grade students.

2. Age equivalents tell us the average performance of students at particular age levels. **Age norms** that show age equivalents accompany standardized intelligence tests. If Ricardo makes a raw score of 74 on his IQ test, one could look in the norms and find, perhaps, that 74 is the score made by the average person when 12 years, 6 months of age. It could then be said that Ricardo has a mental age of 12 years, 6 months, which may or may not be the same as his chronological (calendar) age.

3. Percentile ranks (symbolized *%ile* or *PR*) are converted scores that indicate one's **relative standing** in comparison to others who have taken the same test or have been included in the same measurement. Percentiles have nothing to do with percent correct but instead indicate relative position. Suppose you were informed that your raw score on a graduate aptitude test was 89. That would tell you virtually nothing. But if you were also informed that your score placed you at the 73rd percentile, you would understand that you did as well as or better than 73 percent of all people who had taken the test.

4. Stanines are conversions not into individual scores but into wider bands of scores. The word *stanine* comes from *standard nine,* in which the range of possible scores is divided into nine bands. The first stanine is the lowest, the ninth stanine is the highest, and the fifth stanine normally includes the mean of all scores made. Many raw scores fall into the fourth, fifth, and sixth stanines but few into the first or ninth.

REVIEW OF TERMINOLOGY USED IN STATUS REPORTS

Raw scores   Scores made or numbers involved.

Mean (M or $\overline{X}$)   The arithmetic average.

Median (Mdn or Md)   The midpoint between highest and lowest in an array of scores.

Mode (Mo)   The most frequently occurring score or measure in an array.

Standard deviation (SD or s)   Indicator of the dispersion from the mean for a set of scores.

Grade equivalents   The average scores made by students at particular grade levels.

Age equivalents   The average scores made by students of particular age levels.

Percentile rank (%ile or PR)   Indicator of a given score's standing, relative to others made on the same test or measurement.

Stanines   Nine bands, showing relative position within which all scores are distributed.

The reader is reminded that specific information concerning the calculations of measures of central tendency and diversity—accompanied by sample exercises—has been included in the Appendix.

COMPARISON REPORTS

We have considered some of the statistical and other special terms often employed in research to describe the status of individuals or groups. Now let us consider **comparison reports,** which typically involve the application of inferential statistics in evaluation, causal-comparative, and experimental research. Suppose a researcher compared the levels of self-esteem among various groups of students attending Elmwood Lincoln High School or the levels of reading progress of groups in Elmwood elementary schools. Reports of those studies would likely include comparisons performed using one or more of the following procedures.

Chi-square (χ^2)

You will usually see this term spelled out as a word in the report, then symbolized afterward. Chi-square is a statistical procedure that allows one to determine, when measurements are expressed as categories in the form of frequency counts, whether a difference exists (1) between two groups (known specifically as a **chi-square test of independence**), (2) between before-and-after measurements of the same group (also requiring the use of a chi-square test of independence), or (3) between what is expected for a group compared to what is actually observed for the group (known as a **chi-square goodness-of-fit test**). As an example of the second situation, suppose Mr. Michael wants to improve his students' regard for Algebra II. To determine their present attitude he asks them to respond anonymously by checking one of the following:

_____ I like Algebra II.

_____ I don't like Algebra II very much, but I don't dislike it either. I'm neutral.

_____ I don't like Algebra II.

Mr. Michael tallies responses from his four sections of students and finds that:

- 5 like the class
- 27 are neutral
- 71 dislike the class

After recording these numbers in their proper categories (like, neutral, dislike), he then organizes and presents his classes in a different way he believes will improve student approval. Two months later he asks them to respond as before, with the result that

- 27 like the class
- 42 are neutral
- 34 dislike the class

It seems to Mr. Michael that student regard for the class has improved considerably, but he is uncertain whether the change indicates a real improvement or simply a chance difference in the way students responded. The chi-square test of independence is a procedure that enables Mr. Michael to statistically answer his question. Chi-square compares what one expects to see (measured here as the students' attitudes *prior* to the change in instruction) against what one actually observes (measured as their attitudes *following* the change in instruction). In Mr. Michael's case, a null hypothesis would assume that after the new approach to teaching had been used, one would still expect to find that 5 students like Algebra II, 27 are neutral, and 71 dislike it. But the actual observation is now that 27 like the class, 42 are neutral, and 34 dislike it. The frequencies (or counts) of responses for students' opinions before the instructional change (expected) and after (observed) can be formatted as a table.

	Observed	Expected
Like	27	5
Neutral	42	27
Dislike	34	71

It is from a table like this that chi-square is computed to determine whether the difference between observed and expected frequencies is, or is not, attributable to chance errors made in selecting the participants. The procedure by which this is done, along with a complete example, is provided in the Appendix.

Difference between Means (Using the *t* Test)

You saw that if responses are made by categories, as in Mr. Michael's case, chi-square can be used to determine differences between groups. If, however, responses are obtained as scores or other numerical measurements, the difference between groups can be assessed in terms of group mean scores through an analysis technique called **difference between means.**

Suppose that Ms. Jones, a colleague of Mr. Michael, also teaches Algebra II in Elmwood High School. She has followed with interest Mr. Michael's efforts to improve student regard of his class, but while she admits he might have caused students to like his course better, she doubts his students are learning any more than hers. In fact, she bets Mr. Michael that her traditional way of teaching the class will produce higher student achievement than does Mr. Michael's new approach.

At the end of the grading period, the two teachers give the same final test to their students. They exchange classes, each administering the test to the other's students, and they arrange for impartial scoring. They find that Mr. Michael's class has a mean score of 88 on the exam, while Miss Jones's class has a mean score of 90. She gloats, but Mr. Michael contends that the difference between the groups' scores is not significant, that it is due only to chance or sampling error. Which teacher is right?

The *t* **test** enables us to answer that question. This procedure (called an *independent-samples t test*) analyzes the difference between the means of the two groups, to determine whether the difference is significant—that is, whether the difference of two points can, or cannot, be attributed to chance errors made in selecting the participants. The procedure for computing *t* tests is presented in the Appendix. A variation of this design (called a *repeated-measures,* or *dependent-measures, t test*) allows us to analyze the difference between the means of pre- and postmeasures taken on the same group of individuals, again looking for a significant difference.

Analysis of Variance (ANOVA)

Analysis of variance, or **ANOVA,** is used to test for differences between two groups when the sample sizes are relatively large and unequal, provided the discrepancy between sample sizes is not extreme (Gravetter & Wallnau, 2002), and to compare three or more groups of any size.

Suppose Mr. Michael's efforts to increase students' regard for Algebra II stirred up interest in other Elmwood high schools. While many teachers preferred continuing with their customary teaching approaches, several began changing—some using individualized self-paced teaching, others large-group instruction followed by small-group tutorials, and still others using algebra to solve real-life problems. They decided to ask that the results of their efforts be analyzed statistically. All used the same final examination. They found that the mean score for traditionally taught students was 91; for those taught individually, 89; for those using small-group tutorials, 92; and for students using real-life situations, the mean score was 85.

Differences in test performance seem evident, but even assuming that no intervening variables unduly affected the results, the question remains: Do the mean scores reflect *real* achievement differences—possibly the result of methods of instruction—or are the observed differences simply attributable to chance? ANOVA, considered further in the Appendix, is used to answer that question. Variations of ANOVA include (1) designs with more than one independent variable (**factorial ANOVA,** sometimes referred to more specifically as "two-way ANOVA" or "three-way ANOVA," for example); (2) designs with more than one dependent variable (**multivariate ANOVA, or MANOVA**); (3) designs with variables, known as **covariates,** whose effects are being controlled (**analysis of covariance,** or **ANCOVA**); and (4) designs with covariates and multiple independent variables (**factorial ANCOVA**) or multiple dependent variables (**multivariate ANCOVA, or MANCOVA**) or both (**factorial MANCOVA**). If, while reviewing published research, you encounter any of these variations and believe that they are beyond your understanding, do not panic. You should simply remember that they all have the same underlying purpose—to compare groups.

REVIEW OF TERMINOLOGY USED IN COMPARISON REPORTS

Chi-square (χ^2)   A procedure for determining the significance of differences when data are categorical in nature.

Difference between means   Assessment that uses the *t* test, a procedure for determining the significance of a difference between means obtained from two different groups of participants or from the same group measured twice.

Analysis of variance (ANOVA)   A procedure for determining the significance of differences among means obtained from two or more groups of participants; also used to explore interactions among several variables.

CORRELATIONAL REPORTS

Researchers are always interested in discovering **correlations,** which are relationships between individual performances on two or more measures, such as between intelligence test scores and reading test scores. Such correlations between variables, where measures on one of the variables tend to accompany similar (or inverse) measures on the other, permit greater understanding of observed phenomena. They also permit us to predict either variable from knowledge of the other. Such predictions cannot be made with absolute accuracy because correlations are almost never perfect, but the predictions can be useful nonetheless. Examples of useful but far-less-than-perfect predictions are forecasting weather from humidity, temperature, and air pressure, and predicting overall cardiovascular health from the amount of cigarette smoke inhaled over time.

In education, it is known that intelligence and reading ability are correlated, which enables us to predict one from the other. If we know that Juan, in fourth grade, is an outstanding reader, we can predict with fairly good accuracy that he has above-average intelligence. Or if we give Juan an IQ test and find that he scores above the average, we can predict with fairly good accuracy that he is, or can become, a good reader.

Correlations do not, by themselves, *demonstrate* cause and effect. High intelligence cannot be said to cause one to be a good reader, nor does learning to read well cause one's intelligence to increase. True *cause–effect relationships* are shown when one (independent) variable is manipulated such that a second (dependent) variable then changes as a result of that manipulation. In correlational studies, variables are not manipulated. However, correlations often *suggest* cause–effect relationships, which are then sometimes verified through experimental research.

Correlational reports that you encounter in the literature will prominently feature a term called **coefficient of correlation.** The coefficient is shown as a decimal number that indicates the degree of relationship for the two or more variables being investigated. The coefficient of correlation, symbolized by the italicized letter r, ranges from a possible value of −1.00 to +1.00. Both −1.00 and +1.00 indicate extremely high (actually, perfect) correlations. A coefficient of 0 indicates no correlation—the absence of a relationship.

The coefficient of correlation may be positive or negative. A **negative correlation,** takes a minus sign (e.g., −.48); a **positive correlation** takes no sign (e.g., .48). Positive and negative correlations are of equal magnitude; that is, positive .48 (.48) is not larger or stronger than negative .48 (−.48). Positive and negative simply show the direction of the relationship. In a positive relationship, high scores on one variable tend to accompany high scores on the second variable, while low scores accompany low scores. In a negative relationship, high scores on one variable tend to accompany low scores on the other variable. For example, quality of diet is *positively* correlated with overall health—the better the diet, the better the health. Quality of diet is *negatively* correlated with incidence of disease—the better the diet, the less frequent or serious the incidence of disease. Generally speaking, correlations, whether positive or negative, are considered high if the absolute values are equal to .70 or above, medium if between .40 and .60, and low if below .30.

Similar to advanced techniques that build on basic ANOVA designs, advanced analytical techniques also exist for investigating relationships. **Multiple correlations** measure the common relationship among a set of three or more variables. **Partial correlations** provide measures of the relationship between two variables while controlling for the effects of a third. Linear regression employs a graph of the effect of an independent variable as a means of predicting scores on a single dependent variable. Similarly, **multiple regression** uses the pattern of relationships between *several* independent variables as a means of predicting scores on a dependent variable. Multivariate multiple regression extends this notion one step further by including multiple dependent variables in addition to the multiple independent variables. Finally, **factor analysis** also capitalizes on the relationships among numerous variables (for example, resulting from the administration of a survey) in an effort to reduce the number of variables to a more manageable number of factors, or clusters of variables that share common elements (i.e., are related).

REVIEW OF TERMINOLOGY USED IN CORRELATIONAL REPORTS

Correlation   A relationship that exists between two or more variables, such that individuals' standings on one of the variables tend to be accompanied by similar, or inverse, standings on the other variable(s).

Positive correlation   High standing on one variable tends to accompany high standing on the other variable(s), average standing tends to accompany average, low tends to accompany low.

Negative correlation   High standing on one variable tends to accompany low standing on the other variable(s), average tends to accompany average, and low tends to accompany high.

Coefficient of correlation (r)   A decimal number that indicates the degree of relationship in a correlation; virtually always a decimal value, the coefficient can vary from 0, which indicates an absence of relationship, to 1.0 or −1.0, both of which indicate perfect relationships (which are almost never encountered in research); the positive and negative attributes have nothing to do with strength or closeness of relationship—they only show the direction of the correlation; generally speaking, correlations, whether positive or negative, are considered high if they are ±.70 or more, medium if between .40 and .60 (or −.40 and −.60), and low if between .30 and 0 (or −.30 and 0).

Exercise 5.2

Indicate, for each of the following findings, whether the research expresses (S) status, (C) comparison, or (R) relationship.

_____   **1.** The valedictorians at Elmwood Lincoln High School have been female 37 times.

_____   **2.** Girls score better in reading than do boys at Cutter Elementary School.

_____   **3.** Student grades can be predicted, though not perfectly, from family income.

_____   **4.** The inquiry approach produced higher achievement than did memorization.

THE CONCEPT OF SIGNIFICANCE

The terms *significant* and *significance* appear in a majority of research reports. Two separate meanings are associated with these terms. The first has to do with whether or not the topic being investigated is worth the time and effort involved. We read that the topic was significant, or that the research made a significant contribution.

The second meaning is associated with statistical treatment of data. Quite different from the first, this meaning has nothing to do with importance. To say a finding is "statistically significant" is to say it is very likely the finding exists in the population as well as in the sample—that it has not appeared just because of errors made in selecting a representative sample.

It is this second meaning—**statistical significance**—to which we give attention here. For a finding to be deemed significant, it must meet stringent levels of probability, usually either the .05 level or the .01 level. The .05 level of significance means there is only a 5 percent chance, on average, that a finding of a particular magnitude occurred because of errors made in selecting the sample. The .01 level means there is only a 1 percent chance that the finding is due to sampling error.

Thus, significance tests help us determine whether a finding made in a sample is also characteristic of the population. Suppose a difference or a correlation is found in the sample. How can we know whether the finding for the sample also exists in the population? Or has the finding appeared because a sample was erroneously selected that does *not* mirror the population? Or has something occurred to bring about differences between samples that were once equal, something that would affect the population as well?

If the significance test strongly suggests that the finding cannot be attributed to an error in selecting the sample, the finding is called *significant.* However, if there is even a slight chance (usually just over 5 percent) that the finding is due to sampling error, the finding is deemed *not significant.*

Let us suppose that in a study we have found an apparent relationship between bibliotherapy and student attitude toward school. Our **null hypothesis** stated, "No difference exists in attitude toward school between students who have participated in bibliotherapy and students who have not participated." We know that the sample might, or might not, accurately reflect the population. To determine whether it does, we test the null hypothesis statistically. Gall, Borg, and Gall (2003) point out that, before administering the test of significance, we should have decided on the level of probability we will accept. This is called the **alpha (α) level** when stated in advance. We might have selected the .05 level (odds of 19 to 1 against the results being due to sampling error, shown as $p < .05$) or the .01 level (odds of 99 to 1 against the result being due to sampling error, shown as $p < .01$). If we selected an alpha level of .05 and our test showed a probability level less than that, we **reject the null hypothesis** and call the finding significant. By this process, we can assume that the finding in our sample is probably real—that it reflects the population and is not due to errors made in selecting the sample (Bartz, 1976). Following that conclusion, logic allows us to conclude that improved student attitude was brought about by bibliotherapy.

The .05 and .01 **probability levels** of significance are traditional in research, but there is nothing magic about them. They are very low levels of probability of sample error, and until recently were the two levels commonly shown on probability charts used by researchers. Nowadays, statistics packages for computers can show all probability levels. In any case, researchers want to be very sure that they do not **retain the null hypothesis** when in fact it is not true. Therefore, they set the probability level so it is very unlikely they will make such an error. But even the very strict odds of .05 and .01 (or .001 often seen reported) leave room for some doubt about any finding. That is why researchers never report any finding with absolute confidence.

Shaver (1992) presents a concise summary of what significance testing does and does not do. He says that significance testing *does* provide a statement of probability of occurrence in the long run. He cautions, however, that significance testing *does not* support any of the following conclusions:

- The probability of a given finding's having occurred by chance. (The concept of chance applies to numerous future repetitions of a study, not to one particular instance of the study.)
- That the null hypothesis is true or false. (It only suggests levels of probability.)
- Whether a treatment being studied had an effect. (It only helps rule out the possibility of procedural error.)
- The magnitude of a result. (The result can be very small and still significant or very large and not significant, depending on the number of participants involved—*the more participants, the greater the likelihood of significance.*)

- The importance of a result. (As noted previously, statistical significance has nothing to do with importance.)

In light of these facts, Shaver recommends that researchers minimize their reliance on tests of significance and place emphasis instead on the size of differences or correlations they find.

Exercise 5.3

Explain what the italicized phrases mean.

_____   1. Jones found that girls scored higher than boys on 18 of 30 tasks but that the difference between the groups was *not significant*.

_____   2. Adolescent boys from the Midwest were an average of one-quarter inch taller than boys from other parts of the country. The difference was *highly significant*.

_____   3. *A correlation of –.83* was found between the two variables.

_____   4. The correlation was significant at the *.05 level of significance*.

_____   5. The null hypothesis was rejected.

PEARSON
myeducationlab
for research

Part of being able to effectively review literature is to be able to evaluate various aspects of a study. Go to the "Evaluating a Research Report" section of **MyEducationLab for Research** and then click on *Building Research Skills*. Complete the exercise titled "Evaluating a Published Study" by closely following the directions and reading the included articles.

DEVELOPMENTAL ACTIVITY

Reviewing Published Research

In Chapter 4, you began searching for and reading published research related to your chosen research topic. As you read published research, it is imperative that you *analyze* what you are reading for several reasons, starting with the need for researchers to be critical consumers of research. It is important to see what research has and has not been conducted on your topic, because published research will help guide decisions you will make for your particular study. This activity will help you get started in this process. For the article that you review, respond to items 1 through 10. You should be able to respond to each item, although you may sometimes need to make inferences. After reviewing several research studies, respond to item 11.

1. Purpose of the study

_____

_____

2. The research question(s) stated

_____

_____

3. A *brief* summary of the literature review

_____

_____

4. The hypothesis(es) stated

_____

_____

_____

5. Based on the types of research previously discussed, your classification of this study

_____

_____

6. The type of sampling used

_____

_____

7. Method of data collection

_____

_____

8. Method of assessing the validity and reliability of the data

_____

_____

9. The descriptive or inferential analyses used

_____

_____

10. A brief summary of the conclusions and recommendations

_____

_____

11. Now that you have reviewed several studies related to your topic, draft a preliminary outline for the review of related literature that you will eventually write for your study, highlighting the major sections, or subheadings, of your literature review.

 I. _____

 II. _____

 III. _____

 IV. _____

 V. _____

CHAPTER SUMMARY

When reading research reports, scan quickly to determine (1) the topic, purpose, and importance of the report; (2) the type of report you are reading—status, difference between groups, or correlational; and (3) the report's findings and conclusions. When taking notes on material as you read, be sure to include subject, date, author, summary, and complete bibliographical citation.

Your ability to interpret research reports will increase as you familiarize yourself with some of the statistical terms and concepts you are likely to encounter. In status reports of a qualitative nature, you will find verbal descriptions of findings and conclusions, with little if any use of statistics and few specialized terms encountered. In status reports of a quantitative nature, you are likely to see men-

tion of raw scores, mean, median, mode, standard deviation, grade equivalents, age equivalents, percentiles, and stanines. In reports that focus on differences between or among groups, you are likely to see mention of chi-square, difference between means, and analysis of variance. In correlational reports you are likely to see mention of correlation, coefficient of correlation, positive correlation, and negative correlation.

In reports of correlations and group differences, you are almost certain to encounter the term *significance,* which in statistics refers not to importance but to whether the researcher's hypothesis can be retained or rejected at a given probability level, such as .05 or .01.

LIST OF IMPORTANT TERMS

age equivalents
age norms
alpha (α) level
analysis of covariance, or ANCOVA

analysis of variance, or ANOVA
chi-square goodness-of-fit test
chi-square test of independence
coefficient of correlation

comparison reports
correlational reports
correlations
covariates

difference between means
factor analysis
factorial ANCOVA
factorial ANOVA
factorial MANCOVA
grade equivalents
grade norms
mean
median
mode
multiple correlations
multiple regression

multivariate ANCOVA, or
    MANCOVA
multivariate ANOVA, or MANOVA
negative correlation
norms
null hypothesis
$p < .05; p < .01$
partial correlations
percentile ranks
positive correlation
probability levels
range

raw scores
reject the null hypothesis
relative standing
retain the null hypothesis
standard deviation
stanines
statistical significance
status reports
t test

YOUR CURRENT STATUS

Having earlier learned to locate published research, you are now familiar with procedures, concepts, and terms that help you read, interpret, and summarize quantities of research. That gives you the background necessary to begin planning a research project of your own. But before continuing to that phase of your development, please strengthen your ability by responding to the activities presented here for thought and discussion.

ACTIVITIES FOR THOUGHT AND DISCUSSION

1. Outline the strategy suggested for rapidly assessing the large number of reports you are likely to encounter when reviewing literature on a given topic.
2. List the information you were advised to enter on note cards and where the information should be placed.
3. Why is the concept of significance so often employed in research that explores correlations and differences between groups? If you encountered the following statement: "The coefficient of correlation was significant at the .01 level," what would it mean to you?
4. Explain why knowledge of statistical terms and concepts enables you to interpret research reports more accurately.
5. Recall the information organizer presented at the beginning of the chapter. See if by referring to it you can summarize the chapter contents.
6. Here again are the questions presented at the beginning of the chapter. See how well you can answer them.
   a. Why should research reports be skimmed rapidly before they are read carefully?

   b. What specifically does one look for when skimming reports?
   c. What entries should one make on note cards when annotating published reports?
   d. What are the three general types of research reports encountered in published literature?
   e. What characterizes the three different types of research reports?
   f. What common analysis terminology—verbal and/or statistical—is usually associated with each of the three types of reports?
   g. Why do the different types of research reports utilize different verbal and statistical procedures to analyze their data?
   h. What two different meanings does the term *significance* have in the context of research?
   i. Why is the term *significant* often misleading to uninformed readers of research?

ANSWERS TO CHAPTER EXERCISES

5.1. Discuss responses in class in light of the style manual used at your institution.

5.2. 1. S 2. C 3. R 4. C

5.3. 1. The odds are unacceptably high that the finding does not exist in the population but has appeared because of errors made in selecting the sample.

2. The finding is probably true for the population.

3. A high inverse relationship exists between the two variables.

4. If the study were repeated thousands of times, similar findings would occur at least 95 percent of the time.

5. The finding is probably "real" and not the result of sampling error.

REFERENCES AND RECOMMENDED READINGS

Bartz, A. (1976). *Basic Statistical Concepts in Education and the Behavioral Sciences.* Minneapolis: Burgess.

Edyburn, D. L. (1999). *The Electronic Scholar: Enhancing Research Productivity with Technology.* Upper Saddle River, NJ: Merrill.

Gall, M., Borg, W., & Gall, J. (2003). *Educational Research: An Introduction* (7th ed.). Boston: Allyn & Bacon.

Gay, L. R., Mills, G. E., & Airasian, P. (2006). *Educational Research: Competencies for Analysis and Application* (8th ed.). Upper Saddle River, NJ: Merrill.

Gravetter, F. J., & Wallnau, L. B. (2002). *Essentials of Statistics for the Behavioral Sciences* (4th ed.). Pacific Grove, CA: Wadsworth.

Kutz, E. (1992). Teacher research: Myths and realities. *Language Arts, 69,* 193–197.

Lyne, L. S. (Ed.). (1999). *A Cross-Section of Educational Research: Journal Articles for Discussion and Evaluation.* Los Angeles: Pyrczak.

Pajares, M. (1992). Teachers' beliefs and educational research: Cleaning up a messy construct. *Review of Educational Research, 62,* 307–332.

Patten, M. L. (Ed.). (1991). *Educational and Psychological Research: A Cross-Section of Journal Articles for Analysis and Evaluation.* Los Angeles: Pyrczak.

Publication Manual of the American Psychological Association (6th ed.). (2010). Washington, DC: American Psychological Association.

Shaver, J. (1992, April). *What Statistical Significance Testing Is, and What It Is Not.* Paper presented at the annual meeting of the American Educational Research Association, San Francisco.

Taylor, D. (1998). *Writing a Literature Review in the Health Sciences and Social Work.* Available at www.utoronto.ca/hswriting/lit-review.htm

Vierra, A., & Pollock, J. (1988). *Reading Educational Research.* Scottsdale, AZ: Gorsuch Scarisbrick.

Zeuli, J. (1992, April). *How Do Teachers Understand Research When They Read It?* Paper presented at the annual meeting of the American Educational Research Association, San Francisco.

6

Procedures and Tools for Gathering Data

PREVIEW

All researchers require new information to help answer their research questions, information referred to as data. They plan carefully how to obtain data that meets specific criteria:

- Appropriate for their type of research
- Directed at their research questions or hypotheses

They give meticulous attention to the following steps:

- Identifying fruitful sources of data
- Planning out procedures for obtaining desired data
- Selecting tools to use in data collection
- Selecting samples as data sources, when needed
- Obtaining and organizing the new data

They also do their best to ensure the following:

- The validity of their data
- The reliability of their data

To do so, they use two specific procedures:

- Internal criticism
- External criticism

TARGETED LEARNINGS

In this chapter we explore in greater detail the procedures and tools that researchers use to collect data in their investigations. This exploration begins by identifying once more the typical foci of the different types of educational research, which provide guidance for identifying potential sources of data. Once data sources are identified, one can decide whether a sample is needed from which to obtain data, and if so, what kind of sample would be best under existing circumstances. The attributes of different data sources also suggest procedures for obtaining data and the tools that would be most useful.

As you read the chapter, look especially for information related to the following questions:

1. What are the typical foci of the various types of educational research?
2. Which three types of educational research call for the careful selection of samples?

3. What are the differences among the various types of samples?
4. What is meant by *data source?* How does data source differ from type of research?
5. How do internal criticism and external criticism relate to the quality of data?
6. What are the characteristics of the following data collection procedures: notation, description, analysis, questioning, measurement, and testing?
7. Which tools for collecting data are most likely to be used in each of the collection procedures named in question 6?
8. What is meant by *data collection profile?* Of what value are such profiles?

Although much valuable information can be located in the university library, research usually requires that firsthand data be acquired directly from the settings, objects, behaviors, procedures, animals, or humans being studied. As you gain ability to plan your own research, it is important that you learn to specify the following:

1. The information (data) needed to answer your research questions and/or test your hypotheses
2. The sources from which needed data can be obtained
3. Appropriate procedures for collecting data

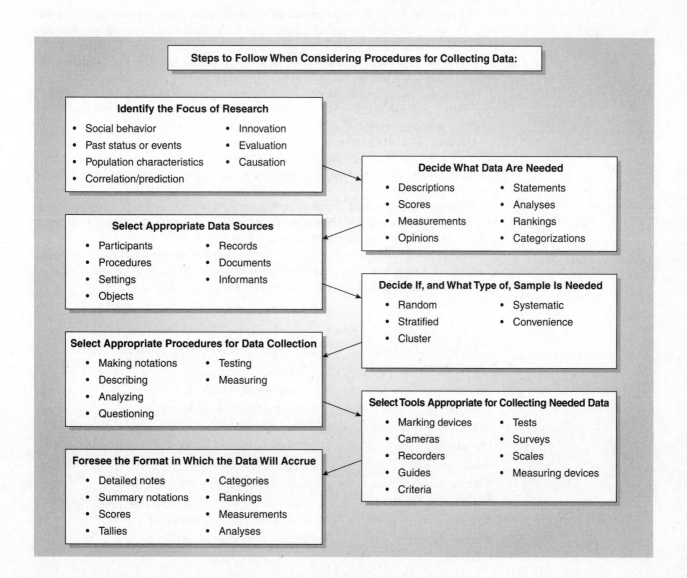

Steps to Follow When Considering Procedures for Collecting Data:

Identify the Focus of Research
- Social behavior
- Past status or events
- Population characteristics
- Correlation/prediction
- Innovation
- Evaluation
- Causation

Decide What Data Are Needed
- Descriptions
- Scores
- Measurements
- Opinions
- Statements
- Analyses
- Rankings
- Categorizations

Select Appropriate Data Sources
- Participants
- Procedures
- Settings
- Objects
- Records
- Documents
- Informants

Decide If, and What Type of, Sample Is Needed
- Random
- Stratified
- Cluster
- Systematic
- Convenience

Select Appropriate Procedures for Data Collection
- Making notations
- Describing
- Analyzing
- Questioning
- Testing
- Measuring

Select Tools Appropriate for Collecting Needed Data
- Marking devices
- Cameras
- Recorders
- Guides
- Criteria
- Tests
- Surveys
- Scales
- Measuring devices

Foresee the Format in Which the Data Will Accrue
- Detailed notes
- Summary notations
- Scores
- Tallies
- Categories
- Rankings
- Measurements
- Analyses

4. Tools useful in collecting data
5. The format in which collected data will accrue

TYPES OF RESEARCH AND THEIR TYPICAL FOCI

Each type of educational research—ethnographic, historical, survey, correlational, causal-comparative, experimental and quasi-experimental, mixed methods, action, and evaluation—has a predominant central focus. Table 6.1 shows the types of research and the typical focus of each.

TYPES OF DATA NEEDED

Each research focus suggests the need for certain kinds of data, such as verbal descriptions, scores, measurements, opinions, statements, and analyses. Although the labels themselves may suggest to some extent the data to which they refer, brief explanations can help clarify their distinctive aspects.

Descriptions are verbal representations of participants, objects, procedures, and settings. They may be given in summary form or in great detail. Ms. Cauthern's explanation of how she assigns homework is a description.

Scores are the numerical values assigned to test performance. The 78 that Jason made on the spelling test is a score.

Measurements are appraisals made with measuring instruments other than tests. They are usually stated numerically, but are sometimes stated verbally. Alicia's height—5 feet, 4 inches—is a measurement.

Opinions are views expressed by participants and informants. Although opinions are often informed and accurate, they may also be uninformed and inaccurate while nevertheless indicating status of thought, attitude, or value. What Mr. Jakes said about school politics is an opinion.

Statements are informed verbal depictions or conclusions, as might be given by authorities or eyewitnesses. What Superintendent Morton said about discipline in Elmwood schools, when interviewed on television, was a statement.

Analyses are clarifications and assessments reached through careful scrutiny and logic. When Mrs. Toler and Mr. Thornton studied the mathematics textbook to determine its attention to problem solving and abstract thought, they performed an analysis.

Table 6.1 Types of Research and Corresponding Foci

Type of Research	Focus
Ethnographic	Human social behavior
Historical	Events or conditions of the past
Survey	Current characteristics of a population
Correlational	Co-relation between variables
Causal-comparative	Existing group differences
Experimental/quasi-experimental	Relationships that show cause and effect
Mixed methods	Topics that require both qualitative and quantitative data
Action	Innovative products or procedures
Evaluation	Quality of programs or operations

SOURCES OF DATA FOR VARIOUS TYPES OF RESEARCH

Data are usually obtained from one or more of the following sources: participants, procedures, settings, objects, records, documents, and informants. The value of a particular source of data depends on the type of research being conducted. Each has distinctive qualities, as demonstrated by the following review of the nature of each of these sources of data.

- *Participants* are the individuals specially selected to undergo scrutiny in research. For example, a student involved in an experiment is a participant. Traditionally participants were, and sometimes still are, called **subjects.**
- *Procedures* are formalized ways of operating in the educational setting. They are the way things are done, such as how lessons are presented and how homework is managed.
- *Settings* are the specific environments in which behavior occurs or is intended to occur. Classrooms, athletic fields, streets, and homes are examples of settings.
- *Objects* are inanimate things, including books, supplies, materials, and artifacts.
- *Records* are highly summarized reports of performance, expenditures, and the like, kept for later reference.
- *Documents* are written papers and reports in their entirety, such as journal articles, technical papers, and curriculum guides. Photographs, drawings, and other illustrations are also considered documents.
- *Informants* are people other than participants in a study from whom opinion, informed views, and expert testimony are obtained. When Mrs. James explained to the researcher how she dealt with the parents of her students, she became an informant.

Exercise 6.1

Indicate the principal data source most likely involved in the eight sentence fragments that follow: (PA) participant, (P) procedure, (ST) setting, (O) object, (R) records, (D) document, or (I) informant.

_____ 1. Mrs. Simpkins said she believed that . . .
_____ 2. The illustrations appear to suggest that . . .
_____ 3. Ted's heart rate just prior to the examination reached . . .
_____ 4. The books had deteriorated . . .
_____ 5. An expert on year-round schools testified . . .
_____ 6. Directions on how to do the activity were given once, then repeated . . .
_____ 7. This information indicates that David has never done very well in school . . .
_____ 8. It was a large urban high school . . .

SAMPLES AND THEIR SELECTION

In research, the sources of data help determine whether a sample should be selected from which to obtain data, and if so, what sort of sample it should be. As you learned previously, a sample is a subgroup of people, animals, or objects selected to represent the much larger population (in its entirety) from which it is drawn.

ARE SAMPLES NECESSARY IN RESEARCH?

Samples are essential in some kinds of research but are not needed in others. For example, in historical research, one does not usually decide in advance to accept data only from selected persons or objects and not from others that might have equal value to the research topic being investigated. In action research, one is concerned only with a particular group in its entirety, such as a class, grade level, or school. In such cases, there is no point in trying to obtain a sample that represents the population.

But where research is concerned with representing a population that is so large it cannot be investigated in its totality, samples are necessary. They should be carefully selected to accurately reflect the distribution of trait variables (e.g., gender, age, socioeconomic status, years of education, and so on) within the population.

CAN SMALL SAMPLES REPRESENT LARGE POPULATIONS?

Small samples can indeed accurately reflect the population, so that findings obtained from the sample can be generalized to the population. To help ensure that samples represent the population, the individuals that comprise them are selected randomly, whenever possible, although other alternative sampling procedures are often required. The various methods of selecting samples are categorized as either probability sampling or nonprobability sampling techniques.

PROBABILITY SAMPLING

Probability sampling is a category of sample selection procedures in which one can state the probability (likelihood) of each member of the population being selected for the sample and in which there is a constant probability of selection for each member of the population. Types of probability sampling include random sampling, stratified sampling, cluster sampling, and systematic sampling.

Random sampling, sometimes called *simple random sampling,* is done in such a way that each individual in the total population has an equal chance of being selected. Random sampling is the best way to obtain a representative sample, although no method guarantees perfect representation. To obtain a sample that would represent all students in Elmwood Lincoln High School, one might put all names on individual slips of paper, thoroughly mix them, and blindly draw out the number desired for the sample. Of course, this would only be a feasible procedure if the population from which you were selecting a sample was small. Random samples were once hand-selected using tables of random numbers. Now, computer programs greatly facilitate the selection process.

Stratified sampling may be used when researchers want to ensure that subgroups within the population are represented proportionally in the sample. The population of Elmwood high school students, for example, contains many different ethnic groups. For the sake of illustration, let us say that the makeup of that population is 33 percent white, 28 percent Latino, 14 percent African American, 9 percent Japanese, 7 percent Korean, and 3 percent Chinese, with several other groups making up the remaining 6 percent. Suppose we wished to conduct a study using a sample with those same exact ethnic percentages. A purely random selection process would give us a sample that might or might not match the ethnic percentages of the population. To ensure an accurate sample, we might decide to use stratified selection. For a sample of 100 students, we would decide in advance that 33 of those students should be randomly selected whites, 28 randomly selected Latinos, 14 randomly selected African Americans, and so on until the sample of 100 participants was filled, thereby ensuring a sample representative of the population with respect to ethnicity. Sampling procedures other than *proportional* representation of the population are possible. Stratified samples may be selected so that various subgroups are represented *equally* in the sample (Gay, Mills, & Aira-sian, 2006). Altering our previous example in this manner would result in a sample consisting of roughly 15 randomly selected students from each of the seven ethnic categories—a sample of 105 students with each ethnic group represented equally.

Cluster sampling involves the random selection of groups that already exist. If we wished to conduct an experiment dealing with a new way of teaching spelling to fourth-grade students, it would be impractical to randomly select a sample of 50 students from the entire fourth-grade population in Elmwood schools and then teach only those 50 students the new spelling method. It would be much more feasible to use entire, intact fourth-grade classrooms. Due to recommendations on sample sizes for classrooms (discussed later in this chapter), at least five classrooms should be selected at random from all Elmwood fourth grades to receive the experimental treatment. But with such cluster sampling, it is improbable that those classrooms would accurately reflect the fourth-grade population of the school district. The convenience or necessity of cluster sampling is thus offset by a greater likelihood of obtaining an unrepresentative sample.

Systematic sampling is often done when all members of the population are named on a master list and the sample is drawn directly from that list. From the list, a name is chosen at random. Following that first selected name, every kth person (that is, every tenth, every fiftieth, every one-hundredth, or whatever) is selected for inclusion in the sample. The value for k is determined by simply taking the total number of subjects in the population and dividing it by the number needed for the sample. Systematic sampling has most of the virtues of random sampling and is usually more conveniently done. However, if the original list of names exists in a predetermined order, it is possible that the resulting sample may be biased. This ultimately results in systematic sampling being classified as a nonprobability sampling technique (see the next section). In this case, it is best to randomize the original list in an attempt to remedy the potential bias in a systematic sample. The various types of probability sampling techniques are depicted in Figure 6.1.

It is also possible to combine two or more probability sampling techniques (or perhaps two or more "stages" of the same technique). Generally speaking, this is known as **multi-stage sampling,** and is often useful when sampling from very large populations. For example, in a hypothetical research study using a two-stage sampling approach, a researcher might first randomly select school districts throughout an entire state (stage 1: cluster sampling), and then from those districts randomly select teachers based on proportional representation by gender (stage 2: stratified random sampling).

NONPROBABILITY SAMPLING

PEARSON
myeducationlab
         for research

Being able to identify aspects of the sampling process within published articles can help you understand how the techniques are used in research. Go to the "Reviewing the Literature" section of **MyEducationLab for Research** and then click on *Building Research Skills*. First, read the article written by Wolcott, then complete the exercise titled "Sampling in a Qualitative Study." As you have read, there are differences between sampling in quantitative and qualitative studies.

Nonprobability sampling is a sampling procedure in which the probability of inclusion for each member of the population cannot be specified. It is used when probability sampling is not feasible. Types of nonprobability sampling include convenience sampling, judgmental sampling, snowball sampling, and quota sampling.

Convenience sampling takes groups of participants that simply happen to be available. Teachers often select convenience samples when doing research, often their own class, or sometimes the classes of two or three fellow teachers. Samples selected in this manner cannot be assumed to represent the population, meaning the results obtained in such studies should only be generalized to the population with great caution.

Judgmental sampling, also known as **purposive sampling,** is a means of selecting certain segments of the population for study. The researcher uses his or her judgment as to which segments should be included. For example, one might wish to do research into the lifestyles of 10 "deviant" students who have a history of chronic misbehavior in school. Or one might wish to investigate the nurturing practices of parents of students named valedictorians of their graduating classes for a particular year. Judgmental sampling, as you can see in these examples, is more appropriate for qualitative research—where making generalizations to the entire population is *not* the focus—than for quantitative research.

Figure 6.1

Graphical
representation of
various probability
sampling techniques

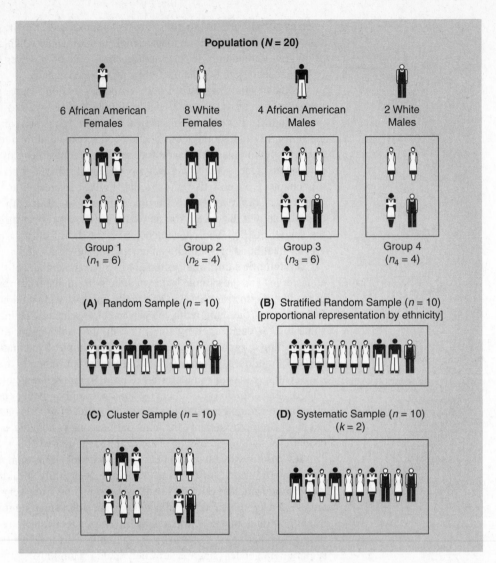

Population (N = 20)

6 African American
Females

8 White
Females

4 African American
Males

2 White
Males

Group 1
($n_1 = 6$)

Group 2
($n_2 = 4$)

Group 3
($n_3 = 6$)

Group 4
($n_4 = 4$)

(A) Random Sample ($n = 10$)

(B) Stratified Random Sample ($n = 10$)
[proportional representation by ethnicity]

(C) Cluster Sample ($n = 10$)

(D) Systematic Sample ($n = 10$)
($k = 2$)

Snowball sampling, also known as **network sampling** or **chain sampling,** is often used in qualitative research endeavors. The basic technique begins with the identification of a few initial participants to be interviewed. Following each interview, the researcher simply asks each participant to recommend other individuals meeting certain criteria who might be interested in participating in the research study. The term *snowball* refers to the accumulation of participants as one progresses through the data collection process. Snowball sampling is useful for getting started when you are unable to identify another means of finding the participants you want; however, it should not be used in isolation as the sole means of sample selection (Glesne, 2006).

Quota sampling, not often found in educational research, is sometimes chosen by an investigator who wants to do research applicable to the population but for whatever reason is unable to draw a proper sample. The investigator may, therefore, intentionally construct a sample that seems to have the same characteristics as the population. If one wished, for example, to study the educational backgrounds of adult members of six different ethnic groups prominent in Elmwood, it might be very difficult to select a sample randomly. However, given existing information about those groups, it might be possible to contact individual members and thus put together a sample that is believed to represent the groups in the population regarding age, gender, socioeconomic status, and other pertinent criteria.

Finally, it should be noted that systematic sampling, previously described as a probability sampling procedure, may also be classified as a *non*probability technique in specific situations. If the list for selecting the sample is "ordered" in some manner (i.e., the names are not randomly arranged), the possibility exists for certain subgroups to be systematically excluded from the sample (Gay, Mills, & Airasian, 2006). For example, certain ethnicities have distinctive last names that may group together when arranged alphabetically. If a sample is being selected from a list arranged alphabetically, it is quite possible that one or more particular ethnic groups might be completely excluded from the sample.

SIZE OF SAMPLES

As indicated earlier, it has been found that samples smaller than 30 are not likely to reflect the trait distributions that exist in the population, a fault that could put one's research findings in doubt. Even when small samples do represent populations accurately, their size reduces the likelihood that research results based on their data will be found statistically significant. A given correlation or difference between means, for example, is more likely to be found statistically significant if obtained from a large sample; significance becomes less likely as the sample size becomes smaller.

How small is too small? A minimum sample size depends on the type of research study being conducted. Statisticians have seemed generally to agree that, as a rule of thumb, samples used in correlational research should be no smaller than 30, those used in experimental or causal-comparative research no smaller than 15 per group involved, and those that involve entire classrooms should include at least five classrooms per different research treatment. For survey research studies, a common recommendation is to sample approximately 10 to 20 percent of the population. With large populations, this can obviously become cumbersome. Gay, Mills, and Airasian (2006) assert that once population sizes of a certain magnitude (about $N = 5,000$) are exceeded, population size becomes irrelevant and a sample size of $n = 400$ will provide adequate representation. Even large samples, if improperly selected, can lead to invalid conclusions. Bartz (1976) maintains that sample size is not nearly so important as sample accuracy. Best and Kahn (2006) agree that care in selecting the sample is more important than increasing the size of the sample.

APPLYING TECHNOLOGY

Probability and Nonprobability Sampling

We again refer you to Dr. Trochim's electronic research methods textbook (http://socialresearch methods.net/kb) for a discussion of probability and nonprobability sampling techniques. On a page titled "Sampling Terminology" (http://socialresearchmethods.net/kb/sampterm.htm), Dr. Trochim provides a brief but excellent general overview of sampling and its related terminology, including

- Populations
- Samples
- Target populations
- Accessible populations

Another page (http://socialresearchmethods .net/kb/sampprob.htm) addresses the concept of probability sampling. Basic definitions and excellent examples with very helpful graphic images are provided for simple random sampling, stratified random sampling, systematic sampling, and cluster sampling. An example of multistage sampling, which involves combining two or more of the preceding probability sampling techniques, is also given.

A third page addresses the various types of nonprobability sample techniques (http://social researchmethods.net/kb/sampnon.htm). Explanations are provided for convenience, purposive, and quota sampling, as well as some lesser used nonprobability techniques.

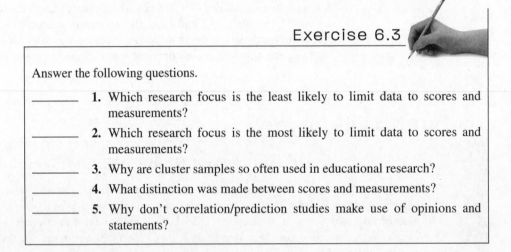

Exercise 6.2

Mark these statements about samples (T) true or (F) false.

_____   1. Samples are not necessary if data can easily be obtained from the entire population.

_____   2. Convenience samples, because participants are included by happen-stance, can be considered equivalent to random samples.

_____   3. You might wish to use stratified sampling if you were studying the differences between males and females.

_____   4. If a convenience sample is as large as 100, we can assume it reflects the population.

_____   5. A carefully selected sample of 25 may well be more indicative of the population than a poorly selected sample of 1,000.

RELATIONSHIPS BETWEEN RESEARCH FOCUS, DATA, SOURCE, AND SAMPLE

We have noted that types of research have particular foci, that those foci suggest kinds of data required and the sources of those data, and that focus and data help indicate whether a sample will be needed when obtaining data. Table 6.2 depicts the relationships between research focus, data required, sources of data, and type of sample that might be indicated.

Exercise 6.3

Answer the following questions.

_____   1. Which research focus is the least likely to limit data to scores and measurements?

_____   2. Which research focus is the most likely to limit data to scores and measurements?

_____   3. Why are cluster samples so often used in educational research?

_____   4. What distinction was made between scores and measurements?

_____   5. Why don't correlation/prediction studies make use of opinions and statements?

VALIDITY AND RELIABILITY IN DATA COLLECTION

Before we consider the general procedures involved in data collection, let us take a moment to review the concepts of data validity and reliability, important considerations for ensuring quality when collecting data.

VALIDITY OF DATA

Validity is essential in research data. The data must be, in fact, what they are believed or purported to be. In other words, did we *actually* measure what we intended to measure,

Table 6.2 Foci, Data, Sources, and Samples

Research Focus	Data Required	Data Source	Type of Sample
Social behavior	Descriptions	Participants Settings	Clustered Judgmental
Past status/ conditions	Descriptions	Settings Records Documents Informants	Usually none
Present status/ conditions	Descriptions Scores Measurements Opinions Statements Analyses	Participants Procedures Settings Objects Records Documents Informants	Random Stratified Clustered Systematic Judgmental
Correlation/ prediction	Scores Measurements Categorizations Rankings	Participants	Random Stratified Clustered Systematic
Causation	Scores Measurements	Participants	Random Stratified Clustered Systematic
Innovation	Descriptions Scores Measurements Opinions Analyses	Participants Procedures Settings Objects Documents Informants	Clustered Convenience
Evaluation	Descriptions Scores Measurements Opinions Analyses Statements	Participants Procedures Settings Objects Documents Informants	Random Stratified Clustered Systematic Judgmental

based on the focus of our research? If you go to a writing clinic expecting to learn how to plot fictional stories but instead find only instruction on how to sell your stories, the information is not appropriate for your purposes. Despite being entirely accurate, the information was not what it was purported to be, or what you believed it would be. Hence, from your perspective, the information was invalid. In the same sense, scores obtained from a test of critical thinking are valid if they represent the ability to think critically, as distinct from knowledge of vocabulary or reading skill. The determination of validity ultimately has a substantial effect on the interpretation of data and the subsequent conclusions drawn from those results.

DETERMINING VALIDITY OF TEST DATA

Presently, validity is seen as a unitary concept (AERA, APA, & NCME, 1999), combining previous descriptions of four distinct types of validity: content, concurrent, predictive, and construct. It is defined as the "degree to which all the accumulated evidence supports the intended interpretation of test scores for the proposed purpose" (p. 11). Validity of data obtained from the administration of tests (usually quantitative data) can be determined through examining various sources of evidence. Although similar to the four outdated types of validity, the five sources of validity evidence are unique in their own right.

Evidence of Validity Based on Test Content

Evidence based on the relationship between the content addressed on a test, or other data collection instrument, and the underlying *construct* (or characteristic) it is trying to measure often includes logical analysis of content coverage on the test, as well as the judgments of experts in the particular content field. This type of evidence was formerly referred to as *content validity.*

Evidence of Validity Based on Response Processes

Examining individual sets of responses from a test for patterns of response or questioning respondents about their performance or strategies they used on a particular test can provide insight into the specific characteristics actually being measured by a set of test items. Patterns of response (for example, having a tendency to agree with certain types of statements and to disagree with others) can reveal underlying characteristics of individual participants or groups of participants (e.g., females). Gathering this type of evidence typically requires the use of advanced statistical analyses.

Evidence of Validity Based on Internal Structure

Analysis of the internal structure of a given test involves an examination of the extent to which the relationships among the test items conform to or parallel the construct actually being measured. Often subsets of test items that on the surface appear to be measuring the construct of interest actually are measuring something slightly or even drastically different. Similar to the former category known as *construct validity,* this form of evidence also requires the use of advanced statistical analyses.

Evidence of Validity Based on Relations to Other Variables

Analyses of the relationships between test scores and other measures of the same or similar constructs can provide evidence of the validity of the scores resulting from the instrument of interest. For example, one might investigate the relationship between college entrance exams (e.g., SAT score) and eventual college GPA. Similar measures might include other tests or inventories or performance (i.e., "hands-on") criteria that purport to measure the same construct. This type of evidence, formerly known as *criterion validity,* involves computations of correlation coefficients (which, in this specific application, are known as *validity coefficients*).

Evidence of Validity Based on Consequences of Testing

Testing, as well as any other type of data collection, is done with the expectation that some benefit will be realized from the intended and appropriate use of the scores. The process of validation should indicate whether these specific benefits are likely to be realized. Examples of benefits include improved academic achievement, enhanced self-esteem, or increased motivation. At a minimum, testing (as well as other forms of data collection) should not have a detrimental effect.

DETERMINING VALIDITY OF NON-TEST DATA

Validity of qualitative data, as well as quantitative data from non-test measurements, is usually determined by experts applying **external criticism** to establish that a given information source is *authentic*. Suppose that in research on the history of Elmwood Urban School District, an informant claims to have been present at a closed school board meeting in 1958 at which scandalous information was purportedly discussed and suppressed. The data from the informant pass the test of external criticism only if the informant's presence at the meeting can be verified. Or suppose that it is reported that participants' temperatures were elevated by 0.5 degrees through a given exercise. The data would be considered valid if authentic thermometers were used in accordance with established procedures.

RELIABILITY OF DATA

Reliability, a second essential characteristic of data, refers not to authenticity but to consistency. If you hear three accounts of the aforementioned closed school board meeting, but each account differs as to what happened, who was involved, and what the results were, you can have little confidence in any of the versions. That is to say, the accounts (the data) are inconsistent and therefore unreliable. If, however, each account is essentially similar, the information you have received is consistent and may be considered reliable.

Similarly, if you administer a certain test repeatedly under identical circumstances but find that you get different results each time, you would conclude that the test is unreliable. If, however, you get similar results each time you administer the test, you would consider the results reliable and therefore potentially useful.

DETERMINING RELIABILITY OF TEST DATA

Reliability of test data is usually established by correlating the test results with themselves. Three different methods can be used: test–retest, equivalent forms, and split-half.

The *test–retest method* involves administering a given test to a group of participants and then, perhaps a week later, again administering the same test to the same people. The scores from the first and second administrations are correlated and the resultant coefficient of correlation provides an index of reliability—the higher the correlation coefficient (i.e., as it approaches 1.00), the more reliable the test.

The *equivalent forms method* of determining reliability is similar to the test–retest method, except that in this case two different forms of the test are available for measuring the same thing. Form A of the test is administered to a group of individuals, and soon thereafter form B is administered to those same individuals. The two sets of scores are correlated and the resultant coefficient serves as the index of reliability. Again, a high coefficient indicates the test has good reliability.

The *split-half method* determines a specific form of reliability known as *internal consistency*. This approach is appropriate when testing a single group on two occasions is not feasible or an alternate form of a test is not available. The split-half method involves dividing a given test into two parts, such as the even-numbered and the odd-numbered items. Two scores are obtained for each person—in this situation, one for even-numbered items and another for odd-numbered items. Those two sets of scores are correlated and the resultant coefficient is the test's index of reliability.

You may come across other measures of internal consistency reliability in the research literature. Two commonly reported measures are Kuder-Richardson (KR) reliability and Cronbach's alpha (α) reliability. Without going into great detail, these two measures are both basically averages of all possible split-half reliabilities. Their interpretations are similar to the split-half reliability coefficient—a high KR reliability or high α both indicate good reliability.

DETERMINING RELIABILITY OF NON-TEST DATA

Reliability of quantitative data is established through consistency. If similar data are found by different but equally qualified researchers, the data are considered reliable. So are data that are similar when acquired before and after a time interval. Reliability of qualitative data, however, is relatively difficult to establish objectively (Vierra & Pollock, 1988). The prime requirement is consistency. Investigators, therefore, attempt to check multiple sources of qualitative data to reassure themselves that the information is consistent, and in addition they think carefully about the procedures used to obtain the data and about the trustworthiness of their sources of informants (Gall, Gall, & Borg, 2005).

In making this effort, investigators are applying **internal criticism** to determine the *credibility* of data. In the example of an informant reporting on a school board meeting held in 1958, even if the informant can substantiate being present at the 1958 board meeting (thereby satisfying authenticity of the source), internal criticism must be applied to determine whether the informant's contentions are reliable. One approach is to compare what the informant says against what is said by other informants, or against records or written accounts. Logical interpretation also plays a strong role in internal criticism, and researchers must answer for themselves pertinent questions. Do these contentions make sense? Could the events have happened? Can persuasive arguments be made for or against them? Although based on logic and examination of documents and records, the judgments necessary in internal criticism require a high degree of subjectivity on the part of the researchers.

RELATIONSHIP BETWEEN VALIDITY AND RELIABILITY

We often think of validity and reliability as two distinct concepts, but in fact they share an important relationship. It is possible for scores obtained from an instrument to be reliable (consistent) but not valid (measuring something other than what was intended). In contrast, scores cannot be both valid and unreliable—if scores measure what was intended to be measured, it is implied that they will do so consistently. Therefore, reliability is a necessary, but not sufficient, condition for validity. When establishing the validity and reliability of your research data, always remember the following adage: *A valid test is always reliable, but a reliable test is not necessarily valid.*

PROCEDURES IN DATA COLLECTION

Suppose an investigator has identified a research topic and located appropriate sources of information. How does he or she now go about collecting the data needed to answer the research questions or test the hypotheses? The general procedures for collecting data that were introduced in Chapter 2 can be considered more fully by examining six methods of data collection: notation, description, analysis, questioning, testing, and measurement.

NOTATION

Characteristics

Notation is the process of making very brief written notes, tally marks, or evaluation symbols about people, objects, settings, or events being observed. All types of research can make use of data collected through notation; descriptive research almost always does so. Notation is tied to observation: You observe and make notes about what is seen or heard, as the name implies.

Tools

No tools other than paper and pencil or other marking device are needed for notation.

Data Format

With notation, you may record data in the sequence they are observed or slot data into categories that correspond to elements receiving special attention in the research. In the first case, one might observe teachers interacting in meetings and attempt to make notes of what occurs at certain times. For example, you might observe ongoing interaction and make tally marks in categories such as who is talking, the nature of what is said, who responds to whom, who defers to whom, constructive comments, destructive comments, and so forth. This notational technique is frequently used in descriptive research.

DESCRIPTION

Characteristics

Description is the process of putting observations into a verbal form that goes beyond notation by attempting to convey complete pictures, replete with detail. Description is used when information cannot be measured but only observed and described, as is typically the case for behaviors, routines, interactions, and linguistic patterns.

Obviously, the descriptive process is usually used in descriptive research, and often in ethnographic and action research. Ethnographic research in particular relies heavily on the richness of observational data, especially detailed descriptions of settings, participants, and phenomena. The data are obtained by a careful observer who enters into a social setting and observes and records as much as possible. The observer ordinarily tries not to influence events or behaviors, but simply records fully what is seen and heard. The investigator's mere presence will for a while influence participants' behavior; some time may pass before group members resume their natural behaviors. Moreover, if the observer becomes a functional member of the group being studied, as sometimes occurs, the group's behavior will be influenced and altered by the investigator's presence.

The investigator usually takes numerous notes, which must later be summarized and organized into an overall picture of occurrences, situations, and contexts. The objective of this data gathering procedure is not simply to present an accurate picture, though accuracy is certainly important, but also to identify topics, categories, and patterns of behavior within the natural setting to be used in answering the research questions.

Although naturalistic observation and description are difficult to do well, this type of research and data gathering is occurring with increasing frequency, especially in educational settings. A kindergarten teacher, for example, might study patterns of personal interaction, dominance, and submission among children on the playground, observing and making careful notes about actions and verbal interchanges while an aide oversees the children. A middle-grades teacher might study changes, over time, in language patterns by students learning English as a second language. An administrative intern might study the dynamics of teacher adjustment to mandated curriculum changes, in an effort to describe and explain the natural patterns of cooperation, resistance, and scapegoating as the changes are implemented.

Tools

No special tools are needed for collecting descriptive data. Many researchers use only pencils and notebooks, while others record with audio and video equipment. Unfortunately, recording devices tend to affect human behavior being observed, thereby distorting the data.

Data Format

The data obtained through written description may fill only a single page or, as often occurs in ethnographic research, may result in voluminous quantities of notes. Structured formats are needed to organize data, either as they are being collected or afterward, to determine how they relate to the research questions or hypotheses.

ANALYSIS

Characteristics

The term *analysis* has three separate meanings in research. One meaning is associated with obtaining data, as in analyzing a book, an article, or an individual's behavior as part of data gathering. In this kind of analysis, objects, documents, procedures, and other behaviors are broken down into constituent parts to determine the nature of those parts, how they relate to each other, and how they function together as a whole.

A second meaning of *analysis* refers to a product—the verbal or written result of the analytical process. For example, you might refer to a completed analysis of the school curriculum or the final analysis of Mr. Baker's teaching methods.

The third meaning involves making sense of data after they have been collected, by applying statistical treatments to quantitative data or logical treatments to qualitative data. You already know something of the terms and meanings used in statistical data analysis, and in Chapter 7 and the Appendix you will find more about analysis of both quantitative and qualitative data.

Here our concern is the first of the three meanings—obtaining data from objects, settings, and procedures. This involves careful scrutiny to discover traits, procedures, meanings, and relationships. Unlike observation, which is broad and all-encompassing, by using analysis you attempt to find specific information to answer specific questions. Journal articles may be analyzed to identify content, treatment, bias, or change over time. Apparatus may be analyzed to assess specific elements of form, function, and quality. Curriculum guides may be analyzed to determine concordance with a school system's stated goals.

Tool

To help ensure the quality of data obtained by analysis, a guide should be used in the process. This analysis guide should stipulate what is being sought and might include criteria and examples for determining the presence and quality of the desired elements. For example, a guide for analyzing a series of elementary school science textbooks might include the following criteria:

- Corresponds to stated goals of the school's science program (which can be listed and checked off)
- Provides clear, unambiguous statements of intended learnings
- Emphasizes a hands-on approach to learning science through classroom activities
- Is written at an appropriate level of difficulty
- Specifies needed materials in teacher's edition and provides suggestions for obtaining and using those materials

The analysis guide would continue in this way, including all the elements being considered in the textbook series.

Data Format

Data resulting from analysis may be either verbal or numerical. Those data should be put into formats that parallel the structure of the analysis guide.

QUESTIONING

Characteristics

Questioning is a prompting process used to elicit and probe responses from participants and informants. In research, questioning is typically done through interview and survey.

The **interview** is conducted in person. The interviewer asks questions directly of respondents, either face-to-face or by telephone. The process involves a one-to-one exchange that permits the interviewer to pose questions and when necessary probe or otherwise follow up to obtain clearer responses in greater depth. Teachers doing graduate research often use interviews for purposes such as obtaining community opinion concerning quality of school programs.

Interviews, however, are time and cost intensive, which limits the number of respondents that can be included in most research projects, especially projects done by graduate students. If too few respondents are interviewed, the data are not likely to represent the population. Investigators, therefore, hope to interview at least 30 respondents, a number that is usually feasible in descriptive research, though historical research sometimes cannot identify more than a few respondents, if any.

Surveys are a second structured procedure for questioning respondents, usually by means of printed questionnaires mailed to large samples, though surveys can also be done by telephone. Surveys are used to obtain data cross-sectionally as well as longitudinally. A **cross-sectional survey** collects data across different segments of the population at a particular time. It shows the status of those segments but cannot clearly depict changes that might be occurring. If one wished to determine the educational levels of parents of Elmwood students, for example, a cross-sectional survey would be appropriate.

In **longitudinal surveys** the researcher obtains data from the same or similar samples over time to reveal changes in opinion or status. If one wished to document changes in residents' evaluations of Elmwood schools, a longitudinal survey, which poses the same questions each time the survey is conducted, would be appropriate. Excellent examples of cross-sectional and longitudinal surveys can be seen in the annual Gallup Poll of the public's attitude toward the schools. This poll, sponsored by Phi Delta Kappa, has been conducted each year since 1969 and published in the journal *Phi Delta Kappan.*

Compared to interviews, surveys tend to be broader in scope and less personal in nature. Surveys do not typically probe responses as do interviews and normally do not provide for additional questioning that could clarify answers or allow respondents to raise concerns.

Survey questions are sometimes open-ended but are more frequently formatted with response choices preselected by the investigator. Asking respondents to select response a, b, or c makes it easier to tabulate and analyze survey results than trying to assess responses to open-ended questions, although this approach may curtail the depth of information being brought to light.

Surveys usually require less time investment per respondent than do interviews, allowing the inclusion of more participants. One might consider mailing written questionnaires to survey 1,000 people, but only under very unusual circumstances could 1,000 people be interviewed personally. On the other hand, interviews provide 100 percent return against the smaller return results from written surveys; respondents are either disinterested or will not take the time to write and return their responses.

Tools

The collection of data through questioning is typically accomplished through interview guides and questionnaires. Interviews are managed with an interview guide, which contains questions sequenced in the order they are to be asked. Follow-up questions should be included for probing or clarifying. Great care should be exercised here, as it is difficult for interviewers to pose questions and probe answers without improperly leading respondents' answers.

The questions in the interview guide can be highly **structured, semistructured,** or **open-ended questions,** as shown in the following examples:

Highly structured question: Of the following three aspects of Elmwood schools, which one do you consider to be highest in quality?

1. Teachers
2. Buildings and grounds
3. Books and equipment

Semistructured question: Elmwood elementary teachers have made an effort to communicate with parents more frequently than in the past. What have you liked best about the communication you have received? What have you liked least about it?

Open-ended question: What suggestions can you make for improving the quality of Elmwood middle schools?

Another useful questioning tool is the **questionnaire,** employed to collect data by means of a written survey. The same types of items appearing on interview guides are included on questionnaires. Because it is essential that the respondents answer and return the questionnaires, the appearance of the instrument must be as appealing as possible. It should be uncluttered and pleasant to look at. Relatively few items should be included, directions should be simple, and responses should be easy to make; otherwise, respondents will put the material aside and neglect to return it. The response rate, always a concern when surveys are used, can be increased by indicating in the cover letter how little time will be required to respond thoughtfully and by stressing the potential value of the responses and the research. Other suggestions for increasing response rate include contacting respondents in advance, expressing appreciation by including a token monetary payment such as a dollar bill, and using follow-up mailings to respondents who do not reply (Clark & Boser, 1989; Hopkins & Gullickson, 1989).

Questionnaire items can take many forms. One of the more common formats is the **Likert scale,** composed of statements that permit responses along an "agree . . . disagree" continuum, such as strongly agree, agree, neutral, disagree, strongly disagree. Likert scale items used in a questionnaire might appear as shown in Figure 6.2. *Likert-type* items also utilize response scales on a continuum, but not the "agree . . . disagree" form of a true Likert item. For example, a Likert-type item might require participants to respond on a scale that examines quality ("excellent . . . poor"), frequency of occurrence ("always . . . never"), or level of comfort ("very comfortable . . . not at all comfortable").

Another common format, the **semantic differential scale,** presents pairs of adjectives related to a word or phrase. A continuum, consisting of up to seven blanks, is given between the pairs of adjectives. Respondents mark the blank along the continuum that represents their view. Figure 6.3 shows a typical semantic differential scale.

Figure 6.2   Format of the Likert scale

Directions: For each statement, circle whether you strongly agree with the statement (SA), agree (A), are undecided (U), disagree (D), or strongly disagree (SD).

1. Teachers in Elmwood school district are, for the most part, overpaid.	SA	A	U	D	SD
2. Elmwood should pass a bond issue to raise money for new school buildings.	SA	A	U	D	SD
3. Racial integration efforts in Elmwood schools reflect community wishes.	SA	A	U	D	SD

Figure 6.3   Format of the semantic differential scale

Directions: Mark an X in the appropriate blank between each pair of words, so that your opinion is accurately expressed.

1. Elmwood's efforts concerning bicultural education

effective	___	___	___	___	___	ineffective
fair	___	___	___	___	___	unfair
too little	___	___	___	___	___	too much
well planned						haphazard

2. Elmwood's treatment of different ethnic groups

considerate	___	___	___	___	___	inconsiderate
ignorant	___	___	___	___	___	knowledgeable
not helpful	___	___	___	___	___	helpful

In both Likert and semantic differential scales, a scoring system can be used that assigns values to the categories, such as 1 for the most negative to 7 for the most positive on the semantic differential, or 1 for "strongly disagree" to 5 for "strongly agree" on the Likert scale. The scoring must be done with care, because items on Likert and semantic differential scales are usually constructed so that their positive and negative sides are not always located in the same place. This forces respondents to think about their responses rather than mark all items the same.

Data Format

Two kinds of responses are obtained in interviews and surveys. Open-ended questions produce unstructured comments, whereas structured questions produce selections from responses provided. The open-ended responses are collated as they are written by respondents, and if categories of response can be foreseen, the responses can be channeled into those categories as they are received. Responses that do not fit any preselected categories must be analyzed and categorized at a later time. Structured responses, on the other hand, can be tabulated as they are received. If relatively few different responses are possible, the tabulations can be made directly on a copy of the interview guide or questionnaire.

TESTING

Characteristics

Testing, as the term is used here, is the process of obtaining data by having participants respond to written or oral examinations. More has been written about test construction, administration, scoring, and interpretation than about all other aspects of educational measurement combined. Researchers like to use tests because the numerical data they offer seem more precise than verbal data. However, proponents of qualitative research generally disagree with that point, contending that a verbal description of Juan's mathematics achievement is more accurate and informative than the numerical scores that might be assigned to his test performance.

Tools

Tests are the tools used in collecting data through testing. Two general types of tests are commonly used in educational research—criterion-referenced tests and norm-referenced (standardized) tests. **Criterion-referenced tests** are constructed so that each test item relates directly to an instructional objective toward which classwork has been directed.

Attainment of such objectives is the goal for both teacher and class, and the ideal result would be for all students to respond correctly to all items. No distribution of scores is desired. Criterion-referenced tests are used to judge the quality of educational programs and to assess minimum proficiency levels for students.

Norm-referenced tests are carefully constructed tests, usually commercial, that are designed not to show the attainment of specific objectives but to show how individuals (and schools and school districts) compare with one another. The score that an individual makes on a norm-referenced test is translated into a converted score, such as a percentile, stanine, or grade-equivalent that enables relative standing to be shown.

Commercial **standardized tests,** typically norm-referenced, are constructed with great precision by professional test makers. These tests are intended to disperse scores across a wide range corresponding to the normal probability curve, thus differentiating among the individuals taking the test. Standardized tests are available in astonishing variety and number; more than 9,000 published and unpublished tests are listed in the Educational Testing Service database.

Standardized tests are accompanied by norms (hence, the label *norm-referenced*) that permit comparisons of individuals, schools, and school systems. The norms are compiled from the responses of thousands of individuals believed to reflect a cross section of the national population. Standardized tests usually have very high levels of validity and reliability.

As mentioned, a great deal has been written about tests, test construction, establishing validity and reliability, using tests properly, and interpreting results correctly. For information about commercial tests, one of the best sources is *The Fifteenth Mental Measurements Yearbook* (Plake, Impara, & Spies, 2003), which includes critical reviews of well over 250 tests, with more than 1,800 references related to the construction, use, and limitations of those tests. A similarly valuable reference is *A Consumer's Guide to Tests in Print* (Hammill, Brown, & Bryant, 1989). Good information on standardized and teacher-made tests can be found in textbooks such as those authored by McMillan (2001) and Mertler (2003).

Data Format

Most of the data obtained through testing are initially raw numerical scores. In some cases they will be rankings or listings by category. Raw scores may be converted into percentiles, stanines, grade equivalents, or other derived scores. Rankings may be placed into ordered position as they are received and tallied. Categorical responses are tallied in the appropriate categories.

MEASUREMENT

Characteristics

Measurement assesses traits and abilities by means other than testing. The assessments are assigned numerical values or can be placed in categories or rankings. Measurement obtains information by comparing participants' performance or status against an established scale, a procedure that first helps determine the extent or quality of a variable trait and, second, permits assigning a value to it.

Testing is sometimes used synonymously with *measurement,* especially in the context of educational research, but the two terms do not have the same meaning. *Measurement* is the broader generic term, widely applicable to human and other natural phenomena. It makes use of measurement scales, which include (1) **interval scales,** consisting of raw numbers (e.g., 34, 43, 48); (2) **ordinal scales,** which show position in rank (e.g., first, fifteenth, thirtieth); and (3) **nominal scales,** which assign individuals to named categories (e.g., fast, medium, slow). As indicated, the value obtained through measurement is most often a cardinal number but may also be an ordinal number or a named category.

APPLYING TECHNOLOGY

Survey Construction

Often researchers have a specific research topic in mind and know what kind of data is needed to answer the related research questions. Unfortunately, there may be no existing survey instrument available to collect these data. The researcher is left to develop a survey that specifically addresses his or her research needs. In his page titled "Constructing the Survey" (http://socialresearchmethods.net/kb/survwrit.htm), Dr. Trochim provides a superb discussion, complete with excellent examples, of

■ The various types of questions that can be used in survey research (http://socialresearchmethods.net/kb/questype.htm)
■ Different methods of structuring response formats (http://socialresearchmethods.net/kb/quesresp.htm)

■ Different ways to word questions in order to avoid misinterpretation (http://socialresearchmethods.net/kb/quesword.htm)
■ Suggestions on where to place specific types of questions within the actual survey (http://socialresearchmethods.net/kb/quesplac.htm)

Developing surveys for research studies is not an easy task, as many people assume. It requires time, practice, and experience. Anyone who is considering collecting data via self-developed surveys is urged to examine the Web pages listed previously for critically important and essential suggestions and recommendations.

Tools

Measurement tools used in data collection are numerous and varied, but all of these tools are scales designed to obtain indices of traits, such as physical characteristics (e.g., weight, height, temperature), physical performance (e.g., speed, accuracy, endurance), or mental acuity (e.g., sees the point, responds appropriately).

When ready-made measuring scales do not exist, researchers often prepare their own. This requires composing a list of traits or task elements, together with a set of scoring criteria. Task elements ensure that overall performance is observed. Scoring may be done in terms of accuracy, time required, or other criteria; the scoring procedures should be specified in advance. An example of such scales are instruments used to assess the performance of teachers and student teachers. In these instruments, assessment takes place in several different categories, such as "relates positively with students" and "is well prepared to teach

APPLYING TECHNOLOGY

Searchable Online Test Locators for Measurement Scales

In many research instances, it is not necessary for researchers to develop their own survey or other data collection instrument. Researchers, as part of previous research studies, may have developed or utilized an instrument that ideally met their needs in terms of desirable data to be collected. Fortunately, several organizations, such as the following, provide searchable databases of tests and other survey materials.

■ TestLink: The Educational Testing Service (ETS) Test Collection (www.ets.org/testcoll/index.html)

■ The Mental Measurements Yearbook's Test Reviews Online (http://buros.unl.edu/buros/jsp/search.jsp)

These databases can be searched by keyword, author, publisher, or acronym. Search results typically provide a description of the instrument (including the authors, publisher, availability, descriptors, and abstract) and how it may be obtained. Both tests, inventories, and surveys that are free and those that are available for a nominal fee are included in the databases.

lessons." Within such categories, an evaluator judges teacher performance against a set of criteria, as in the following example:

Category: Relates positively with students

Criteria: Calls students by name
Makes positive, supportive comments
Takes time to talk with students individually
Gives regular attention to all students

Data Format

Data obtained through measurement are most often numerical, though they may also be verbal, nominal, or ordinal. All are categorized so as to parallel the study's research questions or hypotheses.

Exercise 6.4

From the following list, determine the best response to each of the 10 definitions: (L) Likert scale, (C) criteria, (R) raw score, (Q) qualitative data, (N) nominal scale, (V) validity, (RE) reliability, (T) test, (S) semantic differential, (NO) notation, (A) analysis, (M) measurement, (QS) questionnaire, or (P) percentile.

_____ **1.** A concern raised when a test is not measuring what it is supposed to measure

_____ **2.** Using symbols and tally marks in obtaining data

_____ **3.** A set of standards used in making judgments

_____ **4.** Breaking something down logically into its constituent parts

_____ **5.** Obtaining data through use of a thermometer

_____ **6.** A numerical score that has not been manipulated or converted

_____ **7.** A device for obtaining opinions in written form

_____ **8.** A device that prompts individuals to indicate whether they agree or disagree

_____ **9.** A broad type of data that is difficult to analyze through statistical procedures

_____ **10.** A measurement scale that assigns individuals to categories

TYPES OF RESEARCH AND DATA COLLECTION

In this chapter we have explored types of research, their particular foci, the kinds of data they require, where those data can be found, how the data can be collected, and which tools are most useful in the various procedures of data collection. All of these elements are interrelated. Table 6.3 shows the data collection procedures typically used in different types of research. Table 6.4 presents a juxtaposition of elements and procedures described in the chapter.

Table 6.3   Data Collection Procedures Typically Used in Types of Research

	Data Collection Procedures						
	Research	*Notation*	*Description*	*Analysis*	*Questioning*	*Testing*	*Measurement*
Qualitative	*	*	*		*		
Survey			*		*		
Correlational					*	*	*
Causal-comparative					*	*	*
Experimental					*	*	*
Action		*	*	*	*	*	*
Evaluation		*	*	*	*	*	*

Table 6.4   A Composite of Research Types and Data Collection Procedures

Research	Focus	Pertinent Data	Sources	Collection	Tools
Qualitative	Holistic description	Descriptions Statements	Participants Settings Records Documents Informants	Description Questioning	Recorders Pencil–paper Cameras
Survey	Characteristics of population	Descriptions Opinions Statements Measurements	Participants Informants	Notation Description Questioning Measurement	Questionnaires Measuring devices Scales
Correlational	Relationships Prediction	Scores Measurements	Participants	Testing Measurement	Tests Measuring devices
Causal-comparative	Possible causation	Scores	Participants	Testing Measurement	Tests Measuring devices
Experimental	Causation	Scores	Participants Measurements	Testing Measurement	Tests
Action	Innovation	Descriptions Opinions Analyses Scores Measurements	Participants Procedures Settings Objects Documents	Description Analysis Questioning Testing Measurement	Guides Criteria Questionnaires Tests Scales
Evaluation	Judgments	Opinions Analyses Scores Measurements	Participants Procedures Settings Records Objects	Analysis Testing Measurement	Questionnaires Tests Measuring devices

DATA COLLECTION PROFILES

As you become able to organize and conduct your own research, you will find data collection profiles useful in both the planning and the operational phases of research. The information presented to this point enables you to construct data collection profiles for the different types of educational research. The profiles include focus, data sources, data collection procedures, tools typically used in gathering data, and data formats. The following generic data collection profile for ethnographic research would be completed by supplying the specific information indicated in the parentheses. Data profiles for other types of research would be constructed in the same manner.

> **Generic Data Collection Profile of Ethnographic Research**
>
> *Focus:* Social behavior (of what group?)
> *Data Sources:* Participants (who?), settings (what, where?)
> *Data Collection Procedure:* Description of observations (what is observed?)
> *Tools:* Paper and pencil, camera, recording devices (specify)
> *Data Format:* Detailed written verbal descriptions (of observations made)

DEVELOPMENTAL ACTIVITY

Data Collection Decisions

In this developmental activity, you will begin to make detailed decisions regarding your proposed data collection, specifically with respect to sampling, instrumentation, and quality assurance (i.e., validity and reliability).

1. My research problem or topic

_____

2. The sample for my study

_____

3. The demographic characteristics important in my study *(check all that apply)*

☐ Age
☐ Ethnicity
☐ Gender
☐ Other: _____

4. The type of sampling I will do *(check one)*

☐ Random
☐ Stratified random
☐ Cluster
☐ Systematic
☐ Convenience
☐ Other: _____

5. A brief description of the type of data collection instrument I plan to use

_____

_____

_____

  6. My plan with respect to instrumentation *(check one)*

      ☐ Use an existing instrument
      ☐ Develop an instrument

  7. My independent variable(s)

    _____

    _____

    _____

    Classification *(indicate for each variable listed)*

      ☐ Continuous
      ☐ Discrete

  8. My dependent variable(s)

    _____

    Classification *(indicate for each variable listed)*

      ☐ Continuous
      ☐ Discrete

Based on your response to item 6, respond to either item 9 or item 10.

  9. For an existing instrument, a brief description of the instrument's validity and reliability

    _____

    _____

    _____

    _____

  10. For a self-developed instrument, my plan to ensure the validity and reliability of my instrument

    _____

    _____

    _____

    _____

    _____

CHAPTER SUMMARY

Each type of research has a particular focus—either social behavior, past events, present events, relationships or predictions, innovation, evaluative judgments, or causation. Analyzing the focus helps provide guidance in identifying needed data, which can be obtained in the form of descriptions, opinions, analyses, statements, scores, and measurements. These data are obtainable from participants, procedures, settings, objects, records, documents, and informants, and are collected through procedures of notation, description, analysis, questioning, testing, and measurement. Tools helpful in collecting data include marking devices (pencils), cameras, recorders, guides, lists of criteria, questionnaires, tests, scales (such as the Likert scale), and other measuring devices (such as thermometers or weight scales). The data obtained with these tools and procedures accrue as written verbal descriptions, summarized notations, raw scores, converted scores, categories, and rankings.

Samples are often, but not always, required for data collection. Certain types of research, such as correlational and experimental, depend on samples that accurately represent the population from which they are drawn. Other types of research, such as action and evaluation, use data from the participants and materials available at hand. If a sample is required, a decision must be made concerning whether it is to be random, stratified, cluster, systematic, convenience, snowball, or judgmental.

A further consideration has to do with ensuring validity and reliability of data. For test data, validity and reliability are usually computed through statistical procedures. For qualitative data and non-test quantitative data,

validity and reliability are addressed through external criticism, to establish authenticity of source, and internal criticism, to establish accuracy of the information.

Although many aspects of data collection must be kept in mind, they can be summarized for various types of research by composing data collection profiles that specify focus, data sources, data collection procedures, tools, and formats in which data will accrue.

LIST OF IMPORTANT TERMS

chain sampling
cluster sampling
convenience sampling
criterion-referenced tests
cross-sectional survey
external criticism
internal criticism
interval scales
interview
judgmental sampling
Likert scale
longitudinal surveys

multistage sampling
network sampling
nominal scales
nonprobability sampling
norm-referenced tests
open-ended question
ordinal scales
probability sampling
purposive sampling
questionnaire
quota sampling
random sampling

reliability (of data)
semantic differential scale
semistructured question
snowball sampling
standardized test
stratified sampling
structured question
subjects
surveys
systematic sampling
validity (of data)

YOUR CURRENT STATUS

You now have a solid beginning knowledge of the procedures by which research data are collected. You know the fundamentals of sample selection. You are mindful of validity and reliability of data. You know the foci of the different types of research, the data they require, the sources of those data, the procedures by which those data are ob-

tained, the tools most useful in obtaining them, and the formats into which data are likely to accrue. You are now ready to proceed to Chapter 7, which deals with analyzing research data and presenting findings. But, first, please respond to the following activities.

ACTIVITIES FOR THOUGHT AND DISCUSSION

1. Refer again to Table 6.4, which summarizes most of the information presented in this chapter. Select a research focus and see if you can talk your way through the elements corresponding to that focus.
2. Explain why samples are very carefully selected in some types of research and not in others.
3. Suppose you wish to investigate how nonwhite fictional characters were depicted in children's literature between the years 1900 and 1950. What type of research would this be? What would be its focus? What

sources of data would you use? What would you do about selecting a sample? What data collection tools would you consider appropriate?
4. Explain how validity of test data and non-test data is established.
5. Select three types of research and compose a data collection profile for each. The data collection profile of ethnographic research shown earlier in the chapter can be used for reference.

ANSWERS TO CHAPTER EXERCISES

6.1. 1. I 2. D 3. PA 4. O 5. I 6. P 7. R 8. ST

6.2. 1. T 2. F 3. T 4. F 5. T

6.3. 1. Past status or events

2. Causation

3. For practical reasons—they are what is available without disrupting the educational program unduly

4. Scores refer to test results; measurement is the broader term, referring to data obtained through use of measuring devices other than tests.

5. Verbal data, unless it can be categorized, cannot be correlated mathematically.

6.4. 1. V 2. NO 3. C 4. A 5. M 6. R 7. QS 8. L 9. Q 10. N

REFERENCES AND RECOMMENDED READINGS

American Educational Research Association, American Psychological Association, & National Council on Measurement in Education (AERA, APA, & NCME). (1999). *Standards for Educational and Psychological Testing.* Washington, DC: American Educational Research Association.

Babbie, E. (2001). *The Practice of Social Science Research* (9th ed.). Belmont, CA: Wadsworth/Thomson Learning.

Bartz, A. (1976). *Basic Statistical Concepts in Education and the Behavioral Sciences.* Minneapolis: Burgess.

Best, J., & Kahn, J. (2006). *Research in Education* (10th ed.). Boston: Allyn & Bacon.

Bogdan, R., & Biklen, S. (2003). *Qualitative Research in Education: An Introduction to Theory and Methods* (4th ed.). Boston: Allyn & Bacon.

Clark, S., & Boser, J. (1989). *Seeking Consensus on Empirical Characteristics of Effective Mail Questionnaires: A First Step.* Paper presented at the annual meeting of the American Educational Research Association, San Francisco.

Gall, J. P., Gall, M. D., & Borg, W. R. (2005). *Applying Educational Research: A Practical Guide* (5th ed.). Boston: Allyn & Bacon.

Gay, L. R., Mills, G. E., & Airasian, P. (2006). *Educational Research: Competencies for Analysis and Application* (8th ed.). Upper Saddle River, NJ: Merrill.

Glesne, C. (2006). *Becoming Qualitative Researchers: An Introduction* (3rd ed.). Boston: Allyn & Bacon.

Hammill, D., Brown, L., & Bryant, B. (1989). *A Consumer's Guide to Tests in Print.* Austin, TX: PRO-ED.

Hopkins, K., & Gullickson, A. (1989). *Monetary Gratuities in Survey Research: A Meta-Analysis of Their Effects on Response Rates.* Paper presented at the annual meeting of the American Educational Research Association, San Francisco.

McMillan, J. (2001). *Classroom Assessment: Principles and Practice for Effective Instruction* (2nd ed.). Boston: Allyn & Bacon.

McMillan, J. (2004). *Educational Research: Fundamentals for the Consumer* (4th ed.). Boston: Allyn & Bacon.

Mertler, C. A. (2003). *Classroom Assessment: A Practical Guide for Educators.* Los Angeles: Pyrczak.

Plake, B., Impara, J., & Spies, A. (Eds.). (2003). *The Fifteenth Mental Measurements Yearbook.* Lincoln: University of Nebraska Press.

Trochim, W. M. (2002). *Research Methods Knowledge Base* (2nd ed.). Available at http://socialresearchmethods.net/kb/index.htm

Vierra, A., & Pollock, J. (1988). *Reading Educational Research.* Scottsdale, AZ: Gorsuch Scarisbrick.

Analyzing Research Data and Presenting Findings

PREVIEW

Research can yield two different kinds of data:

- Qualitative data
- Quantitative data

Both types of data must be analyzed as one attempts to do the following:

- Answer research questions
- Test hypotheses

Qualitative data are expressed verbally and analyzed logically, using the following process:

- Identify topics
- Cluster topics into categories
- Form categories into patterns
- Make explanations from the patterns
- Use the explanations to answer research questions

Quantitative data are expressed numerically and analyzed statistically, which usually involves the following steps:

- Making descriptions of the data, using measures of
  Central tendency
  Variability
  Relative standing
  Correlation
- Making inferences about the population, by means of
  Confidence limits
  Significance levels

Once data are analyzed, the results are reported as research findings.

TARGETED LEARNINGS

Chapter 6 explained how original data are obtained in various kinds of research. In this chapter, we explore how those data are typically analyzed to help answer research questions or test hypotheses, and further, how analyzed data are presented as research findings. After examining the differences between analysis of qualitative data and analysis of quantitative data, general approaches used in analyzing both kinds of data are presented. With regard to statistical analyses, we concern ourselves more with the concepts of analysis than with actual statistical calculations, which are treated in greater depth in the Appendix.

As you read the chapter, look especially for information related to the following questions:

1. What is the general purpose of data analysis in all types of research?
2. Why are qualitative data and quantitative data analyzed differently?
3. How are qualitative data analyzed?
4. How are quantitative data analyzed?
5. What are the relationships among populations, parameters, samples, and statistics?
6. What is the difference between descriptive statistics and inferential statistics?
7. What does *significance* mean in statistics?
8. What is the relationship between data analysis and research findings?

Qualitative Data and Quantitative Data

Earlier you learned that research makes use of two kinds of data: *qualitative data,* which are mostly verbal, and *quantitative data,* which are mostly numerical. Sometimes, both kinds are collected and analyzed in the same study. The type of data one obtains is determined by the type of research being conducted. Table 7.1 shows the kinds of data that are most commonly sought in the various types of research.

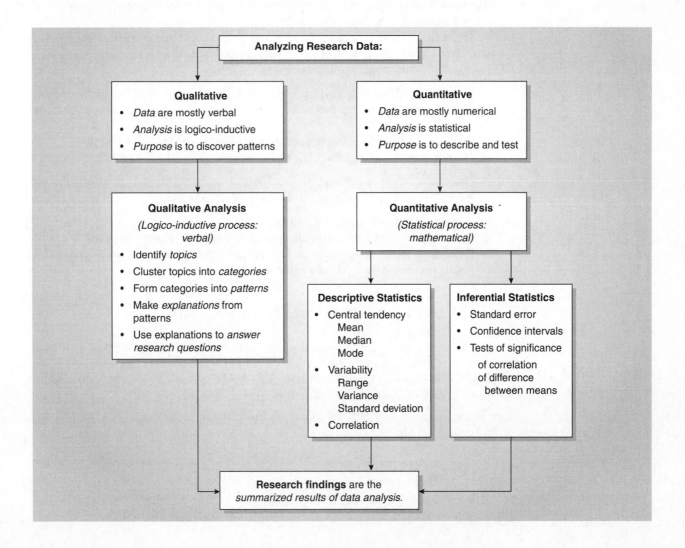

Table 7.1 The Type of Data Analysis Most Commonly Used
in Each Type of Research

Research	Typical Data Analysis Procedures	
	Qualitative	*Quantitative*
Ethnographic	*	
Historical	*	*
Survey	*	*
Correlational		*
Causal-comparative		*
Experimental		*
Mixed-methods	*	*
Evaluation	*	*
Action	*	*

Once collected, both qualitative and quantitative data usually must be analyzed before adequate interpretations can be made. Analysis serves several functions: (1) describes the data clearly; (2) identifies what is typical and atypical among the data; (3) brings to light differences, relationships, and other patterns in the data; and ultimately (4) answers research questions or tests hypotheses.

While all data analysis aims at the same general goals, qualitative and quantitative data are analyzed quite differently. Qualitative data are analyzed logico-inductively, using logic to make sense of observations, in a thought process that

■ Makes observations of behaviors, situations, interactions, objects, and environments
■ Identifies topics from the observations and scrutinizes these topics to discover patterns and categories
■ Induces conclusions from what is observed and states conclusions verbally
■ Uses the conclusions to answer the research questions

Quantitative data, in contrast, are analyzed mathematically, and the results are expressed in statistical terminology. Essentially, statistical analysis

■ Depicts what is typical and atypical among the data
■ Shows degrees of difference or relationship between two or more variables
■ Determines the likelihood that the findings are real for the population as opposed to having occurred only by chance in the sample

AN EXAMPLE OF QUALITATIVE ANALYSIS

Suppose we are conducting historical research into education as it took place in 1935 in Bodie, the California ghost town that was once a mining community (see Chapter 2). One portion of the research has to do with depicting a typical winter day for sixth-grade students attending Bodie School. We pose the following main research question:

What was a typical January school day like for sixth-grade students attending Bodie School in 1935?

To help answer that question, we also pose a number of subquestions, similar to the following examples:

1. What time did school start in the mornings?
2. What would students probably have to do before starting out for school?

3. What was the weather like in January?
4. How did the students get from home to school?
5. How did the morning curriculum usually proceed?
6. What did students do for recess and lunch?
7. How did the afternoon curriculum usually proceed?
8. What was the classroom environment like?
9. What books and instructional materials were used?
10. At what time was school dismissed?
11. What would students probably have to do after being dismissed from school?
12. What sort of homework was assigned, and how much time did it require?

By answering subquestions like these, we should ultimately be able to compile a satisfactory answer to the main research question. Some of the answers to subquestions might be found among the relics left in Bodie School. A class plan book or grade book might help answer questions about the curriculum, as would textbooks and other instructional materials. How students got from home to school and back might be revealed by the presence of skis or snowshoes, and student compositions might be found that would shed further light regarding how they traveled. The mostly verbal data obtained from these sources would be analyzed logically by matching evidence to research subquestions. It is unlikely that any mathematical or statistical treatments would be required.

AN EXAMPLE OF QUANTITATIVE ANALYSIS

Suppose we have been asked by the Bureau of Indian Affairs to help explore various aspects of academic achievement among Native American students attending boarding schools on a large reservation. One of the specific requests concerns information about science achievement among eighth-grade students. Many teachers at reservation schools say their students retain cultural and religious beliefs about natural phenomena that contradict concepts presented in the school science program and that consequently affect science achievement. We are asked to determine whether students do in fact retain such beliefs and, if they do, to investigate whether adherence to those beliefs is related to achievement in science. To guide our research, we state two hypotheses, both in the null form:

Hypothesis 1: No difference exists between eighth-grade students attending schools on the reservation and a matched group of eighth-grade rural white students concerning adherence to cultural beliefs that contradict science concepts taught in school.

Hypothesis 2: No relationship exists between science achievement and adherence to cultural beliefs that contradict science concepts taught in school.

For hypothesis 1, we decide to administer a test designed to reveal the frequency with which students select culture-linked nonscientific responses rather than correct scientific responses to specially designed test items. From this test we can obtain mean scores and patterns of scores for a sample of Native American students and also for a sample of rural white students used for comparison. If differences between the two groups are found, we will test the null hypothesis (tests for this purpose are described later in the chapter). If we are able to reject the null hypothesis—which would mean that any difference we found was probably not due to errors made in selecting the samples but actually represents *real* differences in the population—we could then conclude that the two populations are different in their adherence to nonscientific cultural beliefs.

To test hypothesis 2, we will need to compute correlations between scores made by Native American students on two tests: the science achievement test and the test designed to indicate adherence to nonscientific beliefs. If we are able to reject the null hypothesis of "no correlation," we can conclude that a relationship probably *does* exist in the population between science achievement and adherence to nonscientific cultural beliefs.

ANALYZING QUALITATIVE DATA

myeducationlab
for research

The analysis of qualitative data is a multiphase process. To gain some exposure to this type of analysis, go to the "Qualitative Research: Data Analysis and Interpretation" section of **MyEducationLab for Research** and then click on *Building Research Skills.* Complete the exercise titled "Investigating Data Analysis and Interpretation" to gain some experience in coding, analyzing, and interpreting qualitative data.

The Bodie and Native American illustrations indicate the general difference between approaches to obtaining and analyzing qualitative and quantitative research data. As an example of qualitative data analysis, ethnographic data analysis, however, requires a distinct approach from our historical research example. The reason lies in the nature of ethnographic research, which investigates people and their interactions within social settings. One of its peculiarities is that the questions answered by ethnographic research often emerge after data collection has begun, rather than before, as in other types of research. Pertinent questions in ethnographic research cannot always be foreseen; they may come to light only after considerable data have been collected. Thus, collection of ethnographic data is not necessarily guided by a clearly defined list of questions, in which we only collect data that directly pertain to those questions. Instead, many of the most significant questions emerge during the investigation.

A second unusual trait of ethnographic research is that it attempts to draw conclusions from a broad, rather than limited, picture of human behavior. Voluminous quantities of relatively unstructured data are typically collected in ethnographic research. It is only when preliminary data analysis has narrowed and structured some of the data that the final research questions can be clarified.

To make sense of such unstructured data, researchers employ a systematic process of analysis that involves (1) identification of topics, (2) clustering of those topics into categories, (3) forming the categories into patterns, and (4) making explanations from what the patterns suggest. This process does not occur in straight-line sequence but rather as flux, with ebb and flow, give and take. The process begins with notes and ends with interpretations, as shown in Figure 7.1. In this configuration, the notes that comprise the data should reflect very accurately what has actually been observed. Accuracy requires that the observer be astute in grasping the overall picture while noting significant details. Often video or audio recordings are used instead of pencil-and-paper notes in order to obtain a more detailed and accurate picture.

The analysis of qualitative data involves the *reduction* of large amounts of narrative data (resulting from interview transcripts, observational fieldnotes, existing documents or records, etc.), usually by a process of categorizing and grouping similar types of information. As you read through your transcripts, fieldnotes, and documents, you begin to notice categories of narrative information. You should maintain a running list of each category as it appears, and code your narrative data into these categories. As there is no single correct way to accomplish this, it is important that you find a **coding scheme** that works for you. Some researchers color code with markers, some organize data on 3 × 5-inch index cards, and others physically group together pages of transcripts and fieldnotes. It is important to find some mechanism for coding that works for you.

Once these categories have been developed, data must be reread to code the narrative passages—not an easy process. The coding of qualitative data requires repeated readings

Figure 7.1
Procedure of analysis in ethnographic research

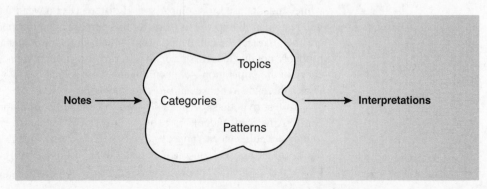

of all your narrative data. You will get to "know" your qualitative data very well during the process of inductive analysis. In some cases, passages may be coded with one or more categories, depending on what is seen or heard, as well as what is *not* seen or heard.

Once the data have been coded, the next step is to *describe* the main features of the categories resulting from the coding. This is an extremely critical stage of the analysis process because this is where connections between the data and the original, or emerging, research questions begin to develop. During this part of the process, it is also important to closely examine data that do *not* support your emerging patterns. This information can provide as much insight as the supportive data.

The final step is to *interpret* the simplified and organized material. During this step, the researcher examines events, behaviors, or other observations—as represented in the coded categories—for relationships, similarities, contradictions, and so on. The key is to look for aspects of the data that answer the research questions, that provide challenges to current or future practice, or that actually may guide future practice. Because the researcher's background, experiences, and expertise will affect the ways in which the data are interpreted, descriptions—or, in some cases, concrete examples—should accompany the interpretations offered. It is important to note that this process is typically not a linear one; often, there are several iterations of rereading, recoding, reanalysis, and reinterpretation. Only when the research questions can be answered satisfactorily should interpretations be put forward as research conclusions. This entire process is referred to as **logico-inductive analysis** or **hypothetico-inductive analysis,** terms that are used synonymously. A thorough example of this process is provided in Chapter 10 ("Qualitative Research Methods").

Exercise 7.1

Among the following research topics, which ones would probably be best analyzed through the notes–topic–categories–patterns–interpretation paradigm of qualitative research?

_____ **1.** A comparison of achievement resulting from two different methods of teaching spelling

_____ **2.** A listing of completion dates and contracting companies in the construction of Elmwood's 157 schools

_____ **3.** Verbal interactions of children on the playground

_____ **4.** The relationship between manual dexterity and learning to type

_____ **5.** The progressive development of dramatic arts abilities among drama students

_____ **6.** The effects of different levels of nitrogenic fertilizer on the growth of turf for football fields

_____ **7.** The comparative achievement of adolescent boys and girls in Spanish I

_____ **8.** What teachers say about administrators behind their backs, and vice versa

_____ **9.** What Mondays are like for high school principals

CAUTIONS AND REMINDERS IN QUALITATIVE DATA ANALYSIS

Both the collection and analysis of qualitative data are prone to errors of subjectivity and imprecision. To counter these concerns, investigators, when collecting data, should strive to be *thoroughly* objective and impartial and to depict contexts and events as realistically as possible (Lancy, 1993). Data analysis is also easily affected by investigator bias. For that reason, great care should be taken to see that prejudices and preconceived notions do not improperly influence perceptions and interpretations.

Finally, when drawing conclusions, it is important to document the evidence on which the conclusions rest. The context should be carefully described as well—the place, the prevailing attitudes, the emotions, the motives, and the existent physical, social, and psychological realities. When making interpretations, investigators should force themselves to look for evidence other than that first noted and to make interpretations that are different from those anticipated or first identified. If alternative explanations can be found that are equally plausible, then questions, data, and interpretation should be reevaluated carefully.

For further information related to the analysis of qualitative data, the reader is advised to consult Miles and Huberman (1994).

Analyzing quantitative data

We have seen that in qualitative research investigators are keenly interested in contexts, values, attitudes, emotions, and social realities that affect human interaction, and that, in order to obtain better data, investigators often involve themselves closely with those they are observing. A different approach is usually taken in quantitative research. There, investigators try to keep themselves apart from participants. They fear that their involvement, or even their presence, might contaminate the study by causing participants to behave differently than they otherwise would. This is not to indicate, however, that quantitative research is value-free. To the contrary, all research is value-laden. Researchers investigate what they believe to be important, and they look for—and certainly hope for—results that can make a practical difference in education.

As shown earlier in Table 7.1, descriptive, correlational, evaluative, action, causal-comparative, and experimental research are all likely to include quantitative data that require statistical analysis. Until recently, students new to research looked on statistics with considerable trepidation, fearful of esoteric formulas and laborious calculations. It is still valuable to understand the processes involved in statistical calculations, but the calculations themselves need cause no fear. Now, computers can do the calculations in the blink of an eye, providing quick and accurate results that might formerly have taken hours or even days. University computer or media centers make such computational services available to graduate students, typically at no cost to the student. With the appropriate software, students can even perform statistical analyses on their home computers.

POPULATIONS AND PARAMETERS; SAMPLES AND STATISTICS

Before proceeding further, let us take a moment to note how populations, samples, parameters, and statistics are related.

A *population* consists of all the individuals who make up a designated group we are interested in studying and, ultimately, drawing conclusions about. If we want to know about sixth-grade students in Alabama, the population consists of all sixth-grade students in Alabama.

A *sample* comprises a small group drawn from a population, carefully selected in order to closely reflect the characteristics of the population. Samples are used in research because it is often impossible and almost always inconvenient—due to financial constraints, time factors, and so on—to study an entire population. If researchers are to suggest that knowledge learned from the sample applies also to the population, samples need to be selected so they represent the population fairly closely.

Parameters are numerical indices that describe a population, such as the number of individuals included, measurements made of them, and descriptions that indicate average, disper-

APPLYING TECHNOLOGY

Software Programs for Analyzing Qualitative Data

The following websites offer several qualitative data analysis software programs. Descriptions of some program features and their sites have been included. If you are interested in learning more about these software programs, we urge you to investigate them further. Be sure to check the computer system requirements before downloading any complete or trial version of a program.

■ NVivo
(www.qsrinternational.com/products_nvivo.aspx)
NVivo is a very flexible software program that allows you to handle rich information where deep levels of analysis on both small and large volumes of data are required. It removes many of the manual tasks associated with analysis, like classifying, sorting, and arranging information, so you have more time to explore trends, build and test theories, and ultimately arrive at answers to questions.

■ ATLAS.ti
(www.atlasti.com)
ATLAS.ti is powerful software for the qualitative analysis of large bodies of textual, graphical, audio, or video information. A free trial version is available at www.atlasti.com/demo.html. As with many of these qualitative analysis software programs, a scaled-down, less-expensive student version is available.

■ AnSWR
(www.cdc.gov/hiv/software/answr.htm)
AnSWR (*Analysis Software for Word-based Records*), developed by the Centers for Disease Control and Prevention (CDC), Division of HIV/ AIDS Prevention, is a software system for coordinating and conducting large-scale, team-based

analysis projects that integrate qualitative and quantitative techniques. AnSWR is downloadable and free of charge in a variety of PC formats.

■ EZ-Text
(www.cdc.gov/hiv/software/ez-text.htm)
EZ-Text, also developed by the CDC, is a software program developed to assist researchers create, manage, and analyze semistructured qualitative databases, especially those resulting from the use of open-ended surveys. Copies of the EZ-Text software and user documentation can be downloaded free of charge from this website.

■ Qualrus
(www.qualrus.com/Qualrus.shtml)
Qualrus, developed by Idea Works, Inc., advertises itself as "the intelligent qualitative analysis program." The complete program costs $399, but there is a free, downloadable trial available at www.qualrus.com/QualrusViewerSignup.shtml.

■ HyperRESEARCH
(www.researchware.com)
HyperRESEARCH, developed by ResearchWare, Inc., bills itself as "an easy to use qualitative data analysis software package enabling you to code and retrieve, build theories, and conduct analyses of your data." The current version permits the integration of advanced multimedia capabilities, allowing you to work with text, graphics, audio, and video sources of data. This is one of the only qualitative analysis programs available in Macintosh formats. HyperRESEARCH sells for $370 but is available in a free trial version (which limits the user to 75 codes and seven cases) at www.researchware.com/hr/downloads.html.

sion, or relationships among those measurements. Parameter indices are usually symbolized with Greek letters, while their sample counterparts are usually symbolized with English or Roman letters. To illustrate, the population mean is symbolized μ, the twelfth letter of the Greek alphabet, pronounced "mew," while the sample mean is symbolized M or $\overline{X}$.

Statistics are numerical indices and procedures that describe the sample and help one make inferences about the population. Statistics (which apply to the sample) are directly analogous to parameters (which apply to the population). Because samples almost never reflect populations exactly, statistics almost never equal exactly the parameters to which they correspond. **Sampling error** is the term applied to this discrepancy between a sample statistic and a population parameter.

Exercise 7.2

For the following, indicate which refers to (P) population, (PR) parameters, (S) sample, and (ST) statistics.

_____   **1.** Thirty-two specially selected girls

_____   **2.** The mean height of all sixth-grade girls in Elmwood schools

_____   **3.** All the students in Elmwood schools

_____   **4.** The mean IQ of 32 selected girls

What statistics are used for

You might recall that the term *statistics* has multiple meanings. One meaning refers to summary indices resulting from data analysis, such as mean, median, standard deviation, and coefficient of correlation. Another meaning refers to the procedures by which data are analyzed mathematically. Statistics—the procedures—are used to describe and treat data in various ways, of which the following are most common:

■ *To summarize data and reveal what is typical and atypical within a group.* Research often yields hundreds or thousands of units of numerical data that, until summarized, cannot be interpreted meaningfully. Suppose you had the raw measurements of heights, weights, and intelligence quotient (IQ) scores for all the adult women in North Carolina. That would give you thousands of pages of numbers that would leave you baffled. Statistics can reduce such masses of data into terms more easily understood by showing what is average, how much difference exists between highest and lowest values, what the most commonly occurring value is, and how spread out the values are. Knowing those factors, you would have a much clearer picture of what adult women in North Carolina are like.

■ *To show relative standing of individuals in a group.* Statistics are frequently used to show where an individual stands for a given measurement in relation to all other individuals in the sample. Such standings are shown through percentile rankings, grade equivalents, age equivalents, and stanines—concepts discussed later in this chapter.

■ *To show relationships among variables.* Investigators are often interested in determining whether correlations exist among variables—for instance, between people's ages and the amount of time they spend watching television or between students' self-concept and their scholastic achievement. Such relationships are often shown by means of statistical correlations.

■ *To show similarities and differences among groups.* Researchers are often interested in determining similarity or difference between groups. For example, they need to make sure, particularly for experimental research, that the two or more groups involved at the beginning of the experiment are approximately equal in the trait being investigated. Then later they must check to see whether a special treatment given to one of the groups has changed it in some way compared to the other.

■ *To identify error that is inherent in sample selection.* Samples are almost always to some extent unlike the population from which they are drawn. This introduces a degree of error—referred to earlier as *sampling error* or simply *error*—into research, so that we can never be sure that a statistical finding is also correct for the population. Error refers to the disparity between a given statistic and its corresponding parameter value—that is, between what is measured in a sample and what exists in the population. Statistical procedures enable one to determine the amount of error associated with measurements, means, correlations, and differences between means. When any error is known, one can specify the "confidence levels" for a particular value or finding. For example, if we find a sample mean of 6.2 and then determine its *standard error*—a quantitative measure of sampling error, defined as the average distance of sample means away from the population mean—we can conclude, with a specified degree of confidence (e.g., 95 percent), that the population mean lies somewhere within a given range, such as between 5.3 and 7.1.

■   *To test for significance of findings.* When researchers discover apparent correlations between variables or differences between means, they apply statistical tests of significance. They determine whether their findings might be based on a sample whose selection, by chance, did not reflect the population or whether, in fact, they represent *real* differences or relationships that exist in the population. If the likelihood turns out to be high that the sample does accurately reflect the population, the researcher will call the finding "significant," meaning that a particular result from sample data is probably also real for the population, rather than one found only in the sample because of chance errors. However, if the test suggests that a finding might not be of sufficient magnitude to override errors in sample selection, the investigator will deem the finding "not significant," meaning that the result might not be real for the population.

■   *To make other inferences about the population.* As noted, researchers are seldom able to investigate an entire population and must, therefore, work with samples. Yet they hope to show that findings for the sample are true also for the population. Thus, when we determine a mean score for the sample, for instance, we wish to say that the same mean score exists in the population as a whole. Of course, since we have not investigated the entire population, we can only make inferences about the population mean. In doing this, we assign probability levels that allow us to say that the sample finding is "probably also correct" for the population, within specified limits.

The actual statistical techniques used to accomplish these ends are presented in the Appendix.

DESCRIPTIVE STATISTICS AND INFERENTIAL STATISTICS

for research

To help you better understand the use of descriptive statistics, go to the "Descriptive Statistics" section of **MyEducationLab for Research** and then click on *Assignments and Activities.* Using the included excerpted article, complete the exercise titled "Computing Descriptive Statistics" to provide some practice in the use of descriptive statistics.

Descriptive statistics are the procedures and associated numerical indices that help clarify data from samples. The following discussion presents the most commonly used descriptive statistics. (The reader should note that, when spelled out, statistical terms are not italicized—mean, median, and so on—whereas symbols and abbreviations used in place of those terms usually are italicized—*M, Mdn.*)

1.   Measures of **central tendency,** including the mean, median, and mode

■   Mean (symbolized $\overline{X}$ or *M*)—the arithmetic average

Example: What is the mean of the following set of scores?

8, 7, 6, 5, 5, 5, 5, 4, 4, 1

(Answer: 5)

■   Median (abbreviated *Mdn* or *Md*)—the midpoint in an array of scores, determined by counting halfway from highest to lowest

Example: What is the median of the following set of scores? (Remember to order the scores from highest to lowest first.)

8, 7, 6, 5, 5, 4, 4, 4, 4, 3

(Answer: 4.5)

■ Mode (abbreviated *Mo*)—the most frequently made score on a test or other measure.

Example: What is the mode of the following set of scores?

8, 7, 6, 5, 5, 4, 4, 4, 4, 3

(Answer: 4)

PEARSON
myeducationlab)
for research

To further your understanding of descriptive statistics, go to the "Descriptive Statistics" section of **MyEducationLab for Research** and then click on *Building Research Skills*. Read the linked article written by Xin et al. and complete the exercise titled "Understanding Descriptive Statistics."

2. Measures of **variability** (amount of spread or dispersion in the scores), including the range, variance, and standard deviation

■ Range—the difference between highest and lowest score or measure

Example: What is the range for the following set of scores?

8, 7, 6, 5, 5, 4, 4, 4, 4, 3

(Answer: 5)

■ Variance (symbolized s^2)—a measure of dispersion; calculated as the average of the squared deviations from a particular value such as the mean (calculation of variance shown in the Appendix)

■ Standard deviation (*SD* or *s*)—a stable and most useful measure of dispersion; calculated as the square root of the variance (calculation of a standard deviation shown in the Appendix)

3. Measures of **relative standing,** including percentile ranks, stanines, and converted or transformed scores

■ Percentile rank (*%ile* or *PR*)—a ranking assigned to a particular score that shows the percentage of all scores falling below that mark

Example: Juan's score fell at the 56th percentile. This percentile ranking means he equaled or excelled 56 percent of all other students who took the test.

■ Stanine—a value from 1 to 9, with 5 being average, that shows where a score stands in relation to others

Example: Mary's score fell in the 6th stanine. This means she was slightly above average among all other students who took the test

■ Converted or transformed score—a value assigned to a raw score, such as the grade-level equivalency, that corresponds to the score a student made on a test

Example: Shawn made a score of 46 on the test, which places him at the seventh-grade, sixth-month level.

4. Measures of **relationship,** including coefficient of correlation

PEARSON
myeducationlab)
for research

To help you better understand the use of inferential statistics, go to the "Inferential Statistics" section of **MyEducationLab for Research** and then click on *Assignments and Activities*. Using the included excerpted article, complete the exercise titled "The Distribution of Means," which will help reinforce the notion of samples of data being used to represent data from an entire population.

■ Coefficient of correlation (the most common of which is called a *Pearson correlation* and symbolized by *r*)—a measure of relationship between two or more sets of scores made by the same group of participants

Example: The correlation between reading ability and achievement test scores was .32. This means there was a modest positive relationship between the two variables.

Inferential statistics are used to make estimates about the population, based on what has been learned from the sample. Investigators can make any of the following inferences about the population from different calculations on the sample data:

1. *Error estimates* that indicate the range within which a given measure probably lies in the population

Example: If the study were repeated many times, the correlation would probably continue to fall between .28 and .36.

2. *Confidence intervals* that indicate the probability that a population value lies within certain specified boundaries

   Example: There is a 95 percent probability that the correlation in the population lies between .22 and .42.

3. *Tests of significance,* which show the likelihood of a finding's having occurred because of sampling error, that is, chance errors made in selecting the sample. Tests include those for correlation, difference between two means, and difference between three or more means.

   ■ *Significance of correlation*

   Example: If the study were repeated hundreds of times, a correlation of this absolute value or larger (e.g., less than $-.83$ or greater than $+.83$) would occur at least 95 percent of the time. This is symbolized by $p < .05$, which means that the probability (p) of the result being due to sampling error, or chance, is less than 5 out of 100.

   ■ *Significance of the difference between means of two samples* (*t* test).

   Example: If the study were repeated hundreds of times, a difference between means of this absolute value or larger would occur at least 95 percent of the time ($p < .05$).

   ■ *Significance of the difference between three or more means* (analysis of variance or *F* test)

   Example: If the study were repeated hundreds of times, a difference between three or more means of this absolute value or larger would occur at least 95 percent of the time ($p < .05$).

Procedures for calculating these inferential statistical indices are presented in the Appendix.

PEARSON
myeducationlab
for research

To further your understanding of inferential statistics, go to the "Inferential Statistics" section of **MyEducationLab for Research** and then click on *Building Research Skills.* Read the article written by Hamre and Pianta and complete the exercise titled "Understanding the Use of Hypothesis Testing" to help demonstrate the connection between hypotheses and inferential statistics.

Exercise 7.3

Supply the appropriate name for each of the following:

_____   **1.** The most frequently made score.

_____   **2.** The relationship between two sets of scores made by the same individuals.

_____   **3.** The arithmetic average of the scores.

_____   **4.** The difference between the highest and lowest score in a group.

_____   **5.** A finding is probably real—not due to sampling error.

_____   **6.** The true measure for the sample probably lies within these boundaries.

_____   **7.** There is a 95 percent probability that the population mean lies within these boundaries.

_____   **8.** Statistics used to make judgments about the population.

_____   **9.** John's score equaled or surpassed 68 percent of all scores.

_____   **10.** Measures that show spread or diversion.

CAUTIONS IN USING STATISTICS

Don't go overboard in using statistics. In your research, specify exactly what it is you want to know—what questions you wish to answer or which hypotheses you intend to test. Then select the statistics that are appropriate for describing your data and performing the

APPLYING TECHNOLOGY

More about Statistics

Statistical analysis of quantitative data often provides graduate students with some of their most difficult challenges. Statistics are frequently likened to a foreign language—new concepts, new terminology, and so on. For Web pages with which readers can supplement understanding of statistical concepts and terminology, we once again refer you to Dr. Trochim's knowledge base. Dr. Trochim has included several Web pages that address various topics related to analysis of quantitative data, briefly described with their URLs in the following list.

■ *Data Preparation* (http://socialresearchmethods .net/kb/statprep.htm)
Information includes discussions of methods of ensuring the accuracy of data, the entry of data into a data file or database, and various examples of simple data transformations

■ *Descriptive Statistics* (http://socialresearch methods.net/kb/statdesc.htm)
Discussions of the general nature of descriptive statistics and an example of univariate analysis, including the development of a frequency distribution, calculations of various measures of central tendency, and calculations of measures of dispersion

■ *Correlation* (http://socialresearchmethods.net/ kb/statcorr.htm)
A discussion of the measure of a relationship between two variables, including graphical representation and sample calculation of the correlation coefficient

Another website providing a multitude of information about statistics has been developed by Dr. David W. Stockburger of Missouri State University. Essentially an online statistics textbook, it can be found at www.psychstat.missouristate.edu/ sbk00.htm. This online version is the actual text used by Dr. Stockburger to teach an undergraduate course in statistics; however, the content and coverage are also appropriate for graduate students taking an introductory course. The following attributes help distinguish this site from others:

■ The concepts are addressed in a brief, but very thorough, manner.
■ It is relatively easy to navigate your way around the text and, therefore, focus on a particular topic by using the Table of Contents.
■ The text incorporates several interactive examples and exercises.

Finally, the text also includes links to numerous additional online resources. By clicking on Bibliography and Web Resources (www.psychstat.missouristate .edu/introbook/biblio.htm) in the Table of Contents, and then clicking on the button

Statistical Resources on the Web

you will find a listing of several categories of resources, including online statistics books, statistical resources, sources for data files, commercial textbooks, research articles, statistical software packages, and online statistics course home pages.

treatments you require. Make sure the statistical analyses contribute directly to the purposes you have in mind. Remember, too, that statistics do not prove anything; in all findings there remains a degree of uncertainty. Confidence intervals and significance levels only help by showing the chances that one might be making an error in judgment.

As for significance, it is possible to determine that a particular finding is significant, statistically speaking, when in fact the magnitude of the finding is so small that it makes no practical difference whatsoever. Such results often occur when a researcher uses very large samples. This points to the very crucial distinction between *statistical significance* and *practical significance.* For example, it might be discovered that in the Elmwood high school population as a whole, students born in January have a mean IQ one point higher than students born in a different month and that the difference is significant. But what possible importance could that minuscule amount have? Conversely, it might be found, in a small sample of 10 students, that mathematics taught through a new method produced 30 percent more achievement gain than did the traditional teaching method. But because the sample is so small, the finding may be deemed not significant. Rather than reject that finding, which might have very important implications, one might wish to repeat the research with a larger sample.

APPLYING TECHNOLOGY

Software Programs for Analyzing Quantitative Data

There are numerous software programs available to assist with quantitative data analysis. Arguably the most popular program in the broad field of education, SPSS (Statistical Package for the Social Sciences, www.spss.com) is a complete statistical analysis package, easily analyzing your data with both descriptive and inferential techniques, including advanced and multivariate analyses. The program can also generate high-quality and detailed graphs and charts. Figure 7.2 shows a sample data file as it appears in SPSS, and Figure 7.3 shows the results of an independent-samples *t* test. A downloadable trial version is available at www.spss.com/registration/index.cfm?Demo_ID=37.

Figure 7.2

Sample data file from SPSS

Source: SPSS for Windows, Rel. 17.0. 2008. Chicago: SPSS, Inc.

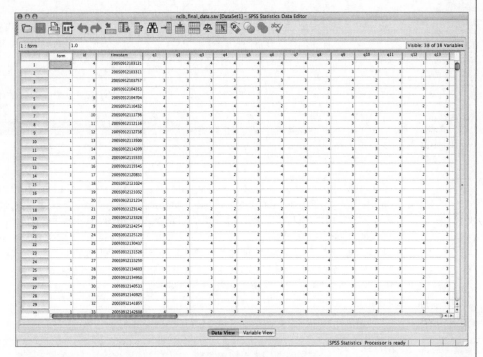

Figure 7.3

Sample analysis from SPSS

Source: SPSS for Windows, Rel. 17.0. 2008. Chicago: SPSS, Inc.

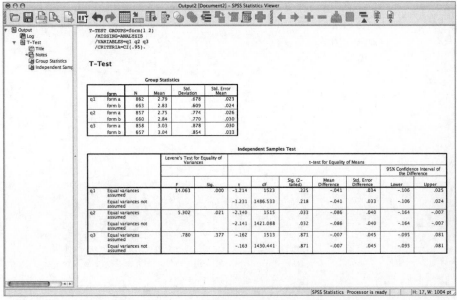

Figure 7.4

Sample data file in Excel

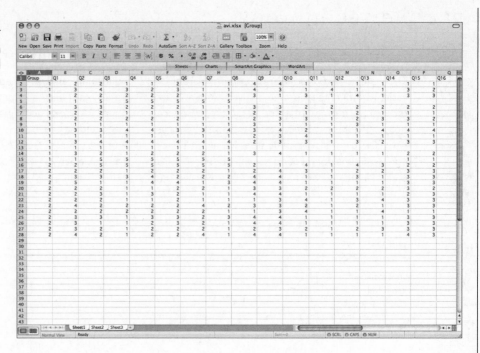

Another relatively accessible program for quantitative analysis is Microsoft Excel, which is part of Microsoft's Office suite of products (along with Word and PowerPoint). Excel is a powerful tool you can use to create and format spreadsheets within a larger process of analyzing and sharing information. It is an excellent program for database management and spreadsheet applications, as well as for statistical analysis and the generation of professional-looking charts. A free 60-day trial version is available online (www.microsoft.com). A sample Excel data file is shown in Figure 7.4, and a chart generated for one variable appears in Figure 7.5.

Figure 7.5

Sample data chart generated in Excel

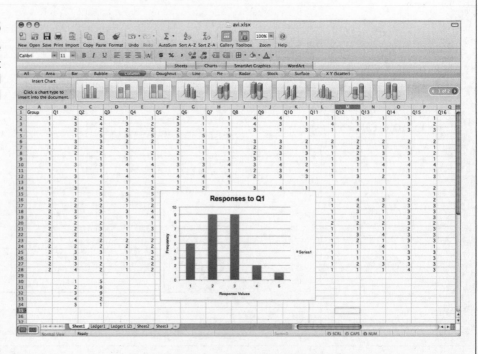

Statistics are used to *assist* logical thought processes. They do not *replace* logic. They help investigators interpret data, answer research questions, and test hypotheses. But they do not make interpretations, nor can they be offered up as the final word in any research matter. So, regardless of how impressive statistics might appear, remember that it is the researcher's thought processes that count most in good research.

PRESENTING YOUR FINDINGS

Research findings comprise the information you bring to light through data analysis. The findings are statements of facts—at least as those facts are represented by the particular sample studied—that the researcher has discovered. They may be accompanied by statements that help readers interpret the findings. Findings help provide answers to research questions and hypotheses and are most appropriately presented in conjunction with those questions or hypotheses.

In historical and descriptive research using qualitative data, the findings will be the summary statements about interactions, situations, environments, objects, and so forth, that have been scrutinized, such as the following examples:

> The school register revealed that 73 students attended Bodie School in 1935.

> The teacher record book contained marks for reading, mathematics, penmanship, history, geography, and spelling.

In the case of ethnographic research based on gathering qualitative data, the findings will be your summary statements about the individuals, environments, and patterns of behavior you have observed. These findings are presented as verbal statements such as the following:

> Gossip was the category of talk most frequently heard in the faculty room.

> Teachers' behavior before school was for the most part work oriented.

On the other hand, in quantitative research, you present your findings statistically, accompanied by verbal statements.

> The mean score for Group A was 45, with a standard error of .38.

APPLYING TECHNOLOGY

Selecting an Appropriate Statistical Test

When analyzing quantitative data, students tend to realize rather quickly that one of the more difficult aspects of the process is determining the applicable statistical test to use. Again, Dr. Trochim has provided a wonderful interactive, Web-based tool designed to aid researchers in deciding on the most appropriate statistical technique for a given situation. Titled "Selecting Statistics" (http://socialresearchmethods.net/selstat/ssstart.htm), the page interactively asks a series of several questions about the design and variables you are trying to analyze. The questions are asked in a specific order, leading you to the appropriate statistical technique.

- How many variables does the problem involve?
- Is a distinction made between a dependent and an independent variable?
- Do you want to treat the relationship as linear?

Depending on the nature of your research design and answers to the questions, there may be additional questions you will need to answer. It is, however, an efficient method of determining an appropriate test—the entire process will take only a minute or two. It certainly is better than the alternative—discovering after the fact that you have conducted the wrong procedure and now must return to your analyses.

The correlation between measures of attentiveness and achievement was −.68, significant at the .01 level.

When you have a number of statistics to report, it is helpful (and customary) to present them in tabular form.

Means and standard deviations for the six groups are shown in Table 1.

Further information on presenting findings and conclusions is provided in Chapter 9.

DEVELOPMENTAL ACTIVITY

Statistical Analysis Decisions

Closely associated with the important decisions about collection of your data that you made in the developmental activity for Chapter 6 are decisions about how you anticipate analyzing your resultant data. In this chapter's activity, you will strengthen choices about analytical techniques that you have likely already begun to consider. Bear in mind that decisions about analyses should focus on the information necessary to enable you to answer your questions or address your hypotheses.

1. My research question(s) or hypothesis(es)

   _____

   _____

2. My main variables and their associated classifications

   _____

   _____

   Variable 1: _____
   ☐ Continuous
   ☐ Discrete
   Variable 2: _____
   ☐ Continuous
   ☐ Discrete
   Others: _____
   ☐ Continuous
   ☐ Discrete

3. The *descriptive* statistics I plan to use to summarize my variables (*check all that apply*)

Statistical Technique	Variable 1	Variable 2	Other
Mean			
Median			
Mode			
Range			
Standard deviation			
Percentile rank			
Stanine			
Correlation coefficient			

4. The appropriate inferential statistical technique(s) for my study

    _____

    _____

5. As I consider again my questions or hypotheses, the reason(s) I chose the foregoing technique(s)

    _____

    _____

6. I ❑ will / ❑ will not *(check one)* perform a significance test

    REASON: _____

    _____

7. I ❑ will / ❑ will not *(check one)* calculate confidence intervals

    REASON: _____

    _____

8. Type of sampling

    _____

    _____

9. Limitations or delimitations on my use of inferential statistics due to the type of sampling

    _____

    _____

CHAPTER SUMMARY

Research data, whether qualitative or quantitative, must be analyzed in order to answer research questions or test hypotheses. Qualitative data, largely verbal in nature, are analyzed verbally through the logico-inductive process. This analysis applies verbal data to research questions and examines the data's persuasiveness in answering related questions.

Quantitative data, largely numerical in nature, are analyzed statistically, in order to describe samples and make inferences about populations. Descriptive statistics include measures of central tendency, variability, relative standing, and correlation. Inferential statistics include measures of standard error and tests of significance. Statistics do not prove anything in themselves, but do assist the logical thought processes of the investigator. Once data have been analyzed, the results are presented as findings, organized according to research questions and hypotheses, and presented clearly so they can be understood easily by others.

LIST OF IMPORTANT TERMS

central tendency
coding scheme
descriptive statistics
hypothetico-inductive analysis

inferential statistics
logico-inductive analysis
parameters
relationship

relative standing
sampling error
statistics
variability

YOUR CURRENT STATUS

In Chapter 6 you learned how to obtain appropriate research data, and in this chapter you have seen how those data, whether qualitative or quantitative, can be analyzed to help answer questions or test hypotheses. For specific statistical procedures, you were directed to explore the contents of the Appendix. You are now ready to learn how to put together a research report.

ACTIVITIES FOR THOUGHT AND DISCUSSION

1. Suppose you conduct research to test student preference among five colors for interior classroom walls. One thousand students are included in your sample. You use chi-square to analyze the data. If one of the colors is chartreuse, based on the null hypothesis how many students do you expect to choose chartreuse?
2. For the nine types of research, indicate which are more likely to involve qualitative analysis and which are more likely to involve quantitative analysis.
3. Here are the questions presented at the beginning of the chapter. See how well you can answer them.
   a. What is the general purpose of data analysis in all types of research?
   b. Why are qualitative data and quantitative data analyzed differently?
   c. How are qualitative data analyzed?
   d. How are quantitative data analyzed?
   e. What are the relationships among populations, parameters, samples, and statistics?
   f. What is the difference between descriptive statistics and inferential statistics?
   g. What does *significance* mean in statistics?
   h. What is the relationship between data analysis and research findings?

ANSWERS TO CHAPTER EXERCISES

7.1. 3, 5, 8, 9

7.2. 1. S 2. PR 3. P 4. ST

7.3. 1. mode 2. correlation 3. mean 4. range
5. significance 6. error estimate 7. confidence interval 8. inferential statistics 9. percentile rank 10. measures of variability

REFERENCES AND RECOMMENDED READINGS

Bartz, A. (1976). *Basic Statistical Concepts in Education and the Behavioral Sciences.* Minneapolis: Burgess.

Best, J., & Kahn, J. (2006). *Research in Education* (10th ed.). Boston: Allyn & Bacon.

Cronk, B. (2004). *How to Use SPSS: A Step-By-Step Guide to Analysis and Interpretation* (3rd ed.). Los Angeles: Pyrczak.

Gall, M., Borg, W., & Gall, J. (2003). *Educational Research: An Introduction* (7th ed.). Boston: Allyn & Bacon.

Green, S., & Salkind, N. T. (2005). *Using SPSS for Windows and Macintosh: Analyzing and Understanding Data* (4th ed.). Upper Saddle River, NJ: Prentice Hall.

Lancy, D. (1993). *Qualitative Research in Education: An Introduction to the Major Traditions.* White Plains, NY: Longman.

Lortie, D. (1975). *Schoolteacher: A Sociological Study.* Chicago: University of Chicago Press.

McMillan, J. (2004). *Educational Research: Fundamentals for the Consumer* (4th ed.). Boston: Allyn & Bacon.

Mertler, C. A., & Vannatta, R. A. (2005). *Advanced and Multivariate Statistical Methods: Practical Application and Interpretation* (3rd ed.). Los Angeles: Pyrczak.

Miles, M. B., & Huberman, A. M. (1994). *Qualitative Data Analysis* (2nd ed.). Thousand Oaks, CA: Sage.

Norusis, M. (1991). *SPSS/PC+ Studentware Plus.* Chicago: SPSS Inc. Software manufacturer is SPSS Inc., 444 N. Michigan Ave., Chicago, IL 60611.

Stockburger, D. W. (1996). *Introductory Statistics: Concepts, Models, and Applications.* Available at www.psychstat.missouristate.edu/sbk00.htm

Trochim, W. M. (2002). *The Research Methods Knowledge Base* (2nd ed.). Available at http://socialresearchmethods.net/kb/index.htm

Vierra, A., & Pollock, J. (1988). *Reading Educational Research.* Scottsdale, AZ: Gorsuch Scarisbrick.

8 Designing a Research Project

PREVIEW

This chapter examines seven tasks to which you must give attention when planning your own research project:

- State topic, problem, and questions and/or hypotheses.
- Outline the library search for related information.
- Identify needed data and their probable sources.
- List steps to be carried out in the study.
- Specify procedures and tools for collecting data.
- Foresee how data can best be analyzed and interpreted.
- Anticipate the appropriate report format for your research.

TARGETED LEARNINGS

This chapter is designed to help you plan a research project of your own. As you complete the chapter exercises, you will simultaneously be preparing a preliminary plan for researching a topic of your choice. Furthermore, you will see how investigations are planned in any of the standard types of educational research. As you proceed through the chapter, make sure to look for information related to the following concerns:

1. Stating a topic and problem, with appurtenant questions and/or hypotheses
2. Identifying the type of research called for in your topic
3. Learning more about the type of research you have selected
4. Organizing a library search for information related to your topic
5. Foreseeing needed data and their potential sources
6. Making a list of steps to be taken in conducting the study
7. Noting the procedures and tools you will require for collecting data
8. Anticipating the kinds of analyses your data will need
9. Drawing up conclusions from your data analysis
10. Selecting the appropriate format for reporting your research

How planning should be done

Authorities offer various suggestions as to how research should be planned. Gay, Mills, and Airasian (2006), for example, say that a research plan should give attention to the following elements:

1. Introduction, including statement of the problem, review of the literature, and statement of the hypothesis
2. Method, specifying participants, instruments, materials/apparatus, design of the study, and procedure
3. Data analysis
4. Time schedule
5. Budget

Wiersma and Jurs (2005) emphasize that planning should be done in accordance with whether the research is qualitative or quantitative, suggesting the following for *qualitative research:*

1. A working design that specifies participants and possible variables
2. A working hypothesis
3. Procedures of data collection such as interview, observation, and document perusal
4. Procedures of data analysis and interpretation, including data reduction, data organization, and description

For *quantitative research,* Wiersma and Jurs maintain that "explaining or controlling variance is an important part of quantitative research" (2005, p. 84). They suggest, therefore, that when planning quantitative research, one should describe not only the participants, hypotheses, and plans for collecting and interpreting data but also the procedures by which variance will be controlled, such as the following:

1. Randomization, which tends to spread a variable evenly across groups being studied
2. Holding factors (e.g., ethnicity of participants) constant, thus reducing the effect that an irrelevant factor might have on the dependent variable

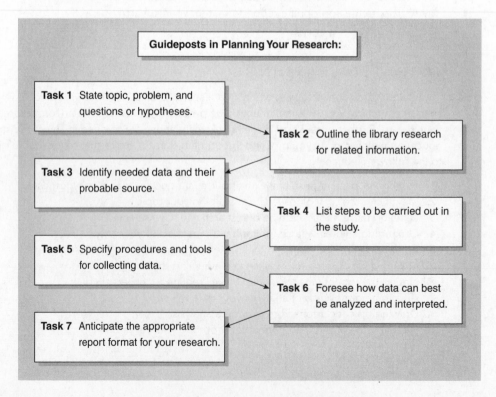

Guideposts in Planning Your Research:

Task 1 State topic, problem, and questions or hypotheses.

Task 2 Outline the library research for related information.

Task 3 Identify needed data and their probable source.

Task 4 List steps to be carried out in the study.

Task 5 Specify procedures and tools for collecting data.

Task 6 Foresee how data can best be analyzed and interpreted.

Task 7 Anticipate the appropriate report format for your research.

Table 8.1 Example of Control of Variables in Quantitative Research

Variable	Control of Variable
Student science background	Random assignments of students to groups
Teacher	An independent variable; each teacher uses different methods
School	A constant; students of only one school are included

3. Making adjustments statistically to remove the effects of an intervening variable such as intelligence

Wiersma and Jurs (2005, p. 85) clarify these points using an example of a study on the effects of different teaching methods on learning high school chemistry, from which Table 8.1 is adapted.

THE APPROACH TO PLANNING ADVOCATED IN THIS BOOK

The planning advice we have just seen is excellent, but experience shows that those new to research appreciate as much guidance as they can get. For that reason, abundant instructions and exercises are provided in this chapter to increase your ability to plan an investigation of your own. In addition to the material presented in this chapter, you will be asked to read at least one of the other chapters presented later that goes into detail about the type of research you wish to plan.

We will now proceed to the tasks you must accomplish when planning your own research. You will be guided through those tasks in order. Instructions are presented for planning each task, and exercises are provided to strengthen your understanding. By completing all the exercises, you will have simultaneously prepared a plan you can follow in researching the topic you have selected.

TASKS TO BE ACCOMPLISHED WHEN PLANNING RESEARCH

Seven major tasks must be completed as you design a workable plan of research. These elements comprise your **research design.**

1. State the title, topic, problem, and questions and/or hypotheses.
2. Identify keywords or descriptors and outline the library search for related information.
3. Identify data you will need and their probable sources.
4. List the steps you will need to carry out in order to complete the study.
5. Specify the procedures and tools you will employ in collecting data.
6. Foresee how data can best be analyzed and interpreted.
7. Anticipate the report format most appropriate for your research.

TASK 1. STATE THE TITLE, TOPIC, PROBLEM, AND QUESTIONS AND/OR HYPOTHESES

To begin your research plan, specify the topic, the problem, and the research questions and/ or hypotheses. For the topic, you should complete the following steps:

1. Select an educational matter that is of personal interest or concern to you.
2. Determine whether the topic is researchable, considering ethics, complexity, and time.
3. Compose a tentative working title for your research.

Exercise 8.1

Identify and jot down a topic (e.g., "student self-concept and reading achievement" or "home laboratories for biology students") that you have a genuine interest in exploring. Compose a tentative working title that describes the topic.

Example

Topic: student self-concept and reading achievement

Working title: The relationship between self-concept and reading achievement among fifth-grade students

Your topic: _____

Working title: _____

Exercise 8.2 can help you decide whether the topic can be researched from a practical standpoint, taking into account ethical considerations, amenability to scientific method, difficulty, time, and cost. If you believe it can be successfully researched, then proceed to the next step. If you find it questionable, go back and revise your initial research topic or select a different one.

Exercise 8.2

Appraise your topic on the following considerations to determine whether it can be researched by a graduate student in education.

- *Ethics.* Can the project be done ethically, or does it have questionable aspects?
- *Scientific method.* Can the topic be investigated scientifically?
- *Difficulty.* Does the project seem too easy, too difficult, or about right?
- *Time.* Does it seem that the project can be investigated in the time you have available?
- *Cost.* Is the investigation likely to entail undue expense?

For stating the problem you should complete the following steps:

1. State the purpose of your intended research.
2. Explain why the topic is of sufficient importance to merit investigative attention.
3. Specify the *limitations* (existing constraints) and *delimitations* (limits you will impose) under which your investigation will be conducted, together with the assumptions you are making, but cannot prove.
4. Define the terms central to your investigation, especially those that have unusual meanings.

Having selected your topic and given it a working title, you next describe the purpose of the study clearly and briefly. Simply state what you want to investigate, discover, or accomplish. This brief description is called the *statement of the problem.* In case you do not remember how to compose a statement of the problem, the following three examples can be used as models:

- The purpose of this study is to determine whether age of entry into kindergarten has an effect on students' subsequent school learning and behavior.
- The purpose of this study is to construct and test an English vocabulary program. The program will be designed for third-grade classrooms and will be field-tested in five selected classes in Elmwood schools.
- The purpose of this study is to explore factors related to achievement levels in English and mathematics among high school students of Filipino, Hispanic, and Caucasian descent.

Exercise 8.3

State the purpose of the proposed investigation for the topic you identified in Exercise 8.1.

_____

_____

Along with the statement of the problem, you will be expected to indicate why the study is worth pursuing. This portion is referred to as the *importance* of the study.

Exercise 8.4

Write a one-paragraph justification of the importance of the study you have identified.

Limitations and delimitations of the study to be undertaken should be specified at this point. Because these concerns are not always immediately clear, you may not be able to state them precisely at this stage of planning—it may be necessary to revisit them later in the development of your study.

In the *limitations of the study* you identify existing restrictions that are outside your control, such as availability of records, problems in selecting a sample, or time allotments. Some common examples of research limitations include the lack of a complete population list from which to select a sample, refusals of parents for children to participate in a study, or denial of access to schools to conduct observations of teachers. Notice how each impediment is out of the control of the researcher. The limitations can usually be presented as a list and then explained further in one or two additional paragraphs.

In the *delimitations of the study* you identify boundaries that you, the investigator, are placing on the study. Here you might state specifically what you will and will not investigate; the number of individuals, classes, or schools to be involved in the study; calendar time to which the study is restricted; or any other boundaries you might wish to impose on the investigation. Some examples of delimitations include constraining your study to include only females, deciding to survey only 300 individuals—as opposed to a larger number—from a large population, or deciding to collect data at the beginning of the school year instead of at the end. These examples represent purposeful decisions made by the researcher. Similarly, delimitations can be presented as a list and further explained in one or two paragraphs.

In this phase of planning you must also define any terms that are not commonly recognized or that you will be using in a special sense.

Exercise 8.5

For your topic, (1) write three limitations, (2) write three delimitations, and (3) define three terms you will use that a lay reader would not readily understand.

Regarding questions and/or hypotheses, you must (1) state the research questions you will attempt to answer, and/or (2) state the research hypotheses or null hypotheses you will use.

You know that some types of research are oriented by questions, others by hypotheses, and still others by both. If you intend to pose questions to guide your research, you should present a main research question supplemented with a number of related subquestions that help answer the main question, as shown in the following example:

Problem: The purpose of this study is to formulate and test a set of procedures for increasing the level of student attention during sixth-grade mathematics instruction.

Main question: Can a set of procedures be devised and implemented that will increase the level of student attention during sixth-grade mathematics instruction?

Subquestions

1. Does evidence indicate that student attention is important during mathematics instruction?
2. What is meant by *paying attention,* and what do students do when paying attention?
3. What materials, techniques, and activities naturally attract and hold student attention?
4. What other factors cause students to pay attention?
5. What have teachers traditionally done to attract and hold student attention during mathematics or other instruction?
6. Can teachers incorporate a planned set of "attention holders" into their lessons?
7. If so, will those efforts produce increases in student attention?

The subquestions are much more limited than the main question. They are also more easily answered and sequenced so that their answers can help answer the main question. Subquestions provide valuable guidance in planning and conducting the investigation.

Exercise 8.6

A. Would you consider the following to be a good or poor main research question?

Are Latino students in Elmwood getting what they should out of school?

You probably see it is a poor question because it is too vague: "getting what they should out of school" has no clear meaning. It is also too broad; even if clarified, it covers too much ground. However, the question would be acceptable if put in this form:

How do Latino students compare to other students in Elmwood high schools regarding achievement and attitude toward school?

The question thus stated directs attention to what the research is to determine. It clarifies the topic and limits it to researchable size.

With these considerations in mind, write a main research question for the problem you have stated.

B. We have noted that answering a main research question is easier when a number of subordinate questions are posed to help answer the main question. The subquestions should be clear and succinct. Evaluate the following subquestions for (C) clarity, (S) succinctness, and (A) answerability.

_____ **1.** Do Latino students goof around a lot after school?

_____ **2.** Why are Latino students so good in math?

_____ **3.** Do Latino students' attitudes toward school differ from the attitudes of other groups of students?

_____ **4.** Do Latino students learn math differently from the way students of Asian descent learn it?

_____ **5.** Given the incredible disadvantages experienced by certain members of the Latino student community, why do Latino students so frequently, and to such a surprising degree, outstrip their peers in so many different academic areas?

Let us appraise the subquestions: Question 5 is not stated succinctly; all the others are sufficiently brief. Questions 2, 3, and 4 are stated clearly, while questions 1 and 5 are not. Only question 3 is readily answerable; the other questions range from difficult to virtually impossible to answer through research.

C. Subquestions should also be arranged in good sequence, either from simple to more complex or so that prior questions furnish beginning points for questions that follow. Given the main question,

> Are Latino students' achievement levels in high school mathematics affected by their parents' support of education?

evaluate the following subquestions. Indicate the five questions that contribute best to answering the main research question. If you find the sequence of questions to be unsatisfactory, rearrange them as you believe appropriate.

_____ **1.** What are the mathematics achievement levels of Latino high school students?

_____ **2.** What do Latino students' parents say about their children's enjoyment of school?

_____ **3.** Does the literature suggest a relationship between parental support and school achievement?

_____ **4.** How does mathematics achievement among Latino students compare with that of students in general?

_____ **5.** Does Latino student achievement in mathematics remain constant through the school years, relative to that of other students?

_____ **6.** Is there a correlation between Latino students' mathematics achievement and their parents' attitude toward education?

_____ **7.** How does Latino high school students' attitude toward school compare with that of other students?

D. Write out five subquestions to help answer the main research question you composed in part A of this exercise.

If hypotheses are used to guide research, they may be _research hypotheses_ (either directional or nondirectional), which state the outcomes the investigator expects, or _null hypotheses,_ which usually are not what the investigator expects to find but are satisfactorily testable within the logic of inferential statistics (examined in Chapter 7 and in the Appendix). To assist you in completing Exercise 8.7, the following examples are provided:

> *Research hypothesis:* Mathematics achievement among Latino high school students is positively related to parental support of education.

> *Null hypothesis:* No relationship exists between mathematics achievement of Latino high school students and their parents' support of education.

Frequently, both types of hypotheses are used in the same study. The investigator states a research hypothesis to orient the study and then a null hypothesis for testing whether a finding can be attributed to errors made in selecting the sample.

Exercise 8.7

A. Which of the following hypotheses are stated suitably for guiding practical educational research?

_____ **1.** No difference exists in grade point average between sixth-grade students of Asian descent and sixth-grade students of Hispanic descent.

_____ **2.** Attitude toward school is better among African American students than among white students.

_____ **3.** No difference exists between students of Japanese descent and students of Korean descent regarding genetic capabilities for learning mathematics.

_____ **4.** All students should be given equal access to educational opportunity.

B. Compose a research hypothesis and a null hypothesis for the problem you stated earlier.

TASK 2. IDENTIFY KEYWORDS OR DESCRIPTORS AND OUTLINE THE LIBRARY SEARCH FOR RELATED INFORMATION

In Task 2, you should accomplish four objectives:

1. Select the terms or descriptors for use in the library search.
2. Identify secondary sources to be searched.
3. Identify guides and directories for searching primary sources.
4. Assemble the materials needed for summarizing and citing references.

Descriptors are terms related to your research topic that can be found in reference indexes such as *Current Index to Journals in Education (CIJE)*. They are helpful when you manually search the indexes and are indispensable when you use the computer for your search. One of the best aids in identifying appropriate descriptors is the *Thesaurus of ERIC Descriptors*. It can be found in the reference section of the library next to the bound volumes of *CIJE*, near the computer terminals used to search ERIC. Additionally, it is included on the ERIC compact disc (if your library has the CD-ROM version of ERIC) and can be accessed online within the searchable ERIC databases. When you consult the thesaurus, identify the descriptor that most closely matches the theme of your study for your initial search. While it might lead to all the references you need, you should list related descriptors as well, as they sometimes lead to unexpectedly valuable resources.

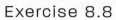

Exercise 8.8

For your topic, write three descriptors that might be appropriate for searching the indexes. To facilitate searching, each descriptor should consist of no more than two words.

Secondary sources, such as yearbooks, research reviews, and encyclopedias, should be checked manually, using the descriptors you have identified. You should consult secondary sources first because it is likely they will summarize existing research in your topic and provide a review of the topic's historical treatment. Secondary sources are also likely to contain critiques and extensive bibliographies but probably will *not* include the most current research.

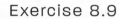

Exercise 8.9

Refer to the list of secondary sources presented in Chapter 4. Write the names of five sources that seem promising for your topic.

Guides such as indexes and directories should be consulted next for indications of documents and journal articles that might contain primary information related to your topic. Plan on using first those that can be accessed by computer, such as *Current Index to Journals in Education, Resources in Education,* and *Dissertation Abstracts International.*

Exercise 8.10

Refer to the indexes and directories listed in Chapter 4. Write the names of four that seem most promising for researching your topic.

You should now plan procedures and materials for summarizing and citing information related to your study. Chapter 5 suggested procedures for surveying quantities of materials and accurately making summaries and bibliographical citations.

As you delve into the literature, you may have to make another decision about your topic, depending on what you find. If your topic has already been researched extensively, answers to your questions may exist in the literature, in which case the topic is probably not a good choice for your project. If references to your topic are few or nonexistent, you may need to think through your topic again; it may have inherent problems that have prevented its being researched.

Assuming you have identified a researchable topic you wish to pursue, you can complete the library search as described in Chapters 4 and 5. Remember to organize the citations so as to present first the information that is more *generally* related to your topic and *earlier in publication date* and then proceed to materials that are more *recent* and more *specific* to your topic. That is, you should organize the references so they proceed

from general → to specific

and from earlier research → to more recent research

The use of research subquestions to guide your research can also help organize your literature review.

Exercise 8.11

Indicate which of the following should probably be presented (E) earlier or (L) later in your review of the literature.

_____   **1.** In 1997 Wilkinson . . .

_____   **2.** Gange's 2005 research showed that . . .

_____   **3.** Historically, research on this topic has dealt with . . .

_____   **4.** Martínez (2000) described research done at the turn of the century . . .

_____   **5.** Present consensus seems to be that . . .

_____   **6.** Garibaldi's 1988 findings are still considered to be the most accurate available . . .

_____   **7.** Of several similar topics investigated, the following are representative . . .

_____   **8.** Of all research, the most pertinent seems . . .

TASK 3. IDENTIFY NEEDED DATA AND SOURCES

A number of elements must be considered within this task and should be carefully organized.

1. Specify events or conditions about which you need data, usually *one* of the following:

   - Human social behavior, individually or in one or more groups
   - Events or conditions of the present
   - Events or conditions of the past
   - Correlations that permit making predictions and sometimes suggest cause–effect relationships
   - Innovative procedures or products
   - Existing group differences and trends
   - Quality of programs or operational units
   - Relationships that strongly indicate cause and effect

   When you identify from the preceding list the event or condition central to the research topic you selected in Exercise 8.1, you have pinpointed the type of research you will undertake. It is important at this point that you read more about the particular type of research you are to pursue in order to gain a greater understanding of what is involved in obtaining and analyzing data.

2. List the kinds of data you need to collect for your research, usually one or more of the following:

   - *Descriptions.* Verbal summaries of observations
   - *Scores or tallies.* Test scores or frequency tallies
   - *Measurements.* Assessments by measuring devices other than tests
   - *Opinions.* What people believe
   - *Statements.* Authoritative pronouncements
   - *Analyses.* Careful logical scrutiny

3. Pinpoint anticipated sources of data, usually including one or more of the following:

   - *Participants.* People participating in the study
   - *Procedures.* Formal ways of doing things

- *Settings*. Physical environments
- *Objects*. Tangible things
- *Records*. Highly summarized notations
- *Documents*. Printed materials, such as articles
- *Informants*. People who provide desired information verbally

Exercise 8.12

Use the following chart to select and read the chapter presented in this book that describes the type of research you have identified for your topic. Select the event or condition central to your topic, note the probable type of research, and then read the suggested chapter. Within that chapter, you will find one or more reprinted research reports that exemplify the type of research described in the chapter. After you have read that chapter, return here to continue your planning.

Central Event or Condition of Your Topic	Type of Research	Pertinent Chapter
Human social behavior	Ethnographic	Chapter 10: Qualitative Research Methods
Events or conditions of the past	Historical	Chapter 10: Qualitative Research Methods
Other qualitative topics	Qualitative	Chapter 10: Qualitative Research Methods
Current characteristics of a population	Survey	Chapter 11: Survey Research
Co-relation between variables	Correlational	Chapter 12: Nonexperimental Quantitative Research
Existing group differences	Causal-Comparative	Chapter 12: Nonexperimental Quantitative Research
Relationships that show cause and effect	Experimental/ Quasi-Experimental	Chapter 13: Experimental, Quasi-Experimental, and Single-Subject Designs
Topics that require both qualitative and quantitative data	Mixed Methods	Chapter 14: Mixed-Methods Research Designs
Innovative products or procedures	Action	Chapter 15: Action Research
Quality of programs or operations	Evaluation	Chapter 16: Evaluation Research

Exercise 8.13

For the topic you have identified for research, first list the kinds of data you will need to collect and then the probable sources of those data.

TASK 4. LIST THE STEPS YOU WILL NEED
TO CARRY OUT TO COMPLETE THE STUDY

1. If you need to select a sample of participants who will furnish data, indicate your choice of the best sample that is also obtainable for your study. Recall that additional information and greater detail for methods of sample selection were provided in Chapter 6.

   Probability Sampling Techniques
   - *Random sample.* Every person in the population has an equal chance of being selected.
   - *Stratified sample.* Sample is specially drawn to fairly represent elements of the population, such as various ethnic groups.
   - *Cluster sample.* Sample consists of existing groups, such as classes or schools.
   - *Systematic sample.* After a random name is drawn from a master list, every *k*th person is selected.

   Nonprobability Sampling Techniques
   - *Convenience sample.* Participants are chosen from an easily accessible group.
   - *Judgmental (purposive) sample.* Specific segments of a given population are selected.
   - *Snowball (network or chain) sample.* Small initial sample is selected; those individuals then provide the names of other participants.
   - *Quota sample.* Construction of a sample is intended to mirror the characteristics of the population of interest.

2. Indicate how you will select the sample.
3. Indicate what the participants, if any, will be expected or required to do. Expectations are normally categorized as one or more of the following:

   - Reorganize or regroup
   - Undergo assessment
   - Receive training, instruction, or other treatment
   - Demonstrate skills or knowledge
   - Interact and behave in their normal fashion

4. Indicate how you will obtain data. In most studies, data are collected by one or more of the following:

   - *Notation.* Observer makes notes of observations.
   - *Description.* Observer makes detailed recordings of observations.
   - *Analysis.* Investigator makes careful logical scrutiny of objects and procedures.
   - *Questioning.* Investigator or assistant conducts interviews or surveys.
   - *Testing.* Participants respond to formal tests.
   - *Measurement.* Assessment is done with measuring devices other than tests.

5. Indicate the tools that will be used in collecting data, usually one or more of the following:

   - *Recording devices.* Pencil, paper, camera, audio and video recorders
   - *Guides.* Structure for procedures and questions, as in interviews
   - *Criteria.* Standards for judging existence or acceptability
   - *Tests.* Commercial standardized tests; sometimes tests constructed by the investigator
   - *Measuring devices other than tests.* Rulers, thermometers, weight scales, and the like

- *Rating scales*. Written prompts to which participants respond, such as Likert scales and semantic differential scales
- *Questionnaires*. Sets of questions to which participants respond in writing

6. Anticipate the form in which data will accumulate (typically one or more of the following):

- Written descriptions
- Numerical summaries
- Categorizations—participants or responses placed in categories
- Hierarchical listings—responses or participants placed in rank order
- Tallies—marks indicating frequency of occurrences of responses

7. Give attention to how you will ensure the quality of your data, such as by

- Determining legitimacy of source by verifying authenticity, credentials of provider, or measures of validity
- Determining accuracy of data via credentials of the provider, preponderance of opinion, logical analysis, and statistical measures of reliability

Exercise 8.14

1. Do you expect to select a sample for your study? If so, indicate the kind of sample and how you will select it.
2. If you use participants in your study, indicate what you will expect them to do.

TASK 5. SPECIFY THE PROCEDURES AND TOOLS YOU WILL EMPLOY IN COLLECTING DATA

This topic was discussed in the preceding paragraphs. You will almost certainly use one or more of the following procedures to obtain data: notation, description, analysis, questioning, testing, and measurement. Depending on the procedures you envision, you will need tools such as recording devices, guides, criteria, tests, measuring devices other than tests, rating scales, and questionnaires.

Exercise 8.15

For the data you anticipate obtaining in your study

1. List the specific steps you will follow and tools you might use in collecting data.
2. Indicate how you expect to organize data prior to analysis.
3. Explain how you will attempt to ensure the quality of your data.

TASK 6. FORESEE HOW DATA CAN BEST BE ANALYZED AND INTERPRETED

Data Analysis

Procedures for analyzing data vary according to type of data and research questions and/or hypotheses. As previously discussed, qualitative and quantitative are the two general types of data and must be analyzed differently. Qualitative data are for the most part narrative or verbal, whereas quantitative data are for the most part numerical. A certain amount of overlap exists between the two types. Either or both of the following steps need to be addressed as part of this task.

1. State how you will perform a **qualitative data analysis** if such analysis is appropriate. This usually involves logically matching data with research questions. In ethnographic studies, analysis involves identifying topics, categories, and patterns that ultimately lead to interpretations, from which conclusions are reached concerning the research questions asked. (Techniques of qualitative data analysis are described in Chapter 10.)
2. State how you will perform a **quantitative data analysis,** if such analysis is appropriate. This usually involves statistical procedures that result in

   - Numerical descriptions of central tendency, variability, correlations, differences, and relative standings
   - Statistical inferences about standard error, probability, and significance

Techniques for analyzing quantitative data are described in Chapter 7 and in the Appendix.

Exercise 8.16

For the data you anticipate

1. Will you need to use qualitative analysis or quantitative analysis? Explain why.
2. If quantitative analysis is indicated, do you expect to explore status of groups, differences between or among groups, or relationships between or among variables?

Analysis Applied to Answering Questions and Testing Hypotheses

Research questions are answered through logic and accumulation of evidence. *Qualitative analysis* requires a strong verbal argument, enough to be very persuasive. *Quantitative analysis* describes data numerically and often requires the application of statistical tests to help determine whether the findings exist in the population as well as in the sample.

Hypotheses, as we have seen, are tested statistically. Statistical tests provide the rationale for either retaining or rejecting your hypotheses, thus suggesting whether or not your findings are probably "real." You also use logic to support the inferences you make about your hypotheses.

Findings

Findings are statements that explain what your data analysis has revealed. Presented verbally, findings are commonly grouped in accordance with the research questions or hypotheses to which they pertain. For example, consider the following research question:

How do Latino students compare to other students in Elmwood high schools regarding achievement and attitude toward school?

You might properly present your findings as follows:

Question 1: How do Latino students compare to other students in Elmwood high schools regarding achievement and attitude toward school?

Findings

1. Latino students' achievement test scores, compared to other students in Elmwood high schools, were . . .
2. Latino students' attitudes toward school, compared to that of all other students in Elmwood high schools, were . . .

Although findings are expressed verbally, it is expected that they should be referenced to the analytical procedures on which they are based, such as the following:

■ Graphic summaries, shown in figures, tables, and graphs
■ Tabular summaries, shown in tables, with appropriate statistical tests applied

Conclusions

Conclusions, which are the interpretations you make of your research findings, are also presented verbally. They comprise your reflections on the meaning, significance, and implications of what you have discovered. Consider the previous example:

How do Latino students compare to other students in Elmwood high schools regarding achievement and attitude toward school?

You might open your conclusion section by writing the following:

Given the findings of this study, the following conclusions appear to be warranted:

1. Latino students in Elmwood high schools . . . *(continue stating your interpretations)*

Exercise 8.17

For the research questions and hypotheses you stated in Exercises 8.6 and 8.7

1. Indicate the general procedures you would use to answer questions and test hypotheses
2. Indicate how you would expect to present your findings and conclusions

TASK 7. ANTICIPATE THE APPROPRIATE REPORT FORMAT FOR YOUR RESEARCH

Relatively little has been said up to now about formats used for research reports, although you have had direct experience with many. (Chapter 9 provides detailed help with report formats.) For the present, simply recognize the existence of a *generic* format and three variations: the *thesis/dissertation* format, the *technical paper* format, and the *journal article* format.

The generic report format includes

1. Specification of the problem
2. Review of related literature
3. Procedures and data collection
4. Data analysis
5. Findings
6. Conclusions

The report format that your institution expects you to follow will be a variation of this generic format. You most likely will be expected to apply the thesis format adopted by your graduate school. Two other variations frequently used by researchers are the technical paper format, specified by agencies that sponsor research, and the journal article format, specified by particular journals that publish research. By now you have seen many examples of the journal format, and you may also have seen some of the technical paper format.

This completes the instruction on how to prepare for your own research. The following case illustrates how one graduate student planned her research.

ILLUSTRATIVE EXAMPLE OF PLANNING A RESEARCH PROJECT

Sheila Holly, an experienced teacher adept at working with student teachers, had for some time been interested in exploring whether success in student teaching could be predicted on the basis of student teachers' personal traits. She planned an investigation to pursue that question, following the research phases outlined in the planning guide you have just completed.

TOPIC AND PROBLEM

The process began when Holly decided she wanted to determine whether student teacher success could be predicted from personal traits. For her working title, she chose "Predicting

APPLYING TECHNOLOGY

More Guidelines for Reports

At several places in this text we have referred the reader to an electronic text authored by Dr. William Trochim of Cornell University (http://socialresearch methods.net/kb). Included in his online text are two pages that provide excellent guidance for planning research and, specifically, the writing of a proposal or final research report. The first of these, titled "Key Elements" (http://socialresearchmethods .net/kb/guideelements.htm), presents an overview of important criteria that must be addressed in any research report. Even though the author focuses on writing up a completed study, his references to and descriptions of several aspects of a report would also apply to writing a research proposal or plan. In "Key Elements," Dr. Trochim addresses the following aspects:

- Introduction
- Methods
- Results
- Conclusion, Abstract, and Reference sections

Included in each of these sections are detailed descriptions of the specific components for each section (e.g., Methods includes descriptions of Sample

Selection, Measurement Issues, and the Research Design and Procedures).

The second page, titled "Formatting" (http:// socialresearchmethods.net/kb/formatting.htm), contains even more detailed descriptions of the specifics of how to format a research proposal or plan. These guidelines follow those provided in the *Publication Manual of the American Psychological Association* (5th edition). Included on this page are descriptions of the contents of individual sections of the research proposal or paper. In addition to the components listed above, Dr. Trochim has also included information on

- Citing references within the text (i.e., within the literature review)
- Formats for citing references in a reference list
- Information on formatting tables, figures, and appendices

Finally, Dr. Trochim has also included the complete text of a sample research paper (http:// socialresearchmethods.net/kb/sampaper.htm), exemplifying many of the guidelines presented within his previously mentioned Web pages.

Success in Student Teaching from Student Teachers' Personal Traits." She then formulated the following problem statement:

> The purpose of this study is to determine whether success in student teaching can be predicted from selected personal traits of student teachers.

Holly included a brief statement about the importance of the study, explaining that student teaching is very costly to taxpayers, that better prediction of success would save money and other resources, that reliable predictors of success in student teaching have not been available, and that there has been speculation but no proof that student teaching success depends more on personal factors than on intelligence or grade point average. She continued by describing the limitations of the study, which had to do with participants available, student teaching placements, and schools and master teachers involved. She also stated the delimitations of the study, which included time duration, personal traits to be investigated, and instruments and procedures that would be used to assess personal traits and success in student teaching. Finally, Holly defined the terms central to her study, including "student teaching," "success in student teaching," "personality," and "personal traits."

Holly incorporated both the following null hypothesis and main research questions in her study.

> No relationship exists between success in student teaching and selected personal traits of student teachers.

> Can personal traits of student teachers be used to predict success in student teaching?

Subordinate to that main research question were the following subquestions:

1. What are some of the personal traits of student teachers that professors and master teachers consider important to success?
2. Can master teachers and professors of teacher education reach consensus concerning a cluster of personal traits that seem to be essential to success in student teaching?
3. If a group of such traits can be identified, can they be reliably observed and rated in student teachers?
4. If a group of reliably observable traits can be identified and agreed on, can those traits be assessed by using an instrument such as a rating scale?
5. If student teachers can be assessed with such a scale, can the overall rating procedure be refined sufficiently to allow accurate predictions to be made from the scale?

EXAMINATION OF THE LITERATURE

With those preliminary tasks completed, Holly went to the library to determine the extent to which her topic had been researched. She examined primary and secondary sources, systematically annotating references that had bearing on her research questions. She found some mention of her topic, but no research or practice that suggested that personal traits could, or could not, reliably serve as predictors. She, therefore, decided to proceed with her study.

REQUIRED DATA AND DATA SOURCES

Holly saw that her study involved two main components. The first was the identification and validation of possible predictors of success that could be built into an assessment instrument. The second was to determine whether a correlation existed between personal traits thus identified and student teaching success. The focus of the first component was *innovation.* The needed data seemed to be expert opinion, and the best source of those data seemed to be experienced teachers and professors of education accustomed to working with student teachers.

The focus of the second component was on correlations for *making predictions*. The needed data seemed to be (1) scores depicting traits of student teachers and (2) measures of candidates' later success in student teaching. Those data would be obtained from participants (i.e., student teachers) involved in the study.

Holly used a cluster sample to obtain data. The cluster consisted of 38 student teachers under her direction during the fall term. She explained the proposed study to those students, and all of them agreed to undergo assessment regarding personal traits and performance in student teaching.

For developing the trait assessment instrument, Holly counted on the help of master teachers and university professors of education. In discussions and interviews with those colleagues, she hoped they could identify a pool of personal traits that they believed important to success in student teaching. If they could do so, Holly would analyze the traits to determine which might be assessable through observation or measurement. She would then incorporate those traits, illustrated with example behaviors, into a rating scale that could be applied by professional educators who were working with student teachers. She planned to have the professionals evaluate the rating scale, suggest modifications, and then use the scale to assess the selected personal traits of the students. Holly intended to assess all 38 student teachers personally as well, and in addition to ask student teachers to assess themselves with the instrument.

Data having to do with success in student teaching would come from the end-of-term evaluations routinely completed for student teachers, plus the professionals' appraisals of where each student teacher seemed to rank among student teachers in general.

Holly planned to obtain both qualitative and quantitative data from the assessments and evaluations. Because she feared that the trait assessment instrument and the final evaluation form might produce unreliable or even misleading numerical data, she intended to have professionals participating in the study keep detailed records of each student teacher's performance.

Holly planned to make a dual analysis of the qualitative and quantitative data to compare the ratings of each student teacher by the master teacher, the university professor, the student, and Holly herself. She would correlate the numerical data from the assessment instrument and the student teaching final evaluation forms. At the same time she aimed to explore qualitatively the correspondence between personal traits and student teaching success.

APPRAISAL OF HOLLY'S PLAN

Holly may or may not be successful in what she proposes to accomplish. She must contend with serious questions about the validity and reliability of the trait assessment instrument she hopes to develop. Also, the reliability of student teacher evaluations is always in question. These factors will leave some uncertainty about any conclusions Holly reaches. Despite these serious concerns, Holly's topic is important and worth exploring. She may well uncover valuable and generalizable findings. But she will have to obtain statistically significant results and build powerful logical arguments if she is to answer her questions convincingly.

AN EXAMPLE OF A RESEARCH PROPOSAL

The following is a brief example of an actual research proposal for the actual study mentioned periodically throughout this book and conducted by its first author. You have already examined various aspects of the study (for example, the cover letter you examined in Chapter 1 also came from this study).

TEACHERS' PERCEPTIONS OF THE INFLUENCE OF NO CHILD LEFT
BEHIND ON INSTRUCTIONAL AND ASSESSMENT PRACTICES
Craig A. Mertler, Ph.D.
Bowling Green State University

PURPOSE OF THE STUDY

The purpose of this study is to describe the extent to which
K-12 teachers believe that NCLB has influenced their assessment
practices, as well as the ways in which teachers deal with
state-mandated testing, as required by NCLB, within their own
classrooms. Additionally, this study seeks to determine if
any differences in these practices existed based on gender,
school level, education level, teaching experience, and school
and district rating. The specific research questions to be
addressed in this study are:

1. What are K-12 teachers' perceptions of NCLB?
2. In what ways do teachers believe that NCLB has influenced
   their instruction and assessment practices?
3. What differences in the perceptions of NCLB's influence on
   assessment practices exist between groups as determined by
   gender, school level, education level, teaching experience,
   and school rating?

BACKGROUND

The No Child Left Behind Act of 2001 (NCLB) requires all states
in the nation to set standards for grade-level achievement and
to develop a system to measure the progress of all students and
subgroups of students in meeting those state-determined grade-
level standards (U.S. Department of Education, 2004). In this
most recent era of high-stakes testing, the amount of pressure
imposed upon teachers has increased immensely. Many leaders
believe that this push for increased test scores has created an
accountability system that tends to cultivate inappropriate and
sometimes unethical behaviors on the part of educators.

Since the implementation of NCLB, research has shown
that teachers do not have favorable perceptions of the law.
In 2004, teachers confirmed that the accountability system
created by NCLB is influencing the instructional and curricular
practices of teachers, but is also producing unintended and
possibly negative consequences. Specifically, teachers reported
that they ignored important aspects of the curriculum, de-
emphasized or completely neglected untested topics, and tended
to focus their instruction on tested subjects, sometimes
excessively (Sunderman, Tracey, Kim, & Orfield, 2004).

Other research has revealed that nearly 60% of teachers
believed that the law is having a negative impact on their
work settings. Forty percent reported that they experience
NCLB implementation pressures that negatively impact teacher
morale and performance. One-tenth reported that teachers are
being forced to divert their attention away from more important
educational issues that could improve teaching and learning. In
contrast, over one-fourth of responding teachers indicated that
the law is having a more positive effect, as evidenced by the

fact that many educators were beginning to think, talk, and act in new ways that could ultimately result in higher levels of student performance (NSDC, 2004).

McMillan, Myran, and Workman (1999) found that teachers did not cover untested areas of the curriculum nearly as much as those areas that were tested, and that they tended to emphasize breadth rather than depth of content coverage. Teachers also reported greater use of multiple-choice formats on their self-developed classroom tests. Many teachers identified accountability and increased pressures as the driving force behind these assessment-related and instructional changes (McMillan et al., 1999). These results have been supported by a more recent, nationwide survey of more than 4,000 teachers (Abrams, Pedulla, & Madaus, 2003).

Research has also examined test preparation practices. While many teachers engage in legitimate test preparation practices, inappropriate practices also abound. The basic problem with these practices is that they focus only on raising scores on a given test without also increasing students' knowledge and skills in the broader subject being tested (Gulek, 2003; Kober, 2002). These types of practices are arguably a result of the stress and pressure experienced by teachers to raise test scores (Mehrens, 1991; Stecher, 2002).

METHODS

PARTICIPANTS & PROCEDURES. The population for this study includes all K-12 teachers in the state of Ohio during the 2005–2006 school year. Participation in the study will be sought through initial contact with superintendents from approximately 150 randomly selected school districts (roughly 25% of the total 614 school districts in the state). Upon agreement, superintendents will be asked to forward an e-mail "cover letter" to respective teachers, containing an embedded link to the NCLB * CAP Survey. Depending on the number of school districts that agree to participate, the researcher may seek an additional random sample of school districts. The survey will be administered during a three-week period extending from mid-September through early-October.

INSTRUMENTATION. An original Web-based survey instrument, titled the NCLB * CAP (Classroom Assessment Practices) Survey, consisting of 22 items, was developed for this study. Teachers will be instructed to respond on a four-point Likert scale, ranging from "strongly disagree" to "strongly agree." Six demographic questions are also asked of respondents for purposes of group comparisons. The initial set of content-based items was adapted from a handful of existing instruments. The survey underwent pilot-testing prior to its implementation. Content evidence of validity was collected, based on reviews from survey research experts, as well as from classroom teachers. An alpha coefficient value equal to .76 was obtained for the instrument's overall reliability.

DATA ANALYSIS.   Proposed data analyses will include descriptive statistics to summarize the overall results. An exploratory factor analysis will also be conducted in order to reduce the number of items for purposes of group comparisons. Analyses of variance will then be used to compare group responses. All ANOVA results will be evaluated at an alpha level equal to .05.

POTENTIAL IMPACT AND EDUCATIONAL IMPORTANCE

The goals of NCLB are admirable, to say the least. However, policymakers need to be aware of how the law is effecting teachers. The increased pressure that has been placed on teachers to raise levels of student academic achievement has made their daily work much more stressful. Furthermore, teachers have been forced to change the ways that they provide instruction to students and assess their resultant academic performance. Additionally, teachers have resorted to spending much more time teaching students how to take standardized achievement tests, perhaps turning to unethical practices in order to achieve higher test scores. Similarly, administrators need to be mindful of these issues as well. They should be aware of these unintended consequences of NCLB and should look for ways to address increased stress levels. They should definitely be cognizant of the potential for their teachers to utilize unethical test preparation practices. Closely examining how teachers are instructing students in the skills of test-taking may be a critical first step. The results of this study may help us to better understand this potential "problem" more completely. We need to better understand what specific techniques are used, why those techniques are used (i.e., what teachers are hoping to accomplish by using them), and the nature of their overall effectiveness. If they fail to improve actual student learning, then their use should be strongly discouraged.

REFERENCES

Abrams, L. M., Pedulla, J. J., & Madaus, G. F. (2003). Views from the classroom: Teachers' opinions of statewide testing programs. *Theory into Practice, 42*(1), 18–29.

Gulek, C. (2003). Preparing for high-stakes testing. *Theory into Practice, 42*(1), 42–50.

Kober, N. (2002). *Teaching to the test: The good, the bad, and who's responsible (TestTalk for Leaders,* Issue No. 1). Washington, D.C.: Center on Education Policy.

McMillan, J. H., Myran, S., & Workman, D. (1999). *The impact of mandated statewide testing on teachers' classroom assessment and instructional practices.* Paper presented at the annual meeting of the American Educational Research Association, Montreal, Canada.

Mehrens, W. A. (1991, April). *Defensible/indefensible instructional preparation for high stakes achievement tests: An exploratory trialogue.* Paper presented at the annual meeting of the American Educational Research Association, Chicago, IL.

National Staff Development Council. (2004). *NCLB: Survey finds many educators experience little positive NCLB impact on professional development.* Retrieved May 20, 2005, from www .nsdc.org/library/policy/NCLBsurvey2_04.cfm

Stecher, B. (2002). Consequences of large-scale, high-stakes testing on school and classroom practice. In L. S. Hamilton, B. M. Stecher, & S. P. Klein (Eds.), *Making Sense of Test-Based Accountability in Education.* (pp. 79–100). Santa Monica, CA: RAND.

Sunderman, G. L., Tracey, C. A., Kim, J., & Orfield, G. (2004). *Listening to Teachers: Classroom Realities and No Child Left Behind.* Cambridge, MA: The Civil Rights Project at Harvard University.

U.S. Department of Education. (2004). A guide to education and "No Child Left Behind." Retrieved September 10, 2005, from www.ed.gov/NCLB/overview/intro/guide/guide.pdf

DEVELOPMENTAL ACTIVITY

Planning for Your Research

This chapter's developmental activity is essentially a compilation of many of the exercises that you have already examined earlier in this chapter but in a more streamlined format. Think about the work you have done in previous chapters' developmental activities and respond to the following:

1. My preliminary research problem or topic

   _____

2. The type of research that seems most appropriate

   _____

3. My research questions and/or hypotheses

   _____

4. My justification for investigating this problem or topic (i.e., why I would argue that it is an important topic to investigate)

   _____

   _____

5. The main variables for my study

   _____

   _____

6. Descriptors that I am using for the identification of related literature

   _____

   _____

7. A potential outline of the major sections of my literature review

   I. _____

   II. _____

   III. _____

   IV. _____

   V. _____

8. My intended sample (who and how many)

_____

9. The type of sampling (if any) that seems most appropriate

_____

10. The type(s) of tool(s) that I plan to use to collect data

_____

_____

11. The statistical techniques that will be used to analyze my data—and ultimately answer my research questions/hypotheses

_____

_____

_____

CHAPTER SUMMARY

Careful advance planning is _extremely_ important if research is to give attention to necessary components, remain focused, and be finalized correctly and expeditiously. Attention must be given to each of the seven tasks discussed in this chapter, because all are essential and critical components of the process of designing and conducting a research study.

LIST OF IMPORTANT TERMS

cluster sample
convenience sample
judgmental sample
null hypothesis

qualitative data analysis
quantitative data analysis
quota sample
random sample

research design
research hypothesis
snowball sample
stratified sample

YOUR CURRENT STATUS

In this chapter, you have seen how research is planned. You are familiar with seven principal tasks to be completed when planning research. By completing the chapter exercises you have outlined a plan for actual research of your own that you should be able to use with confidence.

ACTIVITIES FOR THOUGHT AND DISCUSSION

Using the planning guide, develop an outline, consisting of no more than one page, of an investigation into one of the following topics:

1. Why students such as the members of your class pursue graduate studies in education

2. A comparison of the lecture–discussion method versus the self-guided study method for promoting achievement in classes in educational research

3. Factors that might serve to improve teacher morale and job satisfaction

4. The lines of work teachers believe they would prefer if they had career choices to make over again

REFERENCES AND RECOMMENDED READINGS

Bauman, J., Allen, J., & Shockley, B. (1994). *Research Questions Teachers Ask: A Report from the National Reading Research Center School Research Consortium* (Reading Research Report No. 30). Athens: Universities of Georgia and Maryland, National Reading Research Center.

Best, J., & Kahn, J. (2006). *Research in Education* (10th ed.). Boston: Allyn & Bacon.

Crowl, T. (1993). *Fundamentals of Educational Research.* Dubuque, IA: William C. Brown.

Eisner, E. (1992). A slice of advice. *Educational Researcher, 21*(5), 29–30.

Fleischer, C. (1994). Researching teacher-research: A practitioner's retrospective. *English Education, 26*(2), 86–126.

Gay, L. R., Mills, G. E., & Airasian, P. (2006). *Educational Research: Competencies for Analysis and Application* (8th ed.). Upper Saddle River, NJ: Merrill.

Glass, G. (1992). A slice of advice. *Educational Researcher, 21*(3), 23.

Kagan, D. (1992). Professional growth among preservice and beginning teachers. *Review of Educational Research, 62,* 129–169.

Kutz, E. (1992). Teacher research: Myths and realities. *Language Arts, 69,* 193–197.

McMillan, J. (2004). *Educational Research: Fundamentals for the Consumer* (4th ed.). Boston: Allyn & Bacon.

Padak, N., & Padak, G. (1995). *Guidelines for Planning Action Research Projects: Research to Practice.* Kent State University: Ohio Literacy Resource Center.

Ross, S. (1992). Getting started as a researcher: Designing and conducting research studies in instructional technology. *TechTrends, 37*(3), 19–22.

Schloss, P., & Smith, M. (1999). *Conducting Research.* Upper Saddle River, NJ: Prentice Hall.

Trochim, W. M. (2002). *The Research Methods Knowledge Base* (2nd ed.). Available at http://socialresearchmethods.net/kb/index.htm

Wiersma, W., & Jurs, S. (2005). *Research Methods in Education: An Introduction* (8th ed.). Boston: Allyn & Bacon.

Zeuli, J. (1992, April). *How Do Teachers Understand Research When They Read It?* Paper presented at the annual meeting of the American Educational Research Association, San Francisco, CA.

Preparing a Research Report

PREVIEW

This chapter is designed to help you learn to prepare research reports. Special attention is given to conventions of reporting that have to do with the following:

Format
- Introduction
- Relevant citations
- Procedures followed
- Results found
- Interpretations

Writing style
- Descriptive
- Clear, unemotional
- Third person, passive
- Tentative, not adamant
- Consistency in all

Also included are examples of the sections usually contained in research reports, including the following:

Front material
- Title
- Acknowledgments
- Abstract

Body
- Introduction
- Review of literature
- Procedures
- Findings
- Conclusions

Back material
- Bibliography
- Appendixes

TARGETED LEARNINGS

The purpose of this chapter is to help you learn to write research reports appropriate to your needs. Formats for theses, project papers, and articles are examined, and important conventions of style are described and explained. As you read the chapter, look especially for information related to the following:

1. What is meant by *convention*, and why are conventions important in reporting research?
2. What are the conventions of style regarding person, voice, tense, and consistency?
3. What are the four to six sections usually included in research reports?
4. Which section explains the plan for obtaining data?
5. In which of the sections is the investigator permitted to speculate on meanings and implications?
6. What is meant by *front material* and *back material*?
7. Who ultimately specifies the style and format that graduate students must use when preparing reports required in their programs?

CONVENTIONS IN RESEARCH AND REPORTING

You already know that the research process adheres to certain **conventions,** which are agreed-on procedures that help ensure the accuracy of data and findings. These conventions contribute to the validity of research and increase the confidence one can place in it. When research conventions are not followed, the credibility of the research is brought into question.

The same is true for research reports. They, too, are prepared according to conventions that promote both readability and credibility. It is important that you recognize and follow

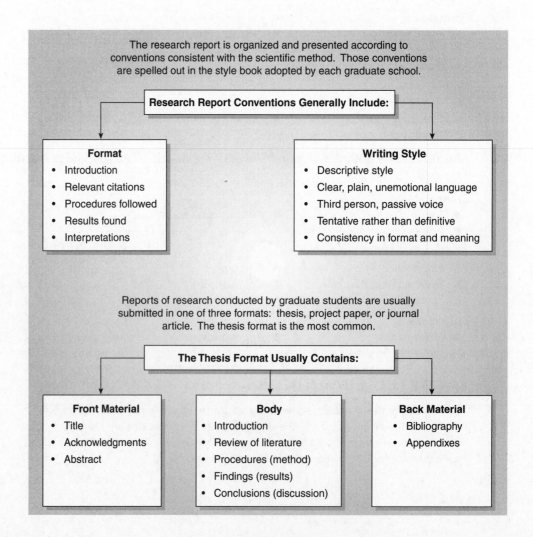

The research report is organized and presented according to conventions consistent with the scientific method. Those conventions are spelled out in the style book adopted by each graduate school.

Research Report Conventions Generally Include:

Format
- Introduction
- Relevant citations
- Procedures followed
- Results found
- Interpretations

Writing Style
- Descriptive style
- Clear, plain, unemotional language
- Third person, passive voice
- Tentative rather than definitive
- Consistency in format and meaning

Reports of research conducted by graduate students are usually submitted in one of three formats: thesis, project paper, or journal article. The thesis format is the most common.

The Thesis Format Usually Contains:

Front Material
- Title
- Acknowledgments
- Abstract

Body
- Introduction
- Review of literature
- Procedures (method)
- Findings (results)
- Conclusions (discussion)

Back Material
- Bibliography
- Appendixes

these conventions when preparing your research report. Failure to do so does not render research invalid, but just as one's credibility as an educator can be damaged by the use of incorrect grammar, so can a researcher's credibility be damaged by using unconventional report styles and formats.

STYLE GUIDES

myeducationlab *for research*

To learn more about APA style, go to the "Preparing a Research Report" section of **MyEducationLab for Research** and then click on *Assignments and Activities*. Complete the exercise titled "APA Reference Style." This exercise consists of a practice tutorial for APA style.

When preparing theses or dissertations, you are expected to follow the **style guide** of the institution through which your work is done. Some colleges and universities have prepared their own guides. Others have adopted existing stylebooks, such as the following well-known and widely used examples:

American Psychological Association. (2010). *Publication Manual of the American Psychological Association* (6th ed.). Washington, DC: American Psychological Association. (Note: This is frequently called "APA style.")

Campbell, W., Ballou, S., & Slade, C. (1990). *Form and Style: Theses, Reports, Term Papers* (8th ed.). Boston: Houghton Mifflin. (Note: This is often referred to as "Campbell.")

Gibaldi, J. (2003). *MLA Handbook for Writers of Research Papers* (6th ed.). New York: Modern Language Association of America. (Note: This is frequently called "MLA style.")

Turabian, K. (1996). *A Manual for Writers of Term Papers, Theses, and Dissertations* (6th ed.). Chicago: University of Chicago Press. (Note: This is often referred to as "Turabian.")

University of Chicago Press. (2003). *The Chicago Manual of Style: The Essential Guide for Authors, Editors, and Publishers* (15th ed.). Chicago: University of Chicago Press. (Note: This is frequently called "Chicago style.")

The APA Manual is arguably the most commonly used style guide in the broad field of education. Many researchers have for years relied on the APA Manual for providing the wide variety of formats for citing references. However, the APA Manual provides much more in the way of stylistic information for researchers, including the following aspects of writing up research:

- Organization and format of a manuscript
- Expressing ideas and reducing bias in written language
- Editorial style (e.g., punctuation, capitalization, abbreviations, headings, quotations, expression of numbers including statistical information within the text)
- Formatting tables, figures, and footnotes
- Reference formats

Specific directions have not been provided in this chapter for preparing front and back material, for citing references, or for presenting tables and figures. Each graduate school or professional journal has adopted a style it prefers; it is important for you to familiarize yourself with the appropriate preferred style. Scholarly journals also have styles they prefer, and when you submit an article for publication you are expected to use that journal's style. Journals will inform you of the required style or send you a style sheet on request; or you can examine published articles to determine the style expected. Style guides, and in particular the APA Manual, are invaluable resources for the educational researcher.

CONVENTIONS OF STYLE

Several conventions of research reporting have to do with writing style, chiefly those concerning (1) titles of reports; (2) person, voice, and tense; (3) tentative and definitive statements; (4) simplicity of language; and (5) consistency of style and meanings. Let us briefly consider these conventions. Keep in mind that none is necessarily a hard-and-fast rule (unless, of course, your graduate adviser says it is), but you cannot go wrong by following conventional approaches.

TITLE

Earlier chapters stressed that the title of a research report should indicate clearly what the report is about. Catchy, clever titles should be avoided unless by chance they happen to describe the topic accurately. Readers of research rely on titles to indicate whether reports deal with topics they particularly wish to read about. For that reason, titles of research reports are sometimes rather long, though writers generally try to limit titles to no more than 15 words.

Exercise 9.1

Suppose you have completed a study of the history of racial integration of students in Elmwood schools. In view of the convention about titles, which of the following would be the best title for your report?

_____ 1. Elmwood Schools—When They Were Trying to Find the Way

_____ 2. Elmwood Schools Dismissed Color as a Criterion

_____ 3. A History of Racial Integration of Students in Elmwood Public Schools

_____ 4. In the Days When Elmwood Schools Learned to Say "No" to Segregation

_____ 5. Desegregation in Elmwood Schools

_____ 6. Elmwood Schools Find They Can Open Their Doors to All Students without the System Collapsing

PERSON AND VOICE

Generally speaking, qualitative research reports are written in the first person. This is done in an attempt to capture individuals' thoughts, feelings, or interpretations of meaning and process, including the thoughts and feelings of the researcher/author. Furthermore, qualitative research reports tend to be written using active as opposed to passive voice. In a sentence using active voice, the subject of the sentence performs the action expressed in the verb: *The student gave her book report to the class.* On the other hand, in a sentence using passive voice, the subject is acted upon, receiving the action expressed by the verb: *A book report was given by the student to the class.*

In contrast, quantitative research reports are typically written in the third person, although this convention is beginning to change. Usually, the authors do not refer to themselves as "I" or "we," but rather as "the author" or "the researchers." This is typically done deliberately, in order to represent the objectivity incorporated into quantitative studies. Also in quantitative research, the passive voice, rather than the active, is used extensively. Researchers write "It was found that . . ." or "The following conclusions were reached . . ." (both passive voice), rather than "The writer found . . ." or "The investigator reached the following conclusions . . ." (both active voice).

TENSE

Research reports are written mostly in the past tense. This is almost exclusively true for sections that report the purpose of the study, the procedures, the findings, and the conclusions. (Note that *research proposals,* unlike reports, tend to use the future tense.) Typical statements in reports might include

The purpose of this study was to . . .

The following steps were taken in obtaining data . . .

It was found that . . .

The data seemed to warrant the following conclusions . . .

Sometimes the present tense is used in the introduction of the report, together with the past tense. For example:

For many years investigators have sought . . . and today they are still seeking . . .

The present tense is used, too, in reports that describe ongoing research, from which additional reports will follow, as in the following example:

The principal implications presently warranted by the data include . . .

TENTATIVE VERSUS DEFINITIVE STATEMENTS

Researchers use tentative statements to report their conclusions. It is not considered correct to present any conclusions as absolutely certain, but rather to show that there always remains some room for doubt, as in the following examples:

The data seem to suggest . . .

The following conclusions appeared to be warranted . . .

The true mean probably lies between . . .

You can be a bit more definite when reporting data and statistics because an accepted margin of error is presumed to exist. It is proper to use statements such as

The mean and standard deviation were . . .

Seventy-two percent of the respondents indicated . . .

The coefficient of correlation was . . .

And, of course, you should be quite definite and precise when describing procedures you followed in conducting the research.

SIMPLICITY OF LANGUAGE

Quantitative research reports should be written in plain language, rather than rhetorical approaches that are more widely accepted in qualitative research. The reporting of qualitative research necessitates highly descriptive language. Its "job," if you will, is to paint a detailed picture of the phenomenon under investigation. Notice the use of adjectives to help describe the intensity of teachers' feelings in the passage below:

Generally speaking, these teachers believed that the intensive two-week workshop on classroom assessment was highly beneficial to their work as classroom teachers. Many of them expressed a great deal of hesitancy at the beginning of the workshop, but felt much more confident following its completion. All of the teachers commented on the overall impact that they believed the workshop had on them, focusing on its intensity and on its importance. A couple of the teachers believed that the most valuable aspect of the workshop was the fact that it "forced" teachers to stop and critically examine what they do in their classes from an assessment perspective.

In quantitative research, you are supposed to get straight to the point, objectively and unemotionally, without attempting to use a "literary style." The following is an example of writing from a quantitative report that contains excessive wordiness:

> The purpose of this extremely involved study was to explore from every conceivable angle the impossible demands that have been placed on the dedicated faculty members of five highly touted middle schools.

More acceptable wording for that same introduction removes the overuse of adjectives and adverbs, as follows:

> The purpose of this study was to investigate the working conditions of classroom teachers in five different middle schools.

Just remember that people read research reports not for entertainment but to make themselves better informed. The bottom line is, of course, that you need to explain your research well enough so that readers can understand your procedures and findings, but while you do so, keep your message clear.

CONSISTENCY

When writing research reports you should strive for consistency in style, word usage, meanings, and special symbols. If you indent direct quotations on each side, do so the same way every time. When using statistical or other special symbols, be sure always to use the same marks in the same way, even though several interchangeable symbols (such as those to indicate standard deviation) are commonly seen. You should also format chapters, sections, headings, charts, tables, and figures in a consistent manner.

Exercise 9.2

Find what needs to be improved in each of the following statements. Reword each statement according to recommended conventions.

1. I decided to undertake this study for two reasons.

_____

2. The data conclusively prove the following:

_____

3. Until a scant two years ago, teachers who clung to the time-treasured ways of motivating their classroom charges were made the objects of derision.

_____

4. The following are the steps I was following in my study:

    a. January 13: I go to the district office to check school records.
    b. I spend January 15 through the 25 making notes of discrepancies in the entries.
    c. On January 26 the investigator meets with the personnel director to discuss the discrepancies.

_____

_____

_____

CONVENTIONS OF FORMAT

Research reports contain four to six major sections, depending on the report, and always include an introduction, a description of the procedures followed, a presentation of findings, and a presentation of conclusions. Often, a short review of related literature is incorporated, and many reports conclude with a discussion of the findings and new questions that have arisen.

These sections are sometimes, but not always, labeled in journal articles, as you have probably seen. Even when they are not labeled, you should not have much difficulty recognizing the sections; they are usually there, according to convention. (You may notice, however, that it is much easier to read reports that contain clear headings.) In theses and dissertations, the principal sections are clearly labeled either with headings or chapter titles. When you write your research report, you will very likely be expected to label the sections in that way.

myeducationlab
for research

To help you better understand the various elements of a research report, go to the "Preparing a Research Report" section of **MyEducationLab for Research** and then click on *Assignments and Activities*. Complete the exercise titled "The Sections of a Research Report." This exercise asks you to list important or typical components of each section of a report.

INTRODUCTION

Introductions specify the topic and tell why it merits attention. In theses and dissertations, the introduction is presented as "Chapter 1." In journal articles and technical reports this section may be labeled "Introduction," but frequently you will simply encounter introductory paragraphs that indicate the topic (which should be made clear in the title), establish its importance, and tell the specific purpose of the research being reported.

In theses and dissertations, the introductory chapter contains additional items not normally found in short reports, such as the following.

Rationale

It is critical to provide a rationale for your research study. In your rationale, you should be prepared to justify *why* the topic is important and worthy of investigation, *who* could potentially benefit from its results, and *how* that group of individuals may benefit.

Statement of the Problem

A concise description of the problem being investigated. In some formats this is simply called "The Problem," and it tells specifically what the investigation was intended to explore. (For example, "The purpose of this study was to explore the relationship between muscularity and running speed among high school basketball players.")

Hypotheses

Hypotheses are conjectures the investigator intends to test. Recall that there are three types of hypotheses: directional research hypotheses, nondirectional research hypotheses, and null hypotheses, each demonstrated in the following examples:

1. More muscular players have a faster running speed than do less muscular players. *(a directional research hypothesis)*
2. A difference in running speed exists between more muscular players and less muscular players. *(a nondirectional research hypothesis)*
3. No difference in running speed exists between more muscular players and less muscular players. *(a null hypothesis)*

Research Questions

Questions may be used instead of hypotheses for orientation in many types of investigation. As you recall, research questions are often organized into one or more main questions and are followed by a number of related subquestions. As subquestions are answered, one hopes to become able to answer the main research question.

Operational Definitions of Terms

This is a section of the report in which operational definitions are given for words, acronyms, abbreviations, names, labels, and the like that are central to the study. In the investigation of the relationship between body weight and running speed among basketball players, for example, you would be expected to define what you mean by the terms *high school basketball players, muscularity, more muscular, less muscular,* and *running speed.*

Limitations and Delimitations

This section describes the limits that *naturally* affect your study (limitations) and limits that you have imposed on your study (delimitations). Limitations on the muscularity–speed study might be that only high school athletes are involved, that they can be measured only at a particular time of the year, and that they have agreed to be tested. Delimitations that you impose might be that the participants are males, that they are of selected ethnic groups, and that they are members of varsity and junior varsity basketball squads.

REVIEW OF RELATED LITERATURE

You are expected to review literature related to the problem of your study for three purposes: (1) determine whether studies already exist similar to the one you propose to do, (2) possibly obtain guidance for the investigation of your topic, and (3) establish a point of departure or a platform on which to build your research.

With the literature review, you inform readers about published research that is related to, but different from, your topic. In theses and dissertations, the review you present is usually quite long; it typically constitutes a separate chapter. If the review is short, it may be included in Chapter 1. Journal articles and technical reports tend to mention in an early paragraph only a few of the most important related studies, as indicated in the following illustration (please note that the citations are fictitious):

> In the later 1990s, discipline continued to rank highest among all teacher concerns (Smith, 1998). In fact, Allison and McCarthy (1998) found discipline problems to be the leading cause of teacher failure and the second leading cause of teacher stress. Concern about discipline has led several investigators to explore alternative discipline systems (Childers, 1997; Harrison, 1998), along with new training programs in behavior management (Paterno, 1997; Sánchez, 1997).

There are no hard-and-fast rules for organizing longer literature reviews, but the following guidelines, presented previously in Chapter 5, facilitate reading and add to the persuasiveness of your report:

1. *Begin with the most general information and end with the most specific.* If you are studying school discipline, you would report studies that indicate it is a widespread problem before you report that it causes stress, and you would report that discipline skills can be taught before reporting on specific training programs.

2. *Begin with older studies and move toward more recent studies.* This progression shows lines of thought and refinement that have occurred over time.

3. *Group your references within the categories you have identified in your research problem.* If you are using research questions and subquestions, a natural organization is to report general findings related to the main question and then specific findings related to each of the subquestions. If you are conducting a historical study, you might group literature by years or decades; if a study is descriptive, you might group by various topics you wish to describe; if it is action research or development, you might group reports according to their similarity to the innovation you have developed and implemented.

4. *When you report what you consider to be particularly important studies, use adjectives that indicate your evaluation.* For example, you might write, "In a landmark study, Jones (1995) . . ." or "Smith's (1996) controversial study."

Exercise 9.3

Suppose you are reporting action research in which you have developed and implemented a new system of discipline in your school. For your review of the literature, you want to report research findings that cluster around certain themes, which are shown in the following list. Number the blanks to indicate the best order for presenting the themes and their related literature:

_____   **1.** Rules and practices that promote good classroom behavior

_____   **2.** The relationship of discipline to achievement

_____   **3.** Support from others that helps teachers enjoy better discipline

_____   **4.** The outcry over what is seen to be lack of discipline in the schools

_____   **5.** Traits and practices of teachers identified as having better behaved classes

_____   **6.** The effects of serious classroom misbehavior on teachers and students

_____   **7.** Elements and emphases in various programs for developing teacher skills in discipline

_____   **8.** Two training programs implemented at schools in other states

PROCEDURES OR METHOD

The third major section of research reports is labeled either "Procedures" or "Method" and typically comprises Chapter 3 in theses and dissertations. Here, the investigator reports step-by-step what was done in the study. Journal articles may or may not use a heading to indicate this section of the report, but, in any case, it can easily be found due to its contents.

There is no prescribed format for recounting procedures, but the following suggestions will make your presentation more easily understood by your readers.

1. In longer reports, especially in theses and dissertations, begin by repeating the purpose of the study (i.e., the problem statement). In short reports, this is not necessary.
2. Describe the design of your study. In this portion, indicate
   a. Hypotheses or questions
   b. Sources of information
   c. People involved and how they were selected
   d. Other important resources used in the study
   e. Tests, measuring devices, and other instruments
   f. Procedures used in data analysis
   In theses and dissertations, the research design should be described in detail. In shorter reports, a brief description is sufficient.

3. Group the procedures into categories—for example: sample, measurement, data analysis. Then describe, step-by-step, what you did in each.

All of this has two purposes: first, to show that in your research you proceeded scientifically and followed established conventions, and second, to enable readers to follow and understand what you did. This also encourages enlightened criticism of your work. You can expect others to ask questions about, or take exception to, the way you have conducted your investigation. It also permits your study to be replicated if someone wishes, which is important in building a reliable body of research evidence and conclusions.

FINDINGS OR RESULTS

The next major section included in research reports is called either "Findings" or "Results" and is usually presented as Chapter 4 in theses and dissertations. Because this portion of the report is so important, it is usually given a heading of some sort, even in shorter papers.

In this section, you summarize the new information you have discovered. If your report is long, you may want to repeat the hypotheses or research questions and then show the results of the analysis of data related to each hypothesis or question.

Results are reported verbally and are usually supported with tables and figures. Tables frequently show numerical data and indicate statistical analyses. Figures illustrate or clarify findings in formats such as graphs, charts, drawings, computer printouts, and the like.

You should use tables and figures whenever they can add clarity to what you are describing. Suppose you are a middle school English teacher doing action research on students' preferences for the writings of Blume, O'Dell, and Bradbury. You could report verbally that out of a sample of 100 boys and 100 girls, a certain number preferred each of the writers, but doing so would require a long paragraph of information that could be confusing. You would do better to present the information in a table, as shown in Table 9.1. (The data in the table are fictitious.) You can see how clearly the information stands out when presented in concise tabular form.

On the other hand, for graphic presentations of data that cannot be presented as rows and columns of numerals, you can use figures to clarify the information. Any sort of graphic depiction, other than rows and columns, can be called a figure. Bar and line graphs are common formats. You could use a bar graph to illustrate the comparative preferences of boys and girls for the writings of Blume, O'Dell, and Bradbury, as in Figure 9.1. (Note that in tables the title is placed at the top; in figures it may be placed either above, below, or to the side of the illustration. To be sure, you should consult the style guide used in your graduate program.)

Verbal descriptions accompany tables and figures to ensure that readers understand correctly what is being shown. To accompany the table in your report, you might write

Table 9.1 shows the preferences of boys and girls for the writings of the three authors. The difference between the two groups was significant at the .01 level, as shown in the chi-square analysis presented in Table 9.2.

Table 9.1   Preferences among 200 Eighth-Grade Students for the Writings of Blume, O'Dell, and Bradbury

	Blume	O'Dell	Bradbury
Girls	42	38	20
Boys	18	33	49

Figure 9.1

The preferences of 200 eighth-grade boys and girls for the writings of Blume, O'Dell, and Bradbury

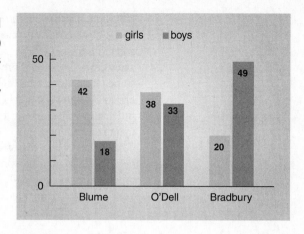

To accompany the figure you might write

> The graph shown in Figure 9.1 illustrates the comparative preferences of boys and girls for the writings of the three authors. Evident is the apparent preference among girls for the works of Blume and the apparent preference among boys for the works of Bradbury.

The information shown in tables and figures should be related to specific hypotheses or research questions set forth in the study. Hypotheses may at this point be either retained or rejected, based on data analysis. If you used research questions instead of, or in addition to, hypotheses, it is at this point that you state answers you judge to be warranted by the data. In answering the questions, you proceed as follows:

- Look at each subquestion separately and select data and the subsequent results related to it.
- Examine the data logically (there are no formulas for this process) and arrive at the answer you deem appropriate.

For example, in a historical study of education in the ghost town of Bodie you might include the question "How did students get to school in the winter?" Based on subquestions, you have obtained the following information: (1) Several pairs of long wooden skis

Table 9.2   Chi-Square Analysis of Differences in Boys' and Girls' Preferences for the Writings of Blume, O'Dell, and Bradbury

	Observed			**Expected**		
	Blume	*O'Dell*	*Bradbury*	*Blume*	*O'Dell*	*Bradbury*
Girls	42	38	20	33.3	33.3	33.3
Boys	18	33	49	33.3	33.3	33.3

o	*e*	*(o − e)*	*(o − e)²*	*(o − e)²/e*
42	30	12.0	144.00	4.80
18	30	−12.0	144.00	4.80
38	35.5	2.5	6.25	0.18
33	35.5	−2.5	6.25	0.18
20	34.5	−14.5	210.25	6.09
49	34.5	14.5	210.25	6.09

$$\chi^2 = 22.14$$
$$df = 2 \quad sig < .01$$

still remain in the cloakroom of the classroom; (2) among the student compositions found in the classroom was one describing coming to school on skis when the snow was deep; and (3) a former Bodie student (now an elderly man) described to you how students used snowshoes or skis but preferred skis because they were faster. From that and the fact that some of the homes had horse corrals, you conclude that "students probably got to school on skis or snowshoes when the snow was deep but walked or rode horses when there was little snow." The answer to each of the individual subquestions contributes to answering the main research question.

In theses and dissertations, you would be obliged to present your data in sufficient detail so that other persons could apply their own logic to answering the questions. If you report your work in a shorter form such as a journal article, others might request sets of your data for further study.

CONCLUSIONS OR DISCUSSION

In the fifth section of most research reports you present and discuss the conclusions you have reached in your investigation. Sometimes, especially in theses and dissertations, this section is called "Conclusions and Recommendations." In shorter reports, it may be labeled "Findings" or "Findings and Implications."

In this final section, you at last have the opportunity to interpret, speculate on, and otherwise discuss the conclusions you have reached. This portion is often quite enlightening because it contains the thoughts of the person most intimately involved in seeking answers and exploring meanings and implications—the researcher herself or himself. Here you may discuss errors you inadvertently made, problems you encountered unexpectedly, your surprise at the findings, or other related matters that help readers understand your research efforts and the conclusions you reached.

More than anything else, it is this portion of the report that allows you to tell what you believe the findings mean, how you have interpreted them, what they imply for education, or what they suggest for further research. This is the one place in the report where you are allowed to speculate a bit, to move a little beyond hard evidence and stringent logic. For the study of education in Bodie, you would be allowed the following analysis:

> A day at Bodie School, while unlike that in today's modern schools, was probably typical of most rural schools in the early 1930s. Everyone—students, teachers, and parents—seemed to have been a bit more resourceful than is now the case, because they had to make do with less. Yet the students still learned their subjects as well as do students today. Teachers had more authority then; their discipline and teaching methods were standardized and were supported by parents. But while they had fewer resources to use in teaching, their concerns about the growth and well-being of their students seem not to have been very different from those of teachers today.

FRONT AND BACK MATERIAL

Front and back material are portions of the report that come before and after the main body. Theses and dissertations contain both. Typical **front material** includes

- Title page
- Signature page (for advisers to sign and date)
- Acknowledgment page
- Table of contents
- List of tables
- List of figures
- Abstract

Typical **back material** includes

- Bibliography (complete list of references and other resources)
- Appendix or appendixes (materials used or produced in the study but that occupy too much space to be included in the body of the report)

Journal articles and other short reports typically have no front material, though some present a very helpful abstract at the beginning of the article. Their back material is usually limited to the list of references cited in the report.

A COMPOSITE OUTLINE OF FORMAT CONVENTIONS

The following outline shows typical format conventions for theses, dissertations, journal articles, technical reports, and occasional papers.

Theses and Dissertations	Articles and Papers
■ Title page	■ Title
■ Signature page	
■ Acknowledgment page	
■ Table of contents	
■ List of tables	
■ List of figures	
■ Title	
■ Abstract (one page)	■ Abstract paragraph, optional
■ Introduction (Chapter 1) Rationale Identify problem Discuss importance Present background State hypotheses/questions Define terms State limitations and delimitations	■ Introductory paragraph(s) Rationale Identify problem Discuss importance Present background State hypotheses/questions
■ Review of literature (Chapter 2) General to specific Older to newer Relate to hypotheses/questions Organize into categories	■ Literature may be reviewed very briefly in introduction
■ Procedures and methods (Chapter 3) Give step-by-step description of research design, participants, instruments, and what was done to collect and analyze data	■ Procedures section Summarize what was done, how, and when, in collecting and analyzing data
■ Findings or results (Chapter 4) Organize by hypotheses or research questions Present in tables and figures Answer questions, test hypotheses	
■ Conclusions (Chapter 5) Present investigator's conclusions Discuss implications	■ Conclusions and discussion Present investigator's conclusions Discuss implications
■ Bibliography List references cited and any used but not cited	■ References List references cited
■ Appendix or appendixes Attach important material used or produced in the study but too lengthy to be included in the body of the report	

SAMPLE PAGES

The following are samples that you can use as general guides or models when preparing research reports. It is critical to remember that each institution and journal has its own approved format that you will be expected to follow. We consider shorter reports first and then proceed to thesis formats.

FOR RESEARCH PAPERS AND JOURNAL ARTICLES

[*fictitious*]
THE APPLICATION OF SELECTED SCHOOL EFFECTIVENESS
FACTORS IN TWELVE REGIONAL SECONDARY SCHOOLS
by
Ira Cartwright
Director of Instructional Improvement
Excellence, Michigan Schools

ABSTRACT

Four selected `school effectiveness factors" were systematically introduced into 12 regional high schools. At the end of the first year, student achievement showed significant improvement over what had been normal for the school. Student attitude toward school improved significantly, as did teacher professional satisfaction.

INTRODUCTION

For the past two decades, student achievement in secondary school has remained static or has declined. Yet at the same time, a number of schools have been identified as highly successful. Many investigators, notably Shumate and Hall (1994), Gromald (1995), Rimes and Cortez (1996), Colbertson (1997), and Khoury (1998), have explored factors that seem to characterize these successful schools and differentiate them from schools considered to be relatively ineffective. Their conclusions have been that highly effective schools show the following characteristics . . . [*continued*]

THE PROBLEM

The purpose of this study was to determine whether selected effectiveness characteristics, when incorporated into ongoing scholastic programs and maintained for one academic year, could raise student achievement and improve the attitudes of students and teachers. In particular, the study was intended to seek answers to the following questions . . . [*continued*]

PROCEDURES

To obtain information for answering the research questions set forth in this study, the following steps were taken:

1. Twelve regional secondary schools were selected for inclusion in the study. The schools were [names]. Approval for involvement was obtained from school board, faculty, and administration.

2. The individuals from whom data were obtained included all the students and teachers in the 12 selected schools who were present on the date of final testing.

3. Four selected effectiveness factors were introduced into the scholastic programs of the participating schools. Those four factors were [*name and define*]. The factors were introduced as follows: [*describe how*]. Training and follow-up sessions were conducted [*describe when and how*].

4. At the end of the school year, student achievement was measured through use of [*name tests*]. The data were analyzed by [*describe*]. Student attitudes and teacher attitude were assessed by means of [*name instruments*]. The data were analyzed by [*describe*].

FINDINGS

Data analysis revealed the following: [*explain in relation to each of the research questions*]. The findings are presented in Table 1, Table 2, and Table 3. [*Show tables and explain contents beneath each table.*] [*continued*]

CONCLUSIONS

Concerning achievement, the findings show growth significantly beyond the levels reached by similar students over the past 10 years and significantly higher than those of students in schools used as controls for this study. This result seems to be due to . . .

The attitude ratings of both students and teachers were also significantly higher than those of students and teachers in the control schools. This seems to have been due to . . . Based on the results of this study, it seems evident that . . . It seems fair to suggest that school districts elsewhere consider . . .

REFERENCES

[*list alphabetically by writers' last names*]

FOR MASTERS' THESES

The following are sample pages that can serve as general guides in preparing graduate theses. The first sample is from a thesis that reported an action research project. The second sample indicates a possible format for theses that report other types of research.

For a Thesis That Reports Action Research

[*title page—one page*]
CHILDREN'S LITERATURE BROUGHT ALIVE:
A LITERATURE PROGRAM TO
ENCOURAGE STUDENTS TO READ

A Paper
Presented to the Faculty of
Excel University in
Partial Fulfillment
of the Requirements for the Degree

Master of Arts in Education
by
Marcella Louise Cox
Spring 1998

[*next page—separate page*]

ACKNOWLEDGMENTS

The writer wishes to express her gratitude to the following people, who encouraged, supported, and assisted in the development of the project: [*list*]

[*new page*]

TABLE OF CONTENTS

[*new single page*]

ABSTRACT

The purpose of this project was to develop and implement a holistic procedure for encouraging intermediate-grade children to develop interest in reading, through exposure to and involvement with a variety of quality children's literature and activities related to it.

The project was designed to call on each student to read storybooks selected from various genres of children's literature. The students were involved in activities related to their reading, including readers' theater, choral reading, creative writing, drama, and art.

The program was put into effect as follows: First, students were assessed to determine their individual levels of reading ability. Second, they were given interest inventories to help in the selection of books. Third, appropriate books were selected for each student. Fourth, each student received a personalized plan that included assignments, schedules, and partners. Fifth, students read their books and participated in associated activities. Sixth, students prepared materials, worked on performances, and presented performances to family members and other classrooms.

Ongoing assessment of student involvement, enjoyment, and progress showed the program to be highly successful.

[*new page*]

CHAPTER I

INTRODUCTION AND STATEMENT OF THE PROBLEM

During the first year that the writer taught a fifth—sixth grade class, she noted how differently students behaved according to what they were asked to do during reading lessons. On the three days per week that they were to work from their grade-level reading books, they groaned and asked, "Do we have to read the whole story today?" and "Do we have to answer all the questions at the end of the story?"

In contrast, on the two days per week they were involved in children's literature, they showed interest and excitement. Typical questions for those days were, "Can we make scenery for readers' theater?" and "Can we make a skit out of the story?"

The writer began to believe that the reading program could contribute much more strongly to building student enjoyment of reading if it were based on selected literature rather than on the grade-level readers.

Such a program would have to be well organized and balanced to include all areas of skill development. This would then permit . . . [*Continue in this vein so as to lead into a statement of the problem, but do not describe anything that was actually done in the project.*]

THE PROBLEM

The purpose of this study was to organize and implement a holistic procedure for helping children develop interest in reading through exposure to and involvement with a variety of children's literature. Such a procedure would include literature of the following genres: picture books, traditional literature, modern fantasy, poetry, contemporary realistic fiction, historical fiction, biography, and nonfiction. Further, it would engage the children in creative and artistic activities, such as painting, designing, acting, pantomiming, and batiking. The program would be balanced to include skill development in word attack, oral and silent reading, and comprehension of theme, character, and meaning.

DEFINITION OF TERMS

Terms central to this study are defined as follows:

Holistic [*define*]

Modern fantasy [*define*]

[*continued*]

DELIMITATIONS

The writer restricted the study as follows:

Program development: The writer selected the books and developed the materials, activities, and guides for the program.

Participants: Participants in the study were the students in the writer's fifth—sixth-grade combination class.

Time period: The time during which the project was planned and implemented was restricted as follows: The project was prepared over a period of four months—September, October, November, and December. The project was implemented and appraised over a period of three months—January, February, and March. [*continued*]

[*new page*]

CHAPTER II
INFORMATION AND RESOURCES

This project relied heavily on the collection of reading materials representing various genres, namely, picture books, traditional literature, modern fantasy, realistic fiction, historical fiction, biography, and nonfiction. It was anticipated by the writer that a minimum of 8 to 10 books within each genre would be required for the project.

The initial list of books developed by the writer contained a minimum of 15 books per category. Several sources, including the local library, children's literature guides, and various school district reading specialists, were contacted in order to develop a preliminary list of books within each category and to determine the local availability of specific books within each category. Following the determination of the local availability of the necessary number of copies of each book, the final list of books to be used in the project was determined. These books, organized by genre, included:[*continued*]

[*new page*]

CHAPTER III
PROCEDURES

The writer began by selecting children's literature in eight genres: picture books, traditional literature, modern fantasy, poetry, contemporary realistic fiction, historical fiction, biography, and nonfiction. Considerations in book selection included variety, overall story quality, depiction of various ethnic groups, balance between boys and girls as main characters, and quality of illustrations.

When the book selection process was completed, a number of different activities were planned for each book and genre. These activities were incorporated into a teacher's guide that consisted of three parts:

1. Assessment instruments to determine reading ability and areas of interest.
2. Contracts, schedules, and notebook formats for students to follow and use.
3. Books students were to read, activities they were to complete, and performances they were to make. The writer then proceeded to collect and make quantities of materials, such as . . .

[*Proceed in this fashion to describe, step-by-step, what was done in the project.*]

[*new page*]

CHAPTER IV
FINDINGS

The writer was successful in producing a literature-based reading program that incorporated writing, art, music, and drama. Compared to the writer's previous reading program, the diversity and quality of these new activities attracted greater student interest and promoted greater degrees of student involvement.

Three problems were encountered when the project was first introduced into the writer's classroom. Those problems were . . . [*list and describe*]

To correct those problems, the following modifications were made in the program . . . [*list and describe*]

Preliminary assessment completed after the program had been in place for three months suggested that student achievement in basic reading skills was as high, or higher, than in the reading program the writer used previously.

[*new page*]

CHAPTER V
CONCLUSIONS

This project demonstrated how a reading program based on children's literature could be organized to include writing, art, music, and drama—a diversity of activity that greatly increases student interest in reading while maintaining necessary emphasis on the acquisition of reading skills.

The enthusiasm that students showed for the activities suggests that the program could be continued indefinitely and could perhaps be spread into other areas of the curriculum as well. [*Continue with observations about the project and thoughts about how it could be improved, expanded, and adopted by other teachers.*]

[*new page*]

APPENDIXES

[*Present here the guides, lists of materials, photographs, and so forth that depict what was developed and implemented in the project. If there is more than one appendix, present a heading for each—e.g., Appendix A: Description of the Project; Appendix B: Teacher's Guide for the Reading Program; Appendix C: Lesson Plans Used in the Program, etc.*]

Thesis Format for Other Types of Research

Theses that report types of research other than action research differ somewhat from the example just presented, in keeping with the characteristics of the research being reported. Let us take as an example a thesis that reports an experiment to determine the effectiveness of "quality school factors" applied in two secondary schools.

[*title page*]

THE EFFECTIVENESS OF QUALITY SCHOOL FACTORS
DETERMINED THROUGH IMPLEMENTATION
IN TWO SELECTED SECONDARY SCHOOLS
[*remainder of page the same as shown previously*]

ACKNOWLEDGMENTS
[*same as shown previously*]

ABSTRACT
[*a one-page summary of the study*]

TABLE OF CONTENTS

[*new page*]

CHAPTER I

INTRODUCTION

[*Begins much the same as the sample provided for action research and development but contains more elements and background information, as indicated in the Table of Contents.*]

[*new page*]

CHAPTER II

REVIEW OF THE LITERATURE

[*Describes literature related to the topic, grouped according to hypotheses and research questions. The presentation is organized to move from general to specific and from older to more recent literature.*]

[*new page*]

REMAINING CHAPTERS

[*Similar to the samples provided for the action research report. See Table of Contents for specific differences.*]

DEVELOPMENTAL ACTIVITY

Preparing to Write Your Report

Writing lengthy, comprehensive scientific reports requires some skill . . . and a great deal of practice. Novice researchers typically find it helpful to anticipate the "look" of their report and to do some degree of preparation *prior* to actually writing the final report. One helpful procedure is to develop a thorough outline of the report, specifying the major headings and subheadings you will use throughout. You then write your report around this outline. Such an outline has been started for you here, with the major section or chapter headings provided. For this activity, complete the outline by specifying the subheadings you anticipate using for your report. Be aware that, depending on your topic and research, you may require fewer or more entries than have been provided; you may also want to use another level of heading.

  I. Introduction

    A. _____

    B. _____

    C. _____

D. _____

E. _____

II. Review of Related Literature

A. _____

B. _____

C. _____

D. _____

E. _____

III. Methodology

A. _____

B. _____

C. _____

D. _____

E. _____

IV. Results

A. _____

B. _____

C. _____

D. _____

E. _____

V. Conclusions and Recommendations

A. _____

B. _____

C. _____

D. _____

E. _____

CHAPTER SUMMARY

Graduate students usually report their research in thesis format and sometimes in formats appropriate for technical papers or journal articles. The reports are done in keeping with conventions of style and format. Although there are differences among types of reports, certain conventions apply to all.

Conventions of acceptable style include descriptive titles, plain language, use of third person, passive voice, use of past tense, consistent organization, and consistent meanings of terminology.

Research formats are organized to include an introduction, statement of the problem, hypotheses or research questions, review of related literature, procedures, findings, and conclusions. Some variation exists in the terminology used to denote these sections of reports.

Reports often include front and back material. Examples of front material are tables of contents and abstracts; examples of back material are bibliographies and appendixes.

LIST OF IMPORTANT TERMS

back material

conventions

front material

style guide

YOUR CURRENT STATUS

You have completed the activities designed to enable you to conduct and report research of your own. The remaining chapters, Chapters 10 through 16, present detailed descriptions of the nature and procedures of the nine types of educational research as determined by the questions asked.

ACTIVITIES FOR THOUGHT AND DISCUSSION

1. Here are the questions listed at the beginning of the chapter. See how well you can answer them.
   a. What is meant by *convention,* and why are conventions important in reporting research?
   b. What are the conventions of style regarding person, voice, tense, and consistency?
   c. What are the four to six sections usually included in research reports?
   d. Which section explains the plan for obtaining data?
   e. In which of the sections is the investigator permitted to speculate on meanings and implications?
   f. What is meant by *front material* and *back material*?
   g. Who ultimately specifies the style and format that graduate students must use when preparing reports required in their programs?

2. Recall the information organizer presented at the beginning of the chapter. For a topic you are interested in researching, see how well you can use the organizer to plan a research report.

ANSWERS TO CHAPTER EXERCISES

9.1. Choice 3 is the best title.

9.2. Each answer is a suggested revision; close variations are acceptable as well as alternate versions that can be justified.
1. This study was undertaken for two reasons.
2. The findings suggest the following conclusions.
3. Prior to [year], teachers who used traditional means of motivating students were considered old-fashioned.
4. The following steps were taken in obtaining data:
   a. Records were checked in the district office.
   b. Notations were made of discrepancies in the records.
   c. A meeting was held with the personnel director to discuss discrepancies.

9.3. The following arrangement would organize topics to proceed from more general to more specific.

5 Rules and practices that promote good classroom behavior

3 The relationship of discipline to achievement

7 Support from others that helps teachers enjoy better discipline

1 The outcry over what is seen to be lack of discipline in the schools

4 Traits and practices of teachers identified as having better behaved classes

2 The effects of serious classroom misbehavior on teachers and students

6 Elements and emphasis in various programs for developing teacher skills in discipline

8 Two training programs implemented at schools in other states

Qualitative Research Methods

PREVIEW

This chapter focuses on the nature, intent, and procedures of qualitative research. Examples of qualitative methods will concentrate specifically on two approaches:

- Ethnographic research
- Narrative research

Other approaches to qualitative research include the following:

- Historical research
- Grounded theory studies
- Phenomenological studies
- Case studies

The strengths of qualitative research include the following:

- Holistic description
- Thoroughness of data collection
- Integration of the researcher into the setting of interest

Major concerns about qualitative research include the following:

- High level of subjectivity
- Possible researcher bias
- Inability to generalize findings

TARGETED LEARNINGS

This chapter deals with qualitative research, a set of approaches that rely heavily on narrative, nonnumerical data. The general purpose of qualitative research is to investigate the quality of a particular topic or activity. These approaches to conducting educational research have some unique characteristics that differentiate them from more quantitative methods. You will learn about these characteristics, the qualitative research process, and several different approaches to conducting qualitative research, with more specificity provided for ethnographic research and narrative research—including samples of published articles. As you read this chapter, look particularly for information related to the following questions:

1. What is the main purpose of qualitative research?
2. What does the term *holistic* mean?

3. What are the distinctive characteristics that differentiate qualitative research from quantitative research?
4. What is the process for conducting qualitative research? How does it differ from that for quantitative research?
5. What is the purpose of ethnographic research?
6. What is the purpose of narrative research?
7. What are the purposes of historical, grounded theory, phenomenological, and case study approaches to conducting qualitative research?

CHARACTERISTICS OF QUALITATIVE RESEARCH

Qualitative research involves the collection, analysis, and interpretation of data, largely narrative and visual in nature, in order to gain insights into a particular phenomenon of interest (Gay, Mills, & Airasian, 2006). The focus of qualitative research tends to be on the *quality* of a particular activity, rather than how often it occurs or how it might be evaluated, which is typically the focus of quantitative research (Fraenkel & Wallen, 2006). Since the focus of qualitative research is on the quality of a specific phenomenon, there is a greater emphasis on *holistic description*—that is, description in thick, rich detail—of the phenomenon, setting, or

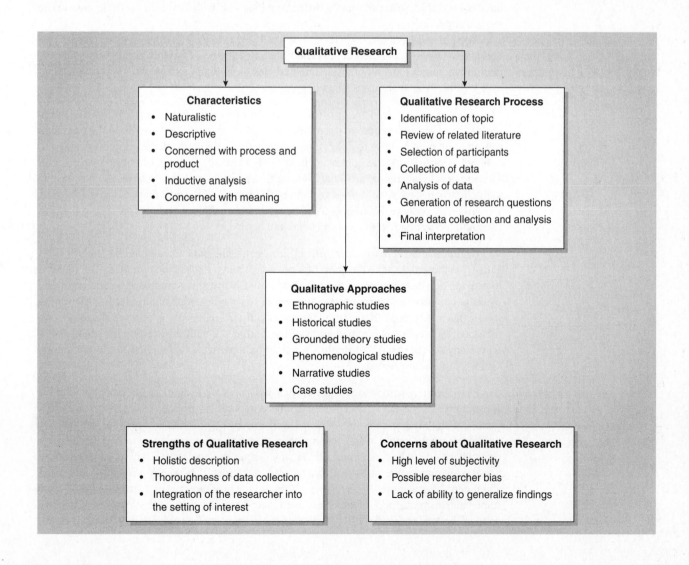

topic of interest. This type of description exists in stark contrast to that resulting from quantitative research, which can be thought of as a "snapshot" of the topic.

It is important to note that the term *qualitative* research is used not necessarily because it describes a specific strategy of inquiry, but rather as a convenient way to differentiate it from other specific strategies of research that we collectively consider quantitative forms of research (Gay, Mills, & Airasian, 2006), such as survey, correlational, causal-comparative, experimental, quasi-experimental, and single-subject research (to be discussed in Chapters 11, 12, and 13). These methods are classified as quantitative forms of research because they all primarily involve the collection and analysis of numerical data. Qualitative research does not incorporate the use of numerical data; in contrast, it involves the collection and analysis of nonnumerical (typically referred to as *narrative*) data, such as observational notes, interview transcripts, transcripts of video and audio recordings, as well as existing documents and records.

It is important to remember that both qualitative and quantitative research methods are valuable in their own respective rights. One is not inherently superior or inherently inferior to the other. Both approaches to research are "scientific" in their own particular ways. Each has its own respective strengths and weaknesses. Since they each contribute important research findings that help us to better understand educational phenomena, most educational researchers would agree that educational problems are best investigated by using whatever method or methods are most appropriate for the research situation (McMillan, 2004). It is best to begin with a topic of interest or specific research questions for which you seek answers and *then* select the method that provides you with the most credible answers to those questions.

Bogdan and Biklen (2003) have described five essential features or characteristics of qualitative research, detailed in the following list. They point out that not all approaches to qualitative research display these characteristics to an equal extent. All approaches, however, exhibit these features to some degree.

1. *Qualitative research is naturalistic.* One of the most distinguishing features of qualitative research is that it occurs in the natural setting. Researchers go directly to the particular setting of interest in order to collect their data because they are interested in observing human behavior in a specific context as it naturally occurs, as opposed to observing or interviewing people in a more "artificial" setting. If we wanted to know how teachers behave in their classrooms, we should observe them in that setting. If we take them out of that setting, we will likely observe different sorts of behaviors from them. In other words, in qualitative research, the setting itself is a direct source of data.

2. *Qualitative research is descriptive.* Simply put, the data, as well as the analytical results from those data, take the form of words or pictures rather than numbers. The intent is to provide rich descriptions of the phenomenon of interest that could not be accomplished by reducing pages of narration into numerical summaries (McMillan, 2004). Oftentimes, the written results contain quotations taken directly from the data in order to illustrate, corroborate, and support the explanation of the findings. Qualitative researchers tend not to ignore any sort of detail that might shed light on a particular topic; nothing in the natural setting is taken for granted.

3. *Qualitative researchers are concerned with process as well as product.* Qualitative researchers are not only concerned with the outcomes or products of a situation or program, but more importantly they are also concerned with *how* and *why* results occur as they do. For example, rather than focusing their attention on academic outcomes, qualitative researchers tend to be more interested in why certain students react positively to an instructional intervention program while others react negatively. They seek answers to questions about people's responses to situations. What did the program mean to students? Why were some students motivated, while others were not? In what ways did the features of the program go beyond the intervention and extend into the rest of a student's school day?

4. *Qualitative researchers analyze their data inductively.* Typically, qualitative researchers do not formulate a hypothesis and then collect data in an effort to either prove or disprove it—a process known as *deductive reasoning.* In qualitative research, the ultimate findings of a study—and the "directions" traveled in order to arrive at them—can occur after some time has been spent collecting and analyzing data. Data are collected and then synthesized in order to generate generalizations—a process known as *inductive reasoning.* It is possible to not even know what one is looking for until after a period of some data collection. This process is important in qualitative research because the researcher wants to be open to new information and new ways of understanding the phenomenon of interest.

5. *Qualitative researchers have a primary concern with how people make sense and meaning out of their lives.* Researchers who engage in qualitative methods are concerned with people's individual perspectives on their lives. Qualitative researchers are typically interested in learning what participants in a study are thinking and why they think as they do. Assumptions, goals, motives, reasons, and values are all of interest and are likely to form the focus of the questions that guide a qualitative researcher's study (Fraenkel & Wallen, 2006).

THE QUALITATIVE RESEARCH PROCESS

In Chapter 1, and again in Chapter 7, we presented a general process for conducting educational research studies. That basic series of steps is fairly consistent across different types of quantitative research, but the steps in conducting qualitative research are not quite as distinct. The steps in a qualitative study may occur out of their sequential order as presented in earlier chapters, may overlap with each other, or may be conducted concomitantly. Although they are typically not followed in linear, sequential fashion, the main steps in the qualitative research process are as follows.

1. *Identification of the phenomenon to be studied.* As with any type of research study, the topic for investigation must first be identified. In qualitative studies, this initial topic is typically quite broad in scope and will be narrowed during the study.

2. *Review of related literature.* As you have learned, related literature is reviewed in order to identify useful strategies for conducting the study, in addition to providing guidance about what has previously been learned about the topic of interest.

3. *Identification and selection of participants.* In qualitative research, participants who will constitute the sample are selected purposefully, not randomly as they are in quantitative studies. Characteristically, there are substantially fewer participants in qualitative than in quantitative research studies.

4. *Collection of data.* Data collection in qualitative studies is a lengthy, ongoing process. Data are typically collected directly from participants through the use of observations, interviews, and other types of records and artifacts.

5. *Analysis of data.* As previously mentioned, qualitative data are analyzed inductively by synthesizing all information collected from various sources into common themes or patterns. The analytical process relies heavily on narrative summary and rich description.

6. *Generation of research questions.* Following an initial stage of data collection and analysis, a preliminary set of research questions is developed. At this point in the process, the questions may appear somewhat broad.

7. *Additional data collection, analysis, and revision of research questions.* This is the key step that differentiates qualitative research from quantitative research. Following an initial stage of data collection, data analysis, and research question generation, the researcher returns to the setting in order to engage in further data collection and analysis. The process of qualitative data collection and analysis may be seen as iterative or cyclical in nature. That is, data are collected and analyzed, and preliminary research questions are developed. More data are collected, combined with the initial data, and then analyzed. The researcher may reexamine the research questions, some of which may be discarded and others revised, based on the "new" data and resulting analyses. This process can continue for extended periods of time and only ends when the researcher is comfortable that he or she is uncovering nothing new through observations and interviews.

8. *Final interpretation of analyses and development of conclusions.* Although interpretation occurs continuously throughout the data collection and analysis process, there is a final stage of interpretation of results. Once the qualitative researcher is sure that nothing new can be learned from further data collection, he or she develops a final, comprehensive interpretation of the data analyses and extends those interpretations into the study's conclusions.

QUALITATIVE DATA COLLECTION TECHNIQUES

PEARSON
myeducationlab
for research

To learn more about data collection through observations, go to the "Qualitative Data Collection" section of **MyEducationLab for Research** and then click on *Assignments and Activities.* Complete the exercises titled "Collecting Data through Observation" and "Developing a Protocol." These exercises will help you think through aspects of observational data collection.

Recall that qualitative data are *narrative;* in other words, the data themselves are words. These words may appear in the form of interview transcripts, observational notes, journal entries, transcriptions of audio or video recordings or as existing documents, records, or reports. They may be collected using a variety of techniques, but it is important to remember that the resulting qualitative data will always consist of descriptive, narrative accounts.

Observations

As human beings, we are constantly observing and taking note of the world around us. Furthermore, as educators, we are constantly observing our students and others with whom we work. However, on a daily basis we typically observe our surroundings in a somewhat haphazard manner—something more akin to "watching" than observing. Observations, as a means of collecting qualitative data, involve *carefully* watching and *systematically* recording what you see and hear in a particular setting. Observations can be extremely useful in certain situations where other forms of data collection simply will not work, such as when teachers want to check for students' nonverbal reactions to events in the classroom or when teachers watch students working in small groups in order to better understand how they interact and communicate with one another.

Classroom observations can range from highly structured to semistructured to unstructured. Structured observations typically require the observer to do nothing else but observe, looking usually for specific behaviors, reactions, or interactions. Because so much is often going on in a given classroom when observations are being made, it is often difficult to conduct structured observations. Unstructured or semistructured observations allow the researcher the flexibility to attend to other events or activities occurring simultaneously in the classroom or to engage in brief, but intense, periods of observation and note taking. In addition, unstructured observations are more typical of qualitative data collection, because they are "free flowing," allowing the researcher to shift focus from one event to another as new, and perhaps more interesting, events arise.

Classroom observations are usually recorded in the form of fieldnotes. Fieldnotes are written observations of what you see taking place in a particular setting. It can sometimes be overwhelming to try to record everything that you see, especially when trying to determine what is important (and, therefore, worth recording) and what is not. As you observe and record what you see, you will undoubtedly begin to focus on more interesting or important occurrences. As you make observations over time, patterns will begin to emerge from the data you have collected.

When recording fieldnotes, you may want to consider dividing each page of your notebook into two columns. You should use the left column for recording your actual observations and the right column for noting preliminary interpretations of what has been observed. Bogdan and Biklen (2003) refer to these interpretations as **observer's comments,** or *OCs*. Observer's comments often shed light on the emerging patterns from your observational data. Including observer's comments in your observation notes is also a way to integrate ongoing analysis into the process of conducting qualitative research. The separation of these two types of commentaries is critical so that *actual* observations are not confused with what you think the observed event *means*. As you know, researchers conducting qualitative studies need to remain as objective as possible in the records kept and data collected. As an aside, this need for objectivity also dictates that you not censor what you record. In addition, interpretations of observations may change over time as you collect more data; having a record of these changing interpretations can be invaluable over the course of your study. An example of a page from a book of fieldnotes recorded several years ago during a study of positive reinforcement in a preschool setting, depicting this two-column format of actual observations and associated observer's comments, is shown in Figure 10.1.

Figure 10.1   A sample fieldnote page, the left column showing actual observations and the right column showing preliminary interpretations

Obs. #3 June 10 10:15–11:00	Observations	Observer's Comments (OC)
Time	There were very few forms of interactions between the children and the teachers. The children were playing, behaving, for the most part. One of the teachers was pushing two girls on swings and the other teacher was sitting near the wading pools, watching the children. Carol said several things to certain children. She repeatedly used phrases such as, "Don't do that," "Don't throw water," "Don't throw that in the pool," and "You're gonna break the sprinkler . . . don't do that!"	I don't think that, in the entire time I was there today, I heard one positive comment or saw one positive gesture. It seemed that the teachers were in only a supervisory role. All they appeared to be doing was supervising the behavior and actions of the children in order to prevent accidents or injuries. I'm not saying that this is wrong; on the contrary, it is necessary when conducting an activity of this nature, especially with very young children. I just expected to hear some positive behaviors being praised in addition to the negative being addressed.
	Several children came close to hurting themselves and/or others. One three-year-old girl tried to pour water over the head of a one-year-old. Two boys were throwing beach balls into the pool and inadvertently hitting smaller children who were playing in the pool.	I began to wonder if this type of activity (i.e., supervisory in nature) did not permit the use of many positive comments. Maybe these teachers leave those types of positive reinforcement for classroom activities. Perhaps activities that require quicker thought and action on the part of the teachers—in order to prevent children from being hurt, or worse—don't allow for positive comments or identification of children to model positive behaviors.
	The children continued to play in the pools, the sprinkler, and the swings. I observed very little verbal interactions between the teachers and the children. Initially, most of what I heard came from Carol. She made several comments to the children, such as "Don't do that" and "You need to ride that bike over there." Carol's daughter picked up a garden hose and began playing with it. Twice Carol told the girl to stop playing with the hose and put it down, but to no avail. The third time she spoke to her, she said, "You better put that down or it will turn into a snake and bite you."	Carol's comment was not in jest. She said it with a firm tone in her voice. I didn't like hearing this. I was always taught never to threaten children, regardless of their age and regardless of how idle the threat. I find myself expecting to see and hear this kind of behavior from Carol and not from Marilyn, as I have not yet heard her say something of this nature.

Written fieldnotes can become problematic, however. They are often insufficient to depict the richness and details of what one is observing. Video can assist as a tool for recording observations, although this format is not without its respective limitations, as well. Background noises may prevent you from hearing what you were hoping to capture on a video. Furthermore, video cameras can only capture what is happening in a given direction (i.e., the direction the camera is facing). Prior to beginning any formal observations, researchers should experiment and become familiar with various methods of recording observations in order to find what works best for the particular setting and situation. It is, however, important to remember that whatever mechanism you use to record your observations, you simply cannot physically record everything that you see or that is happening; it is best not to put pressure on yourself to try to do so.

Interviews

An alternative to observing people is to directly ask them questions. This can be accomplished in several ways. **Interviews** are conversations between the researcher and participants in the study. Interviews can be conducted with individuals or with groups. It is best to prepare an interview guide, containing either specific or general questions to be asked, prior to conducting any interviews.

Similar to observations, interviews are typically classified as being structured, semistructured, or open-ended. In a structured interview, the researcher begins with an interview guide consisting of a specific set of predetermined questions. Those questions—and *only* those questions—are asked of each person being interviewed, which is typically done for the sake of consistency. Interestingly, consistency is usually not a concern when collecting qualitative data; it is typically more desirable for the researcher to have some flexibility and to be able to ask clarifying questions (not initially included on the interview guide), to pursue information not initially planned for, and to seek different information from different people.

When gathering truly qualitative data, interviews are probably best conducted following semistructured or open-ended formats. In semistructured interviews, the researcher asks several "base" questions but also has the option of following up a given response with alternative, optional questions whose use depends on the situation. When developing interview guides, it is best to keep your questions brief, clear, and stated in simple language. For example, if we were interviewing students regarding their opinions of our school, we might ask the following questions, where the italicized questions represent the optional, follow-up, probing questions:

- What do you enjoy most about this school?
  Why do you enjoy that aspect so much?
  Do you think other schools have this particular benefit?

- What are your favorite academic subjects?
  Why is that your favorite subject?
  Do you have any others?
  What about extracurricular activities? Are there any that you participate in?
  Which are your favorites? Why?

- What do you like least about this school?
  Why do you like that so little?
  Is there anything that the principal or teachers could do to improve that aspect?

The semistructured interview guide used in the positive reinforcement study referred to in Figure 10.1 is shown in Figure 10.2, and a portion of a transcript from one interview is shown in Figure 10.3.

Figure 10.2   A sample semistructured interview guide

Semistructured Interview Guide

Interview with the Director

- What type of training and/or certification is held by your classroom teachers?
- Do you have any advice or suggestions for giving positive reinforcement, as discussed with your teachers?
  - How have those suggestions been received by your teachers?
  - Have they attempted to implement them?
- What do you see as acceptable forms of positive reinforcement for children in your school?
- What do you think the meaning of positive reinforcement is for you?
  - Do you think it is the same for your teachers? Why or why not?
  - Do you think it is the same for your students? Why or why not?

Interviews with the Teachers

- Has your director ever provided you with suggestions for giving positive reinforcement?
  - If so, have you used any of them?
  - To what extent have they been successful?
- What do you see as acceptable forms of positive reinforcement for children?
- What do you think the meaning of positive reinforcement is for you?
  - Do you think it is the same for your students? Why or why not?

Open-ended interviews provide the respondent with only a few questions, very broad in their nature. The intent is to gather very different kinds of information from different individuals, depending largely on how each person interprets the questions. For example, an open-ended series of interview questions about school climate might include the following:

- What does "school" mean to you?
- What do you like about school?
- What do you dislike?

Figure 10.3   Portion of a transcript from a semistructured interview, using the guide shown in Figure 10.2

CM: How would you describe positive reinforcement? How would you define that, or what does that mean to you?

"Carol": Positive reinforcement means not yelling at the children. It means talking to them in a positive way. Sometimes you can lose your temper. I try not to use time-out a whole lot. I give them choices. If you're going to throw the blocks, then you're going to pick them up. If you're going to hit someone in the head with that crazy toy, then you're going to go apologize to them. And tell them the difference between right and wrong instead of, . . . take for instance E., who likes to throw toys at everybody. Instead of putting him in the corner and my picking up all the toys he's thrown, I make a game out of it. Instead of "E., pick them up, pick them up," we count them as we put them in. So he's still having to do what he did—you know, having to clean up his mess—but we're making a game out of it. Instead of "this was wrong and you're going to sit in the corner for this."

CM: So they don't see it so much as a punishment. Rather, you try to turn it into something constructive?

"Carol": Right. Like this morning, he punched a little girl in the face, and Gail and I both agreed that he needs to sit out of the group for a little while.

CM: So it really depends on the situation? It would be hard to take that situation and turn it into something positive.

"Carol": Right. It depends on what they've done and if they keep doing it all day long. Then they need time away. That's why we have that carpet out there. If the child needs to leave the room and get away from the other children for 5 minutes, they go out and sit on the quiet rug.

As mentioned earlier, interviews are not only conducted with individuals but also with groups. A **focus group** is the name given to simultaneous interviews of people making up a relatively small group, usually no more than 10 to 12 people. This type of interview typically lasts between one and two hours. Focus groups are especially useful when time is limited and because people often are more comfortable talking in a small group, as opposed to individually. Furthermore, interactions among the focus group participants may be extremely informative due to the tendency for people to feed off others' comments. However, when conducting a focus group interview, it is important to ensure that each participant is provided with the opportunity to speak and share her or his perspective. There can be a tendency for one or two individuals to dominate the discussion; it is the responsibility of the researcher to closely monitor the discussion in order to prevent this from happening. The set of guiding questions used for a study incorporating data collected via a focus group is provided in Figure 10.4.

Journals

Data **journals** may be kept by teachers, students, and others included in your qualitative research site, and can provide valuable information about the workings of a classroom or

---

Figure 10.4   Sample of guiding questions used for a focus group interview

1. (a) What were your overall perceptions of the process used to gather student feedback on your teaching?
   (b) What aspects of the process did you like?
   (c) What aspects did you dislike?

2. (a) How was the feedback you received useful to you?
   (b) How was the feedback not useful to you?

3. (a) What changes have you made to any of your teaching behaviors as a result of the student feedback?
   (b) What behaviors, if any, are you considering changing in your teaching as a result of the student feedback?

4. (a) What unanticipated benefits did you experience as a result of this process of collecting student feedback?
   (b) What negative consequences did you experience as a result of this process of collecting student feedback?

5. (a) Is this method, that of using rating scales, the most appropriate way to collect student feedback?
   (b) What method(s) might work better? Why?

6. (a) For what specific school situations or student groups would this method of collecting student feedback not be appropriate?
   (b) What could be changed to make it more suitable in this context or to these students?

7. (a) Is this process feasible for teachers to conduct on their own?
   (b) If not, what would need to be changed in order to make it more feasible?

8. How often should this information be collected from students?

9. What specific things could be changed to improve the process of collecting student feedback?

10. (a) Based on your experience, will you continue to collect student feedback in this manner?
    (b) If not, will you continue to collect this information but do so by using a different method? Can you describe that method?

*Upon completion of the above questions, explain to the participants that the meeting is about to end. Ask them to take a moment and think about what has been discussed. Then, one by one, ask them if they have any additional comments. If necessary, explore relevant or new comments in greater depth.

school. In a way, student journals provide information similar to homework, in that it is possible to gain a sense of students' daily thoughts, perceptions, and experiences in the classroom. Teacher journals can similarly provide teachers with the opportunity to maintain narrative accounts of their professional reflections on practice. Class journals are another means of incorporating journaling into qualitative data collection. A class journal is a less formal version of a student journal. Students are encouraged to enter their thoughts, ideas, perceptions, feedback, or other forms of response, such as pictures or diagrams, as they wish. Teachers may want to provide some sort of guidelines for making entries into the class journal so that it does not become a "quasi-teacher-approved" form of graffiti that may be offensive to other students.

Existing Documents and Records

Often, qualitative research necessitates the gathering of data that already exist. These data are essentially anything collected for a reason *other* than the research study but are now being used as data for the study. These existing documents and records might take several forms, including (at the individual student level) curriculum materials, textbooks, instructional manipulatives, attendance records, test scores, previous grades, discipline records, cumulative folders, and (at the school or district level) attendance rates, retention rates, graduation rates, newspaper stories about school events, minutes from faculty or school board meetings, and standardized test scores perhaps disaggregated by grade level, gender, or ethnicity. However, a word of caution is in order: Whenever using existing data, it is critical to make sure to follow a given school district's approved procedures for securing access to these various types of data. Their use and the ultimate reporting of the results of any analyses must be done in an ethical manner.

CHARACTERISTICS OF QUALITATIVE DATA: ACCURACY, CREDIBILITY, AND DEPENDABILITY

myeducationlab for research

To help you better identify aspects of qualitative data collection within published qualitative studies, go to the "Qualitative Data Collection" section of **MyEducationLab for Research** and then click on *Building Research Skills*. Read the article and complete the exercises titled "Collecting Data for a Qualitative Study." This exercise will help you better understand qualitative data collection.

When collecting data for qualitative research studies, it is important for researchers to ensure the quality of their data. If data collected for the study are imprecise, or if the researcher has actually measured something other than what was intended to be measured, at a minimum the data will be inaccurate and misleading. **Validity of research data** deals with the extent to which the data that have been collected accurately measure what they purport to measure (i.e., that which we intended to measure). When dealing with the validity of qualitative data, researchers are essentially concerned with the **trustworthiness**—the accuracy and believability—of the data. Trustworthiness is established by examining the credibility and dependability of qualitative data. **Credibility** involves establishing that the results of qualitative research are credible or believable from the perspective of the participant(s) in the research. On the other hand, the concept of **dependability** emphasizes the need for the researcher to account for the ever-changing context within which research occurs. The researcher is responsible for describing the changes that occur in the setting and how these changes have affected the researcher's approach to the study.

Three common practices, which are typical aspects of any qualitative research study, can help to ensure the trustworthiness of your data. The first of these, **triangulation,** is the use of multiple data sources, multiple data collection methods, and perhaps even multiple researchers in order to support the ultimate findings from the study (Glesne, 2006). A given finding is supported by showing that independent measures of it tend to agree with each other or at least do not directly contradict each other. For example, when you observe Susan actually doing something that she has described to you in an interview as a method she employs and that is also indicated on an open-ended questionnaire (see Figure 10.5), you likely will have more confidence in concluding that it is probably an accurate depiction of Susan's practice. In other words, your interview data has been supported by your observation data and by the questionnaire responses. Had any of the three sources of data contradicted each other, you likely would have arrived at a different conclusion, perhaps that Susan was telling you what she thought you wanted to hear, despite in reality not actually practicing it.

A second method that can help to ensure the quality of your data is known as **member checking.** This procedure involves the sharing of interview transcripts, analytical thoughts (such as observation notes with observer's comments), and drafts with the participants of the study. The purpose of sharing these data sources is to make sure that you have represented your participants and their ideas accurately (Glesne, 2006). A third and final procedure involves prolonged engagement and persistent observation. The idea here is that the more time you spend "in the field," so to speak, the more you are able to develop trust with and get to know your participants, learn the culture of their setting (whether it be a classroom or school building), and observe patterns of behavior to the point of being routine (Glesne, 2006). Observing or interviewing only once or twice will not afford you this luxury.

QUALITATIVE DATA ANALYSIS TECHNIQUES

Recall from earlier chapters that the analysis of qualitative data is an **inductive analysis.** That is, when conducting qualitative data analysis, the researcher begins with specific observations (i.e., data), notes any patterns in those data, formulates one or more tentative "hypotheses," and finally develops general conclusions and theories. Also worth reiterating is the fact that the process of analyzing qualitative data attempts to view the phenomenon of interest from a holistic perspective, factoring in not only the data themselves but also the setting, the participants, and anything else that contributes to the uniqueness of the specific context under investigation.

Inductive Analysis

After having gathered potentially voluminous amounts of qualitative data, the researcher may feel a bit overwhelmed with the task that lies ahead, as it can seem a monumental undertaking (Parsons & Brown, 2002). The real challenge in conducting an *inductive analysis* of qualitative data is to remember that you are trying to reduce the volume of information that you have collected, thereby identifying and organizing the data into important patterns and themes in order to construct some sort of framework for presenting the key findings of the action research study. However, you want to be sure that, during this process of data reduction, you do not minimize, distort, oversimplify, or misinterpret any of your data. Parsons and Brown (2002) describe the process of qualitative analysis as a means of "systematically organizing and presenting the findings of the action research in ways that facilitate the understanding of these data" (p. 55). They further describe a three-step process for conducting this analysis: organization, description, and interpretation.

The organizational step of inductive analysis involves the *reduction* of the potentially massive amounts of narrative data in the form of interview transcripts, observational field-notes, and any existing documents or records that you have collected. This is accomplished

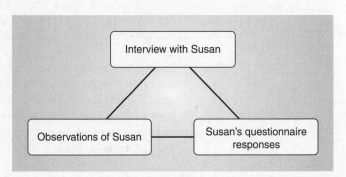

Figure 10.5
Triangulation of three
sources of data

through the development of a system of categorization, often referred to as a **coding scheme,** which is used to group data that provide similar types of information (Parsons & Brown, 2002). As you read through your transcripts, fieldnotes, and documents looking for patterns and themes, you will notice categories of narrative information that begin to emerge. You should make note of each category as it appears and code your narrative data accordingly. This is accomplished by searching for words or phrases that reflect specific events or observations and that begin to repeat themselves throughout your data. Some researchers will do this with different colored markers or by organizing them on 3 × 5-inch index cards; others may actually use scissors to cut apart the pages of transcripts and fieldnotes in order to physically group them together. It is important to find some mechanism for coding that works for you.

Aspects of a study addressing the use of positive reinforcement in a preschool setting have been shared in this chapter. This study involved numerous field observations and interviews with staff members at the preschool visited throughout the study. Once data collection had been completed, it was necessary to begin to wade through fieldnotes, complete with observer's comments, and interview transcripts. This process included the development of the coding scheme that appears in Figure 10.6. Obviously, some categories contained much more data than others. However, at the time, it was important to develop each category, since all categories had an important connection to the research questions.

After developing the categories, the next step was to reread the data in order to code the passages contained in fieldnotes and transcripts. Brief passages from one observation session (see Figure 10.7) and one interview transcript (see Figure 10.8 on page 203) have been included, in order to demonstrate how these samples of data were coded. As you can see from the examples provided, some passages may be coded with one or more of the categories, depending on what is seen or heard, as well as what is *not* seen or heard.

Often, this process of coding data necessitates reading, rereading, and rereading again all of your narrative data. You will get to "know" your qualitative data very well during the process of inductive analysis. Be aware that this process of coding your data is not an easy one; coding schemes are not automatic, nor are they necessarily overtly apparent in your data (Parsons & Brown, 2002). It is truly necessary to spend a good deal of time reviewing the data, both during and following the development of your coding scheme.

The second step in the process of inductive analysis is to *describe* the main features or characteristics of the categories resulting from the coding of the data (Parsons & Brown, 2002). This is the stage of the analysis process where the researcher begins to make connections between the data and the original, or emerging, research questions. The categories need to be reflected on (once again) and described in terms of their connection to or outright ability to answer the research questions. At this point, qualitative researchers should ask themselves the following question: How does the information in this category help me to understand my research topic and answer my research question?

Figure 10.6   Sample coding scheme resulting from data collected as part of a study of positive reinforcement

Coding Categories Used in the Analysis of Data

Desc	Description of Site	MO	Missed Opportunity
TChar	Teacher Characteristics	Modl	Modeling
TQual	Teacher Qualifications	TCRel	Teacher/Child Relationship
Meth	Methodology	Act	Academic/Social Activities
CAct	Child Activity	Sup	Supervisory Role
TBeh	Teacher Behavior	PR	Positive Reinforcement
PInt	Positive Verbal Interactions	NR	Negative Reinforcement
NInt	Negative Verbal Interactions	ChBel	Child Beliefs/Interpretations
ObsAct	Observer's Actions	TBel	Teacher Beliefs
Res	Results of My Presence	TTrng	Teacher Training
CBeh	Child Behavior		

Figure 10.7   Sample page from fieldnotes, with passages coded using the scheme shown in Figure 10.6

One boy asked Carol to push him on the swing and Carol said, "What do you say? What's the magic word?" The boy responded appropriately by saying "Please," and Carol proceeded to push him.

CAct
TBeh
CBeh

> *O/C: Why didn't Carol say anything in response to his correct answer? Especially, when he gave it after being asked only once? What a perfect opportunity to say, "Very good!" or something. She seems to let many "golden opportunities" for giving praise pass her by. I have observed her miss these chances on many occasions.*

MO

Next, I observed Carol's daughter (the girl who has a tendency to misbehave). She wanted to push a bike across the sand, but was having some difficulty. The sand was too deep and the wheels kept getting stuck. She got Marilyn's attention and told her to push the bike for her. Marilyn replied by saying, "Why don't you help me push it?" The girl quickly agreed and they did it together.

CAct
PR

> *O/C: I was very impressed with this brief exchange. Marilyn didn't talk down to the little girl. Instead, she tried to work with her.*

Modl

Immediately after this, I noticed Carol playing with one of the older boys. They were standing about 15 feet apart. Carol threw the football and the boy made a great catch. Carol turned her attention to other children who were nearby.

CAct
TBeh
CBeh
MO

> *O/C: ARGHHH! She didn't even say, "Nice catch." This is frustrating to watch. A short comment like that might have meant a lot to that boy. Yet another apparent missed opportunity.*

As you address the issues of connectedness of your data to your research questions, it is important to also look for information in your data that *contradicts* or *conflicts with* the patterns or trends that have emerged. These discrepant pieces of information often tend to make your interpretations more difficult, but including them in the process will make your findings more accurate and meaningful.

The final step is to *interpret* that which has been simplified and organized. During this step, the researcher examines events, behaviors, or others' observations—as represented in the coded categories—for relationships, similarities, contradictions, and so on (Parsons & Brown, 2002). The key is to look for aspects of the data that answer your research questions, that provide challenges to current or future practice, or that actually may guide future practice. Because the researcher's background, experiences, and expertise will affect the ways in which the data are interpreted, descriptions—or, in some cases, concrete examples—should accompany the interpretations offered (Parsons & Brown, 2002). Figure 10.9 is an excerpt from the final written report of the positive reinforcement study. Notice the discussion of negative comments provided by the teachers toward the children and the frequency of missed opportunities for offering positive feedback to them (which you saw earlier in the coded data appearing in Figures 10.7 and 10.8). Also, you should be aware of the way in which actual data (in the form of interview and observation quotes) supporting the interpretations were incorporated into the written discussion.

APPROACHES TO QUALITATIVE RESEARCH

As with quantitative research, there are numerous approaches to conducting qualitative research studies. The number of approaches differs, depending on the source you consult. Mertens (2005) lists seven approaches to qualitative research, whereas Tesch (1990)

Figure 10.8   Sample excerpt from interview transcript, with passages coded using the scheme shown in Figure 10.6

CM: Can you give me some examples of what you think are acceptable   TBeh
       forms of positive behavior, at least as far as you're concerned—things
       that you would think would be acceptable for you to use with your
       children?

"Marilyn":   That's a hard one. (laugh) Probably, just talk to them.

CM: So, you see positive reinforcement as being mostly a verbal type of   TBeh
       thing?   PInt

"Marilyn":   Yeah.

CM: Can you give me an example of something that you, like a concrete
       example of how or when you would use a verbal type of positive
       reinforcement and what specifically you might say?

"Marilyn":   Well, I would talk like what I used all throughout the play period   CAct
             that we're going to. You're always telling them that maybe they   TBeh
             shouldn't—well, not exactly shouldn't do something—but, you   CBeh
             know . . . I can't explain it. I'm used to talking to 2-year-olds! (laugh)
             Like I said, you go through that all day long, you know, telling them
             what to do and what not to do. Like to pick the toys up, pick this up
             before you go and get something else.

CM: Well, using that as an example, let's say that you asked the child to do   TBeh
       that, to pick up that toy and put it back. Let's take both cases. Let's   CBeh
       say first they didn't do it. What would you say in response to that   PInt
       child if they didn't do what you asked them to do?

"Marilyn":   I would ask them twice, and if they don't do it, I will go and say, "I'm   TBeh
             going to pick them up. Why don't you help me do this?"   Modl

CM: So, you're kind of modeling for them what you want them to do?

"Marilyn":   Yeah.

---

identifies 26 different types. However, in an attempt to provide an overview of qualitative research approaches, we have chosen to focus our descriptions on six of the more commonly used qualitative approaches: ethnographic research, narrative research, historical research, grounded theory research, phenomenological research, and case studies. Brief descriptions of each approach are offered, with greater details provided later in the chapter for ethnographic and narrative research. It should be noted that the in-depth discussions of ethnographic and narrative research are not intended to diminish the importance, relevance, or value of the other approaches to qualitative research.

Ethnographic Research

Ethnographic research, also known as *ethnography,* involves the in-depth description and interpretation of the shared or common practices and beliefs of a culture, social group, or other community. A key assumption for the ethnographic researcher is that by entering directly into—and interacting with—the lives of the people being studied, one reaches a better, more comprehensive understanding of the beliefs and behaviors of those individuals (Mertens, 2005). Therefore, immersion of the researcher into the setting over an extended period of time is necessary. Only through prolonged experience in the natural setting—and establishing rapport with the individuals in that setting—can the researcher gain a complete understanding of the educational phenomenon of interest (McMillan, 2004).

Figure 10.9   Excerpt from final research report documenting the "negative comments" and "missed opportunities" for positive reinforcement

Unfortunately, as she became preoccupied with disruptive, off-task behavior, Carol seemed to forget about those children who were on-task. One of the boys finished his painting and held it up to show Carol. He exclaimed, "Look what I did!" He seemed very proud of himself. Carol replied, "What is it?" The boy looked away and did not answer. She appeared to let opportunities to offer positive reinforcement pass her by—truly a "missed opportunity." For example, she might have responded to the boy's prideful comment by saying something like, "Oh, that's very nice! Can you tell me what you painted?" From my own experience, I know that in situations dealing with disruptive behaviors it is often difficult to remember to do the "little things."

Although many of Carol's comments directed at the children were negative, most of the time they were not made with a harsh tone of voice. Sometimes, they were spoken in an almost "pleasant" tone of voice. It was difficult to understand what she meant when she said something negative but in a positive tone. I found myself wondering if, subconsciously, the children were having the same difficulty (i.e., is she unhappy or not?).

Circle time is an activity where everyone sits on the floor in a circle and discusses daily events, including the day of the week, the month and year, projects they'll be working on that day, and any special events occurring that day. During my observation of Carol's circle time activity, many of the children exhibited negative, off-task behaviors. In nearly every case, Carol responded with negative statements or actions. During the discussion of the day of the week, for example, Carol's daughter began taking things off the calendar. Carol's initial response to the girl was to threaten to send her to time-out. I don't know if Carol would have actually sent her to time-out, but again the situation was dealt with in a negative fashion and with a threat directed toward the child.

It was during circle time that I began to notice something about Carol. She seemed to be focusing only on the negative behaviors exhibited by the children and doing so consistently. For each one that was misbehaving, there were two or three who were following directions. I expected Carol to identify those who were behaving and compliment their actions, perhaps even single them out as models for the others. Unfortunately, I never saw her do this. She only concentrated on the negative displays—more "missed opportunities."

Ethnography is guided either by an explicit educational theory or by an implicit personal theory about how interactions take place within that culture or group setting. Because this approach begins with a theory, the researcher must be willing to abandon or modify a theory that does not "fit" the data, keeping in mind that the data comprise the reality of that culture (Mertens, 2005).

Narrative Research

The purpose of **narrative research** as a methodological approach to conducting qualitative research is to convey experiences as they are expressed in lived and told stories of individuals (Creswell, 2007). Narrative research typically develops as a spoken or written account of an event or action, or series of events, that are chronologically connected. The researcher, while focusing attention on one or two individuals, gathers data through the collection of their stories, reporting individual experiences, and chronologically orders the meanings of those experiences (Creswell, 2007).

Historical Research

The purpose of **historical research** is to describe events, occurrences, or settings of the past in an attempt to better understand them. Historical research is different from many other types of qualitative research because it is oftentimes impossible for data to be collected directly from the "participants" being studied. If the event occurred many years ago, there may be no one who was a direct participant in that setting and time available from whom data can be collected. Therefore, the historical researcher typically relies on existing records, documents, journals, photographs, and the like as the sources of data. Once the data have been collected, however, the process of analysis and interpretation is quite similar to that described earlier.

Grounded Theory Research

The purpose of **grounded theory research** is to discover an existing theory or generate a new theory that results directly from the data. These theories are not generated or stated prior to the beginning of the study, but are developed inductively from the data collected and analyzed during the study itself (Fraenkel & Wallen, 2006). In this sense, the goal of grounded theory research is not to begin with a theory and then set out to collect data that will prove it. In contrast, the goal is to begin with a particular educational phenomenon in mind, and those aspects that are relevant to the phenomenon are permitted to emerge during the study. This is another way of saying that the theory is "grounded" in (or is derived from) the data.

The data for this type of qualitative study are collected primarily through one-on-one interviews, focus group interviews, and participant observation conducted by the researcher (Fraenkel & Wallen, 2006). This is largely because grounded theory studies tend to focus on what happened to individuals, why they believe it happened as it did, and what it means to them (McMillan, 2004). As described earlier in the section outlining the qualitative research process, data collection and analysis are ongoing processes. The analytical process used in grounded theory research involves continually comparing the emerging themes and the developing theory to newly collected data and is known as the *constant comparative method* of data analysis (McMillan, 2004; Mertens, 2005). Data are collected and analyzed, and a theory is proposed; more data are collected and analyzed, and the theory is revised; data continue to be collected and analyzed, and the theory continues to be developed, until a point of saturation is reached.

Phenomenological Research

The intent of **phenomenological research** is to describe and interpret the experiences or reactions of participants to a particular phenomenon *from their individual perspectives* (Fraenkel & Wallen, 2006; Mertens, 2005). The underlying assumption to this approach is that there are multiple ways of interpreting the same experience, as well as multiple meanings that can be derived from that experience (McMillan, 2004). The individual meanings that each participant creates constitute *their* reality; in other words, it is the *essence* of the experience for each individual (Fraenkel & Wallen, 2006; McMillan, 2004). For this reason, the concept of participant perspective is central for researchers using this approach.

Data for phenomenological research are typically collected through the use of in-depth, semi-structured, or unstructured one-on-one interviews. The ultimate goal of the analysis, then, is for the researcher to attempt to identify and describe aspects of each participant's perceptions—and the associated meanings created for each person—in some detail. Phenomenological research is one of the more difficult types of qualitative research to conduct because the researcher must get the participants to accurately relive the experience in their minds, along with their associated reactions and perceptions (Fraenkel & Wallen, 2006).

Case Studies

A **case study** is an in-depth analysis of a single, restricted entity (Fraenkel & Wallen, 2006; McMillan, 2004). A case might consist of one student, one classroom, one school, one program, or one community. Oftentimes, case studies involve both qualitative and quantitative data. The basic purpose of a case study is to develop a highly detailed description and gain an understanding of the individual entity. The methods of data collection, analysis, and interpretation are essentially the same as those that have been discussed up to this point, the lone distinguishing factor being the single case situation. With case studies more than any other type of qualitative approach, generalizability of the findings is a concern. For those who are interested in learning more about case study research, students are directed to *The Art of Case Study Research* by Robert Stake (1995) and to *Case Study Research: Design and Methods* by Robert Yin (2009).

THE NATURE OF ETHNOGRAPHIC RESEARCH

Ethnography (*ethno* refers to human cultures; *graphy* means "description of") is a research process used in the scientific study of human interactions in social settings. Long a predominant research procedure in anthropology, ethnography has in recent years become increasingly popular in educational research. It is used to illuminate in detail the conditions and interactions of individuals and groups as they function within the schools and larger society (Wiersma & Jurs, 2005).

Ethnography is essentially a descriptive approach but is placed in a category of its own because (1) it is unique in focusing on social behavior within natural settings; (2) it relies on qualitative data, usually in the form of narrative descriptions made by an observer of, or participant in, the group being studied; (3) its perspective is holistic—observations and interpretations are made within the context of the *totality* of human interactions; (4) hypotheses and research questions may emerge *after* data collection is well under way, rather than being stated at the beginning of the investigation; and (5) its procedures of data analysis involve **contextualization,** where research findings are interpreted with reference to the particular group, setting, or event being observed.

Ethnographic research can thus be described concisely as follows:

1. *Purpose.* To describe and explain a facet or segment of group social life as it relates to education
2. *Hypotheses and questions.* Initial broad statements about the purpose of the research, which are allowed to emerge more specifically as data are amassed
3. *Data.* Verbal descriptions of people, interactions, settings, objects, and phenomena within the context being studied
4. *Data sources.* The people, settings, and relevant objects being observed
5. *Data collection.* Process undertaken by the researcher through observation, sometimes combined with interview, to gather information
6. *Data treatment and analysis.* Presentation of verbal descriptions or logical analysis of information to discover salient patterns and themes

TOPICS IN ETHNOGRAPHIC RESEARCH

Because ethnographic research studies people in small or large groups in an attempt to understand the groups and how they function, the range of topics is quite broad. The following topics hint at the range of possibilities:

- Faculty interactions in the lounge and workroom
- Kindergartners' behavior on the playground
- The daily regimens of administrative personnel
- Korean American students' lives at school and work
- The lifestyles of top student athletes
- The coping behaviors of students who consider themselves oppressed

The list could go on and on. Virtually any topic involving social behavior that impinges on education can be approached through ethnographic methods.

myeducationlab
for research

To learn more about data collection in ethnographic research, go to the "Ethnographic Research" section of **MyEducationLab for Research** and then click on *Assignments and Activities*. Complete the exercise titled "Taking Field Notes." This exercise will provide you with some practice at developing detailed fieldnotes.

PROCEDURES IN ETHNOGRAPHIC RESEARCH

The following general procedures are followed when conducting ethnographic research:

1. A question or concern worthy of research is formalized.
2. A group is identified as a focus in studying the concern. The group may be very small, consisting of two or three people, or quite large, consisting of hundreds of individuals.
3. The investigator introduces the proposed research to the group and obtains their agreement for involvement.
4. The investigator may function as a **privileged observer** (also known as a *nonparticipant observer*) of the group, who does not participate in its activities, or as a **participant observer,** participating actively as a regular member in all group activities.
5. The researcher's method is to watch and listen attentively, a procedure called *naturalistic observation,* and to record as faithfully as possible all pertinent information. (Note the qualifier *pertinent*—even though the ethnographic approach is holistic, no one can record every detail of events, interactions, objects, settings, and so on. The investigator must exercise quick judgment in deciding what is and is not worth recording.) Although such watching, notetaking, and sometimes audio and video recording take place as the behaviors occur, ethnographers also use informants, whom they interview systematically.
6. The duration of ethnographic research may be as short as a week or two or as long as several years. In educational research done by graduate students, the duration should be adequate to obtain detailed information but usually should not stretch out over more than two months. That being said, typical ethnographic studies require substantial time in the "field"; prolonged engagement at the site, and with those individuals being studied, is critical to a successful ethnographic study.
7. Observations and their recordings produce vast quantities of written notes, which comprise the data obtained in the study.
8. Data analysis, which often requires as much time as does data collection, involves primarily verbal analysis and interpretation. As we have seen, qualitative data do not lend themselves to statistical treatments. Investigators must look instead for patterns of language and behavior that provide insight into the group's concerns and functions. These patterns, once identified, need to be described carefully. Patton (2001) considers this descriptive aspect crucial, believing that if descriptions are good enough, readers can make their own interpretations. However, researchers are also obliged to interpret and explain the findings of their investigation. Reflecting on the following questions may help in formulating interpretations:

   a. What commonalities tie group members together? Do those commonalities or other factors make this group deserving of study?
   b. What seem to be the key life perspectives of this group? Do members feel isolated, put upon, prejudiced against, overworked, misunderstood? Do they feel superior in identifiable ways? Do they seem unusually able to exercise control over their fate?
   c. How do these perspectives, if identified, seem to cause the group to react to opportunity and threat? Do they tend to be aggressive, antagonistic, submissive, escapist? Do they complain, blame, and scapegoat? Do they reach out for greater challenges? Do they attempt to control or dominate?
   d. How does the group attempt to solve or otherwise deal with problems, expectations held for them, or demands made on them? What are the results of their efforts?
   e. What language patterns are associated with identified perspectives and behaviors? What special terms are used and with what meanings?
   f. What are the group's preferred activities? Is there evident linkage between activities and life perspectives?
   g. Which objects within the setting receive major attention (e.g., automobiles, electronic equipment, clothing, printed materials, weapons, sports paraphernalia)?

h. What patterns of leadership, friendship, dominance, and submission are noted within the group? What are the effects of those patterns? What special words or terms are associated with them? What activities, events, or routines seem to strengthen the bonds that hold the group together?

For those who are interested in learning more about the process of conducting ethnographic research, students are directed to several books written by Harry F. Wolcott (1994, 2001), a longtime and leading expert on the topic of ethnographic methods. These books address such topics as how to collect data in the field, how to analyze and interpret ethnographic data, and how to write up the results of ethnographic research studies.

STRENGTHS AND CONCERNS IN ETHNOGRAPHIC RESEARCH

myeducationlab
for research

To learn more about the overall process of ethnographic research, go to the "Ethnographic Research" section of **MyEducationLab for Research** and then click on *Building Research Skills*. Read the article and then complete the exercise titled "Identifying Steps in the Research Process for an Ethnographic Study." This exercise will help you identify key components of an ethnographic research study.

Much of the popularity of ethnographic research in education stems from its holistic nature. Educational practitioners have long expressed dissatisfaction with research findings obtained from investigations that focus on minute aspects of education or personal behavior—findings that appear isolated and unrealistic outside their normal contexts. Ethnography helps satisfy this concern by presenting what educators consider to be realistic pictures of group behavior. Educators often feel they can derive better insights from those realistic portrayals than from traditional research, resulting in more effective ways of working with students under their guidance.

But concerns also exist about ethnography, principally about the reliability of data and, hence, the validity of research conclusions. A major problem is that frequently only a single observer records the descriptions that comprise the data, leaving the research open to questions concerning expertise, consistency, and bias. This exemplifies a major concern about the validity of ethnographic findings, one difficult to resolve even today when two or more observers collect data as a check against one another. An additional problem with ethnographic research has to do with the generalizability of its findings. In far too many cases, it is clear that conclusions drawn from ethnographic research, even though they illuminate the group being studied, do not seem to be applicable to other groups and settings. As you can see, this limits the practical value of the research.

AN EXAMPLE OF ETHNOGRAPHIC RESEARCH

The ethnographic study provided as an example examines the role played by teachers' interactions in working with Spanish-speaking students who are learning English. The authors chose to focus their study on the social nature of these interactions.

Exercise 10.1

As you read the article, see if you can answer the following questions about it:

1. *Problem.* What was the focus and intent of the study?
2. *Time.* Over what length of time was the study conducted?
3. *Subjects or participants.* Who was involved?
4. *Design.* What, specifically, was done to gain access to pertinent data?
5. *Data collection.* What kinds of data were obtained?
6. *Data analysis.* How were the data analyzed, if at all?
7. *Findings and conclusions.* What did the investigators find and conclude?

Influences of Teacher–Child Social Interactions on English Language Development in a Head Start Classroom

Ruth Alfaro Piker
Department of Teacher Education, California State University, Long Beach

Lesley A. Rex
University of Michigan

Abstract

Increasing numbers of Spanish-speaking preschool children require attention to improve the likelihood of success in school. This study, part of a larger 2-year ethnographic study of a Head Start classroom, elaborates the role of teachers' interactions with students who were learning English. Using an interactional ethnography approach, the authors focus on the social nature of these interactions. The study illuminates the kinds of teacher interactions with students that support and hinder the students' language learning. It reinforces the importance of student engagement in social interactions with teachers and with English other than codes of obedience and authority. Finally, it recommends actions teachers can take to provide optimal circumstances for English learning interactions for students.

> The authors are using ethnography to study social interactions in a group (i.e., classroom) setting.

Keywords

- Early childhood education
- English as a second language
- Preschool children
- Social context
- Spanish-speaking children
- Teacher–child interactions

> The literature review summarizes work done on children learning English as a second language, and interactions in a social setting.

The increasing number of Hispanic children learning English as second language (EL2) raises great concern regarding their care and preparation for academic success. A recent report by the Associated Press (2008) states the U.S. birth rate is at a 45-year high since the end of the baby boom in 1961. In 2006, the average fertility rate was 2.1 children per woman in the U.S., and three children per woman among Hispanics, with Mexican-born women having a fertility rate of 3.2 children. In 2003, 21% of children under the age of five were Hispanic (U.S. Census Bureau 2004). For fiscal year 2006, 34% of children served by Head Start were Hispanic (Head Start Bureau 2007), with an estimated quarter of children having Spanish as their primary language.

Source: Piker, R. A., & Rex, L. A. (2008). Influences of teacher–child social interactions on English language development in a Head Start classroom. *Early Childhood Education, 36,* 187–193. With kind permission from Springer Science+Business Media.

Language development is the foundation for building literacy skills and academic success (Dickinson and Tabors 2001), yet the empirical literature regarding second language development for preschoolers is minimal at best compared to older children (Saunders and O'Brien 2006). Some researchers have found that children learning English as a second language (EL2) in a school setting develop English language competencies over time regardless of program types and instruction (Barnett et al. 2007; Winsler et al. 1999; Saunders and O'Brien 2006).

Nevertheless, teachers impact the amount of English language production through their language use and teacher qualifications. Chang et al. (2007) found that the amount of Spanish spoken by the teachers in their cross-national sample affected Spanish-speaking preschoolers' English proficiency, and that classrooms with teachers who spoke more Spanish with the EL2 learners scored higher on English proficiency, even though Spanish-speaking children received less individual attention by their English speaking teachers than other children. Alternatively, Chesterfield et al. (1983) examination of the English development of Spanish-speaking preschoolers found English-speaking teachers initially were the main English source for EL2 learners. The more the EL2 learner interacted with the English-speaking teacher, the more proficient in English the Spanish-speaker. However, they also found that when minimal interactions transpired between the English-speaking teachers and the EL2 children, the EL2 children developed their proficiency from their verbal interactions with their English-speaking peers. Consequently, the more the children interacted with English-speaking peers, the more English proficient the EL2 learners became. Wong Fillmore (1982, 1991) illustrated how four kindergarten teachers' use of English influenced how much English the students in each classroom acquired. She demonstrated that the language opportunities were more important than the structuring of instruction.

Other researchers in education have demonstrated that social communication is critical for oral language development. Interactional ethnographers view teaching and learning as social, interactive communicative processes and study classrooms as cultural settings for understanding how students learn (Green et al. 2002). The ethnographic approach supports attempts to understand the "consequences of membership, and how differential access within a group shapes opportunities for learning and participation" (Green et al. 2002, p. 206). Whereas, by focusing on interaction, researchers seek to understand how, through language routines, social practices in the daily activities of the classroom contribute to gaining access to learning and to the construction of knowledge (Green and Dixon 1994; Rex 2006). This combined focus on the social culture of the classroom and the language interactions is well suited to build upon recent research that suggests the mere exposure to an English-speaker, or speaker of the L2, is not as important as the nature of the interaction (Saunders and O'Brien 2006).

The Interactionist Model (Wong Fillmore 1991) encompasses the reciprocal relationship of the social, linguistic and cognitive processes between the learner, the speaker of the second language (L2) and the social setting. Collectively, the three processes explain the interaction between the learner and the L2 speaker, and the development of the learner's understandings of the grammatical and social structures of the L2. To successfully acquire the L2, the social context must contain three components: learners, who realize they must learn the L2 and are motivated; speakers of the L2, who know the L2 well enough to provide access to the language and help the learner learn it; and social setting, situations that bring learners and speakers into frequent contact. The term *optimal learning opportunity* that is used throughout this paper refers to social contexts that provide these three components.

A recently published study by Early et al. (2007) has found preschool teachers' education is not related to the children's academic gains. However, earlier studies have found that teachers' experiences and knowledge of child development affect how they interact and respond to second language learners, thus influencing second language acquisition (Clarke 1999; Gillanders 2007; Saville-Troike 1987). More knowledgeable and experienced teachers anticipated and responded to learners' questions and needs, which helped the children adjust to the new environment of a classroom. These teachers also scaffold learners' development by building from their prior abilities, and structuring activities in particular ways to address individual needs. Less experienced teachers had more difficulty recognizing discomfort or confusion, and spent most of their time dealing with classroom management and discipline-related issues (Clarke 1999; Saville-Troike 1987). Gillanders (2007) studied one veteran monolingual English-speaking teacher whose methods of developing a trusting relationship, offering consistent and clear routines, incorporating Spanish instructional materials and modeling positive interactions created a social context that provided opportunities for English language development.

With only three studies examining teacher qualifications on second language development, more research is needed. This study is a step in that direction. It is a slice from a much larger ethnographic study of the language practices in a preschool classroom over a two-year period. The larger study described how four representative student cases of preschool-aged second language learners developed their oral production of English

> The literature review also helps to identify a "gap" in the literature, calling for more research on the topic

through their social interactions with their teachers during spontaneous interactions (Piker 2005). That study found that teacher qualification does affect EL2 learners' oral language development. The research questions guiding data selection and analysis were: How did four Spanish primary children's social interactions with their teachers encourage their change in language use? What strategies did the children use to understand the teachers' English inquiries?

> The authors pose two specific research questions to guide their investigation.

METHODOLOGY

Setting and Participants

The classroom is located in a federally funded Head Start center in a Mid-Western section of the United States where more than 90% of the children enrolled produce Spanish as their primary language. The classroom composition included two female classroom teachers and, on average, 17 children (11 girls). The Head Teacher Sue,[1] a European-American monolingual English speaker, had a Bachelor's degree, but no previous experience working in a school setting, nor had she taken courses in child development. The assistant teacher Linda is a Mexican-American bilingual speaker. Her educational knowledge evolved from attending six years of Head Start workshops prior to data collection. The children's ages ranged from 3 to 5 years. Of the 13 children identified as Spanish-Primary, we chose two girls and two boys as our four student cases. Two of the children (Carmen and David) had some experience using English at the beginning of the school year, had older siblings who spoke English, and had been in the program the previous year. The other two children (Rita and Javier) had minimal English experience at the beginning of the school year, and were the eldest children in their families. All four children were expected to enter kindergarten the following academic year.

> Brief, but good, description of the setting, the children, and the teachers.

Procedures and Instruments

Using an ethnographic approach, the first author, who is bilingual—Spanish and English, observed and documented classroom practices twice a week for approximately 3 h a day between October and February, a total of 30 days in the classroom. The authors focused their analysis on the Free Play event. This event promoted spontaneous social interactions among the children and the teachers. The children interacted with their same-language

> Data collection included observations and field-notes for three hours per observation, for a total of 30 observations across several months. The authors clearly note the focus of their observations (i.e., "Free Play event").

peers, different-language peers, and in a mixed-group of same and different-language peers. The children played either alone, in small groups of two to four (either same- or different-language peers), or as a large group of 7–12.

The data collection strategies used are participant observations and video recording. As a participant observer, the first author participated in all classroom activities, including group times and children's play, as well as had multiple jobs, including playing with children and preparing tables for lunch. She also participated in conversations where the teachers and other adults discussed classroom practices, curriculum, children and administrative issues. Because three- and four-year-old children play in multiple size groups and use conversational language, video records enhanced the quality and accuracy of field notes and were instrumental to studying and analyzing classroom interactions. The video-camera data was collected on 24 days.

> On 24 of the visits, the authors also used video cameras to record data.

Data Analysis

The data corpus for analysis was selected from the video-recordings of the Free Play event. We selected two days in December, January and February for each child; and 1 day in October for Rita, 1 day in November for Carmen and Javier, and 2 days in November for David. The days chosen for one child at times differed from the days chosen for another child. The length of time any one child was recorded for each Free Play event differed among the children: for Carmen 26–63 min, for David 13 to 57 min, for Rita 10 to 51 min and for Javier 13–65 min.

> The authors only analyzed a subset of the video recordings.

For the analysis, we proceeded through a series of analytical steps for each child. First, we described each child's behavior during each Free Play event, which totaled 29 descriptions for all four children. Second, a list of all the English words spoken during each event was developed. Third, using a Grounded Theory approach (Strauss and Corbin 1998), we coded the descriptions using line-by-line coding. Each description was divided into scenarios, which represented a time period in which the child participated in an activity or activities in one location. For each scenario, three elements were coded. *Language Use* is the verbal and nonverbal forms of communication being used by the child during the interaction, such as the production of Spanish, English, or a mix of languages. The *Participants Involved* reference the individuals involved in the interaction, such as a same-language peer, a different-language peer, and a teacher. Finally, the *Types of Interactional Moves* are terms that described the interactions between the child and

> Several levels of coding were performed on the data as part of the analysis.

the other individual(s), for example playing, requesting to play, arguing, negotiating, and sharing with peer.

RESULTS

As a result of the cross-case comparison, we ascertained that the four Spanish-primary children's acquisition of English appeared to be influenced in particular ways by their social interactions with their peers and teachers. For this report, we focus on how the classroom teachers' language use affected the types of opportunities available to the children—either optimal or non-optimal—such that they influenced the children's English language development. An optimal learning opportunity refers to the social context that includes the motivated EL2 learner and the L2 speaker, who responded in ways that foster further communication. These social interactions prompt the learners' use and knowledge of English in more complex forms (Wong Fillmore 1982, 1991; Fassler 1998).

Teachers' Language Use

As the school principal and the program goals stated, the Head Start teachers were to support both the children's primary language and their English language development. For the case study children, the teachers' language choice was mostly consistent, such that Sue mostly spoke English and Linda generally spoke Spanish with them. Therefore, it appeared as though each teacher supported one language. However, after closer examination of why and how the teachers interacted with the four children, no evidence emerged of the teachers providing them with optimal circumstances for developing their oral production of English into more complex forms. Nevertheless, we witnessed the teachers supporting the case study children's comprehension of English in other ways. Two similar patterns emerged from observations of how the teachers' language choices, when conversing individually with each child or with the children as a group, may have influenced the children's English language development.

> Many of the authors' results tie directly back to the first stated research question: "How did four Spanish primary children's social interactions with their teachers encourage their change in language use?"

When Addressing a Group of Mixed-Language Children

We noted that Sue and Linda consistently spoke English when addressing a group of children that included a case study child and at least one EP child (David: three instances; Carmen: six instances; Rita: two instances; and Javier: one instance). The teachers appeared to reserve Spanish for translating when necessary. Because their teachers initiated conversation in English, the children may have understood that English was used as the medium of communication between different language individuals. There is research to suggest that students use the language of the curriculum more often within the classroom than another language (Saunders and O'Brien 2006). Thus, the teachers' actions of speaking English and using Spanish for translations most likely privileged English as the important language of teaching, as well as possibly prompting the children to develop their English comprehension skills so as to follow the teachers, but not their oral language skills. The teachers' practices encouraged listening to English more than speaking English.

Teachers' Brief Responses

The second common pattern confirms this interpretation of the teachers' limited support of the four children's oral production of English. All together, the children had 27 interactions with Sue and 48 interactions with Linda; most of these dealt with classroom-related issues (17 and 44, respectively), such as instructing the children to clean up or line up, reprimanding the children for breaking a classroom rule, and asking them to put certain things away that were not related to cleaning up an area. Of the 14 instances when the children attempted to share what they made or to relate a family story, the teachers' brief responses to the children prevented the children from experiencing optimal interactions, which prevented them from developing their oral production of English into more complex forms. The amount of English produced by the children with the teachers was minimal (see Table 1).

Of their combined 75 interactions with the teachers, the children responded nonverbally 37 times and in Spanish 21 times, speaking English with the teachers less than 1/3 of the time (see Table 2). Because they only spoke briefly for a few instances with the teachers, the children were unable to improve their oral production of English into complex forms. The limited language support from the teachers adversely affects both L1 and L2 language development, and general literacy development.

Child's Ability to Understand the Teachers' English Inquiries

The students' readiness to build their comprehension of English, and the teachers' decision to speak English when addressing groups of mixed-language children and when asking or answering the children's inquiries regarding classroom-related issues, required the children to possess a certain level of comprehension for responding appropriately, in verbal and nonverbal ways. Because the children responded appropriately to the teachers'

Discussion of results pertaining to the second research question: "What strategies did the children use to understand the teachers' English inquiries?"

Table 1   The Children's English Production When Communicating with Sue[a]

Child		English words spoken
David	#	the snow
	#	snow ((he points to the white paint))
	#	Mrs. Sue look
	#	Mrs. Sue ((gets her attention))
	#	Lookit (she asks what it is)
	#	A doggie (she asks him to repeat it – donkey or doggie)
	#	A doggie
	#	Mrs. Sue XXX
	#	look Mrs. Sue
	#	Mrs. Sue lookit
	#	lookit Mrs. Sue
	#	I made this XXX
	#	XXX
	#	lookit Mrs. Sue
	#	look Mrs. Sue
	#	look it Ms. Sue (Sue responds – "what")
	#	I make a star (Sue responds – "oh")
	#	me, me, me
Carmen	#	Look, look
	#	Teacher
	#	She got
	#	She got it
	#	(Sue "she what")
	#	she got it
	#	But she put over here ((taps the washer))
	#	Ms. R
	#	Teacher ((goes to Sue))
	#	She hurten me
	#	(Sue – who is?)
	#	Shannon, no her ((points to Tanya))
	#	Today is the party my (p) dad
Rita	#	what
Javier	#	snow
	#	me glue
	#	I don't
	#	I don't want

[a] Carmen, Rita, and Javier did not orally produce English with Linda. David used English with Linda once ("he not a dinosaur, look")

Table 2   The Language Used by the Children When Conversing with Sue and Linda

	Teachers		
Language	**Sue**	**Linda**	**Total**
English	16	1	17
Spanish	2	19	21
Nonverbal	9	28	37
Total	27	48	75

instructions and the teachers accepted their nonverbal responses, the teachers appeared to have no reason to change which language they spoke. Three strategies emerged from the observational data that illustrate the children's perceived comprehension of English.

The teachers strategically asked the children if they understood English. For example, Linda explicitly sent a message to Javier regarding the importance of understanding English. The first observed instance of Linda scolding Javier occurred when he and Carlos were reprimanded for playing rough and running around the room with Shannon. After Linda stated in English that running was not permitted in the classroom and that they should not be playing rough, she asked Javier and Carlos in English if they understood her. Linda made a point to confirm that the boys understood what she had said in English, suggesting that understanding English was important. Javier responded appropriately thereafter when he was reprimanded in English.

The children appeared to use listening as a strategy for comprehension and interaction. They attended to the teachers and others' behaviors and conversations even though they might not physically engage or look at them. For example, while Javier sat at the art table playing with play dough, Linda and Sue, who were sitting and standing elsewhere, announced several times in English that the children had to sit at the table and not walk around the room with play dough in their hands, and they also specifically stated these instructions to Brian and Edgar (EP children). Most of the children physically looked in their respective direction when the teachers made the announcements, except for Javier. David, who had been sitting next to Javier, walked over to where the first author sat to show her what he made out of play dough. Javier warned David that he would get in trouble if he left, indicating he had understood the teachers' instructions.

Lastly, the children used their same-language peers as a resource. The following example demonstrates how Rita turned to her peers to understand how to respond appropriately to Sue's inquiries. Sue asked a group of mixed-language children in English if anyone had to go to the bathroom. Rita responded appropriately by mimicking the other children and teacher. Similarly, when Sue scolded the children for running, Rita attended to how the other children

responded and imitated their actions by also sitting on the carpet. Rita appeared to perceive Sue's intentions and an appropriate response from watching how the other children responded.

DISCUSSION

Our study confirmed that children's social interactions with others are seminal for language development. However, mere exposure to a social context with English speakers is not enough to develop the learners' oral production as was demonstrated with the case study children. Given the current lack of qualified Head Start teachers and barriers to their training (Ackerman 2004), the pairing of the two teachers—one college educated and the other well trained—would appear to be an ideal way of managing the insufficient qualifications of a single teacher (Epstein 1999). Assuming that this type of pairing would have predicted more optimal conditions for children's learning of English, and the recent lack of evidence that teacher education influences academic outcomes (Early et al. 2007), the cases in this classroom caution against jumping to that conclusion. While the SP children's English improved, that development had more to do with English used as the curriculum and procedural language of the classroom than with intentional instruction or encouragement. Other evidence in the larger study confirms that the children attended, mimicked, and acted according to how English was understood by their classmates in order to participate appropriately (Piker 2005). The language they understood was more a code of authority and obedience. Although the children did develop their English skills, the question remains—did they learn enough to be successful at more than obedience in English-only kindergarten classrooms? When the teachers were asked this very question at the end of the year, their unilateral response was "we don't know."

> The authors are connecting their findings back to the body of literature.

What we do know from this study is that while the teachers may not have supported the children's oral production, they did provide opportunities to develop English comprehension, or receptive language. However, that comprehension was limited. Language development includes both receptive and expressive abilities that work closely together. As expert English speakers, through their spontaneous interactions during art and table activities, the teachers could have exposed the children to a more extensive English vocabulary and encouraged them to speak English in different ways and across events (Fassler 1998). Fassler (1998) explains how a teacher consciously linked vocabulary from Group Time activity with Table Activities. These connections between activities equipped the kindergarten children learning English as a second language with materials and vocabulary for successfully communicating with other members of the classroom. But the teachers in our study did not. Head teacher Sue's limited knowledge of child development and lack of experience most likely kept her from understanding what she and Linda could have done to provide a language- and learning-rich environment for the children (Clarke 1999; Gillanders 2007; Saville-Troike 1987). Two alternative explanations may account for the teachers' limited interactions with their charges. First, the teachers may have taken a Maturationist approach to EL2 development and expected the children would naturally acquire English over time. Second, the nature of Free Play events in this classroom offered few required interactions between the children and the teachers. During this event, the children were allowed to play whenever and with whomever they wished. Had we picked another event, such as Circle Time, we may have found more teacher–child interactions that optimally supported the children's English language development. However, given the established patterns of interaction observed between the teachers and students during Free Play time, and the limited development of the children's English over the year, we consider that unlikely.

We posit that even these few cases suggest a number of recommendations for teachers. In light of the evidence that positive social language interactions play an important role in second language development, our main recommendation is that teachers assist English language learners in building social relationships that support and encourage sharing, playing, and spending time with English speakers. Four suggestions for how this may be enacted are suggested by this research. First, teachers could facilitate more optimal circumstances (Wong Fillmore 1982, 1991) that allow the learners to interact with more proficient English speakers, such as themselves and their peers. After observing the classroom play culture and the social relationships that are developing, the teacher can strategically encourage particular students to engage with play groups. Second, teachers could take care to use commonly-spoken language for classroom activity throughout the day. Regularly heard words and phrases for common activities, relationships, and objects—such as "Let's play here"—provide more opportunities for students to associate language with meaning, and build comprehension and vocabulary. Third, teachers could create contexts within their classrooms that make it possible for learners and English speakers to interact in meaningful ways. Play spaces as well as work spaces that focus interaction in a space or around a table could encourage their engagement in socially invested interactions. Finally, teachers could use the learner's same-language peers and different-language peers as resources for assisting the learner in participating in classroom activities, responding appropriately to teachers' inquiries, and providing optimal interactions. Deferring questions to other students whom teachers know can be helpful, asking

> Recommendations for practicing teachers are provided.

children to engage in a common activity the teacher knows one child can do, or encouraging perseverance of a joint activity could make use of available social peer resources. We encourage others to use caution when stating teacher preparation and experience is not a significant indicator of student performance for all children.

Note

1. All the names presented are pseudonyms.

References

Ackerman, D. J. (2004). States' efforts in improving the qualifications of early care and education teachers. *Education Policy, 18*(2), 311–337. doi:10.1177/0895904803262145.

Associated Press (2008). Baby boomlet pushes U.S. birth rates to 45-year high. Foxnews.com. Retrieved 21 January 2008 from http://www.foxnews.com/story/0,2933,323028,00.html.

Barnett, W. S., Yarosz, D. J., Thomas, J., Jung, K., & Blanco, D. (2007). Two-way and monolingual English immersion in preschool education: An experimental comparison. *Early Childhood Research Quarterly, 22*(3), 277–293. doi:10.1016/j.ecresq.2007.03.003.

Clarke, P. (1999). Investigating second language acquisition in preschools: A longitudinal study of four Vietnamese-speaking children's acquisition of English in a bilingual preschool. *International Journal of Early Years Education, 7*(1), 17–24. doi:10.1080/0966976990070102.

Chang, F., Crawford, G., Early, D., Bryant, D., Howes, C., Burchinal, M., et al. (2007). Spanish-speaking children's social and language development in pre-kindergarten classrooms. *Early Education and Development, 18*(2), 243–269.

Chesterfield, R., et al. (1983). The influence of teachers and peers on second language acquisition in bilingual preschool programs. *TESOL Quarterly, 17*(3), 401–419. doi:10.2307/3586255.

Dickinson, D. K., & Tabors, P. O. (Eds.). (2001). *Beginning literacy with language: Young children learning at home and school.* Baltimore, MD: Brookes Publishing.

Early, D. M., Maxwell, K. L., Burchinal, M., Alva, S., Bender, R. H., Bryant, D., et al. (2007). Teachers' education, classroom quality, and young children's academic skills: Results from seven studies of preschool programs. *Child Development, 78*(2), 558–580. doi: 10.1111/j.1467–8624.2007.01014.x.

Epstein, A. S. (1999). Pathways to quality in Head Start, public schools, and private nonprofit early childhood Programs. *Journal of Research in Childhood Education, 13*(2), 101–119.

Fassler, R. (1998). "Let's do it again!" Peer collaboration in an ESL kindergarten. *Language Arts, 75*(3), 202–210.

Gillanders, C. (2007). An English-speaking prekindergarten teacher for young latino children: Implications of the teacher–child relationship on second language learning. *Early Child Education Journal, 35*(1), 47–54. doi:10.1007/s10643-007-0163-x.

Green, J. L., & Dixon, C. N. (1994). Talking knowledge into being: Discursive and social practices in classrooms. *Linguistic Education, 5*(3–4), 231–239. doi:10.1016/0898–5898(93)90001-Q.

Green, J., Dixon, C. N., & Zaharlick, A. (2002). Ethnography as a logic of inquiry. In J. Flood (Ed.), *Handbook for research in the teaching of the English language* (2nd ed., pp. 201–224). Mahwah, NJ: London Lawrence Erlbaum.

Head Start Bureau. (2007). Head Start program fact sheet. U.S. Department of health and human services, Administration for children and families, Retrieved 21 January 2008 from http://www.acf.hhs.gov/programs/hsb/about/fy2007.html.

Piker, R. A. (2005). *Second language acquisition in a head start classroom: The role of play, status, gender, and teachers' language choices.* Unpublished doctoral dissertation, University of Michigan, Michigan.

Rex, L. A. (2006). Acting "cool" and "appropriate": Toward a framework for considering literacy classroom interactions when race is a factor. *Journal of Literacy Research, 38*(3), 275–325.

Saunders, W. M., & O'Brien, G. (2006). Oral language. In F. Genesee, K. Lindholm-Leary, W. Saunders & D. Christian (Eds.), *Educating English language learners* (pp. 14–57). Cambridge, NY: Cambridge University Press.

Saville-Troike, M. (1987). Dilingual discourse: The negotiation of meaning without a common code. *Linguistics, 25,* 81–106.

Strauss, A., & Corbin, J. (1998). *Basics of qualitative research: Techniques and procedures for developing grounded theory* (2nd ed.). Thousand Oaks: Sage Publications.

U.S. Census Bureau. (2004). Hispanic and Asian American Americans increasing faster than overall population. United States Department of Commerce News, Retrieved 21 January 2008 from http://www.census.gov/Press-Release/www/releases/archives/ race/001839.html.

Winsler, A., Diaz, R. M., Espinosa, L., & Rodriguez, J. L. (1999). When learning a second language does not mean losing the first: Bilingual language development in low-income, spanish-speaking children attending bilingual preschool. *Child Development, 70*(2), 349–362. doi:10.1111/1467–8624.t01-1-00026.

Wong Fillmore, L. (1982). Instructional language as linguistic input: Second-language learning in classrooms. In L. C. Wilkinson (Ed.), *Communicating in the classroom* (pp. 283–296). New York: Academic Press.

Wong Fillmore, L. (1991). Second-language learning in children: A model of language learning in social context. In E. Bialystok (Ed.), *Language processing in bilingual children* (pp. 49–69). New York: Cambridge University Press.

ORGANIZING FOR ETHNOGRAPHIC RESEARCH

Elmwood Lincoln High School has in attendance a specific group of students whose record of effort and achievement is very poor. With some exceptions, most of those students seem to relate adequately with others and they cause relatively few disruptions in class. Despite making little or no effort to learn, they continue attending school. Testing has failed to show, for 20 of those students, any psychological or learning problems that would account for a lack of effort and learning. Among those 20 students is a group of six that socializes together on and off campus. Suppose you are asked to conduct research with those six students as participants in order to determine what structures their lives, orients their outlooks, and motivates their activities. The students and their parents grant permission for you to conduct the research. Complete Exercise 10.2 in order to plan your ethnographic research study.

Exercise 10.2

1. Formulate three main questions that you judge you would ultimately need to answer.
2. Formulate three subquestions for each of the main questions.
3. Within which situations and settings, in school and out, would you hope to obtain data?
4. What role would you attempt to assume when collecting data from the group of students—privileged observer, participant, or interviewer?
5. What might you do to encourage students to behave and speak as if you were not present?
6. If the study were supposed to begin in mid-January and end by mid-May, make a preliminary time line (calendar) you would follow in data collection, analysis, and summary of findings and conclusions.

THE NATURE OF NARRATIVE RESEARCH

The general purpose of narrative research is to tell stories, specifically the lived and told stories of individuals. The process of studying one or two individuals by collecting their own stories as the data and reporting those stories in chronological fashion (often through the use of life course stages) is at the heart of narrative research (Creswell, 2007). Among the several forms of narrative research that exist, all tell the stories of lived experiences, but they do so from different perspectives (Creswell, 2007). A **biographical study** is a form of narrative research where the researcher writes and records the experiences of another person's life. An **autobiographical study** is similar, but is written and recorded by the individuals who are the subject of the study. A **life history** portrays an individual's entire life, whereas a **personal experience story** is a narrative study of an individual's personal experience of single or multiple incidents or private situations. Finally, an **oral history** is conducted by gathering the personal reflections of events, as well as implications of those events, from one or several individuals. Additionally, narrative research studies may be guided by a particular lens or perspective (e.g., from a feminist perspective or from the perspective of Hispanic Americans).

PROCEDURES IN NARRATIVE RESEARCH

PEARSON
myeducationlab
for research

To learn more about data collection in narrative research, go to the "Narrative Research" section of **MyEducationLab for Research** and then click on *Assignments and Activities.* Complete the exercise titled "Collecting Narrative Data." This exercise will help you plan or foresee what data collection in a narrative study could look like.

The following general procedures are followed when conducting narrative research (Creswell, 2007). As with many types of qualitative research, the steps should not be viewed as a definitive and linear process, but rather should serve as a general guide.

1. The initial "step" in the process is for the researcher to determine if narrative research is the most appropriate method for investigating the research problem or topic.

2. Identify one or two individuals who have interesting life stories, or experiences, to share. You will want to spend a considerable amount of time with each. It is advised that you collect their stories in multiple ways (e.g., participants can record their own stories in journals, you can observe them and record fieldnotes, stories can be collected through interviews or written accounts with family members or other people who know your participants well, or you can include more "official" data in the form of work-related memos and documents).

3. Closely related to the procedure in item 2, it is critical to collect information on the contexts represented by the various sources of data. It is important to situate the stories in the appropriate context for accurate interpretations later. The experiences of the participants, and their related stories, might be situated in the work place, in a personal family environment, or in a context related to their culture.

4. The participants' stories must then be analyzed and "restoried" into a format that makes sense. The process of **restorying** is largely about organizing the collected personal story data into a presentation that will make sense to the intended audience. Creswell (2007) suggests that this may consist of gathering the stories, analyzing them for thematic patterns, and then rewriting the stories in some sort of chronological sequence.

5. Throughout the process of conducting narrative research, it is important to collaborate with the participants by actively involving them in the process of collecting, analyzing, and rewriting the stories. This allows for clarification and verification of the details of stories. Oftentimes, the meanings of particular events as told in the stories will evolve into meanings negotiated between researcher and participants, an activity that will sometimes lead to epiphanies, or key turning points, in the lives of the participants, as well as perhaps in the life of the researcher.

For those who are interested in learning more about the process of conducting narrative research, you may want to examine Clandinin & Connelly (2000) and Czarniawska (2004).

STRENGTHS AND CONCERNS IN NARRATIVE RESEARCH

The clear advantage of narrative research is its ability to focus in great detail on the events of an individual's life in an attempt to tie events together, examine relationships, and offer explanations and insights into that life within its specific context. Although it is a powerful form of qualitative research, it is not without its challenges. Narrative research constitutes a lengthy process, where the researcher must spend a great deal of time collecting extensive information on the participant. Additionally, there needs to be a clear understanding of the context of the individual's life (Creswell, 2007). The goal is to explain the multiple layers of context and experience that define us as human beings.

AN EXAMPLE OF NARRATIVE RESEARCH

To learn more about the overall process of narrative research, go to the "Narrative Research" section of **MyEducationLab for Research** and then click on *Building Research Skills*. Read the linked article and then complete the exercise titled "Identifying Steps in the Research Process for a Narrative Study." This exercise will help you identify key components of a narrative research study.

The focus of this narrative research study was the life experiences of disadvantaged female graduates of urban Catholic high schools and what these experiences say about the capacity of Catholic education to meet the students' academic, emotional, social, and spiritual needs. The study was conducted with five individuals using a series of in-depth, semistructured interviews.

Exercise 10.3

As you read the following article, see if you can answer the following questions about it:

1. *Problem.* What was the focus and intent of the study?
2. *Time.* Over what length of time was the study conducted?
3. *Subjects or participants.* Who was involved?
4. *Design.* What, specifically, was done to gain access to pertinent data?
5. *Data collection.* What kinds of data were obtained?
6. *Data analysis.* How were the data analyzed?
7. *Findings and conclusions.* What did the investigators find and conclude?

Urban Catholic High Schools and Disadvantaged Females

Corinne R. Merritt
Emmanuel College

> The purpose of this study is for five students to tell the stories of their lives in an urban Catholic high school.

The purpose of this study was to discover the life experiences of disadvantaged female graduates of urban Catholic high schools and what they say about the capacity of Catholic education to meet *their academic, emotional, social, and spiritual needs. Based on narrative inquiry, this study was conducted using a series of in-depth, semistructured* interviews *to elicit the life experiences of 5 participants. Twelve common personal characteristics emerged directly from the narra-*

> Two patterns or themes emerged through the analysis of their narrative data.

tives of the participants and provided the backdrop for two patterns: (a) the importance of education, and (b) the importance of relationships. This study found the high school

Source: Merritt, C. R. (2008). Urban Catholic high schools and disadvantaged females. *Catholic Education: A Journal of Inquiry and Practice, 12*(2), 204–220. © Trustees of Boston College. Reprinted by permission of the author.

experiences met the academic needs of all participants, but the different school sites varied in their ability to meet the emotional, social, and spiritual needs. This study also found four characteristics interacted in creating the Catholic school culture: (a) building relationships, (b) promoting a sense of community, (c) supporting a caring and nurturing environment, and (d) emphasizing respect for all members of the school community.

INTRODUCTION

All schools build, function, and operate based on purposefully written mission statements. The following statements come directly from the mission statements of a number of the Catholic high schools from which participants in this study graduated: "Our school embraces students with differing degrees of academic readiness from diverse ethnic, linguistic, religious, and socioeconomic backgrounds." "Our school seeks to develop a sense of personal dignity, independence, and service . . . [and] promotes the development of the whole person by instilling spiritual values, inspiring love of learning, sharing knowledge, and practicing skills." "Our school offers a rigorous and responsive academic program which includes the mastery and application of basic skills, the assimilation of higher knowledge, and the cultivation of critical and independent thinking." "Our school encourages each young woman to identify and celebrate the presence of God in her personal life and in community with others." "Our school strives to build a curriculum and promote a climate which will inspire students to practice Christian values in a pluralistic society." The

This is an important background statement.

significance of these statements suggests that the role of Catholic education in meeting the academic, emotional, social, and spiritual needs accounts for its success with disadvantaged students.

Background of the Problem

Catholic high schools meet academic needs by providing (a) strict academic structure (Bryk, Lee, & Holland, 1993); (b) an emphasis on high academic achievement (O'Keefe & Murphy, 2000); (c) curriculum

Brief background literature review; gives a framework for what Catholic education and its teachers should provide for its students.

content that reflects the culture of students (Kelly-Stiles, 1999); (d) sensitivity to differences in learning styles (Russo, Adams, & Seery, 1998); and (e) support and encouragement from teachers (Bempechat, 1998; Bryk et al., 1993; Ridenour, Demmitt, & Lindsey-North, 1999).

Bempechat (1998) found that Catholic school teachers "focused on establishing appropriately high expectations for their students, holding each to a high standard, and pro-

viding the academic support that [would] enable students to meet the school's standards" (p. 56). Such focus promoted the belief that all students can learn. In an in-depth study of 7 Catholic high schools, Bryk et al. (1993) found teacher commitment and expectations of excellence resulted in students who responded with "high levels of engagement with classroom activities" (p. 99).

Catholic school teachers perform many roles in the school—instructor, coach, counselor, advocate—and describe their work as ministry (Bryk et al., 1993; Ridenour et al., 1999), suggesting that teachers view themselves as more than instructors of a specific subject. Teachers are also concerned with the kind of person each student will become, resulting in teachers seeing themselves as role models to their students (Bryk et al., 1993; Ridenour et al., 1999). In addition, Catholic school teachers receive lower salaries than public school teachers. Yet, teacher commitment has not suffered (Bryk, 1996; O'Keefe & Murphy, 2000).

Although studies point to the ability of Catholic schools to provide educational practices that promote achievement among disadvantaged student populations (Bempechat, 1998; Ekert, 2000; Kelly-Stiles, 1999; Russo et al., 1998), little research has considered specifically the perspectives of disadvantaged females who graduated from urban Catholic high schools. This study examined five methods for meeting emotional needs: (a) maintaining personalism as a norm of the school community (Bryk et al., 1993), (b) building caring relationships, (c) promoting the belief that all students can learn, (d) providing an environment that promotes student self-esteem, and (e) reflecting the cultural values of the students (Kelly-Stiles, 1999). Personalism occurred when there existed "an extended role for teachers that encouraged staff to care about both the kind of people students become as well as the facts, skills, and knowledge they acquire" (Bryk et al., 1993, p. 301). Similarly, Catholic high schools meet the social needs of students by (a) developing a strong sense of community (Bryk et al., 1993), and (b) providing opportunities for students and teachers to share experiences (Bryk, 1996).

Finally, this study examined three means for meeting spiritual needs: (a) inspirational ideology (Bryk et al., 1993), (b) importance of religious understanding, and (c) a shared belief system (Bryk, 1996). Bryk et al. (1993) described inspirational ideology as "the pursuit of peace and social justice within an ecumenical and multicultural world. . . . It is seen in the explicit content of the shared values that ground the Catholic communal organization—caring and social justice" (p. 303). Similar to inspirational ideology was the idea of a shared belief system: "This set of shared beliefs establishes a common ground which orders and gives meaning to much of daily life for both faculty and students" (Bryk, 1996, p. 29). The importance of religious understanding reflected the aim of

schooling to nurture in students the feeling them apprehend their relations to all that is around them—both the material world and the social world, both those who have come before them and those who will come after. (p. 37)

One central question guided this study: What do disadvantaged female graduates of urban Catholic high schools say about the capacity of Catholic education to meet their academic, emotional, social, and spiritual needs? The findings of this study are expected to add to the existing body of knowledge on current effective Catholic educational practices that seek to meet these needs, as suggested in the mission statements of many Catholic educational institutions. As narratives, the findings provide the reader with the opportunity to reflect on the life experiences of the participants as they relate to his or her own experiences and for the purpose of practical application. The use of female participants gave voice to the needs and issues significant to women.

> There is one guiding research question for the study; it logically follows the literature review.

Research Method

This study used narrative inquiry (Clandinin & Connelly, 2000) to discover the stories and life experiences of 5 disadvantaged female graduates of Catholic high schools located in urban areas. Purposeful sampling was used to select 5 participants representing a variety of socioeconomic and cultural backgrounds. The theories of Bourdieu (1977) and Jencks (1991) assisted in determining the criteria used in this study for selecting participants. The criteria of "disadvantagedness" for the participants in this study came from the fact they were female and from family environments of lower economic status. The participants' parents might not have a steady income or they might have worked at low-paying jobs. For some, their primary language was not English and their culture was other than middle-class American. For some, their parents did not have a college education and lacked the knowledge to direct them through the application and admission process necessary for college entry. Any one or several of these factors could capture the meaning of "disadvantaged" for each participant. In addition, each participant was invited to clarify and describe her personal criteria of "disadvantagedness." The possibility also remained that a participant might not describe herself as disadvantaged.

> This is the appropriately stated methodology for studying life experiences.

> A purposeful sample of five girls was selected.

> The authors provide defining criteria for the purposeful selection of the study's participants.

In-depth, semistructured interviews were used to capture and describe the stories and life experiences of the participants, revealing the extent to which Catholic education met their needs in school. The narratives shed further light on the notion of being disadvantaged, as well as whether or not participants considered themselves disadvantaged. Each participant was interviewed six times for 60 to 90 minutes over the course of 15 months. Using open-ended questions, each of the six interviews focused on a single central topic: background of the participant, including family members, childhood experiences, and early schooling; description of the Catholic high school each participant attended; discussion of experiences relating to academic development; experiences that met emotional needs; experiences that met social needs; and experiences that met spiritual needs. Following each interview, participants were invited to maintain a personal journal in which they could elaborate on interview responses or share any additional stories or life experiences that could enhance or clarify what was shared during the interviews.

> Data were primarily collected through the use of semistructured interviews. Each participant was interviewed six times over the course of more than one year. The interviews were then transcribed.

> Student journals also served as a source of data.

Member checking of all transcripts, research texts, and narrative texts ensured the trustworthiness and credibility of the study (Gall, Gall, & Borg, 1999; Maxwell, 1996; Seidman, 1998). A series of open-ended interview questions provided the means for realizing and understanding the experiences and stories of each participant. A protocol of initial questions provided a framework and direction for all interviews, which produced biographical information of participants, narrative stories, personal experiences, and responses to questions related specifically to this study. Participants read their transcribed responses and had the opportunity to add, delete, or modify any portion of their transcribed responses. Each set of transcripts evolved into a personal narrative with an accurate representation of each participant, as well as the significance of common themes and differences as they related to the purpose of the study.

> Member checking was utilized to confirm the quality of the data collected.

Confirmation of findings resulted from the connection of numerous in-depth, semistructured interviews, individual personal stories created from participant interviews, personal journal entries, and the categorical analysis of responses as they related to the conceptual framework. Multiple member checking with each participant assured reliability of the findings. The findings were based on the analysis of all interviews, journal entries, personal stories, and narratives and corresponded with the conceptual framework to answer the research question for this study. The findings are presented

> The authors used a very comprehensive system for data collection and analysis, and to verify the quality of the data.

in two ways: (a) as descriptions of each participant's life in profiles; and (b) as analyses of responses, narratives, journal entries, and personal stories relating specifically to the research question.

PARTICIPANT PROFILES

Table 1 represents a profile of relevant information on each participant and her high school. The first eight categories present background information of each participant, including the criteria of disadvantagedness for each participant, such as ethnicity, citizenship, family income level, number of parents in household, primary language of the participant, and whether or not the participant was first in her family to attend college. The next eight categories represent details on each participant's high school, such as high school setting, grades serviced by the high school, enrollment size, ethnicity of students and teachers, aver-

> The participants' descriptive information is summarized nicely in this table

Table 1   Matrix of Participant and High School Profiles

Category	Jenny	Julie	Janet	Kelly	Nina
Sex	Female	Female	Female	Female	Female
Ethnicity	African American	Asian (Vietnamese)	Canadian American	Euro American	Latina (Dominican Republic)
Religion	Non-Catholic	Non-Catholic	Catholic	Catholic	Catholic
XCitizenship	American (Mother/African Immigrant)	Immigrant (Mother/ Vietnamese Immigrant)	American	American	American (Mother/ Dominican Immigrant)
Family income	Middle Class	Low Income	Low Income	Low Income	Low Income
Household	Two-Parent Household	Single Parent (Mother)	Single Parent (Mother)	Two-Parent Household	Single Parent (Mother)
Primary language Monolingual/ Bilingual/ Multilingual	English (Mother/ Multilingual Three Tribal Languages)	Vietnamese/First French/Second English/Third	English	English	Spanish/First English/Second
Attended college	Mother	First in Family	First in Family	First in Family	First in Family
High school setting	Coeducational	Coeducational	Coeducational	All girls	Coeducational
Grades serviced by high school	7–12	9–12	7–12	9–12	9–12
Size of high school	Large 1,500	Small 250	Mid size 700	Small 300	Mid size 900
Ethnicity of students in high school (estimate)	White 80% Asian 10% African American and Latinos 10%	African American 80% Haitian 15% Asian 5%	All White	White 40% African American and Haitian 30% Latina 30%	White 60% Latino 30% African American and Asian 10%
Ethnicity of teachers in high school	Mostly White 2 Latinos	Mostly White 2 African American 1 Asian (Chinese) 1 German	All White	Mostly White 1 Asian	All White
Average family income level at high school	Middle-class incomes	Low-income levels	Middle-class incomes	Low-income levels	Mixed-income levels/low-income/middle-class incomes
Grades attended by participant	9–12	11–12	9–12	9–12	9–12
Graduation date	2001	2000	1999	2001	2001

age family income level found at the high school, grades attended by each participant, and year of graduation for each participant. All information for the categories came directly from interviews and journal entries from the participants.

Profiles of Disadvantagedness

Each participant shared her views on whether or not she considered herself to be disadvantaged, according to the criteria of disadvantagedness presented in this study. Jenny's mother was an immigrant from Africa, whose primary language was not English. Her father was a minister, and when Jenny was young, her family lived in a parsonage, a home provided to clergymen and their families by the parish. Although Jenny did not describe her family as having any significant financial problems, she described her first house, the parsonage, as situated in a "very run down" section of the city. She described incidents of crime and violence in their neighborhood. Jenny's father did not earn a large salary; however, his position as a minister placed the family in a high social status in the church community.

A description is provided for each of the five participants, especially in terms of how each saw herself as being disadvantaged.

Jenny stated her disadvantagedness came from the fact that she was a Black female and often felt she had to "prove myself as capable . . . when people label me as an African American. And that Black females are weak [and] sexually promiscuous. As a female, people see me as weaker, not as smart, or very emotional." She also stated she did not see herself as disadvantaged because she had such a "close and supportive family." Jenny's home life, especially her relationship with her father, provided her with emotional security and encouragement to do well in school.

Julie was an immigrant to the United States and disclosed numerous elements of cultural differences. Born in Vietnam, Julie grew up in France and finally emigrated to the United States. She spent most of her life adjusting to cultural and language differences, as well as religious differences. Raised in a single-parent household for most of her life, Julie described her family as the "struggling class":

When my parents arrived in France, they had nothing at all. There was this place that would take care of them through an immigration program. They helped my mom find a job and they sent her to this town. Then she was transferred to [another] little town. You go where you have a job because they [jobs] are very hard to find. When I was 13, my parents divorced. He [father] didn't want to pay support because in Vietnam, men don't do that. Men don't owe anything to anybody, especially not to a woman and her kids.

Left with minimal skills, Julie's mother had to work low-paying jobs to support her family. Although her mother started college in a third world country, she was not able to finish her education, making Julie the first in her family to attend college.

Janet grew up in a single-parent household. Because her mother had a low level of education, she was forced to accept low-paying jobs. Janet described her family as low-income level, "living paycheck to paycheck." She stated she was disadvantaged "financially, always worried about money." Janet stated her family lived in a housing assistance program for low-income families. Like Julie, Janet was the first in her family to attend college. Any guidance in the admission process must come from outside sources, such as the school. Those like Julie and Janet can have difficulties at home with understanding the demands of college life, both academically and socially. Janet also stated she was disadvantaged "being raised in a single-parent family environment, missing that 'dad' relationship. I am lacking in a father figure in a really big way."

Janet explained class issues she experienced in her high school. Like Jenny, Janet transferred to her high school in ninth grade. For both participants, their schools started in Grade 7. Janet provided significant descriptions of the difficulties adjusting to social groups that had already formed in Grade 7: "It was hard to break in. The popular kids had already formed a clique." Janet clearly described the separateness of those with financial resources, the "popular kids," from the "smart girls" like herself, whose families struggled with finances. In addition, Janet made clear distinctions between the types of houses in her neighborhood as the "nice and not so nice" houses. She resented that the school was located in a diverse area of the city where those with low-income lived and that the school bused in the "popular kids" from outside the city where those with middle- and upper-middle-class incomes lived.

Kelly described her family as low-income level. Her father's medical condition put a considerable financial strain on her family. Kelly and her mother had to take on the burden of supporting the family. With minimal education, Kelly's mother was forced to accept lower-paying jobs, such as working in a nursing home or in a bakery, and to work long hours. She described the stress caused by her father's disability and the family's financial needs.

My time is so limited due to family responsibilities, dad out of work and disabled, working for tuition money and living expenses. All my [earned] money goes to helping at home or tuition for college. My family does not understand the pressure this is for me. I have no social life. I have no time to just stay on campus even to study because I have to go home to take care of my father.

Like Janet, Kelly was the first in her family to attend college. Kelly explained her family's disadvantagedness was primarily financial, complicated by her father's inability to work and his personal care needs.

Nina came from a single-parent household. Her mother was an immigrant to the United States and came from a poor family with limited education and job skills. Spanish was the primary language of Nina and her mother. As a single mother with a low level of education, Nina's mother was forced to accept lower-paying jobs to support the family. Like Julie, Janet, and Kelly, Nina was the first in her family to attend college. Nina described her understanding of her disadvantagedness:

> My mother was new to this country. I didn't speak the language [English] at first. My mother was a single parent. I started off with all those disadvantages at first. And also that we just don't have money. But we work for it. . . . We just don't have it. So those are the disadvantages. But my mom worked hard and I am working hard. . . . But the high school that I chose to go to helped me because it is college prep and it prepared me for college. High school reinforced it.

Common personal characteristics emerged directly from the narratives of the participants. All participants were hard-working, smart, good girls. They did well in high school, got good grades, or were considered honor students. All participants stated education was important. All participants shared that as young children they moved from a familiar neighborhood and school and were unhappy with the move. All participants made friends easily, especially in elementary school. They discussed witnessing crime, violence, or danger. Finally, all participants maintained positive attitudes in spite of adversities.

Although not necessarily common to all participants, several additional characteristics emerged from the narratives. Several participants discussed the significance of language. Julie and Nina were either bilingual or multilingual. Jenny, Janet, and Kelly expressed the desire for or appreciation of learning another language. Several participants had support from extended families, including grandparents, aunts, cousins, adult friends, peers, or teachers. Three out of the 5 participants' parents were divorced with single mothers as head of the household, suggesting the need for extended family support. Several participants were non-critical of Catholic education, with significant positive experiences with teachers. Several participants reported making friends in high school. However, two participants attended mid size and large high schools with mostly White student enrollment. These same two high schools served Grades 7 through 12. Both participants attended these schools for Grades 9 through 12 and reported difficulties making friends. Making friends was easier for the three participants who attended smaller high schools serving Grades 9 through 12.

ANALYSIS OF RESPONSES, NARRATIVES, AND JOURNAL ENTRIES

The following description and analysis synthesized the relationship between the narratives and the capacity of each participant's high school to meet her academic, emotional, social, and spiritual needs.

Academic Needs

All 5 participants stated that their Catholic high school experiences met their academic needs. Each participant felt well prepared for the demands of college. All shared that their high schools followed a strict academic structure that was challenging and demanding. Julie and Kelly reported their high schools "had strict guidelines for the college preparatory program; there were no frill courses" offered at their schools. Nina stated teachers and students assumed "college was the next step after graduating from high school."

> This section provides the analysis and results that allow the authors to address and answer their research question.

> All of the students felt that their academic needs were being met.

All stated their high schools emphasized high academic achievement, with their teachers and peers motivating students to excel. Jenny and Julie reported that their teachers held high expectations for all students. Jenny's teachers stressed "excellence in writing and reading and applying what was read." According to Jenny, her advanced placement English teacher applied the subject to real-life situations and "made you think." Julie's English and history teachers were demanding, with "high expectations for research and writing." Although she maintained self-imposed academic excellence, Julie stated she felt "supported and encouraged by teachers and students," which assisted her in adjusting to a new language and culture. Kelly reported that her English courses were "demanding and developed writing and critical thinking." Nina's English teacher encouraged her to move into Honors English and "to share my views through writing and how I saw things as a Latina." In addition, all of the participants stated teachers were always willing to provide extra support. Jenny had difficulties in calculus and physics and her teachers assisted her with their support and extra help after school. Julie stated her teachers and peers were sensitive to her needs as an immigrant, especially in learning a new language. She did not feel "put down," but instead she was "encouraged to move forward." Janet shared that her math teacher "helped her succeed" in math by providing additional tutoring. Not only did her teachers prepare her for college, but they also assisted Janet "through the college application process, completing college applications, requesting recommendations from teachers, and writing college essays." Kelly shared that teachers at her school "adapted their teaching styles to meet the needs of the students in class."

Teacher commitment correlated with the significance of teachers' multiple roles. All participants shared their teachers "were not just teachers but also coaches, advisors," and "someone to talk to when they had any problem." According to Jenny, her English teacher "respected all students and looked out for their general well-being." Julie stated, "My teachers prepared me for American college culture." Kelly stated her school "had two counselors; one for academics and one for personal problems." Because the teachers also directed extracurricular activities, "everyone was close to the teachers. The teachers were more than just teachers." Nina acknowledged students felt comfortable going to teachers with academic and personal concerns. Janet shared, "the strongest quality of the school was the teachers." The narratives reveal that teachers were the most significant factor in meeting the academic needs of all 5 participants.

Emotional Needs

This study found all of the participants experienced personalism among their teachers. Another relevant characteristic in meeting the emotional needs of students was building caring relationships, which all of the participants experienced at their schools.

> Generally speaking, most students felt that the school met their emotional needs.

Jenny and Janet stated the teachers were very supportive and expected all students to do their best. Julie shared that students, as well as the teachers, helped her "both in learning a new language and learning a new culture." Julie stated, the "teachers and students encouraged and supported" her, making her "able to focus on adjusting to a new culture and language." Julie's school also promoted a cooperative form of learning without competition. She shared that "you don't have the cool group and the group of not-so-cool people. You have the smart ones, but they also studied with those who were struggling with their classes. . . . Students helped [me] develop self-love and build self-confidence." This self-confidence and self-love was something Julie had never felt from her former peers in France. Julie's biology teacher told students "everyone can do great things." Kelly stated anyone could "get help from teachers if you needed it. Teachers helped everyone in lots of areas." Nina indicated the teachers expected all the students to graduate and go on to college. In addition, Nina found the "atmosphere of coed students taught me to speak up [for myself]; not be intimidated with male presence."

This study also found that 3 schools reflected the cultural values of the students. Jenny shared that "the values from home lined up with the school values." Julie felt she "had the same academic expectations as the school. Teachers had an understanding of the cultural differences of the students, that [because of financial struggles] the students had jobs, different problems, family issues, and came from poor homes." Julie often stayed for hours after school because the "teachers and students were so warm and inviting, unlike the family" she stayed with when she first arrived in this country. Her biology teacher helped her "find a better place to live" soon after her arrival at the high school. Kelly stated the students were culturally diverse, "but all were respect-

ful to each other. I left 50 best friends [after high school]." Nina was very active in the local Boys and Girls Club. Her high school, in conjunction with the Boys and Girls Club, provided a healthy support system for Nina. The staff at the club worked with the teachers and administration at her high school to encourage Nina and others to excel.

Janet's high school, however, did not meet her emotional needs. According to Janet, the administration seemed to favor the "popular, rich kids." Janet expressed her resentment of the unfair treatment of certain students by the administration. She felt they received this special treatment because many of their parents contributed money to the school. Janet had several friends from her previous elementary school with whom she maintained friendships throughout high school. Because Janet was such a good student, she was liked by the teachers.

Social Needs

> There were somewhat mixed findings related to the extent to which the school met students' social needs.

One way to meet social needs was by developing a strong sense of community. Jenny found the teachers modeled "genuine concern for each other, as well as for the students." Julie shared that since her school was small, "the teachers and administration were very nurturing. Everyone said hello." Kelly, who also attended a small school, stated, "it was like family. Everyone knew each other." Kelly and Jenny also stated their school communities often convened for joyous celebrations, as well as family tragedies and losses. Kelly felt supported through her father's sudden illness. Her teachers understood if she asked for an extension on assignments or if she had to leave school early or come in late so she could take care of her father. Jenny's school collected donations for the families of local firefighters after a tragic fire in the community killed several firefighters. Similarly, Nina's school was small enough so "everyone felt comfortable going to the teachers with problems." Events, like annual retreats, also brought students together in a special way. Kelly, Nina, and Janet reported that although these retreats met their social needs, retreats did not meet their spiritual needs. All 5 high schools observed annual student retreats. On these occasions, students usually went to a retreat house off campus to pray together, to discuss relevant concerns and issues, and to participate in community-building activities and spiritual inspiration. These retreats were also opportunities for personal reflection and prayer, alone or with others.

Both Jenny and Janet stated their high schools had not met their social needs. Both high schools were relatively large schools, which might account for some of the difficulty in creating a sense of community, at least for these 2 individual participants. Janet felt her high school did not meet her social needs in spite of her involvement in several extracurricular activities, such as dance team, service club, yearbook staff, Future Business Leaders of America, and the National Honor

Society. Student cliques neither reached out to others nor let other students in. Janet was close to several teachers who were also her coaches and activity directors. On several occasions, Janet stated "the strongest quality of the school was the teachers and their willingness to help students."

Spiritual Needs

All 5 participants shared involvement in social justice issues and activities. Each of their high schools required students to perform some form of community service. Religion courses included discussions on morality, ethics, homelessness, poverty, nonviolent resolution to conflict, and other social issues. Julie, Kelly, and Nina stated such experiences and discussions "inspired and motivated" them to become involved in the greater school community.

> Students believed that the school met their spritual needs.

Jenny participated in community service as a requirement for senior year religion. Julie was involved "in a leadership program exploring issues like violence, homelessness, and AIDS care" and participated in Christian Service where she worked with young children tutoring in reading and writing. Kelly shared her involvement in "lots of events around homelessness, Oxfam Fasts, and Social Justice Club." Nina's "religion classes focused on social justice issues, morality, racism, sexism, classism, and the treatment of prison inmates." Such discussions of social justice issues encouraged Nina to become involved in her community by working at the Girls' Club as a leader of the younger girls' group. In this role, Nina drew on her own experiences at the club to act as counselor, activity leader, and role model to younger girls.

Jenny stated her school's ideas on morality and relationships were of the same value system as what she learned at home. For her, the values of home and school were coalescent. Julie shared that her Catholic school experience greatly impacted her faith, and the teachers "taught me to see God in everything and everyone." Her teachers "inspired" her by their teachings and behavior. She also stated, "I learned a lot about myself."

All 5 participants stated their schools offered many opportunities for prayer and reflection. All schools began each day with morning prayer over the intercom system. Each of Nina's classes began with prayer. Janet and Kelly stated there were many visible symbols of Catholicism in every classroom. All 5 schools celebrated holy days and special days in community. The schools respected the faith of students who were not Catholic. These students shared their beliefs in class discussions, and they were not expected to participate in liturgies. Jenny stated she "developed an appreciation for other faiths" and "found meaning in all celebrations and services, even though I am not Catholic." All participants stated their schools offered a course in world religions, giving students an ecumenical view of spirituality. Nina shared the atmosphere at her school "fostered my spirituality and strong faith."

All 5 participants also described the significance of annual class retreats. It was while Julie was on a retreat with her peers that she decided to convert to Catholicism. Janet shared how at one retreat she "learned so much from students I wouldn't ordinarily talk with at school." Kelly described her senior retreat as "the most meaningful because it was our last time together. We prayed for each other's safety." Similarly, Nina stated the "memorable junior retreat impacted how I saw my peers and brought us closer together."

Jenny stated, "religion was the foundation of the school and it put a lot of faith and trust in God, which is a foundation for later in life." Julie shared, "high school greatly impacted my faith." Her high school experiences impacted her values and ideas on social justice issues, but she would not necessarily describe herself as a "practicing Catholic." Nina, on the other hand, stated her high school experiences "fostered her spirituality, which grew into a strong faith." Discussions and experiences involving social justice issues moved Nina to become involved in community service and to advocate for the needy in her area.

Janet and Kelly stated their high schools had not met their spiritual needs. Janet received her spiritual direction from her local parish Church where she remained involved. Kelly described herself "as spiritual but not necessarily religious." Nevertheless, Kelly shared that her high school had not met her spiritual needs due, in part, to her disinterest in spiritual matters.

In summary, this study found the participants had varied experiences in urban Catholic high schools. All participants stated their high schools met their academic needs. The data revealed teachers were significant through their support and encouragement and in their capacity to perform multiple roles. Caring and nurturing relationships, as well as shared values and experiences, contributed to a sense of community where individual high schools met the emotional and social needs of the participants.

DISCUSSION

Stanton-Salazar (2001) found support systems in school settings had more meaning in the lives of children from low-income and working-class families than in the lives of children from middle-class families. These support systems primarily come in the form of teachers as instructors and mentors, teachers as coaches and activity directors, and from school counselors. The data from the participants in this study concurred with this finding. Four of the participants described having mentoring relationships with at least one significant teacher, with Nina describing the significance of counselors

> Findings from this study are supported by the related literature.

from the local Girls' Club. Jenny, who described her family background as middle class, was an exception. She identified her family, especially her father and her older sister, as the two support systems in her life. These support systems, which Stanton-Salazar referred to as network systems, can, however, create conflict with a teacher's position of authority, placing the teacher in the position of choosing between advocating for the student and maintaining the established order. In other words, teachers as advocates for students in lower-class status must choose between the best interest of students or keeping social class order and maintaining the status quo. More research is needed to explore how this conflict manifests in urban Catholic high schools serving disadvantaged students.

Bowles and Gintis (1976) stated that schools maintain standards of control by which children internalize the expectations of society. This maintenance occurred in schools where lower- and working-class students had few choices about academics. These schools were characterized by more regulations and procedures in areas of discipline and general behavior, and less freedom for students to explore personal interests. Schools with students from middle-class families had more freedom to explore personal interests, more choices in areas of study, and more freedom to learn through a wide variety of educational opportunities. In this study, all 5 participants revealed their high schools had a strict academic structure and few opportunities for choice in course selection. All students were expected to follow a standard college preparatory program, with the prospects of post secondary education as the norm for graduates of their high schools. Ironically, the "standards of control," as described in Bowles and Gintis, although restricting at the time, enhanced each participant's preparation for the rigors of post-secondary educational experiences. Each participant revealed that her high school prepared her for the demands of college through rigorous coursework and high teacher expectations.

This study emphasizes important areas of professional development needed to support teachers in providing for the academic, emotional, social, and spiritual needs of disadvantaged students. Institutions of higher education need to evaluate their teacher training programs to include coursework and experiences that lead teacher candidates to an understanding of the needs of students from disadvantaged backgrounds. This includes courses on multicultural practices, the significance of language to learning, training in assessing and understanding the individual needs of students beyond academic needs, and training in identifying and addressing a variety of learning styles. The participants in this study indicated the necessity for Catholic educators, as well as teacher training programs in Catholic institutions of higher education, to explore ways to meet the spiritual

> Important recommendation for teacher preparation programs.

needs of all students, especially those from disadvantaged backgrounds. Furthermore, school administrators must provide for ongoing professional development for teachers who lack experience or skills for addressing the needs of students from disadvantaged backgrounds.

Finally, this study suggests the importance of listening to the experiences of students from disadvantaged backgrounds to understand life from their perspectives. The knowledge gained from such stories assists in determining what educational institutions need to provide to ensure the success of disadvantaged students.

IMPLICATIONS FOR RESEARCH

This study raised the possibility of research in several possible areas:

- Regarding the mission of Catholic education in the 21st century, will Catholic education continue to play a role in serving disadvantaged females?

> The authors provide several recommendations stated as implications for future research studies.

- Using similar methods, would the results be the same for males from similar backgrounds who graduated from urban Catholic high schools?
- How do Catholic high school teachers view their roles in meeting the needs of disadvantaged female students?
- Further research could explore follow-up interviews with the same 5 participants in 5 to 8 years to see how things developed for them. Do they feel the same or differently about the capacity of Catholic education to meet their academic, emotional, social, and spiritual needs?
- Further research could include a similar study with five participants from similar backgrounds who graduated from urban public schools.

The 5 participants in this study represent students found in today's urban Catholic high schools, as well as in many urban public schools. Their stories and life experiences shed light on the educational experiences and outcomes of today's disadvantaged students who are served by Catholic schools.

References

Bempechat, J. (1998). *Against the odds: How "at-risk" students exceed expectations.* San Francisco: Jossey-Bass.

Bourdieu, P. (1977). Cultural reproduction and social reproduction. In J. Karabel & A. H. Halsey (Eds.), *Power and ideology in education* (pp. 241–258). New York: Oxford University Press.

Bowles, S., & Gintis, H. (1976). *Schooling in capitalist America: Educational reform and the contradictions of economic life.* New York: Basic Books.

Bryk, A. S. (1996). Lessons from Catholic high schools on renewing our educational institutions. In T. H. McLaughlin, J. M.

O'Keefe, & B. O'Keeffe (Eds.), *The contemporary Catholic school: Context, identity, and diversity* (pp. 25–41). London: Falmer Press.

Bryk, A. S., Lee, V. E., & Holland, P. B. (1993). *Catholic schools and the common good.* Cambridge, MA: Harvard University Press.

Clandinin, D. J., & Connelly, F. M. (2000). *Narrative inquiry: Experience and story in qualitative research.* San Francisco: Jossey-Bass.

Ekert, J. L. (2000). *Ordinary success: Minority adolescent girls managing the demands of their achievement.* Unpublished doctoral dissertation, Harvard University, Cambridge, MA.

Gall, J. P., Gall, M. D., & Borg, W. R. (1999). *Applying educational research: A practical guide* (4th ed.). New York: Longman.

Jencks, C. (1991). Is the American underclass growing? In C. Jencks & P. E. Peterson (Eds.), *The urban underclass* (pp. 28–100). Washington, DC: The Brookings Institution.

Kelly-Stiles, P. (1999). Bridging the cultural divide: Catholic elementary school teachers and professional development in support of culturally responsive pedagogy. *Dissertation Abstracts International, 60*(07), 2339A. (UMI No. 9938907)

Maxwell, J. A. (1996). *Qualitative research design: An interactive approach.* Thousand Oaks, CA: Sage.

O'Keefe, J. M., & Murphy, J. (2000). Ethnically diverse Catholic schools: School structure, students, staffing, and finance. In J. Youniss, & J. J. Convey (Eds.), *Catholic schools at the crossroads: Survival and transformation* (pp. 117–136). New York: Teachers College Press.

Ridenour, C. S., Demmitt, A., & Lindsey-North, J. L. (1999). The experience and meaning of a Marianist education today: A national high school study of mission and school culture. *Catholic Education: A Journal of Inquiry and Practice, 2*(4), 410–428.

Russo, C. J., Adams, S., & Seery, M. E. (1998). Catholic schools and multicultural education: A good match. *Catholic Education: A Journal of Inquiry and Practice, 2*(2), 178–186.

Seidman, I. (1998). *Interviewing as qualitative research: A guide for researchers in education and the social sciences* (2nd ed.). New York: Teachers College Press.

Stanton-Salazar, R. D. (2001). *Manufacturing hope and despair: The school and kin support networks of U.S.-Mexican youth.* New York: Teachers College Press.

APPLYING TECHNOLOGY

More about Qualitative Research

In this chapter about qualitative research, we barely "brush the surface" of the many aspects of qualitative research. For more detail, we have provided several online resources that provide additional information—and even more resources—for you to investigate to learn more about qualitative research methods. Although this is by no means an exhaustive list, it will provide you with valuable resource information.

■ An Introduction to Qualitative Research (www.enquirylearning.net/ELU/Issues/Research/Res1Cont.html)
An online qualitative research text developed by Dr. John Schostak of Manchester Metropolitan University (UK); as stated on the page itself, the guide has been used as an introductory text for master's-level courses aimed at teachers, health professionals, and business consultants; provides an excellent overview of the qualitative approach to conducting research

■ Qualitative Measures (http://socialresearchmethods.net/kb/qual.htm)
Dr. Trochim's introduction and overview of qualitative research

■ Qualitative Approaches (http://socialresearchmethods.net/kb/qualapp.htm)
An introduction to the four major approaches to conducting qualitative research (i.e., ethnography, phenomenology, field research, and grounded theory)

■ Qualitative Methods (http://socialresearchmethods.net/kb/qualmeth.htm)
A discussion of the more commonly used methods of qualitative measurement (i.e., participant observation, direct observation, unstructured interviewing, and case studies)

■ Qualitative Validity (http://socialresearchmethods.net/kb/qualval.htm)
A presentation and discussion of alternative criteria for judging the validity of qualitative research (i.e., credibility, transferability, dependability, and confirmability)

■ Qualitative Research Resources on the Internet (www.nova.edu/ssss/QR/qualres.html)
A page of qualitative research resource sites on the Internet maintained by Ron Chenail of Nova Southeastern University; includes a link to an extensive alphabetical listing of qualitative

research websites, as well as links to individual qualitative research papers, research journals, and research conferences (including the Annual Conference on Ethnographic and Qualitative Research in Education and the Annual Midwest Qualitative Research Conference)

- QSR (Qualitative Solutions and Research) Home Page (www.qsr.com.au)
  The home page for a company that produces a software program for qualitative data analysis called NVivo; the site includes a free, download-

able demo version of NVivo (simply point your browser to www.qsr.com/au/DemoReg/Demo Reg1.asp)

- Research Proposal Evaluation Form: Qualitative Methodology (www.gslis.utexas.edu/~marylynn/ qreval.html)
  An online proposal evaluation form maintained by Mary Lynn Rice-Lively; summarizes 10 essential criteria for developing or evaluating qualitative research proposals

CHAPTER SUMMARY

Qualitative research focuses on the collection and inductive analysis of narrative, nonnumerical data. The resulting research reports typically contain a great deal of rich description of the phenomenon being studied, which is largely due to the holistic and naturalistic nature of qualitative inquiry. Qualitative research tends to be concerned with process as well as product and with the meanings that people attach to specific events, settings, or occurrences.

There are numerous types of qualitative research, depending on the nature of the specific phenomenon under investigation, including ethnographic research, narrative research, historical research, grounded theory research, phenomenonological studies, and case studies. This chapter focuses on two of these types. The purpose of ethnographic research is to gain an understanding of particular groups of people as they function within given settings and conditions. Data are collected primarily through observations and interviews. In narrative research, the researcher writes and records the lived stories of one or two individuals. The perspective from which those stories are told is also an important component of narrative research.

LIST OF IMPORTANT TERMS

autobiographical study
biographical study
case study
coding scheme
contextualization
credibility
dependability
ethnographic research
ethnography
focus group

grounded theory research
historical research
inductive analysis
interviews
journals
life history
member checking
narrative research
observer's comments
oral history

participant observer
personal experience story
phenomenological research
privileged observer
qualitative research
restorying
triangulation
trustworthiness
validity of data

ACTIVITIES FOR THOUGHT AND DISCUSSION

1. Here are the questions presented at the beginning of the chapter. How well can you answer them?
   a. What is the main purpose of qualitative research?
   b. What does the term *holistic* mean?

   c. What are the distinctive characteristics that differentiate qualitative research from quantitative research?

d. What is the process of conducting qualitative research? How does it differ from that for quantitative research?

e. What is the purpose of ethnographic research?

f. What is the purpose of narrative research?

g. What are the purposes of historical, grounded theory, phenomenological, and case study approaches to conducting qualitative research?

ANSWERS TO CHAPTER EXERCISES

Because multiple correct answers are possible for the chapter exercises, no list of "correct" answers is provided here. It is suggested that responses to exercises be made a topic of class discussion.

REFERENCES AND RECOMMENDED READINGS

Bogdan, R. C., & Biklen, S. K. (2003). *Qualitative Research in Education: An Introduction to Theory and Methods* (4th ed.). Boston: Allyn & Bacon.

Clandinin, D. J., & Connelly, F. M. (2000). *Narrative Inquiry: Experience and Story in Qualitative Research.* San Francisco: Jossey-Bass.

Creswell, J. W. (2007). *Qualitative Inquiry and Research Design: Choosing among Five Approaches* (2nd ed.). Thousand Oaks, CA: Sage.

Czarniawska, B. (2004). *Narratives in Social Science Research.* London: Sage.

Fraenkel, J. R., & Wallen, N. E. (2006). *How to Design and Evaluate Research in Education* (6th ed.). Boston: McGraw-Hill.

Gay, L. R., Mills, G. E., & Airasian, P. (2006). *Educational Research: Competencies for Analysis and Application* (8th ed.). Upper Saddle River, NJ: Merrill/Prentice Hall.

Glesne, C. (2006). *Becoming Qualitative Researchers: An Introduction* (3rd ed.). Boston: Allyn & Bacon.

Lincoln, Y., & Guba, E. (1985). *Naturalistic Inquiry.* Thousand Oaks, CA: Sage.

McMillan, J. H. (2004). *Educational Research: Fundamentals for the Consumer* (4th ed.). Boston: Allyn & Bacon.

Mertens, D. M. (2005). *Research and Evaluation in Education and Psychology: Integrating Diversity with Quantitative,* *Qualitative, and Mixed Methods* (2nd ed.). Thousand Oaks, CA: Sage.

Patton, M. Q. (2001). *Qualitative Research and Evaluation Methods* (3rd ed.). Thousand Oaks, CA: Sage.

Parsons, R. D., & Brown, K. S. (2002). *Teacher as Reflective Practitioner and Action Researcher.* Belmont, CA: Wadsworth/Thomson Learning.

Stake, R. (1995). *The Art of Case Study Research.* Thousand Oaks, CA: Sage.

Tesch, R. (1990). *Qualitative Research Analysis Types and Software Tools.* New York: Falmer.

Ulibarrí, H. (1958). *The Effect of Cultural Difference in the Education of Spanish Americans* (Research monograph). Albuquerque: University of New Mexico, College of Education.

Wiersma, W., & Jurs, S. (2005). *Research Methods in Education: An Introduction* (8th ed.). Boston: Allyn & Bacon.

Wolcott, H. F. (1994). *Transforming Qualitative Data: Description, Analysis, and Interpretation.* Thousand Oaks, CA: Sage.

Wolcott, H. F. (2001). *Writing Up Qualitative Research* (2nd ed.). Thousand Oaks, CA: Sage.

Yin, R. (2009). *Case Study Research: Design and Methods* (4th ed.). Thousand Oaks, CA: Sage.

CHAPTER 11

Survey Research

PREVIEW

This chapter focuses on the nature, intent, and procedures of survey research. Modes of survey data collection include the following:

- Direct administration
- Mail surveys
- Telephone surveys
- Interviews
- E-mail surveys
- Web-based surveys

The strengths of survey research include the following:

- Feasibility of data collection
- Versatility of data collection
- Ability to generalize findings to large populations

Major concerns about survey research include the following:

- Potentially low response rates
- Possible time requirements
- Possible financial requirements

TARGETED LEARNINGS

This chapter deals with *survey research*, an approach to conducting research that focuses on describing the characteristics of potentially large groups of people. As you study this chapter, you will learn about the various ways that survey data can be collected, different types of surveys, as well as different types of survey questions. Included in the chapter are examples of survey questions, a complete survey with cover letter, and a published study in its entirety. As you read this chapter, look particularly for information related to the following questions:

1. What is the main purpose of survey research?
2. What are the various types of data collection methods used in survey research? What are their relative advantages and disadvantages?
3. What are the three different types of surveys and how do they differ?
4. What is the basic difference between a closed-ended and an open-ended question?

5. What are the characteristics of demographic, knowledge, attitudinal, and behavioral survey questions?
6. What are the differences between checklists and Likert (or Likert-type) questions?
7. What are some important guidelines to keep in mind when designing surveys?

CHARACTERISTICS OF SURVEY RESEARCH

The central purpose of **survey research** is to describe characteristics of a population (Fraenkel & Wallen, 2006). It is for this reason that survey research is also sometimes referred to as **descriptive research.** Survey research is primarily a quantitative research technique in which the researcher administers some sort of survey or questionnaire to a sample—or, in some cases, an entire population—of individuals in order to describe their attitudes, opinions, behaviors, experiences, or other characteristics of the population (Creswell, 2005).

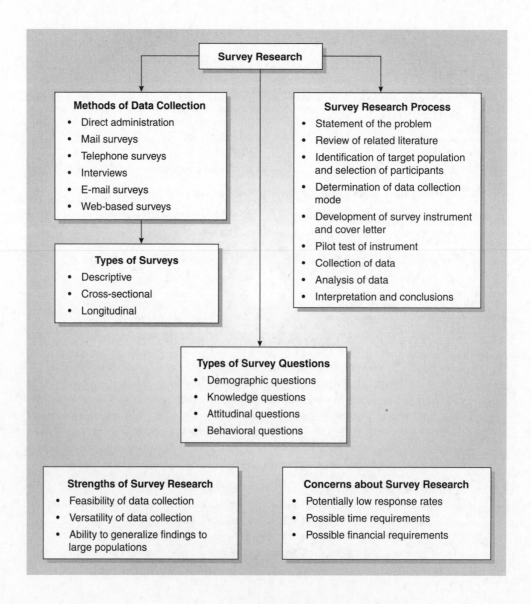

In most cases, it is not possible or feasible to survey an entire population. Therefore, a sample of **respondents** must be selected from the population. Since the purpose of survey research is to describe characteristics of the population, it is imperative that the sample be selected using a probability sampling technique in order to more accurately represent the population. No sampling technique will *guarantee* perfect representation, but probability techniques improve your odds of accurate representation. Accurate representation is necessary because the survey researcher is attempting to describe an entire population by collecting and analyzing data from a smaller subset of the larger group. If the sample does not approximate the population, then the inferences drawn about the population will be erroneous to some degree.

Survey research can be used in a descriptive manner, as has been explained. However, survey research may also be used to investigate relationships between variables (Fraenkel & Wallen, 2006; McMillan, 2004). This involves a combination of survey research and correlational research design (see Chapter 12). Educational researchers use this approach when the purpose of their study is to describe the relationships that exist between variables within a given population. Similarly, survey research may also be used in a comparative research design (McMillan, 2004). For example, if a researcher wished to examine the differences in attitudes between two or more subgroups of a population (e.g., with the subgroupings based on gender, ethnicity, years of teaching experience, or school level), survey research would be an appropriate methodology to use.

When conducting survey research, the researcher has a choice among several modes of data collection, including direct administration of surveys, mail surveys, telephone surveys, interviews, e-mail surveys, and Web-based surveys (Creswell, 2005; Fraenkel & Wallen, 2006; Mertens, 2005). **Direct administration** is used whenever the researcher has access to all, or most, members of a given group who are located in one place. The survey instrument is administered in person by the researcher to all members of the group and usually at the same time. This typically results in a very high rate of response, usually near 100 percent. The cost of this mode is lower than most others; however, the main disadvantage is that it is not always possible to collect an entire group together in the same location at the same time.

Mail surveys involve administering or distributing the survey instrument to the sample by physically sending it to each individual and then requesting that it be returned by mail before a certain date. While the cost can be a bit prohibitive, the researcher does gain access to a wider sampling of individuals than through the use of the direct administration mode. The trade-off, however, is that the response rate is typically much lower. Additionally, it is not feasible to encourage participation when the researcher is not face-to-face with the respondents.

Telephone surveys can be quite expensive because they must be administered individually, as opposed to the simultaneous administration of direct and mail surveys. These surveys essentially require the researcher (and any assistants, who must receive training) to read each survey question to individual respondents. Therefore, data collection can take a good deal of time, depending on the size of the sample. Also, access to some individuals may be substantially limited (e.g., those without telephones, those with unlisted telephone numbers, or those who exclusively use cell phones). However, telephone surveys are very effective at gathering responses to open-ended questions.

Interviews are the most costly type of data collection in survey research, largely because they must be conducted individually in a face-to-face manner. This usually means that either the researcher or the respondent (or possibly both) must travel in order to meet in the same location. The advantage is that it is easier to enlist the participation of respondents and to probe for clarification of their answers, due to the more conversational style of data collection. Somewhat similar to telephone surveys, interviews require that any assistants or staff be trained in the interview protocol, which requires additional time and expense on the part of the researcher.

Finally, the rise of the Internet has resulted in a substantial increase in electronic surveys. Electronic surveys are distributed to potential respondents usually as attachments to e-mail messages or as stand-alone Web pages, each with its own unique URL. **E-mail surveys** are delivered to potential respondents via e-mail and require an e-mailed set of responses in return. Individuals who complete **Web-based surveys** are typically directed to a website through initial contact via e-mail. They complete the survey online and submit their responses over the Internet. The cost and time requirements for these electronic modes of data collection are low. However, both modes require access to technology—e-mail surveys require an active e-mail account, which must also be accessible from some sort of existing database, and Web-based surveys require access to the Internet via a Web browser. The lack of a database for e-mail addresses of larger populations (e.g., all teachers in a given state) often prevents the use of this method. An additional limitation of electronic surveys is that many people are not comfortable using websites or with sending personal information over the Internet. Mertler (2002b), in addition to providing some guidelines for their use, has outlined some of the technological limitations of Web-based and other electronic surveys, including, but not limited to,

- Compatibility issues (e.g., older computers or Web browsers that will not allow the respondent to view or complete the online survey)
- E-mails being redirected to potential respondents' spam folders because they are sent to multiple recipients (thus appearing to be "spam" e-mails)
- The representativeness of the resulting self-selected sample (and ultimately the generalizability of the findings of the study)

Table 11.1 presents a summary of the relative advantages and limitations of the various survey data collection modes.

TYPES OF SURVEYS

There are three basic types of surveys: descriptive, cross-sectional, and longitudinal. It is important to note that a given research topic may be studied using any of the three types of surveys, as you will see in a moment, depending on the purpose of the research. Mertens (2005) explains the **descriptive survey** approach as a one-shot survey for the purpose of

Table 11.1   Relative Advantages and Limitations of Survey Data Collection Methods

	Method of Delivery					
	Direct Administration	*Mail Surveys*	*Telephone Surveys*	*Interviews*	*E-Mail Surveys*	*Web-Based Surveys*
Comparative cost	Lowest	High	High	Highest	Low	Low
Data collection time	Shortest	Short	Long	Longest	Very short	Very short
Response rate	Highest	Low	High	High	Low	Low
Group administration	Yes	Yes	No	Possibly	Yes	Yes
Permit follow-up questions	No	No	Yes	Yes	No	No
Permit random sampling	Possibly	Yes	Yes	Yes	Yes	Yes
Facilities required	Yes	No	No	Yes	No	No
Technology required	No	No	No	No	Yes	Yes
Training required	No	No	Yes	Yes	No	No

Source: Adapted from J. R. Fraenkel & N. E. Wallen. (2006). *How to Design and Evaluate Research in Education* (6th ed., p. 400). Boston: McGraw-Hill.

simply describing the characteristics of a sample at one point in time. In researching students' reading attitudes and behaviors, for example, a descriptive survey study might simply involve randomly selecting students—possibly elementary or middle school students—and surveying them in an attempt to describe their attitudes toward reading, as well as their reading behaviors.

A **cross-sectional survey** involves examining the characteristics of, and possibly the differences among, several samples or populations measured at one point in time. Using the same topic discussed above, a cross-sectional survey study might examine and compare the reading attitudes and behaviors of third-, fifth-, and seventh-grade students. All the students making up the sample would be surveyed at the same point in time. A cross-sectional survey conducted for an entire population, rather than a sample, is known as a **census.**

Finally, in a **longitudinal survey,** individuals in one group or cohort are studied at different points in time. In other words, the same group of participants is studied over an extended period of time, which typically involves the administration of several surveys at particular time intervals. The longitudinal version of our hypothetical study would look somewhat similar in purpose but would address somewhat different research questions. The purpose would again be to examine the reading attitudes and behaviors of students, but this time the researcher would follow the same students over an established period of time. For example, the attitudes and behaviors of third-grade students would be measured. Two years later, the same group of students would again be measured as fifth-graders. Two years later, they would again be surveyed as seventh-grade students.

Generally speaking, there are three main types of longitudinal surveys: trend, panel, and cohort studies (Creswell, 2005). A **trend study** is a longitudinal survey study that examines changes within a specifically identified population over time. An example might be a survey study of ninth-graders' attitudes toward and use of illegal substances between 2005 and 2009 in an attempt to identify trends in those attitudes and behaviors. Different ninth-grade students would be surveyed each year; however, they would all represent the same population (i.e., ninth-grade students).

In a **cohort study,** the researcher studies a subgroup (called the "cohort") within a specified population that share some common characteristic. This subgroup, as defined by the characteristic, is then surveyed over time. Let us now extend our example of studying attitudes toward and use of illegal substances and apply a cohort design to it. If the researcher wanted to begin by studying ninth-graders (i.e., "ninth grade" would be the defining characteristic) in 2005, this same cohort (but not *necessarily* the same people) would be studied as tenth-graders in 2006, eleventh-graders in 2007, and so on. It is important to note that the group studied each year may or may not comprise the same individuals that began the study in 2005; they are *selected* from and *represent* a particular subgroup of a much larger population. In order to be a part of the group studied in each subsequent year, participants must have been in the ninth grade in 2005.

Finally, a **panel study** is most closely aligned with the fundamental description of a longitudinal survey, because the researcher examines the same people over a specified length of time. In applying this design to our current example, the researcher would select and survey a group of ninth-graders in 2005, survey the same students in 2006, then again in 2007, and so on. Therefore, a panel study is somewhat analogous to a cohort design that studies the same people throughout the length of the longitudinal study. The advantage of this type of design is that you are studying the same individuals; the limitation is that some of them may relocate and become difficult or impossible to find. This tendency will likely result in an ever-decreasing sample size.

Cross-sectional survey designs are the most commonly used survey design method, especially when compared to longitudinal designs (Creswell, 2005), largely because they can be conducted in a shorter amount of time. On the other hand, some researchers argue that a longitudinal study provides more meaningful information (i.e., *changes* in reading attitudes and behaviors can be examined for the *same* students). However, the trade-off is the amount of time required for data collection in this type of survey study.

PEARSON
myeducationlab
for research

To learn more about different types of survey items, go to the "Survey Research" section of **MyEducationLab for Research** and then click on *Assignments and Activities*. Complete the exercise titled "Constructing Survey Items." This exercise will give you some exposure to writing your own survey items.

TYPES OF SURVEY QUESTIONS

Researchers can choose from several types of survey questions, based on purpose and format. Purposes can be subdivided into four categories of survey questions—demographic, knowledge, attitudinal, and behavioral. **Demographic questions** allow respondents to indicate personal characteristics (e.g., gender, age, level of education), as shown by the following examples of demographic questions:

What is your gender?

☐ Female
☐ Male

Which of the following is the most appropriate description of the level at which you teach?

☐ Elementary–primary (K–grade 3)
☐ Elementary–intermediate (grades 4–6)
☐ Elementary (K–6)
☐ Middle (grades 6–8)
☐ High (grades 9–12)
☐ Secondary (grades 6–12)
☐ K–12
☐ Other

Which best describes the educational level you have attained?

☐ B.A. or B.S.
☐ M.A. or M.S.
☐ Specialist
☐ Ed.D.
☐ Ph.D.

Knowledge questions seek to determine how much an individual knows about a particular subject (Mertens, 2005). This type of question is typically found on subject-based tests administered in schools. Knowledge questions on surveys have the defect that respondents could look up the answers; therefore, this type of survey is used less than others.

Questions that ask individual respondents to indicate their attitudes or opinions about some topic are known as **attitudinal questions.** The following two questions from a survey about No Child Left Behind (NCLB) and teachers' assessment practices are examples of attitudinal questions.

I believe that I know a lot about the No Child Left Behind (NCLB) Act.

☐ Strongly disagree
☐ Disagree
☐ Agree
☐ Strongly agree

I believe that the overall effect of NCLB on my school has been positive.

☐ Strongly disagree
☐ Disagree
☐ Agree
☐ Strongly agree

Finally, **behavioral questions** are survey questions that seek information about actual behaviors from individuals in the sample group, as demonstrated by the following two sample behavioral questions:

When you use traditional assessments, how often do you use self-developed forms of traditional assessment (e.g., teacher-made chapter tests) for your students?

☐ Never
☐ Not very often
☐ Sometimes
☐ Most of the time
☐ Always

When you use traditional assessments, how often do you use published forms of traditional assessment (e.g., chapter tests from textbooks) for your students?

☐ Never
☐ Not very often
☐ Sometimes
☐ Most of the time
☐ Always

Survey questions can be formatted in a variety of ways, including closed- or open-ended. **Closed-ended questions** (also sometimes called **forced-choice questions**) are the more common type used in written surveys, typically consisting of multiple-choice or other types of items that allow the respondent to select a response from a number of options provided by the researcher directly on the survey. Closed-ended questions may be used to measure opinions, attitudes, knowledge, or behavior. All of the preceding examples provided to you have been of the closed-ended format. **Open-ended questions** allow for more individualized responses, because respondents are not limited to selecting only from a supplied set of options, as in the following example of an open-ended survey question:

What strategies do you employ when you encounter a struggling reader in your class?

Closed-ended questions provide for greater consistency of responses across respondents because all individuals are selecting from the same set of options. Responses are also easier to tabulate and analyze than responses to open-ended questions, which can vary greatly in length and content across respondents. Because they are quicker to answer than open-ended questions, this format tends to be more popular with respondents. On the other hand, they tend to limit the breadth of responses and take more time to construct (Fraenkel & Wallen, 2006).

There are several common types of closed-ended survey questions. The most commonly used types are checklists and Likert (or Likert-type) questions. **Checklists** are questions that consist of a list of behaviors, characteristics, skills, or other criteria that the researcher is interested in studying. A checklist provides only a dichotomous set of response options. Typically, survey respondents indicate that they do or do not possess something, or have or have not observed something, for example. They are characteristically quick and easy to respond to and not too difficult to construct. However, you are limited with respect to the statistical techniques that can be used to analyze the responses. The following checklist question shows a typical example.

In which content areas are advanced placement courses offered in your school (please check all that apply)?

☐ English
☐ Foreign languages
☐ Mathematics
☐ Social studies
☐ Science

As introduced in Chapter 6, a **Likert** (pronounced "lick-kert") **scaled** question begins with a statement and then asks individuals to respond on an "agree–disagree" continuum. The Likert scale typically ranges from strongly disagree to strongly agree. There is no specific rule about the number of points that you must have on a Likert scale, but five points, as shown below, is quite common.

1 = Strongly disagree
2 = Disagree
3 = No opinion
4 = Agree
5 = Strongly agree

There tends to be quite a bit of disagreement among experts in conducting research regarding the appropriateness of including a neutral point on a scale (Mertler, 2006). By including it as a response option, the researcher allows respondents to indicate that they truly are neutral or have no opinion if in fact that is the case for them. However, if provided with a neutral option, there is sometimes a tendency for people to *avoid* thinking about how they truly feel; they simply select the neutral option, which may not represent their true belief (i.e., the data they provide is inaccurate). On the other hand, if individuals *truly* are indifferent or have no opinion, and you do not provide this option—because you are operating under the assumption that no one is truly neutral about anything—you "force" them to a choice that they do not really believe, thus providing inaccurate data once again. There is no right or wrong answer on inclusion of a neutral point on your rating scale, but researchers should consider the implications of including or excluding such an option (Mertler, 2006). In the following Likert questions, notice the format of the Likert-scaled items and that a higher number corresponds to a higher level of agreement with a given statement.

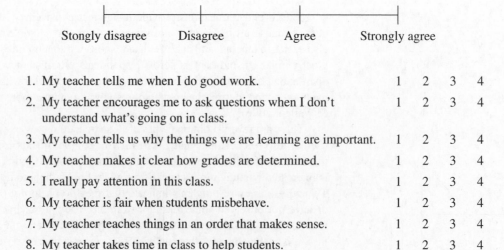

	1	2	3	4
	Stongly disagree	Disagree	Agree	Strongly agree

	1	2	3	4
1. My teacher tells me when I do good work.	1	2	3	4
2. My teacher encourages me to ask questions when I don't understand what's going on in class.	1	2	3	4
3. My teacher tells us why the things we are learning are important.	1	2	3	4
4. My teacher makes it clear how grades are determined.	1	2	3	4
5. I really pay attention in this class.	1	2	3	4
6. My teacher is fair when students misbehave.	1	2	3	4
7. My teacher teaches things in an order that makes sense.	1	2	3	4
8. My teacher takes time in class to help students.	1	2	3	4
9. This class is challenging to me.	1	2	3	4
10. My teacher gives fair tests.	1	2	3	4

Similarly, a **Likert-type scale** also exists on a continuum, but something other than extent of agreement is being measured. For example, a Likert-type item might require participants to respond on a scale that examines quality (ranging from "excellent" to "poor"), frequency of occurrence (ranging from "always" to "never"), or degree of benefit ("very beneficial" to "not at all beneficial"). The following example of a Likert-type scale shows a different possibility.

How would you describe your level of preparation, in terms of assessing student performance, that resulted from your undergraduate teacher education program?

☐ Not at all prepared
☐ Not very well prepared
☐ Slightly prepared
☐ Somewhat prepared
☐ Well prepared

SURVEY DESIGN CONSIDERATIONS

The process of designing a survey should not be taken lightly. Failure to follow some general guidelines for survey development can result in inaccurate data, which will then be followed by inaccurate inferences drawn about the population of interest. Whenever possible, it is imperative to follow these guidelines (Creswell, 2005; Fraenkel & Wallen, 2006; Gay, Mills, & Airasian, 2006; McMillan, 2004; Mertens, 2005):

- *Provide directions that make the respondent's task clear.* For example, indicate whether you want your respondents to circle an item, mark the checkbox, or write a response in the blank provided.
- *Include only questions that relate to the purpose and research questions of the study.* Do not try to collect too much information. Generally speaking, the longer the survey, the lower will be the response rate.
- *If you plan to make comparisons between subgroups, you must remember to include the pertinent demographic questions.* Once your data have been collected, it will be too late to go back and attempt to get this information.
- *Survey questions should be clear and unambiguous.* Avoid using words that are subject to interpretation. For example, "Do you spend a lot of time doing homework?" (where individuals are likely to have different interpretations of "a lot") should be restated to read, "How much time do you spend doing homework?"
- *Avoid asking leading questions, which might suggest that one answer is preferable to another.* For example, the question that begins "Would you agree with most people that . . . ?" could more appropriately be stated as "Do you believe that . . . ?"
- *Keep your questions short with a straightforward focus.* This simply makes the task of providing an answer easier for the respondents.
- *Avoid double negatives and negative wording in general.* Negatives tend to confuse people, especially when they are reading quickly. For example, consider the following question: "Which of the following are not rules that you would not be opposed to in your classroom?" As stated, it is very confusing. Restating the question as follows would undoubtedly clarify the task for the respondent: "Which of the following rules do you believe would be appropriate for your classroom?"
- *Emphasize critical words in the question by formatting them in italics, bold, or underlined print.* This forces potential respondents to read the question more carefully.

■ *Avoid the use of double-barreled questions.* A **double-barreled question** is one that essentially asks two different things. Consider the following question: "My principal is approachable and responsive." Because it is possible to be approachable and not responsive (or vice versa), this is potentially a difficult question to answer. If both components are important in your study, separate them and ask two questions.

■ *Use correct grammar and spelling.* Many people are turned off if incorrect grammar is used or if words are misspelled. This will only serve to lower your response rate.

THE SURVEY RESEARCH PROCESS

As previously mentioned, the basic steps in conducting a quantitative research study are fairly consistent across different types of quantitative research. The steps in conducting a survey research study are no exception, although there are unique aspects to the process.

1. *Identification of the topic to be studied.* As with any type of research study, the topic for investigation should first be identified. The topic is often refined and narrowed during the next step.

2. *Review of related literature.* As you have learned previously, related literature is reviewed in order to identify useful strategies for conducting the study, in addition to providing guidance about what has previously been learned about the topic of interest. Also, in survey research, related literature can be used to guide the development of survey or interview questions as well as data collection protocols.

3. *Identification and selection of participants.* In survey research, the initial activity in the selection of participants is to identify the **target population,** which is the larger group of people to whom the researcher would like to generalize the ultimate results of the study. From that list of people, individuals are randomly selected using a probability sampling technique for inclusion in the sample.

4. *Determining the mode of data collection.* The researcher must decide the most appropriate method of collecting data, whether it be direct administration of a survey, a mail survey, a telephone survey, interviews, an e-mail survey, or a Web-based survey, focusing on the advantages and limitations of each mode.

5. *Drafting the cover letter and instrument.* A **cover letter,** which will accompany a written survey or precede the interview process, explains the purpose of the study and describes what will be asked of participants. In addition, this letter also describes the potential benefits of the study. An example of a cover letter (used in a Web-based survey study) is shown in Figure 11.1. The survey instrument or interview questions must be developed based on the guidelines previously discussed. The survey that accompanied the Figure 11.1 cover letter is shown in Figure 11.2.

6. *Pilot test of the instrument.* A **pilot test** is a trial run of the data collection process. Using a small group (selected from the population of interest), the cover letter and survey are distributed and completed. On completion, the researcher seeks feedback from the participants. This process gives the researcher an idea of how long it might take individuals to complete the instrument. It also provides feedback about specific questions that may need revision prior to actual data collection.

7. *Collection of data.* Data are collected through the administration of the survey instrument or by interviewing participants.

8. *Analysis of data.* Most analysis of survey data will involve the use of statistical procedures. These analyses may involve simple frequency distributions, descriptive statistics, correlations, or group comparisons.

PEARSON
myeducationlab
for research

A cover letter is an important part of a survey study. To learn more about writing a cover letter, go to the "Survey Research" section of **MyEducationLab for Research** and then click on *Assignments and Activities.* Complete the exercise titled "Designing a Cover Letter." This exercise will give you some exposure to developing your own cover letter for a survey.

Figure 11.1

Example of an e-mail cover letter used in a Web-based survey study

Dear Ohio Teacher,

I am currently conducting a Web-based survey research study titled **"The Impact of NCLB on Teachers' Classroom Assessment Practices,"** the purpose of which is to examine how (or if) NCLB has affected the ways in which teachers assess the academic learning of their students.

Your superintendent has granted approval for teachers in your district to participate in the study as one of 150 randomly selected school districts in Ohio. The purpose of this e-mail message is to ask for your participation in the study. I am asking you to participate in the study by simply completing the survey as honestly and openly as you can. The survey should only take about 10–15 minutes to complete. When you have completed the survey, simply click on the **SUBMIT** button located at the bottom of the page to send your responses to me. Please make sure you submit your responses only once! Additionally, please complete the survey by **September 30, 2005.**

Please be assured that your responses will be anonymous. There will be no way for me to determine the origin of your responses. You will not be contacted for any further information. No one other than you will know if you have or have not participated in this study. Additionally, no individual information will be shared; only aggregate results will be reported. Finally, due to the Web-based nature of the survey, there exists a minimal chance that your responses could be intercepted, by individuals not involved with this study, while being transmitted.

Your participation in this study is voluntary. By completing and submitting the survey, you are giving your consent to participate. Please be assured that your decision to participate or not participate in this study will have no impact on your relationship with your respective school district. If you do not wish to participate, simply disregard this message. If you have any questions regarding this survey study, I may be contacted at mertler@bgnet.bgsu.edu. You may also contact the Chair, Human Subjects Review Board, Bowling Green State University, (419) 372-7716 (hsrb@bgnet.bgsu.edu) if any problems or concerns arise during the course of the study.

I would like very much for you to participate in the study by completing the brief survey which can be found by clicking on the following link:

http://edhd.bgsu.edu/mertler/nclbsurveya.php

It is important to note that the survey is best viewed with <u>Internet Explorer (version 5 or higher)</u> or <u>Netscape Navigator/Communicator (version 4.5 or higher)</u>.

In advance, thank you very much for your participation in this research endeavor and best of luck in the remainder of your school year!

Best Regards,

Craig A. Mertler, Ph.D.
Associate Professor of Assessment and Research Methodologies

APPROVED – BGSU HSRB
EFFECTIVE 8/22/05
EXPIRES 8/14/06

9. *Answering research questions and drawing conclusions.* The results of the analyses should permit the researcher to answer the guiding research questions for the study. Once this has been done, inferences about the population may be drawn and conclusions about the study stated.

Figure 11.2 Example of a Web-based survey

Survey of Ohio Teachers' Perceptions of NCLB and Its Impact on Their Classroom Assessment Practices

The purpose of this survey is to explore the impact that the No Child Left Behind Act (NCLB) has had on the ways that classroom teachers assess the academic learning of their students. This survey should take no more than 10 minutes of your time. Your participation in this brief survey is greatly appreciated!

SECTION 1

Please respond to each of the statements below, indicating the extent to which you agree or disagree with each one, using the following scale:

SD = Strongly disagree
D = Disagree
A = Agree
SA = Strongly agree

#	Statement	SD	D	A	SA
1.	I believe that I know a lot about the No Child Left Behind (NCLB) Act.	○	○	○	○
2.	NCLB has forced me to change the focus of my classroom instruction.	○	○	○	○
3.	NCLB has changed the nature of academic motivation for students and has placed more stress on students.	○	○	○	○
4.	NCLB has changed the nature of instructional motivation for teachers and has placed more stress on teachers	○	○	○	○
5.	The importance placed on Ohio's achievement tests and the Ohio Graduation Test (OGT) have led to instruction that violates the standards of good educational practice.	○	○	○	○
6.	I feel more pressure and stress as a result of the increased testing mandates in Ohio and the related need to improve student performance.	○	○	○	○
7.	My students feel more stress as a result of the increased testing mandates in Ohio.	○	○	○	○
8.	NCLB has forced me to change the ways in which I assess my students' academic performance.	○	○	○	○
9.	As a result of NCLB, I create a greater number of my classroom tests such that they mirror the same format and types of questions on the state's achievements tests and/or the OGT.	○	○	○	○
10.	I use multiple-choice classroom tests more frequently than I have in the past.	○	○	○	○
11.	I have substantially DECREASED the amount of time spent on instruction of content NOT tested on the state-mandated tests.	○	○	○	○
12.	I have NOT let NCLB or the state-mandated testing program in Ohio influence what or how I provide instruction to my students.	○	○	○	○
13.	I have substantially INCREASED the amount of time spent on instruction of content that I know is covered on the state-mandated tests.	○	○	○	○

		SD	D	A	SA
14.	I have NOT let NCLB affect how I assess the academic achievement and progress of my students.	O	O	O	O
15.	I spend much more time throughout the year preparing my students for the state-mandated tests.	O	O	O	O
16.	As a result of NCLB, I now spend more time teaching test-taking skills to my students.	O	O	O	O
17.	I have used sample test items from the state tests, approved by the Ohio Department of Education, to help prepare my students to take the tests.	O	O	O	O
18.	As a result of NCLB, I use standardized test data to help guide and improve my instruction	O	O	O	O
19.	In my school, I believe that most teachers are carrying on their work much as they did before NCLB.	O	O	O	O
20.	In my school, I believe that NCLB has forced teachers to divert their attention away from more important issues that can better improve teaching and learning	O	O	O	O
21.	I do not care to know any more about NCLB and its effect on my work as a classroom teacher than I do right now.	O	O	O	O
22.	I believe that the overall effect of NCLB on my school has been positive.	O	O	O	O

SECTION 2

Please respond to each of the following questions:

23. What is your gender?
   O   Female
   O   Male

24. Which of the following is the <u>most appropriate</u> description of the level at which you teach?
   O   Elementary–primary (K–grade 3)
   O   Elementary–intermediate (grades 4–6)
   O   Elementary (K–6)
   O   Middle (grades 6–8)
   O   High (grades 9–12)
   O   Secondary (grades 6–12)
   O   K–12
   O   Other

25. Which <u>best</u> describes the educational level you have attained?
   O   B.A. or B.S.
   O   M.A. or M.S.
   O   Specialist
   O   Ed.D.
   O   Ph.D.

26. <u>Including the current year</u>, how many years of experience do you have as a classroom teacher?
   O   1–5 years
   O   6–10 years
   O   11–15 years
   O   16–20 years
   O   21–25 years
   O   26–30 years
   O   More than 30 years

(continued)

Figure 11.2   Example of a Web-based survey *(continued)*

---

27.   What is the current Ohio Department of Education rating for your <u>school district</u>?
   O   Excellent
   O   Effective
   O   Continuous Improvement
   O   Academic Watch
   O   Academic Emergency
   O   Don't know

28.   What is the current Ohio Department of Education rating for your <u>school building</u>?
   O   Excellent
   O   Effective
   O   Continuous Improvement
   O   Academic Watch
   O   Academic Emergency
   O   Don't know

Click here to submit your responses

Thank you for your assistance!!!

If you have any questions about this survey, please feel free to contact me:
<u>Dr. Craig A. Mertler</u>
Bowling Green State University
Bowling Green, Ohio

PEARSON
myeducationlab 🍎
for research

To learn more about the overall process of survey research, go to the "Survey Research" section of **MyEducationLab for Research** and then click on *Building Research Skills*. Read the article and then complete the exercise titled "Identifying Steps in the Research Process for a Survey Study." This exercise will help you identify key components of a survey research study.

STRENGTHS AND CONCERNS IN SURVEY RESEARCH

As with any research methodology, survey research has its advantages and its limitations. Among its advantages are that survey research provides feasibility in data collection from a large number of people (and can typically do so efficiently), allows for generalizability of results to large populations, and is versatile both in terms of what can be investigated and how (i.e., the various modes of data collection). As you have read in this chapter, the wide variety of design options within survey research allows the researcher to "customize" survey research to meet the needs and goals of a research study (and its associated research questions).

Limitations include issues related to potentially low response rates, as well as the time and financial requirements of some modes of data collection. Low response rates are always a potential concern in conducting survey research. Unfortunately, there is no single, widely accepted standard for rate of survey response, which often depends on the nature of the survey study, the length of the actual survey instrument, and the population being studied. Some methods (such as surveying individuals through a direct administration mode of delivery) will likely be expected to receive nearly a 100 percent return rate. However, when utilizing mail, e-mail, or Web surveys as the mode of delivery, response rates of 50 to 75 percent may be entirely acceptable, and characteristics of the population may result in response rates even lower than this range. For example, some people (and, therefore, some populations) are constantly inundated with requests to complete surveys; educators are not immune to this fact.

APPLYING TECHNOLOGY

More about Survey Research

Because much of this chapter focuses on the design of surveys, the reader is referred back to the Applying Technology feature titled "Survey Construction" in Chapter 6. Helpful information is provided in that section concerning various elements involved in and considerations to be made when developing a survey as a means of collecting data. The methods, techniques, and considerations presented and discussed are appropriate for both descriptive research studies that may include or rely entirely on quantitative data, as well as those whose data results from open-ended questions.

With the increase and potential for Web-based surveys, we provide the following list of websites where researchers can develop surveys, have them published online, and collect data. Most of these sites charge fees, which can vary quite a bit, for hosting the survey and for storing data on their Web servers. The sites have many interesting features and we encourage you to investigate them.

- Insiteful Surveys (www.insitefulsurveys.com)
- SurveyGuru at MyOnlineForms (www.myonlineforms.com/surveyguru)
- SurveyMonkey (www.surveymonkey.com)
- SurveyZ! (www.surveyz.com)
- ZapSurvey (www.zapsurvey.com)
- Zoomerang (info.zoomerang.com)

It is always advisable to "oversample" from the population (i.e., select substantially more individuals for potential participation than you are actually hoping to get), anticipating some degree of nonresponse. Additionally, follow-up mailings for requests to complete the survey are nearly always necessary and will result in improved rates of response. Of course, doing so will add to the monetary cost of implementing the survey study. That being said, Dillman (2000) has stated that engaging in multiple contacts with respondents is the single most effective technique for increasing response rates to surveys.

AN EXAMPLE OF SURVEY RESEARCH

The following survey research study involves a national survey of high school counselors regarding their practice limitations and future training needs related to high school students' use of substances such as alcohol, cigarettes, and marijuana. Included are discussions for counselor training and recommendations for future research into students' substance use problems.

Exercise 11.1

As you read the following report of survey research, discuss your findings concerning the following elements of research studies:

1. Research problem
2. Purpose of the study
3. Method of data collection
4. Methods of data analysis
5. Findings
6. Conclusions
7. Recommendations

Identifying Substance Abuse Issues in High Schools: A National Survey of High School Counselors

Jason J. Burrow-Sanchez
Department of Educational Psychology, University of Utah

Adriana L. Lopez
Department of Educational Psychology, University of Utah

High school students consistently report the use of substances such as alcohol, cigarettes, and marijuana. One of the people they would talk to about a substance use problem is their school counselor. A survey study was conducted with a national sample of 289 high school counselors. Results indicated that participants were clearly able to identify their practice limitations and future training needs in this area. Implications for training and recommendations for future research are discussed.

> In the abstract, the authors begin to provide a rationale for why they chose to survey high school counselors about substance abuse issues.

High school students across the nation consistently report the use of substances as evidenced by data colle cted from the annual Monitoring the Future study (Johnston, O'Malley, & Bachman, 2003). Alcohol is the most commonly used drug among high school students with 35.4% of 10th- and 48.6% of 12th-grade students reported to have used it in the past 30 days. For illicit substances (e.g., marijuana, amphetamines), 20.8% of 10th- and 25.4% of 12th-grade students reported to have used one of these drugs in the past 30 days (Johnston et al., 2003). A small proportion of students who experiment and regularly use substances will go on to develop more severe substance abuse problems that significantly affect their lives (Newcomb, 1995; Shelder & Block, 1990). For example, in 2002 it was estimated that 11.6% of children and adolescents in the United States between the ages of 12 and 17 years were currently using illicit drugs, and 8.9% of this age group could be classified with a diagnosis of substance abuse or dependence (Substance Abuse and Mental Health Services Administration, 2003).

In the school setting, the counselor can be a source of support for students in many areas of their lives, including academic, social, mental health, and substance abuse concerns (Sink, 2005). For example, the school counselor can assist the student with the identification of a problem and referral to appropriate resources. In fact, students report that one of the people they would talk

> Rationale and justification for the study.

Source: Burrow-Sanchez, J., & Lopez, A. L. (2009). Identifying substance abuse issues in high schools: A national survey of high school counselors. Journal of Counseling and Development, 87(Winter), 72–79. © 2009 The American Counseling Association. Reprinted with permission. No further reproduction authorized without written permission from the American Counseling Association.

to about a substance use problem is their school counselor (Mason, 1997; Palmer & Ringwalt, 1988). As such, counselors may be the first professional contact for a student with a substance abuse problem in many school settings. Therefore, it is important to understand the practices and training levels of school counselors for working with students with substance abuse problems.

PRIOR RESEARCH ON SCHOOL COUNSELOR PRACTICES

A review of the research literature reveals that there are few studies that have examined the practices and training levels of school counselors regarding assisting students with substance abuse problems. Specifically, only three studies were found that surveyed school counselors about their perceptions of working with students with substance abuse issues. Vail-Smith and Knight (1995) surveyed a sample ($N = 109$) of elementary school counselors in North Carolina about their practices when working with children of parents who abuse substances. They found that almost all the participants in their sample indicated that it was important that counselors are able to provide counseling and referral services to children of parents who abuse substances. Nevertheless, more than two thirds of their sample (70%) indicated that prior college course work was inadequate in preparing them to work with such students. Furthermore, Vail-Smith and Knight found that their sample reported lack of knowledge and skills as the two most frequent barriers, respectively, to providing services to children of parents who abuse substances.

> The authors begin by identifying a void in the literature, one that will hopefully be filled, at least in part, by their study.

Goldberg and Governali (1995) surveyed a sample of school counselors ($N = 54$) in central New York across all grade levels (i.e., elementary, middle, and high school) about their preparation in the area of substance abuse. These researchers found that slightly less than half of their sample (47%) reported having taken a drug counseling course and slightly more than half (55%) indicated taking a drug education course. Counselors were also asked whether they felt adequately prepared and comfortable to counsel students with substance abuse problems depending on the type of substance used. More than half of the sample (59%) felt adequately prepared and comfortable counseling students about alcohol, whereas only a few (11%) felt the same regarding steroids. In general, counselors felt most prepared and comfortable counseling students when the drugs were alcohol, tobacco, and marijuana. In contrast, counselors felt least prepared and comfortable counseling students when the drugs were inhalants, stimulants, hallucinogens, and steroids. Furthermore, approximately one third of the sample (30%) indicated that they felt neither adequately prepared nor comfortable in their ability to identify students with substance problems. When asked about desiring more information on specific types of drugs, approximately half of the sample wanted more information on alcohol, tobacco, and marijuana and approximately two thirds of the sample wanted more information on substances such as inhalants, stimulants, hallucinogens, steroids, and over-the-counter drugs.

Coll (1995) surveyed a sample of school counselors (N = 124) in one state about their schools' procedures for identifying students with substance abuse problems. More specifically, the researcher indicated that his sample was taken from a population of public school counselors in a Rocky Mountain state. He found that 46% of the counselors in the sample indicated that their school did not have any formalized procedures for identifying students with substance abuse problems, whereas 50.2% of the sample reported that their school did have such procedures. Counselors were also asked about the effectiveness of the prevention programming in their schools for identifying students with substance abuse problems. For this question, 38% of the sample indicated that the programming in their school was not effective in identifying students with substance abuse problems, 20.2% reported being unsure of the effectiveness, and 41.8% indicated the programming was effective in identifying students with substance abuse problems. When asked about the percentage of students in their schools with substance abuse problems, 41.8% of the sample indicated that more than 10% of the students at their school experienced substance abuse problems. Furthermore, 62% of the sample indicated that at least 6% of the students at their school had substance abuse problems.

LIMITATIONS OF PRIOR RESEARCH

The results from the limited number of available studies, reviewed previously, fail to provide an adequate picture of training levels and needs of school counselors for working with students with substance abuse problems. First, each of the prior studies included small samples of school counselors. Thus, it is difficult to obtain accurate estimates of counselor training levels and needs given such small sample sizes. Second, the prior studies only included a sample of school counselors from within a particular state. Given this restricted geographical

Further explanation of this void in the literature, as exemplified by the limitations and delimitations of previous studies.

sampling, the results of the prior studies cannot be generalized to counselors in other parts of the nation. Finally, the results of two of the prior studies included school counselors from all school levels (i.e., primary, secondary). Although it is important to understand what school counselors across school levels know about substance abuse issues, it is likely more important to understand the practices of school counselors at each school level given the variance in student use rates by grade. For example, the national use rates of high school students are greater compared with those of middle school students (Johnston et al., 2003). Therefore, the training levels and needs of counselors working in high schools are important areas for further consideration.

PURPOSE OF THE PRESENT STUDY

To date, there has been no national survey study conducted on school counselors' training levels and needs for working with student substance abuse problems. Furthermore, large numbers of students in Grades 10 and 12 report the frequent use of substances (Johnston et al., 2003). Given these two factors and the paucity of research in this area, there is a great need to further understand how high school counselors perceive their ability to work with student substance abuse problems. Because of the limited prior research in this area, we have developed three general research questions that guided our survey development. For the present study, the following research questions were asked: (a) What are high school counselors' current training levels for working with student substance abuse problems? (b) What training areas do high school counselors identify as being most important for working with student substance abuse problems? and (c) What substances do high school counselors identify as being most common in their schools?

The authors pose three essential research questions to guide their study.

METHOD

Participants

A national mailing list of 1,910 high school counselors was obtained from the American School Counselor Association for use in this study. From this list, a sample of 500 high school counselors were selected and sent survey materials. The final sample consisted of 289 participants, of which data from their surveys were coded and entered for data analysis. A proportional, stratified random sampling procedure was used to select a geographically representative sample of high school counselors. Specifically, participant sampling was based on the percentage of high

A large national population list was used to select the sample, using a proportional, stratified random sampling technique.

school–age children living in each of the nine national divisions identified by the 2000 U.S. Census report. The nine divisions consisted of the following: Pacific, Mountain, West North Central, West South Central, East North Central, East South Central, Middle Atlantic, South Atlantic, and New England. The proportion of high school–age children living in each division was then used to calculate the number of surveys that were mailed to each geographical division. Finally, high school counselors within each of the nine divisions were selected using a random numbers table. A total of 307 surveys were returned (61.4% return rate) by participants. Of the 307 returned surveys, 18 were eliminated from analysis because significant portions of data were missing or the respondent did not identify as a high school counselor.

Participant Demographics

The distribution of percentages for the 500 participants on the initial mailing list by geographical region was as follows: Pacific (16.2%), Mountain (6.8%), West North Central (7.4%), West South Central (12.2%), East North Central (16.4%), East South Central (6.0%), Middle Atlantic (13.2%), South Atlantic (17.2%), and New England (4.6%). Of the 289 participants composing the final sample for this study, the following percentages reflect the distribution by geographical region: Pacific (16.0%), Mountain (6.9%), West North Central (7.6%), West South Central (12.5%), East North Central (20.5%), East South Central (6.3%), Middle Atlantic (11.1%), South Atlantic (16.0%), and New England (3.1%). As for participants' educational levels, the majority of the sample reported having earned a master's degree (94.8%), whereas 5.2% of the participants reported having earned a doctorate degree. For this sample, 76.5% were female and 23.5% were male. The racial/ethnic breakdown was as follows: 87.2% White, 4.2% African American, 3.5% Hispanic, 3.5% multiracial, 1.0% Asian American, and 0.3% other (0.3% did not identify their race/ethnicity). Participants reported being a school counselor for a mean of 10.82 years (SD = 8.42). Two participants indicated that they had retired within the same calendar year as the survey being administered and were included in the analysis. In terms of school size, the mean number of students enrolled across schools was 1,368.64 (SD = 899.48). Finally, counselors reported having a mean student caseload of 362.30 (SD = 185.10) and seeing an average of 16.16 (SD = 26.50) students per year specifically for substance abuse problems.

> Demographic description of the 289 respondents.

Survey Materials

A 36-item survey was developed to obtain information about high school counselors' training levels and needs for working with students with substance abuse problems (a copy of the survey can be obtained from the first author). The survey was developed throughout a validation process. Initially, the survey items were developed by the first author on the basis of the current substance abuse literature. Suggestions were then solicited from a senior researcher in the addictions field and from school personnel familiar with the role of school counselors. Next, the survey was pilot tested with a small group of graduate students (n = 5) in a school counseling program. The survey was refined on the basis of the initial pilot testing and was pilot tested a second time with another group of graduate students (n = 13) in a school counseling program. Final revisions were made to the survey after the second pilot testing.

> A self-developed instrument was created by the authors. There was likely not room to include the survey instrument in the article, but they do make it available to readers.

> The survey went through a thorough process of development, including two pilot tests.

Each item on the survey was categorized into one of the following four sections: (a) background information, (b) assessment and referral, (c) types of substances, and (d) substance abuse training areas. The survey used a variety of question formats, including forced choice, rank order, and checklist (Fink & Kosecoff, 1998). For example, some items asked respondents to indicate whether they thought they had the training necessary to work with students with substance abuse problems in specific competence areas. These items were rated on a 5-point Likert-type scale that included the following choices: 1 = *strongly disagree*, 2 = *disagree*, 3 = *neutral*, 4 = *agree*, and 5 = *strongly agree*. This type of scaling format was also used for other items on the survey.

> This is actually a Likert scale.

Additional items asked respondents to rate and subsequently rank order substance abuse training areas they believed were most important for school counselors. The last page of the survey contained an open-ended question asking participants whether they wanted to provide any additional information or comments. The total time to complete the survey materials was estimated between 10 and 15 minutes.

Procedure

This study used a survey study design composed of an initial mailing and two follow-up mailings in accordance with the tailored design method (Dillman, 2000). The initial mailing packet was sent to 500 randomly selected high school counselors across the nation as described previously. The initial mailing packet included an introductory letter and consent form addressed to the school counselor that briefly described the

> A very thorough survey administration procedure was used, including two follow-up mailings to potential respondents.

purpose of the study and encouraged him or her to participate. Also included in the initial mailing packet were a copy

> They even included an incentive!

of the survey; a self-addressed, postage-paid return envelope; and a bag of tea for participants to drink as they completed the survey. The second mailing was an oversize postcard sent approximately 1 week after the initial mailing to all recruited participants. The purpose of the postcard was to thank those who had already completed the survey and encourage those who had not completed it to do so promptly. A research assistant kept track of returned completed surveys prior to the third and final mailing. A final mailing packet was sent approximately 2 weeks after the reminder postcard to only high school counselors from whom a survey had not been received. The final mailing packet consisted of a letter addressed to the counselor encouraging his or her participation in the study, along with the original introductory letter and consent form; a copy of the survey; a self-addressed, postage-paid return envelope; and a tea bag. After the initial mailing, a small number of packets (n = 17) had not been completed or had been returned either because of the participants contacting the first author and stating that they did not identify as a high school counselor (e.g., elementary counselor) or because of the mailing address on the packet not being deliverable by the postal service. After receiving this information, we immediately replaced these participants from the initial mailing sample with other participants from the original mailing list who were randomly selected from within the same geographical regions.

RESULTS

To answer the initial research question "What are high school counselors' current training levels for working with student substance abuse problems?" we calculated the means of responses for nine items on the survey that addressed current counselor training levels in specific competence areas.

> Results pertaining to the first research question are discussed here.

As can be seen from Table 1, the mean scores ranged from 2.08 to 3.57. Thus, school counselors indicated the highest level of current training in relation to consulting with teachers about students with substance abuse problems. In contrast, counselors indicated the lowest level of current training in relation to providing comprehensive screening or assessment to students with substance abuse problems.

Further analysis was conducted to better understand counselors' perceptions of their training for working with students with substance abuse problems. For example, counselors indicated being neutral (M = 3.09, SD = 1.07, n = 287), on average, about having the current level of training necessary to effectively work with students with sub-

Table 1 Current Levels of Training for Working With Student Substance Abuse (n = 287)

Competence Area	M	SD
Consult with teachers about a student with substance abuse problems	3.57	1.03
Consult with parents about a student with substance abuse problems	3.51	1.02
Identify students with substance abuse problems	3.23	1.10
Work with students from families with a parent who has a substance abuse problem	3.11	1.10
Effectively work with students with substance abuse problems	3.09	1.07
Provide individual counseling interventions to students with substance abuse problems	3.02	1.15
Develop/teach curriculum units on substance abuse prevention	3.01	1.23
Provide group counseling interventions to students with substance abuse problems[a]	2.77	1.14
Provide comprehensive screening or assessment	2.08	1.02

[a]n = 286.

stance abuse problems. Male counselors, however, had a higher mean score on this question (M = 3.46, SD = 0.97, n = 67) compared with female counselors (M = 2.97, SD = 1.07, n = 220). This mean difference between counselors on the basis

> These results are from the use of simple descriptive statistics.

of gender was significant, $t(285) = -3.35$, $p < .01$, $r^2 = .04$. Furthermore, experience as a school counselor (i.e., years of experience) was weakly related to counselors' perceptions of their ability to work with student substance abuse as indicated by a small positive correlation between these two variables $r(285) = .16$, $p < .01$, $r^2 = .03$.

> However, inferential statisical analyses in the form of group comparison analyses (i.e., t tests) and correlational analyses were also conducted.

We also examined data from counselors who indicated that their school participated in a schoolwide substance abuse prevention or intervention program. One hundred counselors indicated that their school participated in a program that addressed substance abuse. On average, the number of years counselors indicated their school had participated in the program was 8.33 (n = 87). In addition, on average, counselors indicated that they were unsure of the effectiveness (M = 2.97, SD = 0.86, n = 84) of the program for preventing or reducing substance use problems in their schools as rated on a 5-point scale.

To answer the second research question "What training areas do high school counselors identify as being most

Figure 1 Most important areas for school counselors to receive substance abuse–related training (*n* = 282)

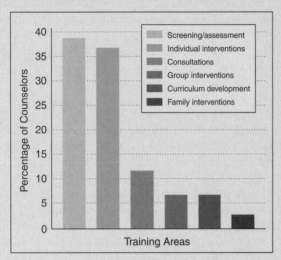

Nice visual representation of results described above.

the number of prior training opportunities their school or district had provided them in the past 3 years, 46.0% indicated none, 27.4% indicated one, 14.4% indicated two, and 12.3% indicated three or more (*n* = 285; percentages do not equal 100% because of rounding). Furthermore, mean scores suggested that counselors strongly agreed that they should receive (*M* = 4.48, *SD* = 0.75, *n* = 287) and would attend (*M* = 4.25, *SD* = 0.80, *n* = 287) training in the area of student substance abuse. Finally, there was no correlation between counselors' caseload size and their willingness to attend a substance abuse–related training, *r*(281) = .10, *p* > .05. This finding indicates that caseload size was not related to a counselor's willingness to attend a future training opportunity on substance abuse issues.

To answer the third research question "What substances do high school counselors identify as being most common in their schools?" we calculated the percentage of counselors indicating which substances had been used by students they had seen for substance abuse problems. The percentage of positive responses by school counselors for each substance is presented in Table 2. As is evident in Table 2, the top three most commonly seen substances used by students were alcohol, marijuana, and cigarettes, respectively. In contrast,

Discussion of results pertaining to the third research question.

important for working with student substance abuse problems?" we examined the areas that counselors believed were most important for school counselors to receive substance abuse–related training. The response of counselors who rank ordered an area as being most important for school counselors to receive training is presented in Figure 1. As can be seen in Figure 1, approximately 38% of respondents indicated that screening and assessment was the most important area to receive substance abuse–related training. Similarly, approximately 37% of respondents indicated individual interventions as being the most important area to receive training. In contrast, fewer than 3% of respondents indicated that family interventions were the most important training area.

Discussion of the analyses pertaining to the second research question.

Further analysis was conducted to better understand counselors' past training experiences and perceptions of future training for working with student substance abuse problems. On average, counselors disagreed (*M* = 2.29, *SD* = 1.07, *n* = 287) that their graduate education had provided them with adequate training to work with students with substance abuse problems. Half of the sample (50.3%) indicated not having taken a substance abuse course in graduate school, 31.8% indicated taking one course, 12.6% indicated taking two courses, and 5.2% indicated taking three or more courses (*n* = 286; percentages do no equal 100% because of rounding). Counselors indicated that, on average, they were neutral (*M* = 2.65, *SD* = 1.31, *n* = 286) about whether their school or district provided them with adequate training opportunities on student substance abuse. When asked about

Table 2 Type of Substance Used by Students Seen by School Counselors

Substance	%[a]	*n*[b]
Alcohol	98.87	266
Marijuana	98.50	266
Cigarettes	96.84	253
Amphetamines	71.79	195
Prescription medications	69.12	204
Over-the-counter medications	66.67	186
Club drugs[c]	62.43	189
Inhalants	61.41	184
Smokeless tobacco	61.40	171
Methamphetamines	60.69	173
Tranquilizers	59.32	177
Cocaine	50.29	171
Crack cocaine	41.46	164
Sedatives	35.95	153
Steroids	30.14	146
LSD	25.17	151
Heroin	22.92	144

[a]Percentage of school counselors responding "yes" to each question.
[b]Total number of school counselors responding either "yes" or "no" to each question. [c]Examples are Ecstasy, gammahydroxybutyrate (GHB), and LSD.

the three least commonly seen substances were steroids, LSD, and heroin, respectively.

Further analysis was conducted to better understand whether school size was related to the number of students that counselors had seen for substance abuse problems. A weak correlation was found between school size (i.e., student census) and the number of students counselors had

> More correlational analyses were conducted here.

seen for a substance-related issue, $r(273) = .15$, $p < .05$, $r^2 = .02$. This finding indicates that there was a small positive relationship between school size and a counselor seeing a student for a substance abuse problem. In addition, a weak correlation was found between school size and the number of students referred by counselors to an outside agency for substance abuse assessment or treatment, $r(270) = .15$, $p < .05$, $r^2 = .02$. Similarly, this finding indicates that there was a small positive relationship between school size and the number of students referred by counselors for a substance use or abuse problem.

DISCUSSION

The results of this study provide important information about the training levels and needs of high school counselors for addressing student substance abuse concerns. First, high school counselors reported differential levels of train-

> Summary of results are provided and are tied back to a void in the literature.

ing concerning specific competence areas for student substance abuse. Second, counselors clearly identified two to three important areas for further training for working with high school students who abuse substances. Third, counselors identified certain substances (e.g., alcohol, marijuana) as being more prevalent with students on their campuses. The results from the present study fill a gap in the literature by providing a more complete picture of the actual training levels and needs for high school counselors and student substance abuse. More specifically, this is the first study to survey a national sample of high school counselors on their training levels and needs related to student substance abuse. Each of the central findings of the present study is further discussed in more detail in the following sections.

Counselor Training Levels

High school counselors reported differences in their training levels for working with student substance abuse issues in their schools. For example, consultation with teachers

> Discussion of three specific areas of findings are presented next.

and parents was endorsed most strongly by counselors. This finding is not surprising given that counselors spend large parts

of their time consulting with other school personnel (e.g., teachers, administrators) and parents regarding the academic, career, personal, and social needs of students (Partin, 1993; Tennyson, Miller, Skovholt, & Williams, 1989). Nevertheless, counselors less strongly endorsed their ability to identify students with substance abuse problems, work effectively with these students, and develop or teach curriculum units on this topic. Unfortunately, these findings are not unexpected given that half of the sample reported not having taken a single course on substance abuse in graduate school, and almost half indicated that their school or district had not provided any training on this topic in the past 3 years. Counselors were least likely to endorse their ability to provide group counseling and screening or assessment for student substance abuse. The lack of training in group counseling for substance abuse was somewhat surprising given that group-based intervention is frequently used in school settings and is a useful format for working with students with substance abuse problems (Burrow-Sanchez & Hawken, 2007). With some additional training, counselors could use their existing group facilitation skills to develop groups that would benefit the needs of students with substance abuse concerns.

Some counselors indicated in the comments section of the survey that they do not have the time or training to provide interventions for students with substance abuse problems and refer such students to specialists, school administration, or an outside community treatment agency. Even if the counselor is simply a referral resource for the student, it is still important for him or her to posses a basic level of training to appropriately identify students with substance abuse problems to facilitate appropriate referrals and a continuation of educational services for the student (Burrow-Sanchez & Hawken, 2007; Lambie & Rokutani, 2002). Furthermore, effectively assisting a student with a substance abuse problem will likely help the student in other areas of his or her life. For example, one counselor stated, "Substance abuse is [the] #1 problem in roadblocks to academic success [high school diploma]." In addition, it is important for school counselors to assist students who transition back into the school system after completing treatment in a community facility.

Needed Training Areas

The counselors in this study clearly identified the most important areas for high school counselors to receive substance abuse–related training. For example, approximately 38% of the sample indicated that screening and assessment was the most important area for high school counselors to receive training. Approximately 37% indicated that individual interventions were the most important area for counselor training. A training need in screening and assessment is not unexpected given that counselors also believed that their training in this area was clearly lacking as described previously. Screening instruments are available that would assist counselors in obtaining more information about an adolescent's level of substance use (see Burrow-Sanchez & Hawken, 2007). Similarly, a training need in individual interventions is also not surprising given that counselors in high school settings identify spending a portion of their time meeting individually with students (Partin, 1993; Tennyson et al., 1989). Individual interventions can be used by school counselors to motivate students to identify problems and seek further treatment (Lambie, 2004). Thus, screening and individual interventions are two needed areas of training for high school counselors for them to effectively work with students with substance abuse problems.

Although counselors in this study identified specific training needs, some also expressed concern about the lack of time in a typical day to meet with students and provide direct services. Some stated that counselors are required to spend much of their day in front of a computer terminal dealing with scheduling issues instead of providing direct services to students. For example, one counselor stated, "Frankly, over the last four years, the school counselors at my school have seen our jobs gradually change from dealing with people to dealing with data/computers." Given these types of statements, we were concerned that, even if counselors were provided with training opportunities in these areas, they would not take advantage of them. We were glad to find, however, that counselors strongly endorsed their willingness to attend training on substance abuse topics. Furthermore, they even more strongly endorsed the position that counselors should receive training in student substance abuse topics. Our findings also suggested that caseload size, as one indicator of counselor workload, was not a factor in their willingness to attend future substance abuse–related training opportunities. Therefore, it seems that the high school counselors in our sample were eager to receive training to further develop their skills in the area of student substance abuse.

Prevalence of Substances

The counselors in this study identified the most prevalent substances used by students they had seen for substance abuse problems as alcohol, marijuana, and cigarettes. These data were obtained by counselors responding to a question asking them to indicate which substances had been used by the students they had seen for substance abuse problems. Thus, each counselor's assessment of type of substance used was based on his or her perception and may or may not have included self-report data from the student. Nevertheless, our findings that these three substances were most prevalent coincide with the national data for high school students (Johnston et al., 2003). Some counselors indicated that they would like to receive more information about the types of substances currently being used by students. One resource for school counselors to obtain more information on

substances of abuse is the National Institute on Drug Abuse Web site (www.nida.nih.gov). This Web site contains current information on substance abuse that is easily accessible to a range of individuals (e.g., students, parents, counselors). A second resource is the Substance Abuse and Mental Health Services Administration Web site (www.samhsa.gov). This Web site features information about substance abuse and mental health as well as a national substance abuse treatment locator. In addition to the aforementioned resources, it is also important that high school counselors receive didactic training (e.g., in service) on the types of substances used by students.

Limitations and Implications for Future Research

The majority of the sample in this study identified as being White (87.2%). A potential limitation of this sample is that it may not generalize to high school counselors from ethnically diverse backgrounds. For example, it is important to understand whether counselors from various ethnic groups share similar or different perspectives on dealing with student substance use and abuse issues in their schools. A secondary issue is to understand how students from different ethnic groups are perceived by school counselors regarding substance use and abuse. This type of information may lead to designing specific prevention or intervention efforts that meet the diverse needs of students instead of assuming that programming interventions work well for all students regardless of ethnic differences. Investigating these cultural issues should be a target for future research in this area.

The authors have provided a good discussion of several potential limitations to the findings of their study. Additionally, they have extended those limitations into discussions of recommendations for future research.

The data we obtained from counselors regarding the types of substances used by students were limited for the reason that they were based on counselor perception and may or may not have included student self-report. Therefore, we cannot be certain that the counselor's assessment of the substances used by students accurately reflected what the students used. Despite this limitation, our data for alcohol, marijuana, and cigarettes were reflective of the use levels reported by students in national samples (Johnston et al., 2003). Future research in this area, however, should focus on more accurately measuring how school counselors make assessments of the type of substances that students are using in their schools.

Our survey included only a few questions asking counselors about any current schoolwide prevention or intervention programs for substance abuse in their schools. Our results indicated that counselors with substance abuse programming in their schools were, on average, not sure of the effectiveness of them. We suggest that it is important for school counselors to be familiar with the effectiveness of any prevention or intervention program in their school that involves them. For example, school district budgets are becoming increasingly tighter around the nation, and school personnel frequently need to justify the inclusion or exclusion of specific programs in their schools. In addition, the school counseling profession has placed greater emphasis on accountability for school counselors, which includes ways to evaluate the impact of their work with students (Davis, 2005; Lapan, 2005). Additional research in this area should examine ways to measure the effectiveness of substance abuse interventions from a school counselor perspective. This issue is important considering that school personnel will likely have more "buy in" for a program when they are aware of evidence that it actually works and can produce empirical data to support its effectiveness.

Recent research in the form of a meta-analysis and literature review have provided a more thorough understanding of the effectiveness or lack thereof for school-based substance abuse prevention programs (see Cuijpers, 2002; Tobler et al., 2000; White & Pitts, 1998). For example, Cuijpers suggested that substance abuse prevention programs selected for use in school or other settings should have demonstrated efficacy in the research literature. Furthermore, he provided a listing of evidence-based criteria (e.g., interactive delivery, peer leaders) that should be carefully considered when implementing a program. The findings from current research also underscore the importance of implementing substance abuse programs in schools that are evidence based and effective rather than popular but ineffective (Clayton, Leukefeld, Harrington, & Cattarello, 1996). Thus, it is important for school counselors and other school personnel to become familiar with ways to assess the effectiveness of prevention programs currently used in their schools as well as establish evidence-based criteria to evaluate new programs prior to adopting them.

This study had a clear focus on understanding the perspectives on student substance abuse issues from counselors at the high school level. Given that national data exist on the prevalence of drug use rates for middle school students, one area for future research is considering the perspectives of middle school counselors. Specifically, data from a recent Monitoring the Future study indicate that students in the 8th grade across the nation report the use of a range of substances (Johnston et al., 2003). In particular, the national data suggest that inhalant use is higher among students in 8th grade compared with students in 10th and 12th grades. This finding highlights the importance that school counselors should be cognizant of differences in substance use depending on the age of the student. A well-known risk factor for substance use and abuse is the age of first using a substance. For example, children who begin using substances at younger ages are more likely to develop problems later in life (Hawkins, Catalano, & Miller, 1992). Furthermore,

school counselors can play a key role in promoting the prevention and intervention programs for students in middle schools. Unfortunately, little data exist on the training levels and needs of middle school counselors related to substance abuse prevention or intervention programming. Thus, the role of middle school counselors related to student substance abuse should be a key area for future research.

References

Burrow-Sanchez, J. J., & Hawken, L. S. (2007). *Helping students overcome substance abuse: Effective practices for prevention and intervention.* New York: Guilford Press.

Clayton, R. R., Leukefeld, C. G., Harrington, N. G., & Cattarello, A. (1996). DARE (Drug Abuse Resistance Education): Very popular but not very effective. In C. B. McCoy, L. R. Metsch, & J. A. Inciardi (Eds.), *Intervening with drug-involved youth* (pp. 101–109). Thousand Oaks, CA: Sage.

Coll, K. M. (1995). Legal challenges in secondary prevention programming for students with substance abuse problems. *The School Counselor, 4,* 35–42.

Cuijpers, P. (2002). Effective ingredients of school-based drug prevention programs: A systematic review. *Addictive Behaviors, 27,* 1009–1023.

Davis, T. (2005). *Exploring school counseling: Professional practices and perspectives.* Boston: Lahaska Press.

Dillman, D. A. (2000). *Mail and Internet surveys: The tailored design method* (2nd ed.). New York: Wiley.

Fink, A., & Kosecoff, J. (1998). *How to conduct surveys: A step-by-step guide* (2nd ed.). Thousand Oaks, CA: Sage.

Goldberg, R., & Governali, J. (1995). Substance abuse counseling and the school counselor: A needs assessment. *Wellness Perspectives, 11,* 19–29.

Hawkins, J. D., Catalano, R. F., & Miller, J. Y. (1992). Risk and protective factors for alcohol and other drug problems in adolescence and early adulthood: Implications for substance abuse prevention. *Psychological Bulletin, 112,* 64–105.

Johnston, L. D., O'Malley, P. M., & Bachman, J. G. (2003). *Monitoring the Future national results on adolescent drug use: Overview of key findings, 2002* (NIH Publication No. 03-5374). Bethesda, MD: National Institute on Drug Abuse.

Lambie, G. W. (2004). Motivational enhancement therapy: A tool for professional school counselors working with adolescents. *Professional School Counseling, 7,* 268–276.

Lambie, G. W., & Rokutani, L. J. (2002). A systems approach to substance abuse identification and intervention for school counselors. *Professional School Counseling, 5,* 353–360.

Lapan, R. T. (2005). Evaluating school counseling programs. In C. A. Sink (Ed.), *Contemporary school counseling: Theory, research, and practice* (pp. 257–293). Boston: Lahaska Press.

Mason, M. J. (1997). Patterns of service utilization for Mexican American majority students who use alcohol or other drugs. *Journal of Health & Social Policy, 9,* 21–27.

Newcomb, M. D. (1995). Identifying high-risk youth: Prevalence and patterns of adolescent drug abuse. In E. Rahdert & D. Czechowicz (Eds.), *Adolescent drug abuse: Clinical assessment and therapeutic interventions* (NIDA Research

Monograph No. 156, pp. 7–38). Rockville, MD: U.S. Department of Health and Human Services.

Palmer, J. H., & Ringwalt, C. L. (1988). Prevalence of alcohol and drug use among North Carolina public school students. *Journal of School Health, 58,* 288–291.

Partin, R. L. (1993). School counselors' time: Where does it go? *School Counselor, 40,* 274–281.

Shelder, J., & Block, J. (1990). Adolescent drug use and psychological health: A longitudinal inquiry. *American Psychologist, 45,* 612–630.

Sink, C. (2005). *Contemporary school counseling: Theory, research, and practice.* Boston: Lahaska Press.

Substance Abuse and Mental Health Services Administration. (2003). *Results from the 2002 national survey on drug use and health: National findings* (NHSDA Series H-22, DHHS Publication No. SMA 03-3836). Rockville, MD: Substance Abuse and Mental Health Administration, Office of Applied Studies.

Tennyson, W. W., Miller, G. D., Skovholt, T. M., & Williams, R. C. (1989). How they view their role: A survey of counselors in different secondary schools. *Journal of Counseling and Development, 67,* 399–403.

Tobler, N. S., Roona, M. R., Ochshorn, P., Marshall, D. G., Streke, A. V., & Stackpole, K. M. (2000). School-based adolescent drug prevention programs: 1998 meta-analysis. *The Journal of Primary Prevention, 20,* 275–336.

Vail-Smith, K., & Knight, S. M. (1995). Children of substance abusers in the elementary school: A survey of counselor perceptions. *Elementary School Guidance & Counseling, 29,* 163–177.

White, D., & Pitts, M. (1998). Educating young people about drugs: A systematic review. *Addiction, 93,* 1475–1487.

CHAPTER SUMMARY

Survey research attempts to describe various characteristics of groups of people. Data are collected from respondents, usually selected through a random sampling technique. Data can be collected through direct administration of a survey, a mail survey, a telephone survey, interviews, an e-mail survey, or a Web-based survey. Depending on the purpose of the study, surveys may be administered using either a descriptive, a cross-sectional, or a longitudinal approach.

Numerous types of questions can be used during a survey research study. Demographic, knowledge, attitudinal, and behavioral questions each provide unique types of data about the selected sample. Questions can also be formatted as either closed-ended or open-ended questions. Furthermore, there are a variety of formats for closed-ended questions, including checklists and Likert (or Likert-type) questions. Designing surveys is not a simple task; novice researchers are advised to follow the guidelines presented in the chapter.

LIST OF IMPORTANT TERMS

attitudinal questions
behavioral questions
census
checklists
closed-ended question
cohort study
cover letter
cross-sectional survey
demographic questions
descriptive research

descriptive survey
direct administration
double-barreled question
e-mail survey
forced-choice question
interview
knowledge questions
Likert scale
Likert-type scale
longitudinal survey

mail survey
open-ended question
panel study
pilot test
respondents
survey research
target population
telephone survey
trend study
Web-based survey

ACTIVITIES FOR THOUGHT AND DISCUSSION

1. Try to answer the following questions, which were presented at the beginning of the chapter.
   a. What is the main purpose of survey research?
   b. What are the various types of data collection methods used in survey research? What are their relative advantages and disadvantages?
   c. What are the three different types of surveys and how do they differ?
   d. What is the basic difference between a closed-ended and an open-ended question?
   e. What are the characteristics of demographic, knowledge, attitudinal, and behavioral survey questions?
   f. What are the differences between checklists and Likert (or Likert-type) questions?
   g. What are some important guidelines to keep in mind when designing surveys?

2. Suppose you wanted to study teachers' job motivation and satisfaction. For this study, state the problem, research questions, and methods you might use for data collection and analysis.

3. Suppose you wanted to research the climate of your local schools from various perspectives. For this study, state the problem, research questions, and methods you might use for data collection and analysis.

4. Locate an example of published survey research in a reputable journal. Compare and contrast it with the article that appears in its entirety in the chapter regarding (a) purpose, (b) organization, (c) data collection and analysis, and (d) conclusions.

ANSWERS TO CHAPTER EXERCISES

Responses to the chapter exercise can vary and still be considered correct for individual students. It is suggested that responses be discussed and evaluated as group activities.

REFERENCES AND RECOMMENDED READINGS

Creswell, J. W. (2005). *Educational Research: Planning, Conducting, and Evaluating Quantitative and Qualitative Research* (2nd ed.). Upper Saddle River, NJ: Merrill/Prentice Hall.

Dillman, D. A. (2000). *Mail and Internet Surveys: The Tailored Design Method* (2nd ed.). New York: Wiley.

Fraenkel, J. R., & Wallen, N. E. (2006). *How to Design and Evaluate Research in Education* (6th ed.). Boston: McGraw-Hill.

Gay, L. R., Mills, G. E., & Airasian, P. (2006). *Educational Research: Competencies for Analysis and Application* (8th ed.). Upper Saddle River, NJ: Merrill/Prentice Hall.

McMillan, J. H. (2004). *Educational Research: Fundamentals for the Consumer* (4th ed.). Boston: Allyn & Bacon.

Mertler, C. A. (2002a). Demonstrating the potential for Web-based survey methodology with a case study. *American Secondary Education, 30*(2), 49–61.

Mertler, C. A. (2002b, April). *Web-Based Surveys: Guiding Lessons for Their Use.* Paper presented at the annual meeting of the American Educational Research Association, New Orleans, Louisiana.

Mertler, C. A. (2003). Patterns of response and nonresponse from teachers to traditional and web surveys. *Practical Assessment, Research & Evaluation, 8*(22). Available at www.pareonline.net/getvn.asp?v=8&n=22

Mertler, C. A., & Earley, M. A. (2002, October). *The Mouse or the Pencil? A Psychometric Comparison of Web-Based and Traditional Survey Methodology.* Paper presented at the annual meeting of the Mid-Western Educational Research Association, Columbus, Ohio.

Mertler, C. A. (2006). *Action Research: Teachers as Researchers in the Classroom.* Thousand Oaks, CA: Sage.

Mertens, D. M. (2005). *Research and Evaluation in Education and Psychology: Integrating Diversity with Quantitative, Qualitative, and Mixed Methods* (2nd ed.). Thousand Oaks, CA: Sage.

Wiersma, W., & Jurs, S. (2005). *Research Methods in Education: An Introduction* (8th ed.). Boston: Allyn & Bacon.

12

Nonexperimental Quantitative Research

PREVIEW

This chapter explains the nature and procedures of two types of research:

- Correlational research
- Causal-comparative research

These two approaches have similar characteristics:

- They are nonexperimental designs
- They require the collection and analysis of quantitative data

Correlational research is used to explore covarying relationships between two or more variables (such as between motivation and academic achievement). The purposes of exploring such relationships include the following:

- To identify variables that relate to each other in this fashion
- To make predictions for values of one variable from another (such as to predict academic achievement from level of motivation)
- To examine the possible existence of causation (such as the influence that motivation might have on academic achievement)

Causal-comparative research is used to further explore the possible existence of cause and effect.

TARGETED LEARNINGS

The chapter explains the purposes and methods of correlational and causal-comparative research and includes reprinted published articles that exemplify these two approaches to conducting research. As you read the chapter, look especially for information related to the following questions:

1. What differentiates correlational research from other types of research?
2. What can correlational research accomplish, and what are its limitations?
3. What elements comprise the method of correlational research?
4. What is meant by *criterion variable* and *predictor variable*?
5. What are some of the different methods of computing coefficients of correlation, and what kinds of data are used in each?

6. How do coefficients of correlation help answer research questions or test hypotheses?
7. Why is it said that causal-comparative research begins by first considering the effect before considering the cause?

In this chapter, we begin to explore research methodologies that investigate cause and effect—or at least the possibility of cause-and-effect—relationships. Both correlational and causal-comparative approaches to conducting research are nonexperimental (meaning that no manipulation to variables is done) and require the collection of quantitative data. There are many conceptual similarities between correlational research and causal-comparative research. However, the primary difference is that in correlational research the researcher is attempting to measure the nature of the *relationship between two or more variables,* while in causal-comparative research the researcher is looking closer at the *possibility of a cause-and-effect relationship between variables* through a group comparison (i.e., differences between groups) approach.

WEATHER AND THE PROCESS OF EDUCATION

Most of us make several observations of the weather every day and exchange comments about it. You would think that after a while we would understand weather, at least well

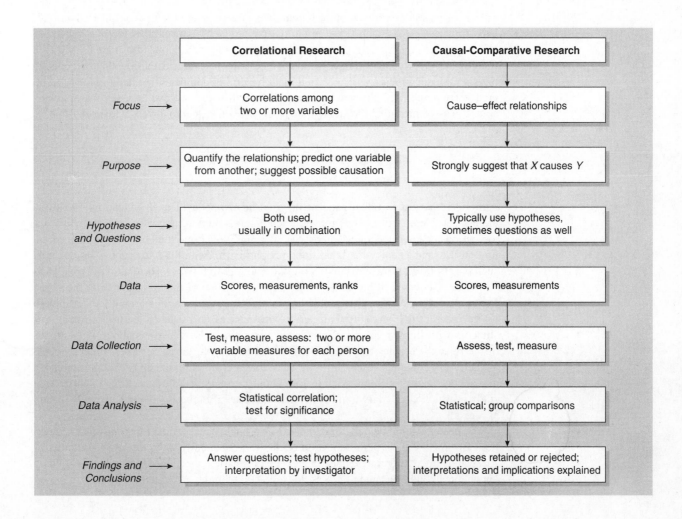

enough to predict wind or rain. But even after a lifetime of observation, commentary, and in some cases advanced study in meteorology, no one can explain much about what "causes" weather.

The process of education is somewhat like weather in that regard. After a lifetime of study, educators can hardly say what causes a person to become educated. They can of course describe conditions that are associated with education, but those particular conditions may or may not produce an educated person, and we know that it is possible to become educated without exposure to the usual trappings of schooling.

These facts are perplexing and sometimes frustrating. The human mind wants to *know*—not only know about things but also to know how and why they function as they do. We would like to know not just that there are clouds in the sky and that it is raining but also what causes clouds to form and precipitation to occur and pressure to change. In a similar sense, we would like to know not only that learning is occurring among seventh-grade students but also what is causing the learning to occur, and why it occurs for some students and not for others.

These questions may or may not be answerable through normal thought processes. Human logical thinking tends to be linear: If X happens, then Y will result; if we drop an apple, it will fall to earth; if the night gets cold, frost will form; if Joshua is taught his number facts, he will be able to do arithmetic. Such linear thinking serves fairly well in hard sciences such as physics and chemistry, but less well in the softer sciences of psychology, learning, and meteorology. If we drop an apple, it will almost certainly fall toward earth (except when weightless in space), but just as cold nights do not always produce frost, neither does teaching number facts always result in arithmetic competence.

Despite our desire to know what causes what, the best we can do in explaining most aspects of weather or education or human behavior in general is to determine what is related to what—to say with some certainty that X (teaching of number facts) is related to Y (competence in arithmetic), or that X and Y (humidity and temperature) are related to Z (precipitation). "Related" simply means that certain conditions occur together and change together. Most of the time, being taught and becoming competent go hand in hand, as do precipitation and humidity and temperature. Scientifically, we can only say that the variables are associated, that they tend to be present together and to covary with each other.

CORRELATIONS

Although clear cause–effect patterns may not be always evident in education, we nevertheless can identify numerous related phenomena—numerous conditions, materials, interventions, teaching methods, and styles of communication—that have to do with when, how much, and under what conditions people learn. Searching for such relationships, such *correlations,* is the purpose of correlational research. When correlations among variables are discovered, it becomes possible to predict one of the variables from the other. For example, if we know that vocabulary competence and school learning are correlated, we can predict that students with better vocabularies will usually learn more than will students with limited vocabularies. Correlations also raise questions about whether one of the related variables may be causing the other to occur and, therefore, suggest fertile areas for experimental research. If we learn that a correlation exists between vocabulary and achievement, we might wish to follow our correlational study with an experimental study in which vocabulary training is provided to see if higher school achievement occurs as a result.

Educators would be delighted to discover reliable cause–effect relationships in education. But for the most part, education occurs too chaotically to be explained in terms of cause and effect. Therefore, educators rely on correlational evidence for much of what they know about conditions and practices that affect education.

THE NATURE OF CORRELATIONAL RESEARCH

The purpose of correlational research is to discover relationships between two or more variables. *Relationship* means that an individual's status on one variable tends to reflect his or her status on the other. Correlational research in education seeks out traits, abilities, or conditions that covary, or correlate, with each other. As we have noted, correlations help us

- Understand certain related events, conditions, and behaviors
- Predict future conditions or behaviors in one variable from what we presently know of another variable
- Sometimes obtain strong suggestions that one variable is "causing" the other

For example, we know that high school grade point average is correlated with subsequent student success in college. The correlation is far from perfect; indeed, perfect correlations are virtually never discovered in education. Nevertheless, we can predict, albeit imperfectly, a person's future college success by the grades he or she earns in high school.

CAUTIONS CONCERNING CAUSE AND EFFECT

Correlations show the extent to which variables are related to each other. It has been explained that correlations do not, in themselves, show that one of the variables causes the other—a conclusion toward which the intellect automatically turns, though often erroneously. For example, certain Native American tribes once believed that toads could call forth rain. That seemed plausible, for the rainy season began at the same time toads went into a frenzy of mating, egg laying, and ceaseless croaking. More rain followed predictably as the toads continued to croak. It could certainly seem that the croaking brought forth rain.

This conclusion is an example of the **post hoc fallacy**—*post hoc ergo propter hoc*—in other words, "after the fact, therefore because of the fact." The fallacy lies in concluding that because it rained after the toads croaked, it therefore rained because the toads croaked. One could as logically, or more logically, say that the rain was causing the toads to croak. Sometimes when we find correlated variables, one of the two does in fact turn out to be the cause and the other the effect.

Such may well be the case in the correlation that medical researchers have found between smoking and lung disease, which is in the news at times and is the scientific basis for recent lawsuits of magnitude. But statistical correlations do not demonstrate cause and effect. It is only through experimental research that causal relationships can be demonstrated convincingly, where purposeful manipulations of independent variables are consistently followed by corresponding changes in dependent variables. The smoking illustration shows the advantage correlational research has over experimentation; we would hardly force people to smoke heavily for years on end to see whether smoking causes them to have lung disease.

TOPICS FOR CORRELATIONAL RESEARCH

Six categories of topics are especially amenable to correlational research in education:

1. Suspected relationships between certain human traits *(X)* and learning or other school behavior *(Y)*
2. Suspected relationships between classroom environment or organizational schemes *(X)* and learning or attitude *(Y)*

3. Suspected relationships between various teaching practices and instructional materials *(X)* and learning *(Y)*

4. Conditions or practices *(X)* that are suspected of interfering with learning or optimal performance *(Y)*

5. Predicting from a given variable *X* (e.g., self-concept) some other variable *Y* (e.g., the future success, adjustment, or difficulties of students, teachers, and other professionals)

6. Establishment of validity and reliability of tests and other diagnostic and assessment instruments

HYPOTHESES AND QUESTIONS IN CORRELATIONAL RESEARCH

Correlational research may be oriented by either research questions or hypotheses, or both. If you wanted to explore a possible relationship between students' overall evaluation of the classes they are taking and the amount of homework assigned in those classes, you might pose a question such as

What degree of relationship exists between high school students' evaluation of their classes and the amount of homework assigned in those classes?

If you decided to guide your study with hypotheses, you might state a hypothesis that contends

High school students give lower evaluations to classes in which larger amounts of homework are assigned.

For statistical testing you might state the hypothesis in the null form:

No relationship exists between (1) the evaluations high school students give to classes and (2) the amount of homework assigned in those classes.

You would then collect data that answer the question or test the hypothesis.

Of course, an actual correlational study would likely be larger in scope than suggested by this example. A genuine study into a topic of this sort might be guided by a main research question such as

What coursework factors do high school students believe to be most closely related to the quality of their classes?

Several subquestions might then be put forth. Some of those questions might be approached through testing null hypotheses, as shown in the following examples:

No relationship exists between students' appraisal of the quality of classes and their liking for the teachers.

No relationship exists between students' evaluation of the quality of their classes and their appraisal of the fairness of discipline regulations.

CORRELATIONAL RESEARCH DESIGN

Correlational research design is relatively simple, and its procedures are uncomplicated. In essence, correlational research is designed as follows:

1. Variables whose relationship is to be explored are identified and clarified.
2. Questions or hypotheses are stated.
3. A sample is selected—with a minimum sample size of 30 individuals.

4. Measurements are obtained from sample members on each of the variables being explored.

5. Correlations between and among variables are computed to determine degrees of relationship.

Suppose you read a report of an investigation into the relationship between carbohydrate intake and the performance of high school cross-country runners. You would find included in the report (1) either questions or hypotheses, (2) a sample of runners selected for inclusion in the study, (3) two measures obtained from each subject—one for carbohydrate intake and the other for running performance, and (4) a coefficient of correlation that has been calculated to show the degree of relationship between carbohydrate intake and running performance.

You can see from this design that data are obtained by testing, measuring, or making judgments and are compiled to pair the measures obtained for each individual. The data are analyzed statistically and the results show the size of the correlation and its direction (whether positive or negative). The coefficient of correlation is then tested for statistical significance.

DATA SOURCES AND COLLECTION

PEARSON
myeducationlab for research

To learn more about data that are appropriate for correlational research, go to the "Correlational Research" section of **MyEducationLab for Research** and then click on *Assignments and Activities.* Complete the exercise titled "Selecting Measures Based on Correlational Data," which will "get you thinking" about correlational data.

Correlational research relies on relatively few sources of data. Those sources are usually individuals in the study sample from each of whom at least two measures are obtained. Those two measures are paired, as pairs of test scores, pairs of ratings, pairs of measures, pairs of dichotomies, or combinations thereof.

The data are collected either by directly measuring the participants (to determine physical characteristics), by sorting participants on the basis of certain criteria (to group them into categories), or by having them respond to tests and rating scales (to obtain sets of scores). Instruments frequently used in data collection include standardized tests; rating scales; and devices or indexes that gauge height, weight, frequency, and the like.

Although in most cases data for correlational studies are obtained through measurement, at times they come from judgments made by researchers, teachers, or other qualified persons. For example, suppose you wanted to explore the relationship between student cooperation and scholastic achievement. You could measure each subject's level of achievement objectively, but participants' degrees of cooperation would have to be determined by qualified judges, such as teachers.

Subjective judgments invariably raise questions about data reliability. When judgment must be used, researchers should be meticulous in spelling out the criteria on which judgments are based. For example, in a study to explore the relationship between personal attractiveness and social acceptance (both of which would have to be determined subjectively), the researcher should express very explicitly the criteria by which attractiveness and acceptance (both nominal data) are to be determined. This is not to suggest that all nominal data present difficulties. It is easy to assign numerical values to certain dichotomies, such as "boy–girl," "tall–short," "pass–fail," and "correct–incorrect." But in cases where gradations exist, as in "adjustment to the group" or "level of attention," clear criteria are especially needed.

WHAT CAN BE CORRELATED AND HOW

Several kinds of variable data can be correlated; the methods described in this section are merely a sampling of the more frequently used types of correlations. As indicated, you must have two measures or ratings for each individual in the sample. (Please remember

for research

Correlational data are often displayed visually. To learn more about graphing correlational data, go to the "Correlational Research" section of **MyEducationLab for Research** and then click on *Assignments and Activities*. Complete the exercise titled "Plotting Correlational Data" to give you some exposure to developing scatterplots for correlational data.

that computer statistical software calculates all these correlations for you and tests their significance.)

PRODUCT-MOMENT CORRELATION

Most commonly, correlational studies explore the relationship between variables expressed in continuous interval or ratio data, such as numerical test scores or numerical measures of physical performance. The **Pearson product-moment correlation**—often called "Pearson *r*" or simply "*r*"—is used to correlate such data.

BISERIAL CORRELATION AND POINT-BISERIAL CORRELATION

At times, one variable can be expressed as continuous interval data while the other variable is expressed as a *dichotomy*—either an **artificial dichotomy** (a dichotomy with an artificial dividing line, such as "happy–sad") or a **natural dichotomy** (a dichotomy that occurs naturally, such as "left-handed–right-handed").

A **biserial correlation** is used to explore the relationship between a continuous variable and an artificial dichotomy. For example, "school achievement," a continuous interval variable, could be correlated with "poverty-level" versus "nonpoverty family income," an artificial dichotomy.

A **point-biserial correlation** is used when one variable is continuous and the other variable is a natural dichotomy. For example, "school achievement," a continuous variable, could be correlated with the "number of parents resident in the family" (either one or two—a natural dichotomy).

PHI CORRELATION AND TETRACHORIC CORRELATION

Some research explores relationships in which both variables are expressed as dichotomies. If the dichotomies are both natural—for example, "handedness" (left–right) and "varsity sports participation" (yes–no)—a **phi correlation** is used. If both variables are artificial dichotomies—for example, "class participation" (high–low) and "family income" (poverty–nonpoverty)—a **tetrachoric correlation** is the appropriate procedure.

CORRELATIONS FROM RANKINGS

Data organized into rankings (i.e., ordinal data), such as "best to worst," "quietest to loudest," or rankings based on grades received, can be correlated through two different procedures—the **Spearman rho** and the **Kendall tau.** Spearman rho is preferable for larger samples; the Kendall tau is preferable for samples smaller than ten.

MULTIVARIATE CORRELATIONS

The types of correlations discussed to this point have been **bivariate correlations**—that is, correlations involving only two sets of scores. Some studies, however, call for explorations of relationships among three or more variables, calling for **multivariate correlations.** Multivariate procedures that investigate correlations include partial correlation, multiple regression, discriminant analysis, and factor analysis.

PARTIAL CORRELATION

Often it is found that the correlation between two variables is affected strongly by a third variable. An example is the high correlation between scores on reading tests and on vocabulary tests; both of these variables are highly related to intelligence. To explore the relationship between reading ability and vocabulary per se, with the influence of intelligence removed, it is necessary to use a procedure that "partials out" the effects of intelligence. This is accomplished by means of the procedure called **partial correlation,** whose coefficient is called *partial r.*

MULTIPLE REGRESSION

Multiple regression is used to determine the degree of correlation between a continuous criterion variable *(Z)* and a combination of two or more predictor variables (*X* and *Y*, etc.). This procedure might be used, for example, in exploring the relationship between school achievement (*Z*, the *criterion variable*) and a combination of intelligence *(X)* and motivation *(Y),* two *predictor variables.*

DISCRIMINANT ANALYSIS

Discriminant analysis is analogous to multiple regression, except that the *Z* or criterion variable consists of two or more categories rather than a continuous range of values. An example might be an exploration of the relationship between class participation (*Z*, categorized as "above average" and "below average") and a combination of self-concept *(X)* and grade point average *(Y).*

FACTOR ANALYSIS

Factor analysis is often used when a large number of correlations have been explored in a given study; it is a means of grouping into clusters, or *factors,* certain variables that are moderately to highly correlated with each other. In studies of intelligence, for example, numerous variables may be explored, and those that are found to be highly correlated with each other are clustered into factors such as verbal ability, numerical ability, spatial orientation, and problem solving.

AN EXAMPLE OF CORRELATIONAL RESEARCH

Following the exercise is a reprinted correlational research report that investigates relationships between factors such as reading attitude and ultimate reading performance.

Exercise 12.1

As you read the report, identify the following:

1. Question or hypothesis
2. Variables whose possible relationship is being explored
3. Sample
4. Data collection
5. Results

School Aggression and Dispositional Aggression among Middle School Boys

Mary E. Ballard
Appalachian State University

Kelvin T. Rattley
Appalachian State University

Willie C. Fleming
Appalachian State University

Pamela Kidder-Ashley
Appalachian State University

Abstract

We examined the relationship between dispositional (trait) aggression and administrative reports of school aggression among 100 adolescent male participants from an urban middle school. Aggression was fairly common among the sample; 58 boys had a record of school aggression, and many of those were repeat offenders. Our hypothesis that those higher in dispositional aggression would have more records of aggression at school was supported. Dispositional aggression was significantly, positively correlated with verbal and physical aggression at school. Regression analyses indicated that dispositional aggression accounted for a substantial amount of the variance in administrative reports of school aggression. Two other factors, family income and age, accounted for a minimal amount of the variance in school aggression.

Great initial summary statement, clearly indicating that the authors used a correlational design.

Aggression is defined as behavior intended to harm another living being, either physically or emotionally (Berkowitz, 1998a; Geen, 1998). School aggression is perpetrated against students or school personnel while at, or traveling to or from, school or school-sponsored events (National School Safety Center, 2000). Aggression is a relatively stable trait, across both time and context (Eron & Huesmann, 1990). Those who experience more aggressive thoughts and feelings behave more aggressively across contexts (Bushman, 1995; 1996; Canary, Spitzberg, & Semic, 1998; Carlo & Roesch, 1998; Dill, Anderson, Anderson, & Deuser, 1997; Dula & Ballard, 2003). We examined if adolescent males with higher levels of dispositional (i.e., trait) aggression were more likely to be cited for instances of school aggression.

Aggression is influenced by a complex interaction of factors (e.g., Berkowitz, 1998b; Geen, 1998; Huesmann, 1994). Anderson and Bushman (Anderson & Bushman, 2001a;

Source: Ballard, M. E., Rattley, K. T., Fleming, W. C., & Kidder-Ashley, P. (2004). School aggression and dispositional aggression among middle school boys. *Research in Middle Level Education Online, 27(1)*. Retrieved August 18, 2009, from www.nmsa.org/Publications/RMLEOnline/tabid/101/Default.aspx. Reprinted with permission from National Middle School Association.

2001b; Anderson & Dill, 2000) have proposed a social cognitive model, the General Affective Aggression Model (GAAM), to explain the interactive effects of learning, environment variables, and personality on behavior. Anderson and Bushman note that children learn aggressive scripts and schemas from the environment (e.g., parents, media) that may be modeled later. Socialization of morals and empathy, as well as the child's personality, mediate affective responses, arousal, and a variety of automatic and controlled decision-making processes in response to specific situational factors (e.g., an anger-arousing stimulus). Anderson and Bushman suggest that an aggressive personality (i.e., high dispositional aggression) serves as an input variable in this model to affect behavioral aggression. According to the GAAM, dispositional aggression affects the internal state of the person (e.g., cognitions, affect, and arousal), which in turn affects appraisal (e.g., perception of a threat) and behavior (e.g., aggressive response). That is, those with high levels of dispositional aggression have more ready access to aggressive scripts, experience more negative affect, and are more easily aroused. Thus, they are more likely to make aggressive attributions for others' behavior and are at increased risk for behavioral aggression (Anderson & Bushman, 2001a; 2001b; Anderson & Dill, 2000).

Individual differences in behavioral aggression manifest in early childhood and predict the likelihood of aggression more than 40 years later (Eron, 1987; Eron & Huesmann, 1990; Huesmann, Eron, Lefkowitz, & Walder, 1984; Huesmann, Moise-Titus, Podolski, & Eron, [2003]; Loeber & Hay, 1997). Dispositional aggression, or the individual's daily experience of aggressive and hostile cognitions and feelings, is viewed as a relatively constant individual difference that affects behavioral aggression across contexts (Anderson & Dill, 2000; Canary et al., 1998; Dula & Ballard, 2003; Eron & Huesmann, 1990; Huesmann et al., in press). Dispositional aggression is measured using questionnaires such as the Interpersonal Behavior Survey (Mauger & Adkinson, 1993) and the Aggression Questionnaire (Buss & Warren, 2000). These instruments survey various facets of aggression, including thoughts, feelings, and reactivity related to physical aggression, verbal aggression, hostility, and anger.

Research indicates a relationship between measures of dispositional aggression and behavioral aggression among

The related literature has indicated a relationship between disposition to display aggression and actual displays of aggression in a variety of contexts.

adolescents and adults across contexts (Coles, Greene, & Braithwaite, 2002; Driscoll, Jarman, & Yankeelov, 1994; Dula & Ballard, 2003; Vance, Fernandez, & Biber, 1998). For example, those who score higher on measures of dispositional aggression are more likely to engage in driver aggression (Deffenbacher, Lynch, Deffenbacher, & Oetting, 2001; Dula & Ballard, 2003). Those high in dispositional aggression are also more behaviorally aggressive after exposure to violent video games (Dill et al., 1997) and violent movies (Kiewitz & Weaver, 2001). Finally, among adult samples, those high in dispositional aggression are more likely to perpetrate spousal abuse (Schumacher, Feldbau-Kohn, Slep, & Heyman, 2001) and workplace violence (Douglas & Martinko, 2001; Neuman & Baron, 1998). Less is known about such correlations among children and adolescents, but children who perpetrate school aggression are likely to have a history of aggression and/or being bullied (Speaker & Petersen, 2000; Vance et al., 1998) and are more likely to have friends who are aggressive (Coie et al., 1999; Dodge, Coie, Pettit, & Price, 1990; Minden, Henry, Tolan, & GormanSmith, 2000). Further, children who are aggressive in mid-to-late childhood are likely to be aggressive in adolescence (Séguin, Arseneault, Boulerice, Harden, & Tremblay, 2002). Perseveration of aggression is related to having a difficult temperament, which is linked to dispositional aggression (Anderson & Bushman, 2001a; 2001b; Séguin et al., 2002).

School-related violence has declined in recent years, and children are more likely to be harmed while away from school than while at school (Mulvey & Cauffman, 2001; *Indicators . . .* , 2001). Even so, school aggression is of concern across cultures, as evidenced by research in Canada (Carter & Stewin, 1999), Finland (Olafsen & Viemeroe, 2000), France (Mallet & Paty, 1999), Germany (Martin, 2000), Turkey (Hatipoglu-Suemer & Aydin, 1999), and the United States (Centers for Disease Control and Prevention, 1997; the National School Safety Center 2000; *Sourcebook . . .* , 1999). School aggression can be physical (e.g., fighting, hair pulling), verbal (e.g., threats, insults), or relational (e.g., alienation, gossip). We chose to focus on physical and serious verbal aggression, as these behaviors were recorded in school records. It should be noted, however, that relational aggression often results in more serious aggressive incidents (Olafsen & Viemeroe, 2000).

STATEMENT OF PROBLEM AND HYPOTHESES

Given the association between dispositional aggression and behavioral aggression described in the literature review, we expected that dispositional aggression, measured using the general aggression subscale of the Interpersonal Behavior Survey, would account for a significant amount of the variance in boys' records of school aggression. Although it is

not central to the thesis, based on past research (Brooks-Gunn & Duncan, 1997) we also expected that factors related to socioeconomic status (e.g., parental education, family income) would account for a significant portion of the variance in boys' school aggression. Further, due to findings regarding the stability and perseveration of aggression into adolescence (Eron, 1987; Eron & Huesmann, 1990; Huesmann et al., 1984; Huesmann et al., in press; Loeber & Hay, 1997; Séguin et al., 2002), we expected that a minority of boys would account for a majority of aggressive incidents. Thus, in addition to fleshing out our understanding of dispositional aggression, these data add to our knowledge of school aggression, in terms of both the factors related to school aggression and descriptive data regarding the incidence of school aggression.

The authors used the related literature to guide their hypothesis regarding the relationship between dispositional aggression and school aggression.

Although not the focus of their study, the literature also led them to hypothesize that SES would have a strong relationship to school aggression.

METHOD

Participants

Participants included 100 adolescent males from a suburban Charlotte, NC, middle school (grades 6–8). Most ($n = 69$) of the participants were White, the remainder ($n = 31$) were Black; this is representative of the school and community (*Population Estimates . . .* , 1998). Participants ranged in age from 11 to 15 years ($M = 12.7$). Participant SES, as evidenced by parental education, ranged from lower class to upper middle class. The working class students were bused from "inner city" Charlotte to an upper middle class neighborhood for school. Participants received a small gift (i.e., candy, toy) for their participation in the study.

Description of the participants; although we do not know how they were selected, the authors state that the breakdown by ethnicity was representative of both the school and the community.

Measures

A demographic questionnaire, completed by the parent or guardian, was used to gather students' age, grade level, self-reported ethnicity, annual family income, marital status of parents, parents' level of education, and the amount of time the student had attended the middle school.

Demographic information was collected from the parents.

Each participant's student record was used to code administrative reports of school aggression. School administrators used a standard coding scheme, developed by administrators based on past aggressive incidents, to record 17 categories of aggression into student records—fist fight, two-on-one fight, hit a teacher/staff member, shoved a student in anger, shoved a teacher/staff member in anger, pushed someone out of the way (instrumental, not hostile), threw an object at a student, verbal harassment of a student, took property from

> Data on school aggression was collected from existing school records.

a student via force, took property from a student via intimidation, kicked a student, bit a student, fought a student with a weapon, made fun of a student's looks, threatened a student with physical harm, threatened a teacher with physical harm, and brought a gun/knife to school. For each of these categories of aggression, the administrator had recorded the number of times each student had engaged in the behavior. None of the boys had been cited for bringing a gun or knife to school, so this item was not used in the analyses. For each student, the number of recorded instances of each of the 16 remaining items was summed for *a total school aggression score.* Four behaviors (verbal harassment, threatened student, threatened teacher, made fun of student) were used to calculate *a verbal aggression score,* and the remaining 12 behaviors were totaled to calculate *a physical aggression score.*

> Dispositional aggression was measured through the use of a self-report questionnaire that consisted of Likert-type scaled items.

The measure of dispositional aggression was drawn from the 34-item, self-report Interpersonal Behavior Survey-Short Form (IBS; Mauger & Adkinson, 1993). The IBS, so labeled to avoid demand characteristics, includes subscales of general assertiveness and denial, in addition to the general aggressiveness subscale. Only the general aggressiveness subscale was used in this study. This subscale measures aggressive feelings and cognitions (e.g., It is never all right

> The authors report reliability values for the subscales of the instrument.

to harm someone else.; There are times I would enjoy hurting people I love.; I enjoy making people angry). Each item is rated on a Likert-type scale from 1 (not at all like me) to 5 (completely like me). Raw scores were converted to T-scores for use in the analyses. The IBS general aggressiveness subscale has excellent test-retest reliability ($r = .81$ for a 10-wk. interval) and internal consistency ($\alpha = .73$) and is moderately correlated with the subscales of the Buss-Durkee Hostility Inventory, which include hostility ($r = .57$), indirect hostility ($r = .50$) and assault ($r = .38$) scales (Mauger & Adkinson, 1993).

Procedure

> The procedures are clearly explained by the authors; they received a relatively low response rate to the parental permission process.

Parents of each male student ($N = 445$) at the middle school were sent a packet containing a cover letter/consent form that explained the study and described the measures, a demographic

form, a release for school records, and a self-addressed, stamped envelope to return the forms. One hundred parents (22% total; 27% of parents of White boys and 14% of parents of Black boys) returned the forms, giving permission for their sons to participate. This is a lower rate of return than typical (33–44%) for school-based surveys (Gillig & Zimmer, 1986), but is a higher return rate than other researchers have obtained in the same area (K. D. Michael, personal communication, July 28, 2002). Follow-up calls made by the second author indicated that many of the children and parents from the school had recently participated in a lengthy survey study and did not want to participate in another study so soon. Thus, non-participation in the study seemed to be related to "study fatigue," rather than to potentially confounding variables such as temperament, ethnicity, or age. After their parents gave consent, participants were scheduled to complete the study. Students were run in small groups (5–8) in the school's media center. They were seated apart for privacy. Each participant signed an informed assent and completed the IBS. They were asked not to discuss the questions or their answers with their peers. The second author monitored the students during each session. The procedure lasted 30 min. After completing the forms, each participant was debriefed and given his choice of candy or a small toy.

RESULTS

Descriptive Statistics

Of the 100 boys, a majority ($n = 58$) had an administrative record of aggressive behavior at school. The most common aggressive behaviors, with number of infractions reported parenthetically, were fist fights ($n = 30$), shoving another student in anger ($n = 27$), pushing someone

> This section of descriptive results summarizes the collected school aggression data.

out of the way ($n = 20$), throwing an object at another student ($n = 19$), verbal harassment ($n = 15$), taking property from another student via intimidation ($n = 14$), and kicking another student ($n = 12$). Aggression directed at teachers, such as hitting ($n = 7$), shoving ($n = 1$), and threats ($n = 2$) was uncommon. Biting ($n = 2$) and threatening students ($n = 6$) were also uncommon.

The total number of recorded acts of school aggression was 402. The overall mean for aggressive acts while attending the middle school was 4.02 ($sd = 5.64$). When the students with no infractions ($n = 42$) were removed from the equation, the boys with a history of school aggression ($n = 58$) had a mean of 6.93 ($sd = 5.89$) aggressive acts. Several of these boys ($n = 13$) had only one citation for aggression, but many ($n = 45$) were repeat offenders. Seventeen of the boys had 5 to 10 citations for aggressive behavior at school, and an additional 14 boys had more than 10 citations for aggression. Thus, a minority (31%) of the boys perpetrated most (86%) of the administratively recorded aggression.

Mean Comparisons

> Boys who had higher incidences of school aggression had significantly higher scores on the measure of dispositional aggression. Additionally, there were no observed differences in aggression between Black boys and White boys.

A median split of administrative citations for aggression was used to divide the boys into *high and low* school aggression groups. A *t*-test was performed, with level of school aggression as the between subjects factor and IBS aggressiveness scores as the dependent measure. The *t*-test was significant, $t(98) = 6.17$, $p < .001$. Boys high in school aggression ($M = 40.00$, $sd = 5.86$) had significantly higher scores on the IBS aggression score than did boys low in school aggression ($M = 33.89$, $sd = 4.01$).

We also used *t*-tests to see if ethnic background was related to mean differences on the variables (i.e., school records of total, verbal, and physical aggression, and IBS aggression sub-scores). There were no ethnic differences (all *p*s >.05). Ethnic differences in each aggressive behavior were examined using *t*-tests; a was set at $p < .01$ to correct for family-wise error. There were no ethnic differences (all *p*s < .03), so we collapsed the data across ethnicity for the analyses.

Correlational and Regression Analyses

Partial correlations were performed to examine the relationship between IBS aggression scores and administrative records of aggression. Length of time enrolled in the middle school served as a covariate. There were strong, significant positive correlations between IBS aggression scores and administratively recorded verbal aggression, physical aggression, and total aggression (see Table 1).

> The authors calculated partial correlations; "length of time in the middle school" was used as the covariate. This means that they removed the impact of "length of time enrolled" from the relationship between aggression scores and actual records of aggression.

Regression analyses were performed with administrative records of overall school aggression, verbal aggression, and physical aggression as the dependent factors. Length of time enrolled in the middle school was entered first into each equation.

> Predictive regression analyses were also conducted.

IBS general aggression scores and demographic variables that have been correlated with aggression (age, family income, and parents' education) were entered as predictor variables in a *stepwise* fashion. See Tables 2, 3, and 4 for additional statistics.

With regard to total school records of aggression, 36% of the variance was accounted for. Length of time enrolled accounted for 3% of the variance, IBS aggression scores accounted for 28% of the variance, and age accounted for 5% of the variance. In terms of verbal aggression, only 15% of the variance was accounted for. IBS aggression scores accounted for 10% of the variance and family income accounted for 5% of the variance. Finally, 36% of the variance in physical aggression was accounted for. Length of time enrolled accounted for 4% of the variance, IBS aggression scores accounted for 27% of the variance, and age accounted for 5% of the variance. The remainder of the factors did not account for a significant portion of the variance in school aggression.

DISCUSSION

The hypotheses that (a) dispositional aggression would predict school aggression and (b) a minority of boys would account for a majority of school aggression were supported. Rates of administratively documented school aggression were strongly, positively correlated to levels of dispositional aggression. Dispositional aggression was a better predictor of behavioral aggression than demographic variables such as age, ethnicity, and socio-economic status. These results add to the evidence that dispositional aggression predicts aggressive behavior across a wide range of contexts.

> The authors' primary hypothesis was supported by their data and resulting analyses.

A majority of the boys sampled had engaged in at least one act of school aggression. Of those who had perpetrated school aggression, most were repeat offenders, displaying the sort of perseveration described by Séguin et al. (2002).

> These are the partial correlations referred to earlier.

Table 1 Partial Correlations between Dispositional and School Aggression

	IBS Aggression	Verbal Aggression	Physical Aggression	Total Aggression
IBS Aggression	—	.31*	.54**	.54**
Verbal Aggression	.31	—	.48**	.64**
Physical Aggression	.54**	.48**	—	.98**
Total Aggression	.54**	.64**	.98**	—

*$p < .01$, **$p < .001$; Years at the middle school served as a covariate.

Table 2 Summary of Predictor Variables Regressed onto School Records of Overall Aggression

Model	R	R^2	R^2 Change*	Unique Variance*
Model 1 (Length of time at school)	.18	.03	.03	>1%
Model 2 (Length of time at school + dispositional aggression)	.56	.31	.28	17%
Model 3 (Length of time at school + dispositional aggression + age)	.60	.36	.05	1%

*R^2 change and unique variance of the predictor variable added at each step.

Table 3 Summary of Predictor Variables Regressed onto School Records of Verbal Aggression

Model	R	R^2	R^2 Change*	Unique Variance*
Model 1 (Length of time at school)	.02	.00	.00	0%
Model 2 (Length of time at school + dispositional aggression)	.32	.10	.10	9%
Model 3 (Length of time at school + dispositional aggression + family income)	.36	.15	.05	4%

*R^2 change and unique variance of the predictor variable added at each step.

Table 4 Summary of Predictor Variables Regressed onto School Records of Physical Aggression

Model	R	R^2	R^2 Change*	Unique Variance*
Model 1 (Length of time at school)	.20	.04	.04	>1%
Model 2 (Length of time at school + dispositional aggression)	.56	.31	.27	17%
Model 3 (Length of time at school + dispositional aggression + age)	.60	.36	.05	1%

*R^2 change and unique variance of the predictor variable added at each step.

Thus, as expected, a minority of the boys were culpable for most of the aggression recorded at this school. Since most boys who perpetrate school aggression do not desist from this behavior during the middle school years, a past history of school aggression may be the best predictor for subsequent school aggression, including bullying (Pellegrini & Bartini, 2000; Solberg & Olweus, 2003).

However, the aggression among these boys was relatively mild. Fist fights, a common method of settling disputes among young adolescent boys (Baron, Forde, & Kennedy, 2001; Lindeman, Harakka, & Keltikangas-Jaervinen, 1997) were the most frequent form of school aggression recorded for this sample. Other minor acts of aggression, such as pushing and shoving, were also common. However, more serious forms of aggression (e.g., biting, fighting with a nonlethal weapon) were uncommon and there was no serious *violence* (e.g., stabbings, shootings) among this sample. These results are consistent with Mulvey and Cauffman (2001), who contend that serious acts of violence are rare at school and, consequently, difficult to predict.

While it may be true that specific incidents of school aggression and school violence are difficult to predict, our results indicate that both dispositional aggression and past history of school aggres-

The authors state that, while school aggression and violence are difficult to predict, their results indicate that dispositional aggression and past history of school aggression are good predictors of school aggression.

sion predicted school aggression. Dispositional aggression was a better predictor of physical aggression than verbal aggression. Thus, while measures of dispositional aggression would not be useful in predicting specific incidents of aggression, they could be useful in predicting which boys are at greater risk for engaging in physical aggression at school. If coupled with data regarding prior aggression, measures of dispositional aggression could be useful for screening adolescents who might benefit from intervention aimed at reducing dispositional and behavioral aggression. School- or community-based interventions for aggression could include cognitive therapies (e.g., Cavell & Hughes, 2000; Larson, Calamari, West, & Frevert, 1998; Robinson, Smith, Miller, & Brownell, 1999), bibliotherapy (Shectman, 1999; 2000), and/or martial arts training (Lamarre & Nosanchuk, 1999; Skelton, Glynn, & Berta, 1991).

At this point, dispositional aggression is not well understood. Further research is needed to examine the factors related to the development of dispositional aggression (e.g., temperament, parenting, media exposure) and to tease apart the physiological, cognitive, and emotional bases of individual differences in behavioral aggression. Some recently proposed models, including the General Aggression Model (Anderson & Bushman, 2001a; 2001b) are useful in conceptualizing the components of aggression, but are inadequate to predict or explain specific incidents of aggression.

Recommendations for further research.

The nature of the data used in this study has both benefits and limitations. On the positive side, the data were collected by school administrators in context and in a standard fashion. However, a potential limitation arises from the use of a pre-established method of recording school aggression into school records. That is, the data are based on a collection of behaviors that was set up by school administrators, rather than a system that was derived from the literature. Conspicuously absent from the coding scheme was rela-

> Over the next several paragraphs, the authors identify limitations of their study.

tional aggression, which aims to harm others socially (e.g., Crick, 1995), perhaps because it is difficult to observe and report social aggression. Further, relational aggression has not been as great a concern to school administrators as physical and verbal aggression.

It is likely that administrators are not privy to much of the aggression that occurs at school. Aggression is likely perpetrated most often out of the view of administrators, and victims may be hesitant to report such incidents, particularly if they were threatened further harm by the perpetrator (Bendixon & Olweus, 1999; Pellegrini & Bartini, 2000). Relational aggression would be even more difficult to observe and intervene in than physical and verbal aggression. However, as boys with a history of aggression are more likely to perseverate in this behavior, they could be monitored more closely by school administrators. Closer supervision might prevent many aggressive incidents and/or ensure that fewer aggressive incidents would go unreported.

The biggest shortcoming of the study is the relatively low response rate—only 22% of parents returned consent forms to allow their sons to participate. The sample was representative of the school in terms of ethnicity and other demographic factors. However, there is no way to evaluate if this subset of students differs in their level of aggression from those who did not participate.

In summary, mild to moderate aggression is common among middle school boys with high levels of dispositional aggression. Dispositional aggression does account for a substantial amount of variance in aggressive behavior at school. Boys who engage in aggressive behavior at school are likely to be repeat offenders, indicating that both screening for dispositional aggression and the individual's history of school aggression could be used to identify boys who might benefit from intervention. Indeed, given that not all aggressive incidents are reported, students with high levels of dispositional aggression might be targeted for preventative intervention, even in the absence of a history of reported school aggression.

References

Anderson, C. A., & Bushman, B. J. (2001a). Effects of violent video games on aggressive behavior, aggressive cognition, aggressive affect, physiological arousal, and prosocial behavior: A meta-analytic review of the scientific literature. *Psychological Science, 12,* 353–359.

Anderson, C. A., & Bushman, B. J. (2001b). Human aggression. *Annual Review of Psychology, 53,* 27–51.

Anderson, C. A., & Dill, K. E. (2000). Video games and aggressive thoughts, feelings, and behavior in the laboratory and in life. *Journal of Personality and Social Psychology, 78,* 772–790.

Baron, S. W., Forde, D. R., & Kennedy, L. W. (2001). Rough justice: Street youth and violence. *Journal of Interpersonal Violence, 16,* 662–678.

Bendixon, M., & Olweus, D. (1999). Measurement of antisocial behaviour in early adolescence and adolescence: Psychometric properties and substantive findings. *Criminal Behaviour and Mental Health, 9,* 323–354.

Berkowitz, L. (1998a). Frustration-aggression hypothesis: Examination and reformulation. *Psychological Bulletin, 106,* 59–73.

Berkowitz, L. (1998b). Affective aggression: The role of stress, pain, and negative affect. In R. G. Geen, & E. Donnerstein (Eds.) *Human aggression: Theories, research, and implications for social policy* (pp. 4972). San Diego, CA: Academic Press.

Brooks-Gunn, J., & Duncan, G. J. (1997). The effects of poverty on children. *The Future of Children, Summer/Fall,* 55–71.

Bushman, B. J. (1995). Moderating role of trait aggressiveness in the effects of violent media on aggression. *Journal of Personality and Social Psychology, 69,* 950–960.

Bushman, B. J. (1996). Individual differences in the extent and development of aggressive cognitive-associative networks. *Personality and Social Psychology Bulletin, 22,* 811–819.

Buss, A. H., & Warren, W. L. (2000). *Aggression questionnaire.* Los Angeles, CA: Western Psychological Services.

Canary, D. J., Spiztberg, B. H., & Semic, B. A. (1998). The experience and expression of anger in interpersonal settings. In P. A. Anderson, & L. K. Guerrero (Eds.) *Handbook of communication and emotion: Research, theory, applications, and contexts* (pp. 189–213). San Diego: Academic Press.

Carlo, G., & Roesch, S. C. (1998). The multiplicative relations of parenting and temperament to prosocial and antisocial behaviors in adolescence. *Journal of Early Adolescence, 18,* 266–290.

Carter, S. P., & Stewin, L. L. (1999). School violence in the Canadian context: An overview and model for intervention. *International Journal for the Advancement of Counseling, 21,* 267–277.

Cavell, T. A., & Hughes, J. N. (2000). Secondary prevention as context for assessing change processes in aggressive children. *Journal of Social Psychology, 38,* 199–235.

Centers for Disease Control and Prevention. (1997). Rates of homicide, suicide, and firearm-related death among children—26 industrialized countries. *Mortality and Morbidity Weekly Report, 46,* 101–105.

Coie, J. D., Cillessen, A. H. N., Dodge, K. A., Hubbard, J. A., Schwartz, D., & Lemerise, E. A. (1999). It takes two to fight: A test of relational factors and a method for assessing aggressive dyads. *Developmental Psychology, 35,* 1179–1188.

Coles, C. J., Greene, A. F., & Braithwaite, H. O. (2002). The relationship between personality, anger expression, and perceived family control among incarcerated male juveniles. *Adolescence, 37,* 395–409.

Crick, N. R. (1995). Relational aggression: The role of intent attributions, feelings of distress, and provocation type. *Development and Psychopathology, 7,* 313–322.

Deffenbacher, J. L., Lynch, R. S., Deffenbacher, D. M., & Oetting, E. R. (2001). Further evidence of reliability and validity for the Driving Anger Expression Inventory. *Psychological Reports, 89*, 535–540.

Dill, K. E., Anderson, C. A., Anderson, K. B., & Deuser, W. E. (1997). Effects of aggressive personality on social expectations and social perceptions. *Journal of Research in Personality, 31*, 272–292.

Dodge, K. A., Coie, J. D., Pettit, G. S., & Price, J. M. (1990). Peer status and aggression in boy's groups: Developmental and contextual analysis. *Child Development, 61*, 1289–1309.

Douglas, S. C., & Martinko, M. J. (2001). Exploring the role of individual differences in the prediction of workplace aggression. *Journal of Applied Social Psychology, 86*, 547–559.

Driscoll, J. M., Jarman, B. J., & Yankeelov, P. A. (1994). Effects of a person's history of aggression on attributions of affect to aggressors. *Journal of Social Behavior and Personality, 9*, 685–700.

Dula, C. S., & Ballard, M. E. (2003). Correlates of aggressive, risky, and emotional driving. *Journal of Applied Social Psychology, 33*, 263–282.

Eron, L. D. (1987). The development of aggressive behavior from the perspective of a developing behaviorism. *American Psychologist, 42*, 435–442.

Eron, L. D., & Huesmann, L. R. (1990). The stability of aggressive behavior—even unto the third generation. In M. Lewis & S. M. Miller (Eds.), *Handbook of developmental psychopathology: Perspectives in developmental psychology* (pp. 147–156). New York: Plenum.

Geen, R. G., (1998). Processes and personal variables in affective aggression. In R. G. Geen & E. Donnerstein (Eds.), *Human aggression: Theories, research, and implications for social policy* (pp. 1–21). San Diego, CA: Academic Press.

Gillig, S., & Zimmer, J. W. (1986). Survey return rate and size of school district. *Psychological Reports, 58*, 381–382.

Hatipoglu-Suemer, Z., & Aydin, G. (1999). Incidence of violence in Turkish schools. A review. *International Journal for the Advancement of Counseling, 21*, 335–347.

Huesmann, L. R. (1994). *Aggressive behavior: Current perspectives.* New York, NY: Plenum Press.

Huesmann, L. R., Eron, L. D., Lefkowitz, M. M., & Walder, L. O. (1984). Stability of aggression over time and generations. *Developmental Psychology, 20*, 1120–1134.

Huesmann, L. R., Moise-Titus, J., Podolski, C. P., & Eron, L. D. (2003). Longitudinal relations between children's exposure to TV violence and their aggressive and violent behavior in young adulthood: 1977–1992. *Developmental Psychology, 39*, 201–221.

Indicators of School Crime and Safety, 2001 (2001). Retrieved December 17, 2001, from http://nces.ed.gov/pubs2002/crime2001.

Keiwitz, C., & Weaver, J. B. III. (2001). Trait aggressiveness, media violence, and perceptions of interpersonal conflict. *Personality and Individual Differences, 31*, 821–835.

Lamarre, B. W., & Nosanchuk, T. A. (1999). Judo—the gentle way: A replication of studies on martial arts and aggression. *Perceptual and Motor Skills, 88*, 992–996.

Larson, J. D., Calamari, J. E., West, J. G., & Frevert, T. A. (1998). Aggression management with disruptive adolescents in a residential setting: Integration of a cognitive-behavioral component. *Residential Treatment for Children and Youth, 15*, 1–9.

Lindeman, M., Harakka, T., & Keltikangas-Jaervinen, L. (1997). Age and gender differences in adolescents' reactions to conflict situations: Aggression, prosociality, and withdrawal. *Journal of Youth and Adolescence, 26*, 339–351.

Loeber, R., & Hay, D. (1997). Key issues in the development of aggression and violence from childhood to early adulthood. *Annual Review of Psychology, 48*, 371–410.

Mallet, P., & Paty, B. (1999). How French counsellors treat school violence: An adult-centered approach. *International Journal for the Advancement of Counseling, 21*, 279–300.

Martin, L. R. (2000). Violence in German Schools: What school counsellors can do. *International Journal for the Advancement of Counseling, 21*, 301–313.

Mauger, P. A., & Adkinson, D. R. (1993). *Interpersonal Behavior Survey manual.* Los Angeles, CA. Western Psychological Services, Inc.

Minden, J., Henry, D. B., Tolan, P. H., & Gorman-Smith, D. (2000). Urban boys' social networks and school violence. *Professional School Counseling, 4*, 95–104.

Mulvey, E. P., & Cauffman, E. (2001). The inherent limits of predicting school violence. *American Psychologist, 56*, 797–802.

National School Safety Center. (2000). *Report on school associated violent deaths.* Retrieved December 17, 2001, from http://www.nssc1.org/savd.

Neuman, J. H., & Baron, R. A. (1998). Workplace violence and workplace aggression: Evidence concerning specific forms, potential causes, and preferred targets. *Journal of Management, 24*, 391–419.

Olafsen, R. N., & Viemeroe, V. (2000). Bully/victim problems and coping with stressing school among 10- to 12-year-old pupils in Aland, Finland. *Aggressive Behavior, 26*, 57–65.

Pellegrini, A. D., & Bartini, M. (2000). A longitudinal study of bullying, victimization, and peer affiliation during the transition from primary school to middle school. *American Education Research Journal, 37*, 699–725.

Population Estimates by Age, Sex, and Race—Mecklenburg County, North Carolina. (1998). Retrieved December 17, 2001, from http://www.govinfo.library.orst.edu/cgi-bin/pe-list?map=01–119.ncc.

Robinson, T. R., Smith, S. W., Miller, M. D., & Brownell, M. T. (1999). Cognitive behavior modification of hyperactivity-impulsivity and aggression: A meta-analysis of school-based studies. *Journal of Educational Psychology, 91*, 195–203.

Schectman, Z. (1999). Bibliotherapy: An indirect approach to treatment of childhood aggression. *Child Psychiatry and Human Development, 30*, 39–53.

Schectman, Z. (2000). An innovative intervention for treatment of child and adolescent aggression: An outcome study. *Psychology in the Schools, 37*, 157–167.

Schumacher, J. A., Feldbau-Kohn, S., Slep, A. M. S., & Heyman, R. E. (2001). Risk factors for male-to-female partner physical abuse. *Aggression and Violent Behavior, 6*, 281–302.

Seguin, J. R., Arseneault, L., Boulerice, B., Harden, P. W., & Tremblay, R. E. (2002). Response perseveration in adolescent boys with stable and unstable histories of physical aggression: The role of underlying processes. *Journal of Child Psychology and Psychiatry, 43,* 481–494.

Skelton, D. L., Glynn, M. A., & Berta, S. M. (1991). Aggressive behavior as a function of tae-kwon-do ranking. *Perceptual and Motor Skills, 72,* 179–182.

Solberg, M. E., & Olweus, D. (2003). Prevalence estimation of school bullying with the Olweus Bully/Victim Questionnaire. *Aggressive Behavior, 29,* 239–268.

Sourcebook for Criminal Justice Statistics. (1999). Tables 3.44; 3.46; 3.64 & 3.65. Retrieved December 17, 2001, from http://www.albany.edu/sourcebook.

Speaker, K. M., & Petersen, G. J. (2000). School violence and adolescent suicide: Strategies for effective intervention. *Educational Review, 52,* 65–73.

Vance, J. E., Fernandez, G., & Biber, M. (1998). Educational progress in a population of youth with aggression and emotional disturbance: The role of risk and protective factors. *Journal of Emotional and Behavioral Disorders, 6,* 214–221.

ORGANIZING FOR CORRELATIONAL RESEARCH

myeducationlab
for research

To learn more about the overall process of correlational research, go to the "Correlational Research" section of **MyEducationLab for Research** and then click on *Building Research Skills.* Read the linked article and then complete the exercise titled "Identifying Steps in the Research Process for a Correlational Study," which will help you identify key components of a correlational research study.

As evident in the foregoing report, you must, when planning and conducting correlational research, give attention to the following:

1. Identification of variables to be explored
2. Hypotheses or questions
3. Means by which variables will be measured or assigned
4. Selection of a sample
5. Collection of data
6. Analysis of data

You will find these tasks illustrated and further clarified as you move through the following procedures on planning correlational research in a specific study. Suppose you wish to identify factors that predict how successful new teachers are likely to be during their first year in the classroom. You call your investigation "Predictors of Success in First-Year Teaching."

SELECTING THE VARIABLES

In prediction studies such as those reflected in this series of exercises, the variable to be predicted is called the **criterion variable,** which in this case is success in the first year of teaching. The other variable is called the **predictor variable** and designates the trait or condition that one hopes will predict first-year teaching success.

The variables to be explored in correlational research are suggested by the problem being investigated. In relationship studies whose main purpose is to describe, you can identify for consideration any two or more variables whose possible correlations you wish to explore, such as reading ability and writing ability. In relationship studies whose main purpose is to predict, the criterion variable is established in the research topic (e.g., success in first-year teaching). The predictive variable is then selected logically and on the basis of previous research—you use knowledge and judgment to identify one or more traits or conditions that seem likely to predict the criterion variable.

Our tentative criterion variable is success in first-year teaching. As stated, however, this variable is vague. You need a criterion variable that can be measured, ranked, or otherwise objectively observed. You might consider such variables as student learning, good evaluations from the principal, popularity with students, popularity with fellow teachers, favorable comments from parents, special contributions to the school program, unusual accomplishments, and the like. The predictor variable(s) can be any measurable or observable trait, behavior, or experience that you believe can forecast success in first-year teaching, such as personality traits, grade point average in college, teacher training background, communication skills, poise, and so forth.

Exercise 12.2

1. Specify a measurable or observable trait or quality that you believe evidences success in first-year teaching.
2. Once you have clarified the criterion variable, identify one or more variables that you believe might predict the criterion variable. As you do so, be sure that your predictor variables can be quantified, ranked, or dichotomized. A possible variable that is easy to quantify would be college grade point average. A possible variable easy to dichotomize would be gender. A variable that might be ranked is teacher popularity with students. In contrast, a variable that would be difficult to quantify, rank, or dichotomize would be an understanding of children.

STATING QUESTIONS OR HYPOTHESES

Once the criterion variable and predictor variable(s) have been clarified, research questions and/or hypotheses are stated as appropriate, such as the following suitable form for an overall research question:

Example 1: Can degree of success in first-year teaching be reliably predicted?

The question takes a different form if only a single predictor variable is involved:

Example 2: To what degree can success in first-year teaching be predicted from the basis of evaluations earned in student teaching?

If more than one predictor variable is involved, a main research question can be posed as in Example 1, followed by a subordinate question for each predictor variable, as shown in Example 2.

Hypotheses, if used, are stated differently. Recall that hypotheses may be stated in the research form or the null form, but you would not use an overall research hypothesis unless exploring a single predictor variable. Instead, you would state a null hypothesis of relationship between *X* and *Y* for each of the predictor variables, as shown in this example:

No predictive relationship exists between success in first-year teaching and evaluations previously earned in student teaching.

Exercise 12.3

Use a predictor variable that you identified in Exercise 12.2 to

1. Formulate a research question
2. Formulate a research hypothesis
3. State a null hypothesis

ASSESSING AND QUANTIFYING THE VARIABLES

Both the criterion variable and the predictor variables must either be assigned scores, given rankings, or placed into dichotomies such as gender, handedness, or high–low. It is preferable, when possible, that all variables be measurable, so they yield continuous interval data that indicate a wide degree of quality or accomplishment. When such measurement is not feasible, *and only then,* should variables be ranked or dichotomized.

If one of the predictors is scores made on initial interviews, existing numerical data are available. If one of the predictors is evaluation by administrators, you will need to decide how such evaluations can be assigned numerical equivalents, dichotomized, or ranked. If one of the predictors is popularity with students, you will have to devise a means of measuring, ranking, or dichotomizing popularity.

Exercise 12.4

1. Indicate how the criterion variable you described in Exercise 12.2 could be quantified. If not quantifiable, indicate how it could be ranked or dichotomized.
2. Indicate how one of the predictor variables you named in Exercise 12.2 could be quantified. If not quantifiable, indicate how it can be ranked or how it can be dichotomized naturally (e.g., on the basis of gender) or artificially (e.g., high–low).

SELECTING A SAMPLE

In the research we have been considering, a sample of teachers must be selected from whom to obtain data. Because the criterion is success in first-year teaching, it is preferable that the teachers be assessed at the end of their first year or early in their second year of teaching. For the sample's correlations to be safely generalizable to the population, the sample should include at least 30 teachers, selected at random. In actual practice such a sample would be difficult to obtain except in costly large-scale research. In most cases, a convenience sample would have to suffice, consisting perhaps of second-year teachers from various school districts.

COLLECTING DATA

Data are obtained from members of the sample, who are tested or otherwise assessed in accordance with the criterion and predictor variables. At least two scores are obtained for each person in the sample—one for the criterion variable and one for each of the predictor variables—and paired as follows:

Person	Predictor	Criterion
Gary	32	47
Ruth	29	43
Sean	33	46

ANALYZING THE DATA

Correlations between predictor and criterion variables are calculated using the correlational procedure appropriate for the type of data obtained, as described earlier.

As discussed, one of the main uses of correlations is making predictions of criterion variable scores from predictor variable scores. The process of predicting a given person's unknown (Y) score from his or her known (X) score is rather involved, but computer software does the task very quickly.

Almost all variables, even those that seem completely unrelated, such as teaching success and number of dental fillings, will show a slight positive or negative coefficient when correlated. Such results may or may not have occurred by chance. Correlations are tested for significance in order to determine whether the observed correlation is likely to have occurred due to errors in selecting the sample. If the correlation is found to be statistically significant, we may rule out sampling error and deem the finding real for the population. Computer software will help you select the appropriate analytical approach, perform the calculations, and test the results for significance.

APPLYING TECHNOLOGY

More about Correlational Research

Dr. AnnMaria Rousey of Cankdeska Cikana Community College (an American Indian Tribal College located in Ft. Totten, North Dakota) has included in her online course in developmental psychology a couple of pages that describe correlational research, and what it does and does not do. The first page, titled "Correlational Research" (www.fractaldomains.com/devpsych/corr.htm), provides a thorough discussion of exactly what correlational research is and incorporates several graphical displays, as in the following sample screenshot from Dr. Rousey's site:

A second page (www.fractaldomains.com/dev psych/corr2.htm) presents an extremely appropriate discussion—especially to the novice researcher—of what a correlation can and cannot tell you, specifically focusing on the issue of implying causation from correlational research. Included is a wonderful example of the positive correlation between shoe size and reading achievement in elementary school students.

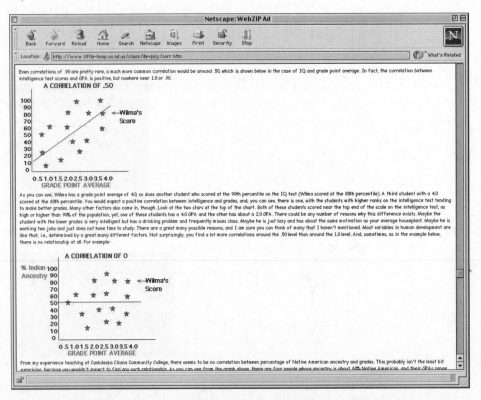

The highest possible coefficient of correlation is 1.0, either positive or negative. From such perfect correlations perfect predictions can be made. That is, if you know Tom's score on the predictor variable plus the range of scores possible on the criterion variable, you can predict the exact score he will make on the criterion variable. However, this level of predictive precision is virtually impossible because perfect correlations are almost never seen in education and the social sciences.

As described earlier, coefficients of correlation are generally considered to be high if ±.70 or above, moderate if between ±.30 and ±.70, and low if below ±.30 (see Figure 12.1 on page 273). The lower the correlation (i.e., the closer it is to zero), the less accurate are the predictions of one variable from the other. The degree of predictive accuracy for correlations is determined by calculating the standard error of estimate, which indicates the range of likely error inherent in predicting one variable from the other. If you know the correlation between X and Y and know Tom's score on the X variable, with your computer you can

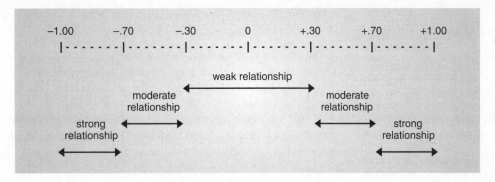

Figure 12.1
General rule of thumb
for interpreting
correlation coefficients

predict his score on the *Y* variable. The higher the correlation between *X* and *Y*, the lower the standard error of estimate; hence, the more accurate the prediction is likely to be.

CAUSAL-COMPARATIVE RESEARCH

Causal-comparative research is used to explore the possibility of cause and effect when neither experimental nor quasi-experimental research (see Chapter 13) can be done. Causal-comparative research does not convincingly demonstrate cause and effect but can strongly suggest it. Such research might be used by medical researchers trying to establish the possibility that smoking causes heart disease. They could not do experimental research because they could not ethically select a group of people and make them smoke heavily to see what happens to their health. They could, however, randomly select groups of heavy smokers and groups of nonsmokers and then assess the groups for incidence of heart disease. If heavy smokers were found to have a higher rate of heart disease, that would be a strong indication, though still not absolute proof, that the disease was being "caused" by smoking.

As another illustration, one might hypothesize that "femaleness," compared to "maleness," causes better student achievement in certain curriculum areas. If researched, achievement would be the dependent variable (**Y variable**) and gender the independent variable (**X variable**). Obviously, gender cannot be manipulated. However, if differences are found in the dependent variable (achievement), it might be inferred that gender is somehow causing those differences. Logic is used to help establish the direction of cause and effect; in this case there can be no confusion—higher or lower achievement could not possibly affect one's gender. Causal-comparative research might, therefore, strongly suggest a cause–effect relationship between gender and achievement in certain areas but could not demonstrate such a relationship unequivocally.

THE NATURE OF CAUSAL-COMPARATIVE RESEARCH

Causal-comparative research explores possible cause and effect, though it cannot demonstrate cause and effect as does experimental research. Its concern is similar to that of experimental and quasi-experimental research, but it differs from them in the following ways:

- In causal-comparative research the independent variable is not manipulated, either because manipulation is impossible or because it is impractical or unethical.
- Of necessity, causal-comparative research focuses first on the effect and then attempts to determine the cause of the observed effect. The basic question it explores is "What is causing this effect that I observe?"

The nature of causal-comparative research might be outlined as follows:

1. First one focuses on the effect—for example, differences in ethnic group achievement.
2. Then one hypothesizes a cause—for example, differences in stability of home life.

PEARSON
myeducationlab
for research

Causal-comparative studies are often difficult to distinguish from experimental studies. To learn more about causal-comparative designs, go to the "Causal-Comparative Research" section of **MyEducationLab for Research** and then click on *Assignments and Activities.* Complete the exercise titled "The Basic Causal-Comparative Design," which will give you some practice at designing causal-comparative studies that match specific designs.

3. Finally, one makes a logical connection that persuasively suggests that the observed effect is being influenced by the hypothesized cause.

You can see in these steps that the independent variable, stability of home life, cannot be manipulated as would be required in experimental research.

You may see causal-comparative research referred to as **ex post facto research.** *Ex post facto* means "after the fact" and simply indicates that one is exploring a suspected "cause" of a condition that already exists. This kind of research can again be illustrated by cardiovascular disease and smoking. One identifies a sample of 70-year-old people who have advanced cardiovascular disease and asks, "What has caused these people to have this disease?" One might hypothesize that the cause is heavy cigarette smoking over a period of years. To explore that hypothesis, one selects another sample of 70-year-old people who do not have cardiovascular disease and investigates both groups' histories of cigarette smoking. This reveals that some individuals with cardiovascular disease have never smoked; some who have smoked heavily all their lives have no cardiovascular disease; many with the disease have smoked heavily for decades; and many without the disease have smoked little if any during their lifetimes.

One examines these findings and applies careful logical thinking to the hypothesis and in so doing perhaps concludes that prolonged heavy smoking does probably tend to cause cardiovascular disease. But because the independent variable (amount of smoking over a long time) cannot be manipulated experimentally, the hypothesis that smoking causes the disease remains open to debate. Indeed, cigarette manufacturing companies for many years claimed that no linkage between smoking and disease could be shown.

Further, because the independent variable cannot be manipulated, some question exists concerning which is cause and which is effect. Could it not be that whatever condition predisposes people to cardiovascular disease might also make them want to smoke? This question shows that the cause–effect linkage explored in causal-comparative research must be argued very persuasively.

How does one make such arguments?

1. You provide examples showing that without the first condition (smoking), the second condition (disease) does not occur, or else occurs differently or less frequently. The first (causal) condition, therefore, must be shown to precede the second (effect) condition.
2. You consider carefully whether the cause you have hypothesized is sufficient in itself or in combination with other factors to have produced the effect.
3. You seriously explore whether there are other conditions or events that might be equally plausible as causes.

Consider how these three elements of persuasive argument would come into play in a study exploring the hypothesis that, with intelligence held constant, family wealth produces higher student achievement.

1. You identify the Elmwood high school students whose family incomes are in the upper 10 percent. You determine the students' achievement levels. You find that several are high achievers, but many are average and a few are low achievers. You then make a search of the records for other high-achieving students who are not from wealthy families. You find that many are from middle-income families and that many others are from low-income families. But you see that a certain level of family income is present in the majority of high-achieving students.
2. You now probe the hypothesized cause—wealth—to see if it seems to be sufficient in itself to produce high achievement. You have already found high-achieving students from poor families and lower-achieving students from wealthy families. This causes you to wonder whether you can support your hypothesis, although you continue to believe that wealth is probably one of the causes of higher achievement.
3. You now seriously explore whether there might be other causes of high achievement as important or more important than family wealth. Because you have used statistical procedures to hold intelligence constant, you explore other potential causative factors

such as family stability, language skills, family belief in the value of education, and individual motivation to excel in school. After considering these possibilities, you may decide that you cannot make a strongly persuasive argument for wealth as the main causative factor in school achievement, even though you still believe it plays a role.

Exercise 12.5

1. Suppose you have noted that girls are more likely than boys to raise their hands before speaking in class discussion.

   a. Hypothesize two possible causes for that difference.
   b. Support each cause with two arguments.
   c. Is there any way you can demonstrate cause and effect for this phenomenon? (To do so you will have to manipulate the independent variable you hypothesize as the cause.)

2. Mr. Simmons claims that students who smoke a great deal are less responsible and considerate than those who do not. He says smoking causes students to lose self-respect. Would you agree or disagree with that assertion? What arguments would you present to support your views?

CONDUCTING CAUSAL-COMPARATIVE RESEARCH

Chapter 3 described a graduate student, Jan, who believed that students who entered kindergarten at age 4 tended to experience social and learning difficulties to a greater degree in later years than did students who entered kindergarten at age 5. To explore her hypothesis, she selected from among sixth-grade students a sample who had begun school at age 4 and a second sample who had begun school at age 5. She used stratified samples to make sure the groups were equivalent in gender, ethnicity, and socioeconomic status. She then examined records and interviewed teachers to compare the achievement levels and social adjustment patterns of the two groups.

Jan's study is an example of causal-comparative research. She was aware of learning and social problems that certain schoolchildren experienced; she believed the cause of their difficulties was immaturity, attributable to age of entry into kindergarten. Appropriately for causal-comparative research, Jan did the following:

1. Identified the dependent variable (social, emotional, and academic difficulties)
2. Defined the independent variable (early age entry into kindergarten), which she hypothesized to be the cause of the problems associated with the dependent variable
3. Selected for comparison two groups that were as similar as possible except for the independent variable
4. Measured both groups to ascertain the level or degree of the dependent variable
5. Analyzed the differences between the groups' dependent variable data
6. Built a logical case to support the hypothesis that early age of entry to kindergarten contributed to later difficulties socially, emotionally, and academically

Jan's conclusions were not airtight. No research conclusions ever are, and any cause–effect linkage suspected in causal-comparative research is always open to question. Although Jan believed a relationship was present between the independent and dependent variables in her study, it is possible that the relationship was not causative. Certainly many early entry students do well throughout their school careers, with no unusual problems. Some other unidentified factor might have brought about the difficulties that drew Jan's attention, such as family makeup, parental strife, nutritional patterns, or presence of younger or older siblings. In Jan's logical analysis of the data, however, she was unable to identify any other causes that in her mind could account for the student problems observed.

PEARSON
myeducationlab for research

To learn more about the overall process of causal-comparative research, go to the "Causal-Comparative Research" section of **MyEducationLab for Research** and then click on *Building Research Skills.* Read the article and then complete the exercise titled "Identifying Steps in the Research Process for a Causal-Comparative Study" to help you identify key components of a causal-comparative research study.

Exercise 12.6

Suppose you conducted a causal-comparative study in which your dependent variable was artistic ability and your independent variable was handedness. In the study you confirmed that left-handed students, on average, tended to be significantly more artistic than right-handed students. Would you, therefore, contend that left-handedness caused artistic ability? Explain. Is it possible that a third factor might be causing both handedness and artistic ability? What other causal variable might you identify?

AN EXAMPLE OF CAUSAL-COMPARATIVE RESEARCH

Following the exercise is a published causal-comparative study examining differences in the sense of community between traditional classrooms, blended courses, and fully online higher education learning environments.

Exercise 12.7

As you read through the report identify the following:

1. Focus of the study—what it is about.
2. What independent variables are considered?
3. What are the hypotheses?
4. Were the data and data analyses mainly quantitative or qualitative?
5. Did the data support or fail to support the hypotheses?
6. What cautions did the investigator advise regarding the conclusions of the study?

Blended Learning and Sense of Community: A Comparative Analysis with Traditional and Fully Online Graduate Courses

Alfred P. Rovai
Regent University, USA

Hope M. Jordan
Regent University, USA

Abstract

Blended learning is a hybrid of classroom and online learning that includes some of the conveniences of online courses without the complete loss of face-to-face contact. The present study used a causal-comparative design to examine the relationship of sense of community between traditional classroom, blended, and fully online higher education learning environments. Evidence is provided to suggest that blended courses produce a stronger sense of community among students than either traditional or fully online courses.

> The authors begin with an important definition for the reader.

Source: Rovai, A. P., & Jordan, H. M. (2004, August). Blended learning and sense of community: A comparative analysis with traditional and fully online graduate courses. International Review of Research in Open and Distance Learning, 5(2). Retrieved August 18, 2009, from www.irrodl.org/content/v5.2/rovai-jordan.html. Reprinted by permission of the authors.

Keywords
Blended learning
Sense of community
Higher education
Online learning
Computer-mediated communication
Faculty training

INTRODUCTION

Times are changing for higher education. From the de-emphasis on thinking about delivering instruction and the concurrent emphasis placed on producing learning, to using technology to expand distance education, to the recognition of the importance of sense of community, we are witnessing a transformation of higher education. A decade ago, Davis and Botkin (1994) wrote:

> [w]ith the move from an agrarian to an industrial economy, the small rural schoolhouse was supplanted by the big brick schoolhouse. Four decades ago we began to move to another economy but we have yet to develop a new educational paradigm, let alone create the 'schoolhouse' of the future, which may be neither school nor house (p. 23).

Today, we appear to be well along the road of creating that new schoolhouse and, as Davis and Botkin predicted, it is not constructed exclusively of bricks and mortar.

Producing Learning

Barr and Tagg (1995) described the first focus of change as a paradigm shift in which universities were re-inventing their purpose and thinking less about delivering instruction and more about producing learning in student-centered environments. According to Barr and Tagg, universities are moving away from a faculty-centered and lecture-based paradigm to a model where learners are the focus, where faculty members become learning environment designers, and where students are taught critical thinking skills. Thus, the role of professors in the new schoolhouse is to serve their students by ensuring student learning is of paramount importance. They support their students by attending to their intellectual growth and self-autonomy, and by instilling in them an awareness of important social issues, thus supporting their ability to become more productive members of society as lifelong learners working toward the common good.

The authors identify three focal points for change in higher education and have organized their literature review accordingly: producing learning, distance education, and the development of a strong sense of community.

Gardiner (1994, 1998) endorsed the need for classroom change to allow students to acquire more significant kinds of cognitive learning, particularly critical thinking skills. He pointed out that research shows the ability of university students to reason with abstractions is strikingly limited. He argued that many university students have not yet reached the formal operational level of cognitive development. Consequently, revisions to curricula, instructional and advising practices, and campus climates are needed to improve student learning and to promote student growth. If we envision a university education as education in the conduct and strategy of inquiry itself, then the university becomes society's unique site where students learn how to think, learn, produce, and evaluate knowledge, providing the basis for lifelong, independent learning (Rury, 1996).

An important implication of this shift is the need for a recommitment to creating an ideal learning environment for students and employing new pedagogies and technologies, where appropriate. In implementing change, one reality seems clear. Universities will face more competition to attract quality-conscious students and thus cannot afford to underestimate the depth and speed of the changes required to remain competitive. Change is not easy, however, and there is considerable pressure from within the university to preserve the status quo, particularly from faculty members. In many cases, professors teach as they were taught and resist change (Gardiner, 1998), often using academic freedom as an academic crutch. Since faculty promotion and tenure, at present, are largely based on research and publication, some professors zealously feel that they should not take away from their research or writing time to change curricula and pedagogy, for the potential rewards are not worth the time or risk to them. Consequently, many professors still use the traditional lecture as their instructional strategy of choice.

Several learning theories are particularly relevant to the learning-centered university classroom. Approaches to learning that promote social constructivism, or learning within a social context, and that feature active group construction of knowledge, rather than transfer of knowledge, provide ideal learning environments for the new schoolhouse. These approaches to learning are highly consistent with the views of Barr and Tagg (1995), who wrote that the new educational paradigm "creates environments . . . that bring students to discover and construct knowledge for themselves" (p. 15).

Distance Education

A second focus of change is the shift from providing exclusively traditional classroom instruction to reaching out to students by delivering courses at a distance using technology. Distance education is already a pervasive element of higher education and it continues to rapidly expand. Research, however, suggests that online courses are not suitable for all types of students and faculty. Collins (1999) noted that students and teachers react to new educational technologies with varied emotions, ranging from enthusiasm to disabling fear. Abrahamson (1998) reported that distance education required students who were self-regulated and independent. Marino (2000) also discovered that some students experienced difficulty adjusting to the structure of online courses, managing their time in such environments, and maintaining self-motivation.

The text-based computer-mediated communication (CMC) that is used by Internet-based e-learning systems for discussion board and email discourse is a powerful tool for group communication and cooperative learning that promotes a level of reflective interaction that is often lacking in a face-to-face, teacher-centered classroom. However, the reduced non-verbal social cues in CMC, such as the absence of facial expressions and voice inflections, can generate misunderstandings that adversely affect learning.

Sikora and Carroll (2002) reported that online higher education students tend to be less satisfied with totally online courses when compared to traditional courses. Fully online courses also experienced higher attrition rates (Carr, 2000). The research is mixed regarding the reasons for these higher attrition rates, however. Hara and Kling (2001), conducting a study of online courses, found that feelings of isolation were an important stress factor for online students, but not the primary factor as frequently mentioned in the professional literature. Rather, "[s]tudents reported confusion, anxiety, and frustration due to the perceived lack of prompt or clear feedback from the instructor, and from ambiguous instructions on the course website and in e-mail messages from the instructor" (p. 68). Thus, it may be that the reason some online courses suffer more dropouts is less related to the course delivery medium and more related to the online course design and pedagogy employed by some online faculty who have limited skills in using CMC to facilitate learning and to nurture sense of community.

Sense of Community

The third major focus of change in higher education is the increased attention given to the importance of a strong sense of community. McMillan and Chavis (1986) offered the following definition of sense of community, "a feeling that members have of belonging, a feeling that members matter to one another and to the group, and a shared faith that members' needs will be met through their commitment to be together" (p. 9). Sergiovanni (1994) stressed the need for authentic community in schools, a tie binding learners and teachers through shared values, ideals, and goals.

Research evidence suggests that low sense of community is related to two student characteristics associated with attrition: student burnout (McCarthy, Pretty, and Catano, 1990) and feelings of isolation (Haythornthwaite, Kazmer, Robins, and Shoemaker, 2000; Morgan and Tam, 1999). Tinto (1975) argued that insufficient interactions of higher education students with peers and faculty and differences with the prevailing value patterns of other students, are also likely to result in dropouts. In other words, students who feel they do not *fit in* and have low sense of community tend to feel isolated and are at-risk of becoming dropouts.

Blended Learning

Blended learning is an important building block of the new schoolhouse that offers students both flexibility and convenience, important characteristics for working adults who decide to pursue postsecondary degrees. According to Colis and Moonen (2001), blended learning is a hybrid of traditional face-to-face and online learning so that instruction occurs both in the classroom and online, and where the online component becomes a natural extension of traditional classroom learning. Blended learning is thus a flexible approach to course design that supports the blending of different times and places for learning, offering some of the conveniences of fully online courses without the complete loss of face-to-face contact. The result is potentially a more robust educational experience than either traditional or fully online learning can offer.

From a course design perspective, a blended course can lie anywhere between the continuum anchored at opposite ends by fully face-to-face and fully online learning environments. The face-to-face component can be either on the main university campus or the professor can travel to a remote site in order to meet with students. Martyn (2003) described a successful blended learning model. It consists of an initial face-to-face meeting, weekly online assessments and synchronous chat, asynchronous discussions, e-mail, and a final face-to-face meeting with a proctored final examination.

Dziuban and Moskal (2001) reported that blended courses at the University of Central Florida replaced face-to-face class time with online learning so that a three-hour course occupied only one hour of actual face-to-face classroom time. Such courses allowed the weekly operation of multiple classes in a classroom previously occupied by only one course, thus making more efficient use of existing university infrastructure. Moreover, they reported that blended courses, when compared to traditional courses, had equivalent or reduced student withdrawal rates as well as equivalent or superior student success rates.

Voos (2003) suggested that it is unlikely that the *blendedness* makes the difference in such courses, but rather the fundamental reconsideration of course design in light of new instructional and media choices and the learning strengths and limitations of each. Joyce Neff (1998), a professor of writing, found that teaching a blended course had profound effects on her teaching. She wrote: "[t]he ways I perceived and manipulated the medium, the ways I imagined the subjectivities of my students, and the ways intermediaries affected my authorities all influenced . . . my writing pedagogy" (p. 154). Privateer (1999) summarized the direction needed with the following passage:

Opportunities for real change lie in creating new types of professors, new uses of instructional technology and new kinds of institutions whose continual intellectual self-capitalization continually assures their status as learning organizations (p. 72).

PURPOSE

Prior research has not examined sense of community in higher education blended learning environments. Consequently, the purpose of the present study was to examine how sense of community differed across fully traditional, blended, and fully online courses. The research hypothesis was that sense of community would be strongest in the blended course. The rationale was that a combination of face-to-face and online learning environments provides a greater range of opportunities for students to interact with each other and with their professor. These interactions should result in increased socialization, a stronger sense of being connected to each other, and increased construction of knowledge through discourse, thus providing stronger feelings that educational goals were being satisfied by community membership.

> The authors identify a void in the literature.

> The authors state a purpose and a research hypothesis about the strength of sense of community across three different instructional delivery modes.

METHODOLOGY

Participants

Study participants consisted of 68 graduate students enrolled in three graduate-level education courses during the same semester. All participants were employed as full-time K-12 teachers seeking a Master's degree in education. The overall volunteer rate was 86 percent. By course, the total number of students enrolled, the number of students who volunteered, and the volunteer rates were as follows: (a) traditional course, 26 enrolled, 24 volunteered, 92.31 percent volunteer rate; (b) blended course, 28 enrolled, 23 volunteered, 82.14 percent volunteer rate; and (c) fully online course, 25 enrolled, 21 volunteered, 84.00 percent volunteer rate.

> The sample of students is split into three preexisting groups; this is a key aspect of causal-comparative research.

Setting

All three courses were presented by a small accredited university located in an urban area of southeastern Virginia. These courses were selected for inclusion in this study because they were each taught by full-time professors of education with reputations for being superb teachers universally well regarded by their students and who valued interaction and collaborative group work. The professors were also noted for possessing such personal qualities as sociability, sensitivity, discernment, concern, and high expectations regarding student achievement.

The traditional course presented instruction on educational collaboration and consultation, and met Wednesday evenings throughout the semester in a classroom on the main university campus. Students resided in the same geographical area. Each class meeting lasted approximately three hours for total face-to-face time of approximately 48 hours. Online technologies were not used in this course. The professor employed a mix of textbook study assignments, lecture with class-wide discussions, some collaborative group work, and authentic assessment tasks requiring individual work. The group work involved two to three students working collaboratively on a single project assigned by the instructor.

> Descriptions are provided for the overall setting and for each of the three courses.

The blended course covered legal and ethical aspects associated with teaching disabled students and consisted of both face-to-face and asynchronous online components. Like the traditional course, students resided in the same geographical area. Assignments emphasized practical application, authentic tasks, collaborative action research, and group projects, all complemented with textbook readings. The course started with an initial face-to-face session followed by two Friday evening and Saturday sessions, spread evenly throughout the 16-week semester, for a total of approximately 14 face-to-face hours. These sessions were conducted either on the main campus or at remote sites, chosen based on their accessibility to students and included activities such as guest speakers, group project presentations, group simulations, interactive videos, and discussions. The online component was delivered using the BlackboardSM e-learning system, which allowed for presentation of online content and the extensive use of student-student and student-professor asynchronous dialogue as extensions of the face-to-face sessions.

The fully online course covered curriculum and instructional design and was delivered entirely online using the BlackboardSM e-learning system. Unlike the other two courses, students were geographically dispersed throughout the U.S. The online professor used a mix of textbook study assignments, collaborative online discussion topics using group discussion boards consisting of 12 to 15 students each, and authentic assessment tasks requiring individual work. The only collaborative group work in the course was the weekly problem-oriented discussion topics posted by the instructor. These topics required students to interact with each other as they moved toward achieving consensus on solutions to the issues raised by the instructor. In order to encourage participation in the discussion boards, active and constructive online interactions accounted for 10 percent of the course grade.

Instrumentation

The Classroom Community Scale (CCS) was used to measure connectedness and learning (Rovai, 2002). This instrument consisted of 20 self-report items, such as *feel isolated in this course* and *feel that this course is like a family*. Following each item was a five-point Likert scale of potential responses: *strongly agree, agree, neutral, disagree,* and *strongly disagree*. The participants check the place on the scale that best reflects their feelings about the item. Scores are computed by adding points assigned to each of the 20 five-point items, with 10 items allocated to each subscale. These items are reverse-scored where appropriate to ensure the least favorable choice is always assigned a value of 0 and the most favorable choice is assigned a value of 4. The connectedness subscale represented the feelings of students regarding their cohesion, community spirit, trust, and interdependence. The learning subscale represented the feelings of community members regarding the degree to which they shared educational goals and experienced educational benefits by interacting with other members of the course. Scores on each subscale can range from 0 to 40, with higher scores reflecting a stronger sense of classroom community.

> The authors use an existing instrument for their data collection. They have included information on how the scales are scored.

The results of a factor analysis confirmed that the two subscales of connectedness and learning were latent dimensions of the classroom community construct (Rovai, 2002). Cronbach's coefficient alpha for the full classroom community scale was .93. Additionally, the internal consistency estimates for the connectedness and learning subscales were .92 and .87, respectively. In the present study, Cronbach's coefficient alpha for the full classroom community scale and the connectedness and learning subscales were .92, .90, and .84, respectively.

> Ample information related to the validity and reliability of the data resulting from the instrument have been provided.

End-of-course student evaluations were also used to obtain anecdotal data regarding student perceptions of their respective courses. These evaluations are voluntary on the part of each student and are submitted anonymously directly to the university. Instructors receive written copies of comments disaggregated by course after course grades are submitted to the university registrar.

> Supplemental data, but not the focus of data collection and analysis.

Procedures

The CCS was completed by the traditional and blended course participants during face-to-face meetings proctored by the course's professor while fully online course participants completed the CCS via an online survey. All participants completed the pretest during the second week of the semester and the posttest during the final two weeks of the semester. Participants were unaware of their final course grades when they completed the CCS.

Design and Data Analysis

A causal-comparative design was used to determine whether the mean differences in sense of community measured at the end of traditional, blended, and fully online graduate courses, as reflected by the composite dependent variable of the two CCS subscales of connectedness and learning, were larger than expected by chance after adjusting for preexisting differences in the two subscales. A multivariate analysis of covariance (MANCOVA) was used to analyze the data in order to provide statistical matching of groups based on the pretest results, since random assignment of participants to groups was not possible in this study. Effect size was calculated using the eta squared (h2) statistic and interpretation was based on Cohen's (1977) thresholds of .01 for a small effect, .06 for a moderate effect, and .14 for a large effect. Assumptions tested and specific statistical procedures used in the analyses are described in the following results section.

> The primary analysis was done using MANCOVA, a variation of ANOVA, for group comparisons. The pretest score served as the covariate. There are two dependent variables: each of two scale scores.

RESULTS

A total of 51 (75.0 percent) of the students were females and 17 (25.0 percent) were males. Overall, 13 students (19.1 percent) reported their age as being 25 years old or less, 16 (23.5 percent) were between 26 and 30, 18 (26.5 percent) were between 31 and 40, 18 (26.5 percent) were between 41 and 50, and 3 (4.4 percent) were over 50 years old. For ethnicity, 53 (77.9 percent) reported being white, 10 (14.7 percent) were African-American, 2 (2.9 percent) were Hispanic, and 3 (4.4 percent) were bi-racial. Chi-square contingency table analysis provided evidence that there were no significant differences in the composition of the three courses by gender, age, or ethnicity. The pooled pretest means (with standard deviations in parentheses) for the connectedness and learning subscales were 28.75 (4.90) and 32.53 (3.66), respectively, while the pooled posttest statistics were 31.57 (6.18) and 34.44 (4.67), respectively. The means and standard deviations for the two subscales by course are displayed in Table 1.

> The authors provide the results of descriptive analyses.

A one-way MANCOVA was conducted on two dependent variables: posttest connectedness and posttest learning. The independent variable was type of course (traditional, online, and blended). The two covariates were pretest connectedness and pretest learning. Data screen-

Table 1 Descriptive Statistics

	Pretest scores		Posttest scores	
Variable	**M**	**SD**	**M**	**SD**
Traditional course (*n* = 24)				
Connectedness	32.63	4.12	32.50	4.85
Learning	34.38	2.39	35.88	3.55
Blended course (*n* = 23)				
Connectedness	26.70	4.10	32.70	4.42
Learning	30.57	2.76	34.26	3.74
Fully online course (*n* = 21)				
Connectedness	26.57	3.83	29.29	8.45
Learning	32.57	4.61	33.00	6.20

Note: N = 68. Scores can range from 0 to 40 for each variable, with higher scores reflecting a stronger sense of classroom community.

> "Connectedness" and "Learning" are the two scales resulting from the instrument.

ing revealed no univariate or multivariate within-cell outliers at $p < .001$. Results of evaluation of normality, linearity, singularity, and multicollinearity were satisfactory. Table 2 displays all Personian bivariate correlations for the dependent variables and covariates. The homogeneity of slopes assumption was tested by examining two interaction effects for each dependent variable: type of course × pretest connectedness and type of course × pretest learning. The assumption was tenable although the partial $\eta^2 = .11$ for the type of course × pretest connectedness interaction associated with posttest connectedness was of medium size, a cause for some concern. The assumption of homogeneity of variance-covariance matrices was not met, Box's $M = 16.06$, $F(6, 96620.57) = 2.56$, $p = .02$. Consequently, Pillai's criterion, instead of Wilks' lambda, was used to evaluate multivariate significance because of its robustness to moderate violations of this assumption.

The MANOVA revealed that the combined dependent variables were significantly affected by course type, Pillai's trace = .23, $F(4, 126) = 4.09$, $p = .004$, partial $\eta^2 = .12$. Tests of

> These results indicate significant group differences.

between-subjects effects were also conducted to investigate the impact of type of course on individual dependent variables. Both connectedness, $F(1,

Table 2 Inter-Correlations

Variable	**1**	**2**	**3**	**4**
1. Pretest connectedness	1.00	.25	.57	.41
2. Posttest connectedness		1.00	.57	.85
3. Pretest learning			1.00	.67
4. Posttest learning				1.00

Note: $p < .05$.

63) = 9.37, *MSE* = 20.70, $p < .001$, partial $\eta^2 = .23$, and learning, $F(1, 63) = 4.74$, *MSE* = 11.06, $p = .01$, partial $\eta^2 = .13$, differed significantly.

The blended course possessed the highest estimated marginal mean (i.e., the adjusted posttest mean) of the connectedness variable ($M = 34.91$), followed by the traditional course ($M = 30.78$) and the online course ($M = 28.83$). Based on these estimated marginal means and the results of Sidak's *t* test, which adjusts the observed significance level for the fact that multiple comparisons are made, participants in the blended course scored significantly higher on the connectedness posttest, after adjustment based on pretest results, than either participants in the traditional course, $p = .04$, or the online course, $p < .001$. The difference between participants in the traditional course and the online course was not significant. The blended course also possessed the highest estimated marginal mean for learning ($M = 36.17$), followed by the traditional course ($M = 34.03$) and the online course ($M = 33.01$). Based on Sidak's *t* test, the participants in the blended course scored significantly higher on learning than those in the online course, $p = .01$, after adjustment based on pretest results. The differences for other pairwise comparisons were not significant.

DISCUSSION

The present study examined the relationship of sense of community between traditional classroom, blended, and fully online higher education learning environments. After adjusting for course pretest differences, the combined dependent variable of connectedness and learning differed

> Summary of results.

significantly among the three courses. The effect size, as measured by partial η^2, was medium. The blended course possessed a significantly higher adjusted mean connectedness score than either the traditional or online courses with a large effect size. The blended course also possessed a significantly higher adjusted mean learning score than the online course, but with a medium effect size.

An examination of the variability of connectedness and learning scores by course, as reflected by their standard deviations as well as by the significant differences found in their variance-covariance matrices, showed that the scores of online course students were substantially more diverse than either the two other courses. Moreover, the distribution of these two community variables among online students revealed a decidedly negative skew. These results suggest the existence of one or more confounding variables. Such variables are likely to be related to student characteristics, such as learning style preference, that facilitate the development of strong feelings of community in some online students, while other students remain at a psychological distance from their peers in the same learning environment.

Often cited characteristics of successful online students include interest in the material taught, self-motivation, independent and self-directed learner, critical thinker, family support, positive and timely feedback, accepts responsibility for own learning, organized, and practical knowledge in the use of computers (Irizarry, 2002). Student deficiencies in any of these factors could possibly result in a weak sense of community and explain the relatively large variability and negative skew of sense of community variables among students in the online course. Since students in the blended course exhibited similar sense of community and variability as students in the traditional course, offering the convenience of fully online courses without the complete loss of face-to-face contact may be adequate to nurture a strong sense of community in students who would feel isolated in a fully online course.

The ability of the blended course to generate stronger feelings of community than the fully online course was expected, based on the frequent online student complaint of feeling isolated (e.g., Haythornthwaite et al., 2000; Morgan and Tam, 1999). Additionally, the frustrations some students feel in fully online courses, particularly those who are dependent learners, are less self-regulated, and need frequent direction and reinforcement from a visible professor, are eased when combined with periodic opportunities for face-to-face interactions. Fully online learning environments also require technological ability and frequency of usage that varies from student to student based on individual characteristics. Accordingly, all these differences influence the benefits that each student derives from online environments and help explain why some students are not fully satisfied with online courses and feel isolated. Likewise, discussions in traditional classrooms, where vocal students can dominate and discussions may be superficial, spontaneous, and limited, can frustrate those students with a more introverted personality and thus help explain why sense of community in the blended course was stronger than in the traditional course.

All student comments regarding the blended course were positive. Many initially expressed concern regarding the online component of the class at the initial face-to-face session. They were not sure that they could handle the technological aspects and the required independent learning. They were also uncertain how they would feel about communicating with other students and the professor online. Nonetheless, students predominantly ended up expressing the benefits of the online portion of their classes. As one student explained in the anonymous end-of course student evaluations of the course, "As a teacher, I would never have made it through this semester without the practical guidance of this course along with the freedom of the online component." Another student wrote: "I feel the experiences this program has given me have better prepared me for the classroom than any lecture I had in my traditional undergraduate work, and I've been teaching for six years."

Students felt that the authentic nature of the assignments tied nicely with what they were doing in their own classrooms

Results of this study are being connected back to the literature throughout this discussion.

everyday as practicing K-12 teachers. One student wrote, "this course was rigorous, yet extremely workable for teaching professionals because the assignments directly impacted my teaching practices during the year." Several blended students also commented that they would not have been able to complete the course without the online component, as they needed to continue working while attending school. They also pointed out, however, that the face-to-face weekend classes were a valuable component both academically and in building professional relationships and a strong sense of community. Students often left class on Saturday and tried a new technique, such as implementing a new behavior management plan or using a new academic strategy, the very next week. Having strategies modeled in class, participating in simulations and group work, as well as face-to-face feedback from peers and instructors, were all considered important to the overall learning experience. Although such behavior may have occurred in the other two courses, students did not mention it in their end-of-course evaluations.

Students provided a mix of negative and positive comments about the fully online course. Negative comments addressed the limitations of the text-based nature of CMC. A typical negative comment was:

> Trying to understand abstract concepts from only printed words in the discussion forums was and is still difficult for me. I have to be able to visualize within a context. I need a more visual approach. I need the professor to draw pictures and diagrams or show slides as he speaks.

Additionally, there were some student-professor misunderstandings, possibly due to the reduced social cues in text-based discussions. One student wrote to the professor: "Some of your responses to other students appeared sharp and frank. So instead of calling you, I just depended on my own wit and received help from my colleagues." The professor's view was that his communicator style was direct, concise, and to the point in order to minimize misunderstandings and manage time in responding to numerous messages each day. There was no evidence of such misunderstandings in the blended or traditional courses, suggesting that the opportunity for face-to-face discussions allowed everyone to become acquainted with each other, which may have assisted in the interpretation of subsequent text-based communication in the online course.

Positive comments regarding the fully online course centered on the value of reflective thinking and the extra time to process information. "I noticed that I process the information better when it is presented online, because I have to analyze it myself before I hear someone else's interpretation of what I am learning," was one online student's comment. The extra time to process information allowed students to give more in-depth answers and promoted critical thinking skills. However, the professor's skills in facilitating online discussions are essential to the success of the course. A comment written by one student underscores this point:

> [The professor] corrected gaps in understanding immediately when they occurred on Blackboard. This was of great ben-

efit, especially to those individuals who spent large amounts of time on Blackboard. We were able to discuss at length with him any misconceptions or errors in lingo. The level of difficulty of this course is such that the instructor must be vigilant, pointed, and on top of the learners each step of the way, if concepts are to be purely assimilated and applied. I feel that face-to-face is ideal for teaching a course as this, but if (and ONLY if) an instructor can master the online format, as our professor has, is it doable as an online course.

Course quality can vary due to a number of factors including available technology and the capabilities of professors who design and teach the courses. While technology has the great potential to enhance student's active learning, the use of technology requires a compatible pedagogy to achieve its benefits. Consequently, within each type of course, sense of community among students is likely to co-vary based on the values and abilities of the professor.

Such findings are suggestive of the need for faculty training and university faculty development centers. A designated university-wide faculty development center with a learner-centered philosophy is essential to the success of any technology-based distance education program (Bakutes, 1998). Additionally, issues such as tenure, merit, and promotion policies, faculty workload, and the changing roles of professors need to be revisited and revised, as needed, based on the new higher education schoolhouse. Faculty promotion and tenure committees need to adapt promotion and tenure criteria based on the learning paradigm. According to Senge (1990), as cited in Barr and Tagg (1995), changes to the university in support of the learning paradigm are as important as the decision or desire to shift towards the learning paradigm. Consequently, all issues regarding change, to include any moves toward increased use of blended learning, need to be addressed by the school's strategic planning process.

The ability to generalize findings beyond the present study is limited because only three courses at the same university were sampled and the learner characteristics, course content, course design, and pedagogy used by the professors in the present study may not be representative of other professors and other settings. Additionally, the researchers exercised no experimental control over the courses examined in the present study and cause-and-effect relationships were not confirmed.

The authors have identified some limitations to their findings.

CONCLUSION

The blended concept of learning is highly consistent with the three areas of change identified in the introduction—thinking less about delivering instruction and more about producing learning, reaching out to students through distance education technologies, and promoting a strong sense of community among learners. Indeed, the concept of blended learning may be a synthesis of these areas as

the learning environment becomes more learning-centered, with emphasis on active learning through collaboration and social construction of understanding. Such a concept is moving toward O'Banion's (1997) vision of a learning college as a place where learning comes first and educational experiences are provided for learners anyway, anyplace, and anytime. Graham B. Spanier, president of The Pennsylvania State University, referred to this convergence of online and traditional instruction as the single-greatest unrecognized trend in higher education today (Young, 2002).

References

Abrahamson, C. E. (1998). Issues in interactive communication in distance education. *College Student Journal, 32*(1), 33–43.

Bakutes, A. P. (1998). An examination of faculty development centers. *Contemporary Education, 69*(3), 168–171.

Barr, R. B., and Tagg, J. (1995). From teaching to learning: A new paradigm for undergraduate education. *Change, 27*(6), 13–25.

Carr, S. (2000). As distance education comes of age, the challenge is keeping the students. *The Chronicle of Higher Education, 46*, A39–A41.

Cohen, J. (1977). *Statistical power analysis for the behavioral sciences* (revised edition). New York: Academic Press.

Colis, B., and Moonen, J. (2001). *Flexible learning in a digital world: Experiences and expectations.* London: Kogan-Page.

Collins, M. (1999). I know my instructional technologies: It's these learners that perplex me! *The American Journal of Distance Education, 13*(1), 8–23.

Davis, S., and Botkin, D. (1994). *Monsters under the bed.* New York: Touchstone.

Dziuban, C., and Moskal, P. (2001). Evaluating distributed learning in metropolitan universities. *Metropolitan Universities, 12*(1), 41–49.

Gardiner, L. (1994). *Redesigning higher education: Producing dramatic gains in student learning.* ASHE-ERIC Higher Education Report 7. Washington, DC: George Washington University.

Gardiner, L. (1998). Why we must change: The research evidence. *Thought and Action, 14*(1), 71–88.

Hara, N., and Kling, R. (2001). Student distress in web-based distance education. *Educause Quarterly, 3*, 68–69.

Haythornthwaite, C., Kazmer, M., Robins, J., and Shoemaker, S. (2000). *Making connections: Community among computer-supported distance learners.* Paper presented at the Association for Library and Information Science Education 2000 conference, San Antonio, TX. Retrieved July 3, 2003, from: http://www.alise.org/conferences/conf00_Haythornthwaite_Making.htm

Irizarry, R. (2002). Self-efficacy and motivation effects on online psychology student retention. *USDLA* Journal, *16*(12), 55–64.

Marino, T. A. (2000). Learning online: A view from both sides. *The National Teaching & Learning Forum, 9*(4), 4–6.

Martyn, M. (2003). The hybrid online model: Good practice. *Educause Quarterly, 1*, 18–23.

McCarthy, M. E., Pretty, G. M. H., and Catano, V. (1990, May). Psychological sense of community and student burnout. *Journal of College Student Development, 31*, 211–216.

McMillan, D. W., and Chavis, D. M. (1986). Sense of community: A definition and theory. *Journal of Community Psychology, 14*(1), 6–23.

Morgan, C. K., and Tam, M. (1999). Unraveling the complexities of distance education student attrition. *Distance Education, 20*(1), 96–108.

Neff, J. (1998). From a distance: Teaching writing on interactive television. *Research in the Teaching of Writing, 33*(2), 136–157.

O'Banion, T. (1997). *A learning college for the 21st century.* Phoenix, AZ: Oryx Press.

Privateer, P. M. (1999). Academic technology and the future of higher education: Strategic paths taken and not taken. *The Journal of Higher Education, 70*(1), 60–79.

Rovai, A. P. (2002). Development of an instrument to measure classroom community. *Internet and Higher Education, 5*(3), 197–211.

Rury, J. (1996). Inquiry in the general education curriculum. *Journal of General Education, 45*(3), 175–196.

Senge, P. (1990). *The fifth discipline: The art and practice of the learning organization.* New York: Doubleday Currency.

Sergiovanni, T. J. (1994). *Building community in schools.* New York: Jossey-Bass.

Sikora, A. C., and Carroll, C. D. (2002). *Postsecondary education descriptive analysis reports* (NCES 2003–154). U.S. Department of Education, National Center for Education Statistics. Washington, DC: U.S. Government Printing Office.

Tinto, V. (1975). Dropout from higher education: A theoretical synthesis of recent research. *Review of Educational Research, 45*(1), 89–125.

Voos, R. (2003). Blended learning: What is it and where might it take us? *Sloan-C View, 2*(1), 2–5.

Young, J. R. (2002, March 22). Hybrid teaching seeks to end the divide between traditional and online instruction. *The Chronicle of Higher Education,* A33.

CHAPTER SUMMARY

Most relationships among variables of interest in education cannot be explained persuasively in terms of cause and effect because of the cumulative influence of countless unidentified variables combined with sources of error endemic to research involving human participants. Nevertheless, a great deal about education can, and has, been learned through investigating relationships in which one variable is found to be correlated with a second.

Such investigations are carried out through correlational research, used when one wishes to explore descriptive or predictive relationships among two or more variables. Relationships may be either descriptive or predictive in nature. Although correlational research cannot, technically, demonstrate cause and effect, it may suggest such relationships strongly and offer grounds for subsequent experimental research.

Correlational research is comparatively easy to conduct. It involves identifying and clarifying variables whose possible relationship is to be explored, stating research questions or hypotheses, selecting a sample from which to obtain data, collecting the data, analyzing the data, presenting findings, and making interpretations. The coefficients of correlation obtained in data analysis are used to help answer research questions or test hypotheses.

Causal-comparative research is aimed at exploring possible cause–effect relationships, though it cannot demonstrate cause and effect as can experimental and quasi-experimental research. Causal-comparative research proceeds by first focusing on an effect (Y = the dependent variable); it then asks what might be causing that effect (X = the independent variable) and then attempts to identify and substantiate a plausible connection between the effect and its cause. The cause–effect linkage must be made logically because it cannot be demonstrated by manipulating the independent variable, as in experimental research.

LIST OF IMPORTANT TERMS

artificial dichotomy
biserial correlation
bivariate correlation
causal-comparative research
criterion variable
discriminant analysis
ex post facto research
factor analysis

Kendall tau
multiple regression
multivariate correlation
natural dichotomy
partial correlation
Pearson product-moment correlation
phi correlation
point-biserial correlation

post hoc fallacy
predictor variable
Spearman rho
tetrachoric correlation
X variable
Y variable

ACTIVITIES FOR THOUGHT AND DISCUSSION

1. Here are the questions presented at the beginning of the chapter. See if you can answer them without looking back.
   a. What differentiates correlational research from other types of research?
   b. What can correlational research accomplish, and what are its limitations?
   c. What elements comprise the method of correlational research?
   d. What is meant by *criterion variable* and *predictor variable*?
   e. What are some of the different methods of computing coefficients of correlation, and what kinds of data are used in each?
   f. How do coefficients of correlation help answer research questions or test hypotheses?
   g. Why is it said that causal-comparative research begins by considering the effect before considering the cause.
2. Suppose you wanted to plan research into a possible relationship between superstition and scientific knowledge among eighth-grade students. Outline the steps you would take and the considerations you would keep in mind.
3. Suppose you have worked for two years to develop a short vocabulary test that you believe to be as good as a long and expensive vocabulary test that you have previously used with your students. You hope to show that your quick test can accurately predict student performance on the long test. How would you determine whether your test actually does so?

ANSWERS TO CHAPTER EXERCISES

Because the chapter exercises call for personal responses, unequivocal answers are not possible. It is suggested that answers to exercises be made a topic of class discussion.

REFERENCES AND RECOMMENDED READINGS

Gall, M., Borg, W., & Gall, J. (2003). *Educational Research: An Introduction* (7th ed.). Boston: Allyn and Bacon.

Mertler, C. A., & Vannatta, R. A. (2003). *Advanced and Multivariate Statistical Methods: Practical Application and Interpretation* (3rd ed.). Los Angeles: Pyrczak.

Rousey, A. M. (2000). *Correlational Research.* Available at www.fractaldomains.com/devpsych

Vierra, A., & Pollock, J. (1988). *Reading Educational Research.* Scottsdale, AZ: Gorsuch Scarisbrick.

13

Experimental, Quasi-Experimental, and Single-Subject Designs

PREVIEW

This chapter examines two closely related types of research:

- Experimental research

The two types are very similar in the following ways:

- Both are used to show cause and effect.
- Both have an independent variable (cause) linked to a dependent variable (effect).
- In both, differences that exist or occur in the independent variable are said to cause (produce, bring about) differences in the dependent variable.

Experimental research can convincingly demonstrate cause–effect relationships; it manipulates (makes changes in) an independent variable, possibly producing corresponding changes in the dependent variable. Quasi-experimental research also shows cause and effect, just as does experimental research, but less convincingly because the participants involved have not been selected at random, thus leaving doubt as to whether the sample properly reflects the population. Single-subject designs involve only one participant, but typically utilize experimental or quasi-experimental methods.

TARGETED LEARNINGS

Experimental and quasi-experimental research have a unique ability to demonstrate cause–effect relationships, where changes in the independent variable produce resultant changes in the dependent variable. Quasi-experimental research differs from experimental research only in that participants are not randomly assigned to treatments as they are in experimental research. Because of the power that cause–effect relationships provide in helping us control events, experimental research is highly valued.

As you read this chapter, look especially for information related to the following questions:

1. What sets experimental research apart from all other types of research?
2. What is the difference between experimental research and quasi-experimental research?
3. What research designs are most frequently used in experimental research?
4. What research designs are most frequently used in quasi-experimental research?
5. What are the main threats to internal and external validity in experimental research and quasi-experimental research?

6. What are the principal data sources in experimental and quasi-experimental research?
7. Which data analysis procedures are most often used in experimental and quasi-experimental research?

THE SEARCH FOR CAUSATION

Researchers are usually delighted when they are able to discover that one factor causes another. Such knowledge, not easy to come by but perhaps the most powerful element in science, provides not only increased understanding of phenomena but also the ability to manipulate conditions to produce changes for the better. Is there a teacher who would not

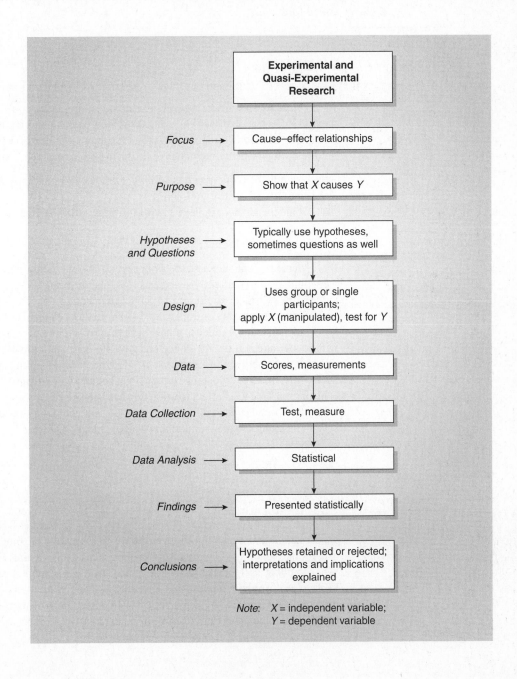

	Experimental and Quasi-Experimental Research
Focus →	Cause–effect relationships
Purpose →	Show that X causes Y
Hypotheses and Questions →	Typically use hypotheses, sometimes questions as well
Design →	Uses group or single participants; apply X (manipulated), test for Y
Data →	Scores, measurements
Data Collection →	Test, measure
Data Analysis →	Statistical
Findings →	Presented statistically
Conclusions →	Hypotheses retained or rejected; interpretations and implications explained

Note: X = independent variable;
Y = dependent variable

change teaching methods if shown that a new method, just as easily used, could substantially increase student learning? Or one who would not adopt a new discipline system if convincing evidence showed the new system improved student behavior and work habits?

Other types of research do not have the power to demonstrate this prized cause–effect relationship. Correlational, action, and evaluation research suggest such a relationship but fail to supply compelling evidence, which is brought forth only when an independent variable can be shown to influence a dependent variable. If we measure how much people in a given group smoke and also measure their overall cardiovascular health, we can very likely find a correlation between smoking and health, which makes us want to say that smoking causes poor health. We have noted, of course, that the correlation itself simply shows that the two are related, not that one causes the other, though we may certainly make inferences about causation. But frequently we look too eagerly and recklessly and believe we see a causative relationship where there is no evidence to show that one in fact exists. Or we may even confuse cause with effect, as did early Native Americans who believed that toads called forth rain.

EXPERIMENTAL RESEARCH

As noted, **experimental research** can demonstrate cause and effect convincingly. Why, then, are correlational, action, evaluation, and causal-comparative research ever used in relation to questions of cause and effect? The answer lies in what experimental research requires, which usually includes the following components of **experimental design.**

- A sample of participants randomly selected and randomly assigned to experimental group(s) and control group(s)
- An independent variable (i.e., **treatment condition**) that can be applied to the experimental group
- A dependent variable that can be measured in all groups

If we wanted to conduct an experiment on sixth-grade classroom discipline, for example, we would need to randomly select and assign sixth-grade students to two or more classes, at least one of which would receive the experimental treatment while another, serving as a **comparison group,** or control group, would not. The experimental treatment (the manipulated independent variable) is a new system of discipline. The dependent variable (which will be measured) is the incidence and severity of student misbehavior. The control group receives no experimental treatment. If, after the new discipline system has been in effect for a while, the experimental group exhibits behavior significantly different from that of the control group, a cause–effect relationship has been discovered—provided that threats to validity have been accounted for. It can then be said with some confidence that the discipline system has caused better (or perhaps worse) student behavior.

QUASI-EXPERIMENTAL RESEARCH

We have seen that experimental research requires random assignment of participants to experimental and control groups. However, researchers, despite their wishes, cannot always make random assignments to groups. This is particularly true in school settings. When random assignment cannot be made, true experimental research cannot be done. In its place, **quasi-experimental research** is used, which embodies the characteristics of experimental research except for random assignment of participants. The label *quasi-experimental* indicates that this type of research is otherwise very much like experimental research.

FUNDAMENTALS OF EXPERIMENTAL AND QUASI-EXPERIMENTAL RESEARCH

CAUSE AND EFFECT

When a cause–effect linkage is suspected, *cause* is a condition or event that exists or occurs prior to the effect. *Effect* is a condition or event that occurs subsequent to the cause.

Cause exists → then → Effect occurs as a result

The linkage between the two is intellectual: Based on evidence, one concludes that had it not been for the causal condition or event (e.g., new discipline system), the second condition or event (e.g., better student behavior) would not have occurred. The cause–effect connection is demonstrated when, by manipulating the independent variable, a resultant change occurs in the dependent variable.

RANDOM SELECTION AND ASSIGNMENT

Random selection of samples and random assignment of sample members to experimental and control groups are essential and distinguishing features of experimental design. The only exception occurs in single-participant experiments, usually conducted on an individual diagnosed as having significant personal problems—for example, obsessive eating or uncontrolled outbursts. **Random selection** is the process of choosing, in random fashion, individuals for participation in a research study. We have previously examined in Chapter 6 several techniques for the random selection of participants, including simple random sampling, stratified random sampling, and cluster sampling. Once participants have been randomly selected to participate in a study, they then undergo **random assignment** to groups (usually treatment and control groups). Random selection and assignment help ensure equivalence of groups and control for many extraneous variables that might otherwise contaminate the results of the investigation. When it is not possible to draw a randomly selected sample of participants (one usually cannot randomly select for research conducted in school settings), one must, if possible, randomly assign students to experimental and control groups. When random assignment cannot be done, what one has is quasi-experimental rather than experimental research.

It is important to note here that, in experimental or quasi-experimental designs, there may be a need or desire to have multiple (i.e., more than two) groups. Clearly, in these cases, the researcher must be able to structure some sort of "alternative" treatment group. This means that there will typically be an experimental or treatment group (that receives the treatment condition), a control group (that receives nothing), and a third comparison group (that receives *something,* but not the treatment of interest). For example, suppose a researcher wanted to investigate the impact that an Internet-based study site has on student performance on a standardized achievement test. The treatment group would receive structured time to work with the online study site. The control group would not receive any form of direct "study" support in preparation for the achievement test. However, the researcher might hypothesize that *any* sort of supplemental study time or effort would be beneficial to student performance, but also would like to compare the effectiveness of this other type of study support against the online site (i.e., the treatment condition), as well as against the complete lack of support (i.e., the control condition). Therefore, the researcher establishes a third "alternative treatment" group that receives a limited amount of study support supplied by the teacher. This group is sometimes referred to as the **comparison group.** The benefit of including a comparison group is that it can provide for the researcher an additional level or type of comparison in order to better explain the effectiveness of the treatment condition.

USE OF EXPERIMENTAL RESEARCH

We have seen that experimental research is done to show that event or condition X (an independent variable) can cause or modify event or condition Y (a dependent variable). If you supply enough heat *(X)*, you can make water boil *(Y)*. If you ask your students certain kinds of questions *(X)*, you can cause them to give more thoughtful and complete answers *(Y)*.

You would, therefore, use experimental research when the following conditions are met:

- You strongly suspect that a cause–effect relationship exists between two conditions or events.
- At least one randomly assigned group is available to participate in the study.
- The independent (causal) variable can be introduced to the participants and modified, regulated, or otherwise manipulated.
- The resulting dependent (effect) variable can be measured in the participants.

Under ideal circumstances, experimental research would involve at least two groups of participants randomly assigned from the sample. The experimental group would receive the experimental treatment—that is, an independent variable would be introduced or modified—while the control group would proceed as usual, that is, would receive no treatment. After a time, the two groups would be tested to see if differences had appeared in the dependent variable.

EXPERIMENTAL DESIGNS

myeducationlab for research

To learn more about the variety of designs in experimental research, go to the "Experimental Research" section of **MyEducationLab for Research** and then click on *Assignments and Activities*. Complete the exercise titled "Designs in Experimental Research," which will give you practice at designing experimental studies that match specific designs.

Several different designs are used in experimental research. The following five are the most common. In addition to describing them in narrative fashion, we will present them in standard experimental design notation, using the following symbols:

X_1 = Unusual or new treatment condition

X_2 = Control condition

O = Observation (pretest or posttest)

R = Random assignment

1. *Single-Group Pretest–Treatment–Posttest Design.* This design, though included here, is technically a "preexperimental design" because it makes use of only a single group of students. Suppose that Mrs. Simpkins believes students learn more when they have to explain their learnings to others. She decides to conduct an experiment in which sixth-grade students explain to their parents or guardians selected mathematics concepts and algorithms learned in school. Her principal agrees at the beginning of the year to assign students to Mrs. Simpkins's classroom randomly from among all sixth-graders at the school. After several weeks of instruction, Mrs. Simpkins tests her class to determine their level of knowledge. She then asks the students to explain what they have learned to adults at home, over a week's time, while providing no new math instruction during that week. She then retests the class to see if their level of knowledge has increased. The design can be diagrammed as follows:

Assigned Group → given a Pretest, then → receives Treatment, then → given a Posttest

Using experimental design notation, this design would appear as:

$$R \quad O \quad X_1 \quad O$$

Although this design is sometimes used by graduate students in education, it is not a strong design, for three reasons: first, it has no control group against whom to make comparisons, second, the pretest may actually instruct students so that they make higher scores on the posttest, and third, the learning effects might be attributable to a trait peculiar to Mrs. Simpkins. There is, therefore, no way to be sure that changes in student knowledge would not have occurred anyway, even without the home teaching.

2. *Two-Group Treatment–Posttest-Only Design.* This design uses two groups, an **experimental group** and a **control group,** with participants randomly assigned to the groups. An independent variable treatment is given to the experimental group, while none is given to the control group. Later, both groups are tested on the dependent variable. This design is illustrated as follows:

Group 1 is given the → Experimental Treatment and later is given a → Posttest

Group 2 → (no special treatment) → Posttest

Using experimental design notation, this design would appear as:

Group 1 $R \quad X_1 \quad O$
Group 2 $R \quad X_2 \quad O$

This was the design Mrs. Simpkins used the following year when she enlarged her study to include Mrs. Almira's next-door sixth-grade class, also randomly assigned, as a control group. She and Mrs. Almira coordinated their teaching so that both classes were taught the same content, but Mrs. Almira's students were not asked to explain the learnings at home. Later, both classes were tested on what they had been taught. This experimental design is sometimes used by graduate students in education, but despite the random assignment, it leaves some question as to whether the two groups are initially equivalent. If they are not, differences that show up on the posttest cannot be attributed with certainty to the effects of the experimental treatment.

3. *Two-Group Pretest–Treatment–Posttest Design.* To establish initial equivalence of the two groups, Mrs. Simpkins next refined her design to include the same pretest for both her class and Mrs. Almira's class. The design can be illustrated as follows:

Group 1 is given a → Pretest, then the → Experimental Treatment, and then a → Posttest

Group 2 is given the → Pretest → (no experimental treatment) → Posttest

Again, using standard notation, this design would be:

Group 1 $R \quad O \quad X_1 \quad O$
Group 2 $R \quad O \quad X_2 \quad O$

This design, which is popular among graduate students in education, is strong because potential sources of error have been reduced.

4. *Factorial Designs.* Up to this point the examples of research designs have included only a single independent variable. At times, two or more independent variables may be included simultaneously in the experimental design. (The variables are in this case referred to as *factors*—hence the name *factorial design.*) This design enables one to determine differential effects, that is, to see if the treatments have different effects on participants according to, for example, their IQ, ethnic origin, or gender. Mrs. Simpkins might decide to explore the effects of two independent variables—students' reteaching to adults versus in-class review—and, further, to determine if the two treatments produce different effects for higher-achieving versus lower-achieving students. To do this, she would enlist the cooperation of Mr. Mohl, the other sixth-grade teacher in her school. After first identifying lower-achieving and higher-achieving students in all three classes, she would use the reteaching treatment in her class while having Mrs. Almira employ the review treatment, with Mr. Mohl's class as the control group. Her 2 × 3 factorial design, with Mr. Mohl's class serving as the control group, might be diagramed as follows:

	Reteaching Group	Review Group	Control Group
Higher achievers	Mrs. Simpkins	Mrs. Almira	Mr. Mohl
Lower achievers	Mrs. Simpkins	Mrs. Almira	Mr. Mohl

Her procedure would be illustrated as follows:

Simpkins's class: Pretest → Reteaching Treatment → Posttest

Almira's class: Pretest → Review Treatment → Posttest

Mohl's class: Pretest → (no treatment) → Posttest

Using standard notation, this factorial design would be:

Group 1 (Simpkins) R O Y_1 X_1 O
                       R O Y_2 X_1 O

Group 2 (Almira) R O Y_1 X_2 O
                       R O Y_2 X_2 O

Group 3 (Mohl) R O Y_1 X_3 O
                       R O Y_2 X_3 O

where Y_1 are high achievers and Y_2 are low achievers.

Mrs. Simpkins would compare the posttest performance of students initially identified as higher and lower achieving and examine the comparative effects of reteaching and in-class review on learning by students of different ability levels. She would have a control group against whom to compare the results. An obvious source of potential error is that each treatment is given by a different teacher, which does not control for differences in teacher skill or personality. The pretest would enable Mrs. Simpkins to deal with the question of initial group differences.

QUASI-EXPERIMENTAL DESIGNS

As mentioned earlier, quasi-experimental research is just like experimental research, except that participants are not randomly assigned to treatments. Three research designs commonly used in quasi-experimental research are (1) posttest only with nonequivalent groups, (2) pretest–posttest with nonequivalent groups, and (3) time series design with a single group.

1. *Posttest Only with Nonequivalent Groups.* This design uses two groups of participants from the same population (such as two established classrooms in the same school system). One group is given the experimental treatment, and then both groups are given the posttest to see if the groups show differences in the criterion variable. This design can be diagrammed as follows:

Group 1 → Experimental Treatment → Posttest

Group 2 → (no treatment) → Posttest

Using the standard notational symbols, this design would be:

Group 1 X_1 *O*
Group 2 X_2 *O*

This is not a strong design because it leaves doubt as to whether the groups are equivalent before the experimental treatment is introduced.

2. *Pretest–Posttest with Nonequivalent Groups.* In this design two groups of participants are used, as in the previous example. The difference is that the groups are given a pretest to help establish their equivalency, prior to introducing the experimental treatment. This is a stronger design and can be diagrammed as follows:

Group 1 → Pretest → Experimental Treatment → Posttest
Group 2 → Pretest → (no treatment) → Posttest

Using standard notation, this design would be:

Group 1   *O* X_1 *O*
Group 2   *O* X_2 *O*

3. *Time Series Design.* This design uses a single group of participants measured over a period of days or weeks. In an interval between two of the measurements, the experimental treatment is introduced. If a noticeable change occurs after introduction of the experimental treatment, that treatment may be judged to have caused the change. This design can be diagrammed as follows:

O   O   O X_1 O   O   O

THE COMMONALITY OF EXPERIMENTAL AND QUASI-EXPERIMENTAL DESIGNS

PEARSON
myeducationlab
for research

To learn more about the overall process of experimental research, go to the "Experimental Research" section of **MyEducationLab for Research** and then click on *Building Research Skills.* Read the article and then complete the exercise titled "Identifying Steps in the Research Process for an Experimental Study." This exercise will help you identify key components of an experimental research study.

The experimental and quasi-experimental designs described in the preceding paragraphs share the following characteristics.

■ A cause–effect relationship is hypothesized, which stipulates that trait or condition X will produce, bring about, or cause trait or condition Y.

■ Participants are selected for the experiment. In experimental designs, participants or classrooms are randomly assigned to experimental and control groups. Occasionally, only a single participant is used. In quasi-experimental designs, participants and classrooms are not randomly assigned to treatments.

■ The experimental treatment is applied. The treatment is an introduction of a new independent variable or else a modification of an existing one—something is added or changed.

■ After the experimental treatment has been completed, all participants are measured to determine the effects, if any, of the experimental treatment.

■ Data are usually obtained in the form of scores made on the posttest. (Single-participant experiments sometimes use qualitative data.) Data analysis includes testing for significance of differences observed in the dependent variable. If a significant difference is found, and if possible errors can be satisfactorily accounted for, the treatment can be said to have caused the observed difference.

SINGLE-SUBJECT DESIGNS

for research

To learn more about single-subject designs, go to the "Single-Subject Experimental Research" section of **MyEducationLab for Research** and then click on *Assignments and Activities*. Complete the exercise titled "Selecting a Single-Subject Design," which will give you some practice at identifying aspects of single-subject designs.

myeducationlab
for research

To learn more about the overall process of single-subject research, go to the "Single-Subject Experimental Research" section of **MyEducationLab for Research** and then click on *Building Research Skills*. Read the article and then complete the exercise titled "Identifying Steps in the Research Process for a Single-Subject Study." This exercise will help you identify key components of a single-subject research study.

Most experimental research is accomplished through the use of groups but as we noted may at times involve only a single participant. Known as **single-subject designs,** such research is seen in studies of exceptional students where it would be inappropriate to administer experimental treatment to participants other than those with special needs. Suppose Mr. Mohl has a student, Jonathan, who chronically misbehaves and does not respond to the disciplinary techniques Mr. Mohl uses with his other students. Mr. Mohl may decide to conduct a single-participant experiment to see if he can improve Jonathan's behavior.

In such a study (typically called a *single-participant measurement–treatment–measurement design*), Mr. Mohl would need to make accurate measurements of Jonathan's behavior before applying the experimental treatment. Mr. Mohl would prepare a chart of misbehaviors and ask an aide to record, over a period of a week or two, the number of times that Jonathan exhibits those misbehaviors, such as shouting out, getting up and wandering about the room, provoking confrontations with other students, and refusing to comply with Mr. Mohl's directions. These notations would serve as a baseline measurement against which to compare Jonathan's behavior during and after receiving the experimental treatment.

Mr. Mohl would then implement the experimental treatment, perhaps a special system of behavior modification. At a designated time, Jonathan's misbehaviors would again be recorded over several days. This process might be repeated several times. Mr. Mohl's single-participant experimental design could be diagrammed as follows:

Participant (Jonathan) → Baseline Measurement → Experimental Treatment → Measurement Repeated → Entire Process Repeated

In standard notation, this design is:

$$O \quad O \quad O \quad O \quad X_1 \quad X_1 \quad X_1 \quad O \quad O \quad O \quad O$$

In this process, the baseline measurements should accurately reflect Jonathan's typical behavior. Jonathan should be carefully observed two or three different times before the experiment is begun. When applying the treatment, Mr. Mohl must be very careful to limit himself to what he intends to do and say, so as to keep the treatment consistent. Even when these conditions are met, the results of single-participant experiments can only be generalized with great caution. When groups are used, individual differences among participants tend to cancel one another out. This is not the case in single-participant experimentation. What works for Jonathan may not work for Christopher, a chronically misbehaving student in another class.

There are several types of single-subject research designs. The simplest form is known as the **AB design.** In this design, a baseline measure ("A") is obtained and then a treatment ("B") is implemented. If there is a change, in behavior for example, then the treatment is said to have had an effect. Although this is a very straightforward design, its results may be subject to numerous competing explanations, making it a very weak design in the long run. As we have already seen with both experimental and quasi-experimental designs, other variations of this simple design introduce ways to control for these alternative explanations.

The **reversal design,** also known as the **ABA design** or measurement–treatment–measurement design, is a much-improved single-subject design when compared to the AB design. The ABA design begins in similar fashion by establishing the baseline ("A") and then introducing a treatment ("B"). However, in the third phase (the second "A"), the treatment is reversed or, in actuality, removed. If the negative behavior returns after removing the treatment, this tends to show that the treatment had an effect. The substantial limitation to this design is that many interventions cannot, or perhaps should not, be reversed, whether for ethical reasons (e.g., involving self-injurious behavior) or perhaps even some practical reasons (they cannot be unlearned, like a skill). The previous example of Mr. Mohl and his student, Jonathan, is an example of an ABA design.

A third single-subject design is the **alternating-treatment design,** which is used to investigate and explain the comparative effects of two treatments. In the application of this design, two treatments are alternated in quick succession and changes as measured in the participant are plotted on a graph to facilitate informal comparisons.

Finally, in the **multiple baseline design,** two or more (often three) behaviors, people, or settings are plotted in a staggered graph where a change is made to one, but not the other two, and then to the second, but not the third behavior, person, or setting. Differential changes that occur to each behavior, person, or in each setting help to strengthen what is essentially an AB design with its problematic competing hypotheses by providing opportunities to examine those hypotheses.

THREATS TO INTERNAL AND EXTERNAL VALIDITY

for research

To learn more about various threats to validity, go to the "Experimental Research" section of **MyEducationLab for Research** and then click on *Assignments and Activities.* Complete the exercise titled "Threats to Validity." This scenario-based exercise allows you to see threats to validity in action.

Validity of research refers to the degree to which research conclusions can be considered accurate and generalizable. Both experimental research and quasi-experimental research are subject to **threats to validity,** both internally and externally. These threats must be controlled or otherwise accounted for so that the potential error they might introduce does not put research conclusions into question.

Internal validity has to do with conditions present in the participants or their environment while the experiment is in progress. Threats to internal validity may include the following (Campbell & Stanley, 1966):

1. *Differential selection of participants.* Participants for the groups are not selected or assigned randomly. (This threat is always inherent in quasi-experimental research.)

2. *History.* When experimental treatments extend over longer periods, such as a semester or year, factors other than the experimental treatment have time to exert influence on the results.

3. *Maturation.* If treatments extend over longer periods of time, participants may undergo physiological changes that produce differential effects in the criterion variable. For example, they may become stronger, better coordinated, better able to do abstract thinking, or have better endurance than before.

4. *Testing.* If pretests and posttests are used, participants may learn enough from the pretest to improve performance on the posttest, even when the experimental treatment has no effect. If equivalent forms of a test are used, despite their being considered equal, one form may in fact be easier than the other.

5. *Attrition.* While the experiment is in progress, there may be a loss of participants for reasons such as illnesses, dropping out, or moving elsewhere.

External validity of research refers to the extent to which results can be generalized to other groups or settings. It is well known that what works in one setting may not work in another. Considerations about the external validity of research (see Bracht & Glass, 1968) include the following:

1. *Population validity.* This refers to the degree of similarity among (1) the sample used in a study, (2) the population from which it was drawn, and (3) the target population to which results are to be generalized. The greater the degree of similarity among the three, the greater one's confidence in generalizing research findings.

2. *Personological variables.* A given research finding can apply well to some people and poorly to others. Individuals differ in what they find acceptable, comfortable, and useful.

Self-directed learning is an example. Some students prefer to work on their own and can do so effectively. Other equally intelligent students require guidance from a teacher and desire the companionship of their peers.

3. *Ecological validity.* This refers to the situation, physical or emotional, that exists during the experiment. An experimental situation may be quite different from a new setting where results are to be applied. For example, some groups of participants, especially when involved in innovations, develop a group spirit that motivates high achievement. Such groups' results may be quite different from results seen in groups that lack a similar group spirit.

Exercise 13.1

Mr. Smith and Mr. Jones have very different ideas about how civics should be taught. They decide to conduct a semester-long experiment to determine which of the two teachers' procedures produces higher student achievement. Indicate what you would suggest they do in their experiment about the following:

1. Selecting and assigning students to be involved as participants
2. Clarifying the experimental treatments (methods and materials) that each intends to use, including equalizing the time commitments for homework expected of students
3. Measuring achievement at the end of the semester
4. Controlling error that might be associated with the teachers—that is, effects attributable to teacher personality and skill, as distinct from the methods and materials in the experimental treatment

AN EXAMPLE OF QUASI-EXPERIMENTAL RESEARCH

Following the exercise is a reprinted report of a quasi-experimental study that examines the effect of computer-assisted instruction (CAI) on eighth-grade mathematics achievement.

Exercise 13.2

As you read the study, be sure to note the following:

1. Focus of the study (what it is about)
2. Research questions, if any
3. Hypotheses, stated or implied
4. Selection of participants
5. Assignment of participants to control and experimental groups
6. The independent (treatment) variable(s) and the dependent (result or criteria) variable(s)
7. Instrument(s) used for measurement
8. Application of the experimental treatment(s) (i.e., introduction or manipulation of an independent variable)
9. Procedures by which data are obtained and analyzed
10. Findings
11. Conclusions

The Influence of Computer-Assisted Instruction on Eighth Grade Mathematics Achievement

Christopher H. Tienken
Seton Hall University
South Orange, NJ

James A. Maher
Maher Consulting
Holmdel, NJ

Abstract

The issue of lower than expected mathematics achievement is a concern to education leaders and policymakers at all levels of the U.S. PK–12 education system. The purpose of this quantitative, quasi-experimental study was to determine if there was a measurable difference in achievement on the mathematics section of the state test for students ($n = 121$) from a middle school in New Jersey who received computer-assisted instruction (CAI) in drill and practice computation related to the eighth grade mathematics curriculum standards compared to students ($n = 163$) who did not receive the CAI. The results suggest that the CAI intervention did not improve student achievement significantly ($p > .05$). In two categories, students who received the CAI performed significantly lower than their peers in the comparison group. Students in the control group who scored in the 25th percentile on the seventh grade CTB/McGraw Hill TerraNova pretest outperformed their peers in the treatment group on the New Jersey Grade Eight Proficiency Assessment (GEPA) mathematics section. Likewise, Asian students in the control group outperformed all other students in treatment and control groups. The results fit within the existing knowledge on the subject of computer-assisted instruction and add support to the idea that practitioners should evaluate curriculum and instruction interventions for demonstrated success before they bring them into the learning environment.

> The purpose of this study is to examine if CAI has an effect on achievement in mathematics. The authors concluded that it does not.

INTRODUCTION

The issue of lower than expected mathematics achievement is a persistent worry to some education leaders and policymakers at all levels of the U.S. PK–12 education system. The 1999 Third International Mathematics and Science Study Report (TIMSS-R) showed an example of the reported weaknesses of mathematics achievement of U.S. students compared to students in other industrialized countries. Grade 8 students in the United States ranked lower than 14 of the 38 participating nations (National Center for Education Statistics [NCES], 2000). In addition, 15-year-old students from the United States ranked between 16th and 23rd of 31 countries that participated in the mathematics portion of the 2000 Programme for International Student Assessment (PISA) administration (Organisation for Economic Co-Operation and Development [OECD], 2004).

On the national level, the 2005 (NCES, 2005) administration of the National Assessment of Education Progress (NAEP)[1] mathematics test indicated only 30% of grade 8 students scored "at or above proficient." While the validity of the NAEP achievement levels has not yet been demonstrated, the results influence policymakers. These achievement statistics raise concerns for some education leaders and policymakers about the mathematics achievement of U.S. middle school students.

Middle school students in New Jersey are not immune to this issue. New Jersey had a greater percentage of its students score proficient (30%) on the 2005 grade 8 NAEP mathematics test than the national average (24%). However, grade 8 NAEP New Jersey scale-score performance gaps exist between subgroups such as students eligible for free or reduced-price lunch and students not eligible for free or reduced-price lunch; 262 scale-score points and 292 scale-score points, respectively. This is a growing issue across the country. For example, the Southern Education Foundation (2007) reported that the percentage of economically disadvantaged students now outnumbers non-economically disadvantaged students in southern states. Childhood poverty rates range from a low of 20% in New Hampshire to a high of 84% in Louisiana. The expanding scourge of childhood poverty across the nation, and the corresponding negative influence on achievement, requires education leaders to use interventions with demonstrated records of success.

> National trends are also paralleled by mathematics achievement of New Jersey students.

Source: Tienken, C. H., & Maher, J. A. (2008). The influence of computer-assisted instruction on eighth grade mathematics achievement. *Research in Middle Level Education Online, 32*(3). Retrieved August 18, 2009, from www.nmsa.org/Publications/RMLEOnline/Articles/Vol32No3/tabid/1810/Default.aspx. Reprinted with permission from National Middle School Association.

REVIEW OF RELATED LITERATURE

Computer-Assisted Instruction and Student Achievement in Middle School Mathematics

We reviewed the results of experimental and quasi-experimental studies on the effect of computer-assisted instruction (CAI) on middle school student achievement in mathematics. An immediate issue with the middle school mathematics CAI knowledge dynamic was that few studies existed that met the federal definition of scientifically based research (SBR) and many of the studies that met the definition were conducted prior to the year 2000. In this section, we provide representative examples of the existing experimental and quasi-experimental studies on CAI drill and practice and achievement in middle level mathematics.

> Since this is a quasi-experimental study, the authors limited their review of related literature to those studies that were either experimental or quasi-experimental in nature.

Roberts and Madhere (1990) found that CAI had a small positive effect on the overall mathematics achievement of 743 elementary and junior high school students. Students who participated gained 3.06 points on their Normal Curve Equivalent scores on a nationally normed standardized test of mathematics compared to students who did not have the CAI. Roberts and Madhere did not report effect sizes. Traynor (2003) found that CAI improved mathematics achievement of regular education, special education, and limited English proficient middle school students ($n = 161$) on a mathematics pretest-posttest when compared to traditional, teacher-directed practice techniques. The students comprised intact groups based on the way the middle school scheduled students into exploratory classes. Results were statistically significant ($p < .001$) with a moderate effect size (d) of 0.47 favoring the treatment group. Social scientists consider an effect size of 0.2 as small, an effect size in the range of $0.2 < d < 0.8$ as moderate, and an effect size greater than 0.8 as large (Cohen, 1988). Plano (2004) found that CAI activities for algebra had a non-significant predictive influence on student achievement overall but had a slightly significant influence on the algebra achievement of English language learners. Tienken and Wilson (2007) conducted a quasi-experimental, pretest-posttest control-group study and found a small, but statistically significant positive effect of CAI drill and practice computation exercises on the mathematics achievement of seventh grade students on the CTB/McGraw Hill TerraNova full battery mathematics test. They reported an effect size (d) of 0.12.

Campbell, Peck, Horn, and Leigh (1987) found no significant difference in the mathematics achievement of third grade students who used CAI drill and practice activities compared to students who used only print drill and practice materials. Rosenberg (1991) found a negative influence of computers on instruction and achievement. He stated that the computer failed to deliver on the promises of increased efficiency (i.e., take less time for students to learn the concept) and effectiveness (i.e., higher student achievement than with traditional paper/pencil methods). Recent studies demonstrated similar results. Baker, Gersten, and Lee (2002) conducted a synthesis of studies on the influence and effect of CAI on mathematics achievement of low-achieving students. They found low achievers did not perform statistically significantly better. They observed an average effect size (d) of 0.01.

The empirical literature on CAI and middle school mathematics achievement is thin and the results are mixed. The findings related to middle school mathematics achievement and the use of CAI is congruent to those found in a recent report by the U.S. Department of Education, Institute of Education Sciences (IES). IES conducted a review of the effectiveness of CAI in mathematics on grade 6 student achievement and found no statistically significant effect, while an algebra CAI program had a positive statistically significant effect ($p < .05$) on student achievement in junior high school. The overall findings suggested mixed effects of CAI on student mathematics achievement (USDOE, 2007).

Theoretical Perspective: Active Learning

Like CAI, active learning is designed to improve student achievement. Cooperstein and Kocevar-Weidinger (2004) noted that active learning occurs when (a) the learner can construct his or her own meaning, (b) current learning is developed on previous learning, (c) the learner is involved in meaningful social interaction, and (d) the learning is built using authentic involvement with the learning materials. Examples of active learning pedagogy include inquiry-based learning, discovery-based learning, hands-on learning, and problem-based learning. The roots of current active learning methodology reach back 200 years beginning with Pestalozzi's Object Teaching and Froebel's Kindergarten, and more recently by Dewey's ideas of experiential learning. Landmark projects during the 1930s and 1940s such as Wrightstone's study (1935), the New York City Experiment (Jersild, Thorndike, & Goldman, 1941), and the Eight Year Study (Aikin, 1942) demonstrated the power of active learning to have a positive effect on student achievement and attitudes toward learning compared to traditional approaches.

Some studies demonstrated that active learning was an effective method of enhancing students' learning. However, a glaring limitation of the recent literature in this area is that in many cases, quasi-experimental and experimental designs were not used, effect sizes were not reported, and overall methodology was suspect. Nonetheless, several studies reported positive outcomes. Hetland (2000) concluded that students' active involvement in music had an effect on the development of their spatial thinking. Wilson,

Flanagan, Gurkewitz, and Skrip (2006) found that students' active involvement in origami resulted in increased problem-solving ability. Cerezo (2004) conducted a qualitative study and reported that active involvement in problem solving enhanced the learning of mathematics for at-risk female students. Huffaker and Calvert (2003) conducted a review of the literature related to active learning through online games and concluded that active learning was particularly useful when used in problem solving with computers. One complaint against active learning is that teachers sometimes mistakenly leave students on their own, and thus, the learning process becomes unguided and disconnected (Kirschner, Sweller, & Clark, 2006).

Purpose

Middle level education leaders search for scientifically based interventions (U.S. Department of Education, 2002) to address issues related to improving mathematics achievement.

> The need and justification for the study is provided.

The knowledge dynamic on the influence or effect of CAI on middle school mathematics achievement is not well developed and the results from previous studies are mixed. The results from this study add to the experimental/quasi-experimental CAI literature available to education leaders.

We present findings from an evaluation of a middle school mathematics intervention implemented during the

> The authors actually refer to this as an evaluation study that utilizes quasi-experimental methods.

2004–2005 school year to improve students' mathematics performance on the New Jersey Grade Eight Proficiency Assessment (GEPA). The purpose of this quasi-experimental study was to determine if there was a measurable difference in achievement on the mathematics section of the GEPA for students from a middle school in New Jersey who received computer-assisted instruction (CAI) in drill and practice computation related to the eighth grade mathematics curriculum standards compared to students who did not receive the CAI.

Problem

The central New Jersey school under study served 895 students in grades 7 and 8 during the 2004–2005 school

> Demographic description of the participants.

year. Almost 34% of the students were eligible for the federal free or reduced-price lunch program and approximately 46% were non-white. The New Jersey Department of Education (NJDOE) rated the school "in need of improvement" *Level 4* during the 2003–2004 school year. Approximately *55%* of the students in grade 8 scored *Partially Proficient* on the mathematics section of the GEPA. *Partially Proficient* is the lowest of three performance cat-

egories developed by the NJDOE. The need for improvement was urgent. Failure to improve could lead to sanctions such as restructuring the school or outsourcing the school to a private company.

Although some controversy exists about the effective use of CAI, particularly with respect to the drill and practice forms associated with simple knowledge development, the literature suggested a small, positive effect of active learning on mathematics achievement. The literature also suggested a positive influence occurred primarily when CAI integrated more complicated kinds of learning, such as open-ended, divergent problem solving. From the research reviewed, it was not clear, however, whether using active learning with simpler CAI processes such as those associated with computation-based drill and practice computer software and websites would have a positive influence on student achievement as measured by the GEPA.

Questions

We examined how the use of a drill and practice CAI in combination with a less complex active learning follow-up exercise, direct instruction of how to use computer presentation software (Microsoft PowerPoint™) to communicate understanding of the drill and practice exercises, influenced student achievement of grade 8 mathematics skills and knowledge.

> Although there are no actual questions stated, the authors explain the focus of the study and what will guide their analyses and results.

This study was guided by our desire to evaluate the influence of mathematics drill and practice CAI combined with the use of multimedia presentation software on mathematics achievement of the following groups of regular education grade 8 students: (a) total population of regular education students; (b) students who received basic skills instruction (BSI) in mathematics, language arts, or in both subjects; (c) various ethnic groups; and (d) socioeconomically disadvantaged (i.e., eligible for federal free or reduced-price lunch program).

METHODOLOGY

We used a quasi-experimental pretest/posttest control-group design because students comprised intact groups and random assignment of students was not possible. The design controlled effectively for most threats to internal validity (Campbell & Stanley, 1963). Internal validity is the extent that the experiment demonstrates

> Specifically, the authors used a quasi-experimental pretest–posttest control group design, explaining that random assignment was not possible.

a cause and effect relationship between the independent

and dependent variables. The design overcomes the threat to internal validity posed by the interaction of selection of participants and maturation, the time between pretest and posttest, because of the large sample sizes of students and the short duration of the study. The pretest-posttest design mitigated further the threat posed by maturation because all participants experienced the pretest and posttest. Theoretically, any influences of maturation would be experienced by both groups, experimental and control, and thus, neutralize the maturation threat to internal validity.

> Good discussion of how the authors addressed potential threats to validity.

We assigned teachers randomly to experimental ($n = 2$) and control ($n = 2$) groups and compared students based upon their pretest mathematics achievement. Because the pretest was part of an existing testing program, the potential threat to external validity posed by the interaction between the pretesting and treatment was reduced.

The study used a sample of eighth grade students and the total population of four eighth grade regular education mathematics teachers from one middle school in New Jersey. The NJDOE categorized the school as "needs improvement" based on lower than expected prior student achievement on the mathematics and language arts sections of the GEPA. The experimental group included 121 students and the control group included 163 students (total $n = 284$). We collected data from all students who met the following criteria: (a) received a valid score on the Grade 7 mathematics section of the TerraNova test (CTB-McGraw Hill, 2007), (b) received a valid score on the GEPA mathematics section, (c) enrolled in the school for the entire seventh and eighth grade years, and (d) enrolled in a regular education program in the school for the entire seventh and eighth grade years. We excluded students who received special education services from the analysis due to the individualized nature of those programs.

Treatment

We assigned randomly the total population ($n = 4$) of eighth grade mathematics teachers to experimental and control groups prior to the start of the study. The teachers in the experimental group used mathematics drill and practice websites and slide presentation software with students.

> The authors thoroughly explain the nature of the experimental treatment condition.

The teachers in the control group used neither the websites nor the presentation software. The purpose of the CAI treatment was to provide students practice with basic mathematics skills related to the Grade 8 New Jersey Core Curriculum Content Standards (NJCCCS). The mathematics websites provided students opportunities for drill and practice of computation in operations, fractions, geometry, data analysis, and algebra based on the NJCCCS and

the school's mathematics curriculum. A site facilitator (i.e., district mathematics supervisor) observed the instruction of the teachers in the experimental group to monitor frequency of implementation, and when necessary, coached the teachers on how to access and use the mathematics websites.

After students became familiar with the CAI, the teachers taught them to use slide presentation software to create a digital "book report" to explain one aspect of mathematics they learned via the CAI. Each student used the slide presentation software to construct an explanation of the material he/she learned from using the drill and practice CAI. Upon completion of the CAI work, the students in the experimental groups presented the information to their classmates. The students used the CAI technology two sessions per week, 45 minutes per session, for 20 weeks. They used the CAI during their regularly scheduled mathematics period. There was no difference in the amount of time that the students in the experimental and control groups participated in mathematics instruction. The CAI was not an add-on and did not result in more mathematics time on task for the students in the experimental group.

The site facilitator ensured that the mathematics content was consistent for all teachers and that the teachers and students in the experimental group were the only ones using the mathematics websites and presentation software. The site facilitator conducted weekly classroom observations of the experimental and control teachers and reviewed lesson plans weekly. Teachers in the experimental group facilitated student creation of slide shows to demonstrate their understanding of mathematics concepts such as adding and subtracting fractions with unlike denominators.

Hypotheses

We examined whether there is evidence to reject one or more of the following hypotheses:

> H_0: There is no difference in mean score achievement between the experimental and control group students on the mathematics section of the New Jersey GEPA for the following subsets of regular education students: (a) students who scored in the same quartile of the TerraNova grade 7 math assessment, (b) students who participated in similar basic skill instruction (BSI) math and/or reading remediation service programs, (c) students who did not participate in BSI math and/or reading remediation service programs, (d) students who were in the same ethnic group, and (e) students who participated in the same level of the school's free or reduced-price lunch program.

> More specifically than their previous "questions," the authors specify their hypotheses.

In addition, we examined if there was evidence that the odds of a student scoring at the proficient or above proficient level on the GEPA mathematics section was higher for the students in the experimental group compared to those in the control group.

ANALYSIS

The purpose of the statistical analysis is an examination of factors expected to explain success or failure on the New Jersey GEPA mathematics test. These factors include the experimental versus control curriculum (i.e., CAI enhanced vs. traditional), student achievement on the TerraNova mathematics pretest; student referral or not to basic skills instruction (BSI) sessions in math, language/ reading, or both mathematics and language; ethnicity; and the student's socioeconomic status (via the level of participation in the school's free or reduce-priced lunch program).

Analysis of variance (ANOVA) methods were used to derive linear models of best fit for the raw data summarized in Tables 1 through 4. A factor was included in an ANOVA model only if the factor was statistically significant at the .05 level of significance or lower. The resulting model was used to estimate the residual variability not explained by the model and then to derive 95% confidence intervals for the predicted GEPA mathematics score for each group of students identified by the cell descriptors. The means of two groups of students are declared statistically significant when their corresponding 95% confidence intervals do not overlap.

Since all hypotheses are based on the comparison of groups, the authors used ANOVAs to analyze their resulting data.

Limitations

The small population of available teachers (*n* = 4) created external validity concerns and limited the ability to generalize results beyond the school in this study. Likewise, the demographic and socioeconomic makeup of the student population limited the ability to generalize student results beyond districts located in lower socioeconomic communities. Results may be different for students in schools located in higher socioeconomic communities. While the design was quasi-experimental and controlled for major threats to internal validity, the statistics used were to determine whether the CAI influenced achievement. Thus, the results do not demonstrate cause and effect, but merely the existence or lack of a relationship between CAI and achievement.

The authors identify and discuss several important limitations.

Strengths

Potential internal validity issues posed by instrumentation were reduced because both groups took the same pretest and posttest assessments. The pretest was the mathematics section of a nationally normed, commercially prepared standardized test with reported full-test reliability estimates of .90 (CTB/McGraw-Hill, 1997). The posttest was the mathematics section of the New Jersey GEPA. The NJDOE reported full test reliability of .91 for the 2005 administration of the GEPA (NJDOE, 2005). Ecological validity issues were limited because the study took place in the school setting under existing constraints. We did not create artificial contexts and we worked within the existing confines (i.e., used only preexisting assessment tools and grading procedures, did not reassign students to alternative groupings, did not reassign staff to different grade levels). The potential external validity threat posed by the Hawthorne effect was mitigated because both groups used the same curriculum and textbook, spent the same amount of time in mathematics classes, and a site supervisor monitored the teachers in each group throughout the process to ensure continuity of instruction and program.

Threats due to maturation were accounted for as stated in the methods section. Issues due to temporal validity were accounted for by comparing achievement of the groups based on their quartile achievement from the grade 7 pretest. That is, achievement of students was not measured solely on a posttest, aggregate basis. We matched student achievement from the pretest quartiles and then compared the posttest achievement of the quartile groups. Thus, we were able to control for prior achievement of the students in each group.

The authors really do an extensive job of discussing threats to both external and internal validity.

CAI is a specific independent variable identified in the knowledge dynamic that can influence student achievement. Other variables that could potentially influence student achievement in mathematics include curriculum, the teacher, professional development, and special instructional programs such as special education, basic skills instruction, or gifted education.

As mentioned earlier, the curriculum, teachers, and professional development remained constant during the period under study. We accounted for special programs by excluding students in special programs from the analyses.

Interpretive validity was strengthened through the quasi-experimental design and the way in which we monitored the implementation of the treatment. Organizational, structural, and instructional conditions other than CAI for the experimental group were remarkably stable during the 20-week period.

RESULTS

Table 1 relates GEPA mathematics test performance for the experimental and control groups of students to the student's performance on the grade 7 TerraNova pretest and provides the mean and standard deviation GEPA math summary statistics for each quartile of student scores on the TerraNova

Table 1   Grade 8 Mathematics GEPA Score Mean/SD vs. Experimental/Control Group Placement & TerraNova Pretest Score Classification for Regular Education Students

Classification	Terra Nova Pretest	Actual Mean/Standard Deviation, (Predicted Mean), (Sample Size), & 95% Confidence Intervals for Mean Predicted Grade 8 Math GEPA Score	
		Experimental	*Control*
Regular Education	25Q	169.0/10.55 (169.0) ($n = 14$) 156.90 – 181.10	211.43/27.60 (211.43) ($n = 21$) 201.55 – 221.30
	50Q	185.4/14.31 (185.41) ($n = 37$) 177.97 – 192.85	199.44/26.51 (199.44) ($n = 25$) 190.39 – 208.49
	75Q	202.25/16.23 (202.25) ($n = 40$) 195.09 – 209.41	206.17/28.42 (206.17) ($n = 53$) 199.95 – 212.39
	UQ	218.87/18.86 (218.87) ($n = 30$) 210.60 – 227.13	206.20/32.47 (206.20) ($n = 64$) 200.55 – 211.86
	Regular Class Statistics	197.37/22.51 (197.37) ($n = 121$) 192.75 – 201.99	205.83/29.63 (205.83) ($n = 163$) 201.85 – 209.81

pretest. The Analysis of Variance (ANOVA) model with a full set of significant interaction terms was used to derive predicted 95% confidence intervals for the mean cells.

Performance on the GEPA mathematics test was correlated with the student's performance on the TerraNova mathematics pretest for regular class students. It is useful to contrast the GEPA test scores of experimental and control groups by comparing students who scored in similar quartiles of the TerraNova mathematics pretest. In Table 1, the 95% mean confidence interval estimates overlap for all comparisons except one. Namely, regular education students in the control group who scored within the 25th percentile of the TerraNova mathematics test, performed higher, statistically significant ($p < .05$), on the GEPA mathematics test than did students in the experimental group. An effect size was calculated using the formula developed by Glass (1976) where the difference of mean of the experimental and control groups is divided by the standard deviation of the control. An effect size of 1.53 favoring the control group students in the 25th quartile was observed.

> This represents a very large effect size.

The first hypothesis stated there is no difference in achievement on the mathematics section of the New Jersey GEPA between regular education students in the experimental and control groups who scored in the same quartile on the grade 7 TerraNova pretest. The results suggest a difference favoring control group students who scored in the 25th percentile on the Terra-Nova pretest in grade 7. Overall, there is not evidence that the CAI program influenced the average achievement of students in the experimental group positively compared to the students in the control group.

> No significant differences were noted between regular education students in the two groups.

Table 2 relates GEPA mathematics performance for the experimental and control groups to whether the student participated in basic skills instruction (BSI) mathematics remediation as well as the student's **quartile** performance on the grade 7 TerraNova pretest. An ANOVA model with two interaction terms (TerraNova pretest score—experimental/control group interaction and a BSI mathematics referral—experimental/control group interaction) was used to derive predicted 95% confidence intervals for the mean cells in Table 2.

Performance on the GEPA mathematics test correlated highly with the student's performance on the TerraNova mathematics test. The data provide evidence that students in the control group not referred for mathematics BSI services scored statistically significantly ($p < .05$) higher on the GEPA mathematics test than did the corresponding experimental group (See the non-overlapping 95% confidence intervals in Table 2 for the No BSI referral group totals of the experimental and control groups). An effect size of

> Students in the control group scored higher than those in the experimental group.

Table 2 95% Confidence Intervals for Mean GEPA Score for BSI Math Referral and Experimental/Control Groups

BSI Math Referral Classification	Terra Nova Pretest	Mean/Standard Deviation, (Predicted Mean), (Sample Size), & 95% Confidence Intervals for Mean Predicted Grade 8 Math GEPA Score	
		Experimental	*Control*
No	25Q	—	215.38/27.39 (216.81) ($n = 18$) 207.43 – 226.18
	50Q	190.30/14.15 (188.91) ($n = 23$) 180.32 – 197.50	209.19/28.14 (212.99) ($n = 16$) 203.99 – 221.99
	75Q	201.87/16.51 (202.72) ($n = 38$) 195.94 – 209.49	214.71/25.34 (213.99) ($n = 42$) 207.89 – 220.07
	UQ	218.87/18.86 (218.87) ($n = 30$) 211.08 – 226.65	216.16/29.72 (215.03) ($n = 49$) 209.38 – 220.68
	No BSI Math Referral: Total	204.55/19.97 (204.55) ($n = 91$) 199.90 – 209.20	214.67/27.53 (214.67) ($n = 125$) 210.70 – 218.64
Yes	25Q	169.0/10.55 (169.0) ($n = 14$) 157.60 – 180.40	187.67/15.88 (179.16) ($n = 3$) 167.61 – 190.71
	50Q	177.36/10.76 (179.65) ($n = 14$) 168.90 – 190.39	182.11/9.82 (175.35) ($n = 9$) 165.40 – 185.29
	75Q	209.5/9.19 (193.45) ($n = 2$) 179.30 – 207.61	173.55/9.47 (176.34) ($n = 11$) 167.71 – 184.96
	UQ	—	173.67/15.31 (177.38) ($n = 15$) 169.27 – 185.49
	No BSI Math Referral: Total	175.6/14.37 (175.6) ($n = 30$) 167.50 – 183.70	176.74/13.08 (176.74) ($n = 38$) 169.54 – 183.93

0.36 favoring the control group students who did not participate in mathematics basic skills was observed.

The data suggest that BSI eligibility is a strong predictor of student achievement on the GEPA mathematics test.

The third hypothesis states that there is no difference in achievement on the mathematics section of the New Jersey GEPA between students in the experimental and control groups who are classified in the same ethnic group. Table 3 relates GEPA mathematics test performance for the experimental and control groups to the student's ethnicity.

An ANOVA model with an ethnicity-experimental/control group interaction was used to derive predicted 95% confidence intervals for the mean cells in Table 3. The data provide evidence that Asian/Pacific Islanders in the control group, on average, outperformed the other ethnic groups on the GEPA mathematics test and whites, on the average, outperformed the blacks. However, the data do not provide evidence that there was a difference between the performance of the black and the Hispanic/Latino groups. In the experimental group, there was not a statistically significant

Table 3   95% Confidence Intervals for Mean GEPA Score for Ethnicity and Experimental/Control Groups

Ethnicity	Actual Mean/SD, (Predicted Mean), (Sample Size), & 95% Confidence Intervals for Mean Predicted Grade 8 Math GEPA Score	
	Experimental Classes	*Control Classes*
Asian/Pacific Islanders	207.2/15.87 (207.20) ($n = 5$) 183.21 – 231.19	237.67/34.40 (237.67) ($n = 6$) 215.76 – 259.57
Black/African American	190.47/17.99 (190.47) ($n = 57$) 183.37 – 197.58	185.41/27.88 (185.41) ($n = 74$) 179.17 – 191.64
Hispanic/Latino	199.18/27.77 (199.18) ($n = 11$) 183.00 – 215.36	197.13/31.41 (197.12) ($n = 24$) 186.17 – 208.08
White	202.36/22.82 (202.36) ($n = 74$) 196.13 – 208.60	199.44/31.30 (199.44) ($n = 135$) 194.82 – 204.05

difference ($p < .05$) in the means of the four ethnic groups in the study. Therefore, we conclude that the data do not provide evidence that any one ethnic group in the experimental population outperformed any other on the GEPA mathematics test. Overall, the data do not provide evidence that the CAI program benefited any ethnic group in the study other than the Asian/Pacific Islander students in the experimental group. Those students scored statistically significantly higher ($p < .05$) than the Asian/Pacific Islander students in the experimental group. An effect size of 0.88 favoring the Asian/Pacific Islander students in the control group was observed.

On average, no significant differences existed among ethnic groups. Only Asian/Pacific Islanders scored significantly higher than any other group.

Table 4 relates GEPA mathematics performance for the experimental and control groups to the student's level of participation in the school's free or reduced-price lunch program. An ANOVA main effects model (no interaction term) was used to derive predicted 95% confidence intervals for the mean cells in Table 4. The fifth hypothesis states that there is no difference in achievement between students in the experimental and control groups based on the level of eligibility for the federal free or reduced-price lunch program.

The data in Table 4 provide evidence that the students in the experimental and control non-subsidized lunch group performed better, on the average, on the GEPA mathematics test than did the students in the free or reduced-price lunch group (see the non-overlapping 95% confidence limits for these groups in Table 4). For example, we observed a statistically significant difference ($p < .05$) in the mean achievement score of students in the experimental group not eligible for free or reduced-price lunch compared to those eligible for free or reduced-price lunch. We observed an effect size of 0.35 favoring students in the experimental group not eligible for free or reduced-price lunch. Likewise, we observed an effect size of 0.56 favoring the students in the control group not eligible for free or reduced-price lunch compared to their group members who were eligible. Overall, the data do not provide evidence that, on average, the CAI program benefited students in any one of the school lunch programs.

Those students not eligible for free or reduced lunches scored significantly higher than those who did qualify.

Table 5 examines the odds of students passing the GEPA math test as a function of the student's BSI language/reading service profile and the student's BSI math service profile. A logistic main effects model (no significant experiment/control group effect and no interaction terms) was used to derive predicted probabilities and odds of passing the GEPA math test for each cell in Table 5. The model was also used to derive 95% confidence intervals for the relative odds of passing the GEPA math test. At the .05 significance level, the logistic model found no statistically significant difference between the experimental and control groups regarding the percentage/odds of a student passing the GEPA math test.

More than half, 56.94%, of the students who were not referred to language and/or reading remediation passed the GEPA math test, compared to 26.47% of those who were referred to language/reading remediation. On the average, of

Table 4   95% Confidence Intervals for Mean GEPA Score for Free Lunch and Experimental/Control Groups

Student's Free Lunch Classification	Actual Mean/SD, (Predicted Mean), (Sample Size), & 95% Confidence Intervals for Mean Predicted Grade 8 Math GEPA Score	
	Experimental Classes	*Control Classes*
Free Lunch	191.61/20.67 (187.45) ($n = 26$) 180.39 – 194.50	185.21/27.00 (186.85) ($n = 66$) 180.92 – 192.79
Reduced-Price Lunch	199.64/21.22 (198.59) ($n = 14$) 189.07 – 208.10	197.4/28.04 (197.99) ($n = 25$) 188.98 – 207.00
Non-Subsidized Lunch	198.90/22.19 (200.05) ($n = 107$) 195.25 – 204.84	200.28/33.02 (199.45) ($n = 148$) 195.25 – 203.65

Table 5   Actual and Logistic Model Predicted Percent and Odds of Students Passing the GEPA Math Test as a Function of the Student's BSI Language/Reading BSI Math Service Profiles

Language or Reading Referral	Math Referral	Actual % (Model Predicted) of Students Passing Math GEPA Test		Actual (Model Predicted) Odds of a Student Passing the Math GEPA Test	
		Experimental	*Control*	*Experimental*	*Control*
No	No	67.57% (68.19%) (n = 74)	68.69% (68.19%) (n = 99)	2.08 (2.14)	2.19 (2.14)
	Yes	9.52% (11.69%) (n = 21)	13.64% (11.69%) (n = 22)	0.11 (0.13)	0.16 (0.13)
	No Language or Reading Referral:	54.74% (56.94%) (n = 95)	58.68% (56.94%) (n = 121)	1.21 (1.32)	1.42 (1.32)
Yes	No	35.29% (39.60%) (n = 17)	42.31% (39.60%) (n = 26)	0.55 (0.66)	0.73 (0.66)
	Yes	11.11% (3.89%) (n = 9)	0.0% (3.89%) (n = 16)	0.12 (0.04)	0.0 (0.04)
	Yes Language and/or Reading Referral:	26.92% (26.47%) (n = 26)	26.19% (26.47%) (n = 42)	0.39 (0.36)	0.35 (0.36)

those referred neither to language/reading nor math remediation, an estimated 68.19%, passed the GEPA math test. Of those students referred to both language/reading and math remediation only an estimated 3.89% passed GEPA math test.

CONCLUSIONS

In summary, the data suggest that the school under study was successful in identifying a large number of students (110 out of 283 regular students) who required language, reading, and/or math basic skills instruction; however, the remediation program in general, with or without CAI, demonstrated limited success in bringing students up to the level required to pass the GEPA math test.

The drill and practice CAI and student multimedia slide show demonstrations did not have a statistically significant positive influence on student achievement on the GEPA mathematics test. The data suggest that CAI may have had a negative influence on student achievement, as only an estimated 68.19% of those students referred neither to language arts nor math-

> Overall, CAI did not have a positive effect on mathematics achievement; in fact, it may have had a negative effect.

ematics BSI passed the GEPA mathematics test. Of students referred to both language arts and mathematics BSI, only an estimated 3.89% passed the GEPA mathematics test.

The CAI drill and practice program was not an effective intervention for increasing achievement on the GEPA. It did not improve the experimental group students' proficiency on the GEPA mathematics test. In two categories, students who received the CAI performed statistically significantly lower than did their peers in the control group. The academically weakest students, those students in the control group who scored in the 25th percentile on the grade 7 TerraNova pretest, outperformed their peers in the experimental group on the GEPA mathematics section. Students in the control group not referred to mathematics BSI remedial instruction outperformed the corresponding group of students in the experimental group.

These findings trouble us for three reasons. First, the teachers used CAI instruction two mathematics periods per week for 20 weeks leading up to the GEPA test. The 90 minutes a week spent on drill and practice CAI may have been better spent

> The results of the study really seemed to confuse the authors.

on problem solving and critical thinking. Half the points on the GEPA mathematics test come from open-ended problem-solving questions (NJDOE, 2005).

Second, more than 35% of the students in the district participated in BSI mathematics programs. CAI did not influence positively the achievement of the regular education students who struggled academically. In fact, the students in the control group who scored in the lowest quartile of the TerraNova pretest significantly outscored their peers in the experimental group. This suggests that the CAI program may have had a negative influence on some of the district's academically weakest students. The drill and practice CAI used during this study did not have a positive influence on the test scores of low-achieving students compared to similar students in the control group, nor did it influence positively the performance of non-Caucasian students.

Third, the CAI program did not improve the performance of the district's neediest students, those eligible for free or reduced-price lunch. Leaders looking for an intervention to increase the achievement of economically disadvantaged students should take note of the findings presented. In this case, drill and practice CAI was not an effective intervention to overcome the debilitating influence of poverty on student learning.

An ancillary finding included that students enrolled in the BSI programs had the lowest odds of passing the GEPA mathematics section and they demonstrated the lowest scale scores as a group on the test. A universal goal of BSI programs in New Jersey, and in fact, the main focus of the federal Title I program, is to improve student achievement for students eligible for free or reduced-price lunch. Furthermore, section 101 of the NCLB Act (No Child Left Behind [NCLB PL 107–110], 2002) calls for closing the achievement gap between subgroups of students. The basic skills program did not help students in the Title I subgroup achieve proficiency (Note: Only 3.89% of the students requiring language/reading and math BSI services passed the math section of the GEPA test.).

Middle school leaders might be well served to revisit the history of their profession to inform future actions related to restructuring traditional basic skills programs. For example, the recommendations from the Cardinal Principles of Secondary Education (Commission on the Reorganization of Secondary Education, 1918) and the results of the Eight-Year Study (Aikin, 1942) suggested the positive influence of problem-based curriculum and instruction over traditional methods such as drill and practice. Middle level leaders should consider retooling ineffective drill and practice basic skills programs and begin to incorporate problem-based instruction or other types of active learning into their programs and in future uses of CAI.

The school in this study was successful in identifying a large number of students (110 of 284 regular students) who required language arts and/or mathematics BSI; however, the schoolwide BSI program demonstrated limited success in bringing the students in the experimental or control groups up to the level required to attain proficiency on the GEPA mathematics test. While both the students' BSI language arts service profile and the students' BSI mathematics service profile were significant predictors of the odds of the student passing the GEPA mathematics test, the students' mathematics service profile was the more discriminating predictor. The CAI drill and practice was unable to influence positively student performance for those students.

While readers should not generalize the results of this study to general forms of CAI used in other middle schools, the results may prompt middle school leaders to evaluate carefully interventions used to improve student achievement against criteria for success before bringing them into the school environment. Interventions should first and foremost do no harm. Ultimately, they should improve student achievement by using effective and appropriate means to achieve an agreed upon, productive, and ethical end. In education, one desired end is to help develop students who can think critically and solve authentic problems. This study provides further evidence that CAI drill and practice activities void of problem solving will not help students achieve that end.

References

Aikin, W. M. (1942). *The story of the Eight-Year Study: With conclusions and recommendations.* New York: Harper and Brothers.

Baker, S., Gersten, R., & Lee, D. (2002). A synthesis of empirical research on teaching mathematics to low-achieving students. *Elementary School Journal, 103*(1), 51–73.

Campbell, D. L., Peck, D. L., Horn, C. J., & Leigh, R. K. (1987). Comparison of computer-assisted instruction and print drill performance: A research note. *Educational Communication and Technology Journal, 35*(2), 95–103.

Campbell, D. T., & Stanley, J. C. (1963). Experimental and quasi-experimental designs for research on teaching. In N. L. Gage (Ed.), *Handbook of research on teaching* (pp. 171–246). Chicago: Rand McNally College Publishing.

Cerezo, N. (2004). Problem-based learning in the middle school: A research case study of the perceptions of at-risk females. *Research in Middle Level Education Online, 27*(1). Retrieved on June 1, 2007, from http://www.nmsa.org/portals/0/pdf/publications/RMLE/rmle_vol27_no1_article4.pdf

Cohen, J. (1988). *Statistical power analysis for the behavioral sciences* (2nd ed.). Hillsdale, NJ: Lawrence Erlbaum.

Commission on the Reorganization of Secondary Education. (1918). *Cardinal principles of secondary education.* Washington, DC: U.S. Bureau of Education, Bulletin No. 35.

Cooperstein, S. E., & Kocevar-Weidinger, E. (2004). Beyond active learning: A constructivist approach to learning. *Reference Services Review, 32*(2), 141–148.

CTB/McGraw-Hill. (1997). *TerraNova Technical Bulletin 1.* Monterey, CA: Author.

CTB-McGraw Hill. (2007). Glossary of Assessment Terms. Retrieved on June 1, 2007, from http:// www.ctb.com/articles/article_information.jsp?CONTENT%3C%3Ecnt_id=10134198673250329&FOLDER%3C%3Efolder_id=1408474395222381&bmUID=1210949935335

Glass, G. V. (1976). Primary, secondary, and meta-analysis of research. *Educational Researcher 5,* 3–8.

Hetland, L. (2000). Learning to make music enhances spatial reasoning. *Journal of Aesthetic Education, 34*(3/4), 179–238.

Huffaker, D. A., & Calvert, S. L. (2003). The new science of learning: Active learning, metacognition, and transfer of knowledge in e-learning applications. *Journal of Educational Computing Research, 29*(3), 325–334.

Jersild, A. T., Thorndike, R. L., & Goldman, B. (1941). A further comparison of pupils in "activity" and "non-activity" schools. *Journal of Experimental Education, 9*, 307–309.

Kirschner, P. A., Sweller, J., & Clark, R. E. (2006). Why minimal guidance during instruction does not work: An analysis of the failure of constructivist, discovery, problem-based, experiential, and inquiry-based teaching. *Educational Psychologist, 41*(2), 75–86.

National Center for Education Statistics (NCES). (2000). *Highlights from the Third International Mathematics and Science Study—Repeat.* Office of Educational Research and Improvement. U.S. Department of Education: Office of Educational Research and Improvement. Retrieved May 3, 2007, from http://nces.ed.gov/pubs2001/2001027.pdf

National Center for Education Statistics (NCES). (2005). *The Nation's Reportcard.* U.S. Department of Education: Institute of Education Sciences. Retrieved May 3, 2007, from http://nces.ed.gov/nationsreportcard/pdf/main2005/2006453.pdf

New Jersey Department of Education. (2005). *Grade eight proficiency assessment. Technical report.* #1505.69. Author.

No Child Left Behind (NCLB). (2002). Act of 2001, P.L. No. 107–110, § 115, Stat. 1425.

Organisation for Economic Co-Operation and Development. (2004). *Learning for tomorrow's world: First results from PISA 2003.* Retrieved May 3, 2007, from http://www.oecd.org/document/55/0,2340,en_32252351_32236173_33917303_1_1_1_1,00.html

Plano, G. (2004). *The effects of the Cognitive Tutor Algebra on student attitudes and achievement in a 9th grade algebra course.* Unpublished doctoral dissertation. Seton Hall University, South Orange, NJ.

Roberts, V. A., & Madhere, S. (1990). *Chapter I resource laboratory program for computer-assisted instruction (CAI) 1989–1990.* Evaluation report. Evaluation report for the District of Columbia Public Schools, Washington, DC.

Rosenberg, R. (1991). Debunking computer literacy. *Technology Review, 94*(1), 58–64.

Southern Education Foundation. (2007). *A new majority: Low income students in the South's public schools.* Retrieved on Nov. 11, 2007, from http://www.sefatl.org/pdf/A%20New%20Majority%20Report-Final.pdf

Tienken, C. H., & Wilson, M. (2007, fall/winter). The impact of computer-assisted instruction on seventh-grade students' mathematics achievement. *Planning and Changing, 38*(3/4), 181–190.

Traynor, P. (2003). The effects of computer-assisted instruction on different learners. *Journal of Instructional Psychology, 30*(2), 137–151.

U.S. Department of Education. (2002). *Proven methods: Scientifically based research.* Retrieved April 14, 2008, from http://www.ed.gov/nclb/methods/whatworks/research/index.html

U.S. Department of Education. (2007). *Effectiveness of reading and mathematics software products: Findings from the first student cohort.* Retrieved May 2, 2008, from http://ies.ed.gov/ncee/pdf/20074005.pdf

Wilson, M., Flanagan, R., Gurkewitz, R., & Skrip, L. (2006, September). *Understanding the effect of origami practice, cognition and language on spatial reasoning.* Paper presented at the Fourth Annual Science, Origami, Mathematics, and Education Conference, at California Institute of Technology, Pasadena, CA.

Wrightstone, J. W. (1935). *Appraisal of newer practices in selected public schools.* New York: Teachers College Press.

Endnote

[1]The following quotes regarding the documented flaws in the NAEP achievement levels are from the 2002 Executive Summary NAEP Reading Report Card (USDOE, 2003):

> "As provided by law, NCES, upon review of a congressionally mandated evaluation of NAEP, determined that achievement levels are to be used on a trial basis and should be interpreted with caution" (USDOE, p. xi).

> "In 1993, the first of several congressionally mandated evaluations of the achievement level setting process concluded that the procedures used to set the achievement levels were flawed . . . In response to the evaluation and critiques, NAGB conducted an additional study of the 1992 reading achievement levels before deciding to use them for reporting the 1994 NAEP results. When reviewing the findings of this study, the National Academy of Education (NAE) panel expressed concern about what it saw as a confirmatory bias in the study and about the inability of the study to address the panel's perception that the levels had been set too high" (USDOE, p. 14).

> "First, the potential instability of the levels may interfere with the accurate portrayal of trends . . . it is noteworthy that when American students performed very well on an international reading assessment, these results were discounted because these results were contradicted by poor performance against the possibly flawed NAEP reading achievement levels in the following year" (USDOE, p. 14).

> "The most recent congressional mandated evaluation conducted by the National Academy of Sciences (NAS) relied on prior studies of achievement levels . . . The panel (NAS) concluded NAEP's current achievement-level-setting procedures remain fundamentally flawed. The judgment tasks are difficult and confusing; raters' judgments of different item types are internally inconsistent; appropriate validity evidence for cut scores is lacking, and the process has produced unreasonable results" (USDOE, p. 15).

Reference

U.S. Department of Education. Institute of Education Sciences. National Center for Education Statistics. (2003). *The nation's reportcard: Reading 2002.* NCES 2003-521, by W. S. Grigg, M. C. Daane, and J. R. Campbell. Washington, DC.

APPLYING TECHNOLOGY

More about Experimental and Quasi-Experimental Research Designs

Dr. William Trochim has again provided an extremely thorough discussion of experimental and quasi-experimental research designs, spanning several Web pages. Initially, in Experimental Designs (www.socialresearchmethods.net/kb/desexper .htm), Dr. Trochim presents an overview of experimental research designs, focusing on the relationship of internal and external validity to those designs. Probably more important, however, are his links to pages that discuss specific types of designs. These pages contain not only narrative information about the various designs but also incorporate wonderful graphic images that strongly support his discussions. Included in his text are the following designs:

- *Two-Group Experimental Designs* (www.social researchmethods.net/kb/expsimp.htm)
- *Factorial Designs* (www.socialresearchmethods .net/kb/expfact.htm)

- *Randomized Block Designs* (www.socialresearch methods.net/kb/expblock.htm)
- *Covariance Designs* (www.socialresearch methods.net/kb/expcov.htm)
- *Hybrid Experimental Designs* (www.social researchmethods.net/kb/exphybrd.htm)

He has also included pages that examine quasi-experimentation (www.socialresearchmethods. net/kb/quasiexp.htm). Specific discussions include the following:

- *The Nonequivalent Control Group Design* (www.socialresearchmethods.net/kb/ quasnegd.htm)
- *Other Quasi-Experimental Designs* (www .socialresearchmethods.net/kb/quasioth.htm)

AN EXAMPLE OF SINGLE-SUBJECT RESEARCH

Following the exercise is a reprinted report of a single-subject research study that was designed to increase the language production and verbal behavior of a 9-year-old boy diagnosed with both autism and Down syndrome.

Exercise 13.3

As you read the study, be sure to note the following:

1. Focus of the study (what it is about)
2. Research questions, if any
3. Hypotheses, stated or implied
4. Description of the participant
5. The independent (treatment) variable(s) and the dependent (result or criteria) variable(s)
6. Instrument(s) used for measurement
7. Application of the experimental treatment(s) (i.e., introduction or manipulation of an independent variable)
8. Procedures by which data are obtained and analyzed
9. Findings
10. Conclusions

A Language Programme to Increase the Verbal Production of a Child Dually Diagnosed with Down Syndrome and Autism

K. A. Kroeger
Division of Developmental Disabilities, The Kelly O'Leary Center for Autism Spectrum
Disorders, Cincinnati Children's Hospital Medical Center, Cincinnati, OH, USA

W. M. Nelson III
Department of Psychology, Xavier University, Cincinnati, OH, USA

Abstract

Background The incidence of children dually diagnosed with Down syndrome and autism is estimated to be as high as 11%. There is a paucity of research investigating linguistic treatment interventions for such children. This single-subject experiment examined a programme designed to increase the language production and verbal behaviour of a 9-year-old dually diagnosed boy who had been receiving a 15-h/week home-based applied behaviour analysis (ABA) programme.

Methods Training principles were derived from previously empirically validated research in discrete trail learning and natural environment teaching, as well as modified incidental teaching procedures. The crux of the language programme involved withholding reinforcement until a spoken request was made.

Results Language production noticeably increased for each target area after the introduction of the language programme and was maintained at a 9-month follow-up session.

Conclusions A combined treatment approach incorporating direct instruction, natural environment teaching and incidental teaching can be effective in increasing and maintaining responsive and spontaneous speech in a child with Down syndrome diagnosed with autism. Replication studies are needed with such multiple dually diagnosed children to further evaluate the effectiveness and generalizability of this combined language programme.

Keywords

Applied behaviour
Analysis design
Autism
Down syndrome
Dual diagnoses
Language programme
Spontaneous language

> The authors note a lack of research on the topic at hand.

Source: Kroeger, K. A., & Nelson, W. M. (2006, February). A language programme to increase the verbal production of a child dually diagnosed with Down Syndrome and autism. *Journal of Intellectual Disability Research 50*, 101–108. © 2006 Blackwell Publishing, Ltd. Reproduced with permission of Blackwell Publishing, Ltd.

Both autism and Down syndrome (DS) are classified as disorders diagnosed early in life that are characteristically pervasive and chronic (American Association on Mental Retardation 1992; American Psychiatric Association 1994). While approximately 50% of individuals with autism fall within the intellectual disability (ID) range, co-morbid autism diagnosis in children with DS was traditionally considered rare, and the two childhood disorders regarded as distinct and separate disorders. The first mention of a child with both DS and autism came as late as 1979, when Wakabayashi (1979) reported this duality to be a fascinating phenomenon in a 7-year-old Japanese boy. Since this case report, the co-morbid occurrence of children with DS diagnosed with autism is estimated at 7% (Kent *et al.* 1999) and could be as high as 11%, which leads to the assumption that these two disorders coexist more commonly than previously suggested (Howlin *et al.* 1995; Kent *et al.* 1999). This increase in the co-morbid diagnosis of autism in children with DS appears to be reflective of the general population increase in children diagnosed with autism over the past 10 years (Baird *et al.* 2000; Centers for Disease Control & Prevention 2000).

Evaluation of traits of the two disorders leads to unique treatment implications. Historically, children with DS were commonly associated with positive personality characteristics such as sociability and cheerfulness (Smith & Wilson 1973); however, current research shows that they are more likely to develop temperaments similar to typical children (Chapman & Hesketh 2000). When speaking of a 'behavioural phenotype', features characteristic of children with DS include diagnosis within the moderate ID range, inherent social strengths and interests, a tendency over time to slow in development of intellectual abilities and adaptive behaviour skills, and noted weaknesses in grammar and speech (Hodapp & Dykens 1996). In addition, primary language deficits for children with DS include a delay in speech (first word at approximately 18 months), weaker (than receptive) expressive language skills and unintelligible speech (Roizen 2002). It could be surmised that the inherent strengths and interests in socialization connect children with DS to others;

the desire to socialize is largely present in this population of children.

The personality correlates of DS contrast those associated with autism, which typify such children as severely socially incapacitated and withdrawn (Bregman & Volkmar 1988; Newsom & Hovanitz 1997). Autism is considered a collective combination of deficits in the areas of socialization, social-communication and cognition (Klinger & Dawson 1996). Approximately 50% of children with autism fail to develop vocal speech (Rutter 1978; Prizant 1996), and those who do have disordered language across linguistic areas including prosody, semantics and pragmatics (Klinger & Dawson 1996). Additionally, in individuals with autism, socialization is pervasively affected with impairments noted in attachment, social imitation, joint attention, emotion perception and expression, and symbolic play (Klinger & Dawson 1996). Therefore, contrary to children with DS, children with autism lack the skills repertoire required for social interactions.

Research has shown that children with both ID and autism characteristically perform inadequately in the domains of socialization and communication (Oswald & Ollendick 1989; Rodrigue et al. 1991; Kraijer 2000). By nature of the diagnosis, children with autism will have impairments in communication (American Psychiatric Association 1994). A necessary component of socialization is usually some form of communication. Therefore, it would appear that research focusing on intervention strategies intended to improve communicative language might greatly benefit children dually diagnosed with DS and autism from the perspective of enriching language and increasing the opportunity for socialization. Unfortunately, this has not been the case. Although research has demonstrated that intensive early behavioural interventions are effective in improving communication in children diagnosed with autism and falling within metal retardation ranges (e.g. McEachin et al. 1993), such interventions have not been empirically demonstrated as effective for children presenting with both DS and autism diagnoses. Considering that children with DS have behaviour specific phenotypes, evidence-based autism therapies may or may not be effective for these youngsters. Likewise, effective communication strategies have been developed for children with DS (e.g. Sanchez-Fort et al. 1995; Kumin et al. 1996; Girolametto et al. 1998), but also not researched on the dually diagnosed population. Researchers recognize the need for distinguishing language phenotypes among the various developmental disabilities (Rice et al. 2005). However, current literature on this dual population is instead still examining the comorbidity and defining common behavioural correlates.

Research investigating linguistic treatment interventions specifically for children with DS diagnosed with autism is non-existent at this time. Therefore, this single-subject experiment examined a programme designed to increase the language production and verbal behaviour of a child with DS diagnosed with autism.

METHOD

Participant

The participant was a 9-year-old boy dually diagnosed with DS and autism. The child developed characteristic for children with DS, however, displayed some hyperlexic tendencies early on and developed speech more similar to children meeting typical developmental milestones than children with DS. Speech and socialization, considered to be normally developing, began to regress after age 2 and shortly after a diagnosis of autism (regressive type) was made by the local children's hospital affiliated developmental programme.

> The single subject of this study is a 9-year-old boy with Down syndrome and autism.

Testing was conducted after the intervention was implemented but before the 9-month follow-up. The child was 10 years, 2 months at the time of assessment. Results on the Peabody Picture Vocabulary Test-Third Edition (PPVT-III, Form III-A; Dunn & Dunn 1997) produced a standard score of 45 (M = 100, SD = 15) with a derived age equivalency (AE) of 3 years, 7 months. The Vineland Adaptive Behavior Scales: Interview Edition (VABS; Sparrow et al. 1984) yielded an Adaptive Behavior Composite score of 30 (M = 100, SD = 15), with an AE of 1 year, 5 months. The participant obtained standard scores of 55 (AE = 1 year, 6 months) on the Communication and 43 (AE = 1 year, 10 months) on the Socialization Domains.

The child was mainstreamed in a regular education second-grade classroom with support from a school-assigned educational assistant. He additionally received 15 h per week of direct instruction in a home-based applied behaviour analysis (ABA) programme; eliciting expressive language was a continual challenge. The child was selected for this study because he carried a dual diagnosis and had a history of limited verbal behaviour. Language production usually took the form of immediate or delayed echolalia, and when requested to speak the child usually answered in one or two word phrases.

Design

Throughout this study, the participant's routine treatments and interventions were held constant and no changes were made to his home ABA programmes or pharmaceutical regimen. The child had been engaged in his home programme for over 3 years and his tutors were aware that another intervention was being tried with the participant, but were blind to the actual targets (language production) and structure of the programme. Additionally, the

> The only changes experienced by the child during the course of the study was the addition of the language program; all other aspects of medical treatment and other forms of care were held constant.

participant was on Valproic acid for over three and a half years for the treatment of autistic symptoms and the dosage remained stable for the entirety of the programme. Therefore, no changes were made to his treatment, nor were any interventions withdrawn during the study time. The purpose of this controlled study was to add an element, the language programme, to his current treatment regimen.

This study employed an ABA (baseline–treatment–treatment withdrawn) single-subject design across behaviour (targeting the increase of verbal behaviour) for the child.

> This study used an ABA design (also known as a "measurement–treatment–measurement" or "reversal" design).

It should be noted, however, that the child was not left on a no treatment phase, as his ABA behavioural treatment programme was ongoing throughout this experimental language programme. Data were collected and the programme was implemented in the child's home after school hours. Baseline and treatment

> The procedures for implementation of the treatment and data collection are explained here.

withdrawn data were collected for seven consecutive days via videotaping the child for 1 hour each day. Taping was conducted for 1-h intervals because of the child's low frequency of verbal production. The language-training programme was conducted for 14 consecutive days, 1 hour each day (also videotaped). A 14-day treatment period was chosen arbitrarily, but deemed long enough to see a true effect should it exist. Additionally, 9-month follow-up data were collected.

From the videotapes, a frequency count of the number of verbal utterances was recorded for each of the sessions. Each time the child spoke, the verbalization was recorded in one of three categories: prompted language, responsive

> Data were collected in the form of videotapes.

language, or spontaneous language. Words spoken together at one time (e.g. multiple word utterances conveying one idea) were included as one unit, and only recorded as one occurrence of verbalizing.

Language was considered to be in one of the three categories: 'prompted language' [defined as occurring each time the child immediately (up to a 15 s delay) responded or spoke after an instructor prompt (verbal, physical or written) was given]; 'responsive language' [defined as occurring when the child immediately (up to a 15 s delay) spoke in response to a directive or question made by the instructor]; and 'spontaneous language' [classified as occurring if the utterance was not echolalia, not a response to the instructor or to prompting]. Spontaneous initiations were spoken speech that requested something desired, labelled things in the environment, or spoken words that seemed to not reference anything; hence, non-responsive functional or non-functional language without prompting or repeating was considered spontaneous. These language categories were chosen based on function and generalization.

Intervention

The teaching and training principles employed were derived from previous empirically validated research on discrete trial training (DTT; Leaf & McEachin 1999), errorless and natural environment teaching (Sundberg & Partington 1996), and modified incidental teaching procedures (Hart & Risley 1980; Haring et al. 1987; Charlop-Christy & Carpenter 2000).

> In this entire section, the authors explain the nature of the language program that was used as the treatment condition.

The crux of this language programme was withholding reinforcement; that is, the child would not receive any desired objects or other reinforcing stimuli without verbalizing. If the child reached for or non-verbally requested stimuli, he was required to label it before receiving the desired object; and if the child verbally requested something, he was required to use more language and elaborate upon the request before receiving reinforcement. Hence, language was encouraged if not spoken by the child, and once the phrase became familiar and used routinely, the phrase then was extended to incorporate more, and/or more sophisticated language. The language training was presented equally in both the natural environment and during structured table time, where opportunities for language production were continually presented.

Language was presented by the instructor modelling the labelling of objects, actions, and events (e.g. 'Look, it's a ball'), prompting for language [ranging from phonetic to full word to written prompts (e.g. a notecard with the prompt written out capitalizing on the child's hyperlexic tendencies)], and creating a reinforcing activity that could not be accessed without language delivered by the child. Reinforcing items and activities were identified by history (i.e. child was known to enjoy it) and reinforcer hierarchy probing (e.g. child showed preference for it by grabbing, moving towards, or refusing to give back after time was up). Hence, each intervention hour the child was continuously presented various tasks that kept him engaged and required the use of language in order to obtain reinforcement. Activities and reinforcement were varied throughout to prevent satiation. Within each session and over the course of the intervention, prompting procedures were faded out and/or minimized, until only incidental teaching was available to attain the reinforcing stimuli (e.g. the instructor would model the appropriate way to request an item and the child would imitate the instructor in some variant).

Multiple activities that were considered reinforcing to the child were set up as teaching modules to first increase the child's language through prompting procedures, and then faded out so that the child would spontaneously request reinforcing stimuli from a large repertoire of language and activities, or respond to the instructor without prompts. A platform swing and commercially produced videotapes were historically high preference activities for the participant. Prior to the intervention, the child had free access to both activities. Once the language programme was initiated, access was restricted and the child had to use language in order to obtain access to these activities.

For example, if the child wanted to be pushed on the swing, the instructor first gave a full verbal prompt for one of the following: push me, pull my legs (or feet) or pull my arms (or hands). Varying the mands for 'push' introduced choice and provided a larger repertoire of language for the child to generalize. Any form of pushing was not delivered until the child requested it, whether the request was on his own and spontaneous (e.g. child said 'push'), a response to the instructor (e.g. 'What do you want?'), or the result of a prompt (e.g. instructor said, 'Tell me, "pull my legs".'). However, consistent with the developed language protocol, once the child was consistently requesting a push (90% of the time), prompts were faded and incidental teaching implemented.

As with the platform swing, language was promoted when the child indicated interest in watching a videotape. Prompts were administered until the target verbal behaviour became part of his language repertoire, and once the child was requesting consistently, prompts were faded. Target verbalizations for the video script included the child vocalizing to turn on the television, put the tape in, and push 'play.' When the child was engaged in watching the videotape, it was paused periodically and questions about the paused screen were asked (e.g. Who is it?; What are they doing?). Once the child answered the question, the videotape was again played as reinforcement for appropriate language usage.

During structure table time, the child typically requested his reinforcement for work by giving a one-word request (e.g. 'cookie'). One-word utterances were extended by initially prompting additional language such as 'I want a cookie' or 'How about a cookie, please' until the child used the extended version with greater unprompted consistency. Once the child consistently used the multiple word mands, prompts were faded and reinforcement was withheld until the child used the multiple word requests.

As with the described activities (i.e. platform swing and videotapes), all interactive play and activities (e.g. a game of chase or tickle, puzzles) were taught the same way through withholding reinforcement and gradually fading prompts.

All activities incorporated multiple mands and language interactions with communicative intent (e.g. look here, chase me, tickle me, come here, play with me).

RESULTS

In regard to frequency recordings of the categorized verbalizations (prompted, responsive and spontaneous language), a data scorer unrelated to the study was trained and interrater reliability was assessed on 10% of the 1-h data videotapes. Three hours of videotape were randomly selected, 1 h from each phase of the study (baseline, treatment, and treatment withdrawn). Frequency counts were conducted on the matched sessions and compared using the exact agreement formula: [agreements (of frequencies) divided by (agreements + disagreements)] multiplied by 100. Interrater reliability was 95% for prompted language, 98% for responsive language, and 97% for spontaneous language, yielding a mean interrater reliability score of 96.26%.

> From the videotapes, frequencies of specific behaviors were tallied and analyzed.

Means of frequencies for each of the language areas (prompted, responsive and spontaneous) were computed for the three phases and reported in Table 1, along with frequency data from the 9-month follow-up. In addition, data for the three phases (baseline, treatment, and treatment withdrawn) and the 9-month follow-up were plotted and visually analyzed for treatment effects (see Figs 1 and 2). As can be seen in Figs 1 and 2, language production was notably stable over the 7-day baseline, so the treatment phase was initiated.

> Description of data collected during the initial "A" phase of the study, done to establish a baseline of behavior for the child.

As demonstrated, verbal production notably increased for each target area after the language programme was introduced (343.11% increase for prompted language, 600.08% for responsive language, and 237.09% for spontaneous language). The frequency of prompted language increased with the introduction of the language programme, and then decreased again as the child became more fluent with manipulating language to obtain reinforcement. After

Table 1 Mean Frequencies of Language Categories for the Three Phases: Baseline, Treatment, and Treatment Withdrawn, and the 9-Month Follow-Up Frequencies

Language category	Treatment phases			
	Baseline	*Treatment*	*Treatment withdrawn*	*Follow-up*
Prompted language	18.86	64.71	18.43	20.00
Responsive language	11.14	66.93	78.43	85.00
Spontaneous language	13.86	32.86	33.14	32.00

Figure 1

Frequency of production for the target language categories (responsive language and spontaneous language) for each 1-h session during the three intervention phases (baseline, treatment, and treatment withdrawn), and the 9-month follow-up.

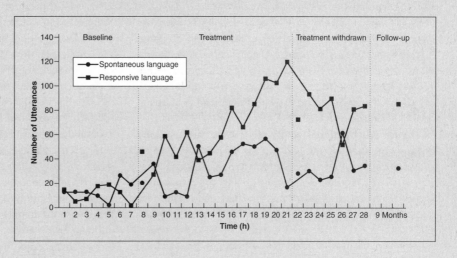

the first few days of the intervention and once the child was demonstrating utilization of learned language, prompts were gradually reduced to the least intrusive manner (e.g. an 'I want . . . ' written prompt was faded to a phonetic 'I' prompt which was then faded to an expectant look from the instructor). Hence, prompts were delivered throughout the intervention, decreased towards the end, and qualitatively differentiated with the passage of time.

> The authors saw huge increases in desirable behavior after introduction of the treatment (i.e., the language program).

DISCUSSION

The results indicate that a combined treatment approach incorporating direct instruction, natural environment teaching, and incidental teaching can be effective in increasing the verbal production (responsive and spontaneous speech) in a child with DS diagnosed with autism. This modified multimodal, continuous language programme appears to hold promise in increasing language production, especially in light of the lack of research on related treatment interventions validated specifically for this dually diagnosed population.

> The authors provide a broad summary statement, followed by a discussion with greater detail.

The observed treatment effects were maintained after direct treatment was discontinued during the return to baseline phase and maintained again after a 9-month interval. By continually modelling and requesting language in the presence of reinforcing activities and stimuli, responsive and spontaneous language may be increased. Such forms of speech are considered to be the basic building blocks

Figure 2

Frequency of production for the prompted language category and the total target language categories (responsive language and spontaneous language frequencies combined) for each 1-h session during the three intervention phases (baseline, treatment, and treatment withdrawn), and the 9-month follow-up.

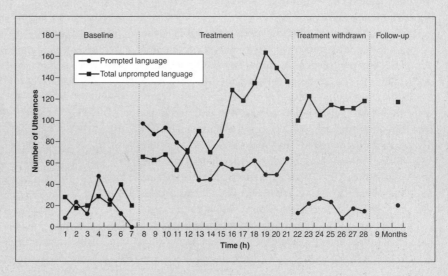

of social communicative language, and the intervention is hopeful in that it appears to have increased these verbal behaviour targets. Because the child's other interventions were held constant throughout the baseline, treatment, and treatment withdrawn phases, increases in verbal production are seemingly attributed to the intervention and the language programme appears to be responsible for the changes in the child's verbal behaviour.

During the treatment withdrawn phase, the language programme was discontinued and the child returned to his previous routine. An interesting trend to note was a slight increase in use of spontaneous language after the programme was discontinued. It appears that the child incorporated his learned language skills by generalizing them to his daily routine with his ABA tutors. Therefore, it appears that increased meaningful communication that occurred during the treatment phase generalized into everyday usage, as reflected in the treatment withdrawn phase data. This is hopeful in that generalization of learned skills is usually a difficult task for individuals in this population (Foxx 1999).

> The authors note that during the second "A" phase (i.e., following removal of the treatment), the child exhibited behaviors learned from the treatment program.

Following the treatment withdrawn phase, the ABA tutors and family were taught the language programme procedures in order to promote the continuation of his increased verbalizations and maintain the treatment effects. Maintenance was evidenced by his language production recorded after the follow-up session 9 months later. (It should be noted that since the child participated in ongoing ABA programming, it is unknown if the treatment effects would have maintained at the observed level if the child was not involved in such intensive programming for the duration of the follow-up period.) Although treatment effects are preliminary given the study consisted of only one child, the language programme appears successful in its intention of increasing verbal behaviour.

> The effective program was maintained even after the formal study ended.

Through this controlled study design, it was planned for changes to occur as a result of the language programme. In a treatment reversal design, exists the risk that the treatment may lead to change initially, but then the behaviour may extinguish. The maintenance of treatment effects is always important in clinical endeavours. It is assumed in this case that the language skills developed were maintained by the natural environment in that the child could, through the intervention, more independently get his needs met, and hence it reinforced the use of language. Such a 'behavioural trap' (Baer et al. 1976) where natural contingencies support the newly acquired verbal behaviours is the key to longer-term treatment gains. For ethical reasons, the investigators did not want to end the study on a no-treatment phase.

Therefore, the tutors and family (after training) continued the language programme following the treatment withdrawn 7-day period. In completing this study, not only was the language programme in place, but it also appeared that the increased language production had become self-reinforcing for the child (able to access reinforcers and accommodate his needs). This appeared validated at the 9-month follow-up where the child was still using comparable (to treatment) levels of responsive and spontaneous speech.

Replication studies with multiple dually diagnosed children, especially those with corresponding levels of ID, are necessary. While the population of children with DS diagnosed with autism is increasing, it is still relatively small, so any intervention should be demonstrated to generalize across children. In addition, the intensity of the treatment programme could be increased to determine whether even greater verbal fluency could be achieved. Not only might this further increase treatment gains, but it may also assist with generalizing the learned verbal skills to other language environments (e.g. school, home, social activities with peers).

> As is typically appropriate with single-subject studies, replications are recommended.

ACKNOWLEDGMENTS

Much gratitude is owed to the study participant and his family. Without their dedication to the research process, this study would not have completed with such success.

References

American Association on Mental Retardation. (1992) *Mental Retardation: Definition, Classification, and Systems of Support.* Author, Washington, DC.

American Psychiatric Association. (1994) *Diagnostic and Statistical Manual of Mental Disorders*, 4th edn. Author, Washington, DC.

Baer D., Rowbury T. & Goetz E. (1976) Behavioral traps in the preschool: a proposal for research. *Minnesota Symposia on Child Psychology* 10, 3–27.

Baird G., Charman S., Baron-Cohen S., Cox J., Sweetenham S., Wheelwright S. & Drew A. (2000) A screening instrument for autism at 18 months of age: a 6-year follow-up study. *Journal of the American Academy of Child and Adolescent Psychiatry* 39, 694–702.

Bregman J. D. & Volkmar F. R. (1988) Autistic social dysfunction and Down syndrome. *Journal of the American Academy of Child and Adolescent Psychiatry* 27, 440–1.

Centers for Disease Control and Prevention. (2000) *Prevalence of Autism in Brick Township, New Jersey, 1998: Community Report.* Department of Health and Human Services, Atlanta, GA.

Chapman R. & Hesketh L. (2000) Behavioral phenotypes of individuals with Down Syndrome. *Mental Retardation and Developmental Disabilities Research Reviews* 6, 84–96.

Charlop-Christy M. H. & Carpenter M. H. (2000) Modified incidental teaching sessions: a procedure for parents to increase spontaneous speech in their children with autism. *Journal of Positive Behavior Interventions* 2, 98–112.

Dunn L. M. & Dunn L. M. (1997) *Peabody picture vocabulary test*, 3rd edn. American Guidance Service, Circle Pines, MN.

Foxx R. (1999) Long term maintenance of language and social skills. *Behavioral Interventions* 14, 135–146.

Girolametto L., Weitzman E. & Clements-Baartman J. (1998) Vocabulary intervention for children with Down syndrome: parent training using focused stimulation. *Infant-Toddler Intervention* 8, 109–25.

Haring T. G., Neetz J. A., Lovinger L. & Peck C. (1987) Effects of four modified incidental teaching procedures to create opportunities for communication. *Journal of the Association for Persons with Severe Handicaps* 12, 218–26.

Hart B. & Risley T. R. (1980) In vivo language intervention: unanticipated general effects. *Journal of Applied Behavior Analysis* 13, 407–32.

Hodapp R. & Dykens E. (1996) Mental retardation. In: *Child Psychopathology* (eds E. J. Mash & R. Barkley), pp. 362–89. Guilford, New York.

Howlin P., Wing L. & Gould J. (1995) The recognition of autism in children with Down syndrome: implications for intervention and some speculation about pathology. *Developmental Medicine and Child Neurology* 37, 406–13.

Kent L., Evans J., Paul M. & Sharp M. (1999) Comorbidity of autistic spectrum disorders in children with Down syndrome. *Developmental Medicine and Child Neurology* 41, 153–8.

Klinger L. G. & Dawson G. (1996) Autistic disorder. In: *Child Psychopathology* (eds E. Mash & R. Barkley), pp. 311–39. Guilford, New York.

Kraijer D. (2000) Review of adaptive behavior studies in mentally retarded persons with autism/pervasive developmental disorder. *Journal of Autism and Developmental Disorders* 30, 39–47.

Kumin L., Goodman M. & Councill C. (1996) Comprehensive speech and language intervention for school-aged children with Down syndrome. *Down Syndrome Quarterly* 1, 1–8.

Leaf R. & McEachin J. (1999) *A Work in Progress: Behavior Management Strategies and a Curriculum for Intensive Behavioral Treatment of Autism*. Pro-Ed, Austin, TX.

McEachin J., Smith T. & Lovaas O. (1993) Long-term outcome for children with autism who received early intensive behavioral treatment. *American Journal on Mental Retardation* 97, 359–72.

Newsom C. & Hovanitz C. A. (1997) Autistic disorder. In: *Assessment of Childhood Disorders* (eds E. J. Mash & L. G. Terdal), pp. 408–52. Guilford, New York.

Oswald D. P. & Ollendick T. H. (1989) Role taking and social competence in autism and mental retardation. *Journal of Autism and Developmental Disorders* 19, 119–27.

Prizant B. M. (1996) Brief report: communication, language, social, and emotional development. *Journal of Autism and Developmental Disorders* 26, 173–9.

Rice M. L., Warren S. F. & Betz S. K. (2005) Language symptoms of developmental language disorders: an overview of autism, Down syndrome, fragile X, specific language impairment, and William's syndrome. *Applied Psycholinguistics* 26, 7–27.

Rodrigue J. R., Morgan S. B. & Geffken G. R. (1991) A comparative evaluation of adaptive behavior in children and adolescents with autism, Down Syndrome, and normal development. *Journal of Autism and Developmental Disorders* 21, 187–96.

Roizen N. J. (2002) Down syndrome. In: *Children with Disabilities*, 5th edn (ed. M. L. Batshaw), pp. 307–20. Paul H. Brookes Publishing Co., Baltimore, MD.

Rutter M. (1978) Diagnosis and definition. In: *Autism: a Reappraisal of Concepts and Treatment* (eds M. Rutter & E. Schopler), pp. 1–25. Plenum, New York.

Sanchez-Fort M. R., Brady M. P. & Davis C. A. (1995) Using high-probability requests to increase low-probability communication behavior in young children with severe disabilities. *Education and Training in Mental Retardation and Developmental Disabilities* 30, 151–65.

Smith D. & Wilson A. (1973) *The Child with Down's Syndrome*. Saunders, Philadelphia, PA.

Sparrow S. S., Balla D. A. & Cicchetti D. V. (1984) *Vineland Adaptive Behavior Scales: Interview Edition*. American Guidance Service, Circle Pines, MN.

Sundberg M. & Partington J. (1996) *Teaching Language to Children with Autism and Other Developmental Disabilities*. Behavior Analysts, Inc., Pleasant Hill, CA.

Wakabayashi S. (1979) A case of infantile autism associated with Down's syndrome. *Journal of Autism and Developmental Disorders* 9, 31–6.

CHAPTER SUMMARY

This chapter has explained the nature and procedures of experimental research and quasi-experimental research. Experimental research is used to identify cause–effect relationships, in which changes in a prior condition or event (X = the independent variable) produce changes in a subsequent condition or event (Y = the dependent variable). The independent variable is considered to be the cause, the dependent variable the effect, and in experimental and quasi-experimental research, the independent variable is manipulated to determine whether, and how, it influences the dependent variable. Closely related to experimental research is quasi-experimental research, which follows the same procedures except that for any number of reasons the researchers are not able to assign participants randomly to treatment groups.

Several factors are known to affect the internal validity (accuracy of results) and external validity (generalizability) of experimental and quasi-experimental research.

Referred to as "threats to validity," those factors must be accounted for satisfactorily if the research is to have credibility and usefulness.

LIST OF IMPORTANT TERMS

AB design	experimental group	random assignment
ABA design	experimental research	random selection
alternating-treatment design	external validity	reversal design
comparison group	internal validity	single-subject design
control group	multiple baseline design	threats to validity
experimental design	quasi-experimental research	treatment condition

ACTIVITIES FOR THOUGHT AND DISCUSSION

1. Here are the questions posed at the beginning of the chapter. How would you answer the questions now?
   a. What sets experimental research apart from all other types of research?
   b. What is the difference between experimental research and quasi-experimental research?
   c. What research designs are most frequently used in experimental research?
   d. What research designs are most frequently used in quasi-experimental research?
   e. What are the main threats to internal and external validity in experimental research and quasi-experimental research?
   f. What are the principal data sources in experimental and quasi-experimental research?
   g. Which data analysis procedures are most often used in experimental and quasi-experimental research?

2. Explain why a researcher might decide to conduct quasi-experimental research rather than experimental research.

3. Suppose educational researchers wanted to try to identify the causes of the behavior pattern typically known as attention deficit disorder (ADD) syndrome. Which type of research would be indicated: experimental, quasi-experimental, or causal-comparative? Would the most appropriate design include groups or be limited to single participants?

4. Suppose medical researchers wished to study the effects of a new medication to deal with attention deficit disorder syndrome in primary-grade children. Which type of research is indicated: experimental, quasi-experimental, or causal-comparative? Of the experimental designs described in this chapter, which would seem most appropriate for this research?

ANSWERS TO CHAPTER EXERCISES

13.1. 1. If a true experiment, ask to have students randomly assigned to the two classes. If a quasi-experiment, use existing class enrollments. If desired, pretest the groups to ensure equivalency. Consider using a fellow teacher's class as a control group.
   2. Write out what they intend to do. Agree to a certain amount of homework and allow the teachers to satisfy themselves that the agreement is being adhered to.
   3. The same test, preferably a standardized test, should be given to all groups involved at the end of the experiment.
   4. The teacher personality and skill variables probably cannot be adequately controlled in this study.

13.2. Answers are found in the article. Discuss the answers in class.

13.3. Answers are found in the article. Discuss the answers in class.

REFERENCES AND RECOMMENDED READINGS

Bracht, G., & Glass, G. (1968). The external validity of experiments. *American Educational Research Journal, 5,* 437–474.

Brown, S., & Walberg, H. (1993). Motivational effects on test scores of elementary students. *Journal of Educational Research, 86,* 133– 136.

Campbell, D., & Stanley, J. (1966). *Experimental and Quasi-Experimental Designs for Research.* Chicago: Rand McNally.

Crowl, T. (1993). *Fundamentals of Educational Research.* Dubuque, IA: WCB Brown & Benchmark.

Gall, M., Borg, W., & Gall, J. (2003). *Educational Research: An Introduction* (7th ed.). Boston: Allyn & Bacon.

14

Mixed-Methods Research Designs

PREVIEW

This chapter focuses on the nature, intent, and procedures of mixed-methods research. Types of mixed-methods designs include the following:

- Explanatory mixed-methods design
- Exploratory mixed-methods design
- Triangulation mixed-methods design

The main strength of mixed-methods research is that it capitalizes on the individual strengths of two types of data analysis:

- Quantitative
- Qualitative

The major concern about mixed-methods research is that researchers must be familiar with both types of data in terms of the following:

- Collection
- Analysis

TARGETED LEARNINGS

This chapter deals with mixed-methods research, an approach to conducting research that combines both quantitative and qualitative data. As you study this chapter, you will learn about various mixed-methods research designs, as well as situations or research purposes that might be appropriate for the use of mixed methods. As you read this chapter, look particularly for information related to the following questions:

1. What is the main purpose of mixed-methods research?
2. What are some reasons why researchers might want to consider using mixed methods?
3. What are the three different types of mixed-methods designs, and how do they differ?
4. How does the process of conducting mixed-methods research differ from other types of research?
5. What are the main strengths as well as limitations of mixed-methods research?

CHARACTERISTICS OF MIXED-METHODS RESEARCH

Researchers are increasingly employing research designs that combine both qualitative and quantitative methods, known as **mixed-methods research designs.** Mixed-methods designs combine qualitative and quantitative approaches to *only* the research methods (i.e., data collection and procedures) portion of the research process. These designs are not to be confused with mixed-model designs (see Tashakkori & Teddlie, 1998), which combine these two approaches across *all* phases of the research process, including their respective underlying philosophical assumptions, methods of generating research questions and hypotheses, and bases for analysis and inference (Tashakkori & Teddlie, 1998). Our focus in this chapter will be on the former, that is, mixed-methods research designs.

Mixed-methods studies are appropriate when a researcher has both quantitative and qualitative data that can—when considered together—provide a better understanding of the research problem than either type of data alone (Creswell, 2005). One of the major benefits of mixed-methods research is that it capitalizes on the strengths of both quantitative and qualitative research. For example, quantitative data yields information that can be analyzed statistically to provide useful information for describing a large number of people. However, qualitative data, such as open-ended interviews, offer the chance for individuals to express their own perspectives on the topic. Combining these two types of data provides very powerful information about the study topic at hand (Creswell, 2005). The researcher is afforded the opportunity to develop a much more complex picture of the phenomenon under study.

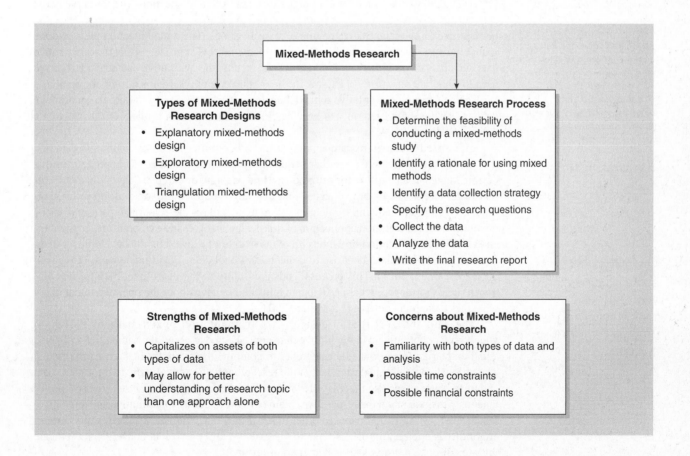

Another situation appropriate for a mixed-methods study occurs when a researcher wants to build from, or extend, one phase of research to another. For example, a researcher may want to first explore qualitative data in order to guide the development of a quantitative survey instrument or to identify variables in order to study them in a subsequent quantitative study. Similarly, the researcher may wish to follow up a quantitative study with a qualitative one in order to collect more detailed information supporting or extending explanations that could be drawn from the results of statistical analyses (Creswell, 2005).

Although the decision to use mixed methods may seem to make common sense (i.e., "Why doesn't everyone use it if it offers a more complete picture of a given research topic?"), it is important to be aware of some limitations to its use. For example, it is absolutely crucial to note that, in order to use this type of research design, one must be *thoroughly* familiar with *both* quantitative and qualitative research methods. Possessing strengths in only one type of research method will not be enough for you to successfully carry out mixed-methods research. At some point, you will struggle with some aspect of each of the three designs we will examine shortly. Additionally, the data collection and analysis procedures tend to be time-consuming and often require more resources than one approach alone (Gay, Mills, & Airasian, 2006).

MIXED-METHODS RESEARCH DESIGNS

Creswell (2005) identifies three main mixed-methods research designs: the explanatory design, the exploratory design, and the triangulation design. The distinguishing factors among the designs are the relative weights given to each type of data and when each method is used (McMillan, 2004). In an **explanatory mixed-methods design**—which McMillan (2004) suggests is the most common type of mixed-methods design—the researcher first collects quantitative data and then gathers qualitative data in order to help support, explain, or elaborate on the quantitative results (Creswell, 2005). The data collection may be done sequentially or in two distinct phases. The rationale for this approach is that the quantitative data and analysis provide the main focus of the results; the qualitative data and analysis are used to elaborate on, refine, or explain the quantitative findings. In this design, the emphasis is placed clearly on quantitative data and analysis (Creswell, 2005). Often, the qualitative data and analysis are used only to provide closer examination of outliers or other extreme cases (McMillan, 2004).

The mixed-methods researcher may want to begin by collecting qualitative data and then collect quantitative data, either sequentially or using a two-phase approach. In this design, known as an **exploratory mixed-methods design,** qualitative data—which are emphasized more heavily—are collected first in order to explore the topic of interest. Quantitative data are subsequently gathered in order to explain the relationships found in the qualitative data. A common application of this design involves the exploration of a phenomenon and the identification of themes (qualitative data), followed by the development of an instrument and its subsequent use to collect additional data (quantitative data) (Creswell, 2005; McMillan, 2004). This process lends credibility to the instrument because its component items stem from what participants think and believe about the phenomenon and not what the researchers believe (McMillan, 2004).

The third and final type of design is the **triangulation mixed-methods design,** in which both quantitative and qualitative data are collected at about the same time and given equal emphasis; this allows the researcher to combine the strengths of each form of data. The rationale behind this design is that the researcher values equally the two forms of data and treats them as such so that they are "merged" and the results of analyses are used simultaneously to understand the research problem (Creswell, 2005). Quantitative and qualitative results are informally compared in order to see if they have yielded similar results. Greater credibility is apparent in the findings to the extent that the two sets converge and indicate the same results, a process known as **triangulation.**

The three mixed-methods designs are depicted in Figure 14.1.

myeducationlab for research

To learn more about designing mixed-methods research studies, go to the "Mixed Methods Research" section of **MyEducationLab for Research** and then click on *Assignments and Activities*. Complete the exercise titled "Reading Programs in the Chicago Public Schools," which will give you some practice at making important design decisions within a mixed-methods study.

Figure 14.1

Depiction of the three types of mixed-methods research designs
(Adapted from Creswell, 2005)

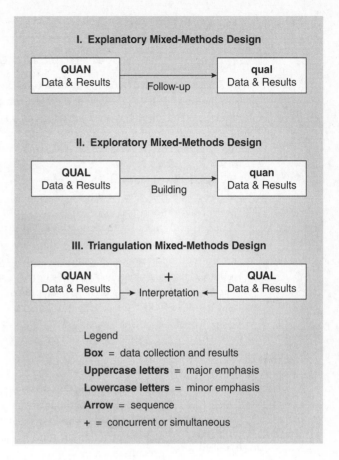

I. Explanatory Mixed-Methods Design

QUAN
Data & Results → Follow-up → qual
Data & Results

II. Exploratory Mixed-Methods Design

QUAL
Data & Results → Building → quan
Data & Results

III. Triangulation Mixed-Methods Design

QUAN
Data & Results → Interpretation ← + QUAL
Data & Results

Legend

Box = data collection and results

Uppercase letters = major emphasis

Lowercase letters = minor emphasis

Arrow = sequence

+ = concurrent or simultaneous

THE MIXED-METHODS RESEARCH PROCESS

myeducationlab
PEARSON
for research

To learn more about mixed-methods designs utilized in published studies, go to the "Mixed Methods Research" section of **MyEducationLab for Research** and then click on *Assignments and Activities*. Complete the exercise titled "Identifying Mixed Methods Research." This exercise will give you some practice at identifying aspects of mixed-methods studies within a published article.

Due to the additional decisions that must be made about methodology, the steps in conducting a mixed-methods research study are somewhat unique, as shown in the following (Creswell, 2005):

1. *Determine the feasibility of conducting a mixed-methods study.* Determining the feasibility of using such designs requires the researcher to make decisions about financial and time resources, as well as familiarity with both quantitative and qualitative approaches to research.

2. *Identify a rationale for using mixed methods.* Assuming that the study is feasible, the researcher must then consider why it is essential to collect both types of data. This rationale should also be included as an essential part of your final research report.

3. *Identify a data collection strategy.* Important decisions must be made with respect to the relative emphasis given to quantitative and qualitative data, the sequence of data collection, and the specific forms of data to be collected.

4. *Specify the research questions.* Once the particular methods have been identified, it is important to specify both quantitative and qualitative research questions.

5. *Collect the data.* Both quantitative and qualitative data are collected, according to the sequence and emphasis specified earlier by the researcher.

6. *Analyze the data.* Both types of data are analyzed, again according to earlier decisions. In explanatory and exploratory studies, quantitative and qualitative data are analyzed separately. In the case of triangulation designs, the analyses are integrated.

APPLYING TECHNOLOGY

More about Mixed-Methods Research

In this chapter, you have been introduced to various mixed-methods research designs and the rationale for their use. The following listed websites can provide additional information and resources to both supplement and extend what you have learned.

■ BRIDGES: Mixed Methods Network for Behavioral, Social, and Health Sciences (www.fiu.edu/~bridges)
A wonderful website that provides links to numerous resources, including a glossary of mixed-methods terms and concepts (www.fiu.edu/%7Ebridges/glossary.htm)

■ The Mixed-Methods Research Special Interest Group (SIG) of AERA (www.aera.net/Default.aspx?id=345)

■ *The Journal of Mixed Methods Research* (www.sagepub.com)

■ User-Friendly Handbook for Mixed Method Evaluations (www.nsf.gov/pubs/1997/nsf97153/start.htm)
The Directorate for Education and Human Resources in the Division of Research, Evaluation and Communication (National Science Foundation) provides this online handbook for mixed-methods evaluations. Although the focus is on evaluation-type studies, the nature of the mixed-methods designs and issues discussed most certainly extend to research studies in general.

myeducationlab *for research*

To learn more about the overall process of mixed-methods research, go to the "Mixed Methods Research" section of **MyEducationLab for Research** and then click on *Building Research Skills.* Read the article and then complete the exercise titled "Identifying Steps in the Research Process for a Mixed Methods Study," which will help you identify key components of a mixed-methods research study.

7. *Write the final research report.* The nature of the final report will also depend on the specific mixed-methods design employed. Explanatory and exploratory studies require that results are written in two separate phases, with findings summarized for each method and later integrated in the report. Triangulation studies integrate both types of findings for each research question.

STRENGTHS AND CONCERNS IN MIXED-METHODS RESEARCH

Quite simply, the major strength of mixed-methods research designs is that these designs capitalize on the individual assets of quantitative and qualitative research. This allows the researcher to potentially create a more multifaceted picture of the phenomenon being studied. Concerns about this methodological approach include the fact that the researcher must be thoroughly familiar with both quantitative and qualitative research methods. Additionally, the methodological procedures tend to be more time-consuming than using one approach alone.

AN EXAMPLE OF MIXED-METHODS RESEARCH

The following mixed-methods research study examines the relationships among resources in three urban public housing neighborhoods, youth perceptions and experiences of resources, and youth reports of neighborhood hassles and cohesion.

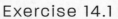

Exercise 14.1

As you read this report utilizing a mixed-methods design, discuss what you find concerning the following elements of research studies:

1. Research problem
2. Purpose of the study
3. Research questions/hypotheses
4. Type of mixed-methods design
5. Methods of data collection
6. Methods of data analysis
7. Findings
8. Conclusions
9. Recommendations

Youth Perceptions of Neighborhood Hassles and Resources: A Mixed Method Analysis

Elizabeth K. Anthony
Corresponding author: University of California, Berkeley

Nicole Nicotera
University of Denver

Abstract

Empirical investigations exploring the processes and mechanisms of neighborhood influences on child and youth development are needed to contribute to the growing body of research on neighborhood as a context for development. Using a mixed method design, this study examined the relationship between structurally identified resources in three urban public housing neighborhoods, youth perceptions and experiences of resources, and youth report of neighborhood hassles and cohesion. Survey data from 153 ethnically and culturally diverse youth between 6th and 8th grade were analyzed using regression analyses; constant comparative analysis was used to code interviews from a subsample of 22 youth. Results indicated an inverse relationship between the number of neighborhood resources and the level of daily hassles youth report. Analysis of mixed method results further highlights the importance of young people's perceptions of neighborhood influences.

This was a mixed-methods study, utilizing survey and interview data collected from sixth-, seventh-, and eighth-grade students.

Keywords

Children and youth
Poverty
Daily hassles
Neighborhood resources
Mixed methods

Source: Anthony, E. K., & Nicotera, N. (2008). Youth perceptions of neighborhood hassles and resources: A mixed methods analysis. Children and Youth Services Review, 30, 1246–1255. © 2008 Elsevier Ltd. Reproduced with permission of Elsevier Ltd; permission conveyed through Copyright Clearance Center, Inc.

1. INTRODUCTION

Ecological theory and research indicate that neighborhood and community transactions play a role in child and youth development (Bronfenbrenner, 1979; Sampson, 2001). A growing interest in contextual factors in adaptation has recently drawn attention to neighborhood level influences (Cauce, Stewart, Rodriguez, Cochran, & Ginzler, 2003; Wyman, 2003). Specifically, studies point to structural characteristics such as poverty, mobility, and differences in social organization impacting levels of risk for children and youth (Brooks-Gunn, Duncan, & Aber, 1997; Gorman-Smith, Tolan, & Henry, 1999). Youth living in impoverished and unstable neighborhoods are often exposed to a number of related risk factors such as high levels of violence exposure and illegal activity.

With an interest in the adaptive characteristics of neighborhoods, other studies examine the availability of resources and positive opportunities such as education and employment as protective factors for children and youth (Brook, Kessler, & Cohen, 1999; Luthar & Cushing, 1999). Access to resources for basic physical and social needs within one's own community is tied to a range of positive outcomes such as motivation to succeed in school and resisting negative peer influences (Hawkins et al., 2007). Further, collective efficacy, or the idea that extra familial social support and a sense of connection impact child development, is a characteristic of "effective neighborhoods" (Fraser, Kirby, & Smokowski, 2004, p. 44). High levels of collective efficacy may minimize the negative effects of risk exposure for some young people.

Examinations of the neighborhood as a context for development have met formidable challenges. In particular, the specific processes and mechanisms of neighborhood influences are poorly understood (Korbin, 2001). Preliminary studies suggest that understanding how youth perceive and experience neighborhood is fundamental to understanding neighborhood as an influential context (Nicotera, 2007, 2008). However, precisely how youth experience neighborhood influences, and individual variation in perceptions and experience, is understudied. Examination of the complex relationship between structural neighborhood variables, subjective experiences of those variables, and developmental outcomes is subsequently hindered by this lack of information. The current study

> The purpose of the study is stated here.

seeks to untangle this complexity by exploring the mechanisms by which neighborhood resources influence youth experiences. Specifically, the study examined the relationship between neighborhood resources, youth perceptions and experience of resources, and youth report of neighborhood hassles and cohesion.

1.1. Neighborhood influences on child and youth development

Of the multiple ecological systems impacting children and youth, the neighborhood context is the least studied and the most poorly understood. Yet, neighborhoods represent an immediate social context for young people. Garbarino, Galambos, Plantz, and Kostelny (1992) note that the neighborhood is an "early and major arena for exploration and social interaction in that it serves as setting for the physical and emotional development of the child" (p. 202). While child and youth adaptation is impacted by broad environmental and social influences such as social norms and laws, neighborhood represents the spatial context of interaction, with various meanings for different young people. One young person might define neighborhood as the block where she/he lives, whereas another might consider the neighborhood to be everyone who goes to the same school. In fact, Burton and Price-Spratlen (1999) point out that children have their own definitions of neighborhood boundaries and meanings related to living and playing within them that do not necessarily match demographic definitions of neighborhoods such as census tracts or block groups.

Research on the effects of neighborhood on child and youth adaptation generally assesses structural characteristics and resources at the neighborhood level. Structural characteristics such as poverty, mobility, and social disorganization interact with family and individual effects in relationship to risk (Brooks-Gunn et al., 1997). For example, Coulton, Korbin, Su, and Chow (1995) found that the following four structural characteristics explained considerable neighborhood variation in rates of child maltreatment reports: (1) impoverishment, (2) child-care burden, (3) residential instability, and (4) proximity to concentrated poverty. Neighborhoods characterized by poverty are associated with a number of negative outcomes for infants, children,

and youth including low birth weight (Coulton & Pandey, 1992), externalizing problem behaviors (Duncan, Brooks-Gunn, & Klebanov, 1994), school dropout (Clark, 1992), and teenage pregnancy, drug arrests, juvenile delinquency, and violent crime (Coulton et al., 1995). Similarly, Shaw and McKay (1942) found that disorganized neighborhoods contribute to risk for children by limiting the opportunities for children to learn skills which enable social, educational, and economic success. Neighborhoods characterized by social disorganization lack important social structures to support children and families in reaching goals and reflect the impact of pervasive poverty and instability.

In contrast, neighborhood resources, both physical resources such as availability of libraries and health care facilities, and socioemotional resources such as social support, contribute to healthy child development. Whereas socially unorganized neighborhoods stifle opportunities, neighborhoods characterized by collective efficacy mobilize social processes to promote opportunities (Sampson, Raudenbush, & Earls, 1997). Opportunities for young people to engage in positive behavior and supportive and collaborative relationships protect youth from other negative influences (Fraser et al., 2004).

Research on neighborhood influences explores the relationship between certain structural risk characteristics such as poverty and protective factors such as collective efficacy and specific outcomes for children and youth. However, studies also suggest that neighborhood influences on developmental outcomes are more complex and diverse than can be accounted for by structural variables alone (Burton, 1991, 1997; Figueira-McDonough, 1998). Therefore, uncovering the relationship between structural neighborhood variables and residents' lived experiences within a neighborhood is an important step in fully comprehending how neighborhood

> The authors have identified a void in the literature.

context influences developmental outcomes. Seidman et al. (1998) point out that "there has been surprisingly little work examining how objective, structural aspects of neighborhoods relate to youths' perceptions or experience of neighborhoods" (p. 260).

1.2. The mechanisms of neighborhood influences

Youth may experience structural characteristics and neighborhood resources in a myriad of ways that existing studies of neighborhood influences do not capture. For example, poverty and lack of opportunity may be operationalized through a set of transactions throughout the day that accumulate into a substantial risk. From this perspective, research on the effect of daily hassles in the lives of children and youth, particularly urban youth, suggests that microsystem-specific transactions in a young person's life impact psychological adjustment (Lazarus & Folkman, 1984; Rowlison & Felner,

1988). Daily hassles, the "irritating, frustrating, distressing demands that to some degree characterize everyday transactions with the environment," are pervasive and complicated for children and youth living in urban poverty (Kanner, Coyne, Schaefer, & Lazarus, 1981, p. 31).

Moreover, a number of studies suggest that neighborhood resources are not always perceived as theorized. In ethnographic interviews, Korbin (2001) found that objective and subjective perspectives on neighborhood resources are not always consistent. For example, objective criteria suggest that a liquor store in the neighborhood is a risk or deficit whereas subjective accounts from participants indicate that a liquor store selling necessities (e.g., toilet paper, juice, and soda) is a strength. Similarly, Spencer (2001) explains how contextual characteristics negotiate subjective experiences of the neighborhood. For example, police presence in the neighborhood may be perceived as a hassle for boys but possibly a resource for girls. Further, differential perceptions of neighborhood by parents may influence children's perceptions and, in turn, developmental outcomes (Spencer, Swanson, & Glymph, 1996).

Accounts of resilient development in youth living in poverty suggest that individual perceptions of neighborhood play an important role in directing individual behavior (Spencer, 2001). Such findings point to the need to understand both the objective characteristics of the neighborhood and the subjective perceptions and experiences of youth living in the neighborhood.

1.3. The current study

The mixed method design of the current study enables examination of the complexity of neighborhood influences on young people's experience. While the literature is unclear about the direction of associations, it is possible to build on prior research that demonstrates variability in youth experiences of neighborhood influences (Figueira-McDonough, 1998; Korbin, 2001) and a relationship between perceptions and behavior (Spencer, 2001). Hence, we hypothesize that structural neighborhood resources influence youth experiences and perceptions which in turn influence a young person's subjective appraisal of hassles and/or cohesion. Specifically, resources available to a young person in the neighborhood were expected to be inversely associated with hassles and positively associated with cohesion. In addition to resources, extra familial support and the young person's sense of fit with neighbors and the neighborhood were expected to be positively associated with cohesion and inversely associated with hassles. These hypotheses were explored through examining the relationships between 3 quantitative variables (structural neighborhood resources, youth reports of daily hassles, and neighborhood cohesion) and qualitative accounts of youth

> The authors restate the purpose of the study and then provide their guiding hypotheses.

perceptions of neighborhood supports and challenges. Prior studies suggest gender and age differences in reports of hassles (higher levels for girls and older youth) but not for cohesion (Anthony, 2008; Seidman et al., 1998); these hypotheses were explored in our quantitative analysis. Finally, while we recognize that broad social and political structures influence these neighborhood conditions, this study is limited to investigating influences that are proximal to youth's daily experiences.

2. METHODS

2.1. Participants

All study participants were residents in 1 of 3 urban, public housing neighborhoods in a western city. Study participants (N = 153) were racially and ethnically diverse; 54% (n = 82) were Latina/o, 16% (n = 24) were African American, 19% (n = 31) were of mixed ethnicity, and 11% (n = 16) were Asian American. The sample was balanced with respect to gender; 51% (n = 78) were female and 49% (n = 75) were male. Youth averaged 11.9 years of age (SD = 1.3). A subsample of 22 young people participated in the qualitative data collection. This subsample included a nearly equal number of boys and girls (males = 10; females = 12) ranging in ages from 10 to 13 with 11 as the modal age. The subsample mirrored the ethnicities of the larger sample with Latinas/os, Asian Americans, African Americans, and mixed ethnicities where Latinas/os were the modal group (63%).

2.2. Procedures and measures

2.2.1. Recruitment procedure

Criteria for participation included being in 6th, 7th, or 8th grade (or equivalent age) and living within the defined public housing boundaries of 1 of the 3 neighborhoods. One hundred sixty-six youth met the sampling criteria during September to November 2005 based on housing lists, although it became apparent during the data collection that the housing lists were not updated. Therefore, youth were permitted to participate if they met the criteria

> Provided here are discussions of the sample and sample sizes for the quantitative portion, as well as for the qualitative portion, of the study.

even if their name was not on the housing list. Extensive efforts were made to interview all eligible participants. Flyers describing the study were distributed throughout the neighborhoods and parents and youth participants were contacted in person by members of the research team. Parental consent was obtained during the recruitment process and youth assent was obtained prior to the interview. Interview questions from the surveys were read aloud and recorded by members of the research team during the individual interview to ensure comprehension due to language barriers and below grade level reading ability and to also minimize missing data. Youth were given the option to complete the survey in Spanish; all youth were English-speaking and bilingual students chose to complete the survey and interviews in English.

A subsample of 22 participants provided the qualitative data for this study through their responses to open-ended questions posed to assess their perceptions of their neighborhoods and neighbors. The subsample was recruited from the Girl's Group and Cub Scout meetings at the after-school program in each of the neighborhoods. Most scholars consider a sample size of 22 to be more than adequate in qualitative analysis. Hill et al. (1997) recommend between 8 and 15 cases for establishing "consistency in findings and providing examples to initially hypothesize about the limits of those findings" (as cited in Franklin & Ballan, 2001, p. 278).

2.2.2. Participant data

We selected measures that were normed on ethnically diverse, urban populations given the ethnic and cultural diversity of the three neighborhoods. The Daily Hassles Microsystem Scale (DHMS) and Neighborhood Cohesion Scale (NCS) (Seidman et al., 1995), were specifically developed and validated as instruments suitable for poor, urban, and culturally diverse adolescents.

> The survey used by the authors was a pre-established instrument. The authors also include information regarding the validity and reliability of the resulting data.

The DHMS consists of 28 items that focus on family, peer, school, and neighborhood hassles. Examples of daily hassles items include, "Not having your own room" and "Being approached by a drug dealer in your neighborhood." Responses to DHMS items range from (1) Hasn't happened this month to (5) A very big hassle. The DHMS total scale demonstrated good reliability, with a Cronbach's alpha of 0.88. The mean score on the DHMS ($N = 153$) was 73.85 (SD = 17.80).

Neighborhood cohesion items specifically focus on the youth's perception of neighborhood dynamics. Participants select a response ranging from (1) Very true to (4) Not true at all to statements such as "If I had the chance, I would like to move out of my neighborhood" and "The relationships I have with my neighbors mean a lot to me." The Cronbach's alpha for the NCS was 0.80. The Neighborhood Cohesion Scale consists of 11 items; the mean score ($N = 153$) was 33.33 (SD = 5.98). Youth were asked as part of the NCS to describe the area they are thinking of when they think of neighborhood. The majority of youth (84%) selected descriptions of neighborhood that more closely resemble a proximal area such as a census block group rather than tract group (i.e., "several apartments or houses around yours" versus "everybody who goes to my school or the shopping center I go to"). Additionally, conversations with a subset of youth during the qualitative data collection confirmed that

they understood the concepts of neighbor and neighborhood to be proximal to their residence.

The qualitative data were derived from participants' written work in response to pre-designed, open-ended questions about their neighborhoods and neighbors, and were collected in the winter and spring of 2005. Participants wrote descriptions of their neighborhoods and neighboring experiences during four time segments of 30–45 min that took place over three to four weeks. Each 30–45 min segment was divided into 10–15 min periods such that participants: (1) spent some time in large group conversations that elicited their understanding of the concepts of neighbor and neighborhood, (2) had opportunities to create colorful drawings of their neighborhoods in reality as well as how they imagined they would like them to be, and (3) completed written responses to the questions noted below. In order to account for difficulties with writing, all participants were offered the opportunity to dictate their ideas in response to each question. In addition, these structured activities were interspersed with game activities to account for the energy levels of the young people.

> Good description of the interview protocol used during the study.

> It appears as if the quantitative data were collected first and that the qualitative data were used to better inform the results of the quantitative data; that would make this an explanatory mixed-methods design. However, some could argue that is more representative of a triangulation design.

To simplify the data collection of written responses, each respondent was provided with a brief worksheet for each question. The worksheets presented each question divided into its logical parts followed by blank lines on which he or she could write a response. Responses varied in length from 6 to 10 sentences. The questions posed in the worksheets are: "A place I like in my neighborhood is . . . I like that place because"; "A place I do not like in my neighborhood is . . . I do not like that place because"; "A neighbor I like is . . . I like that neighbor because . . . Some of the things this neighbor does are. . . ." In addition to these questions, participants were asked to write "letters" in which they could: (1) describe something they would change about their neighborhood and (2) tell a neighbor they like some of the ways they have been helped by them and some of the things they have learned from them. While the atmosphere of the club meetings was not at all similar to a school classroom setting, care was taken to inform the young people that there were no right or wrong answers to the questions.

2.2.3. Neighborhood data

The availability of resources in each neighborhood was assessed by the Neighborhood Resources Measure (Nicotera & Anthony, 2006). The idea for this measure is based on the work of Sheidow, Gorman-Smith, Tolan and Henry (2001). We utilized a systematic recording process to survey each of the three neighborhoods. Using U.S. Census information to map the tract and block groups, the survey involved first driving along the outer street boundaries and then the

> Existing data were also collected on the neighborhoods.

streets within those boundaries while recording each resource (i.e., elementary school, bank, etc.) by name and location, first for the tract and then for the block group of each neighborhood. This process was followed for the 3 census tracts and 3 block groups of the 3 neighborhoods. Despite the fact that census block groups are subsumed in census tracts, driving each as a separate entity allowed for clearer delineation between the number and type of resources in each tract and block group as separate entities. This also provided a check on the consistency of resources found between this overlapping area of each of the 3 tracts and block groups. The general U.S. Census data for these 3 neighborhoods indicates significant levels of unemployment (range from 44% to 56%) and poverty (range from 34% to 51%). The three neighborhoods were somewhat small in comparison to larger city areas based on the number of households. It is also important to note that the public housing units in the neighborhoods consisted of individual, single level apartments rather than a large high-rise complex.

Resources were initially listed without category by name and were later re-coded by resource type such as bank, ethnic market, check cashing service, fast food, etc. Due to the number of different resources, items were collapsed into the following categories:

1. Resident support resources (e.g., social service agency, bank, church/temple, medical/dental facility, school, park, recreation facility)
2. Resident spending resources (e.g., gas station, auto sales/parts/repair, fast food, liquor store, corner store, restaurant, check cashing, beauty supply/parlor, cell phone store)
3. Non-resident resources (e.g., distribution/industry, junk yard, home improvement stores, moving supplies/truck or machine rentals)
4. Legal/financial services (e.g., realtor, bail bonds, insurance/ financial services, attorney)

Categories were established by combining resources with similar characteristics. When a resource did not fit into an existing category, a new category emerged. With a focus on individuals and families living in public housing, the categories were determined based on utility to local residents. For example, resident support resources consist of services that local residents might utilize for health, social, financial, academic, recreational, or spiritual needs. Similarly, resident spending resources include services or goods that are available to local residents to support daily life activities. In contrast, non-resident resources consist of services located in the neighborhood that either are not likely to be used by local residents or are not for the betterment of the community as a whole. For example, a grocery store distribution center

is located in one of the neighborhoods and while it may serve as a place of employment for some residents, there is no major grocery store located in the same neighborhood. Therefore, residents live with the industrial blight of the distribution center, but have to travel outside of the community to get to the stores for consumer use. This is especially difficult for single parents with young children who may have to take one or two buses to reach a grocery store. Additionally, since the families of the young people in this study reside in rental properties with strict housing authority rules they are not likely to access the home improvement stores even though they are located nearby. Lastly, legal/financial services consist of a variety of services located in the community for residents' financial or legal needs. Resources in each category were summed for the tract and block groups for each neighborhood. The mean and standard deviation for each of the resource categories by tract and block group is provided in Table 1.

2.3. Analytic approach

Several analytic techniques were employed to address the study hypotheses. Regression analyses examined the relationship between neighborhood resources as they are grouped and youth report of neighborhood cohesion and hassles. The

> Regression analyses were used to analyze the quantitative survey data.

use of raw numbers rather than rates and the analysis of block group rather than tract group reflect the study's focus on young people's proximal experience in the neighborhood. Additionally, whereas older adolescents may have more mobility beyond the block groups, younger youth are more likely to stay within the immediate neighborhood.

The legal/financial resources category was dropped from the analysis given the lack of such resources in two

Table 1 Resources by Neighborhood Tract and Block Group

Resource category	*M*	(SD)
Resident support		
Tract	24.0	(8.8)
Block	5.3	(3.2)
Resident spending		
Tract	53.0	(39.3)
Block	9.3	(7.0)
Non-resident		
Tract	15.0	(11.1)
Block	8.3	(6.6)
Legal/financial		
Tract	7.0	(5.0)
Block	0.3	(0.5)

of the three neighborhood block groups. Further, resident spending and non-resident resources were highly correlated (r =.94), suggesting these two resources may in fact represent one resource category statistically, even if they represent different qualities for neighborhood residents. Due to this concern about multicollinearity, each resource was entered separately into the analysis. After examining each resource in the model separately, resident spending and non-resident resources were combined to form a category labeled spending resources. While resident spending and non-resident resources are quantitatively correlated, they have important qualitative differences, as we discuss.

All qualitative data were entered into Atlas-Ti 5.0 (Muhr, 2004) for the analysis. Analytic procedures followed the method of constant comparative analysis (Lincoln & Guba, 1985) during which initial codes are developed from the local language (in-vivo codes) of the participants.

> Interview data were analyzed using the constant comparative method of analysis.

The initial use of in-vivo codes is especially important in analysis of data produced by youth to avoid placing an adult lens on the young voices. For example, one of the participants noted a neighbor as a resource who teaches him how to "pump a BB gun" and others noted adult rule enforcers as a hassle. An adult lens would not necessarily consider these as a resource and hassle respectively. However, in order to honor the voices of the young participants in the subsample, these were included in their respective themes.

The second coding assessed the in-vivo codes for commonalities across the participants. At this stage of the analysis four general themes emerged: formal resources; informal resources; people resources; and hassles. Further analysis of the in-vivo codes and quotes for support of these initial themes resulted in maintenance of all 4 with the additional division of people resources into 2 sub-themes, social-emotional resources and instrumental resources. A final round of analysis

examined the codes and quotes in each theme for further commonalities across the 22 participants and all four themes remained. These themes are reported in the next section.

3. RESULTS

Four models were analyzed for daily hassles and neighborhood cohesion, respectively, allowing examination of each neighborhood resource separately. All models were analyzed with the robust option in STATA 9.0 (StataCorp, 2005) that uses the Huber/White/sandwich estimator of the variance. Table 2 reports the regression results predicting daily hassles with each resource separately and then the final model (Model 4) with the combined category, spending.

Model 4 predicted 15% of the variance in youth report of hassles. As predicted, results indicated a gender effect; females were significantly more likely than males to report daily hassles in the final model ($B = 7.0$, $p < 0.01$). Particularly given the developmental transition represented by the age of the young people in the study, higher levels of hassles for girls are consistent with prior findings (Seidman et al., 1995). Age (centered at age 10), however, was not significant in the model. While we expected to find higher levels of hassles in older youth, the results may be due to the limited age range in the sample. We might expect older youth to report more hassles due to their developmental period and perception of age-related hassles as compared to the younger youth who compose our sample.

As shown in Table 2, the number of resident support resources also had a significant effect on daily hassles. As predicted, higher levels of resident support resources were associated with lower levels of daily hassles ($B = -2.53$, $p < 0.001$). Results for nonresident resources, resident spending resources, and the combined spending resource category were non-significant.

Table 2   Regression of Daily Hassles on Individual Characteristics and Neighborhood Resources

	Model 1	Model 2	Model 3	Model 4
	B (SE)	*B* (SE)	*B* (SE)	*B* (SE)
Age	0.85 (1.0)	0.52 (1.1)	0.59 (1.0)	0.96 (0.99)
Gender (female = 1)	6.73 (2.8)*	5.83 (2.8)*	6.0 (2.8)*	7.0 (2.7)**
Resident support	−2.19 (0.49)***			−2.53 (0.54)***
Resident spending		0.38 (0.28)		
Non-resident			−0.28 (0.29)	
Spending (combined)				−0.24 (0.17)
F	9.55	2.26	1.99	8.04
R^2	0.13	0.04	0.03	0.15

Note. $N = 153$.
*$p < 0.05$; **$p < 0.0001$.

Table 3 presents the findings from the regression analyses predicting neighborhood cohesion. Contrary to our prediction, results for resident support resources, spending resources, and non-resident resources were non-significant. Results for age and gender were also non-significant in all models predicting neighborhood cohesion. Table 3 reports results for the final model which included the combined spending category. The qualitative findings assist in further exploration of the results from the regression analyses.

The qualitative analysis uncovered four themes: hassles, people resources, informal resources, and formal resources. The themes are summarized in Table 4 and presented here within the context of the quantitative findings in order to explicate the mixed methods component of the study results. The first theme, hassles, represents social and physical difficulties faced by the participants. Hassles, as measured through the qualitative data, arose from what the youth noted about the presence and absence of particular neighborhood qualities. This theme unpacks the hassles as measured in the survey, dividing them into hassles that result from people and those that, while also the result of human actions, exist as if outside human identities or actions. Hassles perpetrated by people range from concerns about shootings, prostitutes, and gangs to mean neighbors, mean housing managers and homeless people to local bullies and adults who act as rule enforcers in the neighborhood. Hassles that appear to occur outside of human actions include: trash and graffiti and lack of amenities such as banks, malls, public events, and playground equipment. The range of severity of the people hassles is exemplified in the following two quotes: "I would change the murderings, gun shootings, prostitutes, gangs, and fighting" and "You want to live in my neighborhood now because we have no chores to do . . . We would have a lot of fun with no one to boss us around." The range of place hassles is indicated in the following quotes: "I do not like the park. People come and write cuss words on everything,"

and "It's [the neighborhood] different now because I built a sports center—basketball."

The theme people resources consists of neighbors that were described as resources in the participants' lives. The resources associated with this theme can be viewed as instrumental and social-emotional. The instrumental people resources teach some kind of skill or provide some kind of service. For example, one young participant wrote the following about a neighbor, "She taught me how to cook, eggs, pasta, French bread pizza." Another young person noted a neighbor who "tries to teach my mom English because she knows a little Spanish." In contrast, the social-emotional people resources are described as part of the participants' sense of belonging-friendship as well as those which provide humor in their daily lives. This is exemplified in the following quotes about peers "He's really funny, tells jokes, makes me laugh" and "She's fun to be around. I like her family, she likes me, I like to sleep over." While these aspects of people resources are displayed as two separate entities, clearly they can be related in that the young person learning to cook under the tutelage of a neighbor may also acquire a sense of belonging from that same experience. On the whole, this theme provides insight into a type of neighborhood resource not assessed by the structural neighborhood resources measure utilized in the quantitative analysis. The structural neighborhood resources measure does not account for the kind of face-to-face and heart-to-heart resources depicted in the qualitative results, through which the youth develop a connection to neighbors. Additionally, the qualitative data that support this theme uncover more personal details than those assessed in the quantitative measure of cohesion.

The next theme, informal resources, consists of places such as parks, one's own home or yard and fields or other natural areas. It also represents particular characteristics and opportunities that are made available through the informal

Table 3   Regression of Neighborhood Cohesion on Individual Characteristics and Neighborhood Resources

	Model 1	Model 2	Model 3	Model 4
	B (SE)	*B* (SE)	*B* (SE)	*B* (SE)
Age	−0.61 (0.36)	−0.64 (0.36)	−0.64 (0.35)	−0.60 (0.36)
Gender (female = 1)	0.61 (0.94)	0.53 (0.96)	0.53 (0.96)	0.62 (0.94)
Resident support	−0.20 (0.18)			−0.22 (0.19)
Resident spending		0.05 (0.10)		
Non-resident			−0.00 (0.11)	
Spending (combined)				−0.01 (0.06)
F	1.69	1.32	1.19	1.26
R^2	0.03	0.02	0.02	0.03

Note. N = 153.

Table 4   Qualitative Results with Representative Quotes

Theme	Characterization	Quotes
Hassles (people and place)	Gangs, drunks, prostitutes, beggars, bullies, murders-shootings, mean housing manager, accidents, rule enforcers, graffiti-trash, bad smells, no bank, no mall, no sports center, small apartments	"I would change the murderings, gun shootings, prostitutes, gangs, and fighting." "My neighborhood is different now because [they] destroyed 10 houses and built a shopping mall next door to me."
People resources (instrumental and social-emotional)	Teaching skills and/or providing service, providing humor and/or a sense of belonging	"She gave us a plant, let me watch a movie at her house and took us to school." "They are cool. [We] listen to a lot of rap [and] have dance contests.
Informal resources	Own yard, friend's home, field or natural area privacy, active fun, lots of kids, place for conversation, place to relax	"My friend's house. She has 2 rooms that don't have anything but toys and we play in them." "My backyard. I could play games there, keep my privacy and it's not that noisy."
Formal resources	After-school program, Boys and Girls club, learning academics, social skills, technology, freedom, relax	"We help with homework or read a book with you [at the neighborhood after school program]." "I like the [at the neighborhood after school program] cause I can sit around."

> Great idea for the authors to include actual quotes from participants in order to support their resulting themes.

resources such as privacy, access to peers for company, fun, conversation, and relaxation. For example, one participant made this statement about her backyard, "I don't feel lonely there; I can talk to my neighbor; I play around there." Another young person described a natural area in which he liked to play with his peers, "Big hill in our neighborhood. We roll balls down it and go down it on my body."

The last theme, formal resources, represents formal, agency-run resources in the neighborhoods such as the Boys and Girls Club. Similar to informal resources, these formal resources are also noted for their characteristics and opportunities. However, the characteristics and opportunities found within them are different from those noted about informal resources. For example, the young people point out the many things they do when accessing formal resources such as attending groups, getting homework help, and playing on computers. While the actual number of formal neighborhood resources, as counted in the neighborhood resource measure, is limited, it is clear that these few resources provide important support for the young people. This is demonstrated in the following quotes: "At the [name of local neighborhood after school program] there is fun stuff to do, girls group, computer, tutor," and "I like going to that place [Girls and Boys Club] you can do anything you want." The last 2 themes, informal and formal resources, highlight the young people's depiction of the numerous advantages and opportunities available to them in their neighborhoods and demonstrate the potential that these resources can play

in combating other neighborhood risks or deficits. Additionally, while the formal resources exist as a component of the structural neighborhood resource measure, that measure cannot account for their particular influence on the youth as found in the qualitative results.

4. DISCUSSION

The current study explored the relationships between structural neighborhood resources, youth neighborhood experiences and perceptions, and their subjective appraisal of hassles and cohesion. The quantitative analysis demonstrated a clear relationship between structurally identified neighborhood resources and young people's

> In this paragraph, the authors integrate the results of the quantitative and qualitative analyses.

self-reported hassles. A greater number of supportive resources are associated with a reduction in the level of hassles youth experience in daily life. Resident support resources include resources catering to parents (i.e., social service agency or medical facility) and resources for youth (i.e., park and school). Based on these different types of resources we speculate that when parents are less hassled, young people are less hassled. This speculation is bolstered by several quotes from the qualitative results in which youth express concerns about hassles that impact a parent, such as the young person who desires "A nice manager who is not so hard on them if they're poor and the rent is overdue." The qualitative results also provide the nuances of hassles that cannot be detected from the survey questions and suggest that, in addition to an awareness of how their parents are hassled, these young participants are very much aware of the elements through which they personally feel hassled in their neighborhoods. In contrast, the young people's description of the advantages and opportunities available to them via both informal and formal resources in their neighborhoods reflects a heightened awareness of the role neighborhood resources play in combating the hassles (or neighborhood risks or deficits) that youth astutely point out in the qualitative findings.

The association between structurally identified resources and young people's level of neighborhood cohesion was nonsignificant. Several factors may contribute to this finding. Prior analysis with this sample suggests that neighborhood cohesion cannot easily be understood as a risk or protective factor (Anthony, 2008). In the prior study, attachment to the neighborhood (reporting a high level of neighborhood cohesion) appeared to be protective, except when other risk levels (i.e., individual, family, and peer) are high. In these cases, high neighborhood risk exposure may lead to weak psychological connections to neighborhood and community for youth with few individual, interpersonal, and family resources. For youth who have a number of protective factors across levels of influence, neighborhood cohesion may be adaptive. Youth who are protected may think of the social support and other protective factors in their lives when responding to questions about their neighborhood. For other youth, however, responding positively to items such as "I feel like I fit in with the people in my neighborhood" and "The relationships I have with my neighbors mean a lot to me" may not be protective. This arises in the qualitative results when one participant notes that a helpful neighbor is someone who assists him in learning to "pump a BB gun." In neighborhoods where youth are exposed to gang activity and other violent activity as well as drug dealing, it may very well be risky to have high levels of neighborhood cohesion in the absence of other resources.

The fact that the young people in our sample all reside in low-income, public housing neighborhoods combined with the nonsignificant results for cohesion is consistent with Zeldin and Topitzes' (2002) work. They found that urban adolescents (aged 13 to 18) from families with higher incomes reported a stronger sense of community. This suggests that neighborhood cohesion may serve a different function based on other protective factors and resources related to family and neighborhood socioeconomic status. In addition, preliminary studies suggest that neighborhood attachment, though frequently examined as a single construct, is multidimensional (Woldoff, 2002). Our qualitative results for the theme, "people resources," certainly attest to the multidimensionality of neighborhood cohesion. Further studies to clarify the role of neighborhood cohesion in the context of other risk and protective factor patterns are needed.

Finally, we examine the quantitative and qualitative results to consider how young people's responses to open-ended queries about their neighborhood and neighbors as resources compare to survey measures of cohesion, hassles, and structurally identified neighborhood resources. The quantitative measure of neighborhood cohesion poses general questions to discover if respondents feel they fit in with those who live in their neighborhood, if relationships with neighbors mean a lot to them as well as perceptions about neighborhood quality (i.e., gotten worse in past 2 years; better place to live than other nearby neighborhoods; there are people who sell drugs in the neighborhood). The qualitative results indicate the presence of relationships and experiences that promote neighborhood cohesion. These also reflect the latent qualities of cohesion posed in the survey items. For example, one participant noted a neighbor who is "nice [because] she gives us things [and] her friend gives us a ride." Two others suggest closer ties when one notes the following about a neighbor, "She gives us treats, snacks, a free cat, a collar. She lets us play with her dogs. Lets us play inside her house with her kittens. [She] comes to visit us [and] gives us money," and the other points out a neighbor noting that "He give[s] me food and let[s] me use the phone." Participants also described relationships through which they develop skills and garner a sense of belonging, which may also be related to neighborhood cohesion. For example one young person wrote, "[These are some of the things I have learned from you] Is sometimes being more mean [assertive] and to listen in school." Another youth noted the following: "[These are some of the things I have learned from you] How to do things. How to help people with things. [These are some of the ways you have helped me] To take care of K. [a baby]. Helped me with things I can't do." A sense of belonging is noted by the young people who wrote: "I can also talk to my neighbors that I like;" "He is my friend and hangs out with me;" "[A place I like in my neighborhood is] Playground because there are lots of kids that go there and [I] play with my friend, [I like that place because] They have lot of kids that play on there and I could play with my friend," and "[She] takes me to the movies, she pays my sister money for babysitting."

The extra familial social supports and indications of a sense of belonging depicted in the qualitative results along with our quantitative finding that physical resources are not significantly related to neighborhood cohesion, is perhaps an indication that these informal, extra familial resources are more integral to neighborhood cohesion and resulting collective efficacy than tangible neighborhood resources such as access to grocery stores or medical clinics. Future studies that examine the relationship between neighborhood extra familial resources and youth's sense of belonging in neighborhood, along with physical neighborhood resources would assist in untangling this web.

Another layer of the cohesion conundrum can be accessed by considering the neighborhood resources noted in the qualitative results, such as parks and playgrounds that would promote opportunities for cohesion. These resources need to be considered within the context of the reports of hassles related specifically to them and other neighborhood environments. Viewed from this perspective, neighborhood hassles, or neighborhood risk factors, can prohibit the development of cohesion that might ordinarily be accessed through resources such as parks. The qualitative examples that follow reflect the underlying qualities assessed through the quantitative survey items about hassles and how they can prohibit the development of cohesion in places where one would expect it to occur. These hassles are related to school, difficulties with friends, being left out, fears due to presence of unsavory characters in the neighborhood, and lack of spaces for play. For example, a street in the neighborhood where residents can access "resident spending resources" is described by one of the youth in this way, "I don't go their [sic] cause it's scary." Another youth notes the "hill" as a fun place to roll down, but notes, "The hill gets hot. It's itchy—then when I get wet it itches really bad." Still another young person stated that he didn't like school or the playground because "I fall everyday and I don't like to play basketball because everybody pushes me. I don't like school because everybody push[es] me."

There are other more serious hassles that serve to prohibit cohesion such as gangs, shootings, and prostitutes in public spaces like parks and playgrounds. For example, one young person wished to "kick all the bullies out" so that "You won't have to bothered by people who trash your house and put bubble gum on your passenger seat." Another youth points out why the park is more about hassle than cohesion when he refers to, "The bad people who are always drinking beer are there." A third youth notes, "[I don't like] Gangs around my projects. Sometimes they get drunk and they make trouble and accidents. A drunk guy got hit in the head with a shovel. He slipped and broke his neck." In essence, the hassles described in the qualitative results and quantified in the survey items mirror Garbarino's (1995) discussion of the term, social toxicity. He notes the elements of social

toxicity to include, "violence, poverty, economic pressures on parents and their children, disruption of relationships, nastiness, despair, depression, paranoia, alienation—all the things that demoralize families and communities" (pp. 4–5). While the young people in the qualitative subsample readily describe important relationships and environmental opportunities to develop neighborhood cohesion, it may be fair to say that these are outweighed by their experiences of hassles or social toxicities.

The results of this study warrant further exploration of the multidimensional nature of neighborhood cohesion in the context of neighborhood resources and hassles. As noted, our results suggest an association between structural neighborhood resources, a quantitative measure of youth hassles, and their subjective appraisal of neighborhood hassles. However, structural neighborhood resources did not significantly predict youth experiences and perceptions related to neighborhood cohesion as measured quantitatively. The qualitative results, as discussed, assist in unpacking this nonsignificant result. This variation sets the stage for future research as depicted in Fig. 1. This figure suggests that youth's subjective appraisal of neighborhood resources (qualitative themes: people resources, informal resources, and formal resources) influence their perceptions and experiences of neighborhood life which result in levels of neighborhood cohesion in a nested context. This nested context, as depicted in Fig. 1, proposes that parental access to structural neighborhood resources may reduce their hassles, which may in turn leave them with more energy to engage with neighborhood youth, thereby enhancing neighborhood cohesion among youth. This model proposes the adaptive characteristics of neighborhood influences that may mobilize a chain of positive responses to support both adults and youth residing in poverty-level neighborhoods. Furstenberg, Cook, Eccles, Elder, and Sameroff (1999) similarly indicate the influence of a neighborhood's social and material resources on family management and, in turn, adolescent success. As Furstenberg et al. (1999) suggest, neighborhood influences

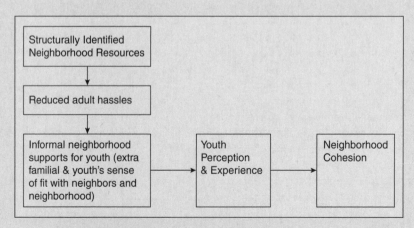

Figure 1
Mechanisms of influence for future study

do not simply cause family management practices that then impact adolescent behavior. Rather, neighborhood influences and family influences interact in complex ways. The model in Fig. 1 echoes this complexity with an emphasis on the importance of extra familial neighborhood supports and a focus on neighborhood cohesion.

4.1. Limitations and future directions

Drawbacks of this study should be noted. First, participants for the subgroup contributing the qualitative data for the study were recruited from the Girl's Group and Cub Scout meetings at the after-school program in each of the neighborhoods. The bias toward young people who may participate regularly in the after-school program therefore exists in this purposive sample, where it does not exist in the larger sample of 153 youth who were recruited broadly from the neighborhood. Prior analyses, however, indicate that youth were distributed across cluster groups of risk and protective factors regardless of participation in the afterschool program, minimizing concerns about differences between the two samples (Anthony, 2008).

Finally, the authors identify limitations to their current study and provide recommendations for future research.

The reliance on youth self-report for cohesion, daily hassles, and perceptions of neighbor and neighborhood, with the exception of the Neighborhood Resources Measure, pose a drawback to the study design. The limitations of youth self-report have been described (Vandell & Posner, 1999) however in this study, youth self-report was necessary for examining the transaction between youth perception and the structural characteristics of the neighborhood. Additionally, studies indicate that young people have a unique way of understanding the proximal neighborhood environment that often eludes objective structural descriptions of a neighborhood. As Prout (2000) points out, " . . . children are social actors, with a part to play in their own representation . . ." (p. xi). The unique perceptions and experiences of youth living in the three public housing neighborhoods were therefore best captured by the mixed method design and reliance on self-report.

In sum, the current study highlights the importance of young people's perceptions of neighborhood influences and the positive role of formal, informal, and people resources in navigating other neighborhood deficits. Our results reflect the complex and varied nature of daily hassles for youth living in urban poverty. While structural characteristics such as poverty and social disorganization impact risk levels for youth, our results suggest considerable variation in how individual youth perceive these influences. Future studies that examine neighborhood resources from an objective and subjective youth-oriented experience would be enhanced by considering the role of parental perceptions

of the neighborhood context. Such studies could examine the nested relationship which suggests that youth of less hassled parents experience less hassles themselves as well as the nested relationships depicted in Fig. 1. Finally, the multidimensional construct of neighborhood cohesion warrants further study.

References

Anthony, E. K. (2008). Cluster profiles of youths living in urban poverty: Factors impacting risk and resilience. *Social Work Research, 32*(1), 6–17.

Anthony, E. K., & Nicotera, N. (2008). Youth perceptions of neighborhood hassles and resources: A mixed methods analysis. *Children and Youth Services Review, 30*, 1246–1255. © 2008 Elsevier Ltd. Reprinted by permission.

Bronfenbrenner, U. (1979). *The ecology of human development: Experiments by nature and design.* Cambridge, MA: Harvard University Press.

Brook, J. S., Kessler, R. C., & Cohen, P. (1999). The onset of marijuana use from preadolescence and early adolescence to young adulthood. *Development and Psychopathology, 1*(4), 901–914.

Brooks-Gunn, J., Duncan, G. J., & Aber, J. L. (1997). *Neighborhood poverty.* New York: Russell Sage Foundation.

Burton, L. (1991). Caring for children: Drug shifts and their impact on families. *American Enterprise, 2*, 34–37.

Burton, L. (1997). Ethnography and meaning of adolescence in high-risk neighborhoods. *Ethos, 25*(2), 208–217.

Burton, L., & Price-Spratlen, T. (1999). Through the eyes of children: An ethnographic perspective on neighborhoods and child development. In A. S. Masten (Ed.), *Cultural processes in child development* (pp. 77–96). Mahwah, NJ: Lawrence Erlbaum Associates.

Cauce, A. M., Stewart, A., Rodriguez, M. D., Cochran, B., & Ginzler, J. (2003). Overcoming the odds? Adolescent development in the context of urban poverty. In S. S. Luthar (Ed.), *Resilience and vulnerability: Adaptation in the context of childhood adversities* (pp. 343–363). Cambridge: Cambridge University Press.

Clark, R. L. (1992). *Neighborhood effects on dropping out of school among teenage boys.* Washington, D.C: Urban Institute.

Coulton, C. J., Korbin, J., Su, M., & Chow, J. (1995). Community level factors and child maltreatment rates. *Child Development, 66*, 1262–1276.

Coulton, C. J., & Pandey, S. (1992). Geographic concentration of poverty and risk to children in urban neighborhoods. *American Behavioral Scientist, 35*(3), 238–257.

Duncan, G. J., Brooks-Gunn, J., & Klebanov, P. K. (1994). Economic deprivation and early childhood development. *Child Development, 65*, 296–318.

Figueira-McDonough, J. (1998). Environment and interpretation: Voices of young people in poor inner-city neighborhoods. *Youth and Society, 30*(2), 123–163.

Franklin, C., & Ballan, M. (2001). Reliability in qualitative research. In B. A. Thyer (Ed.), *Handbook of social work research* (pp. 273–292). Newbury Park, CA: Sage Publications.

Fraser, M. W., Kirby, L. D., & Smokowski, P. R. (2004). Risk and resilience in childhood. In M. W. Fraser (Ed.), *Risk and resilience in childhood: An ecological perspective* (pp. 13–66), 2nd ed. Washington, D.C.: NASW Press.

Furstenberg, F. F., Jr., Cook, T. D., Eccles, J., Elder, G. H., Jr., & Sameroff, A. (1999). *Managing to make it: Urban families and adolescent success.* Chicago: University of Chicago Press.

Garbarino, J. (1995). *Raising children in a socially toxic environment.* San Francisco: Jossey-Bass.

Garbarino, J., Galambos, N., Plantz, M., & Kostelny, K. (1992). The territory of childhood. In J. Garbarino (Ed.), *Children and families in the social environment* (pp. 202–229), 2nd edition. New York: Aldine de Gruyter, Inc.

Gorman-Smith, D., Tolan, P. H., & Henry, D. B. (1999). The relation of community and family to risk among urban poor adolescents. In P. Cohen, L. Robins, & C. Slomskowski (Eds.), *Where and when: Influence of historical time and place on aspects of psychopathology.* Hillsdale, NJ: Erlbaum.

Hawkins, J. D., Smith, B. H., Hill, K. G., Kosterman, R., Catalano, R. F., & Abbott, R. D. (2007). Promoting social development and preventing health and behavior problems during the elementary grades: Results from the Seattle Social Development Project. *Victims & Offenders, 2*(2), 161–181.

Hill, C., Thompson, B., & Williams, E. (1997). A guide to conducting consensual qualitative research. *The Consulting Psychologist, 25*(4), 517–572.

Kanner, A. D., Coyne, J. C., Schaefer, C., & Lazarus, R. S. (1981). Comparison of two modes of stress measurement: Daily hassles, uplifts and major life events to health status. *Journal of Behavioral Medicine, 4,* 1–39.

Korbin, J. E. (2001). Context and meaning in neighborhood studies of children and families. In A. Booth & A. C. Crouter (Eds.), *Does it take a village? Community effects on children, adolescents, and families* (pp. 79–86). Mahwah, NJ: Lawrence Erlbaum Associates, Inc.

Lazarus, R. S., & Folkman, S. (1984). *Stress, appraisal and coping.* New York: Springer.

Lincoln, Y., & Guba, E. (1985). *Naturalistic inquiry.* London: Sage Publications.

Luthar, S. S., & Cushing, G. (1999). Neighborhood influences and child development: A prospective study of substance abusers' offspring. *Development and Psychopathology, 11*(4), 763–784.

Muhr, T. (2004). *User's Manual for ATLAS.ti 5.0, ATLAS.ti Scientific Software Development GmbH, Berlin.*

Nicotera, N. (2007). Measuring neighborhood: A conundrum for human services researchers and practitioners. *American Journal of Community Psychology, 40*(1–2), 26–51.

Nicotera, N. (2008). Children speak about neighborhoods: Using mixed methods to measure the construct neighborhood. *Journal of Community Psychology, 36*(3), 333–351.

Nicotera, N., & Anthony, E. K. (2006). *Neighborhood resources measure.* University of Denver, Graduate School of Social Work.

Prout, A. (2000). Forward. In P. Christensen & A. James (Eds.), *Research with children: Perspectives and practices* (pp. xi–xii). New York: Falmer Press.

Rowlison, R. T., & Felner, R. D. (1988). Major life events, hassles and adaptation in adolescence: Confounding in the concep-tualization and measurement of life stress and adjustment revisited. *Journal of Personality and Social Psychology, 55,* 432–444.

Sampson, R. J. (2001). How do communities undergird or undermine human development? Relevant contexts and social mechanisms. In A. Booth & A. C. Crouter (Eds.), *Does it take a village? Community effects on children, adolescents, and families* (pp. 3–30). Mahwah, NJ: Lawrence Erlbaum Associates, Inc.

Sampson, R. J., Raudenbush, S., & Earls, F. (1997). Neighborhoods and violent crime: A multilevel study of collective efficacy. *Science, 277,* 918–924.

Seidman, E., Allen, L., Aber, J. L., Mitchell, C., Feinman, J., Yoshikawa, H., et al. (1995). Development and validation of adolescent-perceived microsystem scales: Social support, daily hassles, and involvement. *American Journal of Community Psychology, 23*(3), 355–388.

Seidman, E., Yoshikawa, H., Roberts, A., Chesir-Teran, D., Allen, L., Friedman, J. L., et al. (1998). Structural and experiential neighborhood contexts, developmental stage, and antisocial behavior among urban adolescents in poverty. *Development and Psychopathology, 10,* 259–281.

Shaw, C. R., & McKay, H. D. (1942). *Juvenile delinquency in urban areas.* Chicago: University of Chicago Press.

Sheidow, A. J., Gorman-Smith, D., Tolan, P., & Henry, D. B. (2001). Family and community characteristics: Risk factors for violence exposure in inner-city youth. *Journal of Community Psychology, 29*(3), 345–360.

Spencer, M. B. (2001). Resiliency and fragility factors associated with the contextual experiences of low resource urban African American male youth and families. In A. Booth & A. C. Crouter (Eds.), *Does it take a village? Community effects on children adolescents, and families* (pp. 51–77). Mahwah, NJ: Lawrence Erlbaum Associates, Inc.

Spencer, M. B., Swanson, D. P., & Glymph, A. (1996). The prediction of parental psychological functioning: Influences of African American adolescent perceptions and experiences of context. In C. D. Ryff & M. M. Seltzer (Eds.), *The parental experience in midlife* (pp. 337–380). Chicago: University of Chicago Press.

StataCorp (2005). *Stata statistical software (Release 9.0) [Computer software].* College Station, TX: StataCorp LP.

Vandell, D., & Posner, J. (1999). Conceptualization and measurement of children's after-school environments. In S. Freidman & T. Wachs (Eds.), *Measuring environment across the life span: Emerging methods and concepts* (pp. 167–196). Washington, D.C.: American Psychological Association.

Woldoff, R. A. (2002). The effects of local stressors on neighborhood attachment. *Social Forces, 81*(1), 87–116.

Wyman, P. A. (2003). Emerging perspectives on context specificity of children's adaptation and resilience: Evidence from a decade of research with urban children in adversity. In S. S. Luthar (Ed.), *Resilience and vulnerability: Adaptation in the context of childhood adversities* (pp. 293–317). Cambridge: Cambridge University Press.

Zeldin, S., & Topitzes, D. (2002). Neighborhood experiences, community connection, and positive beliefs about adolescents among urban adults and youth. *Journal of Community Psychology, 30*(6), 647–669.

CHAPTER SUMMARY

Mixed-methods research designs combine quantitative and qualitative data and analyses. Often, this methodology can provide a better understanding, or a more complex picture, of the research topic than can one type of data alone. Mixed-methods designs can also be used when a researcher wants to build from or extend one phase of research to another. The three main types of mixed-methods designs are the explanatory, the exploratory, and the triangulation designs. The primary difference among these designs is the point during data collection that the two types of data are collected. The research process itself is relatively straightforward; however, important decisions must be made regarding the feasibility of and rationale behind a decision to use a mixed-methods approach.

LIST OF IMPORTANT TERMS

explanatory mixed-methods design	mixed-methods research designs	triangulation mixed-methods design
exploratory mixed-methods design	triangulation	

ACTIVITIES FOR THOUGHT AND DISCUSSION

1. Try to answer the following questions, which were presented at the beginning of the chapter.
   a. What is the main purpose of mixed-methods research?
   b. What are some reasons researchers might want to consider using mixed methods?
   c. What are the three different types of mixed-methods designs, and how do they differ?
   d. How does the process of conducting mixed-methods research differ from other types of research?
   e. What are the main strengths as well as limitations of mixed-methods research?
2. Suppose you wanted to study a community's satisfaction with its schools. Describe how you might plan your study, including your choice of mixed-methods design.
3. Suppose you wanted to research the climate of your local schools from various perspectives. Describe how you might plan your study, including your choice of mixed-methods design.
4. Locate an example of published survey research in a reputable journal. Compare and contrast it with the article that appears in its entirety in the chapter regarding (a) purpose, (b) research questions/hypotheses, (c) research design, (d) data collection and analysis, and (e) conclusions.

ANSWERS TO CHAPTER EXERCISES

Responses to the chapter exercise can vary and still be considered correct for individual students. It is suggested that responses be discussed and evaluated as group activities.

REFERENCES AND RECOMMENDED READINGS

Creswell, J. W. (2005). *Educational Research: Planning, Conducting, and Evaluating Quantitative and Qualitative Research* (2nd ed.). Upper Saddle River, NJ: Merrill/Prentice Hall.

Gay, L. R., Mills, G. E., & Airasian, P. (2006). *Educational Research: Competencies for Analysis and Application* (8th ed.). Upper Saddle River, NJ: Merrill/Prentice Hall.

Greene, J. C., & Caracelli, V. J. (Eds.). (1997). *Advances in Mixed-Method Evaluation: The Challenges and Benefits of Integrating Diverse Paradigms.* (New Directions for Program Evaluation, No. 74). San Francisco: Jossey-Bass.

McMillan, J. H. (2004). *Educational Research: Fundamentals for the Consumer* (4th ed.). Boston: Allyn & Bacon.

Mertens, D. M. (2005). *Research and Evaluation in Education and Psychology: Integrating Diversity with Quantitative, Qualitative, and Mixed Methods* (2nd ed.). Thousand Oaks, CA: Sage.

Tashakkori, A., & Teddlie, C. (1998). *Mixed Methodology: Combining Qualitative and Quantitative Approaches.* (Applied Social Research Methods Series, Vol. 46). Thousand Oaks, CA: Sage.

15

Action Research

PREVIEW

In this chapter we consider a type of educational research that has a very applied purpose: action research.

Action research is done by educational practitioners, usually at the local level, to resolve matters of concern in their particular setting. Action research is characterized as follows:

- Done by educators rather than professional researchers
- Accomplished in the local school setting
- Intended to resolve local school concerns or questions
- Not intended to be generalized to other groups or settings

TARGETED LEARNINGS

This chapter explores one type of educational research that has a very practical, applied focus. Action research is typically done by teachers or other educational practitioners. It is related to the local setting, such as a classroom, gymnasium, library, or shop, and is intended to resolve a problem for that locale only. As you read this chapter, look especially for information related to the following:

1. Of what value is action research to educational practitioners?
2. What are the key characteristics of action research?
3. What sorts of topics are best approached through action research?
4. What distinguishes action research from other types of research?
5. What are the procedures by which action research is carried out?

Action research

Action research is a catch-all label for research done by teachers, administrators, and other onsite educators to resolve problems at the local level. Mills (2007) has formally defined action research as "any systematic inquiry conducted by teacher researchers, principals, school counselors, or other stakeholders in the teaching/learning environment to gather

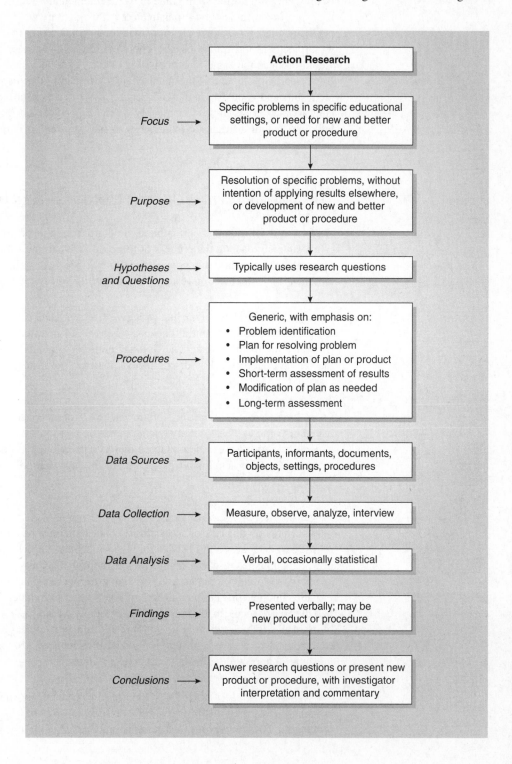

Action Research

Focus → Specific problems in specific educational settings, or need for new and better product or procedure

Purpose → Resolution of specific problems, without intention of applying results elsewhere, or development of new and better product or procedure

Hypotheses and Questions → Typically uses research questions

Procedures →
Generic, with emphasis on:
- Problem identification
- Plan for resolving problem
- Implementation of plan or product
- Short-term assessment of results
- Modification of plan as needed
- Long-term assessment

Data Sources → Participants, informants, documents, objects, settings, procedures

Data Collection → Measure, observe, analyze, interview

Data Analysis → Verbal, occasionally statistical

Findings → Presented verbally; may be new product or procedure

Conclusions → Answer research questions or present new product or procedure, with investigator interpretation and commentary

information about how their particular schools operate, how they teach, and how well their students learn" (p. 5). Its purpose is to develop reflective practice so that educators can effect positive change within their own educational environments; simply put, action research is research done *by* teachers *for* themselves.

Action research usually focuses on the development, implementation, and testing of a new product, plan, or procedure. A team of teachers might wish, for example, to develop and implement a new discipline plan for Elmwood Lincoln High School or a new creative writing program for the sixth grade in Cutter Elementary School. The research designs for these projects would not be sophisticated. Although there would be little hesitation in sharing the results of these investigations with others, any report that did so would explain that the project was illustrative of *one* school's efforts with little certainty that the procedures would produce the same results elsewhere (i.e., that the results would be generalizable). It is important to note that the focus of action research does *not* lie in its ability to generate results and conclusions that are generalizable to other settings or populations. On the contrary, action research focuses only on the immediate setting (e.g., classroom, school building, school district, etc.) and seeks to find answers to immediate problems or questions therein.

THE IMPORTANCE OF ACTION RESEARCH

Because it is for the most part applied in nature, action research has the potential to make a substantial impact on the process of teaching and learning. Action research is a methodological technique that truly connects research to practice. Mills (2007) lists several important means by which action research can impact the practice of education.

■ *Action research is persuasive and authoritative.*   Data collected during action research are persuasive and influential because teachers are invested in the legitimacy and careful collection of those data. The findings and recommendations are meaningful because they are not put forward by disconnected "experts" but instead by the experts in their own classrooms—teachers.

■ *Action research is relevant.*   Often, teachers express concern over the relevance of published research to what actually occurs in their classrooms and schools (i.e., a problem of generalizability). Research conducted by teachers or other educators in their actual work settings with their actual students results in findings that are directly applicable to those settings and individuals.

■ *Action research allows teachers access to research findings.*   Another problem with published research is lack of accessibility. Educators must be familiar with and have access to research databases and libraries that house the countless volumes of academic journals in which published research of interest may appear. Teachers may not have the time or the knack for sorting through hundreds of studies to find relevant information. Action research provides findings that are meaningful to practitioner researchers because *they* have identified the area of focus. In addition, instead of simply reading a study and becoming informed of its results (which typically does not result in positive changes to classroom practices), educators are directly responsible for and have direct access to those findings that are most meaningful in providing insight into *their* problems.

■ *Action research is not a fad.*   Good teaching has always involved systematically examining the instructional process and its effects on student learning. Teachers are always looking for ways to improve instructional practice, whether it be a new approach, new supplemental activities, or new techniques for reinforcement. Educators have seldom referred to this process of reflection, revision, and improvement as *research,* but that is exactly what it is.

■ *Action research can become an integral part of the daily process of teaching.* Once educators become aware of the proportion of time in their professional day that is spent doing this kind of reflection and revision, it becomes more obvious that this investment of time and effort is worth the potential outcomes. By integrating action research into daily teaching practices, educators feel the positive impact on both their personal and professional lives. This idea of reflective practice is part of what it means to be an educational professional.

CHARACTERISTICS OF ACTION RESEARCH

To learn more about designing action research studies, go to the "Action Research" section of **MyEducationLab for Research** and then click on *Assignments and Activities.* Complete the exercise titled "Action Research on the High School Science Club" to give you some practice at making important design decisions within an action research study.

Although a fairly straightforward process, action research is sometimes misunderstood by educational practitioners. Many aspects of action research characterize its uniqueness as an approach to conducting research, as indicated by the following partial list of characteristics describing action research (Mertler, 2009).

- Action research is a process that improves education by change.
- Action research is educators working together to improve their own practices.
- Action research is developing reflection about our teaching.
- Action research is collaborative; that is, it is educators talking and working with other educators in empowering relationships.
- Action research is a systematic learning process.
- Action research is a process that requires that we "test" our ideas about education.
- Action research is open-minded.
- Action research is a critical analysis of our places of work.
- Action research is an emphasis on the particular.
- Action research is a cycle of planning, acting, observing, and reflecting.
- Action research is a justification of our teaching practices.

Although it is important to understand what action research is, it is also important to understand what it is *not,* as shown in the following list also adapted from Mertler (2009).

- Action research is not the *usual* thing that teachers do when thinking about teaching. It is more systematic and more collaborative.
- Action research is not simply problem solving. Again, it is more systematic and involves the specification of a problem, the development of something new (in most cases), and reflection on its effectiveness.
- Action research is not done "to" or "by" other people. Action research is performed by particular educators on their *own* work.
- Action research is not a way to implement predetermined answers to educational questions. Action research explores, discovers, and works to create contextually specific solutions to educational problems.

At this point, you may be asking yourself an important question: "Why should I become involved in an action research project, especially with all the demands and responsibilities placed on me as an educator today?" There are several important reasons to consider involvement in such a project (Dick, 1993). Remember that action research deals with your problems, not someone else's. Second, action research is very timely; it can start now—or whenever you are ready—and provides immediate results. Third, action research provides educators with opportunities to better understand and, therefore, improve their educational practices. Fourth, as a process, action research can also promote the building of stronger relationships among colleagues with whom we work. Finally, and possibly most important, action research provides educators with alternative ways of viewing and approaching educational questions and problems and with new ways of examining our own educational practices.

These answers may have prompted yet another question in your mind: "Why doesn't everyone do action research?" First, although its popularity has increased over the past decade, action research is still relatively unknown compared to more traditional forms of conducting research. Second, although it may not seem the case, action research is more difficult to conduct than traditional approaches to research. Educators themselves are not only responsible for implementing the resultant changes but also for conducting the research itself. Third, action research does not conform to many of the requirements of conventional research with which you may be familiar—it is less structured and therefore more difficult to conduct. Finally, because of the lack of fit between standard research requirements and the process of conducting action research, you may find it more difficult to write up your results.

At this point in our discussion of action research, it is important to include another aspect of this methodology. It is important to remember that research, of any kind, is a scientific endeavor. Quality research must meet standards of sound practice, typically established through the concepts of validity and reliability. Action research, because of its participatory nature, relies on a different set of criteria (Stringer, 2007). Historically, however, one of the "weaknesses" of action research is the *perception* of a lower level of quality. Some people falsely believe that, because action research is conducted by teachers and other educators, and not academicians or researchers, it must be of lesser quality. This is, of course, not true.

It is the responsibility of the action researcher to ensure that the research is sound. The extent to which it reaches a standard of quality is directly related to the usefulness of the research findings for its intended audience. This level of quality in action research is referred to as its *rigor.* In general, **rigor** refers to the quality, validity, accuracy, and credibility of action research and its findings. Rigor is typically associated with the terms *validity* and *reliability* in quantitative studies, referring to the accuracy of instruments, data, and research findings, and with *accuracy, credibility,* and *dependability* in qualitative studies (Melrose, 2001). Many action researchers use the term *rigor* in a much broader sense, referring to the entire research process and not just to its aspects of data collection, data analysis, and findings (Melrose, 2001). Rigor in action research is typically based on procedures of *checking* to ensure that the results are not biased or that they reflect only the particular perspective of the researcher and not those of the participants (Stringer, 2007).

As mentioned, the determination of rigor is often contingent on the intended audience for the action research results. Classroom-based action research can be disseminated to a wide variety of audiences (e.g., teachers, administrators, counselors, parents, school boards, professional organizations), and the usefulness of the results of action research to each often depends on their particular perceptions about rigor; it can have different connotations depending on the particular audience (Melrose, 2001). For example, if the research is intended for limited dissemination (e.g., sharing with members of the action research group or building staff), the necessary level of rigor is much different than if the dissemination is intended for broader scholarly academic output (e.g., formally presenting the results at a national research conference or publishing the study in a journal). It is necessary for the broader dissemination to be concerned more with *generalizability,* meaning that the results of the study will extend beyond its scope to other settings and other individuals.

However, action research intended for more local-level dissemination—most classroom-based action research falls into this category—has a different focus. It is important to remember that participants in action research studies make mistakes and learn from them (Melrose, 2001); this is an inherent part of the action research process. The research questions and design are often emergent, changing as the action researcher works through the process, and therefore unpredictable. There may be no generalizable conclusions at all, as the findings are context specific and unique to the particular participants and their setting and situation. At the end of an action research study or cycle, what typically matters is the improvement of practice, as evidenced by the resulting visible change, not the study's rigor (as defined by its ability to be generalized).

There are numerous ways in which to provide rigor within the scope of teacher-led action research studies. The following list has been adapted from Melrose (2001), Mills (2007), and Stringer (2007).

■ *Repetition of the cycle.* Action research is, by its very nature, cyclical. Most action researchers firmly believe that once through an action research process is simply not enough. In order to develop adequate rigor, it is critical to proceed through a number of cycles, where the earlier cycles are used to help inform the conduct of later cycles (Melrose, 2001). In theory, with each subsequent cycle, more is learned and greater credibility is added to the findings.

■ *Prolonged engagement and persistent observation.* In order to gather enough information to help participants fully understand the outcomes of an action research process, they must be provided "extended opportunities to explore and express their experience" (Stringer, 2007, p. 58) as it relates to the problem being investigated. However, simply spending more time in the setting is not enough. For example, observations and interviews must be deliberately and carefully conducted (Mills, 2007; Stringer, 2007).

■ *Experience with the process.* In many cases, rigor and credibility will depend on the experience of the action researcher(s). A teacher (or other school professional) who has conducted previous studies, or even previous cycles within the same study, can perform confidently and will have greater credibility with respective audiences (Melrose, 2001). However, if the teacher–researcher is a novice, the entire process may benefit from the use of an experienced facilitator in order to help inform and perhaps guide the process.

■ *Triangulation of data.* Rigor can be enhanced during the action research process when multiple sources of data and other information are included (Mills, 2007; Stringer, 2007). This permits the action researcher to cross-check the accuracy of data (Mills, 2007) and to clarify the meanings and misconceptions held by participants (Stringer, 2007). Accuracy of data and credibility of the study findings go hand in hand.

■ *Member checking.* Participants should be provided with opportunities to review the raw data, analyses, and final reports resulting from the action research process (Mills, 2007; Stringer, 2007). The rigor of the research is thus enhanced by allowing participants to verify that various aspects of the research process adequately and accurately represent their beliefs, perspectives, and experiences. It also gives them the opportunity to further explain or extend the information that they have already provided.

■ *Participant debriefing.* Similar to member checking, debriefing is another opportunity for participants to provide insight. However, in this case, the focus is on their emotions and feelings, instead of the factual information they have offered (Mills, 2007; Stringer, 2007). They may address emotions that might have clouded their interpretations of events or inhibited their memories.

Needless to say, rigor in action research is very important, albeit for reasons different from those of more traditional forms of educational research.

AN EXAMPLE

Action research need not be conducted on a schoolwide basis. In fact, it is regularly carried out by classroom teachers singly or in groups, usually in an informal way. An example of such research is illustrated in the following account of teacher Carol Huckaby's attempt to improve her sixth-grade students' library skills.

The Need

Mrs. Huckaby was well liked by her students. After they had completed sixth grade and gone on to junior high, they often returned to visit. She always asked them how they were doing in school, and after a while she began to see that a skill important to their academic success was not being taught in elementary school. The problem she saw was that students were not learning the library skills they were expected to have in junior high school when preparing term papers and other projects.

Obtaining Information

To determine whether the need she identified was widespread, Mrs. Huckaby contacted a number of her former students. They suggested that they did in fact need better preparation in library skills. Huckaby spoke with junior high English teachers who confirmed the students' opinion, agreeing that incoming students knew very little about the purposes of various parts of books or how to locate materials in the library. The teachers also said the students needed more experience completing written projects of the kind expected in junior high.

This need was further substantiated by the Public Information Report distributed in Huckaby's district, which showed that the district's seventh-grade students were below the national average in their ability to locate information in books, encyclopedias, and newspapers. Given this information, Huckaby decided to organize and implement a corrective program in her sixth-grade class. She told her fellow grade-level teachers of her idea, and they asked to be included. In planning the program, Huckaby listed objectives, planned activities, prepared and collected materials, and developed implementation procedures.

Project Objectives

As objectives for the project, Huckaby specified student knowledge of and competence in the following:

For Books, the Ability to Use

1. Table of contents and index
2. Preview page, foreword, and introduction
3. Glossary
4. Chapter titles

For the Library, Knowledge of

1. The system by which books are shelved
2. The organization of the library
3. Use of the *Reader's Guide to Periodical Literature*
4. How encyclopedias and other reference books are shelved, organized, and used

For Finished Written Products, the Ability to

1. Provide sequence organization
2. Use illustrations
3. Cite references
4. Select good titles
5. Make a table of contents

Project Activities, Materials, and Procedures

Huckaby decided to help students achieve the objectives by having them produce an end product—a photo-essay by each student on individually chosen topics. She provided the following specific activities, materials, and procedures:

1. A pretest covering library skills and the purposes of various sections of books
2. An introduction to the photo-essay project
3. A guide to help students complete all aspects of the project
4. A model of a completed photo-essay for student reference
5. Instructions to help students select topics and take appropriate digital photographs
6. Informative talks by the school librarian on how books are shelved, how the Library of Congress system works, and how the books are catalogued
7. Instructive sessions on using the *Reader's Guide to Periodical Literature*
8. Note-taking lessons on how to record bibliographical information, how to write exact quotations, and how to paraphrase and condense
9. Activities in which students practice organizing note cards into a bibliography
10. Student development of rough drafts of their essays to accompany their photographs
11. Individual conferences between teacher and student to determine needs concerning writing, references, and photography
12. Completion of final drafts of photo-essays, to be bound attractively and arranged in a display for parents
13. A posttest covering library skills and the various components of books

Ongoing Monitoring

Huckaby kept a close watch for student difficulties and errors. She helped students and corrected their work appropriately, either by redirecting students or by reexplaining or restructuring activities.

Evaluation

To evaluate the project and its effectiveness, Mrs. Huckaby did the following:

1. Analyzed pretest and posttest scores to determine student growth
2. Analyzed photo-essay projects to determine how well they reflected improvement in stated objectives
3. Asked parents to respond to the following four-item questionnaire (using a five-level rating scale):
   a. How would you rate your child's interest in the photo-essay project?
   b. How would you rate the value of this project?
   c. How difficult do you consider this project to be for your child?
   d. To what degree do you feel positive about the demands the project placed on your own time and resources?

THE ACTION RESEARCH PROCESS

myeducationlab for research

To learn even more about action research studies, go to the "Action Research" section of **MyEducationLab for Research** and then click on *Assignments and Activities*. Complete the exercise titled "Developing an Action Research Project" for additional practice at making important design decisions within an action research study.

The generic research process, which you have seen stated repeatedly, includes a problem statement, hypotheses or research questions, selection of a sample, a design for data collection, analysis of data, presentation of findings, and a statement of conclusions. But for action research aimed at the development of new products or procedures, a somewhat different process is used, as was evident in Carol Huckaby's research. She identified a problem, envisioned a way to resolve it, planned and implemented the solution envisioned, monitored student reactions, identified project strengths and shortcomings, made needed revisions, and assessed the program's overall effectiveness. As exemplified by Huckaby's efforts, the action research and development process can be outlined as follows:

1. Identify a problem or need.
2. Collect information and resources.
3. Prepare the project.
   a. Formulate objectives.

    b. Select activities.

    c. Assemble and prepare materials.

    d. Plan procedures.

4. Introduce and implement the project.

5. Monitor procedures and reactions.

6. Identify strengths and shortcomings of the project.

7. Correct errors, difficulties, and omissions.

8. Appraise the project's ongoing and long-term results.

This eight-step process can be simplified into a four-stage procedure, which would fit any type of action research project. Steps 1, 2, and 3 comprise the preparation for the project (the *planning* stage); step 4 involves the actual application or implementation of the project (the *acting* stage); step 5 requires the collection of data and other forms of information (the *observing* stage); and steps 6, 7, and 8 provide the opportunity to examine the effects of the projects and to develop appropriate revisions (the *reflecting* stage).

Furthermore, the process of action research is not linear; it has historically been viewed as a *cyclical* process. That is to say, whereas action research has a clear beginning, it does not have a clearly defined endpoint. For example, after Carol Huckaby developed and implemented her project, she monitored and evaluated its effectiveness and then made revisions to the program. She would likely implement her program again (perhaps with next year's students), again monitoring and evaluating its effectiveness, followed by the consideration of appropriate revisions and improvements to be implemented next time. One should be able to quickly see that her project may never have a clear end—she may continue to go through subsequent cycles of implementation, evaluation, and revision, spiraling from one year to the next. This process of action research, with its cyclical and spiraling nature, has been depicted in Figure 15.1.

for research

To learn more about the overall process of action research, go to the "Action Research" section of **MyEducationLab for Research** and then click on *Building Research Skills*. Read the article and then complete the exercise titled "Identifying Steps in the Research Process for an Action Research Study," which will help you identify key components of an action research study.

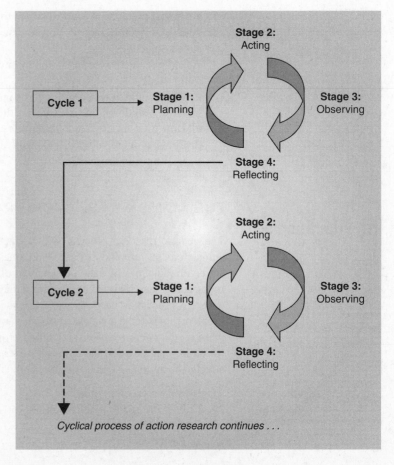

Figure 15.1
The process of action research

Cyclical process of action research continues . . .

AN EXAMPLE OF ACTION RESEARCH

Following Exercise 15.1 is an action research report of a study, conducted by a group of teachers in a rural school setting, that examines the impact of the use of the Japanese lesson study model of professional development.

Exercise 15.1

Indicate where the elements of the action research and development process could be used as headings in the report.

Lesson Study: A Professional Development Model for Mathematics Reform

Ann R. Taylor
Southern Illinois University Edwardsville

Shari Anderson
Carlinville School District

Karen Meyer
Carlinville School District

Mary Kay Wagner
Carlinville School District

Christine West
Carlinville School District

In this action research report 4 teachers and 1 teacher educator use the Japanese lesson study model of professional development for 15 months in rural Carlinville, Illinois. In March 2001, 4 teachers identified a goal to improve their students' understanding of two step word problems in 2nd grade elementary mathematics. Teachers completed three cycles of researching, planning, teaching, evaluating and reflecting. They were motivated, empowered, and found lesson study effective professional development in their rural setting. It focused on the classroom lesson; provided an effective lesson plan and hours of focused professional development; supported attempts to put into practice best professional knowledge of reform mathematics; and developed a professional community among them.

> This action research study was conducted by four classroom teachers and one teacher educator.

Source: Taylor, A. R., Anderson, S., Meyer, K., Wagner, M. K., & West, C. (2005, Winter). Lesson study: A professional development model for mathematics reform. *The Rural Educator, 26*(2), 17–22. With permission of National Rural Education Association.

Recent mathematics reform efforts attempt to unite mathematicians, math educators, administrators, and teachers to focus on two clear goals: (a) to increase mathematical knowledge of teachers, and (b) to improve methods of teaching mathematics. In 2001, the Conference Board of the Mathematical Sciences published their report, *The Mathematical Education of Teachers* (2001), emphasizing the significance of high quality mathematical preparation by teachers in all levels of school mathematics. A year earlier, *Before It's Too Late: A Report to the Nation* from the Glenn Commission (also known as the National Commission on Mathematics and Science Teaching for the 21st Century), identified the solution to the problem of students' low achievement in mathematics as "better mathematics and science teaching" (National Commission on Mathematics and Science Teaching for the 21st Century, 2000, p. 7). To achieve this goal they advocated stronger initial teacher preparation and "sustained, high quality professional development" (p. 5),

> Notice that the background/literature review is much more brief in action research studies than in others that we have looked at. This is not always the case, but many times is true.

which they believe can be facilitated by, among other strategies, "building- and district-level Inquiry Groups . . . for teachers to engage in common study to enrich their subject knowledge and teaching skills" (p. 8).

How can those responsible for professional development in rural areas follow through on such recommendations while facing additional challenges like geographic isolation from large numbers of colleagues and remoteness from specialist professional development opportunities? In this paper, we, four rural elementary teachers and one teacher educator, will first introduce ourselves and our methods and then describe one model for "inquiry groups"—the Japanese "lesson study" model. We then share our 15 month long experience conducting lesson study in rural Carlinville, Illinois, before concluding with some discussion of the strengths of the lesson study model for rural education. We believe lesson study offers a way to systematically address many of our professional development needs.

INTRODUCTIONS AND METHODOLOGY

In January 2001, a teacher education faculty member at the nearest state university, taught a graduate math education class on-site at a public elementary school in Carlinville, Illinois, 50 miles from the university. Carlinville, with a population of 7000, is the seat of Macoupin County in west central Illinois. As such, it is the prosperous center of a largely poor agricultural region. Lesson study was introduced as a small part of that class, and that is how these authors came together to work on this project.

As classroom teachers we represent a profile characteristic of one part of the rural teaching force—stable, hard working, experienced professionals thoroughly embedded in the lives of our communities. We have lived and taught in Carlinville for between 10 and 25 years. Our own mathematical education, mostly in rural schools, was dominated by traditional memory and drill work. One of us particularly enjoyed this approach and was successful through high school, whereas the other three reached a point in junior high or high school where mathematics lessons left us con-

Personal experience is a big factor in action research.

fused, anxious, or bored. Notwithstanding our responses as learners, our own math teaching began by replicating the traditional methods the four of us had experienced. But as serious professionals we began to make changes, and with the help of new textbooks and workshops our teaching began to include connections to literature, use of manipulatives, and integration of writing activities. Change was difficult. Attempts to break away from the text and allow for more discussion and open-ended problem solving work seemed to conflict with the need to cover the curriculum. Pressures of standardized testing kept us from straying too far from our set curriculum. We were generally satisfied with our mathematics teaching prior to taking the graduate course and we did not always think deeply about our teaching. However, we were intrigued by the idea of lesson study and decided to take this on as a class project.

Our work as a lesson study group of four began in March 2001 and continued through May 2002. To document this systematic inquiry into improving classroom practices we used an action research approach (McNiff, 1988; Elliott, 1991; Mills, 2000). Carefully recorded field notes, meeting summaries, video recordings, and interviews provide the data points for this paper. We

The authors are using an action research approach to engage in systematic inquiry into their own teaching for the purposes of improving classroom practice.

write here in a way that includes our collective and individual voices as our narrative of experience (Riessman, 1993; Richardson, 2000), recording some of the richness of our learning about lesson study. The writing was a joint effort reflecting an iterative cycling between university and school personnel that was collaborative and mutually supportive; however, the lesson

They clearly state that their research incorporates a good deal of cyclical iteration, as well as professional reflection.

study work was done exclusively by the four of us, who are currently 2nd and 3rd grade classroom teachers.

We hope we will entice, educate, and stimulate other groups to try this approach. We should add that our understanding of lesson study is deepening all the time but we do not consider ourselves experts, and this paper is not intended to be a definitive statement of the process.

WHAT IS LESSON STUDY?

Lesson study is one component of a system designed for continual professional development in Japan. Introduced to a United States audience during the last 3 to 4 years, the most widely read source on the model is Stigler and Hiebert's *Teaching Gap* (1999), although other scholars are also engaged in independent research on the topic (Fernandez, Chokshi, Cannon, & Yoshida, In press; Lewis & Tsuchida, 1998; Lewis, 2000; Yoshida, 1999). In Japan, lesson studies are either done by teachers across a district, or by teachers within a school.

A brief background on the nature of lesson study is provided.

The topic for the lesson study is chosen by the teachers but is linked to larger national, district, or school goals. For example, as part of a goal to improve children's independent problem-solving, teachers may work on a lesson study topic of subtraction with regrouping. Teachers, usually of the same grade level, meet weekly to design, teach and evaluate one research lesson. Their next steps are to revise the lesson, reteach it, evaluate, reflect on the lesson again, and share their results. This process may take up to a year. Stigler and Hiebert (1999) noted that lesson study empowers individual teachers and leads to steady incremental improvement in teaching, rather than fast reform which is often the unachieved goal of American approaches to change. Stigler and Hiebert (pp. 112–116) summarize lesson study through an eight step problem-solving process, although others divide this process differently (Lewis & Tsuchida, 1998). The next section of the paper describes our work as we proceeded through each of these steps.

LESSON STUDY IN CARLINVILLE

Preparation for Lesson Study

Having chosen to participate in lesson study as part of the graduate class, our group of four set to work. Initially, readings from our graduate class about Japan (Stigler & Hiebert, 1999) and interviews from China (Ma, 1999) made us feel defensive. As experienced teachers

> Action research often allows the teacher–researcher to be very honest with the audience.

who are typically American in outlook, we found the idea that schools and teachers in other countries might be doing a better job teaching mathematics than we were a bit disturbing. As we pursued our study we began to focus on the ideas presented in *The Teaching Gap* (Stigler & Hiebert, 1999).

One aspect of the book that took us some time to accept was the authors' description of teachers in a culture as "homogeneous." We had assumed that the personality of a teacher was what made the difference in a classroom and that the four of us had very different and distinct teaching styles. What we eventually realized, however, was that we were confusing personality with teaching style. Despite our different personal characteristics, we found our teaching styles were more similar than we had expected, in such ways as how we plan our lessons and our expectations of students. Even more interesting to us was the fact that our teaching styles were very similar to the way we were taught as students, despite our belief that we had made significant changes in our math teaching throughout our careers. What we realized was that consistently we have been involved in

> The teachers were already learning a lot about themselves and their practice, early in the study.

superficial changes that did not bring about true reform. As Stigler and Hiebert (1999) described, "American mathematics teaching is extremely limited, focused for the most part on a very narrow band of procedural skills" (p. 10). After struggling with this concept for many months, we agreed that, "teaching is a cultural activity [and that] we learn how to teach indirectly, through years of participation in classroom life, . . . largely unaware of some of the most widespread attributes of teaching in our own culture" (p. 11).

As we continued our dialogue, we came to the realization that Stigler and Hiebert's portrayal of teaching in the United States as limited was a fair representation. However, although we could see the need for change, the idea of spending an entire year focused on one lesson, as recommended in the lesson study literature, seemed impossible. We seriously doubted that real change could take place by studying just one lesson over such an extended period of time, but we were willing to try.

Step 1: Defining the Problem

The first step of lesson study is to decide on a general goal. Over the years, we have found two-step word problems to be both difficult to teach and confusing for many second and third grade students. Typically when we taught two-step word problems in our classrooms, we expected the students to follow steps we designed in a specific order. We decided to use lesson study to shift our methods to better take into account what we had been learning about mathematics teaching and learning. Hence, our goals for our lesson study were: (a) to allow students to do their own thinking and design their own way of solving a two-step word problem; (b) to give students time to share their math thinking with their classmates; and (c) to listen to our students' math thinking and become more flexible in our approaches to teaching two-step word problems.

Step 2: Planning the Lesson

Having decided on the general goal, we moved on to plan the specific lesson we would teach. In March of 2001 we naively expected that it would take about twenty minutes at most to produce a written plan. We joked about the readings' description of Japanese lesson studies lasting an entire year when we could surely produce the same results in a mere fraction of the time. This turned out to be American efficiency—and arrogance—at its finest! An hour and a half into that initial meeting we were still talking math, and we haven't stopped since. We have met regularly, about once a week for the last 15 months, with the sole purpose of discussing this project as well as its implications beyond our own classrooms.

The decision about exactly what lesson to present was, of course, the primary topic of discussion at those early meetings. We spent much time narrowing our focus to one simple problem, a difficult task when we have been accustomed to assigning entire worksheets from a text containing ten or fifteen of those same types of problems. It heightened our awareness that more is not necessarily better, and that one problem in depth could be far more beneficial than a whole page of problems that divide one's attention and effort for the sake of "getting it done." Once we focused on one problem, a two-step story problem, we had further questions. What operations to use in the problem? Should it be printed using numerals or number words? Should the problem use names of our own students and the name of our school to increase interest, or would that sidetrack the easily distracted students?

In addition to the question of what to teach, we discussed many other points, categorized loosely into four groups: logistics, materials, teacher script, and time management. For example, logistics problems included where and when to do the lesson, how to display the problem for the whole group, whether to have the group gather on the rug or stay at their seats for the introduction, whether to have students bring their papers with their solutions to the rug with them, how to pair them up (teacher's choice or students), and numerous other similar discussion points.

Materials to be used created another set of questions to solve. Do we display the problem on the overhead or white board? Do we hand out individual copies to each student? Do we give them scratch paper, and hand out manipulatives, or simply have them available for whomever would choose them? Would large sheets of Post-It paper be better for recording ideas because it could hang on the board and then be moved as needed and saved? Such questions as these led to an amazing amount of discussion over decisions we all, out of the interest of time-efficiency, were accustomed to making instantly and taking for granted every minute in the classroom.

> Note how their steps very closely follow the stages you read about earlier in the chapter: planning, acting or implementation, developing, and reflecting.

Time considerations were heavily discussed. How much time to allow for the entire lesson, and for each section of the lesson? Should students have equal time to work independently and with partners? Is five minutes enough time for the independent work, and again for the partner work? Is fifteen minutes long enough for the class to gather and discuss their solutions at the end of the lesson? Should the teacher cut it off when the allotted time is up, or continue as needed for the flow of the lesson?

The teacher script itself was another area of extreme significance. We agonized over the exact words the teacher would use, and over how necessary it was to even script it so closely. We debated over whether the teacher should read the problem, or whether the students should read it on their own. We eventually decided to do both, which is what we would normally do in the classroom anyway. Should the teacher give clues as students worked? Should she answer questions as she circulated, or just encourage students to keep thinking? Sometimes we simply said we'd just try it one way and change it later if we needed to—which of course is exactly what lesson study is all about! At times we made it harder than it needed to be, probably because we each, in our own ways, are perfectionists, and we wanted to do it "right" the first time. We eventually

learned to accept the fact that it was okay to leave room for improvement in the re-teaching, which helped us relax a bit.

Steps 3 and 4: Teaching and Evaluating the Lesson and Reflecting on Its Effects

With the lesson planned, the next step was to teach and evaluate the lesson, which we completed on March 27, 2001. Shari taught the lesson using the following story problem: "A South School 2nd grade class has been studying about ocean life. They will be taking a field trip to the aquarium. The class will be divided into six groups. Each group has 3 girls and 2 boys. How many more girls than boys are going?" Karen, Mary Kay and Chris observed, took careful notes, and video-taped the lesson to supplement the observations. A video recording cannot adequately capture much of what happens in a classroom, but it did provide a helpful additional source of data for us, particularly as we studied the solutions students shared publicly to the class. Our colleagues covered our classes to enable us to do observe the lesson. We met and discussed our observations immediately after the lesson.

Step 5: Revising the Lesson

We had completed the first four steps of the lesson study process during Winter and Spring semester. With school back in session in August 2001, we moved on to Step 5, which was to revise our original lesson. We began meeting once a week again, reviewing what we had done the previous winter and spring, and planning our reteaching. We felt that we had put so much thought and care into our first scripting of the lesson that we didn't think we would be able to find anything that needed changing for the re-teaching of the lesson. Hah! All it took was one initial question: "Are we going to re-teach the lesson to the same students as last winter, or to our new group of second graders?" and others flowed like syrup on a hot cake! If we teach it to the same students, how many will remember—or *will* they remember?—not so silly a question, knowing some of our students! If we teach it to the same students, how should we change the problem? Keep the same story but change the numbers? Change the story but keep the same numbers and operations? And if we teach it to our new second graders, it will be six months earlier in the year than our first attempt. How do we account for that difference?

What we returned to again and again was this question: What is the purpose of our lesson study? Is it to show growth in our students? Is it to test their ability to follow our directions, to do

> Notice how the teachers seemed to have more questions following the initial cycle of action research.

the thinking, to come up with correct solutions? Or is our purpose at this time to refine our own attempts to provide work that is challenging, thought provoking, and able to develop mathematical thinking. With that question in mind, we made some minor adjustments to the lesson, shifting the time frames involved in each part of the lesson, the way manipulatives were to be used, and our observation methods. We also added a written student reflection.

Steps 6 and 7: Teaching the Revised Lesson and Evaluating and Reflecting Again

In October, we completed the final steps in Stigler and Hiebert's eight step model for lesson study. Shari retaught the lesson on October 4, 2001. Once again, Karen, Mary Kay and Chris observed and took notes. As we evaluated this second teaching we came up with even more changes we would make upon a third teaching of the lesson. This was an epiphany of sorts for the four of us, as we began to realize somewhat sheepishly that the more we teach it, the more we find room for improvement—a far cry from the original "American efficiency" agenda we joked about earlier! As our understanding of lesson study grew, we also realized that rather than having the observing teachers circulate and interact, the lesson study process is designed to enable the teachers to do just the opposite—to stay separate from the concerns of the lesson and carefully observe and record what is happening.

The beginning of the second cycle . . .

From February 2002 through May 2002 we repeated the whole process one more time. This time substitute teachers taught our classes, and we had the benefit of observations and comments from a mathematics educator (Ann) as well as a university mathematician. This significantly enriched our learning. We also understood more clearly the benefits of a detailed lesson plan that included our goals and predictions for students' responses to the problem. This enabled us all to take more detailed observation notes during the lesson, which supported a more thorough debriefing session. As we repeated the lesson study process, we continued to learn more about our teaching, and more about the lesson study process.

. . . and a third cycle. They clearly explain how they continued to learn through subsequent cycles.

DISCUSSION

The lesson study model focuses on one of the areas recommended for math reform, the professional development of teachers, and is one version of an "inquiry group" recommended by the Glenn Commission (National Commission on Mathematics and Science Teaching for the 21st Century, 2000) as a way to improve mathematics teaching. However, providing effective professional development for teachers is a challenge in any setting, urban or rural. We recognized, as a result of our experience with lesson study, that our previous years of professional development, while helpful, had not led us to significantly change our mathematics teaching from what we ourselves had experienced in school. However, through our version of the Japanese lesson study model, we identified a significant number of benefits.

1. Meeting regularly to plan and teach a research lesson focused on an identified classroom need (improving our teaching of two-step word problems) resulted in an **effective detailed lesson plan** that to a large extent achieved its goal of more effective student learning.

2. The lesson study model provided a **highly motivated structure for planning and teaching a lesson** in which we talked for hours about subject matter, curriculum, research, materials, logistics.

3. Given time to reflect and think in the company of other teachers, we were able to **share, interact, question assumptions, and reassess common practices** in light of our best professional knowledge. This enabled us to align our practice more closely with this professional knowledge base.

4. Observing a lesson enabled us to **shift our thinking from a teaching focus to a learning focus** as we recorded and puzzled over our students' mathematical thinking. As observers, we were free to be focused on the actual work the students were doing and the thought processes involved.

5. Focusing on student thinking provided us with more **feedback to support the goals of reform mathematics** that we had been trying to implement. For example, when we added an opportunity for students to write a journal response to the lesson. We were reminded of the importance of really listening to our students. Challenging students, giving them time to solve the challenge, listening to their thinking, allowing them time to share their thinking verbally and in writing takes time, time that we often feel we don't have as we push to complete our given curriculum.

6. Lesson study has **transformed our working relationships** and conversations with each other. In addition to what we learned about mathematics teaching, we found that lesson study has shifted our paradigm completely.

Overall, the lesson study process has empowered and motivated us. Rather than hearing from an outside expert about an ideal situation or a "new method", we have been able to shape our own professional development according to our interests and needs, albeit provoked and guided by research (Ma, 1999; Stigler & Hiebert, 1999). We experienced an immediate impact on our thinking and teaching as we talked and worked with colleagues in our school.

In spite of our success with lesson study, we identified four areas of concern about the use of lesson study in American schools. First, the more we worked on what appeared to be empowering, significant professional ideas for our classroom, the more frustrated we felt about

> Once again, more questions are raised as a result of their classroom-based action research.

the extent to which our professional lives are controlled by external mandates, many of which act counter to the best learning interests of students and the best practices of teachers. Second, the process of shifting our focus from traditional practices to considering new ideas was at times very difficult. Third, understanding the goals of lesson study took time and experience. There were obstacles and we were learning as we went through the process. Finally, administrative support is necessary for lesson study. Although we managed with the help of our colleagues for the first and second lesson teaching, we would strongly recommend having substitute teachers for the day the lesson is taught. This allowed us to really focus on the lesson study and engage fully in the debriefing session afterwards.

To us, as experienced teachers and a teacher educator, lesson study seems very suitable for rural settings because it does not require a complex or expensive infrastructure, either in terms of resources (texts, manipulatives) or personnel. It requires only a group of teachers talking and thinking together. Conversation can be stimulated through the discussion of books, such as *The Teaching Gap* (Stigler & Hiebert, 1999) or *Knowing and Teaching Elementary Mathematics* (Ma, 1999). Supporting materials, videos, and discussion groups are available on the web (see websites), thus enabling rural communities to collaborate with others. The stability of the teaching force and the strong social relationships which often exist in rural areas provides a ready foundation for the close work this model orchestrates. Teachers can extend these existing relationships into systematic professional exchanges. Our case demonstrates how veteran teachers who already "know" a lot, can be reenergized and refocused by using this model.

Clearly, no one single event brings reform to mathematics teaching. However, the lesson study model provides a structure within which small changes gather and flow together to become the substance of new conversations and discussions. Over time, these small changes add up to significant changes in classroom practice. The lesson study structure enabled our group of experienced teachers to engage in significant professional development with a minimum of resources. Lesson study seems to offer possibilities for rural educators to use the resources they already have to further reform elementary teaching of mathematics.

References

Anderson, S., Meyer, K., Wagner, M. K., & West, C. (2002). *Lesson study on two step word problems with second grade students.* Unpublished master's project, Southern Illinois University Edwardsville, Edwardsville.

Conference Board of Mathematical Sciences. (2001). *The Mathematical Education of Teachers* (Issues Mathematics Education v. 11). Washington, D.C.

Elliott, J. (1991). *Action research for educational change.* Milton Keynes: Open University Press.

Fernandez, C., Chokshi, S., Cannon, J., & Yoshida, M. (In press). Learning about lesson study in the United States. In B. M. (Ed.), *New and old voices in Japanese education.* Armonk, New York: M. E. Sharpe.

Lesson Study in Japan-U.S. Science Education. Mills College funded by National Science Foundation. Available 7 May, 2002, from http://www.lessonresearch.net

Lesson Study Research Group (2001). Teachers College Columbia Lesson Study Research Group. Available May 7, 2002, from www.tc.columbia.edu/LESSONSTUDY

Lewis, C. (2000). *Lesson study: The core of Japanese professional development* (Invited Address to the Special Interest Group on Research in Mathematics Education). New Orleans: American Educational Research Association Annual Meeting.

Lewis, C., & Tsuchida, I. (1998). A lesson is like a swiftly flowing river: How research lessons improve Japanese education. *American Educator* (Winter), 14–17, 50–52.

Ma, L. (1999). *Knowing and teaching elementary mathematics: teachers' understanding of fundamental mathematics in China and the United States.* Mahwah, NJ: Lawrence Erlbaum Associates.

McNiff, J. (1988). *Action research: Principles and practice.* New York: Routledge.

Mills, G. (2000). *Action research: A guide for the teacher researcher.* Upper Saddle River, New Jersey: Merrill-Prentice Hall.

National Commission on Mathematics and Science Teaching for the 21st Century. (2000). *Before It's Too Late: A Report to the Nation from The National Commission on Mathematics and Science Teaching for the 21st Century.* Washington, D.C.

Richardson, L. (2000). Writing: A method of inquiry. In N. Denzin & Y. Lincoln (Eds.), *The handbook of qualitative research* (2nd edition ed., pp. 923–948). Thousand Oaks, CA: Sage.

Riessman, C. K. (1993). *Narrative Analysis* (Vol. 30th). Newbury Park, CA: Sage.

San Mateo-Foster City School District. *San Mateo Foster City School District.* Available 7 May, 2002 from http://www.smfc.k12.ca.us

School Renewal Web Center. *Featured Strategy: Lesson Study.* School Renewal Web Center. Retrieved 7 May, 2002, from: http://www.schoolrenewal.org/feature/lesson_study/

Stigler, J., & Hiebert, J. (1999). *The teaching gap: Best ideas from the world's teachers for improving education in the classroom.* New York: Free Press.

REVIEW OF ACTION RESEARCH

In most cases, the purpose of research is to discover new information that can be generalized to other settings. But you have seen that the purpose of action research is not to make generalizable discoveries. It originates with a strongly felt need in a particular situation or setting—usually associated with a difficulty or dissatisfaction—and is carried out in order to resolve the concern. Although its results may prove to be useful in other settings, they are particular to the situation where the concern exists and are not intended to be generalized.

ORGANIZING FOR ACTION RESEARCH

Action research can be characterized by the eight-step procedure noted earlier. The following illustrations are presented to help clarify this process.

The Problem

The statement of the problem in action research takes a form such as the following:

> The purpose of this research was to design an authentic assessment procedure for use in science programs in Aurora school district.

The problem statement alone may provide adequate orientation. Hypotheses are sometimes used, but a series of questions is usually more helpful, such as

> What is authentic assessment, and what does it involve?

> What do educators, particularly teachers, say about the value and practicality of authentic assessment?

> In what situations is authentic assessment being used successfully?

> Can authentic assessment be used in evaluating student progress in science classes?

> What procedures and materials are needed for authentic assessment in science?

> Will Aurora district science teachers accept and make use of authentic assessment?

Desired Outcomes

The outcomes one hopes to achieve through action research are shown in the problem statement and questions. Occasionally, desired outcomes take the form of objectives, as in the Huckaby library skills project.

Information and Resources

Whereas other types of research are often designed to obtain and analyze original data to help answer questions or test hypotheses, existing resources are used in action research to put together a procedure or product that will resolve the problem at hand. For example, most of the questions used in developing a program of authentic assessment can be answered by consulting the literature, and the resources the program might require probably already exist as well. The creative aspect of action research and development lies in the organization, implementation, refinement, and evaluation of the new product or procedure.

Sequence of Research Activities

It is helpful to lay out an anticipated sequence of activities to be undertaken in the course of the project. A calendar should be used to assign dates for completing each activity, and a budget should be prepared, if appropriate.

Refining the Product or Procedure

As the project develops, preliminary field-testing should be done. Here, one tries out the project on a limited scale with real participants, the purposes being to identify what works well and what does not and to gauge participants' reactions. Needed modifications can then be made before the project is implemented on a wider scale.

Evaluating the Product or Procedure

Once refinements have been made, the project is implemented and subsequently evaluated in terms of effects, practicality, and degree of acceptance by participants. The data used for making evaluative judgments about the project may be qualitative or quantitative.

STRENGTHS AND CAUTIONS IN ACTION RESEARCH

Action research provides benefits not often encountered in other types of research. It resolves an immediate problem or can produce a tangible product or useful procedure. In addition to its great potential for bringing about improvements in teaching and learning, it is relatively easy to carry out, and it can help make classroom experiences more enjoyable for students and teachers alike.

But keep in mind certain limitations. Of all types of educational research, action research is the least precise and most subject to errors of bias, reliability, and validity. The findings are limited to the setting where the research was done; if applied elsewhere, the results may well be different.

APPLYING TECHNOLOGY

More about Action Research

In this chapter, you learned about action research. This research methodology has many valuable applications in school settings. By pointing your Web browser to the following sites, you can learn even more about action research.

■ You Want to Do an Action Research Thesis? (www.scu.edu.au/schools/gcm/ar/art/arthesis.html)
Bob Dick of Southern Cross University in New South Wales, Australia, maintains this site, in which he walks the student through the process of conducting and reporting action research. Although very thorough in his approach, the author has developed a manual that is truly a beginner's guide.

■ Research to Practice: Guidelines for Planning Action Research Projects (http://literacy.kent.edu/Oasis/Pubs/0200-08.htm)

This site includes guidelines to help in the planning of action research projects. Nancy Padak and Gary Padak discuss the four stages of the action research process: identifying questions to guide the research, collecting information to answer the questions, analyzing the information that has been collected, and sharing the results with others.

■ Classroom Action Research (www.madison.k12.wi.us/sod/car/carhomepage.html)
This site contains several links that provide assistance in planning and conducting classroom-based action research. Included are links to such topics as what action research is and is not; what teacher researchers do; and guidelines for developing questions, gathering data, analyzing data, and formally writing the results.

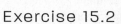

Exercise 15.2

You are made director of a project to improve teacher morale in your school district. Following the elements of the action research process, list the steps you would take. Illustrate each step with a specific example of what you would do or give attention to.

CHAPTER SUMMARY

Action research exemplifies the application of educational research methods to local-level problems or settings. A research methodology that can empower educators to improve their own practice, action research involves systematic investigation and reflection of our own teaching and other educational practices. The process of conducting action research can be summarized as one of planning–acting–observing–reflecting.

LIST OF IMPORTANT TERMS

action research
rigor

ACTIVITIES FOR THOUGHT AND DISCUSSION

1. For Ms. Matheson's spelling program, a description of which follows, see if you can answer the following questions:

   a. What is the problem?
   b. What type of research is Ms. Matheson attempting to conduct?
   c. What would you expect might be her main criterion regarding learning?
   d. Do you think she would list a criterion that does not have to do directly with spelling achievement?
   e. Based on the criteria you gave in (c) and (d), what conclusions might Ms. Matheson draw from her study?

Ms. Matheson is dissatisfied with the spelling program used in her fifth-grade class. Students do not like spelling, and Ms. Matheson does not enjoy teaching the lessons. She believes the program would be more enjoyable and more effective if it were built around the words her students are dealing with in their reading programs. She confers with her principal and receives permission to develop and use a spelling program of the type she envisions for a three-month trial period. She begins by compiling lists of words from the students' reading program. She incorporates the word list into instructional units enhanced with cartoons, rhymes, puzzles, vignettes, and high-interest worksheets.

When preparations are completed, Ms. Matheson introduces the program to her class. She observes carefully to see how students react to the activities, finding that the students are interested in the cartoons and rhymes but have difficulty interpreting the special messages she has tried to build into the vignettes. She begins at once to correct the problem. Before long she realizes that she should build into her lists certain service words such as *danger, poison,* and *flammable.*

As time passes, Ms. Matheson finds that her students seem to enjoy the activities and no longer groan when she tells them it is time for spelling. She finds, too, that students learn to spell their words with little difficulty and remember how to do so. As a check on their progress, she administers two spelling tests from the regular program. Student performance is average on the tests even though they have not had specific instruction on at least half of the words included in the tests.

2. Here are the questions listed with the targeted learnings at the beginning of the chapter. See if you can answer them without looking back in the chapter.

   a. Of what value is action research to educational practitioners?

   b. What are the key characteristics of action research?

   c. What sorts of topics are best approached through action research?

   d. What distinguishes action research from other types of research?

   e. What are the procedures by which action research is carried out?

ANSWERS TO CHAPTER EXERCISES

Because the answers to items in the chapter exercises may vary, it is recommended that these exercises serve as the basis for class discussion.

REFERENCES AND RECOMMENDED READINGS

Brandt, R. (1991). The reflective educator [Special issue emphasizing action research]. *Educational Leadership, 48*(6).

Brown, D. (1991). Secondary teacher's participation in action research. *The High School Journal, 75*(1), 48–58.

Dick, B. (1993). *You Want to Do an Action Research Thesis?* Available at www.scu.edu.au/schools/gcm/ar/art/arthesis .html

Gall, J., Gall, M., & Borg, W. (2005). *Applying Educational Research: A Practical Guide* (5th ed.). Boston: Allyn & Bacon.

Melrose, M. J. (2001). Maximizing the rigor of action research: Why would you want to? How could you? *Field Methods, 13*(2), 160–180.

Mertler, C. A. (2009). *Action Research: Teachers as Researchers in the Classroom* (2nd ed.). Thousand Oaks, CA: Sage.

Mills, G. E. (2007). *Action Research: A Guide for the Teacher Researcher* (3rd ed.). Upper Saddle River, NJ: Merrill.

Santa, C., Isaacson, L., & Manning, G. (1987). Changing content instruction through action research. *The Reading Teacher, 40*, 434–438.

Stringer, E. T. (2007). *Action Research* (3rd ed.). Los Angeles: Sage.

Evaluation Research

16

PREVIEW

In this chapter we consider another type of educational research with a great deal of practical application: evaluation research.

Evaluation research is typically done by school districts to determine the effectiveness of given products, procedures, programs, or curricula. Evaluation research is similar to action research, in several ways:

- Done by educators rather than professional researchers
- Accomplished in the local school setting
- Intended to resolve local school concerns or questions
- Not intended to be generalized to other groups or settings

There are differences between the two types:

- Evaluation research appraises quality while action research develops something new.
- Evauation research tends to be larger in scope than action research.
- Evaluation research is intended for broader application than is action research.

TARGETED LEARNINGS

This chapter explores another type of research that has a high level of practical application, making it somewhat similar to action research. Evaluation research is typically done by school district personnel. Its purpose is to evaluate the quality of school programs, materials, curricula, and the like. As you read this chapter, look especially for information related to the following:

1. What is the purpose of evaluation research?
2. What sorts of topics are best approached through evaluation research?
3. What distinguishes evaluation research from other types of research?
4. What are the procedures by which evaluation research is carried out?

EVALUATION RESEARCH

Evaluation research, synonymously referred to as *program evaluation,* is done to determine the relative merits of various products and approaches used in education. (The term *program* is used very loosely throughout this chapter to include educational programs, curriculum, instructional materials, organizations, as well as administrators, teachers, and

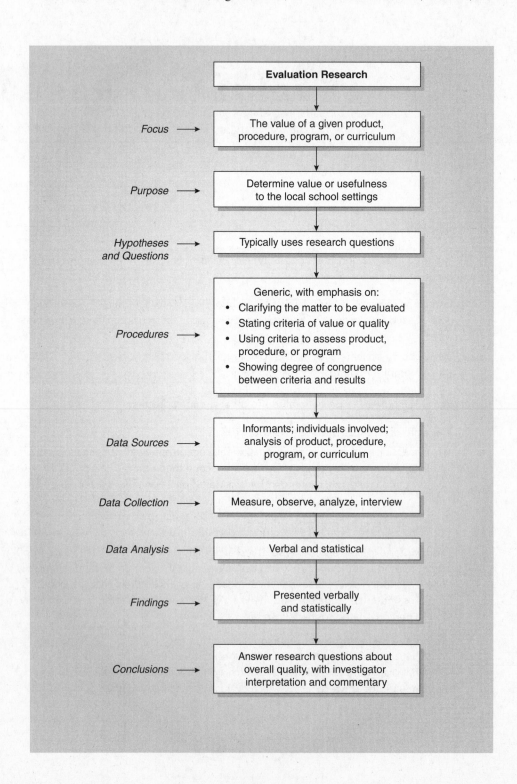

	Evaluation Research
Focus →	The value of a given product, procedure, program, or curriculum
Purpose →	Determine value or usefulness to the local school settings
Hypotheses and Questions →	Typically uses research questions
Procedures →	Generic, with emphasis on: • Clarifying the matter to be evaluated • Stating criteria of value or quality • Using criteria to assess product, procedure, or program • Showing degree of congruence between criteria and results
Data Sources →	Informants; individuals involved; analysis of product, procedure, program, or curriculum
Data Collection →	Measure, observe, analyze, interview
Data Analysis →	Verbal and statistical
Findings →	Presented verbally and statistically
Conclusions →	Answer research questions about overall quality, with investigator interpretation and commentary

students.) Gay, Mills, and Airasian (2009) define evaluation research as the process of collecting and analyzing data about the quality, effectiveness, merit, or value of programs, products, or practices. The main focus of evaluation research is to make decisions about these programs, products, or practices. Often, these decisions may be tied to funding. Administrators may need systematically collected evidence to help them answer important questions such as

■ Should we keep the current math program, or abandon it for something else?
■ Is the newly implemented program focusing on academic motivation as effective as we want it to be? Do its benefits outweigh the time away from direct classroom instruction?
■ Is this new science program really worth the additional cost?

Teachers and administrators may often conduct evaluation research, especially for formally assessing products and processes developed in action research. Gall, Gall, and Borg (2005) identify six aspects of education about which evaluation research is often conducted:

■ Instructional methods
■ Curriculum materials
■ Programs (e.g., social science programs)
■ Organizations (e.g., teachers' organizations)
■ Educators
■ Students

The first three areas can be especially fruitful for research by graduate students, as educators are always concerned about which methods, materials, or programs best meet their needs. On the other hand, teachers should approach evaluative studies of organizations, teachers, or students with caution. Research into those topics can stir up a great deal of emotional controversy and often raise questions of ethics. Unless those cautions can be dealt with adequately, research into such topics should be left to highly trained researchers.

TYPES OF EVALUATION RESEARCH

First of all, and generally speaking, evaluations can be either formative or summative. **Formative evaluation** occurs during the development of a program and continues into its implementation (Gay, Mills, & Airasian, 2009). Its purpose is to provide feedback on the program or product in an attempt to identify its weaknesses and to find ways to improve it while the program is still being implemented. The goal of formative evaluation is to improve specific aspects of a program (Suter, 2006). In contrast, **summative evaluation** focuses on the overall quality of a program, or its overall effectiveness, on completion of the program or product. This is typically determined by comparing the performance of teachers and students, for example, against some predetermined criteria. Suter (2006) notes that summative evaluations can also compare two competing programs in order to determine which is more effective.

Beyond this basic distinction, Worthen and Sanders (1987) have noted well over 50 models of evaluation developed over the past several decades that they have classified into the following six categories:

1. *Objectives-oriented evaluation.* The focus of these types of evaluation studies is on specifying goals and objectives and then determining the extent to which they have been met.
2. *Management-oriented evaluation.* The focus of this category is on identifying and meeting the informational needs of managerial decision-makers.

3. *Consumer-oriented evaluation.* These evaluation models center on developing evaluative information on broadly defined educational "products" for ultimate use by educational consumers (who must choose between competing "programs").

4. *Expertise-oriented evaluation.* These models depend primarily on judgments of professional experts to determine the quality of educational programs.

5. *Adversary-oriented evaluation.* The central focus of these evaluations is on the presentation of opposing points of view from different evaluators (who typically take "pro" and "con" perspectives).

6. *Naturalistic-oriented* and *participant-oriented evaluation.* Naturalistic (i.e., qualitative) inquiry, along with the direct involvement of participants, is key in these models. These stakeholders help determine the criteria, needs, and data for the evaluation study.

EVALUATING METHODS, MATERIALS, AND PROGRAMS

Evaluation studies will typically use other research methods in order to evaluate programs or materials. To learn more about evaluation designs, go to the "Mixed Methods Research" section of **MyEducationLab for Research** and then click on *Assignments and Activities.* Complete the exercise titled "The Ready For School Los Angeles Program." This exercise asks you to consider several important design decisions for implementing an evaluation research study using a mixed-methods approach.

Methods, materials, and programs can be evaluated in various ways. The following methods of evaluation are commonly used because they provide satisfactory results when the researcher can set forth explicit criteria for making judgments.

1. *Comparative content analysis.* The components of a given method, material, or program are identified and analyzed to determine how well they correspond to stated curricular goals, which are clarified as criteria. Those criteria are used in judging the value of the method, material, or program. Evaluation of textbooks, tests, and instructional programs usually involves this process.

2. *Analysis of theoretical, philosophical, or moral tenets.* Methods, materials, and programs are increasingly being scrutinized as to their theoretical, philosophical, and moral underpinnings. Textbooks and programs, especially in natural science, mathematics, language, and social science, can reflect various theoretical views, such as those having to do with the nature and process of science, the procedure of thinking mathematically, the psycholinguistic parameters of language acquisition, or a variety of social values and lifestyles. They also may reflect philosophical views concerning gender equity, racial equity, or cultural understanding and cooperation. Evaluation research is useful in addressing such concerns. Again, it requires stating explicit criteria of quality or worth before scrutinizing materials or curricula, and then compiling and analyzing data obtained from that scrutiny, usually qualitatively.

3. *Teacher acceptance.* The extent to which new curricula, materials, and programs will be implemented depends largely on teachers' favorable or unfavorable reactions. If teachers do not buy into innovations—if they find fault with them or for any other reason resist their use—the innovations have little chance of success. Therefore, it is very important that teacher reactions be evaluated early and regularly as new programs or materials are introduced into schools. Criteria for such evaluation studies tend to be somewhat nebulous, but generally resemble the following:

■ The innovation is educationally sound.
■ The innovation shows promise of improving learning, teaching, or relationships.
■ The innovation can be incorporated into the ongoing program.
■ The innovation will not add unduly to the burdens teachers already carry.

Data are obtained from teachers or others involved directly with delivering the innovation.

4. *Changes produced in teachers.* Many innovative programs that districts attempt to put into place require that teachers undergo in-service training. It is especially important in

those cases to ascertain whether the training effects are being carried over into classroom practice. Even if teachers profess to espouse a new method or set of materials, they may not change their ways of teaching accordingly. Whether or not they make desired changes can be determined through evaluation research. Data can be obtained either by asking teachers what they do differently when using the innovation or by observing and noting their behaviors as they teach. Asking the teachers is by far the easier procedure, but the information obtained may be unreliable. Observing the teachers may yield better data, but such observations may be very difficult for graduate students to arrange, even if they are practicing educators. Whether teachers are interviewed or observed, behaviors relevant to the innovation must be identified and made explicit. Those behaviors might have to do with preparation, delivery of instructions, feedback to students, use of questions to stimulate thought, or procedures of assessing student performance.

For making judgments in this evaluative approach, teacher behavior prior to the innovation can be established as baseline performance. For example, in research into equal opportunity for students to participate in class discussions, an observer could note which students a teacher calls on during discussions over a period of a week. After receiving equal-participation training, that same teacher could again be observed and his or her behavior compared to the baseline behavior. Differences between baseline and subsequent behavior are then explored.

5. *Student acceptance and involvement.* Just as teachers must accept innovations if those innovations are to be successful, so must students accept them and participate willingly. Student reactions to innovations are not difficult to obtain, as students not under threat are usually willing to express their opinions freely. It is also possible to document student behavior in given classes or subject areas before and after the innovation is introduced. Again, appropriate criteria are stated; behavior prior to the innovation establishes a baseline, and behavior subsequent to the innovation allows one to determine the results of the innovation.

6. *Resultant student achievement or behavior.* Changes in achievement and behavior are prime criteria for judging the value of an innovation, but changes in student attitude are important, too. If achievement gains are seen to result from the innovation, the investigator must make sure that the gains have not occurred at the expense of other learnings that would otherwise have taken place. Some innovations consume more time than the activities they replace, so that less instructional time is left for other areas of the curriculum. Achievement in those other areas may suffer as a result.

AN EXAMPLE OF EVALUATION RESEARCH

The following article reports the evaluation of the impact of interactive whiteboards for teaching and learning in primary schools in England.

Exercise 16.1

See if you can answer these questions about the article. What is being evaluated?

1. What is the main criterion of effectiveness?
2. What data figure prominently in the study?
3. What do the data lead investigators to conclude?
4. What additional questions does the research seem to raise?
5. How are those questions explored, and what are the answers determined to be?

Embedding Interactive Whiteboards in Teaching and Learning: The Process of Change in Pedagogic Practice

Cathy Lewin
Manchester Metropolitan University, UK

Bridget Somekh
Manchester Metropolitan University, UK

Stephen Steadman
University of Sussex School of Education, UK

Abstract

This paper draws on research carried out for the UK government during 2004–2006 to evaluate the impact of interactive whiteboards for teaching and learning in primary schools in England. Multilevel modelling showed positive gains in literacy, mathematics and science for children aged 7 and 11, directly related to the length of time they had been taught with an interactive whiteboard (IWB). These gains were particularly strong for children of average and above average prior attainment. Classroom observations, together with teacher and pupil interviews, were used to develop a detailed account of how pedagogic practice changed. Results from the multilevel modelling enabled the researchers to visit the classrooms of teachers whose pupils had made exceptional progress and seek to identify what features of pedagogy might have helped to achieve these gains. It was also possible to examine possible reasons for the lack of impact of IWBs on the progress of low prior attainment pupils, despite their enthusiasm for the IWB and improved attention in class. The IWB is an ideal resource to support whole class teaching. Where teachers had been teaching with an IWB for 2 years and there was evidence that all children, had made exceptional progress in attainment in national tests, a key factor was the use of the IWB for skilled teaching of numeracy and literacy to pairs or threesomes of children. Young children with limited writing skills, and older pupils with special educational needs are highly motivated by being able to demonstrate their skills and knowledge with the tapping and dragging facilities of the IWB. These effects are greatest when they have the opportunity, individually or in small groups, for extended use of the IWB rather than as part of whole class teaching. The IWB is in effect a mediating artefact in interactions between teacher and pupils, and when teachers use an IWB for a considerable period of time (at least 2 years), teachers learn how to mediate the greatly increased number of possible interactions to best aid pupils' learning. The IWB's use becomes embedded in their pedagogy as a mediating artefact for their interactions with their pupils, and pupils' interactions with one another, and this is when changes in pedagogic practice become apparent.

> This is an evaluation study of the impact of a specific instructional tool (i.e., whiteboards).

Keywords

Interactive whiteboards
Pedagogy
Change
Evaluation

1 INTRODUCTION

In 2003–2004 the Primary Schools Whiteboard Expansion project (PSWE), a UK Government initiative, provided £10 million for the acquisition and use of interactive whiteboards (IWBs) within 21 local authorities in England. An IWB has a large touch sensitive screen, linked to the classroom computer, which is visible to a whole class. Thus it can be used by teachers to access still images, moving images and sound, providing a multi-modal portal enabling the needs of whole classes, groups, and individual learners to be addressed. The PSWE funding had a strong pump-priming effect and, with large-scale procurement, many schools were able to fund additional IWBs (approximately double the number funding through the initiative). PSWE also funded an extensive training programme. This included technical training from manufacturers, national training for local authority consultants, and a portal offering resources, forums and additional guidance. Local authorities took responsibility for training staff in their schools and adopted a range of approaches (Lewin et al. in press) but there was no additional funding for this.

> Furthermore, this is an evaluation that is tied to a great deal of financial resources.

Source: Lewin, C., Somekh, B., & Steadman, S. (2008). Embedding interactive whiteboards in teaching and learning: The process of change in pedagogic practice. *Education and Information Technologies,* 13(4) 291–303. © Springer Science+Business Media 2008. With kind permission from Spring Science+Business Media.

The initiative was launched at a time when the UK Primary National Strategy mandated a particular approach to literacy and numeracy: a daily lesson of approximately 1 h for each, with 15–20 min of whole-class teaching, 30 min of group or individual activity and a 10 min plenary session. In addition, all primary classrooms at the time had additional adult support in the form of at least one teaching assistant. These additional staff were not all involved in training but were of course able to observe the classroom teacher's practice. Finally, for the majority of the school day primary school teachers are based in the same classroom and teach most, if not all, of the curriculum to a single group of pupils. This meant that teachers, their teaching assistants and the pupils had exclusive and sustained access to the IWB.

The aims of the evaluation included: assessing the impact of IWBs on attainment, attendance and behaviour; and identifying the effects of such technology on ICT pedagogies, the embedding of ICT across the curriculum and staff professional development. These were addressed using a mixed methods design, which used Multilevel Modelling to look at the impact on attainment and case studies to explore changes in practices. This offered a more sophisticated statistical approach which was sensitive to different contexts and accounted for the shared experiences of pupil cohorts at class level. At the end of the first period of evaluation (after 18 months) there was some tentative evidence to suggest that the IWBs were making an impact but it was clear that an extension would be worthwhile and beneficial. Thus a second phase of quantitative and qualitative data collection and analysis was instigated, extending the evaluation by a further 18 months. The Government, as sponsors of the evaluation, were primarily interested in the impact on attainment. However, it is notable that they also had a strong interest in the development of pedagogy and embedding ICT across the curriculum. This together with a willingness to extend the evaluation represents an enlightened policy, although there were still some naïve expectations of how quickly changes could occur and measurable effects become apparent.

This paper focuses on the process of pedagogical change. We define pedagogy as being the interactive process that goes on between teachers and children, in this case in planned learning. Often evaluations of Government initiatives are too short to reveal evidence of impact; the length of time that it takes for new tools to become embedded in pedagogical practices is not always realistically taken into account. The extension to this evaluation enabled the team to follow the process of change,

> The goals of the evaluation focus on the achievement, attendance, and behavior of the students, as well as the impact across the curriculum and on teacher professional development.

> The focus of this particular paper is on the impact of IWB on teachers' pedagogy.

and investigate the impact of the technology on formal assessments, over a 2 year period. In addition, the design incorporated a substantial element of classroom observation which was digitally recorded. The video data proved to be beneficial for the researchers involved as it facilitated a richer analytical approach. The collection of both quantitative and qualitative data provided opportunities for exploring phenomena in different ways, and for both illuminating and challenging findings. Moreover, it enabled an integrated approach such that qualitative and quantitative strands interacted, each data set informing enquiry and analysis of the other.

> The authors used a mixed-methods design to conduct their evaluation.

The potential of IWB technologies for supporting teaching and learning has been noted by many (Kennewell 2001; Kennewell 2004; Smith et al. 2005). There is a need to provide both technical and pedagogical training (Beauchamp 2004). However, there has been little empirical evidence to date suggesting pedagogical change (e.g. Smith et al. 2006) although IWBs are used effectively to support existing pedagogical practices (e.g. Gillen et al. 2007).

2 METHODOLOGY

The mixed methods approach adopted in this research provided further insights and fresh perspectives for explaining the impact of IWBs on teaching and learning, enhancing knowledge about phenomena and strengthening the findings (Greene and Caracelli 1997; Teddlie and Tashakorri 2003). We agree with Greene and Caracelli (1997, p12) that "[c]ontrasts, conflicts and tensions between different methods and their findings are an expected, even welcome dimension of mixed-method inquiry, for it is in the tension that the boundaries of what is known are more generatively challenged and stretched." As the objectives set by the funders demanded different research approaches, some confirmatory and some exploratory, mixing methods was the only means of achieving this simultaneously (Teddlie and Tashakorri 2003). This could have been achieved by dealing with the questions individually but this would have been foolish; a missed opportunity to extend the analysis and interpretation.

Multilevel modelling (MLM) was used to analyse data on pupils' progress in Mathematics, English and Science at ages 11 and 7. This drew on National Curriculum test data from 100 classes with a total of 2,000 pupils from across the 21 Local Authorities. Multilevel modelling has developed from multiple regression. It takes account of the inevitable 'nesting' that occurs in the school system. Because children in a particular class have the same experience of teaching, particularly in a primary school, than pupils in another class in the same school, their attainment within the group is likely to be similar, and probably different from that in other classes in the same school. Furthermore, there will be differences between schools. There is a need to take this 'non-independence' into account. Otherwise the analysis relates to fewer observations than anticipated (classes rather than pupils).

The MLM analytical approach examines the between class variation and between school variation more explicitly. Prior to MLM, researchers either aggregated data to school level (not accounting for individual variation) or worked with pupil level data but did not take account of contextual variations (thus oversimplifying). MLM enables more statistically efficient estimates of regression co-efficients to be made, but more importantly, standard errors, confidence intervals and significance tests will be more conservative, meaning that findings are more reliable (Goldstein 1983). Moreover, the data can be used to rank classes in relation to the outcome variable (in this case progress in Maths, English and Science) and this affords the opportunity to identify classes which have performed somewhat differently from the cohort of classes overall.

Multi-level-modelling data analysis was undertaken in this project with a two level hierarchical structure of pupil and classroom. This facilitated the tracking of two groups of pupils, aged 11, who took national tests in 2005 and 2006 (Cohort 1 and Cohort 2), enabling combined and separate analyses, using national test data at age 7 as the baseline from which to assess progress. The analysis was based on the length of exposure to IWBs (in months) experienced by pupils. This increased the variance of the measure of exposure. A clear binary distinction of 'taught with IWB' versus 'not taught with IWB' was not possible due to the rapid uptake of the technology in schools that had not been included in the original pilot programme, and because of the variety of experiences that classes of pupils had as a result.

The authors have provided a very thorough discussion of their procedures.

In Phase 1, ten schools were selected as case studies and visited for 2 days on two–three occasions between February 2005 and April 2006. The schools were demographically balanced; had an appropriate mix of ethnic and socio-economic groupings; and included nursery, infant and junior phases. Case study work involved classroom observations which were digitally video recorded, and interviews with learners, staff and managers. The use of video recording offered a powerful means of examining in great detail teaching practices with IWBs.

The analysis of data from the visits was undertaken collaboratively. Three key episodes were selected from each classroom observation and shared with the whole team. This proved to be a very powerful and insightful activity, both stimulating the original researcher's recall and enabling finer grained observations of things not noticed originally. It also enabled others to see important new things from the differ-

ing perspectives that researchers in the team could bring to bear from their individual backgrounds and prior experience. Through this process, the team developed a shared understanding of how to investigate the phenomena, which facilitated progressive focussing from Phase 1 to Phase 2 drawing on grounded theory principles (Strauss and Corbin 1990). The interviews were used to elicit accounts which allowed much tacit knowledge to be inferred, and the data were used to triangulate interpretations. This enabled detailed accounts of pedagogic practice to be developed.

One of the aims of Phase 2 was to track change over an extended period of time. Another was to look for confirmation or disconfirmation of the tentative findings from the analysis of Phase 1 data. For example, the Phase 1 quantitative analysis suggested that pupils with low prior attainment were

The mixed-methods evaluation was explanatory in nature.

not benefiting from being taught with an IWBs; and in Phase 2 we were able to investigate why this might be so. Nine teachers from seven schools were selected as case studies, on the basis that in national tests in 2005 their classes had shown progress (identified through MLM) between the baseline and post-test outcomes that differed from the main trend. However, it was important that the researchers making these visits did not know beforehand whether the classes had fared better or worse than average, so a 'Chinese wall' arrangement operated to prevent foreknowledge.

This arrangement enabled the team to make unbiased observations in classrooms where the use of IWBs had become embedded in teaching and learning with more than 2 years use. It was then possible to develop explanatory theories as to why progress between the baseline and post-test outcomes had been different from the main trend in these classrooms. As in Phase 1, the teachers, groups of their pupils and their headteachers were also interviewed. The nine teachers who participated in the Phase 2 case studies were asked to consider the findings on the use of IWBs identified in Phase 1 and state whether they agreed or disagreed with them. The result of this exercise was a very positive overall agreement. In Phase 2 the researchers gained new insights and were also able to confirm Phase 1 findings through further observations.

Data were analysed through a socio-cultural lens, drawing on the role that tools play in 'mediating' human activity (Vygotsky 1978) whilst acknowledging that the ways in which tools are appropriated and not technologically deterministic (e.g. Fisher 2006). Rather, new tools provide opportunities to create new kinds of activity, but these new kinds of activity are created by the users as they develop skills in using the new tools, not by the tools themselves (Wertsch 1998). Thus we believe that "[t]he development of new social practices will therefore be transformative to varying degrees, depending on the affordances of the tool, the skill with which human agents learn to use them and their ability to imagine new possibilities" (Somekh 2007, p13). Initially, as with all new technologies, teachers explore ways of making the new tool fit their existing practice. Over time, however, where a professional community of practice develops, both formal and informal, within and beyond a school, teachers can learn from each other and help each other to find out new ways of using such technologies (Lewin et al. in press).

3 FINDINGS AND DISCUSSION

3.1 General findings

The take-up of IWBs in PSWE schools was rapid. There was an enthusiastic response from all teachers, leading to integration of ICT use across the curriculum as the IWB was used—albeit to differing extents—in a variety of subject areas. This was unprecedented in our experience. As teachers had technology (IWB and a laptop or desktop computer) in the classroom, available to use whenever they wished to do so, there was a huge increase in teachers' ICT skills over a 2 year period. There was an observable process of continuing professional development through the development of Communities of Practice which generated mutual support (Lave and Wenger 1991), as the IWB was in many cases a whole school phenomenon, or at least installed in all classrooms in a year group, and thus a common experience for all staff or for those working closely together.

Along with ICT TestBed (Somekh et al. 2007a) which also equipped all classrooms in participating schools with technology, the PSWE initiative created a different atmosphere and different attitudes to ICT. For the first time, rather than early adopters struggling to implement technological innovation in isolation, there was a much greater sense of everybody being in it together, sharing ideas and practices over coffee in the staff room. Teachers had continuous access to the school servers and the internet, and so were able to immediately bring up lesson plans, preprepared resources or websites. Teachers either had laptops or memory sticks to use with their classroom workstations, which meant that they could more easily develop resources using IWB software at home if they chose to do so.

There were measurable gains in children's test score results (at age 11) in Mathematics, English and Science when they had been taught with an IWB for more than 2 years. The length of time pupils had been taught with an IWB proved to be a key factor. In Mathematics average and high attaining pupils (both cohorts combined) made greater progress with

> It would have been very helpful if the authors had included actual results of their statistical analyses (e.g., in the form of tables) in order to supplement their discussion.

more exposure to IWBs. Although in Phase 1 there was little effect (but certainly not a detrimental effect) on progress for those pupils who were low attaining, analysis of the disaggregated data (each cohort separately) suggested that once the innovation becomes embedded positive gains are likely to be achieved by all attainment groups. In Science, Cohort 2 (once the IWBs had been embedded) showed benefits for all attainment groups except high attaining girls where there was a ceiling effect. In English there were indications of positive trends but the measures of attainment in this subject are less stable and therefore the results were inconclusive. In Cohort 2, once IWBs were embedded, low attaining boys showed a positive trend in greater progress in writing with more exposure to IWBs. Full results of the quantitative analysis are presented in the project final report (Somekh et al. 2007b).

3.2 Examples of pedagogical change with IWBs

In the case study schools we observed some teachers developing entirely new ways of working by using new skills that draw on possibilities offered by the board. Teaching and learning always involves interactivity between teachers and pupils and learning resources, but as they become skilful in its use the IWB teachers develop new kinds of interactivity with pupils,

> Discussion of the results from the qualitative case studies.

mediated through the IWB. Many teachers adjusted their style to be more inclusive and co-operative in supporting learning. Evidence that the IWB was embedded in teachers' pedagogy came from observing new patterns of teacher behaviour. These were either improvements on previous pedagogical practices made possible by the functionality of the board, or completely new practices. Although these changes had, by the time of the second phase visits, all become routine, instinctive behaviours and part of what is often called 'tacit knowledge', in some cases, during questioning in interviews, teachers were able to give clear accounts of how these new practices helped them to teach more effectively.

Technical facility, that often rests upon confidence with ICT, is not enough by itself. A teacher also has to be able to appreciate what combination of modalities best aids a particular group of pupils to learn the subject matter in a particular area of the curriculum. Another component of the necessary expertise is being able to appreciate that subgroups of pupils, e.g. the gifted, may need a fresh choice of modality, and a different sequence of experiences, if they are to learn as successfully as they can. The point is that, if teaching with IWBs is to work well, IWBs have to be used so that the full potential for them to act as a mediating artefact is realised. This entails the teacher adapting his/her approach so that IWB use fits the purposes of the teaching aims. To do this a teacher has to learn how to mediate the many learning interactions that IWBs can facilitate. If IWBs are used without this level of application, as glorified blackboards, or as occasionally animated passive white boards, then there will be little effect on pupils' learning.

An excellent example came in a Year 6 science lesson on the body's reactions to exercise. The teacher used a CD-Rom resource that allowed three 'characters,' who differed in levels of fitness, to walk, jog and run while their pulse and heart rates were monitored by the IWB/CD-Rom software to provide readings that could be graphed and compared by the class. The teacher introduced the situation, brought pupils up to the board to make choices and start the 'characters' exercising, and simultaneously had her teaching assistant keep a record of the resulting data in a grid on a nearby passive whiteboard. This latter arrangement was for the benefit of the less able pupils in the class. The levels of interaction during the lesson were thus many and varied, and the teacher showed high levels of expertise, not just technically, or even in her knowledge of the subject, but also in her classroom management skills that allowed her to run a well planned and conducted lesson that was centrally based on her enabling pupils' interactivity with the IWB.

Viewing the process of teaching with an IWB in this light, it is clear that, while teachers carry the onus of deciding appropriate modalities and content, they need to allow pupils to interact with the IWB in ways that permit it to function as the main mediating artefact. Both literally and metaphorically teachers have to learn to 'stand away' and allow pupils to fully engage in interaction with what the IWB presents, as the following extract from post-visit analytical notes illustrates.

When the board was in use, the teacher tended to be at the board when he needed to bring up/change to a different screen, when he needed to write something on the board, and when he wanted to point something out. At other times, he seemed to stand 'away' from the board, sometimes moving into the classroom, but often standing just to the side of it at his desk (which was just to the left of the screen). In terms of where the children focused their attention—many of them often seemed to be looking at the screen rather than at the teacher. (Of course, this was not always true and sometimes dependent on what was being talked about/shown etc.). But, as I looked around the room a number of times, I noticed that the children did seem to be looking at the board and not the teacher—interestingly, this was confirmed by the children I spoke with in the interview. They told me that sometimes they found the board was useful for helping them to better understand what was being explained/discussed—or, if they lost track of where they were up to, they could look at the board for reference. Many of them said that sometimes hearing something out loud from the teacher did not explain it clearly to them, *but* looking at the same idea expressed in a different format, i.e. on the IWB, would often help to clarify this for them.

3.2.1 Improvement to an established pedagogic practice

One example of an improvement on an already established practice is the use of the IWB to facilitate a co-learner style of teaching, where teacher and pupils ('we') work together rather than adopting more formal roles as teacher and learner. The IWB as a mediating artefact facilitates this style of teaching very powerfully by allowing the teacher to 'stand off literally and/or metaphorically'. The notes from observation of a lesson in Phase 1 illustrate this:

> Recall that the focus of this paper was on examining pedagogical change; the next several sections discuss these results.

Leading into group work on scientific statements and the difference between conclusions and results type statements, the teacher started group work saying: 'I've given you a set of statements. I want you to decide as a group. But I want us all to come to a class decision.'

When it was time for the first group to feed back, they had to move the statements into the correct box on the IWB, and the first group said they weren't sure where the statement went. So the teacher said, 'Right, where shall we put it then?'

She didn't wield the power by saying something like, 'shall we put it in the middle?' Instead she said, 'Let's talk about it.' There was a class discussion, and she gradually got them all to agree that it went where she wanted it to go. The discussion ended with the pupils all agreeing the correct answer and the teacher smoothly took the power back as she showed them the results on the board.

While this mode of 'shared learning' existed in teachers' behaviour before IWBs were introduced, it takes on an added importance when IWBs are being used because the power of the IWB as a mediating artefact can be fully released when a teacher mediates the interactivity of learning in this way. However, observations also show that the 'teacher as co-learner' stance is adopted most frequently in the infant years, and is less frequent when teaching older children. There are several reasons for this. Older children are expected to take more responsibility for their own learning, and they also have more experience and contextual understandings to draw upon in doing this. They also become more adept at hiding their weaknesses, and have to be challenged more directly if teachers are to assess their levels of understanding accurately.

Another example of improvement on existing practice, arguably amounting to transformation, is the new style of lesson planning whereby resources for teaching and presentations are stored electronically alongside lesson aims and objectives. The plan is thereby transformed from a paper sheet which lists actions to a dynamic 'script' for actions. These scripts are stored from year to year and 'tweaked' to suit different situations. They are often developed collaboratively by a year team and can be used by supply teachers and students on placement.

3.2.2 Emergence of a new pedagogic practice

The first of these comes about precisely because of the way in which the use of structured lesson plans, with associated choices of resources, can now be stored in computer memory, accessible at any time from the IWB, as described immediately above. This allows teachers to work to an invisible 'script' that is embedded in the lesson plans. By 'script' in this sense we imply a more complex idea than the way in which a lecturer or presenter has a script that resides in his or her presentation—or stack of overhead transparency slides. The 'script' that is embedded in the IWB/computer lesson plan, with its interlinking content, is a more complex manifestation because of the higher degree of flexibility in choice of affordance and action that is possible.

Being able to rely on the script of a lesson provides more than an aide-memoire to how the lesson should develop. Its existence enables teachers to multi-task in new ways. More of their mental capacity is released to make observational assessments for learning during whole class teaching. Assured of the shape of the lesson, this frees the teacher who is then able to direct full attention to observing how individual children in the class are responding. And by noting interactions with their TAs, teachers can also assess the progress being made by those children with special needs. Teachers gain time for assessing how individual children are progressing within the lesson. This increased attention to continuous monitoring aids formative assessment and the redirection of teaching as required. The impact this has on personalising learning is illustrated by the quotation below. During a Year 2 lesson on letter and sound combinations, the teacher was able to make direct observations of pupil response and supplement these for the pupils with special needs by noting the kind of interactions going on between these children and their assigned teaching assistant.

> I also knew quite quickly whether they had understood or not because their hands went up before (the SEN TA) had even said anything to them—and then you can see whether she needs to say something to them and re-word and re-phrase and just bring them back a step and help them—and then you can almost see the penny drop, or that she is still going. So you think, 'Right, I won't ask them that question', because they haven't quite got there yet. So sometimes you might pick up—she's still talking to them—and the rest of the class has got to the point where they've answered—(so you go on with the class) then (the SEN TA) will carry on teaching them to that point and then they'll pick up again (with the rest of the class).

The second example of these new pedagogical practices relates to the development of strategies to keep the rest of the class mentally engaged while one child is working at the IWB. In the first year we observed many occasions when the pace of a lesson slowed appreciably when pupils came up to the board, and the rest of the class was left watching but inactive and often visibly bored. Now that IWBs are pedagogically embedded teachers have developed numerous strategies for managing pupil access to the IWB in ways that, at the same time, keep the rest of the class mentally engaged. Sometimes this involves the use of hand-held passive 'wipe' boards onto which pupils must write their an-swers ready to display them if their teacher asks them to. But it can also mean that teachers openly give the pupils new roles. Thus according to the circumstances, pupils may be expected to act as 'scrutineers', responsible for monitoring the work of whichever pupil is at the IWB, or 'commentators' on what the teacher is unfolding at the IWB. Some teachers actively enrol their pupils as 'helpers' when the unexpected happens. With our relatively small samples of classes we are unlikely to have tapped into the full range of practices of this kind that are emerging as parallel developments to changes in IWB teaching practices. But they all imply the creation of different social practices in the IWB classroom.

3.3 Pedagogical approaches for supporting pupils with low prior attainment

While IWBs can dramatically affect motivation for pupils who are not achieving their full potential, and the length of time pupils are taught with an IWB is the major factor that leads to attainment gains, this does not always appear to be the case for those with low prior attainment. However, in classrooms where there had been exceptional gains in attainment in the 2005 national tests (phase 1) for *all pupils* it seemed that a key factor was the use of the IWB for skilled teaching of numeracy and literacy to pairs or threesomes of children. The reason is: if the attainment of relatively small numbers of children at either extreme of the distribution of attainment in a group is lifted, this has a disproportionate effect to raise the average level of attainment within the group as a whole.

This kind of effective teaching of small groups who require additional support can be done by TAs provided they receive training in how to teach numeracy and literacy. Additionally, young children who have not yet acquired writing skills, and older lower attaining pupils, are highly motivated by being able to demonstrate their skills and knowledge with the tapping and dragging facilities of the IWB. These effects are greatest when they have the opportunity, individually or in small groups, for extended use of the IWB rather than as part of whole class teaching. We have seen only limited use of the IWB in this way but in case study schools teachers told us that such use is ideal as a means of assessing pupils' learning.

3.4 A model of pedagogical change

We were able to track the process of pedagogic change over 2 years and derive a three-stage model of its development. The process was one of IWBs becoming integrated with pedagogy as 'an extension of the [teacher's] self' (McLuhan 1964) and 'mediating' the interactivity between teacher/students and student/students (Wertsch 1998;

> The evaluation study was substantial enough to result in a descriptive model of pedagogical change.

Vygotsky 1978). When teachers have used an IWB for a considerable period of time—in this case at least 2 years—its use becomes embedded in their pedagogy as a mediating artefact in their interactions with their pupils, and pupils' interactions with one another. The important process is not one of the IWB mediating teacher–pupil interactions. There is an important distinction here. Rather it is the teacher who, when teaching, mediates all the many kinds of interactivity that an IWB, as a mediating artefact, can facilitate to stimulate and support learning. Once teachers can operate at this level, then they inevitably change their pedagogic practices.

In summary, we identified a three stage model of pedagogic change with an IWB:

■ Stage 1: teachers fitting new technologies into established pedagogies;
■ Stage 2: teachers engaging in collaborative exploration of the new opportunities offered by these technologies;
■ Stage 3: teachers using the IWB skilfully and intuitively in ways that extended or transformed their established pedagogic practices.

This model is grounded in the evidence collected in our research and analysed through a socio-cultural lens. Beauchamp (2004) and Haldane (2005) have developed similar models of teachers' development in their use of IWBs, each with five stages, both also drawing on observational data of classroom practices. Beauchamp presents a framework of transition (black/whiteboard substitute, apprentice, initiate, advanced, synergistic) through themes of system operation, technical skills, software use and pedagogical practices. Haldane's typology (foundation, formative, facility, fluency, flying) presents a similar set of stages arguably with a primary focus on technical development, although also referring to pedagogies. Glover et al. (2007) have also developed a three stage model (supported didactic, interactive, enhanced interactivity) with a particular focus on classroom interaction. As this is not as closely related this third model is not considered further here.

Haldane's (2005) typology proved a useful tool in the early stages of the IWB innovation, as the boards were being introduced and there was, understandably, a great emphasis on gaining the necessary technical ICT expertise to use them. However, in the first phase of the PSWE evaluation it was evident that teacher–pupil and pupil–pupil interactions were crucial. It is now apparent, from the analyses conducted during Phase 2, that once teachers demonstrate consistent facility when using an IWB, they have reached the minimum standard that allows them to mediate the interactivity of the IWB to support learning with great effectiveness. At this point the IWB becomes an integral part of teachers' own interactions with the children.

The argument that excellence in teaching with an IWB is made up from a compound of abilities, almost 'chemical' in their admixture, has been greatly strengthened by this experience of applying the typology in the case study schools. In the mixture that produces 'excellence', the level of a teacher's technical expertise with a board is important but, it is not possible to distinguish between excellent and less effective teachers on this basis alone. Whilst the models presented by Beauchamp (2004) and Haldane (2005) make a valuable contribution to the field, we agree with Jewitt et al. (2007) that the focus should be on the pedagogy rather than the technology. Therefore, we argue that our model provides a simpler (and less prescriptive) tool for understanding changes in pedagogical practice whilst allowing for the complexity of teaching and learning in classroom contexts with technology. Teachers do not necessarily need to develop high levels of technical expertise in order to transform their pedagogical practices.

The situation is still fluid. Manufacturers continue to improve IWBs and add to their modalities, and teachers continue to improve their usage as their experience as IWB users accrues. A sequence is now in train that can be described in almost Piagettian terms—where teachers themselves are the learners. Having had to adopt IWBs and adapt their teaching behaviours to accommodate them, teachers are now in the process of assimilating their knowledge and usage of IWBs. As the sequence proceeds all the various modalities of IWBs as mediating artefacts will become assimilated by teachers as extensions of their teaching capacity. In so doing, leading edge teachers will find ways of using the artefact's affordances that result in new social practices in classrooms.

References

Beauchamp, G. (2004). Teacher use of the interactive whiteboard in primary schools: towards an effective transition framework. Technology. *Pedagogy & Education, 13*(3), 327–248. doi:10.1080/14759390400200186.

Fisher, T. (2006). Educational transformation: is it, like "beauty", in the eye of the beholder, or will we know when we see it. *Education and Information Technologies, 11*(3–4), 293–303. doi:10.1007/ s10639–006–9009–1.

Gillen, J., Kleine Staarman, J., Littleton, K., Mercer, N., & Twiner, A. (2007). A 'learning revolution'? Investigating pedagogic practice around interactive whiteboards in British primary classrooms. *Learning, Media and Technology, 32*(3), 243–256. doi:10.1080/17439880701511099.

Glover, D., Miller, D., Averis, D., & Door, V. (2007). The evolution of an effective pedagogy for teachers using the interactive whiteboard in mathematics and modern languages: an empirical analysis from the secondary sector. *Learning, Media and Technology, 32*(1), 5–20. doi:10.1080/17439880601141146.

Goldstein, H. (1983). *Multilevel statistical models* (3rd ed.). London: Edward Arnold.

Greene, J. C., & Caracelli, V. J. (1997). Defining and describing the paradigm issue in mixed-method evaluation. In J. C. Greene, & V. J Caracelli (Eds.), *Advances in mixed-method evaluation: The challenges and benefits of integrating diverse paradigms* (pp. 5–18). San Francisco, USA: Jossey-Bass.

Haldane, M. (2005). A typology of interactive whiteboard pedagogies. Paper presented at the British Educational Research Association Conference, Glamorgan, September.

Jewitt, C., Moss, G., & Cardini, A. (2007). Pace, interactivity and multimodality in teachers' design of texts for interactive whiteboards in the secondary school classroom. *Learning, Media and Technology, 32*(3), 303–317. doi:10.1080/17439880701511149.

Kennewell, S. (2001). Using affordances and constraints to evaluate the use of information and communications technology in teaching and learning. *Journal of Information Technology for Teacher Education, 10*(1–2), 101–116.

Kennewell, S. (2004) Researching the influence of interactive presentation tools on teacher pedagogy. Paper presented at the British Educational Research Association Conference, UMIST, Manchester, September.

Lave, J., & Wenger, E. (1991). *Situated learning: Legitimate peripheral participation.* Cambridge, New York and Melbourne: Cambridge University Press.

Lewin, C., Scrimshaw, P., & Somekh, B. (in press). The impact of formal and informal professional development opportunities on primary teachers' adoption of interactive whiteboards. *Technology, Pedagogy & Education* (in press).

Lewin, C., Somekh, B., & Steadman, S. (2008) Embedding interactive whiteboards in teaching and learning: The process of change in pedagogic practice. Education and Information *Technologies, 13*(4) 291–303. © Springer Science+Business Media, LLC 2008. With kind permission from Springer Science+Business Media, LLC.

McLuhan, M. (1964). *Understanding media.* London and New York: Routledge and Kegan Paul.

Smith, F., Hardman, F., & Higgins, S. (2006). The impact of interactive whiteboards on teacher–pupil interaction in the National Literacy and Numeracy Strategies. *British Educational Research Journal, 32*(3), 443–457. doi:10.1080/01411920600635452.

Smith, H., Higgins, S., Wall, K., & Miller, J. (2005). Interactive whiteboards: boon or bandwagon? A critical review of the literature. *Journal of Computer Assisted Learning, 21,* 91–101. doi:10.1111/ j.1365–2729.2005.00117.x.

Somekh, B. (2007). *Pedagogy and learning with ICT: Researching the art of innovation.* London and New York: Routledge.

Somekh, B., Underwood, J., Convery, A., Dillon, G., Jarvis, J., Lewin, C., et al. (2007a). Evaluation of the ICT test bed project: final report. Coventry, UK: BECTA.

Somekh, B., Haldane, M., Jones, K., Lewin, C., Steadman, S., Scrimshaw, P., et al. (2007b). Evaluation of the primary schools whiteboard project. Coventry, UK: BECTA.

Strauss, A., & Corbin, J. (1990). *Basics of qualitative research: Grounded theory procedures and techniques.* Newbury Park, CA: Sage.

Teddlie, C., & Tashakorri, A. (2003). Major issues and controversies in the use of mixed methods in the social sciences. In A. Tashakorri, & C. Teddlie (Eds.), *Handbook of mixed methods in social and behavioural research* (pp. 3–50). Thousand Oaks, CA, USA: Sage.

Vygotsky, L. (1978). *Mind in society: The development of higher psychological processes.* Cambridge, MA: Harvard University Press.

Wertsch, J. V. (1998). *Mind as action.* New York and Oxford: Oxford University Press.

ORGANIZING FOR EVALUATION RESEARCH

We have seen that evaluation research is used to determine the worth of a product, procedure, program, or curriculum that has been put into place to serve a particular purpose, or that is being considered for use. *Products* are tangible objects such as series of textbooks or manipulatives for mathematics instruction. *Procedures* are ways of doing things, such as communicating with parents, assigning student grades, or attempting to equalize attention given to individuals in a classroom. *Programs* are organized efforts of broad scope that constitute components of the overall education plan offered by schools. Examples are the social science program, the athletics program, and the music program, each of which is described by its purpose and the classes it includes. *Curricula* are the specifics of instructional programs, including objectives and activities of individual courses and groups of courses. Examples are the biology curriculum, the natural science curriculum, the fifth-grade curriculum, or the middle school curriculum.

Problem

As in other research, the problem statement indicates the purpose of the research:

> The purpose of this investigation is to determine the degree of correspondence between the contents of the Silver Medal Language Series textbooks and the items included on three standardized achievement tests used in Elmwood school district.

Questions or Hypotheses

In evaluation studies, research questions are most often used to guide the investigation. The main research question might parallel the problem statement:

To what degree do the contents of the Silver Medal Language Series textbooks correspond to the contents of the three standardized achievement tests used in Elmwood schools?

This main research question will ordinarily be followed by a number of subquestions:

Regarding Vocabulary Development

1. How much overlap exists between vocabulary development in the textbooks and vocabulary knowledge on the tests?
2. To what extent do textbook activities include the same vocabulary words as do the standardized tests?

Regarding Sentence Structure

1. How much overlap exists between textbook activities on sentence structure and test items involving sentence structure?
2. (and so forth)

However, it is certainly possible to guide the research through hypotheses rather than questions if one so desires. For example, in evaluating student achievement in language arts, one could use the following hypothesis:

The mean language achievement of Elmwood Middle School students does not differ from the mean language achievement of middle school students nationwide.

Design for Obtaining Data

Evaluation research is designed, first, to determine the contents, status, or results of whatever is being evaluated, and second, to compare that assessment against a set of criteria that indicates desired traits. The degree of correspondence between assessment and criteria is used to indicate the worth of whatever is being assessed, and the resultant information is used for making decisions or changes.

Criteria

Criteria are specific indicators of quality. They might have to do with contents or traits or end results. For example, one might evaluate a series of textbooks to determine whether their contents correspond to curriculum objectives and items on standardized tests. Or one might assess student learning occurring in the language arts program. The criteria (or criterion) may be a single factor, such as student achievement. (School districts often evaluate their programs at least partly in terms of how their students stand, on average, in comparison to national achievement norms.) Normally, however, the list of criteria for evaluation studies will include a number of specific elements. For example, criteria used in evaluating a new schoolwide system of discipline might include the following list of specific indicators.

The Discipline System

- Specifies what constitutes misbehavior
- Emphasizes steps for preventing misbehavior
- Indicates clearly what teachers should and should not say and do when correcting misbehavior
- Contains strategies for student motivation and harmonious relationships
- Can stop misbehavior immediately

- Can redirect misbehaving students appropriately
- Contains provisions for fostering goodwill between teacher and students
- Emphasizes the development of student responsibility and self-control

Data

Data may be obtained by testing or interviewing students, teachers, other educators, and parents. They may also be gathered by analyzing tangible objects such as books and materials, or analyzing documents that describe programs, procedures, and curricula, or by observing and noting procedures as they are implemented. Some of the data, such as test scores and ratings, will be numerical. Other data, such as notations, interview responses, and written descriptions, will be largely verbal.

Data Analysis

Data are analyzed either statistically or qualitatively, using procedures that facilitate comparison of data to criteria.

Findings

Findings report the results of data analysis—what is discovered about the products, procedures, programs, or curricula being investigated.

Conclusions

Here the investigator compares findings with the stated criteria used in the study, makes judgments concerning the degree of correspondence between the two, and reports his or her considered opinion concerning meanings and implications.

CHAPTER SUMMARY

Evaluation research involves the application of particular research methods in order to determine the relative merits of or to pass judgment on specific educational programs. On the surface, evaluation studies can be classified as either formative or summative evaluations. Additionally, they can further be classified into one of six categories: objectives-oriented, management-oriented, consumer-oriented, expertise-oriented, adversary-oriented, or naturalistic- and participant-oriented evaluations.

LIST OF IMPORTANT TERMS

adversary-oriented evaluation
consumer-oriented evaluation
expertise-oriented evaluation
formative evaluation
management-oriented evaluation
naturalistic-oriented evaluation
objectives-oriented evaluation
participant-oriented evaluation
summative evaluation

ACTIVITIES FOR THOUGHT AND DISCUSSION

1. Think about a program (or curriculum or instructional material, etc.), at either the school or college level, with which you are familiar. For that program, consider the following questions:

a. What is the purpose of the program?

b. If you were charged with evaluating the program, what specific aspects would you want to include in the evaluation?

c. What types of data would be important to collect?

d. Consider each of the six categories of approaches discussed in the chapter. Could you design an evaluation study for the program using each of these approaches? Why or why not?

e. Which of the six types of evaluations do you think would be most appropriate for evaluating your program?

2. Here are the questions listed with the targeted learnings at the beginning of the chapter. See if you can answer them without looking back in the chapter.

a. What is the purpose of evaluation research?

b. What sorts of topics are best approached through evaluation research?

c. What distinguishes evaluation research from other types of research?

d. What are the procedures by which evaluation research is carried out?

ANSWERS TO CHAPTER EXERCISES

Because the answers to items in the chapter exercise may vary, it is recommended that the exercise serve as the basis for class discussion.

REFERENCES AND RECOMMENDED READINGS

Gall, J., Gall, M., & Borg, W. (2005). *Applying Educational Research: A Practical Guide* (5th ed.). Boston: Allyn & Bacon.

Gay, L. R., Mills, G. E., & Airasian, P. (2009). *Educational Research: Comptencies for Analysis and Applications* (9th ed.). Upper Saddle River, NJ: Merrill.

Suter, W. N. (2006). *Introduction to Educational Research: A Critical Thinking Approach.* Thousand Oaks, CA: Sage.

Worthen, B. R., & Sanders, J. R. (1987). *Educational Evaluation: Alternative Approaches and Practical Guidelines.* New York: Longman.

Appendix

Overview of Statistical Concepts and Procedures

Statistical concepts and procedures were introduced as needed in various chapters. Here they are brought together in an expanded presentation that permits consideration and practice in greater detail, should one desire. Some of the material on the following pages repeats earlier presentations.

This appendix will consider the following aspects of statistics:

- The nature and uses of statistics
- The relationship of statistics to populations and samples
- The difference between parametric and nonparametric statistics
- The calculation and interpretation of descriptive statistics
- The relationship of statistics to the normal probability curve
- Relative standings associated with the normal curve
- The calculation and interpretation of inferential statistics
- Chi-square—its use, calculation, and interpretation
- Calculating and interpreting standard error and confidence limits
- Testing for significance
- Type I and Type II errors

THE NATURE AND USES OF STATISTICS

Statistics are used to describe and analyze numerical data. As pointed out previously, the term *statistics* has two widely used meanings. One refers to summary statements resulting from data analysis, such as mean, median, standard deviation, and coefficient of correlation. The other refers to the procedures by which data are analyzed mathematically. We begin this review by considering the ways statistical analysis is typically used:

■ *To summarize data and reveal what is typical and atypical within a group.* Research often yields hundreds or thousands of items of numerical data that, until summarized, cannot be interpreted meaningfully. Researchers are especially interested in learning what is typical of the group being studied, as well as what individuals do that is atypical.

■ *To show relative standing of individuals in a group.* Statistics can show where an individual stands for a given measurement in relation to all other individuals being studied. Such standings are shown through percentile rankings, grade equivalents, age equivalents, z scores, T scores, and stanines, all discussed later.

■ *To show relationships among variables.* Investigators are often interested in determining whether correlations exist among variables—for instance, between students' family backgrounds and their success in school. Such relationships can be described by means of statistical correlations.

■ *To show similarities and differences among groups.* Researchers are often interested in ascertaining the degree to which groups are similar to or different from each other. For example, in experimental research they need to establish that the two or more groups involved at the beginning of the experiment are approximately equal in the trait being investigated. Then later they need to determine whether the groups have become different from each other, possibly due to the experimental treatment that has been given to one or more of the groups.

■ *To estimate error that may have occurred in sample selection.* Samples almost always differ to some extent from the population from which they are drawn. This difference introduces a degree of error into research, so that one can never be precisely sure that a statistical finding is also correct for the population. Error refers to an estimate of disparity that may exist between a given statistic and its corresponding parameter value—that is, between what is measured in a sample and what exists in the population. Statistical procedures enable one to determine a value called **standard error**—of measurements, means, correlations, and differences between means. When the standard error is known, it is possible to specify the "confidence levels" for a particular value or finding. For example, if we find a sample mean of 6.2 and then determine its standard error, we can conclude with confidence that the population mean lies somewhere within a given range, such as between 7.1 and 5.3.

■ *To test for significance of findings.* When researchers discover apparent correlations between variables or differences between means, they apply statistical tests of **significance.** These tests help determine whether their findings might be due to chance errors that occurred when the sample was selected, which could result in the sample's not reflecting the population. If the finding is sufficiently large to override sampling error, the researcher will call the finding significant. Significance permits one to conclude that a particular finding is probably real for the population rather than a result of sampling error.

POPULATIONS AND SAMPLES

As we proceed into consideration of statistics and their calculation and interpretation, let us acknowledge again the relationships among population, sample, parameters, and statistics. *Population* refers to the totality of individuals or objects that correspond to a particular description. The following are examples of populations:

■ All the females in North America
■ All the girls in Cutter Elementary School
■ All the boys in Cutter Elementary School who qualify for the honor society
■ All the sixth-grade mathematics textbooks published during the past 20 years

Parameters are numerical descriptions of populations. Parameters include such descriptions as the following:

■ The number of individuals in the population
■ The mean (arithmetic average) of various measures made of population members, such as height, weight, or IQ
■ The median (midpoint) in a set of measurements of a particular trait, such as height
■ The standard deviation (an indicator of variability) of various measures made on population members
■ The range of difference between the highest and lowest measures of a particular trait

Samples are smaller groups selected from populations. Samples are used in research when it is not feasible to study the entire population. Because the sample is intended to reflect the characteristics of the population, special care is taken in its selection. Members of the sample are usually selected randomly from the population, a procedure that usually, but not always, yields a sample representative of the population. The following are examples of samples:

■ 1,000 females selected at random from all the females in North America
■ 50 girls selected from among all the girls in Cutter Elementary School
■ Each fifth title from an alphabetized list of all titles of sixth-grade mathematics textbooks published during the past 20 years

Statistics are numerical descriptions of samples. They are the same as parameters, except that they refer to samples rather than populations. The following are examples of statistical descriptions:

- The number of individuals in the sample
- The mean (arithmetic average) of various measures made of sample members, such as height, weight, or IQ
- The median (midpoint) in a set of sample measurements of a particular trait, such as height, weight, or IQ
- The standard deviation (an indicator of variability) of various measures taken from sample members
- The range of difference between the highest and lowest measures of a particular trait

PARAMETRIC STATISTICS AND NONPARAMETRIC STATISTICS

It is important also to distinguish between parametric statistics and nonparametric statistics. Both are useful in research. They are different in that **parametric statistics** are used for analyzing traits that are normally distributed in the population—that is, in a manner that approximates the normal probability curve, shown later in Figures A.3 and A.4. This curve is also known as the *bell-shaped curve* (from its appearance) and as simply the *normal curve.*

Nonparametric statistics, on the other hand, are used to describe and analyze data that are not assumed to be normally distributed in the population. Examples of such nonparametric data are frequency counts (e.g., the number of blue-eyed participants) and rankings (e.g., the order in which runners finished a race). Several nonparametric statistics have been developed for use in analyzing data; the one you are most likely to encounter is the chi-square test, used to analyze data that are classified into categories. Calculation of chi-square is described later.

THE CALCULATION AND INTERPRETATION OF DESCRIPTIVE STATISTICS

You have seen that statistics are used, among other things, to describe data—to show (1) what is typical of the sample, (2) how diverse or spread out the measures are, (3) the relative standings of individual measures, and (4) relationships among variables being studied. Using a practice set of 10 easily handled scores, we will proceed through a few simple exercises to show how these statistical calculations are done. The purpose is to help you develop an understanding of concept and procedure.

MEASURES OF CENTRAL TENDENCY

What is typical for a sample, for any trait being measured, is shown by three statistics referred to as **measures of central tendency**—the mean, the median, and the mode.

The *mean* is the arithmetic average of a set of measures, such as achievement, age, or performance. The mean helps depict what is typical for the group and is a component of many other statistical formulas as well. To calculate the mean, you simply add up the scores and divide the sum by the number of scores. What is the mean of the following practice set of scores?

9, 8, 8, 7, 7, 7, 4, 4, 3, 3 (Answer: $\overline{X} = 6$)

The *median* is a statistic that also indicates typicality. It is simply the midpoint in an array of scores, determined by counting halfway through an array that has been arranged from highest score to lowest. In other words, the median is the score that separates the distribution or array into two equal halves—with 50 percent of the scores above and 50 percent of the scores below that particular value. If there is an odd number of scores in the array, the median falls on the middle score. For an array with an even number of scores, the median lies halfway between the two middle scores.

What is the median for the practice set of scores?

9, 8, 8, 7, 7, 7, 4, 4, 3, 3 (Answer: *Mdn* = 7)

The median is sometimes more valuable than the mean in depicting typicality, especially when the distribution contains a few scores that are extremely high or low. The median is normally used to report such data as average personal income and typical cost of homes, because a few extremely high salaries or extremely expensive homes can produce a mean score that is not reflective of the group.

Although *mode* is included here so you will recognize that it indicates the most frequently occurring score or measurement, the concept of mode has no other application in descriptive statistics. What is the mode for the practice set of scores?

9, 8, 8, 7, 7, 7, 4, 4, 3, 3 (Answer: *Mo* = 7)

MEASURES OF VARIABILITY

Measures of variability show how spread out a group of scores is. Researchers want to know to what extent the scores, overall, vary from the mean of the group of scores. Consider the following sets of scores:

Set A: 9, 10, 10, 10, 10, 10, 10, 10, 10, 11
Set B: 1, 3, 5, 7, 9, 11, 13, 15, 17, 19

What are the mean and median of Set A? (Answer: $\overline{X}$ = 10; *Mdn* = 10)

What are the mean and median of Set B? (Answer: $\overline{X}$ = 10; *Mdn* = 10)

Which set of scores would you guess shows the greatest dispersion or variability, overall, from the mean? (Answer: Set B)

To depict the degree to which scores are dispersed in the two sets, three measures of variability are typically used—range, variance, and standard deviation. *Range* shows the distance from highest score through the lowest score and is calculated as R = highest score − lowest score. Thus, the range for scores in Set A is 2: 11 − 9 = 2. The range for Set B is 18. Although range may be of some interest in itself, it does not present an accurate picture of dispersion among scores. For example, consider the range for the following set of scores:

1, 10, 10, 10, 10, 10, 10, 11, 11, 11

The range is 10, but in fact the overall internal dispersion of scores is quite low. Much more useful indicators of dispersion are variance and standard deviation. Both indicate how much all the scores, when taken into account together, vary from the mean. Both variance and standard deviation are used in formulas for other statistical applications.

Let us calculate the variance and standard deviation of our practice set of scores, using Table A.1, in which $X - \overline{X}$ is the *deviation score* indicating how much each raw score differs from the mean, and $(X - \overline{X})^2$ shows the deviation squared. The mean ($\overline{X}$) for our scores is 6. If you add up the values by which each score deviates from the mean (second column), what total do you get? The total for this column is always zero. To obtain positive values, each deviation $(X - \overline{X})$ is squared. The sum of those squared values (known as the *sum of squares*), when divided by the number of scores, gives us the variance (S^2) of scores. If the scores represent a sample, $N - 1$ should be used instead of N in determining the variance.

Variance in the illustration given above is $46 \div 9 = 5.11$, but that still does not tell us much, for there is nothing in practical experience to which most of us can relate this value because it exists on a squared scale. The degree to which the scores are dispersed is made

Table A.1 Calculation of Variance and Standard Deviation

Raw Score (X)	$(X - \overline{X})$	$(X - \overline{X})^2$
9	3	9
8	2	4
8	2	4
7	1	1
7	1	1
7	1	1
4	−2	4
4	−2	4
3	−3	9
3	−3	9
sum = 60		$46 = \text{sum } (X - \overline{X})^2$
$\overline{X} = 6$		$S^2 = \text{sum } (X - \overline{X})^2/(N - 1) = 5.11$

somewhat more understandable by using the standard deviation of the scores, calculated with the following formula:

$$SD = \sqrt{\frac{\Sigma(X - \overline{X})^2}{(N - 1)}}$$

where Σ = the sum of
$(X - \overline{X})^2$ = the square of the amount by which each score differs from the mean
N = the number of scores

Standard deviation is the square root of the sample variance, which we already determined to be 5.11. The square root of 5.11 gives us a standard deviation of 2.26.

As mentioned, the computer can do all this for you in the blink of an eye. Figure A.1 shows the descriptive statistics for our group of 10 scores, calculated using the *Statistical*

Figure A.1

Computer-analyzed descriptive statistics, using SPSS

Source: SPSS for Windows, Rel. 17.0. 2008. Chicago: SPSS, Inc.

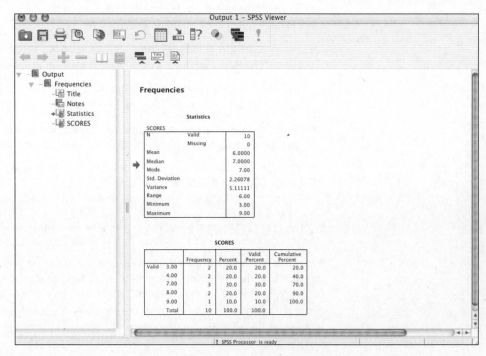

Package for the Social Sciences (SPSS), version 17.0, a complex but easy-to-use statistical software package—very popular with educational researchers—on which descriptive and inferential statistics can be calculated.

Exercise A.1

For practice in the statistical calculations presented so far, try your hand at the following:

1. Compute the mean of the following set of scores:

     1, 4, 4, 5, 8, 8, 9, 9, 9, 10

2. Determine the median of this set of scores:

     1, 2, 2, 2, 3, 4, 6

3. Give the median of this set of scores:

     1, 2, 2, 2, 3, 4, 6, 6

4. Find the range of this set of scores:

     5, 7, 8, 9, 9, 9, 10, 10, 11, 12

5. Find the mean and median of the scores in item 4.

Descriptive statistics are also used for showing relative position and measures of relationship.

RELATIVE POSITION

Common statistics that show **measures of relative position** are percentile rank, stanines, and converted scores.

■ *Percentile rank (%ile* or *PR)* is a ranking assigned to a particular score showing the percentage of all scores that fall below that particular score.

   Example: Juan's score fell at the 56th percentile. This means that he equaled or excelled 56 percent of all other students who took the test.

■ *Stanines* are nine bands of scores with values from 1 to 9 (where 5 represents the average), which show where a score stands in relation to others.

   Example: Mary's score fell in the 6th stanine. This means she was slightly above average among all similar students who took the test.

■ *Converted scores* are values assigned to raw scores, such as the grade-level equivalency that corresponds to the score a student made on a test.

   Example: Shawn made a score of 46 on the test, which places him at the seventh-grade, sixth-month level.

RELATIONSHIPS

Measures of relationships are shown statistically through correlations. The numerical value that indicates the degree of covarying relationship between two or more variables is called the *coefficient of correlation.* A coefficient of correlation (the most commonly used correlational procedure—the Pearson product-moment—is symbolized by the letter *r*) is a measure of relationship between two or more sets of scores made by the same group of participants.

Example: The correlation between reading ability and achievement test scores was +.32. This means there was a modest positive relationship between the two.

Research regularly explores relationships between such traits as self-concept and achievement, motivation and achievement, active class participation and achievement, listening ability and achievement, communication and attitude, and so on. The public generally believes that correlations show cause and effect, but as noted previously, such is not the case. The correlation between intake of saturated fat and incidence of heart disease does not, itself, prove that either causes the other. But it is fair to say that correlations often strongly *suggest* cause and effect and can sometimes lead to experimental research showing that one factor does in fact "cause" another.

Data for correlational research must be obtained in the form of two sets of measures for each individual in the sample. That is, each participant is measured for trait X (perhaps attitude toward school) as well as trait Y (perhaps grade point average). Then the pairs of measurements are correlated statistically. The resultant coefficient of correlation (r) indicates the degree of relationship between the variables, as shown in Figure A.2.

Correlations are most commonly calculated from interval data (such as scores) but can also be computed from nominal data (such as categories) or ordinal data (such as rankings). Computers can instantly calculate coefficients of correlation. For that reason, and because the hand calculation of r is laborious to the point of exhaustion, the procedure for deriving r is not shown here.

The following should be kept in mind concerning correlations:

1. Correlations vary in magnitude from 0 (absence of relationship) to extremes of ±1.0 (a perfect correlation). Coefficients of 0 and ±1.0 are virtually never encountered in research.
2. Correlations may be either positive or negative. In positive correlations, high marks on one variable tend to accompany high marks on the other variable, average accompany average, and low accompany low. You would expect to find a positive correlation between body weight and caloric intake. In negative correlations, high marks on one variable tend to accompany low marks on the other, average accompany average, and low accompany high. You would expect to find a negative correlation between body weight and frequency of aerobic exercise.
3. Positive and negative correlations have equal value in making predictions.

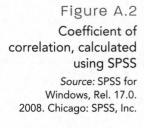

Figure A.2

Coefficient of correlation, calculated using SPSS

Source: SPSS for Windows, Rel. 17.0. 2008. Chicago: SPSS, Inc.

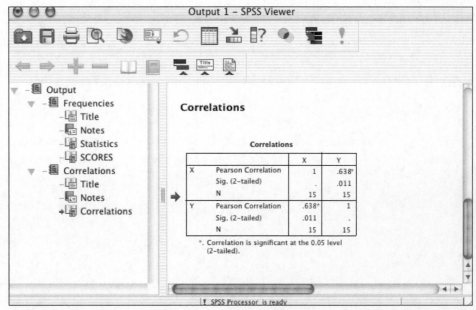

4. Correlations discovered in education and the social sciences rarely exceed ±.70. Nonetheless, lower correlations are often useful and enlightening.

DESCRIPTIVE STATISTICS AND THE NORMAL PROBABILITY CURVE

Reference has been made to the **normal probability curve,** and parametric statistics were described as related to traits that are normally distributed. At this point, we examine the relationships of statistical concepts to the normal curve.

Note that in Figure A.3 the mean is located at the centermost part of the curve. The curve is deepest there, indicating that more measures fall at that point than anywhere else along the baseline. Progressing along the baseline to the right, where measures are higher than the mean, the frequencies become progressively fewer until none occurs. Similarly, to the left-hand side, which depicts measures lower than the mean, the frequencies again become progressively fewer until there are no more.

Figure A.3 also shows where standard deviations fall in a normal distribution and indicates the proportion of the population bracketed by standard deviations. You see that the area beneath the curve bracketed by the lines at −1 and +1 standard deviations includes 68.26 percent—roughly two-thirds—of all the measures. By going out to −2 to +2 standard deviations, we account for 95.44 percent of all measures, and at −3 to +3 standard deviations, 99.75 percent of the population measures are accounted for.

Be sure to take into account, too, that 95 percent of all the population scores are included in the area bracketed by +1.96 standard deviations down to −1.96 standard deviations. These areas beneath the curve depict the .05 level used for expressions of confidence and tests of significance—the α-level. The area bracketed by +2.58 down to −2.58 standard deviations includes 99 percent of all scores, which equates to the .01 probability level.

Figure A.3   The normal curve, showing the mean, standard deviations, and percent of cases throughout the distribution

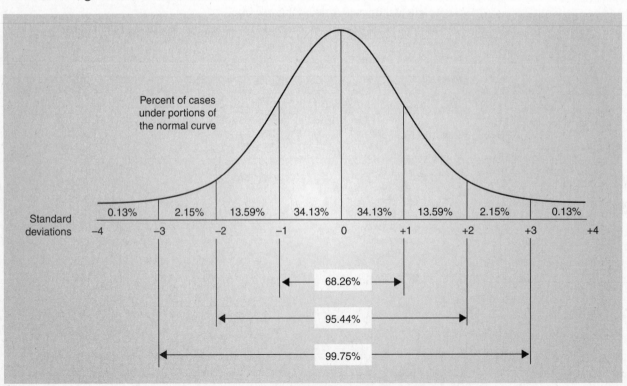

RELATIVE STANDINGS ASSOCIATED WITH THE NORMAL CURVE

Relative standing, which shows the placement of an individual in relation to others measured in the same way, is typically indicated by percentile rankings and occasionally by stanine rankings, which we have explored, and by z scores and T scores as well. These relationships are shown in Figure A.4.

PERCENTILE RANKINGS

Suppose Steve has taken a science aptitude test and is told his performance places him at the 73rd percentile. This means that Steve's score was as high as, or higher than, 73 percent of all people similar to Steve who had taken the test. This does not mean that Steve responded correctly to 73 percent of the test problems but simply that he performed better than 73 percent of others of his status who have taken the test. Note the words *similar to Steve*

Figure A.4   The relationship of standard deviations, as well as several other indicators of relative position, to the normal curve

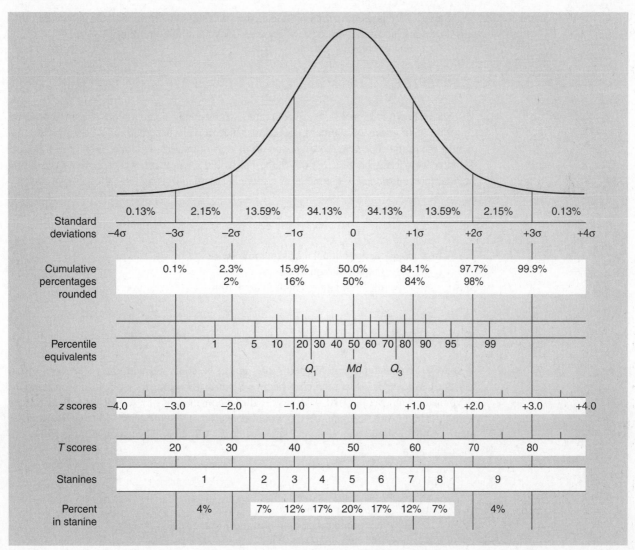

and *of his status.* Those qualifiers indicate that Steve, in sixth grade, is not to be compared directly with Frank, who is in 11th grade. They might have made the same raw score on the test, but Frank might have reached only the 49th percentile, because eleventh-grade students make higher scores than do sixth-grade students. The population that includes Steve is all sixth-grade students. Frank is in a different population—all 11th-grade students.

As you can see in Figure A.4, percentile rankings range from a low of 1 (1st percentile) to a high of 99 (99th percentile). There is no 0th percentile or 100th percentile; the assumption is made that there could always be a lower or higher score. The mean and the median in a normal distribution both fall at the 50th percentile.

STANINES

Look beneath the curve in Figure A.4 to where stanines are represented. Stanines (as mentioned earlier in the text, the name comes from "standard nine") are bands of scores used for convenience. They begin at the mean, with the middle stanine, the fifth, covering the area from +0.25 standard deviation to –0.25 standard deviation. Except for the first and the ninth stanines, each stanine covers one-half of a standard deviation, the fourth, third, and second progressively downward, and the sixth, seventh, and eighth progressively upward. The first stanine includes all scores below the second, and the ninth stanine includes all scores above the eighth.

Steve's 73rd percentile ranking falls in the sixth stanine. Notice that his percentile ranking shows his placement more precisely than does his stanine ranking.

Z SCORES

Z scores (shown in Figure A.4) are converted scores that indicate a score's relative position in terms of fractions of standard deviations. If Ann were assigned a *z* score of +0.5, that would mean that her raw score was one-half of a standard deviation above the mean. If Heather were assigned a *z* score of –0.35, that would mean that her raw score was 0.35 of a standard deviation below the mean. A *z* score is calculated using the following formula:

$$z = \frac{X - \mu}{\sigma}$$

where X = the individual's original raw score
μ = the population mean
σ = the population standard deviation

T SCORES

T scores (another type of converted score, not to be confused with the *t* test) correspond perfectly to *z* scores, except that they begin with an artificial mean of 50, with each standard deviation given a value of 10. *T* scores are direct conversions of *z* scores but with all values being positive. Ann's *z* score of +0.5 would convert to a *T* score of 55, whereas Heather's *z* score of –0.35 would convert to a *T* score of 46.5. A *T* score is calculated in the following manner:

$$T = 50 + 10z$$

where 50 = the mean of the *T* score scale
10 = the standard deviation of the *T* score scale
z = the individual's *z* score

In practice, z scores and T scores are not widely used, although they represent relative standings as accurately as do percentile rankings and much more accurately than do stanine rankings.

CALCULATING AND INTERPRETING INFERENTIAL STATISTICS

Inferential statistics are used to make inferences about the population, based on what has been learned about the sample. They include the following:

1. Error estimates that indicate the range within which a given measure probably lies

   Example: If the study were repeated many times, the correlation would probably continue to fall between .28 and .36.

2. Confidence levels that indicate the probability that a population value lies within certain specified boundaries

   Example: There is 95 percent probability that the population value lies between .22 and .42.

3. Tests of significance, which indicate whether a finding is sufficiently strong to outweigh the effect of chance errors that might have been made in selecting the sample. Frequently seen tests of significance include

   - Significance of correlation

     Example: If the study were repeated hundreds of times, errors made in selecting the sample would account for a correlation of this magnitude less than 5 percent of the time. This is symbolized $p < .05$.

   - Significance of difference between means of small samples (*t* test)

     Example: If the study were repeated hundreds of times, a difference of this magnitude could be attributed to sampling error in fewer than 5 percent of the cases ($p < .05$).

   - Significance of difference between or among means (analysis of variance **F test**)

     Example: Same as for difference between means.

Exercise A.2

Use the normal curve shown in Figure A.4 to answer the following:

1. What percentages of population measures fall

   _____ between 0 and +1 standard deviations?

   _____ beyond +3 standard deviations?

   _____ between 0 and –2 standard deviations?

2. What are the stanine equivalents of

   _____ 50th percentile?

   _____ 15th percentile?

   _____ 90th percentile?

If the test of significance leads us to believe (usually at 95 percent probability or greater) that a particular finding has not occurred because of errors we made in selecting the sample, we call the finding "significant." In this case we may conclude that the finding is probably real for the population. If, on the other hand, the probability level is unacceptably high (usually greater than 5 percent) that our finding might have occurred because of errors we made in selecting the sample, we deem the finding "not significant." In this case we would conclude that the finding is probably not real for the population.

Exercise A.3

Supply the appropriate name for each of the following:

1. The most frequent score
2. The relationship between two sets of scores made by the same individuals
3. The arithmetic average of the scores
4. The difference between the highest and lowest score in a group
5. A finding is probably real for the population—not attributable to sample error
6. The true measure for the sample probably lies within these boundaries
7. There is a 95 percent probability that the population mean lies within these boundaries
8. Statistics used to make judgments about the population
9. John's score equaled or surpassed 68 percent of all scores
10. Measures that show spread or diversion

CHI-SQUARE—ITS CALCULATION AND INTERPRETATION

Chi-square is a nonparametric inferential statistical procedure frequently used in research. The descriptive and inferential statistics discussed to this point have all been parametric procedures, involving variable interval data (e.g., scores) that are presumed to be distributed normally in the population. As you recall, nonparametric statistics such as chi-square are applied to data that are not assumed to be normally distributed in the population. Chi-square is frequently used when data can be placed into categories. To elaborate on an earlier example, suppose that you wish to determine which of three courses—geometry, English, or biology—Elmwood students consider most valuable in their daily lives. You randomly select from the eleventh-grade Elmwood population a sample of 30 students who took the three courses when in 10th grade. You state a null hypothesis that 11th-grade students see no differences in value among the geometry, English, and biology courses they took in 10th grade. If the null hypothesis is true, then students will show no pattern of preference; they will choose the three courses equally—perhaps 10 selecting geometry, 10 selecting English, and 10 selecting biology. This equality of choice is what you expect to observe if the null hypothesis is correct.

But suppose that when the 30 students are asked to indicate which of the courses they believe most valuable, they respond as follows: 3 select geometry, 19 select English, and 8 select biology. Those response choices are what you actually do observe.

By statistically comparing what you expect to observe against what you actually do observe, it is possible to determine whether differences between the two are significant by calculating and interpreting chi-square. Using the example figures and the formula for chi-square shown below, we can complete calculations by hand.

$$\chi^2 = \Sigma\ \frac{(f_o - f_e)^2}{f_e}$$

where χ^2 = chi-square
Σ = sum of
$(f_o - f_e)^2$ = the square of the difference, for each category, between the observed frequencies and those that were expected. Each square is divided by the appropriate expected frequency, and the results are then summated.

Let us proceed to Table A.2 for a concrete example. Having obtained a chi-square value of 13.4, we determine its level of significance by consulting a table of critical values for chi-square, presented in Table A.3. The degrees of freedom *(df)* for our example is 2 (the number of categories minus 1). Check Table A.3 for 2 *df* and read across to the right. You can see that our 13.4 surpasses the critical value at the .01 level of significance. Based on that, we can reasonably reject the null hypothesis of no difference in course preferences.

Table A.2   Calculation of Chi-Square

Course	Observed	Expected	$(f_o - f_e)$	$(f_o - f_e)^2$	$(f_o - f_e)^2/f_e$
Geometry	3	10	−7	49	4.9
English	19	10	9	81	8.1
Biology	8	10	−2	4	0.4
					χ^2 = 13.4

Table A.3   Table of Critical Values for Chi-Square

df	0.05	0.01	df	0.05	0.01
1	3.841	6.635	16	26.296	32.000
2	5.991	9.210	17	27.587	33.409
3	7.815	11.345	18	28.869	34.805
4	9.488	13.277	19	30.144	36.191
5	11.070	15.086	20	31.410	37.566
6	12.592	16.812	21	32.671	38.932
7	14.067	18.475	22	33.924	40.289
8	15.507	20.090	23	35.172	41.638
9	16.919	21.666	24	36.415	42.980
10	18.307	23.209	25	37.652	44.314
11	19.675	24.725	26	38.885	45.642
12	21.026	26.217	27	40.113	46.963
13	22.362	27.688	28	41.337	48.278
14	23.685	29.141	29	42.557	49.588
15	24.996	30.578	30	43.773	50.892

Source: Adapted from Table IV, p. 47, of Fisher and Yates: *Statistical Tables for Biological, Agricultural and Medical Research,* published by Longman Group Ltd., London (previously published by Oliver and Boyd, Ltd., Edinburgh).

CALCULATING AND INTERPRETING STANDARD ERROR AND CONFIDENCE LIMITS

We know that samples are almost never exactly like the populations from which they come. Therefore, we must accept that means, correlations, and other statistical values and findings in the sample are not exactly the same as their parametric counterparts in the population.

In order to estimate how closely a statistic matches its corresponding population parameter, we employ a concept called *standard error*. Standard error can be understood as follows: Suppose we have a population for which we know a parameter. Let us say the population comprises all 11th-grade students in the state of Kansas, and the parameter that we know is those students' mean grade point average. If we obtained a number of samples from that population and for each sample computed a mean grade point average, we would find that most of the sample means differed somewhat from the population mean, some by tiny amounts and a few by larger amounts. If we plotted those differences we would find that they formed themselves into a distribution shaped like the normal probability curve. In other words, the differences between sample values and their corresponding population values are normally distributed and can, therefore, be analyzed by means of parametric statistics. We can compute a mean of those differences and a standard deviation of those differences, just as if they were raw scores.

Now, let us suppose that we have selected a random sample from a population whose parameters we do not know—let it be a sample of 50 male students from the population of all 11th-grade male students in the state of Nebraska. This time we measure the heights of those 50 students and calculate a mean and standard deviation. We can obtain a good estimate of how closely this mean approximates that of the population, even though we do not know the population mean, through use of the following formula for determining the standard error of the sample mean:

$$SE_{\overline{X}} = \frac{SD}{\sqrt{N}}$$

where $SE_{\overline{X}}$ = standard error of mean
SD = standard deviation of the sample
N = size of sample

Suppose the mean height for our sample is 69 inches, with a standard deviation of 2 inches. The standard error of our sample mean equals 2 (the sample standard deviation) divided by 7.07 (the square root of 50), which gives a standard error of 0.28 inches. Now if we say that the real (population) mean does not differ from the sample mean by more than +2.01 or –2.01 standard errors from the sample mean, we have a 95 percent probability of being correct. In other words, the chances are that if we selected another 1,000 samples from the population, in about 95 percent of those samples the mean height would be between 69.56 inches—our sample mean of 69 inches plus (0.28 inches × 2.01)—and 68.44 inches—our sample mean of 69 inches minus (0.28 inches × 2.01).

The upper level of 69.56 and the lower level of 68.44 in this case are used to state *confidence limits*. We can "confidently" say that if we repeated the study thousands of times, we would find a mean height between 69.56 inches and 68.44 inches at least 95 percent of the time.

Standard error can be computed for several measures other than the mean, most notably single measurements (e.g., one person's score on a test), differences between means, and correlations. To determine the standard error of a single measurement we must know the reliability coefficient of the measuring scale or test. The formula is

$$SE_M = SD \sqrt{1-r}$$

where SE_M = standard error of the measurement
SD = standard deviation of test
r = reliability coefficient of test

The result obtained from this calculation is applied just as was the standard error of the mean.

A similar procedure is used to determine the standard error of the difference between means. In studies that involve comparisons, researchers administer a test to two or more groups and then analyze the differences in mean performance of those groups. Suppose after drawing two 50-student samples from the population of 11th-grade boys in Nebraska, we had given one of the samples two weeks' training in muscle stretching and then tested both groups for the number of chin-ups they could do to find a difference of 0.5 chin-ups between the mean of group X and the mean of group Y. We know that if the study were repeated many times, the difference between the means would vary from study to study. Therefore, we wish to find the standard error of the difference between means. However, before we can calculate the standard error, we must first pool the variances of the two samples, which is accomplished through the use of the following formula:

$$s_p^2 = \frac{SS_X + SS_Y}{df_X + df_Y}$$

where s_p^2 = pooled variance
SS = sums of squares (for each group)
df = degrees of freedom ($n - 1$, for each group)

Once we have calculated the pooled variance, we can use its value and the following formula to calculate the standard error of the difference between means:

$$SE_{dM} = \sqrt{\frac{s_p^2}{n_X} + \frac{s_p^2}{n_Y}}$$

where SE_{dM} = standard error of the difference between the means
s_p^2 = pooled variance
n = sample size (for each group)

Suppose that the pooled variance for the two groups was equal to 10. Substituting this value into the equation for the standard error would result in a value equal to 0.63. If this study were repeated hundreds of times, about 95 percent of those repetitions would reveal mean differences within a range of -1.25 and $+1.25$ (i.e., 0.63 times ± 1.98, which is the critical value for t) from the difference between the means observed in this study.

In all of these cases, you can see that the standard error is inversely proportional to the number of participants in the sample. In other words, the larger the sample, the smaller the standard error. As the sample size approaches that of the population, the standard error shrinks to zero.

TESTING FOR SIGNIFICANCE

Findings such as correlations and differences among means are routinely tested for significance. Significance of the coefficient of correlation is determined by consulting a table of critical values for r, as presented in Table A.4. You will notice that the table calls for **degrees of freedom** (df). Degrees of freedom in correlational analyses equal the number of pairs of scores minus 2. If you had 50 participants involved in a correlation, you would have 50 pairs of scores. Therefore, $N - 2$ would be 48 degrees of freedom. Suppose you have found a coefficient of correlation of .25 and you had specified an alpha level of .05.

Table A.4   Table of Critical Values for Correlation Coefficients (for Both One- and Two-Tailed Tests)

Example: When N is 52 and (N – 2) is 50, an r must be > 0.273 to be significant at the .05 level, and > 0.354 to be significant at the .01 level.

Degrees of Freedom (N – 2)	Level of significance for one-tailed test		Degrees of Freedom (N – 2)	Level of significance for one-tailed test	
	.025	.005		.025	.005
	Level of significance for two-tailed test			Level of significance for two-tailed test	
	.05	.01		.05	.01
1	.997	1.000	24	.388	.496
2	.950	.990	25	.381	.487
3	.878	.959	26	.374	.478
4	.811	.917	27	.367	.470
5	.754	.874	28	.361	.463
6	.707	.834	29	.355	.456
7	.666	.798	30	.349	.449
8	.632	.765	35	.325	.418
9	.602	.735	40	.304	.393
10	.576	.708	45	.288	.372
11	.553	.684	50	.273	.354
12	.532	.661	60	.250	.325
13	.514	.641	70	.232	.302
14	.497	.623	80	.217	.283
15	.482	.606	90	.205	.267
16	.468	.590	100	.195	.254
17	.456	.575	125	.174	.228
18	.444	.561	150	.159	.208
19	.433	.549	200	.138	.181
20	.423	.537	300	.113	.148
21	.413	.526	400	.098	.128
22	.404	.515	500	.088	.115
23	.396	.505	1000	.062	.081

Source: From Garrett, Henry E. (1947). *Statistics in Psychology and Education,* Longman, p. 299. Reprinted by permission.

Fifty participants were involved in your study. According to Table A.4, does the coefficient of .25 reach the .05 level of significance?

See Figure A.2 for a sample correlation. For an alpha level of .01, check Table A.3 to determine whether or not this correlation is significant ($df = 11$).

Significance of the difference between means, when only two groups are being compared, can be determined by applying a *t* test and then consulting a table of critical values for *t,* as shown in Table A.5.

The formula for the *t* test is

$$t = \frac{\overline{X} - \overline{Y}}{SE_{dM}}$$

where $\overline{X}$ = mean of group X
           $\overline{Y}$ = mean of group Y
           SE_{dM} = standard error of the difference between means

Suppose you find a difference of 5.0 between two means, with a standard error of the difference between means of 2.0. Degrees of freedom are the total number of participants in both groups minus 2. Suppose there were 25 participants in each group. Degrees of freedom would, therefore, be 50 minus 2, or 48. Now check Table A.5 at approximately 48 degrees of freedom. Is the difference significant at the .05 level? At the .01 level?

When data from three or more groups are being analyzed for differences among means, analysis of variance (abbreviated ANOVA) should be used. The use of ANOVA is also appropriate in place of a t test when the samples are relatively large and unequal, provided the discrepancy is not extreme. Earlier you saw the relationship between variance and standard deviation: Variance is the square of standard deviation, and standard deviation the square root of variance.

In analyzing variance to explore difference among means, the variance that exists between groups is compared with the variance that exists within groups. Dividing between-groups variance by within-groups variance, we obtain an F ratio:

$$F = \frac{s^2_{between\text{-}group}}{s^2_{within\text{-}group}}$$

Table A.5 Table of Critical Values for t (for Both One- and Two-Tailed Tests)

Degrees of Freedom	Proportion in one tail		Degrees of Freedom	Proportion in one tail	
	.025	.005		0.25	.005
	Proportion in two tails			Proportion in two tails	
	.05	.01		.05	.01
1	$t = 12.71$	$t = 63.66$	20	2.09	2.84
2	4.30	9.92	21	2.08	2.83
3	3.18	5.84	22	2.07	2.82
4	2.78	4.60	23	2.07	2.82
5	2.57	4.03	24	2.06	2.80
6	2.45	3.71	25	2.06	2.79
7	2.36	3.50	26	2.06	2.80
8	2.31	3.36	27	2.05	2.77
9	2.26	3.25	28	2.05	2.76
10	2.23	3.17	29	2.04	2.76
11	2.20	3.11	30	2.04	2.75
12	2.18	3.06	35	2.03	2.72
13	2.16	3.01	40	2.02	2.71
14	2.14	2.98	45	2.02	2.69
15	2.13	2.95	50	2.01	2.65
16	2.12	2.92	60	2.00	2.66
17	2.11	2.90	70	2.00	2.65
18	2.10	2.88	80	1.99	2.64
19	2.09	2.86	90	1.99	2.63

Source: Garret, Henry E. (1947). From *Statistics in Psychology and Education,* Longman, p. 464. Reprinted by permission.

The resultant F ratio can be checked manually against a table of critical values of F (not provided here) to determine its significance level, but it is much easier to let the computer do it for you when it calculates analysis of variance.

TYPE I AND TYPE II ERRORS

As you know, hypotheses are frequently stated in the null form for greater ease in applying tests of significance. In light of a significance test you have applied, you may reject your null hypothesis and conclude that your finding is real for the population, not due to error made in selecting the sample. Or else you may retain your null hypothesis and conclude that a particular finding is probably due to sampling error and thus is not real for the population. In either case, the statistical procedures you have used make you feel fairly confident about your decision. Still, you never know for sure whether you are right.

It may be that the null hypothesis is correct—that, for example, there is no difference between means or no correlation—but based on your statistical analysis you reject the hypothesis. When you reject a null hypothesis that is in reality true, you are said to have made a **Type I error.** Conversely, if you retain a null hypothesis when it is in reality false, you are said to have made a **Type II error.**

Type I error: You conclude that there is a correlation or a difference when in actuality there is not. (You wrongly reject the null hypothesis.)

Type II error: You conclude that there is not a correlation or a difference when in reality there is. (You wrongly retain the null hypothesis.)

The likelihood of your making Type I and Type II errors depends on the significance levels you set. Researchers do not wish to make errors of any kind, but generally speaking they would rather make a Type II error than a Type I error—that is, they would rather conclude that no correlation or difference exists (although one does) than to conclude that a correlation or difference exists when it does not. This preference is in keeping with the philosophy of science, which is to require a preponderance of proof before a new finding is accepted.

REVIEW OF STATISTICAL TERMINOLOGY

Descriptive Statistics	Inferential Statistics	Nonparametric Statistics
Central tendency	*Standard error*	*Proportions*
Mean	Of measurement	Chi-square
Median	Of mean	
Mode	Of differences between means	
Variability	*Tests of significance*	
Range	Of correlation	
Variance	Of difference between means	
Standard deviation		
Relative standing	*Analysis of variance*	
Percentile ranking		
Stanines	*Type I error*	
Grade equivalents	*Type II error*	
Age equivalents		

LIST OF IMPORTANT TERMS

degrees of freedom

F test

measures of central tendency

measures of relationship

measures of relative position

measures of variability

nonparametric statistics

normal probability curve

parametric statistics

significance

standard error

T scores

Type I error

Type II error

z scores

ANSWERS TO EXERCISES

A.1. 1. 6.7   2. 2   3. 2.5   4. 7   5. $\overline{X} = 9$, *Mdn* = 9

A.2. 1. 34.13, 0.13, 47.72   2. 5, 3, 8

A.3. 1. Mode   2. Correlation   3. Mean   4. Range
5. Significant   6. Error estimate   7. Confidence
level   8. Inferential statistics   9. Percentile rank
10. Measures of variability, such as range, variance, standard deviation

AB design   A single-subject research design where a baseline measure ("A") is obtained, and then a treatment ("B") is implemented

ABA design   A single-subject research design where the baseline ("A") is established, a treatment ("B") is introduced, and in the third phase (the second "A"), the treatment is reversed or, in actuality, removed

Abstract   A short summary, presented at the beginning of a research report

Action research   Research done to develop or improve a product, procedure, or program in a particular setting, with no intention of generalizing the results

Adversary-oriented evaluation   Type of evaluation whose focus is on the planned opposition in points of view offered from different evaluators (who typically take "pro" and "con" perspectives)

Age equivalents   Converted scores that indicate the mean raw scores made by persons at different age levels on standardized tests. Example: John's raw score equals eighth year, sixth month

Age norms   Values accompanying certain standardized tests that indicate mean performance of subjects at different age levels (*see* Age equivalents)

Alpha (α) level   The probability level (significance level) that a researcher establishes as acceptable before conducting a test of significance

Alternating-treatment design   Single-subject research; two treatments are alternated in quick succession and changes as measured in the participant are plotted on a graph to facilitate informal comparisons

Amorphous topic   A research topic that is too vague and needs to be clarified, refined, sharpened

Analysis   The verbal or statistical treatment of research data to help answer questions and test hypotheses; also, the process of obtaining information through critical examination of an entity or its various elements

Analysis of covariance (ANCOVA)   ANOVA designs where the effect of a variable (called the "covariate") is controlled for

Analysis of variance (ANOVA)   A statistical method for testing the null hypothesis when differences between two or more groups are involved, done by comparing between-groups variance against within-groups variance

Applied research   Research done for the express purpose of solving an existing problem

Artificial dichotomy   An either–or classification of data, based on judgment (e.g., tall–short; above average–below average)

Assent   Process of minors giving their agreement to participate in a research study

Assumption   Something believed to be true, but not actually verified; important assumptions are usually listed in theses and dissertations

Attitudinal questions   Survey questions that ask individual respondents to indicate their attitudes or opinions regarding some topic

Autobiographical study   Type of narrative research that is written and recorded by the individuals who are the subject of the study

Back material   Material placed after the body of a thesis or dissertation, such as bibliography and appendix

Basic research   A type of research done merely to gain knowledge, without regard for practical application

Behavioral questions   Survey questions that seek information about actual behaviors from individuals in the sample group

Biographical study   Form of narrative research in which the researcher writes and records the experiences of another person's life

Biserial correlation   A correlation between variables when one variable is expressed as continuous variable data, such as test scores, and the other as an artificial dichotomy, such as poor–wealthy

Bivariate correlation   A correlation that involves two variables

Broad topic   A research topic that is too large in scope for time or resources available

Case study   A detailed investigation centered on a single participant

Causal-comparative research   A type of research used to explore possible cause–effect relationships in which the independent (causal) variable cannot be manipulated, as would be the case for gender, handedness, ethnicity, and the like

Cause–effect relationship   A relationship between two or more variables in which changes in one variable (the cause) produce changes in a second variable (the effect)

Census   Type of cross-sectional survey that is conducted for an entire population

Central tendency   A statistical concept referring to what is typical for a group; measures of central tendency include mean, median, and mode

Chain sample   A sample resulting from initial participants who identify other individuals to participate in a study (*see also* Snowball sample *and* Network sample)

Checklists   Survey format that consists of a list of behaviors, characteristics, skills, or other criteria that the researcher is interested in studying

Chi-square goodness-of-fit test   A nonparametric statistical procedure used to determine the significance of differences between what is expected for a group compared to what is actually observed for the group

Chi-square test of independence   A nonparametric statistical procedure used to determine the significance of differences between groups when data are nominal and placed in categories, in a process that compares what is observed against what was expected

CIJE *Current Index to Journals in Education,* an index that lists and summarizes journal articles related to education

Clarifying the topic Process of changing the wording of a topic statement to make it understandable

Closed-ended question Format of survey question that consists of multiple-choice or other types of items that allow the respondent to select a response from a number of options provided by the researcher directly on the survey (also known as forced-choice question)

Cluster sample A sample consisting of one or more groups already in existence, such as the fourth-grade classes at Cutter Elementary School

Coding scheme System, developed by the researcher, used to group qualitative data that provide similar types of information

Coefficient of correlation The numerical expression of the degree of relationship between two or more variables, varying in magnitude from 0 (no correlation) to 1.0 (perfect correlation) (may be positive or negative)

Cohort study Type of longitudinal study in which the researcher studies a subgroup (called the "cohort") within a specified population that share some common characteristic; this subgroup, as defined by the characteristic, is then surveyed over time

Comparison group A group, sometimes called a control group, against which an experimental group is compared

Comparison report A general type of research report that compares one or more groups against each other (other general types of research reports are status reports and relationship reports)

Conclusions The investigator's interpretations of research findings

Confounding variable A variable, other than those being explored in a given study, that affects the research outcomes

Consent Willingness of an individual to participate in research; must appear in writing

Constant A characteristic that is the same for all subjects involved in a study—it might be that all are female or all attend the same school, and so forth

Consumer-oriented evaluation Type of evaluation focused on developing evaluative information on broadly defined educational "products," for ultimate use by educational consumers (who must choose between competing "programs")

Contextualization The process of interpreting research findings with reference to a particular group, setting, or event

Continuous variable A quantitative variable that can assume a large number of different values; most tests yield continuous variable data

Control group A group in an experimental study that receives no treatment, against which the experimental group is compared

Convenience sampling A procedure of selecting a sample consisting of whomever happens to be conveniently present (e.g., a group at a playground)

Conventions Agreed-on way of doing things, as procedures in research

Correlation A covarying relationship between two or more sets of data, as between measures of height and weight

Correlational report A research report that depicts a covarying relationship between two or more variables

Correlational research A type of research used to explore correlation between two or more variables, as between IQ and reading ability

Covariate Variable whose effect is being controlled

Cover letter Written letter that accompanies a written survey or precedes the interview process; explains the purpose of the study and describes what will be asked of participants

Credibility Process of establishing that the results of qualitative research are believable from the perspective of the participant(s) in the research.

Criterion-referenced test A test whose items are directly linked to specific objectives of instruction

Criterion variable In prediction studies using correlations, the variable that one attempts to predict

Cross-sectional survey A survey that obtains data from several different groups of subjects at the same time

DAI *Dissertation Abstracts International,* a publication that provides abstracts of doctoral dissertations done in the United States and Europe

Data Basic information obtained in research; the word is traditionally used in its true plural sense (e.g., the data are . . .)

Database Indexed reference sources and other resources, usually accessible by computer

Degrees of freedom The number of observations that are free to vary; used in determining levels of probability

Delimitations Restrictions that researchers impose in order to narrow the scope of a study

Demographic questions Survey questions that provide the opportunity for respondents to indicate personal characteristics about themselves (e.g., gender, age, level of education)

Dependability Process of establishing that the results of qualitative research are valid, emphasizing the need for the researcher to account for the ever-changing context within which research occurs

Dependent variable The "effect" variable in a cause–effect relationship; example: a new method (the independent or causal variable) being used to improve learning of algebra (the dependent or effect variable)

Descriptive research A type of research used to depict present-day people, conditions, settings, and events

Descriptive statistics Numerical values that describe subjects and their behavior; also the mathematical procedures used in establishing those values

Descriptive survey Form of survey research viewed as a one-shot survey for the purpose of simply describing the characteristics of a sample at one point in time

Descriptor A term that is used to locate information in the ERIC references or other cataloguing materials

Dichotomous variable A categorical variable consisting of only two characteristics—either–or

Difference between means One of the methods used to show the difference between traits or performances of two groups of subjects

Direct administration Mode of survey administration; used whenever the researcher has access to all, or most, members of a given group who are located in one place

Directional research hypothesis   A hypothesis that states what the researcher actually expects to find, as regards both magnitude and direction (e.g., girls will perform better than boys)

Discrete variable   A variable that may assume only a limited number of values (e.g., ethnic group affiliation)

Discriminant analysis   A correlational procedure that predicts, from two or more predictor variables, a criterion variable that is expressed as two separate categories

Double-barreled question   A survey question that essentially asks two different things

Educational research   The careful, patient, systematic investigation of topics related to education

E-mail survey   Mode of survey administration; survey is delivered to potential respondents via e-mail messages and requires an e-mailed set of responses in return

ERIC   Educational Resources Information Center, a clearinghouse of information related to education

Ethnographic research   A type of research used to describe group behavior and interactions within social settings

Ethnography   Research process used to study human interactions in social settings

Evaluation research   A type of research used to determine the relative value of products, procedures, and programs

Experimental design   A plan for research to determine what effect manipulation of an independent variable might have on the dependent variable; there are several different experimental designs

Experimental group   The group in an experiment that receives a new treatment, the effects of which are being explored

Experimental research   A type of research used to explore possible cause–effect relationships in which the independent variable is systematically varied to determine the resultant effects on a dependent variable

Expertise-oriented evaluation   Type of evaluation that depends primarily on judgments of professional experts to determine the quality of educational programs

Explanatory mixed-methods design   Most common type of mixed-method design; the researcher first collects quantitative data and then collects qualitative data in order to help support, explain, or elaborate on the quantitative results

Exploratory mixed-methods design   Type of mixed-method design; the researcher first collects qualitative data and then collects quantitative data, either sequentially or using a two-phase approach

Ex post facto research   (from Latin—"that which was done afterward") The effect under investigation has already occurred, but the cause is not clear; another name for causal-comparative research, in which the independent variable cannot be manipulated

External criticism   The careful scrutiny of qualitative data to determine authenticity of the source

External validity   The extent to which findings of a particular study can be generalized elsewhere

Extraneous variable   A physical or environmental confounding variable that is usually temporary, such as fatigue, distraction, or nervousness

Factor analysis   A process that identifies clusters of correlated variables, referred to as factors, and then correlates those factors with the criterion variable

Factorial ANCOVA   ANCOVA designs with more than one independent variable and covariates

Factorial ANOVA   ANOVA designs with more than one independent variable and more than one dependent variable (and, possibly, covariates)

Factorial MANOVA/MANCOVA   ANOVA designs with more than one independent variable and more than one dependent variable (and, possibly, covariates)

Findings   The principal discoveries made in research

Focus groups   Simultaneous interviews of people making up a relatively small group, usually no more than 10 to 12 people

Forced-choice question   Format of survey question that consists of multiple-choice or other types of items that allow the respondent to select a response from a number of options provided by the researcher directly on the survey (also known as closed-ended question)

Formative evaluation   Evaluation research that occurs during the development of a program and continues into its implementation, for purposes of finding ways to improve it

Front material   Material that is placed before the body of a thesis or dissertation, such as table of contents and list of figures

_F_ test   A test for determining the probability that differences among two or more means occurred by chance

Grade equivalents   Scores that indicate grade level, converted from mean raw scores made by students at various grade levels

Grade norms   Values accompanying certain standardized tests that indicate mean scores made by students at different grade levels (_see_ Grade equivalents)

Grounded theory research   Type of qualitative research; goal is to discover an existing theory or generate a new theory that results directly from the data

Historical research   A type of research that explores people, events, conditions, and settings of the past

Hypothesis   A testable statement of a predicted relationship or difference among certain variables

Hypothetico-inductive analysis   A thought process used in qualitative research that constructs meaning from data obtained through observation; synonymous with logico-inductive analysis

Independent variable   The causative variable in a cause–effect relationship; the independent variable is intentionally manipulated, when possible, to observe the effects it might bring about in the dependent variable

Inductive analysis   _See_ Hypothetico-inductive analysis

Inferential statistics   Numerical procedures for determining how closely sample statistics match their corresponding population parameters; also, the values that result from those procedures

Interim analysis   Data analysis that sometimes occurs in qualitative research, especially ethnographic research, before all the data are collected

Internal criticism The careful scrutiny of qualitative research data, done to determine accuracy and trustworthiness of the data

Internal validity The degree to which the effects of extraneous variables have been controlled in a study

Interval scales Measurement scales expressed in equal numerical units, but not having a true zero point (examples: achievement tests, aptitude tests); scores made on interval scales can be added and subtracted accurately, but not divided or multiplied

Intervening variable A variable that alters the relationship that would otherwise exist between certain variables; example: motivation might be an intervening variable between method of teaching and student achievement

Interview A method of obtaining data from subjects by orally asking them selected questions

Journal Means of self-reporting data in qualitative research; types include student journals, teacher journals, and class journals

Judgmental sampling A procedure for drawing a sample of only certain segments of the population, such as high achievers or deviant students

Kendall tau A method of correlating two sets of measures shown as rankings, when the number of pairs is less than 10

Knowledge questions Survey questions that seek to determine how much an individual knows about a particular subject

Life history Type of narrative research that portrays an individual's entire life

Likert scale A scale used to assess attitude or opinion; subjects respond by indicating how strongly they agree or disagree with the statements provided

Likert-type scale A scale used to assess items on a continuum other than an agree–disagree scale

Limitations (on research) Natural conditions that restrict the scope of a study and may affect its outcomes

Logico-inductive analysis A method of analyzing qualitative data by applying logical thought processes

Longitudinal survey Research that collects data from the same group of subjects over months or years, usually to document changes that occur over time

Mail survey Mode of survey administration; the survey instrument is administered to the sample by physically sending it to each individual and then requesting that it be returned by mail before a certain date

Management-oriented evaluation Type of evaluation focused on identifying and meeting the informational needs of managerial decision-makers

Mean The arithmetic average of a set of scores

Measurement Obtaining data by using tests, scales, and other measuring devices

Measures of central tendency Summary numerical values that indicate what is typical for a group of scores

Measures of relationship Numerical values that indicate the degree of relationships between two or more sets of scores made by the same group of participants

Measures of relative position Numerical scores that indicate the location of an individual when compared to the population

Measures of variability Summary numerical values that indicate the internal spread of a group of scores

Median The midpoint in an array of scores arranged from highest to lowest; if there is an even number of scores, the median is the mean of the two middle scores

Member checking Process of sharing summarizations of analyzed qualitative data with participants in order to gauge the accuracy of the interpretations made by the researcher

Method (of the study) The procedures followed in planning research and obtaining and analyzing research data

Mixed-methods research designs Research designs that combine both qualitative and quantitative methods

Mode The most frequently occurring test score or measurement

Multiple baseline design Single-subject design where two or more (often three) behaviors, people, or settings are plotted in a staggered graph where a change is made to one, but not the other two, and then to the second, but not the third behavior, person, or setting

Multiple correlation Measure of the common relationship among a set of three or more variables

Multiple regression A correlational procedure in which a criterion variable is predicted from a combination of two or more predictor variables

Multistage sampling Combination of two or more probability sampling techniques

Multivariate ANCOVA (MANCOVA) ANCOVA designs with more than one dependent variable

Multivariate ANOVA (MANOVA) ANOVA designs with more than one dependent variable

Multivariate correlation A covarying relationship among three or more sets of data

Narrative research Type of qualitative research where the purpose is to convey experiences as they are expressed in lived and told stories of individuals

Natural dichotomy An either–or categorization that occurs naturally, such as male–female

Naturalistic-oriented evaluation Type of evaluation where naturalistic (i.e., qualitative) inquiry is key

Negative correlation A correlation in which high scores on one measure tend to accompany low scores on the other, average tend to accompany average, and low tend to accompany high

Network sample A sample resulting from initial participants who identify other individuals to participate in a study (*see also* Snowball sample and Chain sample)

Newspaper Abstracts A database accessible by computer that summarizes articles contained in a number of different newspapers

Nominal scales Measurement scales that classify data into two or more verbal (name) categories, indicating that the data are different but not quantifying the difference

Nondirectional research hypothesis A type of hypothesis that states that a difference or correlation will be found, but makes no further stipulations about the difference or correlation

Nonexperimental research   Research that does not involve the manipulation of an independent variable to ascertain its effect on a dependent variable

Nonparametric statistics   Statistics, particularly tests of significance, that do not involve variable or ratio data and do not make assumptions about how data are distributed

Nonprobability sampling   A sampling procedure in which the researcher cannot specify the probability of individuals in the population being selected for the sample

Normal probability curve   The bell-shaped curve to which the frequency of many variable traits corresponds and to which most statistics are related

Norm-referenced test   A test that compares individuals' performance against the performance of a great many others

Norms   Numerical summaries of test performances of a great many other individuals; norms usually accompany standardized tests

Notation   A method of obtaining data by jotting down what is observed

NSSE Yearbooks   Reviews of research on selected topics, published annually by the National Society for the Study of Education

Null hypothesis   A hypothesis that states that no difference or relationship exists among specified variables

Objectives-oriented evaluation   Type of evaluation focused on specifying goals and objectives and then determining the extent to which they have been met

Observer's comments   Written, interpretive comments made by the researcher alongside actual fieldnotes

Open-ended questions   Format of survey question that allows for more individualized responses, because respondents are not limited to selecting only from a supplied set of options

Operating rules of research   The ground rules that investigators observe in order to maximize credibility (*see* Principles of . . .)

Oral history   Type of narrative research that is conducted by gathering the personal reflections of events, as well as implications of those events, from one or several individuals

Ordinal scale   A scale that expresses data as rankings, rather than scores

Organismic variable   A physical condition (e.g., poor eyesight) that influences a relationship between other variables

$p < .05$; $p < .01$ Levels of probability (significance) most frequently used by researchers when testing hypotheses in which the .05 level indicates a less than 5 percent chance that a finding is occurring because of sampling error and the .01 level indicates a less than 1 percent chance

Panel study   A longitudinal study in which the researcher examines the exact same people over a specified length of time

Parameters   Numerical values that describe populations, in the same way that statistics describe samples

Parametric statistics   Statistics or statistical tests involving variable or ratio data and based on the assumption that the sample reflects a normal distribution in the population

Partial correlation   A covarying relationship that remains after the influence of one or more confounding variables has been removed mathematically (such as the relationship between vocabulary and reading ability, with the effects of intelligence removed)

Participant observer   An ethnographic researcher who participates actively and completely in all activities of the group being studied

Participant-oriented evaluation   Type of evaluation in which the direct involvement of participants is key

Participants   The people from whom data are collected in a research study

Pearson product-moment correlation   A covarying relationship between sets of measures that are expressed as continuous interval data, such as test scores

Percentile rank   A converted score that indicates the percentage of all scores that have been equaled or surpassed by a given performance (e.g., Sue's score ranked at the 63rd percentile; she did as well as or better than 63 percent of the people who took the test)

Periodical Abstracts   A database that provides abstracts of articles from a number of popular magazines

Personal experience story   Type of narrative research; a study of an individual's personal experience as related to single or multiple incidents, or private situations

Phenomenological research   Type of qualitative research; goal is to describe and interpret the experiences or reactions of participants to a particular phenomenon from their individual perspectives

Phi correlation   A covarying relationship between sets of data when both sets are expressed as natural dichotomies

Pilot test   Trial run of the data collection process, particularly in survey research

Point-biserial correlation   A covarying relationship between sets of data when one is expressed as continuous variable data (such as test scores) and the other as a natural dichotomy (such as male–female)

Population   The total group, represented by the sample, to whom research findings are to be generalized

Positive correlation   A correlation in which high scores on one test tend to accompany high scores on the other, average tend to accompany average, and low tend to accompany low

Post hoc fallacy   The unwarranted conclusion that because one event follows another, the first has caused the second

Predictor variable   In correlations, the variable (e.g., motivation) used in attempting to predict the criterion variable (e.g., rate of learning)

Primary data   Data that come from direct observation, measurement, eyewitness accounts, or firsthand reports

Primary sources   Eyewitnesses of events, firsthand accounts by originators of works and behavior, or the books, articles, and documents in which firsthand accounts are reported

Principle of accurate disclosure   Individuals participating in research are to be informed accurately about the nature of the research and any unusual procedures or tasks in which they will be involved

Principle of beneficence   Research is not done to harm individuals but to promote understanding, opportunity, quality, and improvement

Principle of confidentiality   The anonymity of subjects involved in research is to be maintained

Principle of credibility   Research must be believable; this is accomplished by following established conventions and giving close attention to data validity and reliability

Principle of generalizability   The applicability of research findings to other groups and settings should be as wide as possible

Principle of honesty   All research data are to be obtained, analyzed, and reported without bias or omission

Principle of parsimony   Other things being equal, the simpler the research design, the better

Principle of probability   All research conclusions are considered to be probabilities, not certainties

Principle of protection   Research must not subject individuals to physical, mental, or emotional harm

Principle of replicability   Proper procedures must be followed, and proper records kept, so that a given study can be repeated by other investigators elsewhere

Principle of researchability   Research topics must be approachable through the scientific method and must take into account practical matters such as time, distance, and expenditures

Principle of rival explanations   Research conclusions must remain open to, and be judged against, alternative explanations

Principle of significance   The findings of research should likely contribute to human knowledge

Privileged observer   An ethnographic researcher who is allowed to mingle with the group being studied

Probability levels   Values that indicate degree of likelihood that a finding has occurred due to chance errors made in selecting a sample that does not reflect the population; researchers most often use the .05 and .01 probability levels when testing for significance, values that are also called significance levels and confidence levels

Probability sampling   Any sampling procedure that specifies the probability that each member of the population has of being selected for the sample

Problem   The topic being investigated, once it has been refined

Problem statement   A sentence or paragraph that explains the purpose of a given investigation

Procedures   The steps followed in a study to obtain, analyze, and interpret data

Purposive sampling   Intentionally selecting, in a nonrandom fashion, subjects who are likely to be able to furnish needed information

Qualitative data analysis   The analysis of verbal data through use of certain procedures of logical thinking

Qualitative research   Research that yields extensive narrative data, which are analyzed verbally

Quantitative data analysis   The analysis of numerical data through statistical procedures

Quantitative research   Research that explores traits and situations from which numerical data are obtained

Quasi-experimental research   A type of research very similar to experimental research, except that subjects are not randomly selected or assigned to groups

Questioning   A means of obtaining data from subjects by posing questions that elicit responses

Questionnaire   A formal set of written questions to which subjects respond in writing

Quota sample   A sample selected to contain exact predetermined numbers (quotas) of people with specific characteristics, such as ethnicity or gender (e.g., 20 boys and 20 girls)

Random assignment   A procedure of assigning subjects to groups so that every subject has an equal chance of being placed in any of the groups

Random sample   A group drawn from the population, with every member of the population having an equal chance of being selected

Random selection   Process of selecting a random sample

Range   A statistic defined as highest score in an array minus lowest score; a rough indicator of the spread of scores

Raw score   A test score or numerical measurement that has not been converted in any way

Reject the null hypothesis   Concluding that the evidence obtained does not adequately support the stated hypothesis

Relationship   The tendency for the scores on one variable to reflect the scores on another variable

Relative standing   Where one individual's score or measure stands in relation to those of all other individuals similarly measured

Reliability (of data)   An index of the consistency of data or test results; to be considered reliable, results must be very nearly the same, time after time

Reliability (of research)   An estimate of the consistency of research conditions and procedures

Research   A careful, systematic, patient investigation, using the scientific method, undertaken to discover or verify facts and relationships

Research design   The overall, detailed plan for obtaining, analyzing, and interpreting data

Research hypothesis   A statement of differences or relationships among variables that the investigator expects to discover

Research method   The procedures used to obtain, analyze, and interpret data

Research problem   An educational concern that has been clarified and stated clearly

Research question   The fundamental question or questions that a research project is designed to answer

Respondents   Members of the sample, selected from the population, who ultimately respond to a survey

Restorying   Process of analysis in narrative research; largely about organizing a good deal of personal story data into a presentation that will make sense to the intended audience

Retain the null hypothesis   Concluding that the evidence one has obtained adequately supports the stated hypothesis

Reversal design   *See* ABA design

RIE   *Resources in Education,* a publication of ERIC that contains research reports and related documents that have not been published in journals

Rigor   The quality, validity, accuracy, and credibility of action research and its findings

Sample   A group selected from a much larger population, usually with the objective that the sample distribution be similar to that of the population; findings made for the sample are often generalized to the population

Sampling error   Expected chance variations in the selection of samples that cause the sample to differ somewhat from the population

Scientific method   A procedure commonly used in science that consists of defining a problem, stating the main question or hypothesis, collecting relevant data, and then analyzing those data so as to answer the question or test the hypothesis

Scientific research   A procedure of investigation used to establish facts verifiable through observation and to discover testable relationships among those facts

Secondary data   Information coming not from original sources or eyewitness accounts, but from secondhand reports

Secondary source   Secondhand accounts of events, including scholarly interpretations of work done by others

Semantic differential scale   A scale that presents statements or concepts and calls on respondents to select among seven degrees of difference between pairs of bipolar adjectives such as "effective–ineffective" or "too little–too much"

Semistructured questions   Questions framed to allow respondents some leeway in stating their responses (e.g., "How well do you think schools are meeting the needs of diverse ethnic groups?")

Significance   The odds conventionally used by researchers in tests of significance; those odds are set at 5 chance recurrences of the finding out of 100 repetitions, on average (the .05 probability or significance level), and 1 chance recurrence of the finding out of 100 repetitions, on average (the .01 probability or significance level)

Single-subject design   An experimental or quasi-experimental design involving only one participant

Single-theme books   Scholarly books in which the author's original research and commentary are reported

Snowball sample   A sample resulting from initial participants who identify other individuals to participate in a study (*see also* Chain sample *and* Network sample)

Spearman rho   A statistical procedure for determining the correlation between sets of data given in the form of rankings

SSCI   *Social Sciences Citation Index,* an index that lists articles that make reference to specific studies previously done; this indicates importance of the work cited and provides additional literature that investigators might wish to review

Standard deviation   A stable measure of dispersion of scores from the mean; in a normal distribution, 68.26 percent of all scores lie in the area between plus one standard deviation and minus one standard deviation from the mean; 95.40 percent are included between +2 and –2 standard deviations from the mean; and over 99 percent are included between +3 and –3 standard deviations from the mean

Standard error   The standard deviation of the sampling distribution (assuming hundreds of repetitions); standard error indicates the probable differences between sample measures and their corresponding population values

Standardized tests   Carefully constructed tests accompanied by norms that permit comparisons of individuals

Stanine   A conversion of raw scores into nine bands, or stanines, with the fifth stanine being average, the ninth stanine the highest, and the first stanine the lowest; the conversion is done to give comparative meanings to raw scores

Statistical significance   The very low probability that a particular research finding has occurred because of chance errors made in selecting the sample; findings that very likely have not occurred by chance are called "significant"

Statistics   Numerical values that describe subjects and their behavior or else make inferences about population parameters; also, the mathematical procedures used in making those descriptions and comparisons

Status report   A general type of research report that describes people, conditions, and events as they now are, or once were (other general types of reports are difference reports and relationship reports)

Stratified sample   A sample selected to reflect accurately the proportions of certain segments of the population, such as gender and ethnic groups; the population segments (strata) are identified and then subjects are randomly selected from them

Structured questions   Questions carefully framed to obtain specific information and reduce the diversity among responses (e.g., "Do you think today's schools are better, worse, or about the same as they were 20 years ago?")

Style guide   A document that explains the style requirements of graduate schools or publishing houses

Subjects   A term frequently used to refer to participants in a study, people from whom information is directly obtained

Subquestions   Research questions subordinate to the main research question; as subquestions are answered, they contribute to answering the main question

Summative evaluation   Evaluation research that focuses on the overall quality of a program on its completion

Survey   A procedure that uses interviews or questionnaires to assess opinions, beliefs, and attitudes

Survey research   Type of research; purpose is to describe characteristics of a population

Systematic sampling   A procedure for obtaining a sample by selecting every *n*th name from a master list of the population

Target population   Larger group of people to whom the researcher would like to generalize the ultimate results of the study

Telephone survey   Mode of survey administration; requires the researcher (and any assistants) to read each survey question to individual respondents

Tetrachoric correlation   A covarying relationship between sets of data when both are expressed as artificial dichotomies

Theory   An overall explanation of how large-scale events and relationships probably are, were, or will be, or how and why they came to be as they are

Thesaurus of ERIC Descriptors   A publication that lists key terms to facilitate the search of library literature

Threats to validity   Conditions or events that may weaken the validity of data. Examples of threats to validity are improper selection of subjects, maturation of subjects over time, and confounding variables that exert undetected influence on the research variables.

Treatment condition   The independent (X) variable in experimental research; experimental research determines whether the treatment variable produces an effect in the criterion (Y) variable (also known as treatment variable)

Trend study   A longitudinal survey study that examines changes within a specifically identified population over time

Triangulation   Process in which quantitative and qualitative results are informally compared in order to see if they have yielded similar findings

Triangulation mixed-methods design   Type of mixed-method design; both quantitative and qualitative data are collected at about the same time, and the two types of data are given equal emphasis

Trustworthiness   Assessment of the validity of qualitative data; established by examining the credibility and dependability of qualitative data

***T* scores**   Conversions made from raw scores that indicate how much a given raw score differs from the mean, in terms of standard deviations; the mean is arbitrarily set at 50 and each standard deviation assigned a value of 10, so all that all T values are, therefore, positive

***t* test**   A statistical procedure used to determine the significance of an observed difference between two means; it compares the difference between means against the standard error of that difference

Type I error   Erroneous rejection of the null hypothesis, which leads to the conclusion that a difference or relationship exists among variables when in fact one does not

Type II error   Erroneous retention of the null hypothesis, which leads to the conclusion that a difference or relationship does not exist among variables, when in fact one does

Validity (of data)   A quality of data that indicates authenticity—that is, the data are in fact what they are purported to be

Validity (of research)   A quality of research determined in part by its adherence to conventions that make it easily interpretable, and in part by its generalizability to other groups and settings

Variability   The spread that exists within an array of scores or other measurements; measures of variability include range, standard deviation, and variance

Variable   Any characteristic that tends to differ from individual to individual (e.g., height)

Web-based survey   Mode of survey administration; respondents are typically directed to a website through initial contact via e-mail message

***X* variable**   The independent (causal, treatment) variable

***Y* variable**   The dependent (effect, criterion) variable

***z* scores**   Conversions made from raw scores that indicate how much individual raw scores differ from the mean, in terms of standard deviations; z scores have a mean of zero and a standard deviation of 1 and can, therefore, have positive or negative values

Name Index

Subject Index